The Political Economy of Food System Transformation

The Political Economy of Food System Transformation

Pathways to Progress in a Polarized World

Edited by

DANIELLE RESNICK
AND
JOHAN SWINNEN

OXFORD
UNIVERSITY PRESS

Great Clarendon Street, Oxford, OX2 6DP,
United Kingdom

Oxford University Press is a department of the University of Oxford.
It furthers the University's objective of excellence in research, scholarship,
and education by publishing worldwide. Oxford is a registered trade mark of
Oxford University Press in the UK and in certain other countries

Published in the United States of America by Oxford University Press
198 Madison Avenue, New York, NY 10016, United States of America

Data available

Library of Congress Control Number: 2023943204

ISBN 9780198882121

DOI: 10.1093/oso/9780198882121.001.0001

Printed and bound by
CPI Group (UK) Ltd, Croydon, CR0 4YY

Links to third party websites are provided by Oxford in good faith and
for information only. Oxford disclaims any responsibility for the materials
contained in any third party website referenced in this work.

Any opinions stated in the book are those of the
author(s) and are not necessarily representative
of or endorsed by IFPRI.

MIX
Paper | Supporting
responsible forestry
FSC® C013604

Contents

List of Figures   ix
List of Tables   xi
Preface   xii
Acknowledgments   xiii
List of Contributors   xv

1. Introduction: Political Economy of Food System Transformation   1
   Danielle Resnick and Johan Swinnen
   1.1 Introduction   1
   1.2 The Complexities Underlying Food System Transformation   3
   1.3 Political Economy Drivers of Policy Choices   10
   1.4 Summary of the Book   17
   1.5 Conclusions   23
   References   23

2. Facts, Interests, and Values: Identifying Points of
   Convergence and Divergence for Food Systems   32
   Koen Deconinck
   2.1 Introduction   32
   2.2 Facts   33
   2.3 Interests   37
   2.4 Values   39
   2.5 Interests versus Values   41
   2.6 Policy Controversies   46
   2.7 Conclusion   48
   References   49

3. The Political Economy of Reforming Agricultural Support Policies   54
   Rob Vos, Will Martin, and Danielle Resnick
   3.1 Introduction   54
   3.2 Current Agricultural Support and Its Impacts   55
   3.3 Political Economy Framework for Reform   60
   3.4 Case Studies of Agricultural Support Policy Reforms   64
   3.5 Conclusions   72
   References   75

4. From Re-instrumenting to Re-purposing Farm Support Policies   80
   Kym Anderson and Anna Strutt
   4.1 Introduction   80
   4.2 Evolving Objectives of Agrifood Policy Instrument Choices   82
   4.3 Basic Welfare Economics of Agrifood Policy Instruments   87

4.4 Contributions of Various Policy Instruments to National
     Producer and Consumer Support Estimates   90
4.5 Contributors to the Global Costs of Present Forms of
     Support to Agriculture   96
4.6 How Best to Re-purpose Current Agrifood Policies   100
4.7 Conclusion   104
References   105

5. Policy Coalitions in Food Systems Transformation   111
   Johan Swinnen and Danielle Resnick
   5.1 Introduction   111
   5.2 Policy Coalitions and Effectiveness of Collective Action   113
   5.3 Vertical Policy Coalitions Along the Value Chains   115
   5.4 Cross-Issue Coalitions   121
   5.5 Globalization and Transnational Coalitions   125
   5.6 Conclusions   127
   References   128

6. Government Response to Ultra-Processed and Sugar
   Beverages Industries in Developing Nations: The Need to
   Build Coalitions across Policy Sectors   133
   Eduardo J. Gómez
   6.1 Introduction   133
   6.2 The Politics of Policy of the Food Sector: Multiple Streams
        Analysis and Future Insights   134
   6.3 Contrasting Global Attention and Support for NCD Policies   135
   6.4 Conclusion   148
   References   149

7. Ultra-Processed Food Environments: Aligning Policy
   Beliefs from the State, Market, and Civil Society   155
   Jonathan Mockshell and Thea Nielsen Ritter
   7.1 Introduction   155
   7.2 Research Methods   159
   7.3 Identification of Policy Discourse Coalitions   163
   7.4 Discussion   170
   7.5 Conclusion   176
   References   177

8. Asymmetric Power in Global Food System Advocacy   184
   Jody Harris
   8.1 Contrasting Food Policy Objectives   184
   8.2 Combining Theories of Public Policy   184
   8.3 Evolving Ideas in the International Nutrition Space   188
   8.4 Bringing the Global to the Local   191
   8.5 Conclusion   200
   References   201

9. The Political Economy of Bundling Socio-Technical
   Innovations to Transform Agri-Food Systems   206
   Christopher B. Barrett
   9.1 The Imperative and Challenge of Agri-Food Systems Transformation 206
   9.2 Why Socio-Technical Bundles?   208
   9.3 Building Coalitions for Bundling: Insights from the
       Kaldor-Hicks Compensation Principle   211
   9.4 The Roles of Institutions, Power, Information, and Trust   213
   9.5 Some Empirical Illustrations   218
   9.6 Conclusion   225
   References   226

10. Sustainable Food and Farming: When Public Perceptions
    Depart from Science   230
    Robert Paarlberg
    10.1 The Political Economy of Science Acceptance in Farming   230
    10.2 Defining Sustainable Food   232
    10.3 Case 1: "Green Revolution" Farming   233
    10.4 Case 2: Industrial Farming   237
    10.5 Case 3: Organic Food   239
    10.6 Case 4: Genetically Modified Organisms (GMOS)   242
    10.7 When Will Popular Resistance Block Uptake?   246
    10.8 Will CRISPR Crops Become GMO 2.0?   248
    10.9 Conclusion: Even Unpopular Science Reaches Farmers,
         Most of the Time   250
    References   251

11. Enabling Positive Tipping Points in Public Support for
    Food System Transformation: The Case of Meat Consumption   256
    Lukas Paul Fesenfeld and Yixian Sun
    11.1 Introduction   256
    11.2 Existing Literature on Public Opinion on Sustainable
         Food Policy   257
    11.3 Theoretical Argument   260
    11.4 Methods Used in Survey-Embedded Experiments   264
    11.5 Results   269
    11.6 Combined Framing and Policy Design Effects   271
    11.7 Discussion and Research Outlook   279
    11.8 Conclusion   281
    References   282

12. Urban Food Systems Governance in Africa: Toward a
    Realistic Model for Transformation   288
    Gareth Haysom and Jane Battersby
    12.1 Introduction   288
    12.2 Governance of African Urban Systems and Food Systems   289

12.3 Food Governance in African Cities 292
12.4 Disrupting Food and Urban Governance—
Misalignment in Global Processes 292
12.5 Emerging Global Urban Food Governance Processes 294
12.6 Combining Authorizing and Activating Environments 300
12.7 Conclusion 304
References 305

13. The Political Economy of Food System Transformation in
the European Union 310
*Alan Matthews, Jeroen Candel, Nel de Mûelenaere, and
Pauline Scheelbeek*
13.1 Introduction 310
13.2 Food Systems Transition in the EU—State of Play 312
13.3 Political Economy Explanations for Change (or the Lack
of It) 319
13.4 Opportunities to Catalyze the Transition 329
References 333

14. Tracking Progress and Generating Accountability for
Global Food System Commitments 338
Stella Nordhagen and Jessica Fanzo
14.1 Introduction 338
14.2 The Need for Transformation, Commitments, and Accountability 339
14.3 Prior Work on Food Systems Accountability and Monitoring 341
14.4 Gaps in Food Systems Monitoring Work 345
14.5 Efforts to Fill These Gaps 347
14.6 Moving from Data and Information to Accountability 349
14.7 Conclusion 353
References 354

15. Conclusions 360
Danielle Resnick and Johan Swinnen
15.1 Reconciling Trade-Offs Generated by Different
Incentive Structures 360
15.2 Mixed Modes of Mobilization 363
15.3 Addressing Divergent Coalition Preferences through
Strategic Policy Design 364
15.4 Policy Adaptation and Implementation 365
15.5 Conclusions, Limitations, and Ways Forward 367
References 369

Index 371

List of Figures

1.1. Political economy considerations for food system reforms 11

2.1. Prioritization of environment versus economic growth within and across countries 41

3.1. Agricultural producer support by main types of support, 2019–2021 (billions of US$ per year) 55

3.2. Agricultural producer support by main countries and country groupings, 2019–2021 (billions of US$ per year) 56

3.3. Global implications of repurposing domestic support (% change relative to baseline projections for 2040) 59

3.4. Identifying political economy influences on policy options 61

3.5. China's support to agriculture, 1981–2017 68

4.1. Nominal rates of border protection and of overall assistance to agriculture (grey solid and black dotted lines) and agricultural consumer tax equivalent (grey dashed line), OECD Countries, 1955–2020 (%) 91

4.2. Component shares of PSE in Japan, EU, USA, and all OECD, 1986/88, 2001/03 and 2018/20 (%) 93

4.3. Relative rate of assistance to agriculture vs non-agriculture, high-income countries and developing countries, 1955–2018 (%, five-year averages) 95

8.1. Timeline of Zambian food and nutrition policy since independence 192

8.2. Changing national nutrition policy focus over time 193

8.3. Advocacy coalitions in Zambia's food policy subsystem 194

8.4. Mechanisms and power of policy transfer through advocacy coalitions 197

11.1. A framework of framing, design and feedback for food system transformation 264

11.2. Willingness to pay more (in %) by adding a tax to reduce meat consumption 270

11.3. Average policy support to reduce meat consumption and promote different types of meat alternatives in China, Germany, and the United States 271

11.4. Effects of policy design and framing attributes on respondents' support rating (China) 272

11.5. Effects of policy design and framing attributes on respondents' support rating (Germany) 273

11.6. Difference in marginal means between the control and framing conditions for different tax levels on meat (Germany) 274

11.7. Effects of policy design and framing attributes on respondents' support rating (United States) 275

11.8. Difference in marginal means between the control and framing conditions
for different tax levels on meat (US)   276

11.9. Most stringent policy package proposals in China, Germany, and US
receiving clear public support (i.e., a rating of 5 or higher on a 7-point scale)   277

12.1. Stylized view of urban food governance through activating and authorizing
environments   302

14.1. The accountability cycle   340

14.2. Examples of data presented in high-level reports (top) and online
dashboards (bottom)   342

14.3. Framework for the Global Food Systems Countdown to 2030 Initiative   348

List of Tables

2.1. Three sources of disagreement and potential policy approaches   35

3.1. Comparison of political economy dynamics   73

4.1. Agricultural nominal rates of assistance by country, 1986/88, 2001/03, 2017/19, and 2020 (%, weighted average using value of production without assistance as weights)   92

4.2. Component shares of agriculture's PSE, by country, 2019 (%)   94

4.3. Elasticities of real incomes of farmers and industrial capitalists to changes in the prices of their products in a poor agrarian economy and a rich industrial economy   96

4.4. Subsidies and import tariffs in the updated GTAP Data Base, primary agriculture, processed foods, and non-agrifood goods, 2017 (%)   98

4.5. Simulated changes in real GDP from the elimination of domestic subsidies, import tariffs and export subsidies on all agricultural and food products, 2017 (US$ million and %)   99

4.6. Distribution of changes in real GDP from regional and global elimination of domestic subsidies, import tariffs and export subsidies on agricultural and food products, 2001 and 2017 (%)   99

4.7. Shares of domestic subsidies, import tariffs and export subsidies in the regional and global GDP effects of full liberalization of agricultural and food policies, 2001 and 2017 (%)   100

4.8. Changes in real output of selected foods from the elimination of domestic subsidies, import tariffs and export subsidies on all agricultural and food products, 2017 (%)   100

7.1. Interviewed stakeholders for in-depth interviews   162

7.2. Participants in the discourse coalitions (identified by cluster analysis) (N = 22)   164

7.3. Food environment policy beliefs identified by factor analysis   165

8.1. Study design framework   185

11.1. Overview of policy design attributes in the conjoint experiment   267

13.1. Green Deal food system objectives   311

Preface

The current structure of the global food system increasingly is recognized as unsustainable. In addition to the environmental impacts of agricultural production, unequal patterns of food access and availability are contributing to non-communicable diseases in middle- and high-income countries and inadequate caloric intake and dietary diversity among the world's poorest. To this end, there have been a growing number of academic and policy initiatives aimed at advancing food system transformation, including the 2021 UN Food Systems Summit, the Sustainable Development Goals (SDGs), and several UN Climate conferences. Yet, the policy pathways for achieving a transformed food system are highly contested, and the enabling conditions for implementation frequently are absent. Furthermore, a broad range of polarizing factors affect decisions over the food system at domestic and international levels—from debates over values and (mis)information, to concerns over food self-sufficiency, corporate influence, and human rights.

This edited volume explicitly analyzes the political economy dynamics of food system transformation with contributors who span several disciplines, including economics, ecology, geography, nutrition, political science, and public policy. The chapters collectively address the range of interests, institutions, and power in the food system, the diversity of coalitions that form around food policy issues and the tactics they employ, the ways in which policies can be designed and sequenced to overcome opposition to reform, and processes of policy adaptation and learning. Drawing on original surveys, interviews, empirical modeling, and case studies from around the world, the book touches on issues as wide ranging as repurposing agricultural subsidies, agricultural trade, biotechnology innovations, red meat consumption, sugar-sweetened beverage taxes, and much more.

Acknowledgments

This book would not have been possible without funding from the CGIAR's research program of Policies, Institutions, and Markets (PIM), which was led by the International Food Policy Research Institute (IFPRI) from 2012 to 2021. Special thanks in particular to the PIM Director, Frank Place, for supporting and encouraging the work. We also acknowledge the David M. Rubenstein fellowship of the Brookings Institution, which partially supported the time of one of the editors (D. Resnick) to work on this volume.

We are also grateful for the feedback from anonymous reviewers at Oxford University Press and from IFPRI's Peer Review Committee, which collectively strengthened the volume's key messages. We thank Gillian Hollerich at IFPRI for her excellent editorial assistance as well as Michael Go at IFPRI and Adam Swallow at OUP for believing in the concept of the book. Victoria Sunter at OUP helped shepherd the book through the publication process, and the team at Integra provided invaluable copyediting services. Where relevant, individual chapter authors also acknowledge at the outset of their chapters specific funders and colleagues who helped strengthen their contributions to this volume.

Some parts of a few chapters have appeared in different formats in alternative publications. For Chapter 2, we thank the Organization for Economic Cooperation and Development (OECD) for allowing the reproduction of analytical material that originally appeared in their publication, *Making Better Policies for Food Systems* (2021). For Chapter 3, we thank IFPRI for allowing the reproduction of some material that appeared in IFPRI's 2022 *Global Food Policy Report: Climate Change and Food Systems*. We are grateful to OUP for allowing the re-production of Figures 8.2 and 8.3 in Chapter 8, which originally appeared in *Health Policy and Planning* ("Advocacy Coalitions and the Transfer of Nutrition Policy to Zambia"). Additional permissions were provided for reproducing Table 11.1 in Chapter 11, which first appeared in *Nature Food* ("Policy Packaging Can Make Food System Transformation Feasible"), and Figure 11.9, which the authors originally produced for the 2021 *Meat Atlas,* published by the Heinrich Böll Stiftung, Friends of the Earth Europe, and Bund für Umwelt and Naturschutz under a Creative Commons (CC BY 4.0) license. In Chapter 14, several figures were reproduced from open access resources. These include Figure 14.1 from the Accountability Pact (2021), as well as the different panels in Figure 14.2 from the Food and Agricultural Organization (State of Food and Agriculture Report 2021), Development Initiatives

(Global Nutrition Report 2020), GAIN and Johns Hopkins University (Food Systems Dashboard 2020), and the Institute for Health Metrics and Evaluation at the University of Washington (GBD compare 2021).

List of Contributors

Kym Anderson is the George Gollin Professor Emeritus in the School of Economics and Public Policy at the University of Adelaide, Australia, an Honorary Professor in the Arndt-Corden Department of Economics at the Australian National University in Canberra, and a Research Fellow in the Center for Economic Policy Research (CEPR).

Christopher B. Barrett is the Stephen B. and Janice G. Ashley Professor of Applied Economics and Management and International Professor of Agriculture at the Charles H. Dyson School of Applied Economics and Management, and a Professor in the Jeb E. Brooks School of Public Policy, all at Cornell University, USA.

Jane Battersby is an urban geographer based in the Department of Environmental and Geographical Science at the University of Cape Town, South Africa.

Jeroen Candel is an Associate Professor of Public Administration and Policy at Wageningen University, the Netherlands.

Koen Deconinck is an Economist at the Organization for Economic Co-operation and Development (OECD) in Paris, France.

Nel de Mûelenaere is an Assistant Professor of History at Social and Cultural Food Studies (FOST) at the Vrije Universiteit Brussel, Belgium.

Jessica Fanzo is the Professor of Climate and Food, the Director of the Food for Humanity Initiative, and the Director of the International Research Institute for Climate and Society at Columbia University's Climate School, New York, USA.

Lukas Paul Fesenfeld is an environmental governance and political economy researcher at the Oeschger Centre for Climate Change Research and Policy Analysis and Environmental Governance group at the University of Bern, as well as a lecturer at ETH Zurich, Switzerland.

Eduardo J. Gómez is a Professor and Director of the Institute for Health Policy and Politics at Lehigh University, Pennsylvania, USA.

Jody Harris is senior food systems researcher at the World Vegetable Center in Thailand, and an Associate Research Fellow at the Institute of Development Studies in the UK.

Gareth Haysom is a Researcher at the African Centre for Cities at the University of Cape Town, South Africa.

Will Martin is a Senior Research Fellow in the Markets, Trade, and Institutions Division of the International Food Policy Research Institute (IFPRI), Washington, DC, USA.

Alan Matthews is Professor Emeritus of European Agricultural Policy in the Department of Economics at Trinity College, Dublin, Ireland.

Jonathan Mockshell is a Research Scientist–Agricultural Economist at the International Center for Tropical Agriculture (CIAT), Cali, Colombia.

Stella Nordhagen is a Senior Technical Specialist at the Global Alliance for Improved Nutrition (GAIN), Geneva, Switzerland.

Robert Paarlberg is an Emeritus Professor of Political Science at Wellesley College, an Associate in the Sustainability Science Program at the Harvard Kennedy School, and an Associate at Harvard's Weatherhead Center, USA.

Danielle Resnick is a David Rubenstein Fellow at the Brookings Institution in the Global Economy and Development Program and a Non-Resident Fellow with the International Food Policy Research Institute (IFPRI), Washington, DC, USA.

Thea Nielsen Ritter is an Agricultural Economist Consultant at the International Center for Tropical Agriculture (CIAT), Cali, Colombia.

Pauline Scheelbeek is an Associate Professor in Nutritional and Environmental Epidemiology at the London School of Hygiene and Tropical Medicine, UK.

Anna Strutt is a Professor of Economics at the University of Waikato, New Zealand.

Yixian Sun is an Assistant Professor in International Development at the University of Bath, UK.

Johan Swinnen is Director General of the International Food Policy Research Institute (IFPRI), and Global Director of the Systems Transformation Science Group at CGIAR, Washington, DC, USA.

Rob Vos is the Director of the Markets, Trade, and Institutions Division (MTID) at the International Food Policy Research Institute (IFPRI), Washington, DC, USA.

1

Introduction

Political Economy of Food System Transformation

Danielle Resnick and Johan Swinnen

1.1 Introduction

In August 2022, the *Razoni* cargo ship, laden with 26,000 tons of grain, navigated a narrow corridor of mined waters outside Ukraine's port of Odessa. After Russia's February 2022 invasion of Ukraine exacerbated rising food prices, threatening to plunge millions into hunger, the *Razoni* was the first ship allowed out of Ukraine under the UN-brokered Black Sea Grain Initiative. The ship's journey symbolized the world's dependence on grain from the Black Sea—which supplies 30 percent of the world's wheat exports and constitutes the source of 12 percent of globally traded calories (Glauber and Laborde 2022)—and revealed the vulnerability of countries to dependence on concentrated supply sources (IPES 2022). Moreover, it underscored that food security and food systems are rarely the byproduct of agriculture policy alone but often intertwined with a broad set of political objectives. The impacts of the Ukraine war reverberated far and wide in 2022, amplifying weaknesses in many countries' agricultural and food strategies and generating citizen demands for government accountability. From massive food protests in Tunisia that threatened the country's fragile democracy to the siege of Ecuadorean cities by indigenous groups demanding more affordable food, global unrest reminded the world of the centrality of political economy to food systems at the international, national, and local levels.

Of course, food security and political economy have been closely linked since the early days of history (Swinnen 2018). In many places and times, food shortages triggered political unrest and revolts, from the French Revolution in the late 18th century to the Arab Spring in the early 21st century. Conversely, providing sufficient "bread for the masses" has conferred legitimacy and support for many political rulers and regimes over the centuries. For instance, the dramatic gains in agricultural productivity at the start of the reforms in China increased rice supplies and food security in rural and urban areas and provided popular support for the broader reforms that transformed China into a global powerhouse (Rozelle and Swinnen 2004). Yet, while there have been many studies on the

Danielle Resnick and Johan Swinnen, *Introduction*. In: *The Political Economy of Food System Transformation*. Edited by: Danielle Resnick and Johan Swinnen, Oxford University Press. © Danielle Resnick and Johan Swinnen (2023). DOI: 10.1093/oso/9780198882121.003.0001

political economy of food prices and subsidies and how they relate to hunger, malnutrition, and global food production and consumption, addressing today's food challenges necessitates a broader perspective that accounts for both the growing diversity of actors within the food system and an expansive set of policy objectives beyond just providing sufficient calories.

Consequently, this edited volume delves into the extensive range of political economy factors that affect food system transformation and identifies pathways toward enhancing the political feasibility of necessary policy interventions. The term *food system* refers to the complex web of actors and processes involved in growing, processing, distributing, consuming, and disposing of agricultural commodities, including food but also traditional export crops such as cotton, tea, and coffee. Today, only a minor part of consumer spending on food goes to farmers; the average share is less than 10 percent in rich countries and around 30 percent in many lower- and middle-income countries (Barrett et al. 2022). While agriculture's contribution in terms of employment is larger, it is crucial to integrate the rest of value chain actors and food system participants more broadly into our analyses. A systems lens provides a holistic perspective on these actors, including their interlinkages with one other and with a wider set of development objectives (Eriksen et al. 2010; von Braun et al. 2021).

The focus on *transformation* reflects a growing consensus that current food system objectives must fundamentally expand to improve human and planetary health and resilience (Caron et al. 2018; GLOPAN 2020; Benton et al. 2021; Fanzo 2021; Yates et al. 2021). The rise of non-communicable diseases (NCDs) and obesity combined with stubborn micronutrient deficiencies reflects dietary patterns dominated by ultra-processed foods (Pagliai et al. 2021). Intensive use of fertilizer, pesticides, and herbicides to increase crop output can undermine groundwater quality and create toxic risks to farming communities (El-Nahhal and El-Nahhal 2021; Martínez-Dalmau et al. 2021; Haggblade et al. 2022). Land use expansion often affects biodiversity habitats and greenhouse gas emissions (GHGs), worsening the effects of climate change (Lade et al. 2020). These challenges co-exist with a range of other development imperatives, including creating decent jobs for the millions of un- or underemployed, mitigating gender inequalities, and tackling the economic and socio-political marginalization of certain communities. Consequently, there have been a growing number of high-level initiatives to advance food system transformation, including the 2021 UN Food Systems Summit during which 147 countries committed to ensuring their food systems collectively achieve the Sustainable Development Goals (SDGs) by 2030.

Catalyzing food systems transformation entails, at a minimum, policies that improve one objective (e.g., health, incomes, environment) without worsening others, and, at best, advancing progress on multiple objectives simultaneously. Doing so, however, requires anticipating the distribution of winners and losers from certain policy interventions and how those groups might propel or derail implementation. Such considerations long have been a central focus of extant scholarship on the political economy of agriculture and food policy (Birner and Resnick 2010; Anderson et al. 2013; Pinstrup-Andersen 2015; Swinnen 2018). This volume builds on these insights by applying them to food systems while also extending them to incorporate more interdisciplinary perspectives and diverse methodologies. The applications of political economy analysis in this book encompass input subsidies, genetically modified organisms (GMOs), trade, meat consumption, sugar-sweetened beverage taxes, and ecosystem services, among others. The book's global range of country case studies further allows for probing how political economy factors vary across disparate levels of economic development and political systems.

1.2 The Complexities Underlying Food System Transformation

The need for a political economy lens for the contemporary food system transformation agenda derives from several factors. First, the dynamic, complex, and comprehensive nature of the agenda necessitates concordance and coordination among multiple objectives and actors. Second, due to growing issue linkage, the boundaries of food system decisions are fuzzy, touching on non-traditional areas such as human rights and justice. Third, the influencers on decision making processes are simultaneously more expansive and more polarized due to a growing dependence on social media for information, increased density and discord within transnational advocacy networks, and populist impulses that denigrate evidence-based policymaking. Finally, the norms and institutions of multilateralism have become increasingly stressed in recent years, undermining coordinated efforts to address food system issues that transcend borders and leading instead to a variety of multi-stakeholder initiatives that may lack accountability mechanisms. Each of these issues are discussed in more detail below.

1.2.1 Dynamic and Multi-faceted Nature of Food System Transformation

Food systems are rarely static, but the pace of change for food systems has accelerated in recent decades, with several "revolutions" in livestock, aquaculture, and food retail (Garlock et al. 2020; Reardon et al. 2003; Reardon 2015; Béné 2022). In low- and middle-income countries, agri-food value chains have undergone notable changes, including more expansive food safety standards, greater vertical integration between large processors, supermarkets, and restaurant chains, and more diversity of the food services sector (Barrett et al. 2022). Disruptive technologies have resulted in the emergence of plant-based protein alternatives to meat, improved food traceability systems, and more targeted use of agriculture inputs (Rowan 2021). In some regions, the Covid-19 pandemic spurred adaptations by food industries that may ensure food systems are more resilient to future shocks (Reardon et al. 2021).

This dynamism in agriculture value chains and food industries holds tremendous opportunities but also engenders a more complex set of political economy considerations. For instance, while traditional political economy dichotomies that contrasted producer interests against those of consumers were always too simplistic, this has become truer in recent decades due to the growth of chemical, finance, insurance, and standards companies in the food industry, among others (Anderson et al. 2013; Swinnen 2015). This has resulted in a more varied set of interest groups, leading to unexpected alliances among actors in some cases and often requiring a broader range of veto players whose concordance is needed to generate policy change. Complicating this landscape is that political parties and politicians are sometimes among these veto players, especially if they are directly involved in agriculture and food industries through, for instance, direct company ownership or seats on company boards (Behuria 2020; Whitfield et al. 2015). For instance, in Maharashtra, India, a majority of private sugar mills historically have been owned by "sugar barons" who are also members of the Congress Party, ensuring that the industry has retained political support despite the negative health and environmental concerns of sugar consumption and production (Lee et al. 2020; Sukhtankar 2012).

Moreover, since food system transformation increasingly is expected to address a wide range of development objectives, it explicitly involves multi-sectoral policy interventions, spanning agriculture, health, environment, trade, finance, and social protection. Coherence across such a broad swath of policy domains not only is challenging but also leads to trade-offs in policy prioritization (Sachs 2015). The sugar sector again offers a case in point. In South Africa, the sector directly and indirectly contributes to the livelihoods of almost half a million people, including many women in deep rural areas (South Africa, Department of Trade, Industry, and Competition 2020). Nonetheless, it is highly water-intensive and contributes to the country's rising obesity levels (Hess et al. 2016; Myers et al. 2017). In 2018, the government through the Ministry of Health adopted a Health Promotion Levy, which prompted food and beverage processors to switch to sugar alternatives. Subsequent declines in sugar production, however, prompted the Department of Trade and Industry to launch the Sugar Industry Value Chain Masterplan, which aims to increase domestic sugar production and retain jobs for small-scale growers through tariff protection (Sikuka 2021; Gabela 2022). In other words, different ministerial and development goals can be difficult to reconcile, and moving toward healthier food systems can sometimes threaten industrial competitiveness and employment prospects for poor populations.

The spread of decentralization initiatives over the last two decades (Rodden and Wibbels 2019) requires policy coherence across scale as well. Local governments increasingly have both greater political autonomy from national authorities and more responsibility for agriculture and health functions (World Bank 2014; Kyle and Resnick 2019; Resnick 2022a). Efforts such as the C40 initiative and the Milan Urban Food Policy Pact have given greater visibility to cities, many of which are forging their own food and environmental goals through deliberative platforms (e.g., food policy councils) that bring together local governments, the private sector, and civil society (Moragues-Faus and Morgan 2015; Cohen 2022). Yet, while such initiatives are important for addressing issues related to food environments and urban agriculture, they are less able to address cross-jurisdictional issues in the food system, such as water consumption, soil depletion, and pesticide and fertilizer use (Cohen 2022).

1.2.2 Issue Linkage and Transnational Advocacy Networks

While agri-food systems are most centrally concerned with improving livelihoods and nutrition, they have become entangled with a broader range of societal goals due to the expansion of transnational advocacy networks and issue linkage. Issue linkage refers to the inter-dependencies among policy domains that might not be immediately apparent. Transnational advocacy networks transcend national boundaries and rely on frames—strategic modes of conveying ideas and norms—to mobilize seemingly disparate groups of people, experts, and organizations for a common purpose (Keck and Sikkink 1999). Some of these advocates on environmental or labor issues have gained greater lobbying power than traditional agricultural interest groups, upending historical forms of policy negotiation and consensus.

Several frames related to food systems have gained resonance among advocacy networks. One is corporate social responsibility (CSR), which focuses on the need for companies to base their value on not only financial considerations but also ecological and social dimensions (Bair and Palpacuer 2015). As part of the rapid expansion of food standards in recent decades by private companies and public regulators to ensure food safety and quality (Swinnen 2015), CSR led to a range of standard certifications to ensure food is produced ethically and to serve as a form of market differentiation to attract consumers (Utting 2015). These standards may exacerbate inequality among smaller and poorer smallholders unable to meet standard requirements, but they can also serve as a mechanism to upgrade poor farmers into higher value chains (Maertens and Swinnen 2009; Swinnen 2018; Hidayati et al. 2021; Barrett et al. 2022). Maier (2021) notes, however, that because CSR depends on an environment of open deliberation that allows for public concerns around issues such as labor conditions or environmental pollution, they have been constrained among businesses operating in authoritarian contexts.

Moreover, as industrial governance in agriculture value chains becomes more complex, so too does the governance of global norms around CSR.

Another frame that motivates transnational advocacy revolves around the "right to food." Development, humanitarian, and nutrition organizations have clustered together in recent decades to elevate access to food as a human right. The 1948 Universal Declaration of Human Rights provided the basis for the 1976 International Covenant on Economic, Social, and Cultural Rights (ICESCR), which underscores the right of everyone to be free from hunger. Transnational advocates drew on the ICESCR to legitimate mobilization toward including "right to food" provisions in country constitutions, which more than 30 countries currently have (FAO 2019). However, Jurkovich (2020) examines the imperfect nature of the frame: the right to food varies from traditional human rights norms because the latter largely depends on holding governments accountable while the range of actors involved in the food system—and the structure of international law—complicates enforcement of right to food provisions.

The rights frame has been leveraged by the food sovereignty movement, which emerged through the advocacy of the Via Campesina movement during the 1996 World Food Summit. Sovereignty has been invoked by nation-states for centuries as a justification for protecting national industry from international trade and competition through subsidies, tariffs, and non-tariff barriers and remains one of the top defenses countries use when they oppose a World Trade Organization (WTO) ruling (Sutherland et al. 2004). The food sovereignty movement largely has similar objectives—protecting local production and livelihoods and often critiquing the WTO—but its rationale and organization are qualitatively different from historical antecedents in several ways. First, the movement's advocacy does not center on promoting national sovereignty but often on empowering local communities to define their own food policies and practices as a democratic right (Patel 2009). Second, the movement transcends the boundaries of the nation-state and has allies beyond the farm, including urban-based civil society. Third, the movement goes beyond trade to critique certain scientific advancements, such as biotechnology and large-scale food fortification, as solidifying control of food and agribusiness corporations over smallholders (Nestle 2013; Rock 2022). Although it is not always clear what specific types of policies members of the movement would support (Burnett and Murphy 2014), the movement has expanded citizen engagement in the food system, particularly in the Global South, and has elevated introspection about the potential impacts on the poor of corporate power in the food system.

Overall, the growth and inclusion of civil society actors and transnational advocacy networks fosters richer policy dialogues, expands the food systems agenda, and augments the importance of accountability for policy choices. However, the motivations of such stakeholders are often nuanced and complex. While they may be primarily interested in promoting a broad range of societal goals, advocacy organizations—like private industry and the public sector—typically rely on mobilizing financial resources to be effective and visible, which can often shape the choice of issues and framings that they target (Arvidson et al. 2018; Resnick et al. 2022).

1.2.3 Populism, Disinformation, and the Threat to Evidence-Based Policymaking

The landscape for engaging on food system policy issues is further mediated by the global wave of populism that began to surge in the 2010s (Moffitt 2016; Plattner 2019; Bauer et al. 2021). The roots of the current populist wave are tied to both demographic transitions and partisan de-alignment whereby traditional class, ethnic, racial, and geographic divides can no longer be easily mapped along a left-right ideological spectrum (Goodwin 2018; Goldberg 2020; Garzia et al. 2022). Grievances with, and declining trust in, traditional parties facilitated the rise of personalistic leaders reliant on Manichean "us" versus "other" worldviews, promising to restore the welfare of the masses and to counter the power of a "corrupt elite." The extremist views pushed by populists, and the growth in social media and non-traditional news networks, have worsened political polarization (Carothers and O'Donohue 2019; Persily and Tucker 2020; Kubin and von Sikorski 2021). In turn, this has created more opportunities for disinformation and bias in the policymaking sphere, reducing the impact of evidence-based analysis on decisions.

The impacts of such dynamics are readily apparent for the food system. Partisan de-alignment means that historical alliances between established parties and particular interest groups, such as farmers, have become weaker in some countries. On the one hand, dislocation, neglect, and decline have affected rural livelihoods and identities in many developed countries, increasing the appeal of populism and alternative movements (Scoones et al. 2018). On the other hand, dissatisfaction with mainstream parties has also favored increased support for green parties, who are now in governing coalitions or national legislatures in at least 24 countries (Bennhold 2019; McBride 2022). Where both these trends have occurred, polarization between environmental goals and farmer interests can be particularly intense.

For instance, in many European countries, the traditional links between farmers, their associations and Christian parties have eroded over time, creating the space for new modes of representation. An example is from the Netherlands where the Farmers Defense Force (FDF) emerged as a new political force in 2019, encompassing agribusiness groups, large entrepreneurial farmers, farm workers, and small-scale family producers. The political movement is guided by a populist discourse that portrays its members as a marginalized underclass due to the rising prominence of food consumer groups, environmentalists, and animal welfare activists (van der Ploeg 2020). The group relies on large-scale protests and theatrical antics, such as bringing cows to parliament, and questions the government's nitrogen emissions estimates. The farmers have received support from the newly created Farmer-Citizens Movement (Boer Burger Beweging, BBB) party as well as right-wing groups, such as the Forum for Democracy, which declares "there is no climate crisis" (Moses 2022). The FDF helped spur highly disruptive road blockades after the Dutch government announced plans in June 2022 to reduce nitrogen emissions by 50 percent by 2030, and the BBB shocked the political establishment by winning several legislative seats in the Netherlands' 2023 provincial elections.

Opportunities for disinformation and bias are particularly pronounced for issues such as climate change, red and processed meat consumption, GMOs, and genome editing—issues that are especially tied to political ideology and partisanship (Huber 2020). Despite the scientific community highlighting the negative health and environmental impacts of producing and consuming red and processed meat, this message has been filtered through an ideological prism. An analysis of media reports in the US, UK, Australia, and New Zealand revealed that public views on red and processed meat consumption are polarized between "meat lovers" and vegans, with the former viewing the latter as imposing their worldviews and lifestyles on others (Sievert et al. 2022a, 2022b). Michielsen and van der Horst's (2022) analysis of Dutch social media on the same topic revealed that those with right-wing affiliations viewed the anti-meat/alternative protein movement through a populist lens, i.e., driven by a detached and unrepresentative elite that contradicts the preferences of the masses. Similar caricatures have also been leveled at both pro- and anti-supporters of GMOs, particularly in Europe. With the growing sophistication of artificial intelligence capabilities, further possibilities for disinformation on controversial food issues are likely to be on the horizon (Hsu and Thompson 2023).

Data and policy interventions to promote greater nutrition are likewise affected by populist impulses to dismiss evidence and promote misinformation. Soon after his 2019 inauguration, Jair Bolsonaro—Brazil's former right-wing populist president—abolished the National Food and Nutrition Security Council (CONSEA), which was established in 2003 to monitor the country's food security, nutrition labeling, and genetically modified (GMO) foods and had facilitated the inclusion in 2010 of the right to food in Brazil's federal constitution. Bolsonaro claimed the body was no longer useful and dismissed as "lies" data from the UN's Food and Agriculture Organization showing that more than five million Brazilians were undernourished (AFP 2019; FIAN 2019). In Australia, an analysis of Twitter accounts of prominent ultra-processed food industry actors revealed that similar discursive tactics have been used by industry to dismiss public health concerns or policy proposals, such as sugar-sweetened beverage (SSB) taxes. These include referring to health experts as "elites" and supporters of a "nanny state," labeling food taxes as "discriminatory" for the poor, and heralding their credentials as job creators for local communities (Hunt 2021). Public relations companies can fuel these divides by flooding the policy landscape with alternative facts via well-placed opinion pieces, sponsored events, and newsletters (Aronczyk and Espinoza 2021).

Partisanship even affects consumers' food choices. Consumer boycotts have long been a way to signify discontent with industry stances while buycotts reward companies for certain behaviors and practices (Copeland 2014). Recent research though highlights the rise in corporate political engagement whereby food industry leaders explicitly take partisan stances that generate consumer preference polarization (Schoenmuller et al. 2022). For instance, Liaukonyte et al. (2022) find that after the CEO of Goya beans expressed support for former President Trump, the company experienced a sales boost in heavily Republican counties in the US.

1.2.4 From Multilateralism to Multi-stakeholderism

The multilateral world order that emerged after World War II was largely based on the norm of liberal internationalism supported by pillars such as trade openness, commitment to rules-based relations, security cooperation, multilateral institutions, and democratic solidarity. However, the retreat of liberal democracy and the rise of populism and nationalism in the US and elsewhere, as well as the growing weight of middle powers (Brazil, India, South Africa, Turkey) excluded from major decision-making, has led many scholars to raise alarm bells about the continuation of this order (Ikenberry 2018; Wright 2021). Sluggish, disconnected, and nationalistic responses to the Covid-19 pandemic and vaccine distribution, stalled multinational peace operations in the Sahel and East Africa, and an inability of international organizations to navigate new challenges, like cybertechnology and artificial intelligence, contribute to questions about the relevance and legitimacy of extant multilateralism (Dworkin and Gowan 2019).

Multilateral institutions, including the United Nations and its food agencies (FAO, IFAD, and WFP), the World Bank, and the World Trade Organization (WTO) have been central in inter-governmental negotiations over agricultural policy issues that have interjurisdictional implications (e.g., subsidies, tariffs, climate). Moreover, several multilateral initiatives are at the heart of food systems commitments, including the Paris Climate Change Agreements and the UN's Sustainable Development Goals (Lele 2021). However, multilateral engagement has been under strain for some time, most notably with the collapse of the 2005 Doha Round trade negotiations of the WTO over agricultural issues. A more polycentric institutional setting now exists for intergovernmental decisions around food. The forum of the BRICS countries (Brazil, Russia, India, China, and South Africa) in 2010 resulted in the club's own declaration on agriculture and agrarian development (McKeon 2015) while the G20 has also made food security issues a central part of their agenda (Clapp and Murphy 2013). These new sets of actors and forums complicate the prospects of negotiating agreements among countries.

In addition, multilateralism increasingly has been replaced by multi-stakeholderism. The latter relies on individuals representing different "stakeholder" groups, including academia, business, civil society, and government, to arrive at a consensus on relevant issues. As such, its decisions are not necessarily dependent on actions by inter-governmental organizations (Gleckman 2018). Such multi-stakeholderism has become predominant in many spheres, including food systems. Take, for instance, the 2021 Food Systems Summit. Historically, UN food summits, such as in 1996, 2002, and 2009, were multilateral events and nation-states were the featured participants, though they coincided with parallel civil society events (McKeon 2015). The 2021 Summit adopted an explicit multi-stakeholder organization that revolved around national stakeholder dialogues that incorporated views from public, private, and civil society sectors.[1] While this modality increased inclusion and participation to some extent, one of the criticisms of the Summit is that the substantive policy outcomes tied to such broad participation were unclear (Canfield et al. 2021). Indeed, one of the downsides of multi-stakeholderism is that diverse stakeholders are integrated on an ostensibly even playing field despite sizeable power asymmetries that may exist among them. As Gleckman (2018) notes, these asymmetries are different than those between developed and developing nation-states because stakeholders' source of power may be in different domains (e.g., financial, moral, human capital, legitimacy) and also hierarchically ordered (e.g., international NGOs and corporations have more power than local ones); this leads to internal tensions over issues, framing, and actions. Moreover, because participants in multi-stakeholder platforms are not required to report to, or receive direction from, the intergovernmental community of nation-states, they often lack clear and binding rules over rights, obligations, and accountability for decisions (Manahan and Kumar 2021). Consequently, trade-offs between inclusion of diverse voices and implementation of complex reforms can become even more intense.

1.3 Political Economy Drivers of Policy Choices

These debates within the food system, as well as shifting political and institutional dynamics beyond the food system, provide the backdrop to this current volume. Indeed, the book recognizes that food system transformation is not simply the by-product of improved technology and innovation but rather requires also grappling

---

[1] The UNFSS website notes that 1,676 dialogues were announced with more than 100,000 participants.

with the above, underlying political context. Different political economy traditions and methods are interwoven to uncover various dimensions of food system transformation from global, regional, national, and local case perspectives spanning high-, medium-, and low-income economies. Collectively, the contributions to the book reveal that transforming agri-food systems requires a comprehensive analysis of four, interconnected "spaces" that shape the prospects for policy reform over time, geography, or sector: incentives, mobilization, design, and adaptation. The term "space" connotes both a domain of focus and the degree of maneuver with respect to a particular policy issue (Jackson 2021). Figure 1.1 illustrates these spaces and their relationships with each other.

1.3.1 Incentives Space

The incentives for reform in any policy sphere require considering the costs and benefits of potential policy reforms, different actors' interests, ideas, and values, as well as the structure of institutions in a given context. The distribution of costs and benefits typically reflects the nature of the policy instrument under consideration to advance reforms. Different instruments have disparate impacts on who is affected, for how long, and to what degree (Swinnen 2018). They also though have different degrees of public salience, meaning that some policies, such as income taxes, capture the attention of the public more than others, such as corporate

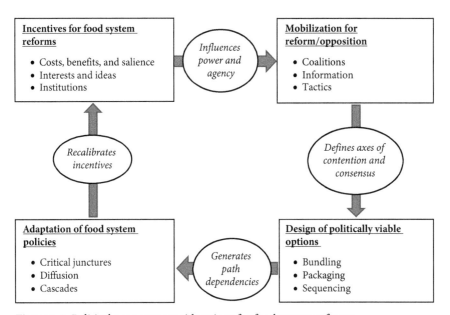

Figure 1.1 Political economy considerations for food system reforms.

governance regulations, because the implications are more readily understandable and more directly felt (Culpepper 2010).

Whether different groups identify a policy issue as salient to them and whether they perceive costs as acceptable or unjustified often depends on their interests, ideas, and values. Vested interests, whether by political elites, private enterprises, or voters, are at the heart of political economy and influenced seminal works on food and agriculture, such as Bates (1981). Interests typically derive from one's place in the political and economic sphere. For example, if profit maximization is the main interest of private sector entities, then they will lobby for policies that support those goals, such as tariff protection (Grossman and Helpman 1994) or against ones that threaten them, such as removing production subsidies. If politicians' main interest is staying in office and winning votes, then they will prioritize policies that maximize that likelihood regardless of potential negative externalities. For instance, despite potential negative environmental impacts and middling efficacy, fertilizer input subsidies have sometimes been driven by politicians' interests to retain support of sizeable voting constituencies (Dionne and Horowitz 2016; Mason et al. 2017).

In addition to interests, which primarily capture how policies may affect these materialist concerns, political economists have long recognized the importance of ideas as drivers or barriers to policy change (Hayek 1949). Ideas affect perceptions of viable and unacceptable policy orientations involving, for instance, the role of the state versus the market, nationalism versus globalism, and nature versus technology. They often derive from inter-subjective understandings of the world based on historical experience, cultural traditions, views of one's identity, and even familial upbringing (Blyth 1997; Abdelal 2009). Such ideas, for instance, can shape consumer willingness to pay taxes on certain foods or to accept GMO or fortified foods as well as influence national governments' decisions about agricultural trade policies (see Schonhardt-Bailey 2006).

Institutions condition expectations about outcomes, thereby influencing interests, ideas, and values, as well as shaping which voices prevail in the policy arena. Organizational institutions, such as business lobbies or farmers' associations, can enhance lobbying efforts. Political institutions, such as electoral rules, constitutions, or regulations, delineate the range of veto players who need to be on board with a policy in order for change to occur (Tsebelis 2002; Olper and Raimondi 2010). Media institutions, including mass media and social media corporations, structure the types of interests and ideas that are communicated to the public, often with a bias toward negative news and "echo chamber" effects that tend to exacerbate fears about food science innovations (McCluskey et al. 2016) and sometimes worsen political polarization (Bail 2021). Global and regional institutions, such as the WTO, Codex, European Union (EU), NAFTA, and others can bind countries' trade, investment, and fiscal policy decisions. The binding effects of institutions has led to a growing debate about whether an Intergovernmental Panel for Food, similar to that for climate change, is needed to keep governments accountable for their food system commitments (von Braun and Birner 2017; Clapp et al. 2021). Outside of crisis periods, institutions are difficult to reform and typically only change incrementally through institutional layering, which involves grafting new elements onto an extant institutional framework (Mahoney and Thelen 2010).

Collectively, these components of the incentives space can influence the degree of power of different policy stakeholders. Power conveys both a relational dynamic whereby one actor causes another to do something (i.e., power *over*), and an aspirational dynamic whereby one actor has the agency to bring about a particular outcome (i.e., power *to*) (Dowding 1996). The role of relational power in the food system has received increased attention in recent years (Leach et al. 2020; Baker et al. 2021). Such power can be encapsulated by the degree of economic concentration in certain parts of an agricultural value chain, which shapes different value chain actors' access to inputs and distribution of profits. For instance, several studies focus particularly on growing corporate power in the global agri-food system due to numerous business mergers in recent years (Clapp 2021, 2022; Clapp and Fuchs 2009; McKeon 2015), affecting everything from fertilizers and seeds to animal pharmaceuticals to food and beverage industries (IPES 2017). As noted earlier, there are other sources of power among stakeholders, such as ideational power exerted by epistemic communities in the donor, academic, and development communities (Haas 1992). Power can also manifest via decision-making structures within the public administration, such as when certain ministries have more clout and resources than others, and within a country's political settlement when particular elites within political parties exert more influence. At the same time, incentive structures can facilitate certain interest groups' aspirational power, contributing to their agency to mobilize either in favor of food system reforms or in defense of the status quo.

1.3.2 Mobilizational Space

The mobilizational space captures how stakeholders converge and lobby to either achieve their policy goals within the agri-food system or prevent others from doing so. Coalitions are at the heart of many agriculture and food policy reforms. As noted earlier, the range of coalitions related to agri-food system issues is increasingly complex, related to greater diversity of actors along global value chains and the expansion of transnational networks on health and nutrition, labor rights, and environmental justice. Some of these coalitions are complementarity in their interests, such as European farmers concerned about unfair trading practices by processors and retailers (Swinnen et al. 2021). Others may share similar values—such as improved nutrition or market reforms—but disagree over which policy instruments are needed to achieve these outcomes.

Information is a powerful tool for coalitions to advance their positions and, as noted earlier, can be conveyed through mass media and social media tools, as well as dissemination of empirical analyses. Indeed, there has been a flurry of support around evidence-based policymaking over the last decade (Cairney 2017). Improving access to information and awareness of different coalitions' concerns could reveal opportunities for policy alignment. Yet, as noted earlier, sometimes facts and evidence, even from rigorously designed research studies, are accepted or rejected based on how well they resonate with one's values and experiences as well as even one's partisan views (MacKillop and Downe 2022). Moreover, some people may avoid accessing information if they feel overwhelmed with conflicting messages or have strong ideological biases.

Coalitions often use multiple tactics to convey information and their policy positions. These include strategic framing of issue areas that re-formulate the policy problem or policy solution (Chong and Druckman 2007) and downplaying certain facts while highlighting others. To achieve this, some actively work with professional public relations firms (Aronczyk 2022). For instance, in Nigeria, the 2021 Finance Act include a sugar-sweetened beverage tax that reflected a coalition of national civil society groups supporting public health and working with Gatefield public relations and media group to frame their message accordingly.[2] Aggressive media campaigns for and against sugar taxes, well-organized protests against market procurement reforms, and annual flagship reports against food pesticides are just some of the tactics described by authors in this book. In other cases, coalitions rely on "quiet politics" behind closed doors to negotiate concessions from governments (Culpepper 2010; Gaventa 2006).

1.3.3 Design Space

The ways in which different groups form coalitions, employ different types of information, and engage in other strategic tactics collectively define the axes of contention and consensus vis-à-vis the relevant policy issue and informs which policy designs might be most politically viable. The design space elaborated on in this book focuses on three design features: bundling, packaging, and sequencing. Bundling involves concurrently combining several socio-technical innovations in recognition that no single intervention will be sufficient to tackle today's agri-food system challenges. At the same time, this approach has a political rationale since potential opponents to a one-off reform may be otherwise appeased with concessions embedded within a broader policy bundle. Indeed,

---

[2] See   https://advocacyincubator.org/2022/01/19/nigerian-advocates-celebrate-sugar-sweetened-beverage-tax-signed-into-law/.

just like a crowded legislative bill, a policy intervention with multiple, intersecting dimensions becomes more difficult for interest groups to assess how they may be materially disadvantaged by the interventions and therefore more difficult to oppose.

Although a similar concept, policy packaging is more narrowly focused on one particular policy problem, such as reducing meat consumption or increased use of conservation farming techniques. The packaging approach relies on identifying the combination of taxes, regulation, subsidies, and information campaigns that the public would be most willing to accept to tackle that policy problem. There will be variations in acceptable policy packaging across countries due to differing cultural values, policy framing, and trust in government capacity.

Policy sequencing refers to the order in which policies are implemented and the time required to achieve impact. Because mandates for different segments of the agri-food system typically fall under different government entities, policies rarely can be implemented simultaneously. Moreover, some policies are administratively easier to implement than others and are therefore prioritized. Research on policy feedback loops and path dependency reveals that poor execution of certain policy bundles or packages can increase public resistance to subsequent portions of such interventions (Bruch et al. 2010; Lerman and McCabe 2017). If public backlash and (mis)information can gain a foothold, then pro-reform coalitions may lose momentum or fragment.

Precisely because bundling, packaging, and sequencing involve combining multiple instruments in a particular way and/or building pro-reform constituencies from several different groups, they can become hard to unravel. Over time, these configurations of policies or coalitions can become path dependent and difficult to upend, even in the face of new policy challenges and interest groups. Yet, as noted earlier, food systems historically have been dynamic, demonstrating that they can adapt under the right conditions.

1.3.4 Adaptive Space

The adaptive space enables policies to shift as a result of new dynamics across geographies and time. Historically, slower moving changes, such as urbanization, economic industrialization, and technological innovation have reconfigured major agricultural policy decisions by shifting land ownership patterns and the weight of different interest groups (e.g., Schonhardt-Bailey 2006; Swinnen 2011; Samuels and Thomson 2021). In this volume, we focus on other drivers of policy adaptation, focusing on critical junctures, diffusion, and cascades, all of which ultimately reconfigure the original incentive structures. Critical junctures are turning points that may be generated by a shock, such as an economic, environmental, political, or health crisis (Collier and Collier 1991). For instance, food safety crises have precipitated improved food quality regulation in many countries (Swinnen 2017) while the impacts of COVID-19 and the Ukraine war necessitated shifts in many countries' agricultural and food policies. Critical junctures can also be less dramatic and involve the opening of a window of opportunity due to, for example, a shift in a political administration (Kingdon 1995). Indeed, the emergence of green parties, especially in Europe, has created a window of opportunity to press forward with food system reforms intended to promote biodiversity (OECD 2017).

Policy diffusion refers to the transfer and adoption of policy ideas and options through epistemic communities and transnational advocacy networks and through bureaucrats and industrial leaders seeking lessons about what policy tools have been used in similar settings or for similar issues (Weyland 2005; Berry and Berry 2007; Graham et al. 2013). The growing shift to promoting dietary diversity rather than solely caloric intake, the emergence of models for ecosystem payment services, food fortification, and the spread of sugar-sweetened beverage taxes are just a few examples of policy diffusion across borders. Similarly, despite some of their weaknesses, multi-stakeholder platforms and food policy councils continue to gain greater salience across countries to address food system challenges, especially at the local level (Resnick 2022b).

Another form of policy diffusion includes accountability mechanisms such as citizen scorecards, peer review mechanisms, and corporate transparency metrics (see Lewis 2015; Kelley 2017). Past and current efforts in the arena of food and nutrition security include Hunger and Nutrition Commitment Indices, the Enabling the Business of Agriculture Index, and the Africa Agriculture Transformation Scorecards. The intention of such efforts is to publicize or shame government or companies for good or bad performance, therefore acting as an incentive to improve. As such, these accountability initiatives assume that governments or industries care about their reputations and will be compelled to change their behaviors.

Policy cascades occur when information and knowledge is successively passed on, gaining momentum along the way. Like water, cascades gain their potency from some commanding heights (Braithwaite and D'Costa 2018), whether a strong political executive or agency or supranational body. The African Union's Comprehensive Africa Agriculture Development Program (CAADP) initiative on agricultural spending, the EU's Farm to Fork Strategy, or the hundreds of national food system policy dialogues set up via the UN Food Systems Summit (UNFSS) are all forms of policy cascades whereby decisions made at a higher level are anticipated to percolate downward. The efficacy of such cascades can depend on congruence with nation-states' legal systems, regulatory structures, and financial resources.

1.4 Summary of the Book

One or more of the above elements from Figure 1.1 permeates each of the chapters of this volume, which are organized into four parts. Part I examines in greater depth the various components of the incentives space. Chapter 2 by Koen Deconinck nicely sets the scene on this topic by differentiating between facts, interests, and values, noting that the latter is the most intractable for reform efforts. Disagreements over facts can be rectified potentially with more evidence or better communication, and contention over interests can be fixed through bargaining. Yet, disagreements over values can reflect more fundamental differences in cultural background, psychology, and even views on morality. As Deconinck emphasizes, some people attach more value to natural foods, others place a premium on supporting family farms, while still others may find government intervention in food decisions problematic. He offers several ways of dealing with differences over values in the food system, including drawing on deliberative processes whereby citizens with disparate values use various fora, such as citizens' assemblies with skilled facilitators, to discuss their policy preferences and where those preferences originate.

Interests, institutions, and ideas are common dimensions in both Chapters 3 and 4. In Chapter 3, Rob Vos, Will Martin, and Danielle Resnick examine the challenge of repurposing agricultural support policies, especially subsidies. Currently, governments provide over US$800 billion annually in transfers to agriculture, but there are concerns about how such transfers accelerate greenhouse gas (GHG) emissions from agriculture, exacerbate inequalities among farmers and across countries, and undermine dietary diversity. Repurposing such support was strongly emphasized during the 2021 UNFSS, and global modeling scenarios suggest that repurposing subsidies toward agricultural research and development as well as rural infrastructure would improve productivity and diminish GHG emissions. However, the political economy of agricultural repurposing is the major bottleneck. They demonstrate how interests, ideas, and institutions intersect through four cases of agricultural support policy reform, including failed efforts at market procurement in India, successful shifts to increased agricultural research and development in China, successive reforms of the EU's Common Agricultural Policy (CAP), and unintended consequences of support for the US biofuels mandate.

In Chapter 4, Kym Anderson and Anna Strutt further examine agricultural support policies with a specific focus on how such policies have evolved over time in advanced economies, moving from mostly price support at the border (e.g., import tariffs, licenses and quotas, export subsidies) to increasingly more direct payments to farmers and priced ecosystem services. Anderson and Strutt estimate the contemporary welfare costs of these different supports for agriculture using a global, economywide Global Trade Analysis Project (GTAP) model and compare the costs of those policies to estimates from 2001. They find that full liberalization of the agriculture and food sectors in 2017 would have led to an increase in almost $50 billion globally per year, mostly from tariff removal and then domestic subsidy removal. While part of the benefits from this liberalization would accrue to advanced economies, an equivalent share would also go to developing countries—a contrast from 2001. This means that developing countries are also supporting their farmers much more than at the start of the Doha Round of the WTO, suggesting that reforms via that multilateral institution are increasingly unlikely. However, Anderson and Strutt see some potential in domestic alliances among farmers and environmentalists, at least in advanced economies, to push for policy instruments at the national level that can support both farmer welfare and the environment.

Part II encompasses chapters that more directly focus on coalitions that mobilize for or against reform. In Chapter 5, Johan Swinnen and Danielle Resnick note that coalitions often are viewed as a panacea and were elevated as part of the UNFSS. Yet, historically, political economy analyses of coalitions have defaulted to simplistic models whereby producers' interests are pitted against those of consumers. In reality, processes of economic development and globalization have led to the rise of many more interest groups in the food system, including animal feed supplies, insurance providers, food processors, distributors, and retailers, and sometimes lead to alliances among unlikely actors. Drawing on global examples, they examine vertical, cross-issue, and transnational coalitions. Vertical coalitions occur along the value chains and sometimes result in producers and agro-processors being aligned on certain issues while consumers and food retailers may be united on others, such as food safety. Cross-issue coalitions tie agricultural production to broader concerns about the environment as well as food quality and nutrition and can vary both cross-nationally and sub-nationally. Transnational coalitions refer to those among domestic agricultural and food groups with international organizations, social movements, multinational corporations, and other sovereign governments. Swinnen and Resnick discuss how coalitions formed to push similar policy instruments but for different policy goals (e.g., profit versus planetary health) are often unsustainable. They further explore some of the institutional prerequisites for coalition formation and why some coalitions shift over time.

One area where transnational coalition formation has been relatively successful is with respect to sugar-sweetened beverage taxes. While taxes are a common policy instrument for trying to alter consumption behavior of certain types of unhealthy foods, they are typically opposed by powerful opponents from food and beverage industries. In Chapter 6, Eduardo Gómez addresses this political economy challenge by examining how the governments of three middle-income countries with high levels of non-communicable diseases (NCDs)—India, Mexico, and

South Africa—were able to implement sugar-sweetened beverage taxes despite intense opposition from powerful corporations. He highlights several factors that generated supportive coalitions, including the importance of transnational advocacy in each country as well as governments' interest in generating more revenue from the tax. By contrast, regulatory measures to regulate the soda and snack food industries have been less accepted by the same governments because such coalitions are weaker, regulation is less likely to generate the same level of public contestation and visibility (i.e., salience), and the prospect for generating government revenue is less pronounced.

Beyond South Africa, rising NCDs are also problematic in other parts of Africa, which is rapidly urbanizing and where affordable ultra-processed foods are increasingly available. In Chapter 7, Jonathan Mockshell and Thea Ritter apply the Advocacy Coalition Framework (ACF) to the case of Ghana, drawing on primary interviews with a diverse set of stakeholders in several Ghanaian cities, including Accra, Cape Coast, Kumasi, and Koforidua. In the ACF, actors with similar perception, values, and beliefs form a discourse and advocacy coalition to address a policy problem. Likewise, Mockshell and Ritter uncover commonalities and differences among public, private, and civil society coalitions vis-à-vis ultra-processed foods. Their discourse analysis reveals shared beliefs among all coalitions around high food prices and the need for more regulation. In addition, there are independent beliefs that vary by stakeholder on the motivation of profits, production incentives, and state capacity, as well as divergent policy beliefs across coalitions on public awareness, education, and advocacy. The analysis helps identify opportunities for the types of coalition alignment reviewed by Swinnen and Resnick and a starting point for the types of deliberative approaches discussed by Deconinck.

In Chapter 8 Jody Harris likewise employs the ACF, along with policy transfer theory, and the power cube approach to understand the diffusion of international ideas on nutrition to the domestic policy context in Zambia. Drawing on an extensive number of in-depth interviews in the country, she finds that international advocates pushed a nutrition agenda around stunting that increasingly shaped the country's health and agriculture sectors, displacing national policymakers' priority around food security. This international policy agenda was transferred to the domestic sphere through normative evidence, global social norms, treaty obligations, and funding—and with different forms of power working in different policy spaces shaping each of these mechanisms. Notably, citizen voice is largely absent from these national policy processes in low-income countries, raising important questions about the legitimacy of certain food system agendas and often reflecting asymmetric power relations. Consequently, her chapter calls for explicit analysis of structural power in food policy research and action and suggests existing practice-friendly frameworks that can be used for this purpose.

Part III delves more into design spaces. In Chapter 9, Chris Barrett highlights three benefits to bundling socio-technical innovations for agri-food systems.

First, most scientific, technical innovations—whether alternative protein sources or genetic advances in rice during the Green Revolution—were transformative precisely because they were complemented by a suite of institutional and cultural innovations as well. Second, no intervention can entirely solve food system problems, especially when accounting for diversity in priorities both across and within countries. Third, as noted earlier, bundles help defuse resistance to innovation across risk-averse interest groups by broadening the policy agenda and therefore facilitating the potential for progressive coalitions to unite. This is particularly due to the Kaldor-Hicks compensation criterion, which suggests that innovations are desirable if and only if they meet Pareto conditions, i.e., the losers can be compensated in a way that the winners still remain better off. Bundling can help satisfy this criterion by finding multiple Pareto improvements that provide net gains greater than under just one policy intervention alone. Barrett illustrates his argument through case studies of the success of China's Science and Technology Backyards program, differential acceptance of genetic improvements in rice, and the adoption of Bt brinjal in Bangladesh but not India.

In Chapter 10, Robert Paarlberg demonstrates the role of policy sequencing by examining four important food production innovations that have been favored by scientists but opposed by influential swathes of the public. This includes Green Revolution farming, industrial agriculture, the use of synthetic fertilizers and pesticides versus organic farming, and genetically engineered crops (e.g. GMOs). In Paarlberg's view, popular critics see these innovations as putting nature at risk, even though agricultural scientists view them as more nature-protecting than the methods they replaced. Notably, while three of the four innovations remain in widespread use despite civil society opposition, GMOs are not; the world's most important food crops, such as wheat, rice, potato, and nearly all fruits and vegetables, are not being commercially grown anywhere today in GMO form. Policy sequencing is one reason because activists raised strong objections early with respect to GMOs, before the seeds were in wide use, and therefore most farmers never had a chance to enjoy and then defend the benefits. Gene-edited crops, a more recent biotechnology innovation, have also met early resistance prior to wide deployment, suggesting a parallel threat to future uptake. However, Paarlberg observes offsetting factors, including the absence of foreign DNA in most genome-edited crops, that may make wide deployment more likely.

Policy packaging is a major focus of Chapter 11 by Lukas Fesenfeld and Yixian Sun. They look at meat consumption, especially in high-income countries, which is viewed as one of the key factors affecting environmental sustainability. Nevertheless, government policies aiming to effectively reduce meat consumption and redesign the food system face potential public backlash given that such policies often intervene in people's everyday life and consumption habits, i.e., targeting the values discussed by Deconinck. Therefore, Fesenfeld and Sun examine the role of public opinion in food system transformation through representative surveys of almost 5,000 respondents in Germany, China, and the US. They find that citizens' support for policy packages to transform the food system strongly depends on policy packaging, i.e., combining policy instruments to foster innovations and adoption of meat alternatives (e.g., discounts for meat alternatives) with policies to reduce meat consumption (e.g., higher taxes on meat). While drawing on framing tactics can also have positive effects on public opinion, these are much smaller than those of policy design. Fesenfeld and Sun further suggest that policy sequencing of protein alternative options with taxes on meat is likely to create feedback effects, enabling what they term "positive tipping points" in public support for policies to reduce meat consumption; in other words, as the public gains more experience with novel meat substitutes, it further increases public support for taxes on meat.

Part IV examines adaptive spaces in more depth, with a particular focus on implementation of food system reform at local, regional, and global scales. In Chapter 12, Gareth Haysom and Jane Battersby focus on the local level, considering how to enhance urban food governance processes in African cities. Indeed, urban food systems in many African cities are governed by multiple municipal entities with minimal coherence and who often lack sufficient administrative and fiscal autonomy to address the food needs of local communities. Moreover, colonial legacies result in a production bias that still dominates food and nutrition security governance frameworks in the region. Operationally, this results in local governments adopting an orientation toward food availability while disregarding structural and policy food system challenges that impact access, utilization, and stability. In addition, urban food governance activities are complicated by the fact that different scales of government all engage different external actors— particularly multilateral organizations, donors, and transnational civil society organizations—who may advocate redundant or contradictory policy interventions. Such external actors can stimulate the diffusion of policy examples implemented elsewhere, such as multi-stakeholder food policy councils. However, these models are sometimes incongruent with the limited resources, capacities, and functional mandates of African city governments as well as perpetuate some of the challenges of multi-stakeholderism discussed above. Recognizing these issues, the authors advance a framework to help consider more contextually appropriate strategies for governing urban food systems, drawing on examples from Cape Town, South Africa.

In Chapter 13, Alan Matthews, Jeroen Candel, Nel de Mûelenaere, and Pauline Scheelbeek focus on cross-jurisdictional implementation at the regional level, particularly among countries within the EU. The EU is a system of multi-level governance where policy competencies are shared between the Union level, Member States, and regions and local governments, and it acts as a venue for policy cascades. The EU has set ambitious goals for the transformation of its agricultural and food systems in the European Green Deal and plans to introduce legislation on a sustainable food systems framework in 2023. While there has been widespread support for the expressed policy objectives embodied in these initiatives, disagreements exist on the strategies to achieve these policy goals and on the pace of change. The authors argue that political leadership is needed to avoid the unraveling of these plans for food system transformation, noting that while the EU Commission has provided this leadership in formulating the Green Deal package, national governments more exposed to the vagaries of electoral fortune are often more hesitant. Moreover, while EU food policymaking has for a long time been low in salience and left to a closed policy community, the recent emergence of new players and views marks its rise to the top of EU political agendas. Therefore, a central challenge will be to avoid the spread of identity politics and disinformation, and preventing what Matthews and co-authors refer to as "dialogues of the deaf" and an erosion of basic rules of the game, such as respecting scientific evidence and legal commitments.

Chapter 14 adopts a global perspective to implementing food systems commitments in a world increasingly characterized by multi-stakeholderism. Stella Nordhagen and Jessica Fanzo emphasize that the world is at a critical juncture to move toward a food system that provides healthy diets from sustainable nature-positive supply chains that support equitable livelihoods. At the same time, they observe that there is less than a decade until the SDG deadline and while many commitments and goals have been set to improve food systems, such efforts will have no impact if they are not followed by concrete, near-term action by key actors (including governments, donors, and the large variety of private-sector organizations). Reflecting the essence of policy diffusion, they draw on the growing trend of using data and performance metrics to enhance accountability for progress on food systems transformation at the global level. After reviewing several reports and tracking mechanisms that currently exist for various sub-aspects and outcomes of food systems, they conclude that none is comprehensive enough to address all the diverse outcomes of food systems. Instead, they provide details about what such mechanisms would need to encompass to effectively enhance accountability of public and private sector actors to their constituents.

Chapter 15 by Danielle Resnick and Johan Swinnen provides concluding remarks, drawing together common points from across the chapters relevant to the political economy framework presented in this introduction. For instance, in terms of incentive structures, they highlight the range of trade-offs—between interests and ideas, societal welfare and individual gain, and short-term certainty and long-term risks—that emerge when trying to reconcile different development objectives and policy instruments for the food system. In the mobilizational space, coalitions feature heavily in the volume, especially transnational ones. These coalitions can bolster the efforts of domestic allies through resources and visibility but, due to power asymmetries, can sometimes lead to the imposition of external preferences on local partners. Policy narratives, framing techniques, and provocative marketing are just some of the tactics that the contributors identify such coalitions employing to advance their causes. Bundling can help overcome political opposition by linking policies that disparate groups support while packaging taps into the right framing to resonate with possible reform dissenters. Deliberate sequencing can facilitate incremental reforms while unintended sequencing may foreclose certain policy opportunities. Finally, certain dynamics in the adaptive space, especially fiscal and food price policy shocks, have helped shift policy path dependencies. Other adaptive drivers, such as policy diffusion and policy cascades, are equally powerful in facilitating reforms but need to be congruent with relevant capacities and institutional mandates to result in effective implementation. The authors further identify several areas for future research to advance political economy analyses on food systems transformation, including how partisan dynamics affect the tactics of negotiation between interest groups and decisionmakers, processes to establish trust to ensure broad reform buy-in, and how to build political constituencies for low visibility public goods, such as agricultural research and development.

1.5 Conclusions

Food holds disparate meanings to so many different constituencies—as a source of profit, a provider of nutrients, and a conduit of cultural traditions—and often epitomizes a vast network of political, financial, and global decisions about how it is produced, where it is sourced, and what it costs. Consequently, while few disagree with high-level goals of a transformed agri-food system, the policy pathways for achieving such a vision are inevitably contested, and the enabling conditions for implementation frequently absent. By bringing together a global group of interdisciplinary and applied scholars examining different political economy elements as they relate to the food system, this book demonstrates how incentive structures, mobilizational modalities, policy designs, and drivers of adaptation intersect and shape the menu of viable options to advance the ambitious transformation agenda.

References

Abdelal, R. 2009. "Constructivism as an Approach to International Political Economy." In *Handbook of International Political Economy*, ed. M. Blyth, 51–71. London: Routledge.

AFP (Agence France Presse). 2019. "Bolsonaro Says Claims of Hunger in Brazil 'a Big Lie.'" *France 24*, July 19.

Anderson, K., G. Rausser, and J. Swinnen. 2013. "Political Economy of Public Policies: Insights from Distortions to Agricultural and Food Markets." *Journal of Economic Literature* 51 (2): 423–477. https://doi.org/10.1142/9789813274730_0016

Aronczyk, M. 2022. "How PR Firms Captured the Sustainability Agenda." *Foreign Policy*, February 17. https://foreignpolicy.com/2022/02/17/climate-crisis-activism-edelman-pr-sustainability/

Aronczyk, M., and M. Espinoza. 2021. *A Strategic Nature: Public Relations and Politics of American Environmentalism*. Oxford, UK: Oxford University Press.

Arvidson, M., H. Johansson, R. Scaramuzzino. 2018. "Advocacy Compromised: How Financial, Organizational, and Institutional Factors Shape Advocacy Strategies of Civil Society Organizations." *Voluntas: International Journal of Voluntary and Non-profit Organizations* 29: 844–856.

Bail, Chris. 2021. *Breaking the Social Media Prism: How to Make Our Platforms Less Polarizing*. Princeton, NJ: Princeton University Press.

Bair, J., and F. Palpacuer. 2015. "CSR Beyond the Corporation: Contested Governance in Global Value Chains. *Global Networks* 15 (Suppl 1): S1–S9.

Baker, P., J. Lacy-Nichols, O. Williams, and R. Labonté. 2021. "The Political Economy of Healthy and Sustainable Food Systems: An Introduction to a Special Issue." *International Journal of Health Policy and Management* 10 (Special Issue): 734–744. https://doi.org/10.34172/IJHPM.2021.156

Barrett, C., T. Reardon, J. Swinnen, and D. Zilberman. 2022. "Agri-food Value Chain Revolutions in Low- and Middle-Income Countries." *Journal of Economic Literature* 60 (4): 1316–1377.

Bates, B. 1981. *Markets and States in Tropical Africa*. Berkeley: University of California Press.

Bauer, M., B.G. Peters, J. Pierre, K. Yesilkagit, and S. Becker. 2021. "Introduction: Populists, Democratic Backsliding, and Public Administration." In *Democratic Backsliding and Public Administration: How Populists in Government Transform State Bureaucracies*, eds. M. Bauer, B.G. Peters, J. Pierre, K. Yesilkagit, and S. Becker, 1–21. Cambridge, UK: Cambridge University Press.

Behuria, P. 2020. "The Domestic Political Economy of Upgrading in Global Value Chains: How Politics Shapes Pathways for Upgrading in Rwanda's Coffee Sector." *Review of International Political Economy* 27 (2): 348–376. https://doi.org/10.1080/09692290.2019.1625803

Béné, C. 2022. "Why the Great Food Transformation may not happen – A deep-dive into our food systems' political economy, controversies and politics of evidence." *World Development* 154 (June). https://doi.org/10.1016/j.worlddev.2022.105881

Bennhold, K.2019. "Greens are the New Hope for Europe's Center. For the Far Right, They're Enemy No. 1." *The New York Times*. July 14. Available at: https://www.nytimes.com/2019/07/14/world/europe/greens-yellow-vests-germany-europe-populism.html

Benton, T., J. Beddington, S. Thomas, D. Flynn, S. Fan, and P. Webb. 2021. "A 'Net Zero' Equivalent Target is Needed to Transform Food Systems." *Nature Food* 2 (12): 905–906.

Berry, F.S., and W.D. Berry. 2007. "Innovation and Diffusion Models in Policy Research." In *Theories of the Policy Process*, ed. P. Sabatier, 223–260. Boulder, CO: Westview Press.

Birner, R. and D. Resnick. 2010. "The Political Economy of Policies for Smallholder Agriculture." *World Development* 38 (10): 1442–1452.

Blyth, M. 1997. "Any More Bright Ideas? The Ideational Turn of Comparative Political Economy." *Comparative Politics* 29: 229–250.

Braithwaite, J., and B. D'Costa. 2018. *Cascades of Violence*. Canberra, Australia: Australian National University Press.

Bruch, S., M.M. Ferree, and J. Soss. 2010. "From Policy to Polity: Democracy, Paternalism, and the Incorporation of Disadvantaged Citizens." *American Sociological Review* 75 (2): 205–226.

Burnett, K. and S. Murphy. 2014. "What Place for International Trade in Food Sovereignty?" *The Journal of Peasant Studies* 41(6): 1065–1084.

Cairney, P. 2017. "The Politics of Evidence-Based Policy Making." In *Oxford Research Encyclopedia of Politics*, 1–9. Oxford, UK: Oxford University Press. https://doi.org/10.1093/acrefore/9780190228637.013.268

Canfield, M., M.D. Anderson, and P. McMichael. 2021. "UN Food Systems Summit 2021: Dismantling Democracy and Resetting Corporate Control of Food Systems." *Frontiers in Sustainable Food Systems* 5: 661552. https://doi.org/10.3389/fsufs.2021.661552

Caron, P., G. Ferrero Y de Loma-osorio, D. Nabarro, E. Hainzelin, M. Guillou, I. Andersen, T. Arnold, et al. 2018. "Food Systems for Sustainable Development: Proposals for a Profound Four-Part Transformation." *Agronomy for Sustainable Development* 38 (4): 41. https://doi.org/10.1007/s13593-018-0519-1

Carothers, T., and A. O'Donohue. 2019. "Introduction." In *Democracies Divided: The Global Challenge of Political Polarization*, eds. T. Carothers and A. O'Donohue, 1–13. Washington, DC: Brookings Institution.

Chong, D., and J.N. Druckman. 2007. "Framing Theory." *Annual Review of Political Science* 10 (1): 103–126. https://doi.org/10.1146/annurev.polisci.072805.103054

Clapp, J. 2021. "The Problem with Growing Corporate Concentration and Power in the Global Food System." *Nature Food* 2: 404–408.

Clapp, J. 2022. "Concentration and Crises: Exploring the Deep Roots of Vulnerability in the Global Industrial Food System." *The Journal of Peasant Studies* 50 (1): 1–25.

Clapp, J., M. Anderson, M.Rahmanian, and S. Monsalve Suarez. 2021. "An 'IPCC for Food'? How the UN Food Systems Summit Is Being Used to Advance a Problematic New Science-Policy Agenda." *Proceedings of the National Academy of Sciences of the United States of America* 113 (17): 4570–4578. https://doi.org/10.1073/pnas.1601266113

Clapp, J., and D. Fuchs. 2009. *Corporate Power in Global Agrifood Governance*. Cambridge, MA: MIT Press.

Clapp, J., and S. Murphy. 2013. "The G20 and Food Security: A Mismatch in Global Governance?" *Global Policy* 4 (2): 129–138. https://doi.org/10.1111/1758-5899.12039

Cohen, N. 2022. "Roles of Cities in Creating Healthful Food Systems." *Annual Review of Public Health* 43: 419–437. https://doi.org/10.1146/annurev-publhealth-052220-021059

Collier, R. and D. Collier. 1991. *Shaping the Political Arena: Critical Junctures, the Labour Movement, and Regime Dynamics in Latin America*. Princeton, NJ: Princeton University Press.

Copeland, L. 2014. "Conceptualizing Political Consumerism: How Citizenship Norms Differentiate Boycotting from Buycotting." *Political Studies* 62 (S1): 172–186. https://doi.org/10.1111/1467-9248.12067

Culpepper, P. 2010. *Quiet Politics and Business Power*. Cambridge, UK: Cambridge University Press.

Dionne, K., and J. Horowitz. 2016. "The Political Effects of Agricultural Subsidies in Africa: Evidence from Malawi." *World Development* 87: 215–226. https://doi.org/10.1016/j.worlddev.2016.06.011

Dowding, K.M. 1996. *Power*. Minneapolis: University of Minnesota Press.

Dworkin, A., and R. Gowan. 2019. *Three Crises and an Opportunity: Europe's Stake in Multilateralism*. Berlin: European Council on Foreign Relations. https://ecfr.eu/publication/three_crises_and_an_opportunity_europes_stake_in_multilateralism/

El-Nahhal, I., and Y. El-Nahhal. 2021. "Pesticide Residues in Drinking Water, Their Potential Risk to Human Health and Removal Options." *Journal of Environmental Management* 299: 113611. https://doi.org/10.1016/j.jenvman.2021.113611

Eriksen, P., B. Stewart, J. Dixon, D. Barling, P. Loring, M. Anderson, and J. Ingram. 2010. "The Value of a Food System Approach." In *Food Security and Global Environmental Change*, eds. J. Ingram, P. Eriksen, and D. Liverman, 25–45. Bristol, UK: Earthscan Publications Ltd.

Fanzo, J. 2021. *Can Fixing Dinner Fix the Planet?* Baltimore, MD: Johns Hopkins University Press.

FAO (Food and Agriculture Organization of the United Nations). 2019. *FAO's Work on the Right to Food*. Rome: FAO.

FIAN Brasil (Organization for the Human right to Adequate Food and Nutrition). 2019. *Human Right to Adequate Food and Nutrition Report 2019: Authoritarianism, Hunger and Denial of Rights*. Brasília, Brazil: FIAN Brasil.

Gabela, M. 2022. "Scrap the Sugar Tax That Harms Black Women Canegrowers in Particular." *Mail and Guardian*, February 21. https://mg.co.za/news/2022-02-21-scrap-the-sugar-tax-that-harms-black-women-canegrowers-in-particular/

Garlock, T., F. Asche, J. Anderson, T. Bjorndal, G. Kumar, K. Lorenen, and T. Ragnar. 2020. "A Global Blue Revolution: Aquaculture Growth Across Regions, Species, and Countries." *Reviews in Fisheries Science and Aquaculture* 28 (1): 107–116.

Garzia, D., F. Ferreira da Silva, and A. de Angelis. 2022. "Partisan Dealignment and the Personalisation of Politics in West European Parliamentary Democracies, 1961–2018." *West European Politics* 45 (2): 311–334.

Glauber, J. and D. Laborde. 2022. "How Will Russia' Invasion of Ukraine Affect Global Food Security?" *IFPRI Blog Issue Post*, February 24. https://www.ifpri.org/blog/how-will-russias-invasion-of-ukraine-affect-global-food-security

Gleckman, H. 2018. *Multistakeholder Governance and Democracy: A Global Challenge*. London: Routledge.

GLOPAN (Global Panel). 2020. *Future Food Systems: For People, Our Planet, and Prosperity*. London: GLOPAN.

Goldberg, A.C. 2020. "The Evolution of Cleavage Voting in Four Western countries: Structural, Behavioural or Political Dealignment?" *European Journal of Political Research* 59 (1): 68–90. https://doi.org/10.1111/1475-6765.12336

Goodwin, M. 2018. "The Party Is Over." *Foreign Policy*, October 24. https://foreignpolicy.com/2018/10/24/the-party-is-over-populism-europe-far-right-afd-five-star-sweden-social-democrats-cdu-merkel-decline/

Graham, E.R., C.R. Shipan, and C. Volden. 2013. "Review Article: The Diffusion of Policy Diffusion Research in Political Science." *British Journal of Political Science* 43 (3): 673–701. https://doi.org/10.1017/S0007123412000415

Grossman, G., and E. Helpman. 1994. "Protection for Sale." *American Economic Review* 84 (4): 833–850.

Haas, P.M. 1992. "Introduction: Epistemic Communities and International Policy Coordination." *International Organization* 46 (1): 1–35. https://www.jstor.org/stable/2706951

Haggblade, S., A. Diarra, and A. Traoré. 2022. "Regulating Agricultural Intensification: Lessons from West Africa's Rapidly Growing Pesticide Markets." *Development Policy Review* 40: e12545. https://doi.org/10.1111/dpr.12545

Hayek, F.A. 1949. "The Intellectuals and Socialism," The University of Chicago Law Review 16 (3): 417–433.

Hess, T.M., J. Sumberg, T. Biggs, M. Georgescu, D. Haro-Monteagudo, G. Jewitt, M. Ozdogan, et al. 2016. "A Sweet Deal? Sugarcane, Water and Agricultural Transformation in Sub-Saharan Africa." *Global Environmental Change* 39: 181–194. https://doi.org/10.1016/j.gloenvcha.2016.05.003

Hidayati, D.R., E. Garnevska, and P. Childerhouse. 2021. "Sustainable Agrifood Value Chain—Transformation in Developing Countries." *Sustainability* 13 (22): 12358. https://doi.org/10.3390/su132212358

Hsu, T. and S. Thompson. 2023. "Disinformation Researchers Raise Alarms about A.I. Chatbots." *The New York Times*, February 8, 2023.

Huber, R.A. 2020. "The Role of Populist Attitudes in Explaining Climate Change Skepticism and Support for Environmental Protection." *Environmental Politics* 29 (6): 959–982. https://doi.org/10.1080/09644016.2019.1708186

Hunt, D. 2021. "How Food Companies Use Social Media to Influence Policy Debates: A Framework of Australian Ultra-processed Food Industry Twitter Data." *Public Health Nutrition* 24 (10): 3124–3135. https://doi.org/10.1017/S1368980020003353

Ikenberry, G.J. 2018. "The End of Liberal International Order?" *International Affairs* 94 (1): 7–23. https://doi.org/10.1093/ia/iix241

IPES-Food (International Panel of Experts on Sustainable food Systems). 2017. *Too Big to Feed: Exploring the impacts of mega-mergers, concentration of power in the agri-food sector.* Brussels: IPES-Food.

IPES-Food (International Panel of Experts on Sustainable food Systems). (2022). *Another Perfect Storm? How the Failure to Reform Food Systems Has Allowed the War in Ukraine to Spark a Third Global Food Price Crisis in 15 years, and What Can Be Done to Prevent the Next One.* Brussels: IPES-Food.

Jackson, R. 2021. "The Purpose of Policy Space for Developing and Developed Countries in a Changing Global Economic System." *Research in Globalization* 3: 100039. https://doi.org/10.1016/j.resglo.2021.100039

Gaventa, J. 2006. "Finding the Spaces for Change a Power Analysis." *IDS Bulletin* 37 (6): 23–33. https://doi.org/10.1001/jama.1896.02430960015001d

Jurkovich, M. 2020. *Feeding the Hungry: Advocacy and Blame in the Global Fight against Hunger.* Ithaca, NY: Cornell University Press.

Keck, M.E., and K. Sikkink. 1999. *Transnational Advocacy Networks in International and Regional Politics.* Malden, MA: Blackwell Publishers.

Kelley, J. 2017. *Scorecard Diplomacy: Grading States to Influence their Reputation and Behavior.* Cambridge, UK: Cambridge University Press.

Kingdon, John. 1995. *Agendas, Alternatives, and Public Policies.* London, UK: Longman.

Kubin, E., and C. von Sikorski. 2021. "The Role of (Social) Media in Political Polarization: A Systematic Review." *Annals of the International Communication Association* 45 (3): 188–206. https://doi.org/10.1080/23808985.2021.1976070

Kyle, J., and D. Resnick. 2019. "Nepal's Changing Governance Structure and Implications for Agricultural Development." In *Agricultural Transformation in Nepal:
Trends, Prospects, and Policy Options*, eds. G. Thapa, A. Kumar, and P.K. Joshi,
573–600. Washington, DC: International Food Policy Research Institute (IFPRI).

Lade, S., W. Steffen, W. de Vries, S. Carpenter, J. Donges, D. Gerten, H. Hoff, T.
Newbold, K. Richardson, and J. Rockstrom. 2020. "Human Impacts on Planetary Boundaries Amplified by Earth System Interactions." *Nature Sustainability* 3:
119–128.

Leach, M., N. Nisbett, L. Cabral, J. Harris, N. Hossain, and J. Thompson. 2020. "Food
Politics and Development." *World Development* 134: 105024. https://doi.org/10.
1016/j.worlddev.2020.105024

Lee, J.Y., R.L. Naylor, A.J. Figueroa, and S.M. Gorelick. 2020. "Water-Food-Energy
Challenges in India: Political Economy of the Sugar Industry." *Environmental
Research Letters* 15 (8): 084020. https://doi.org/10.1088/1748-9326/ab9925

Lele, U. 2021. "Introduction." In *Food for All: International Organizations and the
Transformation of Agriculture*, eds. U. Lele, M. Agarwal, B. Baldwin, and S.
Goswami, 1–8. Oxford, UK: Oxford University Press.

Lerman, A.E., and K.T. McCabe. 2017. "Personal Experience and Public Opinion: A
Theory and Test of Conditional Policy Feedback." *Journal of Politics* 79 (2): 624–641.
https://doi.org/10.1086/689286

Lewis, J. 2015. "The Politics and Consequences of Performance Measurement." *Policy
and Society* 34 (1): 1–12. http://dx.doi.org/10.1016/j.polsoc.2015.03.001.

Liaukonyte, J., A. Tuchman, and X. Zhu. 2022. "Spilling the Beans on Political Consumerism: Do Social Media Boycotts and Buycotts Translate to Real Sales Impact."
Marketing Science, in press. https://doi.org/10.1287/mksc.2022.1386

MacKillop, E., and J. Downe. 2022. "What Counts as Evidence for Policy? An Analysis
of Policy Actors' Perceptions." *Public Administration Review*, in press. https://doi.
org/10.1111/puar.13567

Maertens, M. and J. Swinnen. 2009. "Trade, Standards, and Poverty: Evidence from
Senegal." *World Development* 37(1):161-178.

Mahoney, J., and H. Thelen. 2010. "A Theory of Gradual Institutional Change." In
Explaining Institutional Change: Ambiguity, Agency, and Power, eds. J. Mahoney and
H. Thelen. Cambridge, UK: Cambridge University Press, 1–37.

Maier, A-L. 2021. "Political Corporate Social Responsibility in Authoritarian Contexts."
Journal of International Business Policy 4: 476–495.

Manahan, M.A., and M. Kumar. 2021. *The Great Takeover: Mapping of Multistakeholderism in Global Governance.* Amsterdam: TNI on behalf of the People's Working
Group on Multistakeholderism.

Martínez-Dalmau, J., J. Berbel, and R. Ordóñez-Fernández. 2021. "Nitrogen Fertiliza-
tion. A Review of the Risks Associated with the Inefficiency of Its Use and Policy
Responses." *Sustainability* 13 (10): 5625. https://doi.org/10.3390/su13105625

Mason, N., T. Jayne, and N. van de Walle. 2017. "The Political Economy Fertilizer Subsidy Programs in Africa: Evidence from Zambia." *American Journal of Agricultural
Economics* 99 (3): 705–731. https://onlinelibrary.wiley.com/doi/pdf/10.1093/ajae/
aaw090

McBride, J. 2022. "How Green-Party Success Is Reshaping Global Politics." *Council
on Foreign Relations*. May 5. Available at: https://www.cfr.org/backgrounder/how-
green-party-success-reshaping-global-politics#chapter-title-0-9

McCluskey, J., N. Kalaitzandonakes, and J. Swinnen. 2016. "Media Coverage, Public Perceptions, and Consumer Behavior: Insights from New Food Technologies." *Annual Review of Resource Economics* 8: 467–486.

McKeon, N. 2015. *Food Security Governance: Empowering Communities, Regulating Corporations.* London: Routledge.

Michielsen, Y.J.E., and H.M. van der Horst. 2022. "Backlash against Meat Curtailment Policies in Online Discourse: Populism as a Missing Link." *Appetite* 171: 105931. https://doi.org/10.1016/j.appet.2022.105931

Moffitt, B. 2016. *The Global Rise of Populism: Performance, Political Style, and Representation.* Redwood City, CA: Stanford University Press.

Moragues-Faus, A., and K. Morgan. 2015. "Reframing the Foodscape: The Emergent World of Urban Food Policy." *Environment and Planning A* 47 (7): 1558–1573. https://doi.org/10.1177/0308518X15595754

Moses, C. 2022. "Dairy Farmers in the Netherlands Are Up in Arms over Emission Cuts." *New York Times*, August 20. https://www.nytimes.com/2022/08/20/world/europe/netherlands-farmers-protests.html

Myers, A., D. Fig, A. Tugendhaft, J. Mandle, J. Myers, and K. Hofman. 2017. "Sugar and Health in South Africa: Potential Challenges to Leveraging Policy Change." *Global Public Health* 12 (1): 98–115. https://www.tandfonline.com/doi/full/10.1080/17441692.2015.1071419

Nestle, M. 2013. *Food Politics: How the Food Industry Influences Nutrition and Health.* Berkeley, CA: University of California Press.

OECD. 2017. *The Political Economy of Biodiversity Policy Reform.* Paris: OECD.

Olper, A., and V. Raimondi. 2010. "Constitutional Rules and Agricultural Policy Outcomes." In *The Political Economy of Agricultural Price Distortions*, ed. K. Anderson, 358–392. Cambridge, UK: Cambridge University Press.

Pagliai, G., M. Dinu, M.P. Madarena, M. Bonaccio, L. Iacoviello, and F. Sofi. 2021. "Consumption of Ultra-processed Foods and Health Status: A Systematic Review and Meta-analysis." *British Journal of Nutrition* 125 (3): 308–318. https://doi.org/10.1017/S0007114520002688

Patel, R. 2009. "What Does Food Sovereignty Look Like?" *Journal of Peasant Studies* 36 (3): 663–706. https://doi.org/10.1080/03066150903143079

Persily, N., and J. Tucker. 2020. *Social Media and Democracy.* Cambridge, UK: Cambridge University Press.

Pinstrup-Andersen, P (ed). 2015. *Food Price Policy in an Era of Market Instability: A Political Economy Analysis.* Oxford: Oxford University Press.

Plattner, M.F. 2019. "Illiberal Democracy and the Struggle on the Right." *Journal of Democracy* 30 (1): 5–19. https://doi.org/10.1353/jod.2019.0000

Reardon, T. 2015. "The Hidden Middle: The Quiet Revolution in the MIdstream of Agrifood Value Chains in Developing Countries." *Oxford Review of Economic Policy* 31 (1): 4563.

Reardon, T., C.P. Timmer, C.B. Barrett, and J. Berdegué. 2003. "The Rise of Supermarkets in Africa, Asia, and Latin America." *American Journal of Agricultural Economics* 85 (5): 1140–1146.

Reardon, T., A. Heiman, L. Lu, C.S.R. Nuthalapati, R. Vos, and D. Zilberman. 2021. "'Pivoting' by Food Industry Firms to Cope with COVID-19 in Developing Regions: E-commerce and 'Co-pivoting' Intermediaries." *Agricultural Economics* 52 (3): 459–475.

Resnick, D. 2022a. "Does Accountability Undermine Service Delivery? The Impact of Devolving Agriculture in Ghana." *European Journal of Development Research* 34 (2): 1003–1029. https://doi.org/10.1057/s41287-021-00408-x

Resnick, D. 2022b. "Food Systems Transformation and Local Governance Chapter 2." In *Global Hunger Index Report 2022*. Bonn, Germany and Dublin, Ireland: Welthungerhilfe and Concern Worldwide. https://www.globalhungerindex.org/issues-in-focus/2022.html

Resnick, D., K. Anigo, and O. Anjorin. 2022. "Advocacy Organizations and Nutrition Policy in Nigeria: Identifying Metrics for Enhanced Efficacy." *Health Policy and Planning* 37 (8): 963–978.

Rock, J. 2022. "We Are Not Starving: The Struggle for Food Sovereignty in Ghana." *Culture, Agriculture, Food and Environment* 41 (1): 15–23. https://doi.org/10.1111/cuag.12147

Rodden, J., and E. Wibbels, eds. 2019. "Introduction." In *Decentralized Governance and Accountability: Academic Research and the Future of Donor Programming*, eds. J. Rodden and E. Wibbels, 5–14. Cambridge, UK: Cambridge University Press.

Rowan, N. 2021. "Introduction to Food Disruptions." In *Food Technology Disruptions*, ed. C. Galanakis, 1–36. London, UK: Elsevier.

Rozelle, S. and J. Swinnen. 2004. "Success and Failure of Reform: Insights from the Transition of Agriculture." *Journal of Economic Literature* 42(2): 404-456.

Sachs, J. 2015. *The Age of Sustainable Development*. New York: Columbia University Press.

Samuels, D., and H. Thomson. 2021. "Lord, Peasant ... and Tractor? Agricultural Mechanization, Moore's Thesis, and the Emergence of Democracy." *Perspectives on Politics* 19 (3): 739–753.

Schoenmuller, V., O. Netzer, and F. Stahl. 2022. "Polarized America: From Political Polarization to Preference Polarization." *Marketing Science Frontiers*, forthcoming.

Schonhardt-Bailey, C. 2006. *From the Corn Laws to Free Trade: Interests, Ideas, and Institutions in Historical Perspective*. Cambridge, MA: MIT Press.

Scoones, I., M. Edelman, S.M. Borras, R. Hall, W. Wolford, and B. White. 2018. "Emancipatory Rural Politics: Confronting Authoritarian Populism." *Journal of Peasant Studies* 45 (1): 1–20. https://doi.org/10.1080/03066150.2017.1339693

Sievert, K., M. Lawrence, C. Parker, C.A. Russell, and P. Baker. 2022a. "Who Has a Beef with Reducing Red and Processed Meat Consumption? A Media Framing Analysis." *Public Health Nutrition* 25 (3): 578–590. https://doi.org/10.1017/S1368980021004092

Sievert, K., M. Lawrence, C. Parker, and P. Baker. 2022b. "What's Really at 'Steak'? Understanding the Global Politics of Red and Processed Meat Reduction: A framing Analysis of Stakeholder Interviews." *Environmental Science and Policy* 137: 12–21. https://doi.org/10.1016/j.envsci.2022.08.007

Sikuka, W. 2021. *Sugar Semi-Annual Report*. Pretoria, South Africa: US Department of Agriculture Foreign Agricultural Service. https://apps.fas.usda.gov/newgainapi/api/Report/DownloadReportByFileName?fileName=Sugar%20Semi-annual_Pretoria_South%20Africa%20-%20Republic%20of_10-01-2021.pdf

South Africa, Department of Trade, Industry, and Competition. 2020. *South African Value Chain Master Plan 2030*. Pretoria, South Africa

Sukhtankar, S. 2012. "Sweetening the Deal? Political Connections and Sugar Mills in India." *American Economic Journal: Applied Economics* 4 (3): 43–63. https://doi.org/10.1257/app.4.3.43

Sutherland, P., J. Bhagwati, K. Botchwey, N. FitzGerald, K. Hamada, J. Jackson, C. Lafer, and T. de Montbrial. 2004. *The Future of the WTO: Addressing Institutional Challenges in the New Millennium.* Geneva, Switzerland: WTO.

Swinnen, J. 2011. "Agricultural Protection Growth in Europe, 1870–1969." Chapter 6 in K. Anderson (ed.), *The Political Economy of Agricultural Price Distortions.* Cambridge, UK: Cambridge University Press, 81–104.

Swinnen, J. 2015. "Changing Coalitions in Value Chains and the Political Economy of Agricultural and Food Policy." *Oxford Review of Economic Policy* 31 (1): 90–115. https://doi.org/10.1093/oxrep/grv008

Swinnen, J. 2017. "Some Dynamic Aspects of Food Standards," *American Journal of Agricultural Economics* 99 (2): 321–338.

Swinnen, J. 2018. *The Political Economy of Agricultural and Food Policies.* New York, NY: Palgrave Macmillan.

Swinnen, J., A. Olper, and S. Vandevelde. 2021. "From Unfair Prices to Unfair Trading Practices: Political Economy, Value Chains and 21st Century Agri-food Policy." *Agricultural Economics* 52 (5): 771–788. https://doi.org/10.1111/agec.12653

Tsebelis, G. 2002. *Veto Players: How Political Institutions Work.* Princeton, NJ: Princeton University Press.

Utting, P. 2015. "CSR and the Evolving Standards Regime: Regulatory and Political Dynamics." In *Corporate Social Responsibility in a Globalizing World*, eds. K. Tsutsui and A. Lim, 73–106. Cambridge, UK: Cambridge University Press.

van der Ploeg, J.D. 2020. "Farmers' Upheaval, Climate Crisis and Populism." *Journal of Peasant Studies* 47 (3): 589–605. https://doi.org/10.1080/03066150.2020.1725490

von Braun, J., K. Afsana, L. Fresco, M. Hassan, and M. Torero. 2021. "Food Systems—Definition, Concept and Application for the UN Food Systems Summit." Paper presented at the UN Food Systems Summit, New York, September 23. https://sc-fss2021.org/

von Braun, J., and R. Birner. 2017. "Designing Global Governance for Agricultural Development and Food and Nutrition Security." *Review of Development Economics* 21 (2): 265–284. https://doi.org/10.1111/rode.12261

Webb, P., Benton, T.G., J. Beddington, D. Flynn, N.M. Kelly, and S.M. Thomas. 2020. "The Urgency of Food System Transformation is Now Irrefutable." *Nature Food* 1 (10): 584–585. https://doi.org/10.1038/s43016-020-00161-0

Weyland, K. 2005. "Theories of Policy Diffusion: Lessons from Latin American Pension Reform." *World Politics* 57 (2): 262–295.

Whitfield, L., O. Therkildsen, L. Buur, and A.M. Kjaer. 2015. *The Politics of African Industrial Policy: A Comparative Perspective.* Cambridge, UK: Cambridge University Press.

World Bank. 2014. *The Evolution of Kenya's Devolution: What's Working Well, What Could Work Better.* Washington, DC: World Bank.

Wright, T. 2021. *Advancing Multilateralism in a Populist Age.* Washington, DC: Brookings Institution.

Yates, J., S. Gillespie, N. Savona, M. Deeney, and S. Kadiyala. 2021. "Trust and Responsibility in Food Systems Transformation. Engaging with Big Food: Marriage or Mirage?" *BMJ Global Health* 6 (11): e007350. https://doi.org/10.1136/bmjgh-2021-007350

2

Facts, Interests, and Values

Identifying Points of Convergence and Divergence for Food Systems

Koen Deconinck

2.1 Introduction

Better policies offer significant potential to meet the challenges facing food systems, but policy reform has often proved difficult. This chapter argues that the
difficulty lies in disagreements over *facts, interests, and values*—alone or in combination.[1] For Sunstein (2018), politically contentious issues "are fundamentally
about facts rather than values," and "[i]f we can agree on the facts, we should
be able to agree on what to do—or at least our disagreements should be narrowed greatly." By contrast, a considerable literature on political economy has long
emphasized the importance of tensions between the public interest and special
interests (Rausser et al. 2011), while a third perspective emphasizes the importance
of (differences over) values (Thacher and Rein 2004; Inglehart and Welzel 2005;
Stewart 2006; Enke 2020). In reality, all three are likely to play a role, although
their relative importance will vary by issue.

Understanding the different sources of disagreement can help policymakers
anticipate risks and identify the most promising approaches. For instance, if disagreements are limited to the facts, this suggests that additional evidence, or
better communication of the existing evidence, can help. If disagreements are
due to diverging interests, then policymaking will involve an element of bargaining. Such tensions are unavoidable in diverse societies, and much of political
decision-making involves a search for compromises or grand bargains. But diverging interests can become problematic if there is no "level playing field"—that
is, if one interest group has disproportionate influence over political decision-
making. In such cases, achieving better policies will require efforts to ensure open
and equitable access to policy-making processes, and to safeguard integrity in

---

[1] This contribution is a summary of Chapter 3 in OECD (2021), "Achieving better policies", in:
Making Better Policies for Food Systems, OECD Publishing, Paris, https://doi.org/10.1787/4d4643d6-
en. The additional opinions expressed and arguments employed herein do not necessarily reflect the
official views of the Member countries of the OECD.

Koen Deconinck, *Facts, Interests, and Values*. In: *The Political Economy of Food System Transformation*.
Edited by: Danielle Resnick and Johan Swinnen, Oxford University Press. © Koen Deconinck (2023).
DOI: 10.1093/oso/9780198882121.003.0002

decision-making. If disagreements are over values, the above approaches will not work. Additional evidence, or efforts to "buy off" interest groups through compensation, are not effective when people disagree over what constitutes the public good. In some cases, it may be possible to find creative solutions by focusing on specific actions which can be supported by people with different values. When such solutions are not available, deliberative approaches can help to build societal consensus.

Moreover, disagreements in one area can spread to other areas. For example, motivated reasoning can lead people to interpret evidence in a way which is consistent with their interests or values; and interest groups may deliberately distort facts. In the resulting policy controversies, opposing camps hold different "worldviews," that is, incompatible sets of mutually reinforcing factual beliefs, interests, and values (Rein and Schön 1993).

This chapter examines how facts, interests, and values intersect with food systems, identifying when there are opportunities for alignment and when there are not. After reviewing each component and highlighting approaches to deal with discord in each of these domains, the chapter focuses on policy controversies where facts, interests, and values compete with each other.

2.2 Facts

Food systems face important evidence gaps and disagreements over the facts. Several best practices exist to ensure that policies are based on the best available evidence. Yet evidence by itself is rarely sufficient: on the one hand, societal choices always depend on the interests and values at stake; on the other hand, the role of interests and values also means that facts may become distorted or interpreted in ways consistent with people's prior views.

For many policy issues facing food systems, developing an effective policy response is made difficult by evidence gaps regarding the extent of a problem, its causal mechanisms, the effectiveness and distributional effects of various policy measures, or the magnitude of synergies and trade-offs between different policy goals (Deconinck et al. 2021). For example, policies for healthier food choices require information on the food environment, food products (e.g., nutritional composition, prices), consumers' food choices (purchases, individual intake, household waste) and the determinants of those choices. This information is not always available, or exists in disparate databases with inconsistent definitions and methodologies and which are in many cases privately owned (Giner and Brooks 2019).

Policy discussions are also complicated by misconceptions. For example, it has been claimed that due to soil erosion, the world only has "about 60 years of topsoil left" (World Economic Forum 2012). This claim has been repeated over time in major news outlets, yet it has no factual basis (FAO and ITPS 2015; Wong 2019).

There may also be gaps between public perceptions and the evidence. A study by the Pew Research Center demonstrated substantial gaps between the views of U.S. citizens and scientists on a range of scientific topics, with the largest gaps found in views on food safety. For example, while 88 percent of scientists agreed that genetically modified foods are safe to eat, only 37 percent of the broader U.S. public thought so. Similarly, while 68 percent of scientists thought that food produced with pesticides is safe to eat, only 28 percent of the broader public agreed (Pew Research Center 2015). Such gaps between perceptions and evidence create tensions when policymakers attempt to design evidence-based policies.

As highlighted in Table 2.1, there are several approaches that can improve the evidence base underlying policy decisions. These include regulatory impact assessments, input from scientific advisory bodies, stakeholders, and policy research organizations, as well as more experimental approaches through "learning by doing." International best practices recommend the use of Regulatory Impact Assessments. These should cover economic, social, and environmental impacts, ideally in a quantified and (where possible) monetized form (OECD 2012). A range of methods can be used to collect evidence and information relevant to such ex-ante assessments. Scientific and technical input into policy processes typically comes from three main sources: scientific advisory bodies such as the Joint Research Centre of the European Commission; academic institutions such as the Centre for Food Policy at the City University of London; or individual advisors in formal or informal roles. In the European Union, the European Commission Group of Chief Scientific Advisors recently commissioned a systematic review on sustainable food systems from a consortium of European academies of science (SAPEA 2020).

Stakeholder consultations can also be a powerful tool for policymakers to learn about policy issues and about how proposed policies might affect different groups in society. Examples include Canada's open consultation on dietary guidelines (Health Canada 2018), as well as France's "Estates General of Food" (France, Ministère de l'Agriculture et de l'Alimentation 2020). Stakeholder consultation is not without its complexities, however, as not all stakeholders are equally organized or vocal. Consultations may ignore a "silent majority," or may disproportionately feature certain well-organized groups (see below). Moreover, stakeholder views are not necessarily factually accurate. One fruitful approach is therefore to use impact assessments as part of the consultation process (OECD 2012).

Think tanks, foundations, and government policy research departments occupy an intermediate place between scientific advice and stakeholder input. These organizations are often an important source of information and policy ideas but may also be pushing a particular viewpoint. Research from authoritative, non-partisan institutions trusted across the political spectrum can have an important impact.

Table 2.1 Three sources of disagreement and potential policy approaches

	Types of disagreement	Potential policy approaches
Facts	• Evidence gaps about the extent, causes, and characteristics of policy issues; about synergies and trade-offs; and about policy effectiveness • Gaps between public perception and scientific evidence	• Build a shared understanding of the facts through regulatory impact assessments, incorporating insights from scientific advisory bodies, etc. • Stakeholders can be a source of information, but not all stakeholders equally well represented, and stakeholders' views not necessarily evidence-based; therefore good to use regulatory impact assessment as input in stakeholder consultation
Interests	• Most policies create winners and losers • Interest groups can provide valuable information to policymakers, and the political system can act as a mechanism to balance diverging interests • However, there is a risk that special interests capture policy processes	• Institutions and policy processes should promote transparency, accountability and a level playing field to minimize the risk of policy capture • It may be necessary to mobilize a countervailing coalition
Values	• Many food system issues are marked by differences over values (e.g., genetically engineered organisms, animal welfare). In contrast with interests, it is hard to "buy off" value-based opposition with compensation	• Creative problem-solving: policies can sometimes be adjusted so they are acceptable to people with different values • Making difficult decisions through deliberative processes so that choices have legitimacy
All of the above	• A *policy controversy* combines all of the above and is difficult to resolve due to incompatible worldviews	• Difficult to solve, although some approaches can help (e.g., ensure communication by experts with diverse values to reduce polarization) • Important to prevent their emergence in the first place by embedding the best practices for facts, interests and values into institutions and policy processes, thus building trust

Note: See main text for detailed discussion on each of these items.
Source: OECD (2021), Chapter 3.

International organizations can play this role through collecting internationally comparable data and providing research and recommendations (Tompson 2009). For instance, to support international negotiations on agriculture, governments preferred that data would be gathered by an institution at arms' length from domestic policymakers and trade negotiators, leading to the OECD's efforts in measuring agricultural producer support (Legg 2019).

Another method is "learning by doing," for example, through the use of pilot projects. For example, in France a network of experimental farms was set up to explore possibilities to reduce pesticide use; this network, known as Dephy, currently counts around 3,000 farms spread across France.[2] In these cases, it is important to have mechanisms which allow for timely feedback and for any necessary course corrections.

Whichever method is used, achieving a shared understanding of policy issues is an important precondition for developing successful policies, as uncertainty can greatly complicate policymaking. Clarity on the likely distribution of costs and benefits is of particular importance, as uncertainty is likely to create resistance to reform (Tompson 2009). At the same time, waiting for more data can lead to "paralysis by analysis" as complete information is rarely available, in part because scientific insight continues to evolve.

While evidence describes the way things are, policy debates also consider how things should be. The importance of evidence-based policymaking should thus not obscure the fact that evidence alone is never sufficient to make policy choices, which almost always involve some trade-off between competing interests and values (Parkhurst 2017).

Moreover, the availability of information, and the types of facts that are considered relevant, depend themselves on the interests and values at stake. For example, data on gender implications will be collected only if at least some participants in a policy debate consider gender issues important. Statistical indicators may also implicitly include value judgments, especially when different variables are aggregated into a composite indicator. The selection of variables, and their relative weights, depend on a judgment of which aspects of a problem are most important and how a good performance on one dimension can compensate for a worse performance elsewhere. Some aspects of a problem also lend themselves more easily to measurement. An appeal to evidence-based policymaking could thus mask an attempt to circumvent a debate over interests and values (Parkhurst 2017).

Interests and values affect the role of evidence in other ways. Research in psychology has long documented how people exhibit "motivated reasoning": faced with evidence and arguments, people tend to arrive at the conclusion they prefer to

---

[2] See https://ree.developpement-durable.gouv.fr/themes/economie-verte/activites-de-l-economie-verte/pratiques-agricoles-respectueuses-de-l-environnement/article/vers-la-transition-agro-ecologique

arrive at (Flynn et al. 2017). People's worldviews can influence this process. Beliefs on unrelated issues tend to "cluster" in ways which are difficult to explain rationally but which make sense given individuals' worldviews (Kahan and Braman 2006). For example, people attracted to a more egalitarian worldview find it easier to believe that economic activities are causing societal harm, whereas people with a more individualist worldview are more likely to dismiss such claims (Kahan et al. 2010). Moreover, while people recognize that others' beliefs are not consistent with the facts, they may not recognize the same mechanisms at work in influencing their own beliefs (Cohen 2003). These mechanisms affect not only stakeholders, but also experts and policymakers (World Bank 2015).

Information by itself is thus not sufficient to change people's minds, especially on polarized issues. Yet some approaches can help. A first approach is to present information in a way which affirms the values held by the audience. For instance, people with an egalitarian worldview would probably be more positive about new technologies if information is provided on how these technologies could help in environmental protection (and not only on their potential use in reducing costs, for example) (Kahan 2010). A second approach is to ensure that information is communicated by experts with diverse values; this increases the probability that people will hear the message from someone they identify as a trusted source (Cohen et al. 2007).

Interests and values affect not only how people interpret evidence but can also lead to distortions in communication around evidence. Interest groups may deliberately spread misinformation or biased information to influence policy debates, as discussed in the section on "policy controversies" below. For these reasons, the task of building a shared understanding of the facts is made difficult by disagreements over interests and values.

2.3 Interests

Most public policies have distributional consequences. Even if a policy reform increases overall welfare, there are likely some who will lose; conversely, a policy with negative effects on society as a whole may benefit some. In the context of the food system, influence over policies has been ascribed to farm lobby groups, agricultural input suppliers, food processing companies, and non-governmental organizations (NGOs), among others. In some cases, disproportionate influence has been well-documented; in other cases, evidence is more anecdotal.

Policies affecting the incomes of agricultural producers in both the developing and the developed world show a number of systematic patterns which are difficult to explain as a socially optimal response to market failures, but they are best understood as the result of pressures exerted by various interest groups (Anderson et al. 2013; Swinnen 2018). Other actors in the food system similarly exert pressure to influence policies. For example, food and drinks companies engage in a variety of "corporate political activities" such as disseminating information; providing financial incentives to politicians, political parties, and other decision makers; proposing voluntary initiatives or self-regulation as an alternative to public policies; or challenging proposed policies in court (Mialon et al. 2015). Such activities have also been documented for other food chain actors such as retailers or biotech firms (Clapp and Fuchs 2009). Many of these activities are not illegitimate; neither are they unique to the agro-food sector. Yet there exists a "gray area" in-between legitimate and illegal influence-seeking activities. In this gray area, advocacy activities can lead to increased risks of policy capture (OECD 2017).

There is no doubt that such mechanisms exist and can lead to policies favoring special interests at the expense of the public interest. However, as pointed out by Carpenter and Moss (2014), "observers are quick to see capture as the explanation for almost any regulatory problem," even though many claims in the literature about policy capture turn out to be poorly supported by the evidence. What complicates the analysis is that policies can have positive efficiency effects while at the same time creating important gains for some groups at the expense of others (Swinnen 2018).

Smaller groups with more concentrated interests at stake tend to be better organized than larger groups with more diffuse interests. In fact, the latter may even be "rationally ignorant" when the costs of being informed and politically engaged outweigh the potential benefits (Downs 1957). Similarly, major policy reforms tend to impose clearly identifiable costs on specific groups while benefits may be less certain and spread out over the wider population. In such a context, groups which stand to lose could block the proposed reforms (Tompson 2009). Successful reform may then require compensating those who lose or mobilizing a countervailing coalition (see Chapters 3 and 5 of this volume).

A number of strategies have been proposed to prevent policy capture (OECD 2017). For example, policy processes should strive to "level the playing field" by engaging diverse stakeholders in an inclusive decision-making process. This requires policies to foster integrity and transparency in lobbying activities and political finance, and policies to promote stakeholder engagement and participation. However, stakeholder engagement has its limitations, especially when some interests are not well-organized or difficult to represent (e.g., future generations).

A related strategy is to create greater transparency about how policy decisions are made and who was consulted during the policy process, for example, by making information available on meetings with external stakeholders, disclosing private interests of relevant public officials, publishing background studies, stating explicitly the rationale underlying a policy decision, and publishing evaluation reports and stakeholder comments. For example, in the case of the Canadian dietary guidelines mentioned earlier, Health Canada made available not only a summary of comments from stakeholders (Health Canada 2018) but the content of all correspondence between lobbyists and the government.[3]

While these strategies can help in mitigating risks of policy capture, they may not be sufficient. Surveying a set of major policy reforms in OECD countries, Tompson (2009) found that successful reforms typically found a way to win over potential opponents, for instance by exempting some groups from the reforms; by providing long transition periods or concessions; by involving potential opponents in the post-reform system (e.g., by allowing trade unions to administer pension funds in the case of pension reforms); or in some cases, by adopting policies in other domains to offset the cost of reform for some groups. In several cases where agricultural support policies were abolished, producers received compensation (Alston 2007).

There is often little mobilization of interest coalitions in *support* of agricultural sector reform (Tompson 2009). A notable exception is created through the reciprocity principle in trade negotiations, which implies that domestic exporters can get improved market access abroad only if foreign producers are granted more market access at home. This creates a countervailing interest group of exporters favoring trade liberalization (Irwin 2015). Historically, the adoption of reciprocity as a basic principle in U.S. trade policy fundamentally changed the political dynamics, leading to greater political support for trade liberalization (Bailey et al. 1997). A related strategy is *issue linkage*, where negotiations on various topics form part of a package deal where "nothing is agreed until everything is agreed." This approach was taken during the Uruguay Round, during which developed countries agreed to an unprecedented reduction in barriers to agricultural imports in exchange for greater market access for their industrial and service exporters. Agricultural interests in developed countries were opposed to liberalization, but industrial and service firms lobbied their governments to compromise. Issue linkage thus created countervailing interest groups in favor of agricultural trade liberalization (Davis 2004).

Outside of trade negotiations, mobilizing such a countervailing coalition may be difficult for policymakers. However, civil society actors committed to change can try to create such a coalition, for example through awareness-raising campaigns among the broader public (see Chapters 5 and 6 of this volume).

2.4 Values

Even if there is a shared understanding of the facts and no policy capture, people may still differ in the values they emphasize. Differences over values are a relatively neglected aspect of policymaking, and some authors dismiss values as

---

[3] See   https://www.canada.ca/en/services/health/campaigns/vision-healthy-canada/healthy-eating/transparency-stakeholder-communications-healthy-eating-initiatives.html.

merely convenient covers for the pursuit of self-interest (Stewart 2006). Yet, there is growing evidence on the importance of values in policymaking.

Food and agriculture are intimately connected to people's values. This is the case for religiously prescribed food consumption patterns or behaviors (e.g., dietary restrictions or fasting), but the role of values also holds for new phenomena such as organic foods (Paarlberg 2013). People differ in the values they hold relative to food and agriculture, and these value differences correlate with their behavior as consumers and as citizens. For example, people who attach a greater value to naturalness, fairness, and the environment are more likely to buy organic food (Lusk and Briggeman 2009), and consumers may be willing to pay a price premium for local and organic food in part because of a concern with farmers' incomes (Chang and Lusk 2009; Toler et al. 2009). In the United States, people with a preference for maintaining family farms and for preserving the environment tend to favor government intervention in agriculture (Moon and Pino 2018); and people's policy preferences on food and agriculture are correlated with their overall political outlook (Lusk 2012). It has also been suggested that the negative attitudes of non-experts toward genetically modified food are to an important extent value based, reflecting a preference for "naturalness" (Scott et al. 2018).

There appear to be some systematic patterns in the values people generally emphasize. Drawing on cross-cultural research in moral psychology, Haidt (2012) distinguishes six "moral foundations": *care versus harm, liberty versus oppression, fairness versus cheating, loyalty versus betrayal, authority versus subversion,* and *sanctity versus degradation.* Individuals, cultures, and political traditions differ in the relative importance they attach to these moral foundations. The moral foundations also appear to be relevant to food and agriculture. Mäkiniemi et al. (2013) asked people in Finland, Denmark, and Italy to engage in a word-association task, where they wrote down the first five words, ideas, or concepts that came to mind when thinking of "ethical food" or "morally right food" on the one hand, and "unethical food" or "morally wrong food" on the other hand. These answers revealed a particularly strong influence of the "care versus harm" foundation (e.g., the suffering of animals), the "sanctity versus degradation" foundation—chemical free, pure, clean, natural—and the "fairness versus cheating" foundation such as fair trade, good working conditions, human rights. The study also found systematic differences in response by gender, country, and political orientation.

Value differences similarly exist around broader societal issues with relevance to the food system. This is illustrated in Figure 2.1 using data from the World Values Survey, a large-scale project to quantify cross-country differences and trends over time in people's values and attitudes. While specific questions about food are not available, one of the questions included in the 2011–14 survey asked whether protecting the environment should be the priority, or whether economic growth and jobs should be prioritized. In some countries (e.g., Nigeria, Romania, the United States, Spain) a majority of respondents prioritizes economic growth and

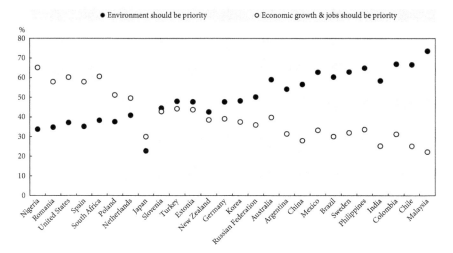

Figure 2.1 Prioritization of environment versus economic growth within and across countries.

Note: Respondents in nationally representative surveys were asked to indicate which of the following two statements comes closer to their personal view: "Protecting the environment should be given priority, even if it causes slower economic growth and some loss of jobs" or "Economic growth and creating jobs should be the top priority, even if the environment suffers to some extent." Responses for selected countries only. In Japan, 47 percent of respondents either gave a different answer or stated they did not know. Surveys conducted between 2011 and 2014.
Source: Inglehart, R., C. Haerpfer, A. Moreno, C. Welzel, K. Kizilova, J. Diez-Medrano, M. Lagos, P. Norris, E. Ponarin, and B. Puranen et al. (eds.). 2014. World Values Survey: Round Six—Country-Pooled Datafile Version: http://www.worldvaluessurvey.org/WVSDocumentationWV6.jsp. Madrid: JD Systems Institute.

jobs, while in some other countries (e.g., Colombia, Chile, Malaysia) a majority of respondents prioritizes the environment. In yet other countries (e.g., Slovenia, Turkey, Estonia, New Zealand) the shares of respondents are roughly evenly matched. Interestingly, there is only a weak correlation between responses and countries' level of economic development. Moreover, even in countries with a clear preference for either option, there is typically a large minority choosing the other option; a national consensus is rare.[4]

2.5 Interests versus Values

The design of policies for food systems is likely to encounter disagreements over values. Such disagreements are harder to resolve than situations where interests

---

[4] Among the 59 countries for which the WVS collected this information in 2011–14, the most unanimous response was found in Haiti (not shown in the chart) where 93 percent of respondents prioritized economic growth and jobs, with only 4 percent prioritizing the environment. The next country is Egypt, where 69 percent of respondents prioritized economic growth and jobs.

diverge: while those who lose financially from a policy change could in principle be compensated, the violation of cherished values is much more difficult to "compensate."

The distinction between interests and values is not always clear-cut, but a first characteristic is that interests are self-regarding while values are other-regarding. For example, people may vote to pay higher taxes because they value equality; people may thus vote against their own interests because of their values. Otherregarding values are not necessarily altruistic or cosmopolitan: moral foundations such as loyalty versus betrayal, or authority versus subversion, could lead to nationalist or ethnocentric attitudes.

A growing body of evidence shows that other-regarding motivations are important drivers of decision-making (Fehr and Schmidt 2006; Cooper and Kagel 2016). Studies of voters' preferences on international trade suggest that these preferences partly reflect considerations of how liberalization would affect others, or the country in general (Mansfield and Mutz 2009; Rho and Tomz 2017). Opinion surveys also often find strong support among the public for agricultural subsidies and tariffs, despite the fact that these harm them as taxpayers or consumers (Naoi and Kume 2011; Jensen and Shin 2014; Moon and Pino 2018).

A second distinction is that interests are usually material (e.g., income) while values are usually non-material and hard to translate into a material equivalent (e.g., liberty). This makes interests "commensurable" (stakeholders could be compensated) while values are in principle "incommensurable." Winship (2006) describes efforts to build a dam in Arizona which would have had considerable economic benefits but which would have flooded the ancestral lands of the Yavapai Indians. The government was willing to pay compensation, but the Yavapai were not interested at any price, arguing that selling the land would be akin to selling one's mother.

In a conflict involving interests, numerous solutions may be possible, as stakeholders can usually be compensated in one domain in return for compromising in another. By contrast, in a value-laden debate, "[c]ompromise, in its most pejorative sense, means abandoning deeply held beliefs, values, or ideals. To negotiate away values is to risk giving up one's identity" (Susskind 2006). As Goldgeier and Tetlock (2008) observe, "the very willingness to consider certain categories of trade-offs is taken as a sign in many political cultures that one is not adequately committed to core cultural values and identities." They distinguish three types of trade-offs, depending on whether the trade-off involves interests or values.[5] A *routine* tradeoff involves a choice between two interests, as is often the case in private economic decision-making or negotiation. A *taboo* trade-off pits values (e.g., human rights) against interests (e.g., profits). A *tragic* trade-off, meanwhile, pits two values against each other.

---

[5] Goldgeier and Tetlock (2008) use the terms "secular values" and "sacred values."

The difference between commensurable interests and incommensurable values bears some similarities to that between goods with a market price and those without, although the mapping is not exact. A good may have a market price, yet its owner may not be willing to accept any compensation to part with it; the case of the Yavapai Indians is an example. On the other hand, some desirable goods don't have a market price (e.g., reductions in crime) but can be valued in monetary terms indirectly by assessing consumers' implicit willingness to pay (e.g., assessing by how much real estate prices are lower in areas with higher crime rates). Hence, some desirable ends could at least partly be translated into a monetary equivalent.

Such techniques are commonly used in cost-benefit analyses and can translate diverse outcomes into a common metric, which facilitates comparisons between policy options.[6] If all costs and benefits of a policy can be expressed in monetary terms, then we can identify the option with the highest net benefit; and if net benefits are positive, we can in theory design transfers from those who gain to those who lose, so that everyone is at least as well off as before.[7] However, there is no consensus on the scope and limits of these techniques, with many questioning the idea that all relevant aspects of a problem can be translated into monetary terms (Wolff and Haubrich 2006). In its strongest form, cost-benefit analysis can be seen as an attempt to translate all policy problems into routine trade-offs, an attempt which strikes many as taboo.

The distinction between those aspects which are commensurable and those which are not is thus best thought of as a continuum. Where highly incommensurable values are at stake, disagreements will be harder to resolve.

There are several ways of dealing with differences over values, not all of them wholly satisfactory. Stewart (2006) identifies six mechanisms used in practice:

- *Structural separation*: responsibilities for different values are assigned to different institutions or departments (i.e., a "silo" approach).
- *Hybridization*: policies with different underlying values coexist, often because a new set of policies is layered on top of existing policies with different underlying values.
- *Casuistry*: choices are made on a case-by-case basis instead of making a general decision on how different values should be prioritized.
- *Incrementalism*: small, gradual steps are made instead of enacting larger changes.
- *Bias*: Some values are implicitly privileged over others.
- *Cycling*: policymakers focus sequentially on different values; policies may "oscillate."

---

[6] For an introduction to "non-market valuation" techniques, see Baker and Ruting (2014).
[7] This idea is known as the Kaldor-Hicks criterion (for more on this concept, see Chapter 9 of this volume).

Agricultural policymaking historically often relied on structural separation and bias. In most developed countries, the post-war period was characterized by "agricultural exceptionalism," with agricultural policies made by closed policy networks of agriculture ministries and farm groups, with a near-exclusive focus on raising farm income and productivity. This suppressed some values while privileging others, giving the impression that value differences had been resolved (Daugbjerg and Swinbank 2012). Similar dynamics have historically been at work in fisheries policy (Delpeuch and Hutniczak 2019).

While common in practice, the approaches above have obvious shortcomings: value differences will often show up as incoherent policies or as policies with little legitimacy. More promising approaches exist. Meijer and De Jong (2019) identify *problem-solving* (where policies are re-designed to accommodate different values) and *deliberation* (where stakeholders discuss why certain values are important in an attempt to clarify and potentially resolve value differences).[8] These hold the promise of a coherent approach, either because tension is removed through a creative solution or because agreement is reached on how different values should be prioritized.

Policy decisions rarely pit values against each other directly; decisions are typically about actions, which are interpreted by stakeholders in terms of values. Modifying the specifics of a policy can thus increase its compatibility with different values through creative problem-solving (Rein 2006; Winship 2006). For example, Ehrlich (2010) found that many voters are opposed to free trade not because of how it would affect them personally, but because of sincere concerns about labor and environmental conditions abroad. If opposition is motivated by such values, conventional approaches to provide compensation (e.g., job training) will not be effective. A creative policy solution might be the inclusion of, for example, labor or environmental side agreements in trade agreements.

Unfortunately, not all issues lend themselves to such elegant solutions. In principle, persistent disagreement could be resolved through decision rules such as voting, but such mechanical decision rules have severe shortcomings. First, they can lead to inconsistent societal choices or other undesirable outcomes even if people are well-informed (Arrow 1951). Second, with contentious issues a decision based on numerical strength could foster resentment rather than legitimacy, making it harder to implement the policy afterward (Susskind 2006). An alternative approach therefore emphasizes *deliberative mechanisms*. Rather than taking people's beliefs, values, and preferences as given, this approach focuses on the process of discussing policy options, where participants can exchange their views, argue in favor or against courses of action, and persuade or be persuaded (Dryzek and List 2003). Ideally, deliberation helps to resolve value differences by building consensus or at least finding compromises with widespread support.

---

[8] Meijer and De Jong (2019) use the term "reconciliation" rather than problem-solving.

A growing number of jurisdictions have been experimenting with forums where citizens can deliberate about important policy issues. Many initiatives use random selection or other approaches to ensure that participants represent the larger population, to guarantee an inclusive process, and to avoid disproportionate influence of stakeholders with vested interests (OECD 2020). Proponents argue that these experiences demonstrate that ordinary citizens are willing and able to engage in high-quality deliberation. Other potential benefits include overcoming polarization and populism, and the ability to generate innovative solutions and move beyond impasse (Dryzek et al. 2019). Empirical research finds qualified support for these claims (Ryfe 2005; Thompson 2008). The quality of deliberations is improved when they include balanced information, expert testimony, and oversight by a facilitator (Dryzek et al. 2019).

Many deliberative initiatives have covered food (Ankeny 2016). A prominent recent example is the Irish Citizens' Assembly. Established in 2016, this body consists of a chairperson and 99 citizens, randomly selected to be representative of the population. The Citizens' Assembly has considered a number of issues, such as legalization of abortion, population ageing, and climate change. The Citizens' Assembly also made several recommendations on how Irish agriculture could contribute to climate change mitigation, including a tax on agricultural emissions with revenues to be reinvested in climate friendly agriculture and incentives paid to farmers for sequestering carbon. A committee with representatives from Ireland's political parties considered these recommendations but did not endorse taxing agricultural emissions. In France, the *Convention Citoyenne pour le Climat* similarly used random selection to bring together 150 citizens to define initiatives to reduce greenhouse gas emissions. Several of the decisions of the Convention related to food systems, such as encouraging a shift toward a diet with less meat and dairy and more fruits and vegetables, as well as providing consumers with information on the environmental impacts on food products (Convention Citoyenne pour le Climat 2020). At the international level, Food Systems Dialogues constitute another example of deliberative approaches to food and agricultural policies.

An important concern is that some people are considerably more interested and more vocal than others. This is the case for food and agriculture, where "foodies" may see themselves as more knowledgeable than the general public (Ankeny 2016). Moreover, people who take an interest in food policy are also likely to have more social and economic power, creating "subtle forms of social domination," which can undermine the attempts to foster deliberation (Ankeny 2016). This problem is particularly pronounced where participants are recruited on a voluntary basis, as "foodies" are considerably more likely to volunteer for deliberative processes around food policies.

Successful reconciliation and deliberation approaches require careful preparation and are neither easy nor cheap. Such mechanisms may therefore not be practical for all policy decisions, although they could be a powerful tool to move forward in the face of important differences over values—at least when their recommendations are taken to heart by policymakers.

2.6 Policy Controversies

The most sensitive policy issues combine disagreements over facts, interests, and values. For example, as discussed further in Chapters 9 and 10 of this volume, policy controversies over genetically modified organisms (GMOs) involve not only potential benefits and risks of the technology, but also claims that biotech firms or NGOs have disproportionate influence over policy processes, and differing views on the role of technology, small farmers, or corporations.

With policy controversies, disagreement in one area (e.g., values) may reinforce disagreements in another area (e.g., facts) through several mechanisms. One such mechanism, motivated reasoning, was discussed earlier. Another example is the deliberate spread of biased or misleading information by interest groups, for example through funding research. Industry-funded research affects research priorities (Fabbri et al. 2018) and leads to conclusions more favorable to the funder (Lundh et al. 2017). Similar dynamics are at work in food systems. For example, a review of more than 200 nutrition-related articles showed that industry-funded studies were four to eight times more likely to report results favorable to the industry (Lesser et al. 2007). Similar results were found by Mandrioli et al. (2016), Bes-Rastrollo et al. (2013), and Massougbodji et al. (2014).

The damage done by industry influence extends beyond these specific topics; it may lead citizens to dismiss *any* scientific study which contradicts their prior beliefs. One possible reason why consumers in many countries remain skeptical about GM crops may be that the public trusts environmental NGOs more than scientists and the private sector, as NGOs are perceived as not having a hidden agenda (Qaim 2020). Industry funding is not problematic per se; it can enable important research, especially in a context of scarce public funding. But clear governing principles are needed to safeguard the public interest, such as rules on the disclosure of funding and conflicts of interest, and transparency regarding data and methods.[9]

Interest groups also invoke values in policy debates: farm groups are likely to describe their goal as a *fair* income rather than simply a higher income. Similarly, agricultural input firms are likely to describe their goals as improved sustainability, better lives for farmers and healthy food, rather than profit alone. In response to initiatives to tax sugar-sweetened beverages, the American Beverage Association organized a campaign with the message that "[e]lected officials and pro-tax advocacy groups should not be dictating what you can and can't eat or drink. These

---

[9] See https://www.cos.io/initiatives/top-guidelines.

choices are yours, and yours alone."[10] These values are invoked for self-serving reasons, but the values themselves are real, and cherished by many. Framing policies in terms of values can help interest groups to move the debate in a desired direction.

The distinction between routine, taboo, and tragic trade-offs is again relevant here. Opponents may frame a policy as involving a taboo trade-off, surrendering a deeply held value for money or convenience, with the effect of portraying proponents as unprincipled or immoral (Goldgeier and Tetlock 2008). Disagreements over facts can also worsen conflicts over interests and values. Uncertainty over the distribution of gains and benefits of reform leads to greater resistance (Tompson 2009). Conversely, *creating* uncertainty over the facts is a useful tactic for opponents of reform.

These interactions between facts, interests, and values can create what Rein and Schön (1993) have labeled "policy controversies." Policy controversies involve competing "frames" which combine facts and theories, interests, and values to make sense of a complex reality. As long as disagreements relate to facts, interests, or values but not all three at once, there remains some common ground for resolving disagreement; but policy controversies and their competing frames are more problematic as they involve fundamentally different worldviews.

An example of such contrasting worldviews is offered by Mann (2018), who distinguishes between "wizards" and "prophets." Wizards emphasize technological progress as a way to achieve sustainability, while prophets emphasize the need for reductions in consumption (including through lower population growth). In Mann's telling, the two worldviews are diametrically opposed: prophets see wizards' faith in technology as unthinking, arrogant, and a recipe for disaster, while wizards see prophets' insistence on reducing consumption as backward, indifferent to the poor, and unnecessarily apocalyptic. Prophets accuse wizards of prioritizing corporate profits, while wizards accuse prophets of racism (as poverty, hunger, and population growth are concentrated in non-Western countries). If participants in food systems debates indeed hold such diametrically opposed worldviews, constructive policymaking is difficult.[11]

Unfortunately, political science does not offer much practical advice on how to manage policy controversies. Rein and Schön (1993) themselves advocated for "frame-reflectiveness," that is, an awareness of the frames being used, a willingness to identify their sources and consequences, and an openness to reassess. However, the authors noted that "there are very few examples of such processes" (Rein and Schön 1993). Another strategy is to search for "frame-robust" policies

---

[10] Americans for Food and Beverage Choice. 2020. "Your Cart, Your Choice." https://yourcartyourchoice.com/your-cart-your-choice/.
[11] See also Thompson (2017), who identifies productionist, agricultural stewardship, true cost of food, and holistic worldviews.

that are acceptable to stakeholders with different frames, similar to the creative problem-solving outlined earlier.

The difficulty of resolving policy controversies underscores the importance of *preventing* policy controversies from emerging in the first place. This imposes a responsibility on participants in policy debates to commit to using rigorous evidence, to be forthcoming about potential conflicts of interest, to acknowledge different values at stake, and so on. But individual responsibility is unlikely to be sufficient. Rather, the various approaches to deal with disagreements over facts, interests, and values need to be embedded institutionally. A large literature confirms the importance of the "rules of the game" in shaping political and economic outcomes. This institutional view suggests we can "improve the *substance* of public policy choices by improving the *procedures* used to make these choices" (Immergut 2006). To the extent that the best practices described in this chapter are firmly embedded in the policy-making process, the obstacles should be greatly diminished. Robust processes should also contribute to public trust, reducing the suspicion that, for instance, evidence provided in a policy debate is biased by conflicts of interest. Disagreements around facts, interests, and values are not specific to food systems, so neither are the relevant best practices. Those concerned with achieving better policies for food systems should thus in the first place support general principles of good governance and policy-making.

2.7 Conclusion

On the path to better policies for food systems, policymakers can expect to encounter disagreements over facts, interests, and values. The most problematic policy controversies involve disagreements over all three. Achieving better policies thus requires processes to build a shared understanding of the facts, to balance diverging interests (or compensating those who stand to lose from reform), and to resolve differences over values.[12]

This chapter has identified several options for dealing with conflicts over facts, interests, and values. For instance, regulatory impact assessments are a way of building a shared understanding of facts, policies that create a "level playing field" through transparency and accountability help limit the risk of policy capture by interest groups, and deliberative approaches are useful for resolving disagreements over values. None of these, however, are quick fixes. Rather, these examples

---

[12] Much of this chapter focused on domestic policymaking. Yet similar difficulties arise at the international level. International organizations can build a shared understanding of the facts. The role of interests and values is harder to assess, as the behaviors of national governments derive from domestic processes as well as strategic interactions with other states (Putnam 1988). It is not always clear whether a country's negotiating position reflects its assessment of domestic welfare and/or deeply held values; lobbying of domestic interest groups; or a mix of those.

underscore that achieving better policies will require embedding the best practices highlighted in this chapter into institutions and policy processes. This can build trust and confidence in the approaches used to gather and assess facts, to balance diverging interests, and to resolve differences over values. In turn, this should make it less likely that disagreement in one domain spills over into others, creating intractable policy controversies.

References

Alston, J. 2007. "Lessons from Agricultural Policy Reforms in Other Countries." In *The 2007 Farm Bill and Beyond*, eds. B. Gardner and D. Sumner, 83–86. Washington, DC: American Enterprise Institute.

Anderson, K., G. Rausser, and J. Swinnen. 2013. "Political Economy of Public Policies: Insights from Distortions to Agricultural and Food Markets." *Journal of Economic Literature* 51 (2): 423–477.

Ankeny, R. 2016. "Inviting Everyone to the Table: Strategies for More Effective and Legitimate Food Policy via Deliberative Approaches." *Journal of Social Philosophy* 47 (1): 10–24.

Arrow, K. 1951. *Social Choice and Individual Values*. Hoboken, NJ: John Wiley & Sons.

Bailey, M., J. Goldstein, and B. Weingast. 1997. *The Institutional Roots of American Trade Policy: Politics, Coalitions, and International Trade*. Cambridge, UK: Cambridge University Press.

Baker, R., and B. Ruting. 2014. "Environmental Policy Analysis: A Guide to Non-Market Valuation." Productivity Commission Staff Working Paper. Australian Government Productivity Commission, Canberra, Australia. https://www.pc.gov.au/research/supporting/non-market-valuation/non-market-valuation.pdf

Bes-Rastrollo, M., M. Schulze, M. Ruiz-Canela, and M. Martinez-Gonzalez. 2013. "Financial Conflicts of Interest and Reporting Bias Regarding the Association between Sugar-Sweetened Beverages and Weight Gain: A Systematic Review of Systematic Reviews." *PLoS Medicine* 10 (12): e1001578.

Carpenter, D., and D. Moss. 2014. *Preventing Regulatory Capture*. Cambridge, UK: Cambridge University Press.

Chang, J.B., and J. Lusk. 2009. "Fairness and Food Choice." *Food Policy* 34 (6): 483–491.

Clapp, J., and D. Fuchs. 2009. *Corporate Power in Global Agrifood Governance*. Cambridge, UK: MIT Press.

Cohen, G. 2003. "Party over Policy: The Dominating Impact of Group Influence on Political Beliefs." *Journal of Personality and Social Psychology* 85 (5): 808–822.

Cohen, G., D. Sherman, A. Bastardi, L. Hsu, M. McGoey, and L. Ross. 2007. "Bridging the Partisan Divide: Self-Affirmation Reduces Ideological Closed-Mindedness and Inflexibility in Negotiation." *Journal of Personality and Social Psychology* 93 (3): 415–430.

Convention Citoyenne pour le Climat. 2020. *Les Propositions de la Convention Citoyenne pour le Climat*. Paris: Convention Citoyenne pour le Climat. https://propositions.conventioncitoyennepourleclimat.fr/pdf/ccc-rapport-final.pdf

Cooper, D., and J. Kagel. 2016. "Other-regarding Preferences: A Selective Survey of Experimental Results." In *The Handbook of Experimental Economics*, eds. J. Kagel and A. Roth, Ch. 4, 217–289. Princeton, NJ: Princeton University Press.

Daugbjerg, C., and A. Swinbank. 2012. "An Introduction to the 'New' Politics of Agriculture and Food." *Policy and Society* 31 (4): 259–270.

Davis, C. 2004. "International Institutions and Issue Linkage: Building Support for Agricultural Trade Liberalization." *American Political Science Review* 98 (1): 153–169.

Deconinck, K., C. Giner, L.A. Jackson and L. Toyama. 2021. "Overcoming Evidence Gaps on Food Systems." OECD Food, Agriculture and Fisheries Papers No. 163. OECD Publishing, Paris. https://doi.org/10.1787/44ba7574-en

Delpeuch, C., and B. Hutniczak. 2019. "Encouraging Policy Change for Sustainable and Resilient Fisheries." OECD Food, Agriculture and Fisheries Papers No. 127. OECD Publishing, Paris. https://dx.doi.org/10.1787/31f15060-en

Downs, A. 1957. *An Economic Theory of Democracy.* New York: Harper & Row.

Dryzek, J., A. Bächtiger, S. Chambers, J. Cohen, J.N. Druckman, A. Felicetti, J.S. Fishkin, et al. 2019. "The Crisis of Democracy and the Science of Deliberation." *Science* 363 (6432): 1144–1146. https://dx.doi.org/10.1126/science.aaw2694

Dryzek, J., and C. List. 2003. "Social Choice Theory and Deliberative Democracy: A Reconciliation." *British Journal of Political Science* 33 (1): 1–28. https://dx.doi.org/10.1017/S000712340300001

Ehrlich, S. 2010. "The Fair Trade Challenge to Embedded Liberalism." *International Studies Quarterly* 54 (4): 1013–1033.

Enke, B. 2020. "Moral Values and Voting." *Journal of Political Economy* 128 (10): 3679–3729.

Fabbri, A., A. Lai, Q. Grundy, and L. Bero. 2018. "The Influence of Industry Sponsorship on the Research Agenda: A Scoping Review." *American Journal of Public Health* 108 (11): e9–e16.

FAO (Food and Agriculture Organization of the United Nations) and ITPS (Intergovernmental Technical Panel on Soils). 2015. *Status of the World's Soil Resources.* Rome: FAO and ITPS. http://www.fao.org/3/a-i5199e.pdf

Fehr, E., and K. Schmidt. 2006. "The Economics of Fairness, Reciprocity and Altruism – Experimental Evidence and New Theories." In *Handbook of the Economics of Giving, Altruism and Reciprocity*, eds. S.C. Kolm and J. Ythier, Ch. 8, 615–691. Amsterdam: North Holland.

Flynn, D., B. Nyhan, and J. Reifler. 2017. "The Nature and Origins of Misperceptions: Understanding False and Unsupported Beliefs about Politics." *Political Psychology* 38: 127–150.

France, Ministère de l'Agriculture et de l'Alimentation. 2020. *#EGalim: Tout Savoir Sur la loi Agriculture et Alimentation.* Paris, France. https://agriculture.gouv.fr/egalim-tout-savoir-sur-la-loi-agriculture-et-alimentation

Giner, C., and J. Brooks. 2019. "Policies for Encouraging Healthier Food Choices." OECD Food, Agriculture and Fisheries Papers No. 137. OECD Publishing, Paris. https://www.oecd-ilibrary.org/agriculture-and-food/policies-for-encouraging-healthier-food-choices_11a42b51-en

Goldgeier, J., and P. Tetlock. 2008. "Psychological Approaches." In *The Oxford Handbook of International Relations*, eds. C. Reus-Smit and D. Snidal, Ch. 27, 462–480. Oxford, UK: Oxford University Press.

Haidt, J. 2012. *The Righteous Mind: Why Good People Are Divided by Politics and Religion*. New York: Pantheon Books.

Health Canada. 2018. *Canada's Food Guide Consultation—Phase 2 What We Heard Report*. Ottowa, Ontario: Health Canada. https://www.canada.ca/en/services/health/publications/food-nutrition/canada-food-guide-phase2-what-we-heard.html

Immergut, E. 2006. "Institutional Constraints on Policy." In *The Oxford Handbook of Public Policy*, eds. R. Goodin, M. Rein, and M. Moran, Ch. 27, 557–571. Oxford, UK: Oxford University Press.

Inglehart, R. and C. Welzel. 2005. *Modernization, Cultural Change, and Democracy: The Human Development Sequence*. Cambridge, UK: Cambridge University Press.

Irwin, D. 2015. *Free Trade Under Fire: Fourth Edition*. Princetone, NJ: Princeton University Press.

Jensen, N., and M.J. Shin. 2014. "Globalization and Domestic Trade Policy Preferences: Foreign Frames and Mass Support for Agriculture Subsidies." *International Interactions* 40 (3): 305–324.

Kahan, D. 2010. "Fixing the Communications Failure." *Nature* 463 (7279): 296–297.

Kahan, D., and D. Braman. 2006. "Cultural Cognition and Public Policy." *Yale Law & Policy Review* 24: 147–170.

Kahan, D., D. Braman, G. Cohen, J. Gastil, and P. Slovic. 2010. "Who Fears the HPV Vaccine, Who Doesn't, and Why? An Experimental Study of the Mechanisms of Cultural Cognition." *Law and Human Behavior* 34 (6): 501–516.

Legg, W. 2019. "Tim Josling's Legacy—The Gold Standard to Measure Agricultural Support." *EuroChoices* 18 (2): 47–48.

Lesser, L., C. Ebbeling, M. Goozner, D. Wypij, and D. Ludwig. 2007. "Relationship between Funding Source and Conclusion among Nutrition-Related Scientific Articles." *PLoS Medicine* 4 (1): e5.

Lundh, A., J. Lexchin, B. Mintzes, J. Schroll, and L. Bero. 2017. "Industry Sponsorship and Research Outcome." *The Cochrane Database of Systematic Reviews* 2 (2): MR000033.

Lusk, J. 2012. "The Political Ideology of Food." *Food Policy* 37 (5): 530–542.

Lusk, J., and B. Briggeman. 2009. "Food Values." *American Journal of Agricultural Economics* 91 (1): 184–196.

Mäkiniemi, J., A. Pirttilä-Backman, and M. Pieri. 2013. "The Endorsement of the Moral Foundations in Food-Related Moral Thinking in Three European Countries." *Journal of Agricultural and Environmental Ethics* 26 (4): 771–786.

Mandrioli, D., C. Kearns, and L. Bero. 2016. "Relationship between Research Outcomes and Risk of Bias, Study Sponsorship, and Author Financial Conflicts of Interest in Reviews of the Effects of Artificially Sweetened Beverages on Weight Outcomes: A Systematic Review of Reviews." *PLoS ONE* 15 (3): e0230469. https://dx.doi.org/10.1371/journal.pone.0162198

Mann, C. 2018. *The Wizard and the Prophet: Two Remarkable Scientists and Their Dueling Visions to Shape Tomorrow's World*. New York: Knopf.

Mansfield, E., and D. Mutz. 2009. "Support for Free Trade: Self-interest, Sociotropic Politics, and Out-Group Anxiety." *International Organization* 63 (3): 425–457.

Massougbodji, J., Y. Le Bodo, R. Fratu, and P. De Wals. 2014. "Reviews Examining Sugar-Sweetened Beverages and Body Weight: Correlates of Their Quality and Conclusions." *The American Journal of Clinical Nutrition* 99 (5): 1096–1104.

Meijer, A., and J. De Jong. 2019. "Managing Value Conflicts in Public Innovation: Ostrich, Chameleon, and Dolphin Strategies." *International Journal of Public Administration* 43 (11): 977–988.

Mialon, M., B. Swinburn, and G. Sacks. 2015. "A Proposed Approach to Systematically Identify and Monitor the Corporate Political Activity of the Food Industry with Respect to Public Health Using Publicly Available Information." *Obesity Reviews* 16 (7): 519–530.

Moon, W., and G. Pino. 2018. "Do U.S. Citizens Support Government Intervention in Agriculture? Implications for the Political Economy of Agricultural Protection." *Agricultural Economics* 49 (1): 119–129.

Naoi, M., and I. Kume. 2011. "Explaining Mass Support for Agricultural Protectionism: Evidence from a Survey Experiment during the Global Recession." *International Organization* 65 (4): 771–795.

OECD. 2012. *Recommendation of the Council on Regulatory Policy and Governance.* Paris: OECD Publishing.

OECD. 2017. *Preventing Policy Capture: Integrity in Public Decision Making.* OECD Public Governance Reviews. Paris: OECD Publishing.

OECD. 2021. *Making Better Policies for Food Systems.* Paris: OECD Publishing.

OECD (Organization for Economic Co-operation and Development). 2020. *Innovative Citizen Participation and New Democratic Institutions: Catching the Deliberative Wave.* Paris: OECD Publishing.

Paarlberg, R. 2013. *Food Politics: What Everyone Needs to Know.* Oxford, UK: Oxford University Press.

Parkhurst, J. 2017. *The Politics of Evidence: From Evidence-Based Policy to the Good Governance of Evidence.* London: Routledge.

Pew Research Center. 2015. "An Elaboration of AAAS Scientists' Views." Accessed March 11, 2020. https://www.pewresearch.org/science/2015/07/23/an-elaboration-of-aaas-scientists-views/

Putnam, R. 1988. "Diplomacy and Domestic Politics: The Logic of Two-Level Games." *International Organization* 42 (3): 427–460.

Qaim, M. 2020. "Role of New Plant Breeding Technologies for Food Security and Sustainable Agricultural Development." *Applied Economic Perspectives and Policy* 42 (2): 129–150.

Rausser, G., J. Swinnen, and P. Zusman. 2011. *Political Power and Economic Policy: Theory, Analysis, and Empirical Applications.* Cambridge, UK: Cambridge University Press.

Rein, M. 2006. "Reframing Problematic Policies." In *The Oxford Handbook of Public Policy,* eds. R. Goodin, M. Rein, and M. Moran, Ch. 18, 389–405. Oxford, UK: Oxford University Press.

Rein, M., and D. Schön. 1993. "Reframing Policy Discourse." In *The Argumentative Turn in Policy Analysis and Planning,* eds. F. Fischer and J. Forester, 145–166. Durham, NC: Duke University Press.

Rho, S., and M. Tomz. 2017. "Why Don't Trade Preferences Reflect Economic Self-Interest?" *International Organization* 71 (S1): S85–S108.

Ryfe, D. 2005. "Does Deliberative Democracy Work?" *Annual Review of Political Science* 8 (1): 49–71.

SAPEA (Science Advice for Policy by European Academies). 2020. *A Sustainable Food System for the European Union.* Berlin: SAPEA.

Scott, S., Y. Inbar, C. Wirz, D. Brossard, and P. Rozin. 2018. "An Overview of Attitudes Toward Genetically Engineered Food." *Annual Review of Nutrition* 38 (1): 459–479.

Stewart, J. 2006. "Value Conflict and Policy Change." *Review of Policy Research* 23 (1): 183–195.

Sunstein, C. 2018. *The Cost-Benefit Revolution.* Cambridge, MA: MIT Press.

Susskind, L. 2006. "Arguing, Bargaining, and Getting Agreement." In *The Oxford Handbook of Public Policy*, eds. R. Goodin, M. Rein, and M. Moran, Ch. 13, 269–295. Oxford, UK: Oxford University Press.

Swinnen, J. 2018. *The Political Economy of Agricultural and Food Policies.* New York: Palgrave Macmillan.

Thacher, D., and M. Rein 2004. "Managing Value Conflict in Public Policy." *Governance* 17 (4): 457–486.

Thompson, D. 2008. "Deliberative Democratic Theory and Empirical Political Science." *Annual Review of Political Science* 11 (1): 497–520.

Thompson, P. 2017. *The Spirit of the Soil: Agriculture and Environmental Ethics.* London: Routledge.

Toler, S., B. Briggeman, J. Lusk, and D. Adams. 2009. "Fairness, Farmers Markets, and Local Production." *American Journal of Agricultural Economics* 91 (5): 1272–1278.

Tompson, W. 2009. *The Political Economy of Reform: Lessons from Pensions, Product Markets and Labour Markets in Ten OECD Countries.* Paris: OECD Publishing.

Winship, C. 2006. "Policy Analysis as Problem Solving." In *The Oxford Handbook of Public Policy*, eds. R. Goodin, M. Rein, and M. Moran, Ch. 5, 109–123. Oxford, UK: Oxford University Press.

Wolff, J., and D. Haubrich. 2006. "Economism and Its Limits." In *The Oxford Handbook of Public Policy*, eds. R. Goodin, M. Rein, and M. Moran, Ch. 37, 746–770. Oxford, UK: Oxford University Press.

Wong, J. 2019. "The Idea That There Are Only 100 Harvests Left Is Just a Fantasy." *New Scientist*, May 8. https://www.newscientist.com/article/mg24232291-100-the-idea-that-there-are-only-100-harvests-left-is-just-a-fantasy/

World Bank. 2015. "The Biases of Development Professionals". In *World Development Report 2015: Mind, Society and Behaviour*, Ch. 10, 180–191. Washington, DC: World Bank.

World Economic Forum. 2012. "What If the World's Soil Runs Out?" *Time*, December 14. https://world.time.com/2012/12/14/what-if-the-worlds-soil-runs-out/

3

The Political Economy of Reforming Agricultural Support Policies

Rob Vos, Will Martin, and Danielle Resnick

3.1 Introduction

In both developed and developing countries, agricultural support policies provide enormous transfers of resources to agriculture—about US$817 billion per year worldwide in the 2019–2021 period (OECD 2022).[1] Some agricultural support policies, such as input subsidies, have boosted global food production, particularly of staple crops, thereby reducing hunger and poverty. Yet, there are serious concerns about their impacts on achieving sustainable, healthy, and inclusive food systems. Redirecting or "repurposing" agricultural subsidies toward investments that support both increased production and greater sustainability—such as agricultural research and development (R&D) and rural infrastructure—has the potential for win-win-win gains for people, planet, and prosperity.

This chapter first considers how shifts in agricultural support would affect global efforts to promote healthy, inclusive, and sustainable food system transformation. Since such reforms are contingent on political economy considerations, the chapter subsequently presents a framework for analyzing how interests, institutions, ideas and information, and policy characteristics intersect to facilitate or stymie reform efforts. Case studies of attempted reforms from different regions are presented that highlight the relevance of the framework. The chapter concludes by summarizing some potentially enabling political economy conditions for repurposing agricultural support policies.

---

[1] This chapter draws on material that was included in IFPRI (2022: Ch. 2). It is an abridged version of a longer paper prepared for the Food System Economic Commission (see Vos, Martin, and Resnick 2022). The authors are grateful to Jikun Huang, Bharat Ramaswami, and Johan Swinnen for their inputs into the case study material presented in this chapter. The authors are further grateful for research funding received from the EAT Foundation and the OneCGIAR research initiative "Rethinking Food Markets and Value Chains for Inclusion and Sustainability."

Rob Vos, Will Martin, and Danielle Resnick, *The Political Economy of Reforming Agricultural Support Policies*. In: *The Political Economy of Food System Transformation*. Edited by: Danielle Resnick and Johan Swinnen, Oxford University Press.
© Rob Vos, Will Martin, and Danielle Resnick (2023). DOI: 10.1093/oso/9780198882121.003.0003

3.2 Current Agricultural Support and Its Impacts

3.2.1 Current Support

Current agricultural support goes largely to agricultural producers, primarily in forms that affect market prices and distort incentives for producers and con-sumers. Agricultural support (provided by 54 countries for which comparable data are available) amounted to $817 billion per year, in 2019–2021 (OECD 2022). Individual producers received $611 billion per year in positive support (that is support excluding taxes on exports), representing 17 percent of gross farm receipts in OECD countries and 13 percent in the 11 emerging economies for which data are available. Of this support to producers, more than half, or $317 billion per year, took the form of support through higher market prices paid by consumers ("market price support"), while the remaining $293 billion was paid by taxpayers through farm payments (Figure 3.1), of which $74 billion in the form of subsidies coupled to output levels or input use and $.200 billion in decoupled payments to farmers. Direct subsidies to consumers totaled $100 billion per annum during 2019–2021 and $106 billion was for "general services," which include expenditures on agricultural R&D, rural infrastructure, and extension services.

Not all of this support comprises the use of government budget resources. The market price support (MPS) involves implicit transfers from consumers to pro-ducers by creating a price gap between domestic market prices and border prices for specific agricultural commodities. Border measures include tariffs, tariff rate quotas, or import licenses that raise domestic prices, benefiting the farm sector. Some emerging and developing countries, including Argentina, India, Indonesia, Kazakhstan, Russia, and Vietnam, implicitly tax producers of certain agricultural commodities through export taxes or export restrictions, which depresses the domestic prices of these products. This "negative" market price support amounted

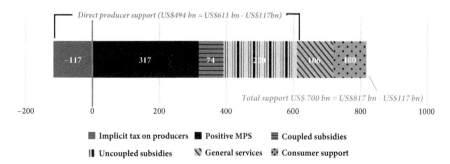

Figure 3.1 Agricultural producer support by main types of support, 2019–2021 (billions of US$ per year).

Source: Compiled from data from OECD 2022.

to $117 billion per year (Figure 3.1), but rose significantly in 2022, as many countries responded with such measures to the global food, feed, and fertilizer market impacts of the war in Ukraine.

Support measures requiring fiscal expenditures amounted to $500 billion per year in 2019–2021. As mentioned above, these include the direct transfers to producers in the form of coupled and decoupled farm payments amounting to $293 billion per year, consumer subsidies ($100 billion) and the general services support ($106 billion). Thus, only a limited portion of total support (about 12 percent) is for R&D and agricultural innovation systems, infrastructure, and other general services for the sector, with only 4 percent of total support allocated specifically to R&D in 2019–2021.

In absolute terms, agricultural support is concentrated in a few large economies (Figure 3.2). The European Union (EU) and the United States (US), both large agricultural producers, jointly account for two-thirds of the total support provided by rich countries, amounting to around $230 billion per year by far most of which is in the form of direct farm payments. The support in the non-OECD developing countries increased to $360 billion per year in 2019/21, of which China alone provided about $280 billion per year mostly in the form of market price support to farmers. Other non-OECD developing countries provide most support in the form of coupled direct payments to farmers and general services. For this group as whole, MPS is negative, meaning a net tax on producers, mainly on account of India's policy stance.

For the discussion on repurposing of the present support, the focus of this chapter, three important points can be made: (a) agricultural support is huge and much takes the form of market distorting measures; (b) repurposing of this

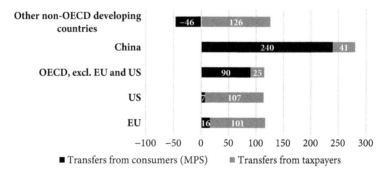

Figure 3.2 Agricultural producer support by main countries and country groupings, 2019–2021 (billions of US$ per year).

Notes: Transfers from consumers refer to market price support; transfers from taxpayers include coupled and uncoupled payments to farmers and general service expenditures.
Source: Compiled from data from OECD 2022.

support involves not only reallocation of budgetary resources, but importantly also changing price incentives through reform of MPS; and (c) degrees of support vary greatly across countries but concentrated among a few large economies, implying that an even-handed repurposing agenda serving global objectives will require international cooperation and overcoming domestic political economy constraints to achieve that cooperation. Before turning to the nature of the desired policy reform and the political obstacles to such reform at the national level, we first assess the impacts of the current support.

3.2.2 Impacts of Current Support

Support coupled to output or input use increases output, leading to increased greenhouse gas (GHG) emissions from agricultural production and land conversion for agriculture. Some types of support—such as fertilizer subsidies—also encourage the use of production techniques that increase emissions per unit of output. Support provided through trade barriers, however, may reduce global emissions because it couples incentives to increase output with higher prices to consumers. The strong focus of many agricultural support policies on promoting staple crops has improved access to basic calories but has done much less to improve dietary diversity. Moreover, social impacts of support are often regressive—benefiting wealthier, commercial farmers, while denying poorer farmers access to markets—and raising the cost of nutritious food and harming poor consumers.

Government support to agriculture usually is justified by perceived needs to protect farm incomes, ensure food availability, and promote agricultural productivity. However, its efficiency in delivering benefits to farmers is low, providing a return to agriculture of 35 cents for every dollar spent (Gautam et al. 2022); with the remainder either shared with consumers or dissipated as economic waste. Much of those 35 cents are likely capitalized into land values (Ciaran et al. 2021). Only a small share of support is in the form of fully decoupled transfers despite their potentially much higher transfer efficiency. Similarly, only a small share of total support is invested in public goods, including R&D and rural infrastructure, although both the private and social returns of such investments are estimated to be very high. Many interventions create trade conflicts between countries and very few help reduce the GHG emissions that are driving climate change, despite the threat of devastating climate change impacts on agriculture, especially in tropical zones.

The need for reforms is now well recognized (see e.g., OECD 2021, 2022), and the urgency of reducing GHG emissions and adapting to climate change has added impetus to the calls for reform. However, recent studies have shown that simply eliminating all existing support would not greatly reduce GHG emissions, but would depress farm incomes, increase poverty, and increase the cost of healthy diets (Searchinger et al. 2020; FAO, UNDP, and UNEP 2021; Laborde et al. 2021; Gautam et al. 2022). Public discourse, including at the 2021 United Nations Food Systems Summit and during the climate discussions at COP26 and COP27, thus has shifted to how existing support might be repurposed to create better incentives for producers and consumers.[2]

3.2.3 Global Scenario Analysis: Removing All Support

To understand the impacts of current support, a series of recent studies estimated the impact of a complete withdrawal of current agricultural support on GHG emissions, farm output, poverty, food security, and diets (Laborde et al. 2020, 2021; FAO, UNDP, and UNEP 2021; Gautam et al. 2022). The results show that current measures have only a small influence on the global overall volume of agricultural production (see Figure 3.2), although they do have important impacts in individual countries. The small impact on the current level of output should be understood in the context of decades-long sustained support to the buildup of present systems, and that the removal of such support now would not lead producers to suddenly reverse all they have built up in capacity with the support. Moreover, at the global level, withdrawal of domestic subsidies and border measures offsets impacts on production and emissions. Removing subsidies reduces both global food output and emissions, but removing border protection, which acts as a tax on demand, slightly increases global output and emissions. The combination of removing both subsidies and border support slightly reduces global output and GHG emissions from agriculture (see Figure 3.3), lowers farm output, and raises the costs of healthy diets.

The impacts of removing all agricultural subsidies also differ substantially between rich and poor countries. As reported in Gautam et al. (2022), the drop in per worker farm income would be four times larger in developed countries than in developing countries. In contrast, farm employment would decline in developed countries but increase in developing countries, where higher world prices would induce a supply and employment response. However, global poverty would rise as higher food prices push more people below the poverty line. GHG emissions would fall by over 6 percent in the developed countries, but by only 1.5 percent globally. The distributional impacts, if the scenario analysis is deemed credible, would suggest that crude policy reform undoing existing support is bound to face strong opposition from those having to pay a price for, at best, very minor gains toward one societal goal only.

---

[2] See: https://https://foodsystems.community/game-changing-propositions-solution-clusters/repurposing-public-support-to-food-and-agriculture-2/

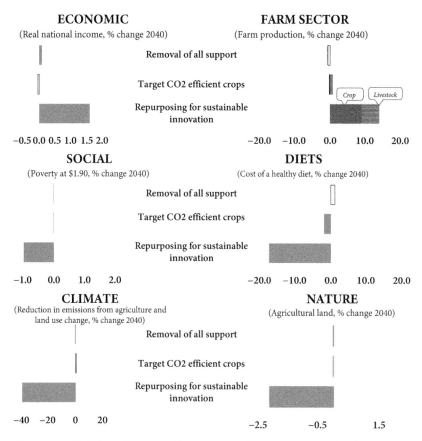

Figure 3.3 Global implications of repurposing domestic support (% change relative to baseline projections for 2040).

Note: **Dark-shaded** bars indicate movement toward societal goals; **white** bars indicate movement away from societal goals.
Source: Gautam et al. (2022).

3.2.4 Global Scenario Analysis: Repurposing Support

Given the above results, how can the substantial resources that support agriculture be repurposed in ways that simultaneously provide strong incentives to reduce GHG emissions, improve food system efficiency and farm productivity, and help combat poverty, hunger, and malnutrition? Additional model-based analysis (Gautam et al. 2022) indicates that investing an additional 1 percent of agricultural output value (or about $45 billion in 2021 prices) in R&D for technologies that both increase the efficiency of production and reduce emission intensities, complemented by incentives to farmers to adopt those technologies, could achieve greater gains with fewer trade-offs than simply eliminating subsidies.

This scenario involves countries repurposing about 15 percent of 2016/18 domestic support into R&D that generates green innovations which reduce emission intensities by 30 percent while raising productivity by 30 percent. These improvements are consistent with those reported for key innovations, such as modified diets for ruminants and alternate wetting and drying for rice. The scenario results are promising: global welfare and food output increase; food prices fall, making food and healthy diets more affordable for many people; and poverty rates fall worldwide (Figure 3.3). Global GHG emissions from agriculture and land use change would drop by about 40 percent, both because of the direct reduction in emissions from crop production and because higher productivity reduces the need for agricultural land. Farm incomes would fall with the removal of subsidies, although returns to farm labor would rise if policy reform were combined with rural development policies to reduce the barriers to movement of labor out of agriculture.

Such a win-win-win scenario could suggest there should be a straightforward road to reform. Yet, political obstacles may well emerge, as farmers may be more uncertain about the productivity and net income gains of innovations than the model scenario assumes and may not be persuaded to accept reform for gains obtained at some distance from their farms (i.e., poverty reduction in other parts of the world or containing climate instability globally in a distant future). Hence, when assessing options for reform and their political feasibility, a deeper dive is needed into factors behind resistance to reform.

3.3 Political Economy Framework for Reform

As the modeling results illustrate, reforms to, and repurposing of, agricultural support policies could produce significantly better outcomes for poverty reduction, for food security and nutrition and for the natural environment, especially if carried out in an internationally coordinated manner. However, achieving outcomes that will be socially optimal for the planet in the longer-term require policy shifts that may face considerable political resistance in the short term, especially if certain groups perceive that they may lose out or face considerable adjustment costs. Moreover, not all optimal policies can be feasibly implemented in a particular country context. International coordination therefore requires first understanding possible sources of domestic resistance or support for a reform agenda and be calibrated to extant state capacities.

To do so, we provide a framework in Figure 3.4 to show how interest groups, institutions, ideas, and information, and policy characteristics combine to delineate who exercises leverage, opportunities for debate and deliberation, influences on policy design, and capacities for implementation. Where those different elements intersect is the win-set, which refers to the range of alternative instruments

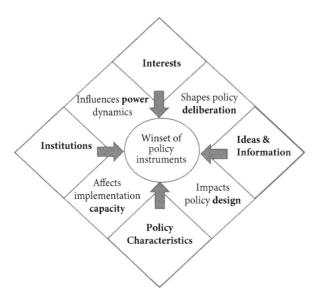

Figure 3.4 Identifying political economy influences on policy options

Source: Authors' depiction.

that a majority of stakeholders prefer compared to the status quo. In other words, the win-set encompasses the most politically feasible policy instruments for repurposing agricultural support, which may include re-allocating subsidies for agricultural R&D, removing price supports, or attaching environmental conditionalities to subsidies. The framework is then used to review recent reform attempts in different national and regional settings in order to draw broader political economy lessons.

3.3.1 Interest Groups

Interest groups play a central role in the political economy of agricultural support policies. Some individuals derive their interests from material goals based on either their position in the economy or in the political arena. The opportunity to secure profits, votes, job security, and prestige, among others, may all shape who favors which policies. For instance, political economy analyses of fertilizer subsidy programs hypothesize that politicians favor these programs because they maximize their chances of re-election (Dionne and Horowitz 2016; Mason et al. 2017). The growing emphasis on food systems, rather than agriculture alone, upends traditional fault lines across interest groups because it requires considering a more complex array of interests and coalitions (Anderson et al. 2013; Swinnen 2015).

Just like individuals, countries have their own interests. For instance, countries may attempt to protect national food security by restricting exports of staple foods or lowering import tariffs on such products (as happened, for instance, in response to global food price crisis during 2022), even though this may end up exacerbating price increases in global markets (Martin and Minot 2022; Glauber et al. 2023).

3.3.2 Institutions

Not all interest groups have equivalent influence and power to secure their objectives (Grossman and Helpman 1994). More concentrated interest groups are frequently able to harness the support from policymakers to gain distortions that narrowly benefit them, even at considerable economic, environmental, and social costs to the economy (Anderson 1995; Olson 1965). In rich countries, for instance, farmers can organize much more easily than in poor countries and have historically been able to secure much more support than farmers in poor countries. And farmers in industries that are geographically concentrated and require close coordination for processing—such as dairy and sugar—tend to get higher protection than those more geographically spread and sold without substantial processing, such as fruits and vegetables.

The structure of institutions largely shapes both whose interests gain traction with policymakers and the prospects for policy coordination and implementation. The importance of institutions spans a wide range of modalities, including domestic regime types (e.g., democracies, autocracies, anocracies), parliamentary and presidential systems, federal or unitary settings, the World Trade Organization (WTO), and international conventions. Sometimes, decisions on agricultural policy may be controlled by a small but politically powerful constituency, epitomized by military involvement in wheat flour milling in Sudan, fertilizer production in Pakistan, or agricultural extension in Uganda (Resnick 2021a, 2021b). Attention to such institutions also underscores the "two-level games" (Putnam 1988), or simultaneous negotiations at national and international levels. In such instances, the gains from international cooperation are diffuse but the costs are concentrated among certain interest groups and sectors who may have substantive domestic influence to block reform.

3.3.3 Ideas and Information

Ideational concerns can also shape interests (see Chapter 1). In this view, policy preferences are derived from historical experience, cultural norms, and societal expectations (Blyth 1997; Abdelal 2009). This may lead policymakers and citizens to, for instance, favor the market over the state, food security over dietary diversity, or nationalism over multilateralism. A particularly salient ideational view adopted by many governments is that food self-sufficiency is tantamount to food security (Sen 1981). Such aspirations can contribute to autarkic practices, such as Nigeria's year-long border closure with Benin in 2019 to increase domestic production of rice. Often, ideational and material interests intersect; concerns about self-sufficiency can provide justification for policies that ultimately support a country's material interests in creating jobs for farmers or ensuring lower food prices for consumers.

Information derived from empirical analysis, media outlets, or learning of policy experiences from other contexts can, like ideas, cause interest groups and policy actors to update their preferences. Despite the conventional wisdom that evidence should inform policymaking, there are disparate understandings of what constitutes evidence. The credibility of the source, the means of diffusion and the background of decisionmakers all determine how information is perceived and whether it is acted upon (MacKillop and Downe 2022). The credibility of the source and the means of diffusion do, however, play a key role in determining how information is perceived and whether it is acted upon. As discussed in Chapter 1, this is especially true in more polarized political environments that can result in even high-quality information being dismissed if it does not resonate with extant biases of policymakers (Kosec and Wantchekon 2020). Moreover, the way in which information is disseminated can influence which policy instruments may be more viable. On the one hand, mass media may ensure that a larger set of affected stakeholders are aware of a policy's distributive implications (Olper and Swinnen 2013). On the other hand, decisionmakers may obfuscate the details of instruments to avoid alienating groups that may stand to lose the most (Swinnen 2018).

3.3.4 Policy Characteristics

Policies have different characteristics, including the dispersion and concentration of costs and benefits, time to demonstrate impact, visibility to the public, and different degrees of sophistication in implementation (see Swinnen 2018). For instance, pollution taxes have a key advantage over regulatory approaches in encouraging adjustment on a wide range of margins—such as choice of production techniques, level of output, and creation of incentives for innovation—perhaps leading to entirely new and unanticipated ways to reduce pollution. Taxes are usually easier to administer than regulatory policies, which require a certain degree of enforcement capacity. Yet, pollution taxes tend to be very unpopular, particularly if imposed on powerful interest groups.

Other instruments include the use of conditionality or incentive subsidies to induce behavioral change by tying practices with desirable social or environmental outcomes, such as low-carbon management practices, to the receipt of a benefit

(Searchinger 2020). Several studies in Southern Africa have found that incentive subsidies increased farmers' adoption of conservation agriculture methods (Bell et al. 2018; Ngoma et al. 2018; Ward et al. 2018). These instruments are a category of distributive policies and less likely to generate contention among stakeholders because while the resources may be collected from diffuse groups (e.g., taxpayers), the benefits are concentrated on just a few actors (Lowi 1972). At the same time, they require strong oversight to ensure farmer compliance with program conditions, making them administratively demanding. Even if compliance can be achieved, such policies need to be carefully evaluated for their impact on productivity. For instance, if the proposed technology is expected to be less productive than the techniques that farmers would have otherwise chosen, it could require farmers to expand land under cultivation with possible adverse environmental impacts.

Regulatory policies restrict the activities of individuals or groups under certain conditions and at risk of some penalty. These types of policies, such as imposing limits on GHG emissions or mandating producers to use organic practices, are much more contentious because they concentrate costs on specific interest groups (Lowi 1972). The viability of regulation depends on the power of such interest groups. These approaches have had some success in particular cases like ozone-depleting refrigerants (Montreal Protocol), where an alternative technology is available. But they proved much less effective than tradable quotas in dealing with acid rain spillovers between the US and Canada. Establishing regulation can be difficult in low-capacity settings since enforcement is essential to policy efficacy. By contrast, de-regulation is considered a quintessential "stroke of the pen" reform (Grindle 1999) because it requires governments to desist from doing something, such as managing quantitative controls on trade or overseeing price controls.

The degree of resistance to removal of subsidies or to imposition of commodity taxes can depend on whether distinct constituencies benefit from the measure, or whether the redistribution of revenues results in investments in public goods of benefit to the affected interest groups. For instance, in Côte d'Ivoire and Kenya, export levies on certain agricultural commodities are intended to be used for reinvestment into agricultural research (Stads and Doumbia 2010; Andae 2021). The success of proposals such as that suggested by Gautam et al. (2022) to invest part of current agricultural support into R&D designed both to reduce emission intensities and to raise productivity will thus depend heavily upon whether the affected interest groups recognize the potential to raise productivity and hence increase farm incomes.

3.4 Case Studies of Agricultural Support Policy Reforms

Each of the key variables discussed in the framework above has demonstrated an important impact on the success or failure of policy reform efforts in several key case study settings. Below we focus on four cases—in India, China, the US, and the EU—that vary not only with regards to political institutions but also with respect to interest group dynamics and policy priorities. This comparative case study approach allows for elucidating which political economy factors have played a more prominent role over time, offering important insights about when and why certain policy options become more feasible and in particular the options suggested in Section 3.2.

3.4.1 Challenges of Market Reform in India

India's agricultural policies have long had twin goals, resulting in supporting farmers through input subsidies (fertilizer, electricity, and hence groundwater) while frequently reducing domestic food prices below world levels to benefit consumers. In addition, the Public Distribution System provides a safety net for poorer consumers through sales of food at concessional prices. Moreover, strong ideational objectives have underpinned interventions, such as the goal of national self-sufficiency in staple foods and price stabilization for key staples. Both input subsidies and minimum support prices for wheat and rice help maintain output levels. However, agriculture does not provide a viable livelihood for most Indian farmers, with 86 percent of farms working less than 2 hectares and mostly growing staple foods (India, Directorate of Economics and Statistics 2020).

Subsidies have also contributed to environmental degradation and GHG emissions; most notably, methane emissions from rice cultivation are sustained through rice price supports and electricity subsidies. Depletion of valuable water resources is also aggravated by support policies, both directly (through electricity subsidies that promote groundwater withdrawal) and indirectly (through output subsidies that promote overproduction of water-intensive rice). Much of the policy debate on environmental damage stemming from agriculture has focused on air pollution rather than reducing GHG emissions; crop-residue burning—a common practice in the paddy-wheat crop rotation sustained by support prices (Kumar et al. 2015)—is a major contributor to poor air quality in northern India.

Resolving trade-offs between supporting livelihoods and food security, on the one hand, and environmental sustainability on the other is a challenge. Current agricultural subsidies amount to about 2 percent of GDP, but account for about 20 percent of farm income (Ramaswami 2019). Any repurposing of support, including toward R&D and promotion of climate-smart policies, could thus cause hardship for poor farmers.

In the past decade, successive Indian governments have experimented with reforms. Historically, procurement of rice and wheat has been a major mechanism to provide minimum support prices to farmers. This system is costly and analysis suggests that simpler approaches could achieve the same goals at lower cost (Gouel et al. 2016). For some other crops, policymakers have used price deficiency payments, which are easier to administer despite being expensive and reproducing some of the market distortions of the procurement system. Some policymakers

increasingly see direct (uncoupled) transfers as an alternative to these distortionary subsidies. Progress has been made in financial systems to facilitate such
payments, but gaps remain in reaching all farmers, in part because of poor land
records and insufficient digital connectivity.

Agricultural policy reform would serve India's national interests and potentially
make an important global contribution to climate change mitigation but lacks
political ownership and is likely electorally costly. In addition, the country's federal
structure gives state governments considerable influence over agricultural policies, which can make policy reform challenging but not necessarily impossible—as
became evident with India's successful implementation of a goods and services
tax that has substantially reduced the costs of transporting goods across state
borders (Rao 2019). These factors all contributed to the difficulties of implementing three market-friendly reforms introduced by India's Finance Minister in May
2020.[3] The first allowed farmers to sell outside of the government-regulated *mandis* (wholesale markets), engage in barrier-free inter- and intra-state trade of farm
commodities, and provide a framework for e-trading of agricultural produce. This
was seen as a way to overcome fragmented supply chains created by the mandis.
The second aimed to de-regulate commodities such as cereals, pulses, oilseeds,
onion, and potato, by no longer allowing them to be exposed to stock-holding
limits, except under extraordinary circumstances. The third sought to allow farmers to engage in contract-pricing schemes with agro-processors that would reduce
price risk to the farmers and encourage private sector investment in agricultural
inputs and technology. The latter was viewed as especially beneficial to producers of perishable fruits and vegetables who appeared to be losing out by relying
on slow-moving government agencies to procure and distribute them (Singh and
Rosmann 2020).

On June 3, 2020, the Union Cabinet approved the policy resolutions and two
days later, the Ministry of Law and Justice issued three ordinances, or farm laws,
that corresponded with the resolutions. The farm laws were then passed by the
majority Bharatiya Janata Party (BJP) Parliament in September 2020, despite resistance from all of the countries' main opposition parties who claimed that the
bills were against the interests of small and marginal farmers and that they had
been pushed forward using emergency powers under COVID-19 with minimal
legislative discussion (Jadhav and Bhardwaj 2020).

In fact, their resistance reflected opposition by different interest groups about
the implications of the laws. While the ability to sell outside Agricultural Produce
and Livestock Market Committee (APMC) *mandis* could improve competition
and reduce transportation costs, concerns emerged about the ability of small farmers to negotiate good prices with large buyers. In addition, there was opposition

---

[3] The announcement on May 15 of that year was part of a five-day set of measures announced as
part of the Self-Reliant India Special Economic Packages (see Singh 2020).

from the commission agents in the mandis, known as "*arhatiyas*," who are influential with farmers and who would potentially lose commissions from the reforms. State governments have been concerned about the loss of tax revenue as a result of anticipated declines in the fees that typically are collected from levies on trade outside the APMC markets. The provision allowing contract farming further raised suspicions that this would result in small farmers losing access to their land and enabling large agribusinesses to dominate markets (Sahoo et al. 2020).

In addition, the disputes over the reforms revealed deeper tensions between the states and the center, across states, and among different farmer groups. For instance, in BJP-controlled Gujarat, Madhya Pradesh, Uttar Pradesh, and Karnataka, state governments had already approved amendments to the APMC Acts in early May that de-regulated trade outside the mandis (Kaur 2020). By contrast, in opposition-controlled Punjab and Rajasthan, disgruntled farmers were supported by their state governments, which refused to adopt the three farm bills (Bhatia 2021).

Starting in October 2020, opposition protests were organized by farmers' unions that were predominantly from Punjab, Haryana, and Rajasthan—major wheat producing states—and often led by the Bharatiya Kisan Union (Indian Farmers' Union). They feared the reforms would ultimately lead to the elimination of subsidized crop prices and make them susceptible to takeover by large corporations. By late November, opposing farmers marched to New Delhi. In December, farmers' unions under the All India Kisan Coordination Committee from other states, including Bihar, Kerala, Tamil Nadu, and Telangana, expressed their support for the farm reforms. Eight rounds of talks between the government and the opposing farmers did not lead to a resolution of concerns. In January 2021, India's Supreme Court temporarily suspended the new agricultural laws to allow further time for negotiation and to build consensus (Sharma 2020).

3.4.2 Shifting Agricultural Priorities in China

The Chinese setting is notably different due to more centralized political institutions that permit substantial policy changes once policy makers are convinced of the need for change. China's agricultural performance has been impressive—averaging 4.5 percent annual sectoral growth and 7 percent annual growth in farm incomes since the 1980s—while substantially diversifying production. Yet, the rural–urban income gap has widened, and agricultural expansion has come at the cost of natural resource degradation and high greenhouse gas (GHG) emissions (Huang and Yang 2017).

Achieving self-sufficiency in staple foods and stability of domestic food prices are policy priorities in China. The Chinese government implicitly taxed agriculture until the early 1990s by keeping urban food prices low. This policy was reversed in the mid-1990s as concerns grew about the expanding rural–urban income gap and urban consumers became less concerned about food prices. The government allowed domestic prices to rise above world market prices and began providing direct payments to farmers—thus shifting from taxation of producers to protection of domestic production. As a result, the nominal rate of protection (NRP) in agriculture increased from −50 percent in 1981 to around +13 percent in recent years, with direct payments adding 5 percentage points (as reflected in the nominal rate of assistance, NRA; see Figure 3.5).

The transformation of China's agricultural policies might have been even greater if it had not been limited by the country's commitment to multilateral trading rules. For instance, protection of domestic rice production would likely have been higher if not for China's commitment to a tariff binding (cap) of 65 percent at the WTO. While the country's policymakers remain committed to ensuring grain self-sufficiency, they managed to do so without substantially raising protection for rice, in contrast with earlier high-growth economies in the region, such as Japan, where rice protection reached over 800 percent, and Korea, where it reached over 400 percent (Anderson 2009). WTO disciplines have also contributed to China shifting to less distortionary forms of support (Swinnen 2018: Ch. 7).

To support farm incomes, the Chinese government introduced a direct payment scheme in 2004 largely decoupled from agricultural production and increased support through crop procurement schemes. Despite the huge fiscal cost, these reforms had only a modest effect on average farm incomes, and benefits from

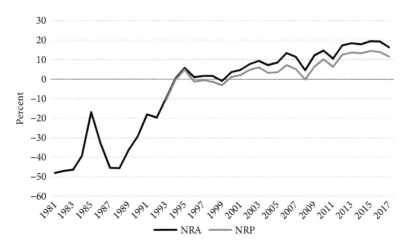

Figure 3.5 China's support to agriculture, 1981–2017

Note: Nominal rate of protection (NRP) is calculated as support from border protection divided by the value of agricultural production at world prices. Nominal rate of assistance (NRA) is calculated as support from all sources divided by value of agricultural production at world prices.
Source: Data compiled from Huang et al. (2010) and OECD (2021).

procurement were unequally shared. As a result, the government phased out public procurement of all commodities, except for rice, wheat, and cotton, and converted all farm subsidies to lump-sum income transfers to farmers in 2015.

Environmental concerns and international commitments to reducing GHG emissions led the Chinese government to enhance its Store Grains (Food) in Land (SGiL) and Store Grains (Food) in Technology (SGiT) programs to raise productivity, enhance food security, and promote sustainable production. The program enlargement, introduced in 2015, included large-scale investments in "high-standard farmland," defined as land with a high degree of resilience to impacts of droughts and floods, water-saving production practices, high yields, and soil improvement. Through the SGiT, public expenditure on agricultural R&D was raised to RMB26 billion (about $4.1 billion), overtaking US spending and making China the world's largest public investor in agricultural R&D (Chai et al. 2019). The additional R&D is primarily focused on biotechnology and digital technology.

In 2016, the Chinese government also introduced a special project to reduce fertilizer and pesticide use and a subsidy program to promote organic fertilizers. In 2018, Technical Guidelines on Green Agricultural Development were issued, promoting low-carbon and circular-economy technologies to raise productivity, reduce GHG emissions, and enhance carbon sequestration. This strategy is part of China's effort to comply with its commitments under the Paris Agreement to reduce GHG emissions by 2030 and achieve carbon neutrality by 2060. This exemplifies how institutions (international agreements, in this case) can drive national policy reform.

3.4.3 CAP Reform in the European Union

European policy reforms between the 1980s and the early 2000s illustrate how even policies that are rooted in long-held ideas, like food self-sufficiency, and heavily supported by powerful interest groups can sometimes be fundamentally changed. In particular, when the European Union (EU)'s Common Agricultural Policy (CAP) was designed in the 1960s, it featured administratively determined market price support and import barriers. Farm organizations lobbied for this system to protect them against internal and external competition. The policy also resonated with the public given concerns about food self-sufficiency in the wake of World War II.

High support prices ignited a strong supply response and turned the EU into a major commodity exporter by the 1980s. The farm support required export subsidies, provoking the ire of other agricultural exporters, particularly the United States, which responded with its own program of export subsidies. As world agricultural prices fell to unprecedented lows during the mid-1980s, pressures from other countries and budgetary pressures increased, with rising costs of export subsidies and storage. Unsold stocks accumulated in embarrassing "butter mountains" and "wine lakes."

Agricultural exporters pushed hard for reform of global agricultural trade during the Uruguay Round of global trade negotiations (1986–1993). Given European desire to contribute to the Uruguay Round and the internal problems with the price support system, important CAP reforms were introduced in 1993, including reducing and replacing support prices with direct payments to farmers (Swinbank 2016).

Several concurrent pressures resulted in subsequent reforms. These included food safety and animal welfare crises in the 1990s, as well as the prospect of ten Eastern European countries with large agricultural sectors acceding to the EU in the 2000s. Expectations were that, unless the CAP was further reformed, it would lead to exploding budgets, a massive inflow of cheaper Eastern agricultural products, and a conflict with WTO agreements. Institutional changes within the EU facilitated reform since decisions no longer required unanimous agreement of EU member states, removing the veto power of reform opponents. These factors contributed to the 2003 reform that decoupled farm subsidies from production decisions, while maintaining the overall level of farm support, and allowing the gradual integration of the Eastern countries into the CAP (Swinnen 2008).

Environmental goals also have been further integrated into Europe's agricultural policies over the past 30 years, with budget allocations shifted accordingly (OECD 2017). However, the global food price spikes in 2008–2011 weakened pro-environment reforms that aimed to restrict input use and production (Swinnen 2014). More recently, the EU has attempted to build a Farm-to-Fork strategy as part of the European Green Deal that is designed to make Europe the first climate neutral continent by 2030 (EC 2020a, 2020b). As discussed more in chapter 13 of this book, the reforms include payments to farmers conditional on reduced use of pesticides and fertilizers, a shift to organic farming practices, and adoption of new technologies that reduce GHG emissions from agriculture. A possible trade-off is that shifting to organic farming practices could reduce productivity which, in turn, could drive agricultural land expansion and potentially lead to increased global GHG emissions from either land-use change or a shift to regions with higher emission intensities (Gautam et al. 2022). Just as in 2008–2011, high food prices on global markets in 2022 are also triggered similar political economy reactions, reinforcing lobby pressure from farmers and agribusiness against environmental policies that would reduce productivity and the EU's potential to produce food.

3.4.4 Biofuel Policies in the United States

Biofuel policies in the United States are an energy and agricultural strategy with important environmental dimensions. Biofuel policies were first introduced in the 1970s to replace expensive petroleum-based fuels and lead-based additives then used to improve engine performance. Their introduction was supported by farmers and ethanol producers keen to increase demand for their products. As concerns about global greenhouse gas (GHG) emissions increased, biofuels were increasingly justified on environmental grounds (Lawrence 2010).

Support for biofuels initially was provided via a tax credit (Tyner 2008). Reforms in 2005 and 2007 introduced a mandate for the use of biofuels, with targets rising from 13 to 36 billion gallons between 2010 and 2022. This policy was enormously popular with ethanol distillers and blenders, who otherwise would face substantial uncertainty about profitability and throughput.

These policies responded to new concerns about the environment and health as well as traditional desires to expand demand for farm products, but several concerns have emerged. First, a binding mandate makes the demand for feedstock unresponsive to changes in corn prices, hence contributing to grain price volatility. Second, due to concerns that transferring large shares of grain output to biofuels production would raise food prices (Wright 2014), the mandate required only a 25 percent increase in conventional biofuels but a twentyfold increase in advanced biofuels, mainly from plant-based matter unsuitable for human consumption. However, due to a lack of substantive technological innovations, advanced biofuel output has only increased sixfold (CRS 2022). Third, while bioethanol use may decrease fossil fuel emissions relative to use of fossil fuels, its production increases emissions through the land use change required to grow bioenergy crops (Searchinger 2008; EPA 2018). Recent estimates suggest that US ethanol has a higher GHG intensity than oil-based gasoline (Lark et al. 2022).

Several lessons can be drawn from the policy innovation represented by biofuels. One is that environmental goals, and particularly mitigation of climate change, may provide important pressure for change. A second is that it may be helpful to build coalitions, including among interest groups with different but potentially compatible goals—such as energy self-sufficiency and farm income support—to achieve rapid, widely supported reform. However, there is a risk of policies being captured by some members of the coalition and ending up not achieving their social goals. Third, no single instrument such as biofuel policy can hope to achieve multiple goals, reinforcing the message on policy bundling discussed In Chapter 9 of this volume. Finally, simply mandating a goal, such as a major expansion of output using new technologies, is unlikely to be successful unless it is backed by investments in targeted R&D.

3.4.5 Summary

Table 3.1 draws on the framework in Figure 3.4 to synthesize key political economy factors that affected policy reforms in the preceding cases. Despite institutional variations, similar policy instruments were implemented in China and the EU to create incentives rather than penalties for more environment-friendly practices. In addition, outlays of agricultural investments for R&D, which are usually seen as low visibility to voters and therefore marginalized by policymakers in democratic countries (Mogues 2015), have been a distinguishing feature of China's recent agricultural strategy. By contrast, the US relied on regulatory mandates for biofuels without sufficient corresponding R&D investments. India's agricultural market reform attempt, which required buy-in at both the federal and state levels and from powerful farmers unions and middlemen, was a much broader and complex undertaking that ultimately failed.

3.5 Conclusions

Climate change is an existential threat to food systems globally, and the scenario analysis for repurposing existing agricultural support presented in Section 3.2 showed that international cooperation for such policy reform should be expected to achieve superior outcomes on all environmental, economic, and social dimensions for all countries compared with current non-cooperative agricultural support policies. Existing government agricultural support budgets offer a potential source of public finance for innovations and incentives to producers and consumers. Currently, only an eighth of total government support to agriculture is invested in R&D, inspection and control systems, and rural infrastructure—all areas where the private sector tends to under-provide—while three-quarters is allocated to individual producing firms, many of which are commercial and large-scale operations, thus reinforcing inequality.

Nonetheless, agreeing on a common approach internationally is difficult partially because of political-economy constraints at the domestic level. Undoubtedly, current beneficiaries will resist policy reforms, while potential winners may be uncertain about the benefits or insufficiently organized to mobilize for change. Most policy reforms therefore emerge from first understanding the confluence of interest, institutions, and ideas that shape the status quo and then uncovering policy instruments that neutralize losses to potential opponents that also account for capacity constraints.

In this regard, the current chapter points to some promising paths and some dead ends for repurposing. For instance, the full abolition of current support is likely neither to find political support nor to generate more than modest reductions in emissions. Moving away from market-distorting price support or subsidies coupled to production levels or input use, and toward providing incentives through direct payments to farmers, is sensible from an efficiency perspective. Such direct payment schemes would need to be clearly targeted, and any conditionality attached to such payments be linked to verifiable farm targets and food systems objectives. Importantly, reforms often have unintended consequences;

Table 3.1 Comparison of political economy dynamics

Country	Interest groups	Institutional factors	Ideas & Information	Policy instruments and outcomes
India	Subsidy, trade, and procurement policies are electorally popular and benefit well-organized cereal farmers	Federal system results in concurrent powers over agriculture between the national and state governments, creates many veto players	Food self-sufficiency still predominant over environmental concerns	Stalled efforts at market procurement reforms in 2020/2021
China	Concern over rural-urban wage gaps increased importance of farmers and agriculture in national investment strategies	WTO commitments and international climate agreements Political regime less beholden to popular interests	Food self-sufficiency but growing desire to assert role in global governance, including on environment	Adoption of lump-sum income transfers to farmers, Conditional subsidies to promote organic fertilizers Increased investment in agriculture R&D
EU	Strong farm lobbies but budgetary burden from subsidies and pressures from trading partners	WTO negotiations at Uruguay Round, reform decisions no longer require unanimous agreement of EU member states	Growing norms about environmental sustainability	Two rounds of CAP reforms, decoupling farm subsidies from production decisions, payments conditional on reduced pesticide and fertilizer use Progress on Green Deal slowed due to 2022 food price crisis
US	Farmers and ethanol plant investors saw income benefits from biofuels and forged unlikely coalition for reform	Environmental Protection Agency	Growing norms about environmental sustainability	Subsidies and mandates to improve ethanol now reconsidered due to ethanol's impacts on land use change

approaches that impose certain types of "green" conditionality to farm support, like the reduced usage of fertilizers and pesticides as proposed as part of EU's CAP reforms, might lower land productivity and thereby induce conversion of new land for agriculture and increase emissions.

Even with green conditionality, resistance is still possible, as seen in the farmer protests in The Netherlands in 2022 over proposed restrictions on nitrogen emissions to meet EU directives (Ortega Froysa 2022). When resistance by farmers or other organized groups is anticipated, the process of negotiation and engagement becomes just as important as the policy instrument under consideration. As learned from the case of India, where attempted reforms announced rapidly as part of Covid-19 measures alienated farmers, it is essential to engage stakeholders early on and iteratively in the process of designing policy reform to build trust and a common agenda.

Another promising approach emphasized in this chapter is reallocating part of existing support to R&D focused on innovations that both increase productivity and lower emission intensities. Reallocation of resources in this way is expected to produce major societal gains, including benefits for those farmers who benefit from current support. However, the gains from innovation in sustainable production methods may be perceived as uncertain and adoption may come at a cost to producers in the short run. Compensatory payments to losers and to offset adoption costs for producers could help win political support. Importantly, appropriate regulations, such as mandates on the use of renewable energy or limits on the conversion of land for farming, may be essential to overcome the resistance of some agricultural producers to more environmentally sustainable reforms.

More broadly, the modeling scenarios presented in this chapter show that international cooperation for repurposing agricultural support achieves superior outcomes on all environmental, economic, and social dimensions for all countries compared with current non-cooperative agricultural support policies. Notwithstanding recurrent threats to multilateralism, an internationally concerted reform agenda bolstered by the WTO, the Paris Climate Agreement, and platforms such as the G20 is critical to deal with the cross-border impacts of climate change driven by agricultural policies (Vos et al. 2022). Such coordination will require intense dialogue, informed by continuous and credible assessments of the gains to be obtained and the trade-offs to be confronted. Moreover, given great differences across countries in the amount of agricultural support provided, a concerted global repurposing agenda would require creating transnational constituencies facilitating equitable diffusion of technologies and financial resources to enable all countries to even-handedly engage in agriculture policy reform and reap the global benefits for people and planet.

References

Abdelal, R. 2009. "Constructivism as an Approach to International Political Economy." In *Handbook of International Political Economy (IPE): IPE as a Global Conversation*, ed. M. Blyth, 62–76. New York: Routledge

Andae, G. 2021. "Horticulture Exporters Sue to Block New Levy." *Business Daily*. August 20. https://www.businessdailyafrica.com/bd/markets/commodities/horticulture-exporters-sue-to-block-new-levy-3517654

Anderson, K. 1995. "Lobby Incentives and the Pattern of Protection in Rich and Poor Countries." *Economic Development and Cultural Change* 43 (2): 401–423.

Anderson, K. 2009. *Distortions to Agricultural Incentives: A Global Perspective*, Palgrave Macmillan and the World Bank, Washington DC.

Anderson, K, G. Rausser, and J. Swinnen. 2013. "Political Economy of Public Policies: Insights from Distortions to Agricultural and Food Markets." *Journal of Economic Literature* 51 (2): 423–477.

Bardsley, P. 1996. "The Collapse of the Australian Wool Reserve Price Scheme." *Economic Journal* 104: 1087–1105.

Bell, A.R., T.G. Benton, K. Droppelmann, L. Mapemba, O. Pierson, and P.S. Ward. 2018. "Transformative Change through Payments for Ecosystem Services (PES): A Conceptual Framework and Application to Conservation Agriculture in Malawi." *Global Sustainability*. 1: e4.

Bhatia, V. 2021. "Who Are the Punjab, Haryana Farmers Protesting at Delhi's Borders?" *Indian Express*, January 30. https://indianexpress.com/article/explained/punjab-haryana-farmer-protests-explained-delhi-chalo-farm-laws-2020/

Bjornlund, V., H. Bjornlund, and A.F. van Rooyen. 2020. "Exploring the Factors Causing the Poor Performance of Most Irrigation Schemes in Post-Independence Sub-Saharan Africa." *International Journal of Water Resources Development* 36 (Suppl 1): S54–101. https://doi.org/10.1080/07900627.2020.1808448

Blyth, M. 1997. "Any More Bright Ideas? The Ideational Turn of Comparative Political Economy." *Comparative Politics* 29 (2): 229–250.

Chai, Y., P.G. Pardey, C. Chan-Kang, J.K. Huang, K. Lee, and W.L. Dong. 2019. "Passing the Food and Agricultural R&D Buck? The United States and China." *Food Policy* 86: 101729.

Ciaian, P., E. Baldoni, d'A. Kancs and D. Drabik. 2021. "The Capitalization of Agricultural Subsidies into Land Prices" *Annual Review of Resource Economics* 13: 17–38.

CRS (Congressional Research Service). 2022. "The Renewable Fuel Standard (RFS): An Overview." Congressional Research Service Report R43325. CRS, Washington, DC.

Dionne, K.Y., and J, Horowitz. 2016. "The Political Effects of Agricultural Subsidies in Africa: Evidence from Malawi." *World Development* 87: 215–226. http://dx.doi.org/10.1016/j.worlddev.2016.06.011

EPA (United States Environmental Protection Agency). 2018. *Biofuels and the Environment: Second Triennial Report to Congress, EPA/600/R-18/195F*. Washington, DC: EPA.

European Commission. 2020a. "How the Future CAP Will Contribute to the EU Green Deal" Factsheet. Brussels: European Commission.

European Commission. 2020b. *Farm to Fork Strategy: For Fair, Healthy and Environmentally Friendly Food System*. Brussels: European Commission.

FAO, UNDP, and UNEP (United Nations Environment Programme). 2021. *A Multi-Billion-Dollar Opportunity. Repurposing Agricultural Support to Transform Food Systems*. Rome: FAO.

Gautam, M., D. Laborde, A. Mamun, W. Martin, V. Piñeiro, and R. Vos. 2022. *Repurposing Agricultural Policies and Support: Options for Transforming Agriculture and Food Systems to Better Serve the Health of People, Economies, and the Planet*. Technical Report. Washington DC: World Bank and IFPRI.

Glauber, J., D. Laborde, and A. Mamun. 2023. Food Export Restrictions Have Eased as the Russia-Ukraine War Continues, But Concerns Remain for Key Commodities. IFPRI Blog. January 23. https://www.ifpri.org/blog/food-export-restrictions-have-eased-russia-ukraine-war-continues-concerns-remain-key

Gouel, C., M. Gautam, and W. Martin. 2016. "Managing Food Price Volatility in a Large Open Country: The Case of Wheat in India." *Oxford Economic Papers* 68 (3): 811–835. https://doi.org/10.1093/oep/gpv089

Grindle, M. 1999. "In Quest of the Political: The Political Economy of Development Policy Making," CID Working Papers 17A. Center for International Development at Harvard University, Cambridge, MA.

Grossman, G., and E. Helpman. 1994. "Protection for Sale." *American Economic Review* 84 (4): 833–850.

Huang, J., Y. Liu, W. Martin, and S. Rozelle. 2010. "Agricultural Trade Reform and Rural Prosperity." In *China's Growing Role in World Trade*, eds. R. Feenstra and S-J. Wei, 397–428. Cambridge, MA: National Bureau of Economic Research.

Huang, J.K., and G.L. Yang. 2017. "Understanding Recent Challenges and New Food Policy in China." *Global Food Security* 12: 119–126.

Hussain, S. 2020. "Farm Laws: Potential for Positive Outcomes." *International Growth Centre Blog*, October 15.

IFPRI (International Food Policy Research Institute). 2022. *2022 Global Food Policy Report: Climate Change and Food Systems*. Washington, DC: IFPRI. https://doi.org/10.2499/9780896294257

India, Directorate of Economics and Statistics. 2020. *Agricultural Statistics at a Glance*. Directorate of Economics and Statistics, Department of Agriculture and Co-operation. Ministry of Agriculture, Government of India.

Jadhav, R., and M. Bhardwaj. 2020. "India's Protesting Farmers Hold Key to Self-reliance in Edible Oils." *Reuters*, December 31. https://www.reuters.com/world/india/indias-protesting-farmers-hold-key-self-reliance-edible-oils-2020-12-31/

Kaur, P. 2020. "Changes in Agricultural Marketing Laws across States." *PRS Blog*, May 19. https://prsindia.org/theprsblog/changes-in-agricultural-marketing-laws-across-states

Kosec, K., and L. Wantchekon. 2020. "Can Information Improve Rural Governance and Service Delivery?" *World Development* 125: 104376.

Kumar, P., S. Kumar, and L. Joshi, eds. 2015. *Socioeconomic and Environmental Implications of Agricultural Residue Burning*. New Delhi: Springer.

Laborde, D., A. Mamun, W. Martin, V. Piñeiro, and R. Vos. 2020. "Modeling the Impacts of Agricultural Support Policies on Emissions from Agriculture." IFPRI Discussion Paper, No. 1954. International Food Policy Research Institute and the World Bank, Washington, DC. https://doi.org/10.2499/p15738coll2.133852

Laborde, D., A. Mamun, W. Martin, V. Piñeiro, and R. Vos. 2021. "Agricultural Sub-sidies and Global Greenhouse Gas Emissions." *Nature Communications* 12: 2601. https://doi.org/10.1038/s41467-021-22703-1

Lark, T., N. Hendricks, A. Smith, N. Pates, S. Spawn-Lee, M. Bougie, E. Booth, C. Kucharik, and H. Gibbs. 2022. "Environmental Outcomes of the US Renewable Fuel Standard." *Proceedings of the National Academy of Sciences of the United States of America* 119 (9): e2101084119. https://doi.org/10.1073/pnas.2101084119

Lawrence, R. 2010. "How Good Politics Results in Bad Policy: The Case of Bio-fuel Mandates." Mossavar-Rahmani Center for Business and Government Working Paper 2010-12. Cambridge, MA: Harvard University.

Lowi, T. 1972. "Four Systems of Policy, Politics, and Choice." *Public Administration Review* 32(4): 298–310.

MacKillop, E. and J. Downe. 2022. "What counts as evidence for policy? An analysis of policy actors' perceptions." *Public Administration Review*. https://doi.org/10.1111/puar.13567

Martin, W., and N. Minot. 2022. "The Impacts of Price Insulation on World Wheat Markets during the 2022 Food Price Crisis." *The Australian Journal of Agricultural and Resource Economics* 66(4): 753–774. https://doi-org.ifpri.idm.oclc.org/10.1111/1467-8489.12498

Mason, N.M., T.S. Jayne, and N. Van De Walle. 2017. "The Political Economy of Fertilizer Subsidy Programs in Africa: Evidence from Zambia." *American Journal of Agricultural Economics* 99 (3): 705–731.

Mogues, T. 2015. "What Determines Public Expenditure Allocations? A Review of Theories, and Implications for Agricultural Public Investments." *European Journal of Development Research* 27 (3): 452–473.

Ngoma, H., N.M. Mason, P. Samboko, and P. Hangoma. 2018. "Switching up Climate-Smart Agriculture Adoption: Do 'Green' Subsidies, Insurance, Risk Aversion and Impatience Matter?," IAPRI Working Paper 146. Indaba Agricultural Policy Research Institute (IAPRI), Lusaka, Zambia.

OECD. 2021. *Agricultural Policy Monitoring and Evaluation 2021*, Paris: OECD Publishing. https://doi.org/10.1787/2d810e01-en

OECD. 2022. *Agricultural Policy Monitoring and Evaluation 2022*. OECD Publishing, Paris,

OECD (Organization for Economic Co-operation and Development). 2017. *Evaluation of Agricultural Policy Reforms in the European Union: The Common Agricultural Policy 2014-20*. Paris: OECD Publishing.

Olper, A., and J. Swinnen. 2013. "Mass Media and Public Policy: Global Evidence from Agricultural Policies." *The World Bank Economic Review* 27(3): 413–436.

Olson, M. 1965. *The Logic of Collective Action: Public Goods and the Theory of Groups*. Cambridge, MA and London, UK: Harvard University Press.

Ortega Froysan, D. 2022. Unpacking the 2022 Dutch Farmers Protests. *European Student Think Tank*. August 31. https://esthinktank.com/2022/08/31/unpacking-the-2022-dutch-farmers-protests/

Putnam, R. 1988. "Diplomacy and Domestic Politics: The Logic of Two-Level Games." *International Organization* 42 (3): 427–460.

Ramaswami, B. 2019. *Agricultural Subsidies*. New Delhi: Finance Commission, Government of India.

Rao, G. 2019. "Goods and Services Tax in India: Progress, Performance, and Prospects," Deepak and Neera Raj Center on Indian Economic Policies Working

Paper no. 2019-02. Columbia University, New York. https://indianeconomy. columbia.edu/sites/default/files/content/201902-Govinda%20Rao%20-%20GST. pdf

Resnick, D. 2021a. "Embracing Political Economy to Enhance Policy Influence: Lessons from PIM Research." PIM Synthesis Brief. International Food Policy Research Institute, Washington, DC. https://pim.cgiar.org/2021/06/24/embracing-political-economy-to-enhance-policy-influence-lessons-from-pim-research/

Resnick, D. 2021b. "Political Economy of Wheat Value Chains in Post-revolution Sudan," Sudan Strategy Support Program Working Paper No.1. International Food Policy Research Institute, Washington, DC. https://www.ifpri.org/publication/political-economy-wheat-value-chains-post-revolution-sudan

Sahoo, J.P., K.C. Samal, and D. Behera. 2020. "The Reasons behind the Protests." *Biotica Research Today: An International E-Magazine* 2 (10): 985–987.

Searchinger, T., R. Heimlich, R.A. Houghton, F. Dong, A. Elobeid, J. Fabiosa, S. Tok-goz, D. Hayes, and T-H. Yu. 2008. "Use of U.S. Croplands for Biofuels Increases Greenhouse Gases through Emissions from Land Use Change." *Science* 319 (5687): 1238–1240. https://dx.doi.org/10.1126/science.1151861

Searchinger, T., C. Malins, P. Dumas, D. Baldok, J. Glauber, T.S. Jayne, J. Huang, and P. Marenya. 2020. *Revising Public Agricultural Support to Mitigate Climate Change.* Washington, DC: World Bank.

Sen, A. 1981. *Poverty and Famines: An Essay on Entitlement and Deprivation.* Oxford, UK: Clarendon Press.

Sharma, A., 2020. "India: Supreme Court Puts Contentious Farms Laws on Hold." *Deutsche Welle,* January 13. https://www.dw.com/en/india-supreme-court-puts-contentious-farms-laws-on-hold/a-56208301

Singh, S. 2020. *COVID-19 in India—GOI's Economic Package for Self-Reliant India— Food and Agriculture Items Report.* New Delhi, India: Global Agricultural Information Network (GAIN) and the US Foreign Agricultural Service.

Singh, S., and Rosmann, M. 2020. *Government of India Issues Three Ordinances Ushering in Major Agricultural Market Reforms.* New Delhi, India: Global Agricultural Information Network (GAIN), US Foreign Agricultural Service.

Stads, G-J., and S. Doumbia. 2010. "Côte d'Ivoire: Recent Developments in Agricultural Research." World Bank Press Release No. 2021/154/AFR, June 4. https://www.worldbank.org/en/news/press-release/2021/06/07/cote-d-ivoire-increased-commitment-to-the-development-of-the-agri-food-sector

Swinbank, A. 2016. *The Interactions between the EU's External Action and the Common Agricultural Policy.* Report for the European Parliament's Committee on Agriculture and Rural Development. Brussels: European Commission.

Swinnen, J. 2008. *The Perfect Storm: The Political Economy of the Fischler Reforms of the Common Agricultural Policy.* Brussels: Centre for European Policy Studies.

Swinnen, J. 2014. "The Political Economy of the 2014-2020 Common Agricultural Policy: Introduction and key conclusions." In *The Political Economy of the 2014-2020 Common Agricultural Policy: An Imperfect Storm,* ed. J. Swinnen. Chapter 1, 1-30. London, UK: Rowman & Littlefield International Ltd.

Swinnen, J. 2015. "Changing Coalitions in Value Chains and the Political Economy of Agricultural and Food Policy." *Oxford Review of Economic Policy* 31 (1): 90–115.

Swinnen, J. 2018. *The Political Economy of Agricultural and Food Policies.* London and New York: Palgrave/Macmillan.

Tyner, W. 2008. "The US Ethanol and Biofuels Boom: Its Origins, Current Status, and Future Prospects." *Bioscience* 58 (7): 646–653.

Vos, R., J. Glauber, D. Laborde, W. Martin, D. Resnick, V. Piñeiro, M. Sanchez, M., et al. 2022. "G20 Framework for Repurposing Agricultural Policy Support to meet Global Climate and Food Security Goals." T20 Policy Brief for Task Force 4 on Food Security and Sustainable Agriculture. Jakarta: T20. https://www.t20indonesia.org/tf4/g20-framework-for-repurposing-agricultural-policy-support-to-meet-global-climate-and-food-security-goals/

Vos, R., W. Martin, and D. Resnick. 2022. "The Political Economy of Reforming Agricultural Support Policies." IFPRI Discussion Paper 02163 (Paper prepared for the Food Systems Economic Commission). Washington DC: International Food Policy Research Institute. https://doi.org/10.2499/p15738coll2.136545

Ward, P.S., A.R. Bell, K. Droppelmann, and T.G. Benton. 2018. "Early Adoption of Conservation Agriculture Practices: Understanding Partial Compliance in Programs with Multiple Adoption Decisions." *Land Use Policy* 70: 27–37.

Wright, B. 2014. "Global Biofuels: Key to the Puzzle of Grain Market Behavior." *Journal of Economic Perspectives* 28 (1): 73–98.

4

From Re-instrumenting to Re-purposing Farm Support Policies

Kym Anderson and Anna Strutt

4.1 Introduction

The world's agrifood systems have served society well since 1798 when Malthus anonymously published *An Essay on the Principle of Population.* That is especially so since the 1950s, when famines became a thing of the past except where deliberately contrived by a country's leaders or rebels for local political purposes (Ravallion 1987, 1997). Yet global food supplies have not been produced very efficiently, equitably or sustainably, especially during the past seven decades. Nor has food been consumed so as to optimize individuals' nutrition and health. Institutions and policies have contributed to this unsatisfactory outcome, particularly insofar as they distort incentives facing producers and consumers, and thereby dampen investor incentives. Moreover, numerous communities are calling out for a major overhaul of agrifood systems and policies, demanding among other things that they do more to improve nutrition and human health and ease natural resource and environmental stresses, particularly in the face of changing climates (United Nations 2021; Gautam et al. 2022; FAO et al. 2022).

Food production has been globally inefficient partly because too many resources have been employed in agriculture in high-income countries, where farmers have received government assistance in various forms, and too few in those low-income countries where governments have heavily taxed exports of many of their farmers (Anderson 2009). The net effect of those policies in the 1980s was to over-produce farm products globally and thus depress their international prices (Tyers and Anderson 1992). That was still the case (though to a lesser extent) even in the mid-2000s following complete implementation by members of the World Trade Organization (WTO) of the multilateral Uruguay Round Agreement on Agriculture (Anderson and Martin 2005, 2006). As well, irrigation water institutions and policies have been poorly designed, leading to excessive water use by farmers in some settings and under-utilization in others (Rosegrant, Ringler, and Zhu 2009; Wheeler 2021). Subsidies to purchase farm inputs such as chemical fertilizers and pesticides have distorted input use on farms too—and have added to pollution. Yet malnutrition remains prevalent in many parts of the world (Masters,

Kym Anderson and Anna Strutt, *From Re-instrumenting to Re-purposing Farm Support Policies.* In: *The Political Economy of Food System Transformation.* Edited by: Danielle Resnick and Johan Swinnen, Oxford University Press.
© Kym Anderson and Anna Strutt (2023). DOI: 10.1093/oso/9780198882121.003.0004

Finaret, and Block 2022). Meanwhile, there has been global under-investment in agricultural research, as indicated by the persistence of extremely high marginal social rates of return and social benefit/cost ratios from such investments (Rao, Hurley, and Pardey 2020).

Early this century, agricultural price-distorting policies accounted for more than three-fifths of the global economic welfare cost of all goods' trade-related policies, three-quarters of which was due to the farm policies of high-income countries (Anderson, Valenzuela, and van der Mensbrugghe 2010)—even though agriculture accounts for less than 3 percent of their economies. Among those welfare-reducing agricultural policies, import market access restrictions (mostly tariffs) were responsible for 93 percent of that global welfare cost, while export subsidies and domestic support policies contributed just 2 percent and 5 percent, respectively (Anderson, Martin, and Valenzuela 2006). Export subsidies were outlawed by the WTO in 2015 and so almost all were removed by 2017, while domestic supports—potentially less market distorting than border policies—have grown in importance.

The political economy reasons behind these and other features of past policies affecting the world's agricultural and food markets are the subject of an extensive review by Anderson, Rausser, and Swinnen (2013), and so will be mentioned only briefly in what follows so this chapter can focus more on the economics and political economy of evolving agrifood policy instrument choices of advanced economies: away from mostly price support at the border (import tariffs, licences and quotas, and export subsidies) to also domestic output and input price supports, then to somewhat-decoupled payments, to direct income payments to farmers, and to more-concerted payments to farmers for their co-provision of public goods.

The policy dynamics in this chapter are predominantly in the incentives space, as defined in Chapter 1 of this volume. In particular, the chapter recognizes that the relative power of various vested interests and the differing values of various groups have important influences on institutional and policy formation and reform, but that conceptual and empirical economic analyses and ideas also can and do inform those processes.

The chapter begins by summarizing the evolving stated objectives of agrifood policy instruments chosen by high-income countries. It then draws on standard welfare economics of open economies to rank the chosen policy instruments in terms of their efficiency in raising the mean and reducing the variance in farm household incomes, and simultaneously contributing (positively or negatively) to equity, national food and nutrition security, and sustainable economic growth. That exposes the political economy behind the sub-optimal instrument choices, as many agrifood policy instruments are shown to have been far from economically optimal for attaining those objectives of high-income countries in the past. They will be even less appropriate for efficiently attaining the even broader range of "non-economic" objectives of today's societies (to use a term popularized by Bhagwati 1971), suggesting the need for further reform. New estimates of the global economic welfare cost of supports to agriculture in 2017 (i.e., prior to Trump-inspired tariff "wars" and COVID-19), using the Global Trade Analysis Project (GTAP) model, are then summarized. The contributions to that global cost in 2017 from import tariffs and domestic supports are shown to be little different from those estimated for 2001. However, the agricultural policies of emerging economies are now responsible for the majority of that cost, suggesting recent political economy forces at work there may be similar to those that operated earlier in advanced industrial economies. The final sections conclude by discussing what might be done to ensure re-purposing of farmer assistance in high-income and emerging economies is directed to more-efficient, more-equitable, healthier, and more environmentally friendly policy instrument choices to better meet societies' evolving objectives and the UN's Sustainable Development Goals.

4.2 Evolving Objectives of Agrifood Policy Instrument Choices

Two fundamental facts characterize agriculture. One is that its production is subject to weather, so in free markets the prices of outputs and the earnings of farmers inevitably will fluctuate. The other is that the agricultural sector typically declines in growing economies. The price of farm relative to non-farm products tended to decline over the past century's course of long-term economic growth, and hence so too did the shares of agriculture in total output and employment (for reasons summarized in Anderson and Ponnusamy 2023). Indeed, the absolute number of farmers has declined in high-wage economies as profitable labor-saving technologies became available and were widely adopted and thus lowered farm product prices. Since an exit by farmers from agriculture often requires re-locating to an urban area, delays/procrastination in doing so are inevitable. Relatively poor-quality education in rural areas adds to the difficulty of securing a lucrative-enough non-farm job, such that the average education of those remaining on farms falls further behind that of urban workers. All this means that, in the absence of government intervention, farm household incomes tend to not keep up with rising incomes of non-farm households in growing economies.

   Given those two facts, it is not surprising that over the past century farmers have sought government assistance aimed at stabilizing and raising prices of farm products and thereby also farm household incomes. In response, governments have sought ways to assist such that the marginal political benefit to politicians from doing so is more than the loss of political support from tax-paying non-farm households and businesses (Rausser 1982; Gardner 1983; Swinnen 1994, 2018). For a long period that political support calculus worked in favor of farm price supports in rich industrial countries (Anderson 1995; Gründler and Hillman

2021); but, with the agrifood sector's share of the economy and of voters ever-shrinking, a threshold eventually is or could be reached when such inefficient and inequitable provision of social welfare is challenged (Hillman 1982; Cassing and Hillman 1986). That point was reached in the 1980s in Australia and New Zealand, for example, although there the policy reforms were part of broader microeconomic reform programs that included also phasing down government support to import-competing manufacturers (Anderson et al. 2009; Anderson 2020).

The most prominently used instruments aimed at both raising and stabilizing farm product prices have been import restrictions such as variable tariffs and occasionally prohibitions. For example, in 1906 Japanese rice farmers succeeded in their lobbying for a tariff to be applied to rice imports, and that broadened into an imperial rice self-sufficiency policy embracing also Japan's then-colonies of Korea and Taiwan (Anderson and Tyers 1992). And when low agricultural prices hit in the late 1920s, and the US introduced the Smoot-Hawley tariff hikes of June 1930, governments elsewhere responded with beggar-thy-neighbor protectionist trade policies that together helped drive the world economy into depression (Hynes, Jacks, and O'Rourke 2012). Real prices of farm products in international markets slumped, initially from oversupply because of a recession and then from increases in trade barriers (see Findlay and O'Rourke 2007, pp. 447–448 and references cited therein).

Meanwhile, in agricultural-exporting countries where import tariffs would do little to raise or even stabilize farm prices, alternative measures were used. In Denmark import restrictions were placed on just grain while export-focused livestock producers received domestic subsidies (subject to production quotas to avoid encouraging oversupply). In the United States, counter-cyclical land retirement programs were made available from 1936 (Swinton 2022). In Australia, so-called home consumption pricing schemes were used from the 1920s: instead of subsidizing exports from the treasury, these schemes raised average producer prices via state marketing boards that were given monopoly control of supplies to allow them to charge domestic consumers well above the export price in the domestic market and to ban imports (Mauldon 2021).

The first attempts to reverse that growth in farmer assistance in advanced economies were discriminatory, benefitting Europe's colonies at the expense of other trading partners (Anderson and Norheim 1993). By the end of the 1930s, protectionism was far more entrenched than in the late 19th century when only non-discriminatory tariffs had to be grappled with. Indeed, nontariff trade barriers were so rife as to make tariffs almost redundant unless and until "tariffication" of those barriers occurred.

Out of the interwar trade policy experience, many in Britain and the United States were convinced that liberal world trade required a set of multilaterally agreed rules and binding commitments based on non-discriminatory principles. An International Trade Organization was proposed but, after much negotiation, the US was unwilling to do more than sign on, in 1947, to a General Agreement on Tariffs and Trade (GATT). The GATT was signed by a total of 23 trading countries—12 high-income and 11 developing—who at the time accounted for nearly two-thirds of the world's international trade. The GATT provided a forum to negotiate subsequent tariff reductions and changes in rules, plus a mechanism to help settle trade disputes. Eight so-called rounds of negotiations were completed in the subsequent 46 years, as a result of which many import tariffs on at least manufactured goods were progressively lowered in most high-income countries. Global merchandise trade grew faster in the half century following the coming into force of the GATT than in any other half century in history. But following Prebisch/Singer advice, many developing countries chose not to participate. That thwarted their trade growth, especially with former colonizers (Head, Mayer, and Ries 2010), and it also weakened the demand by agricultural exporters for reform of agricultural trade-related policies. It was only the last of those GATT negotiations, the Uruguay Round (1986–1994), that culminated in agreements to liberalize agricultural trade (and to replace the GATT's Secretariat in Geneva with the WTO in January 1995).

In the interim, the European Economic Community (EEC, later to enlarge and become the European Union) from its inception in 1957 used variable import levies to both raise and stabilize domestic prices of farm products, while the United Kingdom (UK) (before it joined the EEC in 1973) generated a similar outcome for farmers with its deficiency payments (in place from 1919) being transformed into price guarantees in the UK's 1947 Agriculture Act. That deficiency payment method of domestic support to farmers—unlike import quotas, tariffs and variable import levies—avoided also raising domestic consumer prices in the UK that would have added more harm to farm exports from current and former British colonies and dominions (Josling 2009). An argument invoked to bolster political support for these protectionist measures in Europe was food security. Based on the experiences of drastic food shortages in two world wars during the first half of the 20th century, this was often interpreted as requiring food self-sufficiency (Anderson and Swinnen 2009).

Meanwhile, as real international food prices continued to fall after World War II, agricultural-exporting countries such as Australia used marketing boards to prop up producer receipts, under the guise of "price stabilization." While sometimes being dressed up as necessary for improving the efficiency of domestic resource use by reducing farmer uncertainty and countering import protection for manufacturers, they served mainly as an excuse for paying above market price in what were deemed to be low-price years. When that generated surpluses as for wheat in the late 1960s, production quotas were introduced to prevent further supply expansion (Edwards and Watson 1978). Only when international wheat prices spiked upward in 1973/74, such that the ceiling of the price stabilization band was breached for the first time, did Australia's wheat growers vote to abandon their price stabilization scheme. Attention then turned to more-directly address farm income fluctuations and risks (IAC 1978).

Assistance to farmers everywhere became less necessary during that high food price crisis of the mid-1970s. But thereafter tariff protection rose again through to the mid-1980s in Western Europe and to the mid-1990s in Japan and Korea. The rise was so great in Europe that it and technological improvements generated food surpluses that had to be disposed of with the help of export subsidies from the early 1980s. That triggered a food export subsidy "war" across the North Atlantic, which in turn stimulated non-subsidizing food-exporting countries to form the so-called Cairns Group and demand that the next General Agreement on Tariffs and Trade (GATT) round of multilateral trade negotiations (launched in Punte del est, Uruguay in 1986) have agricultural policy reform high on its agenda.

That so-called Uruguay Round took eight years to conclude, and implementation of its agreements took another decade. However, from the outset it was anticipated that agricultural import restrictions would have to be tariffied, bound, and gradually reduced, and export subsidies phased down as well. Since that could stimulate policy re-instrumentation, disciplines on domestic support measures, especially producer price subsidies, also were demanded by the Cairns Group and many developing countries.

The United States had begun re-instrumenting in the 1980s away from price supports to direct payments to farmers and decoupling them from production and prices. The European Union began to follow that trend with the McSharry reforms of 1992, as did Switzerland (Josling 2009). In the case of the EU, internal budgetary pressure to reduce the Common Agricultural Policy's support for farmers came with the EU's gradual expansion from the 1980s to absorb poorer, more-agrarian southern countries (Greece, Portugal, and Spain) and then ten eastern countries in 2004 (Anderson, Rausser, and Swinnen 2013). Similar programs to Australia's operated in post-World War II Canada through to the 1980s following its Agricultural Stabilization Act of 1958. Canada's farm assistance rates grew more rapidly than and to well above those in the US, and for six years longer until 1991, when Canada introduced its Farm Income Protection Act. Thereafter Canada's programs became more like those in the US, gradually focusing more on stabilizing gross revenue of farmers—a form of subsidized farm income insurance (Gardner 2009).

In response to the political pressure to further reduce agricultural protection and even limit domestic supports, farmers' lobbying in the latter 1990s took a new turn: protected farmers claimed not only to be good stewards of their land and animals but also to contribute to "non-economic" objectives of society by providing a stream of non-marketed ecosystem services. A new term was coined to capture the latter notion, namely farming's "multifunctionality." The claim was that agricultural production was multifunctional in that it provided positive externalities and public goods for which farmers were not being compensated. Among the examples pointed to were food security, environmental protection, and the economic via-bility of rural areas (OECD 2008). Such claims did not stand up well to scrutiny, however, as they ignored the negative externalities from farming (and farm input subsidies) listed above, and there were more-efficient instruments for achiev-ing those social objectives than narrowly focused measures that support farm prices, reduce trade, and benefit the largest farmers/landowners most (Anderson 2000).

More recently, governments of advanced economies have come under politi-cal pressure from other groups to meet an ever-widening set of societal demands. The following are among the ones most pertinent to agriculture's social licence to operate: mitigating climate change, slowing biodiversity loss, reducing chem-ical and ruminant animal pollution of air, soil and water, improving food safety and quality in addition to basic food and nutrition security, and enhancing ani-mal welfare. Ruminants (most notably beef and dairy cattle plus sheep) are major contributors of the greenhouse gas methane (IPCC 2020, 2021, 2022), land clear-ing for monocropping is a major contributor to biodiversity loss (Dasgupta 2021), farm chemical inputs are perceived not only as pollutive but also as potentially diminishing food safety and nutrition, and intensive livestock raising is seen as harmful to animal welfare. All this, plus the need for farmers to adapt to cli-mate change, has contributed to calls for major changes to food systems to ensure they can contribute more efficiently, equitably and sustainably to national and global economic growth and human health, and do less harm to the natural environment.

One response by farm groups has been to transform the most plausible of the environmental protection component of those earlier "multifunctionality" claims into ones that, via alliances with some environmental groups, could be supported more strongly by governments. This can and has been done by rebadg-ing requests for assistance as payments for "ecosystem services," deemed to be necessary to ensure society gets closer to the optimal use of its natural capital. An example has to do with carbon sequestration in soils, demand for which will be greater the higher the taxation of carbon emissions and the more developed the market for tradable emission permits nationally and abroad (Simone et al. 2017).

To see how agrifood policies might be best re-purposed to meet these chang-ing societal demands, the next section draws on basic welfare economics to rank policy instruments in terms of their efficiency in meeting these various objectives, and then Section 4.4 summarizes changes in key policy instruments' estimated contributions to producer and consumer support estimates in high-income and developing countries.

4.3 Basic Welfare Economics of Agrifood Policy Instruments

Welfare economics provides economists with the ability to rank policy instruments for meeting various policy objectives, be they economic (e.g., improving efficiency of resource allocation), environmental (e.g., reducing pollution), or social (e.g., reducing income or wealth inequality and variance through time). In this section, we discuss the agrifood policy instruments used for achieving the following societal objectives in advanced industrial economies: raising the mean and lowering the variance of farm household incomes, reducing inequality, increasing food sovereignty and national food and nutrition security, and boosting agriculture's net contributions to sustainable economic growth and improvements in the natural environment.

4.3.1 Raising the Mean and Lowering the Variance of Farm Household Incomes

As noted early in the previous section, tariffs on imports have been the most common policy instrument for raising farm incomes. The economics of lowering import tariffs are well understood by trade negotiators: gains from opening to trade can come from exchange when consumer preferences at home are different from those abroad; from production specialization when relative factor endowments or technologies differ between the countries involved and when economies of scale are present; from intra-industry trade when seasons or product qualities or product varieties differ; and from increased competition from abroad driving down monopolistic pricing domestically. The gains from production specialization are becoming even greater as global value chains increase in importance.

A potentially important exception to the gains-from-trade arguments has to do with whether the environmental damage from greater transportation when importing food is more or less than the pollution from producing abroad instead of locally. This argument has motivated many of the "food miles" campaigns and "eat local" / "locavore" advocacy efforts. However, in a comprehensive global study by Avetisyan, Hertel, and Sampson (2014), transport costs are shown to be important in the case of dairy products but, overall, environmental benefits from differences in domestic emission intensities of production outweigh transport costs in about 90 percent of the country/commodity cases they examine, thereby undermining one of the rationales for the local food movement.

Distortionary policies such as import tariffs or quotas, or export subsidies, diminish the benefits from trade by raising domestic prices above the border prices of affected goods for not only producers but also consumers. Hence a switch from a trade measure to a domestic producer subsidy at that same rate would eliminate the consumer-distorting half of the trade measure without reducing assistance to farmers—assuming there are no greater costs associated with collecting tax revenue by means other than import tariffs, and no costs of dispersing some of it as a producer subsidy (see Bhagwati 1971; Corden 1997). That shifts the ranking from third best to a second best policy instrument.

The gains from switching from a trade measure to a domestic producer subsidy would be greater if, in the process of reform, the variance of rates of assistance among industries within the farm sector were reduced (Lloyd 1974). Furthermore, if trade barriers are managed by inefficient institutions such as distributors of import or export quota licenses, the gains from removal of such barriers will be larger than those from removing standard trade taxes or subsidies (Khandelwal, Schott, and Wei 2013). Also, a switch from subsidizing a sub-set of farm inputs to spending that outlay on farm output price subsidies would reduce distortions to farm input use and so shift it from third best to second best, assuming the cost of dispersing those payments by those two alternative means are similar.[1]

Domestic producer price subsidies are a more-inefficient way to raise the mean and lower the variance of farm household incomes than direct income supplements decoupled from production, because the latter but not the former can also compensate for weather-induced production fluctuations from year to year. That is what many non-farm households have access to in hard times, in the form of generic social safety nets—or, better still, trampolines that help struggling households bounce back and become more resilient to future shocks.

4.3.2 Reducing Income and Wealth Inequality

Import tariffs or export subsidies on farm products, together with home consumption price schemes that set domestic consumer prices of food above export prices, are inequitable in two respects: they benefit farmers and landowners in direct proportion to their output and land holding size and so raise the incomes and wealth of large farmers/landowners most, with tenants gaining little because their rents are raised (Floyd 1965; Ciaian et al. 2021); and they hurt the poorest domestic consumers most in proportional terms, because the share of disposable income spent on food is higher the poorer the household. A switch from border measures to direct producer subsidies removes the consumer effect of the border measures and so reduces the extent of that contribution to real income inequality.

---

[1] Analysis by Warr (1977) and others of the inefficiency of fertilizer subsidies in Australia led to their eventual phasing out.

4.3.3 Increasing Food Sovereignty and National Food and Nutrition Security

Greater openness is seen as harming national food sovereignty by those who equate the latter with reducing the share of domestic consumption supplied by imports (i.e., with raising the nation's food self-sufficiency rate). Import protection is not an efficient way to boost food sovereignty though, and may also be inequitable. It is inefficient in that the optimal policy intervention to reduce import dependence is not an import tariff that eliminates food imports (and thus raises no government revenue) but rather a lower tariff plus a tariff-revenue-funded domestic producer subsidy (Nettle, Britten-Jones, and Anderson 1987). The optimal tariff rate is that which equates the marginal social benefit from allowing some imports with the perceived marginal social cost of the resulting degree of dependence on imports. Import protection also is inequitable in those settings where the domestic households that are farm owner-operators or owners of farmland they rent to tenants (and hence beneficiaries of that protection) have more real income or wealth than the domestic households that are net buyers of food (whose cost of living rises with a restriction on food imports).

Food security is perceived by some as being related to food self-sufficiency. However, it is defined by FAO as the condition in which all people, at all times, have physical, social, and economic access to sufficient, safe, and nutritious food to meet their dietary needs and food preferences for an active and healthy life. Improving food security requires improving the three interrelated elements of food availability, access, and utilization, as well as reducing market instability.

How much access households have to the available food supplies depends heavily on their income, assets, remittances, or other entitlements. How well household heads utilize the foods that are accessible to them depends on their knowledge and willingness to ensure a healthy and nutritious diet for all members of their household. That in turn depends on the level of education in the household, particularly of adult females, which again is closely related to household income and wealth or other entitlements. Thus, food insecurity is a consumption issue that is closely related to household poverty.

Any initiative whose net effect is to raise real incomes, especially of the poorest households, may also therefore enhance food and nutrition security. Since openness to trade raises national income (and increases food diversity, quality, and safety), it should be considered among the food policy options available to national governments. If all countries were open to international trade and investment, that would optimize the use of resources devoted to producing the world's food, maximize real incomes globally, and minimize fluctuations in international food prices and quantities traded. Openness thus contributes to three components of food security: availability, access, and market stability. Yet some countries continue to restrain food imports because enough of their voters place a high value on national food self-sufficiency.

4.3.4 Boosting Agriculture's Contributions to Sustainable Economic Growth and the Natural Environment

Opening up to trade does more than just provide a single step up in the level of a country's income. Far more importantly it generates dynamic gains from trade, raising *the rate of increase* in future living standards. This is a further reason for governments to shy away from both trade measures and domestic subsidies that raise producer prices. In their place are numerous policy options capable of raising instead of lowering the contribution agriculture can make to sustainable national and global economic growth and environmental enhancement.

Sustainability refers to more than just ensuring long-term economic security. Increasingly, affluent societies value the sustainable use of natural resources and the sustainability of the natural environment. Insofar as market production or consumption would alter the stock of natural resources (e.g., native forests) or the quality of the natural environment (e.g., biodiversity loss), optimal environmental policies need to be in place and enforced such that the marginal social value of that marketed production or consumption equals the marginal social value foregone in terms of the environment. Opening up to trade would still be beneficial (Ch. 2 of Anderson and Blackhurst 1992), but it would require the level of environmental intervention to be altered in order to remain optimal for that country. However, in cases where the environmental damage spills over to other countries or is global, the calculus is necessarily more complex and the politics much less tractable. There remains a place for trade openness, but typically international agreements are needed to achieve globally optimal outcomes.[2]

4.4 Contributions of Various Policy Instruments to National Producer and Consumer Support Estimates

The inverted-U trend since the mid-1950s in nominal rates of border protection and overall assistance to farmers in high-income countries is depicted in Figure 4.1. Peaks and troughs around that trend are when international prices of farm products slumped or spiked up, respectively. The growth in protection to the mid-1980s and its even-more-dramatic fall in the subsequent 20 years has been followed by no further decline in the most-recent 15 years.

---

[2] For a thorough review of the subtle literature on trade and the environment, see Copeland and Taylor (2004) and Copeland, Shapiro and Taylor (2022).

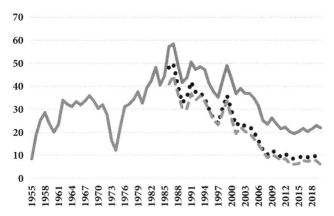

Figure 4.1 Nominal rates of border protection and of overall assistance to agriculture (grey solid and black dotted lines) and agricultural consumer tax equivalent (grey dashed line), OECD Countries, 1955–2020 (%).
Source: Data from Anderson and Nelgen (2013) to 1985, OECD (2021) thereafter.

Also shown in Figure 4.1 is the consumer tax equivalent of agrifood policies: that it so closely traces the nominal rate of border protection to farmers reflects the fact that the majority of the farmer support had come from trade measures until recently, especially import tariffs which are equivalent to a producer subsidy and a consumer tax at the same rate.

Table 4.1 shows the changes in nominal rates of assistance to farmers by the individual member countries of the OECD, plus for key emerging economies. What is clear from that ordering of countries is that the high-income ones' NRAs are spread over the full spectrum from just 1 percent for New Zealand to more than 100 percent for Norway and Switzerland in 2020; but that is far smaller than the range—peaking at more than 300 percent—in the late 1980s.

Accompanying that reduction in producer assistance has been substantial change in the instruments providing support. Figure 4.2 summarizes that for all OECD members and for its three biggest contributors, namely Japan, the EU, and the US. Most of the assistance to Japan's farmers continues to be via market price supports. This is mostly due to very high tariffs on rice but also restrictions on imports of livestock products. However, in recent years domestic payments based on current production have been added. In the US, output and input supports have accounted for half or more of farmer assistance, with payments based on current production making up most of the rest, although payments based on non-current production have been added this century.

It is the EU that has changed most its mix of policy instruments: having relied almost entirely on trade measures (tariffs and export subsidies) in the late 1980s, tariffs contributed only half the support by 2001/03 and only 20 percent by

Table 4.1 Agricultural nominal rates of assistance by country, 1986/88, 2001/03, 2017/19, and 2020 (%, weighted average using value of production without assistance as weights)

	1986/88	2001/03	2017/19	2020
Norway	247	238	145	104
Switzerland	328	196	95	108
Korea	165	95	86	91
Japan	135	111	71	69
Philippines[a]	na	23	37	37
Indonesia[a]	na	10	30	25
UK	na	na	26	26
European Union	63	43	24	24
Turkey	29	33	22	24
US	26	21	13	12
Colombia[a]	na	28	14	15
China[a]	na	7	16	14
Mexico[a]	na	31	11	11
Russian Federation[a]	na	12	12	7
Canada	53	23	9	11
Kazakhstan	na	3	5	3
Costa Rica	na	8	6	8
Australia	11	4	3	2
South Africa[a]	na	8	4	3
Ukraine[a]	na	1	1	1
Chile[a]	na	6	3	3
Brazil[a]	na	8	2	1
New Zealand	12	1	1	1
India[a]	na	−5	−5	−7
Viet Nam[a]	na	8	−6	−6
Argentina[a]	na	−13	−17	−16

Note: [a] In the 1986–88 column, the estimates for developing countries are for 1985–89 and the estimates for Russia and Ukraine are for 1992–95, all from Anderson (2009).
Source: Compiled from OECD (2021) and Anderson (2009).

2018/20 while export subsidies were phased out. Input support has gradually risen over those three decades. Payments based on current production rose to two-fifths of the EU total by early this century, but by 2018/20 payments based on non-current production were equally important.

So, for the OECD as a whole, the contribution of output supports has shrunk from about 90 percent to 40 percent of the total, input support has grown from a little under to a little over 10 percent, and the share of direct payments based on current production has more than doubled, to 20 percent.

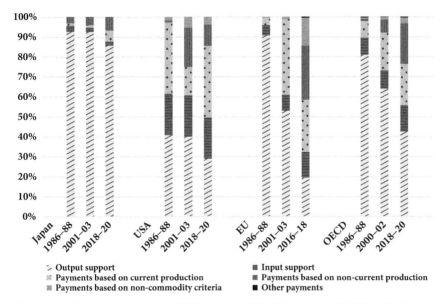

Figure 4.2 Component shares of PSE in Japan, EU, USA, and all OECD, 1986/88, 2001/03 and 2018/20 (%).
Source: Compiled from OECD (2021).

Table 4.2 shows those breakdowns of instrument contributions by country as of 2019. Particularly noticeable is the unimportance to date of payments for environmental services, with their share being non-trivial only for the EU, Switzerland, and Mexico. This is a striking fact: despite all the hype about increasing support to farmers for providing better environmental outcomes, inefficient and inequitable market price supports continue to play by far the most dominant role in assisting farmers in advanced economies.

Two other stylized facts that were revealed in the World Bank's study of distortions to agricultural incentives (Anderson 2009) and that remain true today for high-income countries are that (a) assistance to agriculture is greater in agrifood-importing than in agrifood-exporting countries, and (b) a wide dispersion of rates of farm assistance persists across industries within each of those two agricultural sub-sectors of each country. In particular, a strong anti-trade bias in agrifood policies remains in countries regardless of whether they are net exporters or net importers of agricultural products. The political economy reasons for this are complex but in one respect they are the same in agriculture as they are in manufacturing: import tariffs (or export taxes) *raise* government revenue and are less likely to be scrutinized in each year's government budget whereas export subsidies *deplete* government coffers and so are more exposed in the budget papers each year.

Table 4.2 Component shares of agriculture's PSE, by country, 2019 (%)

	Output support (A)	Input support (B)	Payments based on current production (C)	Payments based on non-current production (D+E)	Payments for environment services and resource conservation (F)	Other payments (G)	TOTAL
Argentina	101	−1	0	0	0	0	100
Australia	0	55	23	21	1	0	100
Brazil	3	92	5	0	0	0	100
Canada	46	12	35	6	0	1	100
Chile	2	92	6	0	0	0	100
China	67	10	15	7	1	0	100
Colombia	90	10	0	0	0	0	100
Costa Rica	92	8	0	0	0	0	100
EU28	19	14	26	27[a]	14[a]	0	100
India	276	−145	0	−29	0	−2	100
Indonesia	89	11	0	0	0	0	100
Japan	85	3	5	7	0	0	100
Kazakhstan	−7	102	5	0	0	0	100
Korea	91	3	3	4	0	0	100
Mexico	56	22	1	9	12	0	100
New Zealand	86	14	0	0	0	0	100
Norway	51	6	31	11	0	0	100
Philippines	97	3	0	0	0	0	100
Russian Fed	50	33	10	0	0	8	100
South Africa	70	29	1	0	0	0	100
Switzerland	46	2	17	20	12	4	100
Turkey	77	9	13	0	0	0	100
UK	25	12	10	47	1	5	100
Ukraine	67	12	21	0	0	0	100
US	21	17	46	12	4	0	100
Viet Nam	113	−11	−2	0	0	0	100

Note: [a] The EU's Greening Payments (PHNRI2) in E have been shifted to F.

Historically, farmers are assisted relative to manufacturers in rich industrial economies (RIEs), and the opposite bias has prevailed in poor agrarian economies (PAEs). However, many countries have transitioned from taxing to subsidizing farmers relative to manufactures as their economies grow (Figure 4.3). To understand why, it is helpful to look at the way government price supports alter the incentives those two sets of producers face. Anderson (1995) calibrates the simplest numerical economy-wide model (two tradables sectors plus nontradables, three sector-specific factors plus intersectorally mobile labor) to such economies and estimates the elasticities of real incomes of farmers and industrial capitalists to changes in the prices of their products. As shown in Table 4.3, in the PAE the elasticity of the industrialists' incomes with respect to the price of farm products is 10 times that of farmers, and with respect to the price of manufactures it is more than 20 times that of farmers. By contrast, in the RIE the elasticity of the industrialists' incomes with respect to the price of farm products or manufactures is one-fifth or less that of farmers. While this is only one determinant of the altering political economy of sectoral support in growing economies (differing costs of collective action by pertinent interest groups is another), it suggests emerging economies may be facing political economy forces at work that are similar to those that operated earlier in advanced industrial economies.

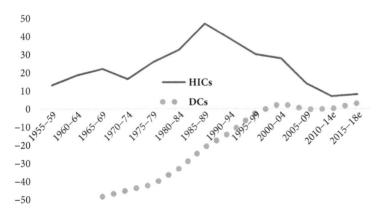

Figure 4.3 Relative rate of assistance to agriculture vs non-agriculture, high-income countries and developing countries, 1955–2018 (%, five-year averages)[a].

Note: [a]RRA is defined as $100 * [(100+NRAag^t)/(100+NRAnonag^t)-1]$, where $NRAag^t$ and $NRAnonag^t$, respectively, are the nominal rates of assistance (NRAs) for the tradable segments of the agricultural and non-agricultural goods sectors. The NRA is the percentage by which gross returns to producers in a sector are raised because of government sectoral or trade policies.
Source: Data from Anderson and Nelgen (2013) to 2011 updated using nominal rates of protection from www.ag-incentives.org (accessed January 2019).

Table 4.3 Elasticities of real incomes of farmers and industrial capitalists to changes in the prices of their products in a poor agrarian economy and a rich industrial economy

Elasticity with respect to the price of:	Poor agrarian economy		Rich industrial economy	
	Farmers	Industrial capitalists	Farmers	Industrial capitalists
Farm products	0.4	−4.0	2.3	−0.3
Manufactures	−0.2	4.5	−2.0	0.4

Source: Anderson (1995).

4.5 Contributors to the Global Costs of Present Forms of Support to Agriculture

To estimate the global costs of present farm-support policies, we use the latest version of the GTAP model (Hertel 1997; Corong et al. 2017) and its latest Data Base (pre-release 4 of Version 11) which is calibrated to 2017 (updated from Aguiar et al. 2019). The Data Base has been aggregated to 56 countries/regions and 30 sectors in our new modeling. In particular, it distinguishes primary agricultural sectors from processed food sectors, since the latter are becoming increasingly important in both production and trade as incomes grow and value chains lengthen (Gollin and Probst 2015; Barrett et al. 2022; Bellemare, Bloem and Lim 2022).

This version of the GTAP Data Base draws on domestic support estimates from the OECD (2021). It includes payments based on output (A2), intermediate input payments (B1+B3) and factor payments (B2, C, D, and E).[3] Payments vary in the extent to which they are decoupled from current production, and some of them may even be welfare-improving for society (such as rewards for providing ecosystem services), in which case they likely fall into the WTO's "Green Box." For subsidies not tied to specific sectoral output, integration in the GTAP Data

---

[3] As shown above in Table 4.2, the OECD classifies policy measures into seven broad categories, A to G, based on whether the basis is explicitly linked or not to current outputs or inputs and whether production is a prerequisite for receiving the payment (OECD 2021). Category A1 covers product market price support, A2 covers payments based on output, B covers payments based on input use, C covers payments based on current production, D covers payment based on non-current production with production required, E covers payments based on non-current production with production not required, F covers payments based on non-commodity criteria, and G is miscellaneous payments (see OECD 2021 for details). The GTAP Data Base does not include OECD data for categories F and G, and market price support (A1) is excluded to avoid double counting with tariffs already in the GTAP Data Base (Boulanger, Philippidis, and Jensen 2019). We follow Anderson et al. (2023) in adjusting the GTAP Data Base to better account for primary factor subsidies.

Base requires that assumptions be made to allocate these subsidies across sectors (Boulanger et al. 2019; Huang and Aguiar 2019).[4]

The scenario reported here involves full removal from the 2017 GTAP Data Base of all domestic agricultural supports and agrifood import tariffs and remaining export subsidies in all countries. The extent of domestic support to farmers and the average applied import tariff equivalents at the border as a percent of imports in the updated GTAP Data Base are shown in Table 4.4, which reveals that agrifood tariffs are more than twice those of other goods, and that farm subsidies nearly double the support provided by tariffs to farmers (i.e., "primary agriculture," while raising the support to food processors only slightly). Our purpose here is to report firstly how costly are agrifood policies of high-income countries to the world compared with those of developing countries, and then how costly are agrifood tariffs and export subsidies versus farm domestic support measures of high-income countries versus developing countries to those country groups and to the world. It is those costs that could be lowered greatly by re-purposing agrifood policies to better serve the transition of the world's food systems.

The results, reported in Table 4.5, suggest that full liberalization of agriculture and food sectors in 2017 would have led to a 0.06 percent increase in real GDP, equivalent to almost US$50 billion globally per year. Of this, almost $46 billion is due to tariff removal, with removal of domestic subsidies contributing most of the rest ($3 billion). Liberalization in high-income countries contributes $21 billion (42 percent) to global GDP, almost all of which is due to reform of their own policies. Developing country liberalization contributes a little more ($28 billion or 58 percent) to global GDP, of which again almost all is due to reform of their own markets. Thus, developing countries would have benefitted somewhat more from complete liberalization of global agrifood policies in 2017 than high-income countries—in contrast to 2001, when three-quarters of the benefit would have come from high-income country liberalization (bottom row of Table 4.6). This means there are more developing countries likely to be resistant to reforming their agricultural policies now than was the case two decades ago when the WTO's Doha Development Round was launched. It may be partly why the WTO membership has struggled to get traction in multilateral negotiations in its Agricultural Committee, and so has narrowed its focus in recent years to just domestic support policies.

Yet of those potential total global real GDP gains as of 2017, the results suggest that just 6 percent is from removal of domestic subsidies, it being very similar for high-income countries as for developing countries. That contribution of domestic support removal is not much higher than that of earlier global estimates of 5

---

[4] We modify the GTAP model code to separate primary factor subsidies from primary factor taxes, enabling us to directly target reductions in primary factor subsidies rather than subsidies net of any taxes on primary factors, as in the standard GTAP model code (Anderson et al. 2022).

Table 4.4 Subsidies and import tariffs in the updated GTAP Data Base, primary agriculture, processed foods, and non-agrifood goods, 2017 (%)

Region	Domestic subsidies, 2017[a]			Tariffs, 2017[b]			
	Primary agriculture	Processed foods	Total Ag&food	Primary agriculture	Processed foods	Total Ag&food	Non-ag&food
HICs	10.7	0.2	3.3	3.1	6.2	5.1	1.3
DCs	3.7	0.6	2.0	7.1	7.8	7.5	3.6
WORLD	5.3	0.4	2.5	5.7	7.1	6.6	2.5

Note: [a] Average subsidy to production (including total subsidy payments on outputs, intermediate inputs and primary factor inputs), weighted by the value of output at market prices.
[b] Average tariff, weighted by imports at cif prices, excluding intra-EU trade.
Source: Authors' calculations from the adjusted GTAP v11p4 2017 Data Base.

Table 4.5 Simulated changes in real GDP from the elimination of domestic subsidies, import tariffs and export subsidies on all agricultural and food products, 2017 (US$ million and %)

Contributions from:	US$m change in GDP			% change in GDP		
	HICs	DCs	World	HICs	DCs	World
Domestic subsidies:						
Primary factors	814	−503	311	0.00	0.00	0.00
Intermediate inputs	126	2,160	2,286	0.00	0.01	0.00
Outputs	359	162	521	0.00	0.00	0.00
Total	1,298	1,819	3,118	0.00	0.01	0.00
Import tariffs	19,437	26,152	45,589	0.04	0.07	0.06
Export subsidies	−28	11	−16	0.00	0.00	0.00
TOTAL	**20,707**	**27,983**	**48,690**	**0.04**	**0.08**	**0.06**
HIC liberalization	18,716	1,931	20,646	0.04	0.01	0.03
DC liberalization	1,992	26,052	28,044	0.00	0.07	0.03

Source: Authors' GTAP model simulation results.

Table 4.6 Distribution of changes in real GDP from regional and global elimination of domestic subsidies, import tariffs and export subsidies on agricultural and food products, 2001 and 2017 (%)

	Shares of effect in 2001 on:			Shares of effect in 2017 on:		
	HICs	DCs	World	HICs	DCs	World
HIC liberalization	61	12	73	38	4	42
DC liberalization	14	13	27	4	54	58
Global liberalization	75	25	100	42	58	100

Source: Authors' GTAP model simulation results as reported in Table 4.4 above and Table 4.4 of Anderson and Martin (2005).

percent in 2001 (Table 4.7). The reason for the slightly higher share estimates due to domestic support in 2017 versus 2001 is mainly because tariffs in most countries were reduced over that period, but also because of the growth of domestic supports in high-income countries and, notably, China.

The GTAP model is also able to shed some light on the impact such reform would have on the environment, poverty, and human health. According to the FAO, methane emissions and manure from cattle and sheep are responsible for three-quarters of agriculture's global contribution to greenhouse gas emissions (Gautam et al. 2022; IPCC 2022; Chapter 3 of this volume). Furthermore, in many countries feedgrains and oilseed meal are the dominant feed for those ruminant animals, which raises the price of staple foods for the world's poorer consumers.

Table 4.7 Shares of domestic subsidies, import tariffs and export subsidies in the regional and global GDP effects of full liberalization of agricultural and food policies, 2001 and 2017 (%)

	Shares of effect in 2001 on:			Shares of effect in 2017 on:		
	HICs	DCs	World	HICs	DCs	World
Domestic supports	5	4	5	6	7	6
Import tariffs	88	108	93	94	93	94
Export subsidies	7	−12	2	0	0	0
TOTAL	**100**	**100**	**100**	**100**	**100**	**100**

Source: Authors' GTAP model simulation results as reported in Table 4.4 above and Table 4.5 of Anderson and Martin (2005).

Table 4.8 Changes in real output of selected foods from the elimination of domestic subsidies, import tariffs and export subsidies on all agricultural and food products, 2017 (%)

	Beef and sheepmeat contribution of:			Dairy products contribution of:			Fruit and vegetables contribution of:		
	Subsidies	Tariffs	Both	Subsidies	Tariffs	Both	Subsidies	Tariffs	Both
HICs	−2.2	−1.0	−3.2	−2.6	1.3	−1.3	−5.1	0.2	−4.9
DCs	0.0	0.8	0.8	0.4	−1.4	−0.9	0.6	−0.1	0.5
World	−0.9	0.1	−0.8	−1.2	0.0	−1.1	−0.4	−0.1	−0.4

Source: Authors' GTAP model simulation results.

Meanwhile malnutrition would be reduced if fruit and vegetables were more accessible to poor households. Our results suggest that removing all farm tariffs and subsidies globally would reduce pollution by shrinking the world's output of ruminant meat by 0.8 percent and of dairy products by 1.1 percent (Table 4.8). However, Table 4.8 also reveals that, in developing countries, the output of fruit and vegetables would *rise* (by 0.5 percent), as would that of ruminant meat (by 0.8 percent), thereby potentially improving human health of poor consumers there.

4.6 How Best to Re-purpose Current Agrifood Policies

The task for governments challenged with demands to meet multiple policy objectives is becoming more complex as the voices of ever-more single-focused interest groups become louder via the megaphone of social media, and as concerns grow for the global commons. It is in this environment that there have been calls for transforming the world's food systems to make production more sustainable, consumption safer and healthier, and both more resilient and inclusive and less damaging to natural resources and the environment (see, e.g., Fan et al. 2021). That would require major re-purposing of food policies in both high-income and developing countries (FAO et al. 2022; Gautam et al. 2022). We conclude by outlining several ways in which that could be done, bearing in mind the political economy forces at work.

4.6.1 Lowering Trade Barriers

Reform should begin by lowering trade barriers, since they are still by far the most dominant form of assistance to farmers globally. Even though they have declined slightly in importance relative to more-direct support measures over the past two decades, they still contribute around 94 percent of the economic welfare cost of all agricultural support policies globally, according to the above GTAP Model results.

Since one of the thorniest sectors to deal with at the WTO has been agriculture, Cahill et al. (2021) suggest new pathways for agricultural negotiations that, if taken up, could re-invigorate other parts of the WTO's long-inactive Doha Development Agenda. Consistent with the above GTAP model results, that note argues first for significant tariff reductions, with the extent being greater the higher are current tariffs. Second, it argues the highest rates of domestic supports also be lowered most. Certainly, those two moves would generate bigger economic gains nationally than flat across-the-board cuts. Just as certainly, such reforms are likely to be resisted by the groups that had the political influence on their national government to get them implemented in the first place. But mass media offers a potential counter pressure to those vested interests, and has been shown to have a helpful influence in high-income countries (Olper and Swinnen 2013).

The complexity of reaching multilateral trade agreements has been made more difficult by the fact that the global effects of international trade on the natural environment and resource sustainability are also under scrutiny (Copeland, Shapiro, and Taylor 2022), including via agricultural trade (Baylis, Heckelei, and Hertel 2021). Also, biodiversity loss (Matthews and Karousakis 2022) and biosecurity threats (Campbell et al. 2017) are becoming key foci in multilateral negotiations (Kehoe et al. 2019; Fan et al. 2021). Since agriculture is considered a major contributor to greenhouse gas emissions, future global trade analyses will need to draw on models that better integrate economic and environmental systems. Results from such models would help in anticipating future policy demands of left-behind groups and the complementary policy adjustments that might be needed in response.

Should the Cahill et al. proposal for multilateral trade negotiations prove elusive, as suggested at the most-recent WTO Trade ministerial meeting in mid-2022, agricultural policy reform reliance in the coming years will need to be mostly on unilateral actions, supplemented by bilateral and regional preferential agreements. As argued above, unilateral lowering of food trade barriers could bring gains not just in efficiency terms but also in terms of reducing inequality and especially poverty, food insecurity, malnutrition, and ill-health. Openness is also the best national insurance against unexpected shocks to markets. The long-term decline in costs of trading internationally, and the consequent strengthening of global value chains (Barrett et al. 2022), add to that potential for openness to increase the trend rate of economic growth and to reduce its fluctuations, and to boost affordable access to healthy food as populations and incomes grow. Making those benefits from greater openness clearer to voters is one way to alter the political economy in their favor.

Since global warming and extreme weather events are becoming more damaging to food production in many regions (Jägermeyr et al. 2021), climate change is a further reason for nations to be open to international food markets so trade can buffer seasonal fluctuations in domestic production. The more countries that do so, the less volatile will be international food prices (Tyers and Anderson 1992; Martin and Anderson 2012).

4.6.2 Ensuring Optimal National Environmental Policies Are in Place

The best option for national governments dealing with local natural resource and environmental issues is to directly target local market frictions and market failures that currently lead to inefficiency, inequality, and environmental damage. That can be done via better education for the next generation of leaders, and also for those likely to be otherwise left behind by forthcoming technologies (Colantone, Ottaviano, and Stanig 2022). The OECD's Trade and Agriculture Directorate's analyses and advocacy efforts are examples of efforts to boost leaders' understanding of these and related issues.

Specifically, to reduce the risk of back-tracking on the trade reforms of recent decades and to increase the prospect of continuing down the reform path, attention should turn to strengthening the measures that will make firms and households more resilient in the face of uncertainties, and more assured that optimal domestic policies and institutions are in place to deal with externalities and to supply needed public goods. For example, taxing greenhouse gas emissions would add to costs of production, and more in agriculture than many other sectors, but it would also potentially stimulate new environmentally friendlier technologies. That could provide other income streams for some landholders in the form of carbon sequestration options or the provision of priced ecosystem services (see Section 4.6.5 below).

4.6.3 Ensuring Property Rights Are Encouraging Optimal Investments in all Forms of Capital

The national economic welfare gains from trade opening will be greater, the more there are complementary first-best domestic policies and institutions in place for encouraging optimal accumulation of various forms of capital (natural, human, knowledge, financial, physical), for providing national public goods, and for offsetting local environmental and other externalities and risks. Key institutions that can boost optimal investments in primary production are well-established and enforced land, water, forest, and fishery property rights, in addition to those for minerals and energy raw materials. And social costs associated with households and firms being more exposed to uncertain international markets and new innovations can be lowered with better-functioning financial and insurance markets (Jensen and Barrett 2017; Robles 2021), income tax systems, and generic social safety nets/trampolines. The latter also facilitate the adjustments by firms and households to reductions in trade barriers and subsidies, especially if those reforms are pre-announced and phased in over time.

4.6.4 Boosting Public Investments in Rural Infrastructure, R&D, Education, and Health

An efficient way to compensate today's farmers for reducing their import protection would be to boost the current underinvestment in rural infrastructure (to lower transport and communication costs involved in getting to market farm products, especially nutritious but perishable fresh fruits and vegetables) and in agricultural R&D (to lower farmers' costs of production or raise the quality and thus price of their product). Both of those initiatives would benefit food consumers as well as producers. Rural education and health services often are inferior to those in urban areas, so they could be improved too. That would boost human capital of farm families, enabling them to become more resilient as farmers, or to more easily take up more lucrative non-farm activities. Boosting such public investments is often not a high priority for elected politicians though, because the benefits may not be evident to voters until well beyond the current election cycle (Mogues 2015). More dissemination to voters, bureaucrats, and politicians of the results of analyses that point to those future long-term benefits would help, but it continues to be a hard sell.

In the case of agricultural R&D, there continues to be a reluctance in many countries to allow the production or import of genetically modified (GM) seeds for local production and even the importation of GM foods for local consumption. This is unfortunate, since GM crops can be bred specifically to help mitigate climate change, reduce local pollution, and improve nutrition. Indeed, wider adoption in Europe of already-existing GM crops could result in a reduction equivalent to 7.5 percent of the total agricultural greenhouse gas emissions of Europe, according to Kovak, Blaustein-Reito, and Qaim (2022). Moreover, the latest genome editing technologies could speed R&D's contributions to the environment and human health. While differences in values continue to make this issue politically contentious in Europe and hence its developing country trading partners, China at least is actively exploring these opportunities (see Chapter 9 in this volume by Barrett et al.).

4.6.5 Encouraging Markets for Ecosystem Services

Much of the environmental protection component of those earlier "multifunctionality" claims by farmers has been recently rebadged as payments for "ecosystem services." These are deemed necessary to ensure society gets closer to the optimal use of its natural capital. Where a contestable market can be developed such that the community can express its willingness to pay for such services, it would then be up to farmers to demonstrate that they are competitive suppliers of those services. That may well boost demand for targeted research on how best to design and implement institutions and policies in this space.

One example has to do with carbon sequestration in soils, demand for which will be greater the higher the taxation of carbon emissions and the more developed the market for tradable emission permits nationally and internationally (Simone et al. 2017). For individual farmers the first task is to estimate whether the upfront cost of changes in land management practices is more than offset by the subsequent flow of benefits from selling carbon credits (White, Davidson, and Eckard 2021). Scientists have cautioned that the scientific basis for such payments is often not sound, so some have proposed a set of guidelines and principles to assist this process (Naeem et al. 2015). As well, much remains to be learned about the effectiveness of various schemes that have been tried (Börner et al. 2017). Their success to date has been hampered by inadequate design and implementation leading to adverse self-selection, poor administrative targeting, and noncompliance in the wake of limited willingness/organizational capacity to pay for environmental services (Wunder et al. 2020).

4.7 Conclusion

The per capita cost of global distortions to agricultural and food markets has fallen somewhat in recent decades with the reduced dependence on border measures, and their distributional consequences may now be less inequitable than in the past. Yet the policy instruments currently used are still far from being the most efficient, equitable, and sustainable ones available. The preceding section exposes some of the ways society could be better served through further changes in policy instrument choices. It remains to be seen whether political circumstances will allow such reforms to take place. While major reform via the WTO on its own seems unlikely in the foreseeable future, the prospect of pressure on national governments to contribute to mitigation of greenhouse gases (and biodiversity loss but to a much smaller extent) may add to domestic pressures from environmental groups for better environmental policies. That in turn might trigger new alliances between farm and environmental interest groups in high-income countries that could lead to more re-purposing of current supports to farmers away from inefficient and inequitable price-distorting policy instruments and toward instruments that support not just farmer welfare but also the natural environment. The research that has been triggered by the World Bank and IFPRI (Gautam et al. 2022) is one contribution that economists together with environmental scientists can make toward farm policy reforms that boost national and global environmental and social outcomes in addition to standard economic ones.

References

Aguiar, A., M. Chepeliev, E.L. Corong, R. McDougall, and D. van der Mensbrugghe. 2019. "The GTAP Data Base: Version 10." *Journal of Global Economic Analysis* 4 (1): 1–27.

Anderson, K. 1995. "Lobbying Incentives and the Pattern of Protection in Rich and Poor Countries." *Economic Development and Cultural Change* 43 (2): 401–423.

Anderson, K. 2000. "Agriculture's 'Multifunctionality' and the WTO." *Australian Journal of Agricultural and Resource Economics* 44 (3): 475–494.

Anderson, K. (ed.). 2009. *Distortions to Agricultural Incentives: A Global Perspective, 1955-2007*. London: Palgrave Macmillan and Washington, DC: World Bank.

Anderson, K. 2020. "Trade Protectionism in Australia: Its Growth and Dismantling." *Journal of Economic Surveys* 34 (5): 1044–1067.

Anderson, K., and R. Blackhurst (eds). 1992. *The Greening of World Trade Issues*, Ann Arbor, MI: University of Michigan Press.

Anderson, K., E. Corong, A. Strutt, and E. Valenzuela. 2023. "The Relative Importance of Global Agricultural Subsidies and Tariffs, Revisited." *World Trade Review* 22 (forthcoming).

Anderson, K., Corong, E. L., and A. Strutt. 2022. "The GTAP-DS (Domestic Support) Model." Presented at the 25th Annual Conference on Global Economic Analysis, June 8–10.

Anderson, K., R. Lattimore, P.J. Lloyd, and D. MacLaren. 2009. "Australia and New Zealand." In *Distortions to Agricultural Incentives: A Global Perspective, 1955–2007*, ed. K. Anderson, Ch. 5, 221–256. Washington, DC: World Bank and Palgrave Macmillan.

Anderson, K., and W. Martin. 2005. "Agricultural Trade Reform and the Doha Development Agenda." *The World Economy* 28 (9): 1301–1327.

Anderson, K., W. Martin, and E. Valenzuela. 2006. "The Relative Importance of Global Agricultural Subsidies and Market Access", *World Trade Review* 5 (3): 357–376.

Anderson, K., and S. Nelgen. 2013. "Updated National and Global Estimates of Distortions to Agricultural Incentives, 1955 to 2011." Spreadsheet last updated June 2013. World Bank, Washington, DC. www.worldbank.org/agdistortions

Anderson, K., and H. Norheim. 1993. "From Imperial to Regional Trade Preferences: Its Effect on Europe's Intra- and Extra-regional Trade." *Weltwirtschaftliches Archiv (now Review of World Economics)* 129 (1): 78–102.

Anderson, K., and S. Ponnusamy. 2023. "Structural Transformation Away from Agriculture in Growing Economies." *Agricultural Economics* 54 (1): 62–76.

Anderson, K., G. Rausser, and J.F.M. Swinnen. 2013. "Political Economy of Public Policies: Insights from Distortions to Agricultural and Food Markets." *Journal of Economic Literature* 51 (2): 423–477.

Anderson, K. and J.F.M. Swinnen 2009. "Eastern Europe and Central Asia." In *Distortions to Agricultural Incentives: A Global Perspective, 1955–2007*, ed. K. Anderson, Ch. 6, 259–288. London: Palgrave Macmillan and Washington, DC: World Bank.

Anderson, K., and R. Tyers. 1992. "Japanese Rice Policy in the Interwar Period: Some Consequences of Imperial Self Sufficiency." *Japan and the World Economy* 4 (2): 103–127.

Anderson, K., E. Valenzuela, and D. van der Mensbrugghe. 2010. "Global Welfare and Poverty Effects: The Linkage Model." In *Agricultural Price Distortions, Inequality and Poverty*, eds. K. Anderson, J. Cockburn and W. Martin, Ch. 2, 49–86. Washington, DC: World Bank.

Avetisyan M., T.W. Hertel, and G. Sampson. 2014. "Is Local Food More Environmentally Friendly? The GHG Emissions Impacts of Consuming Imported Versus Domestically Produced Food." *Environmental and Resource Economics* 58 (3): 415–462.

Barrett, C.B., T. Reardon, J. Swinnen, and D. Zilberman. 2022. "Agri-food Value Chain Revolutions in Low- and Middle-Income Countries." *Journal of Economic Literature* 60 (4): 1316–1377.

Baylis, K., T. Heckelei, and T.W. Hertel. 2021. "Agricultural Trade and Environmental Sustainability." *Annual Review of Resource Economics* 13: 379–401.

Bellemare, M.F., J.R. Bloem, and S. Lim. 2022. "Producers, Consumers, and Value Chains in Low- and Middle-Income Countries." In *Handbook of Agricultural Economics, Vol. 6*, eds. C.B. Barrett and D.R. Just, Ch. 89, 4933–4996. Amsterdam: Elsevier.

Bhagwati, J.N. 1971. "The Generalized Theory of Distortions and Welfare." In *Trade, Balance of Payments and Growth*, eds. J.N. Bhagwati, R.W. Jones, R.A. Mundell, and J. Vanek, 69–90. Amsterdam: North-Holland, 69–90.

Börner, J., K. Baylis, E. Corbera, D. Ezzine-de-Blas, J. Honey-Rosés, U.M. Persson, and S. Wunder. 2017. "The Effectiveness of Payments for Environmental Services." *World Development* 96: 359–374.

Boulanger, P., G. Philippidis, and H.G. Jensen. 2019. "Domestic Support in the European Union." In *The GTAP Data Base: Version 10*, eds. A. Aguiar, M. Chepeliev, E.L. Corong, R. McDougall, and D. van der Mensbrugghe, West Lafayette, IN: Global Trade Analysis Project. https://www.gtap.agecon.purdue.edu/resources/res_display.asp?RecordID=5948

Cahill, C., S. Tangermann, L. Brink, S. Fan, J. Glauber, A. Gonzalez, et al. 2021. *New Pathways for Progress in Multilateral Trade Negotiations in Agriculture.* https://newpathwaysagric.files.wordpress.com/2021/05/new-pathways.pdf

Campbell, B.M., D.J. Beare, E.M. Bennett, J.M. Hall-Spencer, J.S.I. Ingram, F. Jaramillo, R. Ortiz, V. Ramankutty, J.A. Sayer, and D. Shindell. 2017. "Agriculture Production as a Major Driver of the Earth System Exceeding Planetary Boundaries." *Ecology and Society* 22 (4): 8.

Cassing, J.H., and A.L. Hillman. 1986. "Shifting Comparative Advantage and Senescent Industry Collapse." *American Economic Review* 76 (3): 516–523.

Ciaian, P., E. Baldoni, D.A. Kancs, and D. Drabik. 2021. "The Capitalization of Agricultural Subsidies into Land Prices." *Annual Review of Resource Economics* 13: 17–38.

Colantone, I., Ottaviano, G., & Stanig, P. 2022. "The Backlash of Globalization." In *The Handbook of International Economics, Volume V,* edited by G. Gopinath, E. Helpman, and K. Rogoff, Ch. 7, 405–477. Amsterdam: Elsevier.

Copeland, B.R., J.S. Shapiro, and M.S. Taylor 2022. "Globalization and the Environment." In *The Handbook of International Economics, Volume V,* edited by G. Gopinath, E. Helpman, and K. Rogoff, Ch. 2, 61–146. Amsterdam: Elsevier.

Copeland, B.R. and M.S. Taylor. 2004. "Trade, Growth, and the Environment." *Journal of Economic Literature* 42 (1): 7–71.

Corden, W.M. 1997. *Trade Policy and Economics Welfare* (Second Edition). Oxford: Clarendon Press.

Corong, E.L., T.W. Hertel, R. McDougall, M.E. Tsigas, and D. van der Mensbrugghe. 2017. "The Standard GTAP Model, Version 7." *Journal of Global Economic Analysis* 2 (1): 1–119.

Dasgupta, P. 2021. *The Economics of Biodiversity: The Dasgupta Review.* London: HM Treasury.

Edwards, G.W., and A.S. Watson. 1978. "Agricultural Policy." In *Surveys of Australian Economics,* ed. F.H.Gruen, Ch. 4, 187–239. Sydney, Australia: Allen and Unwin.

Fan, S., D. Headey, C. Rue, and T. Thomas. 2021. "Food Systems for Human and Planetary Health: Economic Perspectives and Challenges." *Annual Review of Resource Economics* 13: 131–156.

FAO, IFAD, UNICEF, WFP, & WHO. 2022. *The State of Food Security and Nutrition in the World 2022: Repurposing Food and Agricultural Policies to Make Healthy Diets More Affordable.* Rome, FAO. https://doi.org/10.4060/cc0639en

Findlay, R., and K.H. O'Rourke. 2007. *Power and Plenty: Trade, War, and the World Economy in the Second Millennium.* Princeton, NJ: Princeton University Press.

Floyd, J.E. 1965. "The Effects of Farm Price Supports on the Returns to Land and Labor in Agriculture." *Journal of Political Economy* 73 (2): 148–158.

Gardner, B.L. 1983. "Efficient Redistribution through Commodity Markets." *American Journal of Agricultural Economics* 65 (2): 225–234.

Gardner, B.L. 2009. "United States and Canada." In *Distortions to Agricultural Incentives: A Global Perspective, 1955–2007,* ed. K. Anderson, Ch. 4, 177–220. London: Palgrave Macmillan and Washington, DC: World Bank.

Gautam, M., D. Laborde, A. Mamun, W. Martin, V. Piñeiro, and R. Vos. 2022. *Repurposing Agricultural Policies and Support: Options to Promote Sustainable Development,* World Bank Report No: AUS0002236. Washington, DC: World Bank and IFPRI. https://openknowledge.worldbank.org/handle/10986/36875

Gollin, D., and L.T. Probst. 2015. "Food and Agriculture: Shifting Landscapes for Policy." *Oxford Review of Economic Policy* 31 (1): 8–25.

Gründler, K., and A.L. Hillman. 2021. "Ambiguous Protection." *European Journal of Political Economy* 68: 102009.

Head, K., T. Mayer, and J. Ries. 2010. "The Erosion of Colonial Trade Linkages after Independence." *Journal of International Economics* 81 (1): 1–14.

Hertel, T.W. (ed.). 1997. *Global Trade Analysis: Modeling and Applications.* Cambridge and New York: Cambridge University Press.

Hillman, A.L. 1982. "Declining Industries and Political-Support Protectionist Motives." *American Economic Review* 72 (5): 1180–1187.

Huang, H., and A. Aguiar. 2019. "Agricultural Domestic Support." In *The GTAP Data Base: Version 10*, A. Aguiar, M. Chepeliev, E.L. Corong, R.McDougall, and D.van der Mensbrugghe. West Lafayette, IN: Global Trade Analysis Project. https://www.gtap. agecon.purdue.edu/resources/res_display.asp?RecordID=5946

Hynes, W., D.S. Jacks, and K.H. O'Rourke. 2012. "Commodity Market Disintegration in the Interwar Period." *European Review of Economic History* 16 (2): 119–143.

IAC (Industries Assistance Commission). 1978. *Report on Rural Income Fluctuations*, Canberra, Australia: IAC.

IPCC. 2021. *Climate Change 2021: The Physical Science Basis.* Geneva: IPCC.

IPCC. 2022. "Food, Fibre, and Other Ecosystem Products." In *Climate Change 2022: Impacts, Adaptation, and Vulnerability*, eds. H-O. Pörtner, D.C. Roberts, M. Tignor, E.S. Poloczanska, K. Mintenbeck, A. Alegría, M. Craig, S. Langsdorf, S. Löschke, V. Möller, A. Okem, and B. Rama, Ch. 5. Cambridge and New York: Cambridge University Press, 713–906.

IPCC (Intergovernmental Panel on Climate Change). 2020. *Climate Change and Land.* Geneva: IPCC.

Jägermeyr, J., C. Müller, A.C. Ruane, J. Elliott, J. Balkovic, O. Castillo, et al. 2021. "Climate Impacts on Global Agriculture Emerge Earlier in New Generation of Climate and Crop Models." *Nature Food* 2: 873–885. https://doi.org/10.1038/s43016-021-00400-y

Jensen, N., and C.B. Barrett. 2017. "Agricultural Index Insurance for Development." *Applied Economic Perspectives and Policy* 39: 99–219.

Josling, T. 2009. "United States and Canada." In *Distortions to Agricultural Incentives: A Global Perspective, 1955–2007*, ed. K. Anderson, Ch. 3, 115–176. London: Palgrave Macmillan and Washington, DC: World Bank.

Kehoe, L., T. Reis, M. Virah-Sawmy, A. Balmford, K. Kuemmerle, and 604 signatories. 2019. "Make EU Trade with Brazil Sustainable." *Science* 364 (6438): 341.

Khandelwal, A.K., P.K. Schott, and S-J. Wei. 2013. "Trade Liberalization and Embedded Institutional Reform: Evidence from Chinese Exporters." *American Economic Review* 103 (6): 2169–2195.

Kovak, E., D. Blaustein-Reito, and M. Qaim. 2022. "Genetically Modified Crops Support Climate Change Mitigation." *Trends in Plant Science* 27 (7): 627–629. https://doi.org/10.1016/j.tplants.2022.01.004

Lloyd, P.J. 1974. "A More General Theory of Price Distortions in an Open Economy." *Journal of International Economics* 4 (4): 365–386.

Martin, W. and K. Anderson. 2012. "Export Restrictions and Price Insulation During Commodity Price Booms." *American Journal of Agricultural Economics* 94 (2): 422–227.

Masters, W.A., A.B. Finaret, and S.A. Block. 2022. "The Multiple Burdens of Malnutrition: Dietary Transition and Food System Transformation in Economic Development." In *Handbook of Agricultural Economics, Vol. 6*, eds. C.B.Barrett and D.R. Just, Ch. 6. Amsterdam: Elsevier.

Matthews, A., and K. Karousakis. 2022. "Identifying and Assessing Subsidies and Other Incentives Harmful to Biodiversity: A Comparative Review of Existing National-Level Assessments and Insights for Good Practice." OECD Environment Working Paper No. 206, Paris: OECD.

Mauldon, R.G. 2021. "Early Analytical Agricultural Economics in Australia." *Australian Economic History Review* 61 (1): 45–63.

Mogues, T. 2015. "What Determines Public Expenditure Allocations? A Review of Theories, and Implications for Agricultural Public Investments." *European Journal of Development Research* 27 (3): 452–473.

Naeem, S., J.C. Ingram, A. Varga, T. Agardy, P. Barten, G. Bennett, et al. 2015. "Get the Science Right When Paying for Nature's Services." *Science* 347 (6227): 1206–1207. https://doi.org/10.1126/science.aaa1403

Nettle, R.S, M. Britten-Jones, and K. Anderson. 1987. "Optimal Policy Intervention to Reduce Import Dependence." *International Economic Journal* 1 (4): 101–106.

OECD. 2021. OECD Producer and Consumer Support Estimates. https://stats.oecd.org/Index.aspx?QueryId=114551

OECD (Organization for Economic Co-operation and Development). 2008. *Multifuctionality in Agriculture: Evaluating the Degree of Jointness, Policy Implications*. Paris: OECD.

Olper, A., and J.F.M. Swinnen. 2013. "Mass Media and Public Policy: Global Evidence from Agricultural Policies." *World Bank Economic Review* 27 (3): 413–436.

Rao, X., T.M. Hurley, and P.G. Pardey. 2020. "Recalibrating the Reported Returns to Agricultural R&D: What If We All Heeded Griliches?" *Australian Journal of Agricultural and Resource Economics* 64: 977–1001.

Rausser, G.C. 1982. "Political Economic Markets: PERTs and PESTs in Food and Agriculture." *American Journal of Agricultural Economics* 64 (5): 821–833.

Ravallion, M. 1987. *Markets and Famines*. London and New York: Oxford University Press.

Ravallion, M. 1997. "Famines and Economics." *Journal of Economic Literature* 35 (3): 1205–1242.

Robles, M. 2021 "Agricultural Insurance for Development: Past, Present and Future." In *Agricultural Development: New Perspectives in a Changing World*, eds. K. Otsuka and S. Fan, Ch. 17, 563–594. Washington, DC: IFPRI.

Rosegrant, M.W., C. Ringler, and T. Zhu. 2009. "Water for Agriculture: Maintaining Food Security under Growing Scarcity." *Annual Review of Environmental Resources* 34: 205–222.

Simone, T.E., D.M. Lambert, I. Cuvaca, and N.S. Eash. 2017. "Soil Carbon Sequestration, Carbon Markets, and Conservation Agriculture Practices: A Hypothetical Examination in Mozambique." *International Soil and Water Conservation Research* 5: 167–179.

Swinnen J.F.M. 1994. "A Positive Theory of Agricultural Protection." *American Journal of Agricultural Economics* 76 (1): 1–14.

Swinnen, J.F.M. 2018. *The Political Economy of Agricultural and Food Policies*. London and New York: Palgrave Macmillan.

Swinton, S.W. 2022. "Precision Conservation: Linking Set-Aside and Working Lands Policy." *Applied Economic Perspectives and Policy* 44 (3): 1158–1167.

Tyers, R., and K. Anderson. 1992. *Disarray in World Food Markets: A Quantitative Assessment*. Cambridge and New York: Cambridge University Press.

United Nations. 2021. *Tokyo Nutrition for Growth Summit & UN Food Systems Summit: Joint Statement*. United Nations, New York, September 23. https://nutritionforgrowth.org/wp-content/uploads/2021/09/N4G_UN_FoodSysSummit_9.23.pdf

Warr, P.G. 1977. "Tariff Compensation via Input Subsidies." *Economic Record* 53 (144): 508–516.

Wheeler, S.A., ed. 2021. *Water Markets: A Global Assessment*. London: Edward Elgar.

White, R.E., B. Davidson, and R. Eckard. 2021. "An Everyman's Guide for a Landholder to Participate in Soil Carbon Farming in Australia." Occasional Paper 21.01. Australian Farm Institute, Sydney, Australia. https://www.farminstitute.org.au/publication/a-landholders-guide-to-participate-in-soil-carbon-farming-in-australia/

Wunder, S., J. Börner, D. Ezzine-de-Blas, S. Feder, and S. Pagiola. 2020. "Payments for Environmental Services: Past Performance and Pending Potentials." *Annual Review of Resource Economics* 12: 209–234.

5

Policy Coalitions in Food Systems Transformation

Johan Swinnen and Danielle Resnick

5.1 Introduction

Coalitions—or a set of individuals and groups with shared policy preferences—lie at the heart of political economy.[1] They are also often considered central to policy change. For instance, in 1999, the president of the World Bank argued that many of the world's most intractable development issues could only be tackled by marshaling "coalitions for change" (Wolfensohn 1999). The implied positive potential of coalitions was reiterated during the 2021 UN Food Systems Summit, where coalitions were seen as a fundamental tool for addressing the multi-sectoral and multi-scalar nature of food systems transformation. In fact, more than two dozen coalitions were formed to address various elements of the food system, from halting deforestation to improving data to enhancing wages for food system workers.[2]

Coalitions matter for at least two reasons. First, interest groups that share similar goals often exert more influence on policymakers and greater visibility to the public when they combine to forge a larger partnership. Policymakers may ignore small interest group demands or find it too time-consuming to deal with each one separately. Coalitions, however, provide more tractable partners for negotiation and compromise. Second, coalition members can benefit from the consolidation of their different types of resources and legitimacy. In other words, some may have financial leverage or geographical reach, others may have political connections, while still others may hold a respected reputation with the broader public. Forming coalitions thereby provides a greater basis for mobilizing and sustaining pressure on decision makers and shaping the policy discourse in desired ways.

Historically, coalitions played a central role in agriculture and food policies, especially with respect to trade and price interventions, such as import tariffs and price support measures (Anderson 2009, 2016). The use of tariffs and trade

---

[1] This chapter includes abridged material from Swinnen (2015, 2018).
[2] See https://foodsystems.community/coalitions-in-the-context-of-the-food-systems-summit/. These were almost entirely formed by multilateral agencies, international non-governmental organizations, and academics.

Johan Swinnen and Danielle Resnick, *Policy Coalitions in Food Systems Transformation*. In: *The Political Economy of Food System Transformation*. Edited by: Danielle Resnick and Johan Swinnen, Oxford University Press. © Johan Swinnen and Danielle Resnick (2023). DOI: 10.1093/oso/9780198882121.003.0005

restrictions goes back centuries and are the key component of many countries' agricultural and food policies today. These policies affect producers, consumers, and taxpayers and as a result, many studies only focus on these three agents to understand the impacts on agricultural policies and political incentives. Theoretically, such a simplified approach is didactically useful by avoiding unnecessary complications in deriving policy effects and identifying equilibria. Empirically, the absence of disaggregated information of policy impacts on various agents within (or outside) the value chain necessitates focusing on a narrow set of actors.

Yet, in reality, there are many other agents involved in these processes, including input suppliers (such as landowners, seed and agro-chemical companies, or banks), traders, food processors, retail companies, and environmental and food advocacy groups. These different agents can join forces and form coalitions with farmers or with final consumers to influence policy makers in setting public policies. The expanded agenda on food systems transformation increases the complexity of these agents and their interactions. Consequently, the breadth and diversity of policy coalitions has become even more apparent.

This chapter therefore provides greater nuance about contemporary coalitions for food systems transformation, focusing on three broad types of coalitions. Specifically, vertical coalitions encompass the range of actors within particular food value chains. How they coalesce or fracture often depends on both the policy instrument under consideration and where in the value chain the policy intervention is most proximate. Cross-issue coalitions consider a wider range of interests that different stakeholders possess beyond prices, costs, and profitability. Such interests can include food safety, the environment, and nutrition. Transnational coalitions consider how interest groups—whether governments, corporations, or social movements—create allies that encompass both domestic and international members. Such coalitions may be either outward looking and thereby aimed at influencing policy dynamics at the global scale, or inward looking by drawing on international discourses and resources to shift domestic policy. Importantly, these three types of coalitions are not mutually exclusive; vertical coalitions may, for instance, intersect with transnational ones, especially when considering policies related to global value chains.

As the chapter illustrates, coalitions are not static; their membership, influence, and goals can shift over time for several different reasons. First, traditional power structures within value chains may change as some (sub)sectors grow and others decline as economic development proceeds. For example, farming accounts for two-thirds of value added in food value chains in poor countries but for less than 20 percent in rich countries (Holtemeyer et al. forthcoming). New technologies may bring new players into the value chains and new policy instruments may be introduced. For instance, in the 1970s, there was no pro- or anti- lobby with respect to genetically modified (GM) crops. Yet, with advances in biotechnology and the growing promotion of such crops, a range of new vested interests emerged around this issue. Other examples include biofuels, which emerged in recent decades as an important factor in agricultural markets and food policy with rising oil prices and the growing urgency to find renewable energy sources.

Second, the promotion of policy innovations can foster the entry of new interest groups into the food systems arena. Crop insurance subsidies, for example, have brought insurance companies into the lobbying game for farm support programs. Third, income growth in developed countries and globalization has invigorated old concepts, such as food sovereignty, with renewed resonance. Consumers are demonstrating more enthusiasm for eating locally produced foods while farm groups can draw on sovereignty claims to both market their products and protect trade. In turn, this has generated tensions in trade negotiations over regulations on geographical indications (GI)—labels that identify a product as coming from a particular territory (e.g., champagne as sparkling wine from the Champagne region in France) that is equated with quality (Josling 2006; Meloni and Swinnen 2018).

Fourth, the influence of coalitions can shift with the rise and fall of what McAdam's (1996) refers to as "political opportunity structures." Such structures may shift due to an unexpected crisis or loss of longstanding policy champions, including politicians, political parties, and bureaucrats. In some countries, the ouster of an agricultural minister or president through elections may affect the political opportunity structure. In countries with a history of well-institutionalized parties, the preferences of certain interest groups—such as those of workers, farmers, or business—may have long been incorporated into policy programs. However, shifting demographics, the rise of populism, and new economic goals may cause parties to try to incorporate new constituents and abandon others.

The following section briefly reviews the importance of coalitions for collective action. Subsequently, the chapter discusses vertical, cross-issue, and transnational coalitions and their role in food system transformation. In doing so, the chapter underscores that while coalitions are widely viewed as essential for policy change, the diversity of such coalitions for food systems is rarely examined, nor are the ways in which the goals of disparate coalitions may complement or contradict each other. Such a holistic perspective is needed to understand who champions or opposes transformative policy change and where there are prospects for issue linkage and compromise.

5.2 Policy Coalitions and Effectiveness of Collective Action

Research on the political economy of agricultural policies was heavily influenced by Mancur Olson's (1965) seminal work on the "logic of collective action."[3] From his insights, the size, concentration, and wealth of vested interests all affect their

---

[3] Other work looking at the narratives and frames used by coalitions draw on Sabatier's (1998) advocacy coalition framework as their starting point. Chapters 10 and 11 of this volume examine advocacy coalitions in more detail.

influence in the policy process. In order to effectively influence policy choices, interest group members must act in unison. They must form an organization that can mobilize resources and direct individual action. The greater the number of politically active members in an organization and the more resources at its disposal, the greater its political power base.

However, as Olson argues (1965), individuals in the group often prefer to free ride. Several factors can mitigate against free riding and thereby enhance a coalition's political leverage. These include the geographic concentration of group members, a strong commitment to a broadly shared ideology, and low communication costs as a result of, for instance, operating via trade and professional associations that contribute to coalition cohesion while decreasing organizational set-up and maintenance costs. By logical implication, as the costs of collective action shift, the political influence of the coalition should shift as well.

Olson's insights have been widely applied in studying the political economy of agricultural and food policies and to predict changes in the political equilibrium over time (Anderson et al. 2013). In poor countries, food consumers are often concentrated in cities with lower costs to coordination relative to farmers, who are dispersed in rural areas. However, as the economy develops, and especially as the share of agriculture in employment declines and rural infrastructure improves, the cost of political organization for farmers decreases. This cost reduction is likely to increase the effectiveness of farmers' representation of their interests and, consequently, of their lobbying activities.[4]

However, changes in relative collective-action costs alone cannot explain major changes in agricultural policies (de Gorter and Swinnen 2002). Although rural infrastructure and information have improved significantly as countries have developed, even in developed countries, there remain a very large number of farmers. The persistence of such large numbers of farmers, whose interests are not necessarily aligned, might imply that collective action obstacles still exist. Structural changes in the economy as well as market fluctuations and commodity specifics also affect political economy dynamics (Swinnen 1994, 2018). Farmers are also not a homogeneous group and often segmented into different commodities—some more export-oriented and others import-competing—and therefore their policy preferences are not automatically aligned.

More significantly, economic and technological development have expanded the range of relevant interest groups involved in food and agricultural policy

---

[4] The nature of agricultural structures also may determine the effectiveness of collective political action, but there may be offsetting effects. Traditional arguments predict that a sector with mainly large-holding farmers can more easily overcome collective action problems because its members are typically fewer and its collective-action costs lower compared to the political rents they receive. However, La Ferrara (2002) argues that inequality among farmers may make it harder for collective action to succeed because small and large farmers have conflicting incentives and because free riding is likely to be more common in a heterogeneous group setting. Historical evidence from Europe also supports this result (Schonhardt-Bailey 2006; Swinnen 2009).

decisions. Other agents in the value chain, such as food processors, retail companies, and agribusinesses tend to be less fragmented and more capitalized than the farms. Consequently, they may be more effective in organizing for political action, disproportionately so at the global level (Clapp 2021).

In some cases, the same agent is involved in multiple elements of the value chain, such as the four dominant global agricultural trading firms, Archer Daniels Midland, Bunge, Cargill, and Louis-Dreyfus. As observed by Clapp (2015), these firms—known as the ABCDs—operate as cross-sectoral value chain managers that have interests in land, insurance, finance, storage, and transport and increasingly draw on blockchain and artificial intelligence technologies. Several mergers in recent years have further consolidated agribusiness companies providing seeds and herbicides as well as within the food retail industry (McKeon 2015). An examination of vertical policy coalitions elucidates axes of alignment and divergence along elements of the value chain, taking into account not only producers and consumers but also input suppliers (e.g., animal feed suppliers, seed, fertilizer, and pesticide companies, landowners, rural credit organizations), food processors, wholesalers, retailers, importers, and exporters.

5.3 Vertical Policy Coalitions Along the Value Chains

Agricultural and food policies typically intervene in specific parts of the value chain. The type of instrument used, and the "location" of intervention, has a major impact on the possible political coalitions. The nature of the policy instrument will determine whether the interests of farmers and processors or other agents are aligned or conflictual, often making the choice of the policy instrument the subject of lobbying itself. Import tariffs may be imposed on processed food products (e.g., pasta or specific cheeses) or on (raw) agricultural products (e.g., cereals or milk). In case import tariff and price interventions are on raw agricultural products, the food processors (buyers of cereals or milk) may have opposing interests to the farmers. More specifically, such tariffs can protect agricultural producers but may increase the costs of production for processors, even if the latter can nonetheless pass on part of the increased costs on to final consumers.[5]

However, agricultural policies (such as tariffs, import quota, or price interventions) often do not apply to the raw agricultural products as they are sold by the farmers, but to products which have undergone a certain level of processing or marketing. For example, it is typically not the raw milk or the sugar beets that are traded or purchased by government agencies but processed products such as milk

---

[5] A few studies have tried to disentangle these policy effects along the value chain. For example, Briones Alonso and Swinnen (2016) analyze the wheat–flour chain in Pakistan and find important impacts for all agents, including grain traders and milling companies. Other examples are Ivanova et al. (1995) and Swinnen (1996) analyzing the wheat-bread value chain in Bulgaria.

powder, cheese, or sugar. Hence, interests of food processing companies involved in early-stage processing will often be aligned with those of farmers, while those of further processing may be opposite. In this case, coalitions will emerge that include farm organizations and early-stage processors, which may lobby for import tariffs, while retailers, traders, and final consumers may oppose such tariffs. Such coalitions not only organize around tariffs but also on product standards or other type of regulations. For example, an interesting current discussion relates to names of plant-based alternatives to meat products, and whether the word "burger" can be used for them—a discussion where the meat industry and livestock farmers are joint in a coalition trying to restrict such broad use of names.

Take the case of sugar: the "production side" includes sugar processing companies and the farmers producing sugar cane or sugar beet (and other agents, such as landowners and agribusinesses supplying inputs to the farmers). The "consumer side" also includes food companies. Some sugar is "consumed" directly by households, but most is sold to the food industry, which uses the sugar in various products sold to retailers and only then do households consume the sugar. This separation is well illustrated by the debate in the European Union (EU) in recent years on ending the sugar production quotas, which ultimately occurred in September 2017. The EU's beverage and confection industries and sweetener companies lobbied the EU decision-makers against the extension of the EU sugar quota, which kept production low and prices high; by contrast, the sugar processing companies were lobbying to keep the system and its higher sugar prices.

But even if the policy applies to unprocessed products, such as cereals, many other sectors are affected and involved. Commodity traders (often large multinational companies) and large food processing and retailing companies are affected by farm policies and will actively lobby for or against them. History provides many examples of the importance of policy coalitions in this process. For example, the often-heralded period of free trade in the 19th century comes to an end when cheap overseas grain floods West European markets after 1875. Reactions of governments in Europe differ because of different policy coalitions (Swinnen 2009). The governments of France and Germany introduced import tariffs to protect their grain farms. Both countries were characterized by a large agricultural population, little industrialization, and a large crop sector. In contrast, countries such as the United Kingdom (UK) and Belgium did not impose import tariffs for grain because both countries were already quite industrialized and grain tariffs were opposed by a broad coalition. This coalition encompassed workers who benefited from low food prices, industrial capital who wanted to maintain low wages, the transport industry and the coal mines where horse power was key and thus cheap grain was important, the brewing industry, the harbor managers who opposed any tariffs that would limit trade volume, and livestock farmers who benefited from low feed prices.

Importantly, changes in these coalitions can affect policy outcomes because market power structures are often quite different along the value chain. For example, the growth of agricultural protection in many OECD countries in the second half of the 20th century was associated with the growth of cooperative agribusiness and food-processing companies. The growth and concentration of agribusinesses and food-processing companies created a strong political coalition with farm interests in lobbying for agricultural policies (Anderson 1995). Farm-related cooperatives and business organizations in the agri-food sector became important interest groups, with, for example, agricultural credit cooperatives, dairy and sugar processing companies joining farm unions in actively lobbying for government support and import protection for their sectors. Since farm lobbies and agribusiness interests were increasingly well capitalized and concentrated, they became an important force in orchestrating public policies that benefited their interests (Gawande and Hoekman 2006; López 2008).

Interests and power relations on the consumer side of the value chains have also changed over time. The growth of food processing and marketing companies created new, powerful, often international players with strong vested interests. Growing concentration in the retail sector have made the retail sector a more powerful sector in the value chain (Swinnen and Vandeplas 2010). This may benefit consumers since for many agricultural and food policy issues—such as food safety—consumer and retailer interests are aligned and may be reinforced by growing retail concentration.[6] The following sections examine several specific areas of coalition formation and fractionalization, focusing on landowners, biotechnology, and biofuels.

5.3.1 Landowners and Farmers

Landowners and farmers have always had a complex relationship. In countries where farmers own most of their land, such as in much of Latin America, their interests mostly coincide. During the 1990s and 2000s, agrarian elites in places such as Chile and El Salvador built conservative parties to represent their interests in Congress while in Brazil, they created their own parliamentary caucus to support the congressional aspirations of landowners. The Brazilian Agrarian Caucus has, over time, pushed for a relaxation of regulations on deforestation and genetically modified organisms (GMOs) (Milmanda 2019).

---

[6] In response to concerns on abuse of market power and unfair practices in the food supply chain emerged in the EU, the European Commission establishment the *High Level Forum for a Better Functioning Food Supply Chain*, which includes different stakeholders from the food supply chain. The Forum agreed on a set of principles of good practices in vertical relationships and launched a voluntary framework for implementing the principles of good practice (the Supply Chain Initiative). Regulations differ significantly between EU member states. (Swinnen and Vandevelde, 2019).

However, in many parts of the world, farmers rent a considerable part of their land (either through sharecropping or cash rent contracts)—and there have been considerable changes on this through history (Swinnen et al. 2014). At the end of the 19th and early 20th centuries, landowners and tenant farmers throughout Europe fought over land rental conditions. These conflicts resulted in a series of policy changes that shifted land rents from large landowners to family farmers (Swinnen 1999). In some countries, such as Ireland, governments forced landlords to sell land to their tenants, creating a large group of land-owning small holders. In others, such as Belgium and the Netherlands, the government imposed strict rental regulations, including fixed prices, benefiting smallholders who continued to lease land. In the UK, the government increased land and inheritance taxes, triggering land sales to farmers by landlords.

More recently, political relations between landowners and farmers in Europe, the United States (US), and Canada are very different. In some cases, they join forces to lobby for agricultural subsidies. Farm subsidies, either linked to production or to land use, have spilled over into high land prices and rents, creating a coalition between farmers and landowners. Studies in the US and Canada have demonstrated significant increases in land prices as a consequence of farm payments (Kirwan 2009; Vyn et al. 2012). In recent EU policy discussions, landowners have not opposed moving from trade-distorting price support toward non-trade-distorting decoupled farm payments, since the payments are still linked to land use and thus keep land prices high (Salhofer and Schmid 2004; Ciaian and Swinnen 2009; Ciaian et al. 2014). Empirical studies (Ciaian et al. 2018) suggest that a large share of agricultural subsidies in the EU end up with landowners. Hence, not surprisingly, landowners are active lobbyists in favor of farm subsidies in these situations.

Similar coalition dynamics apply to other farm inputs beyond land, such as agricultural machinery, fertilizer, seeds, and water rights.[7] Agribusiness and input owners have a lot at stake, even indirectly, in agricultural policy. For example, agribusiness has joined forces with farm organizations in opposing recent attempts to set land aside and reduce input use in EU policy reforms. These measures were introduced as part of the EU's Green Deal in 2021. Yet, in the wake of the 2022 Ukraine war and associated high food prices, this coalition was able to mobilize against some of these proposed reforms (for more details, see Chapter 13 of this volume).

5.3.2 Biotechnology

As elaborated in more detail in Chapter 10 of this volume, coalitions have played a crucial role in differences in technology regulations as well. A well-documented

---

[7] Political economy issues are also important in optimal water allocation and (clean) water rights distributions in many countries in the world (see e.g., special issues of Choices Magazine in 2017 edited by Madhu Khanna and David Zilberman).

and striking case is the difference in regulations of genetically modified (GM) agricultural products (Pinstrup-Anderen and Schioler 2001; Paarlberg 2001; Qaim 2009, 2016). While the US and other countries such as Canada and Brazil have approved the use of GM in agriculture, the EU has followed a precaution-ary approach in establishing new legislation to regulate GM technology. For some time, this led to a de facto EU moratorium on the approval of GM products both for imports and for domestic production. The restrictions on imports have been reduced since 2003, but the staunch opposition of consumers and anti-GM activist groups in combination with the institutional set-up of the EU's decision-making procedure on GMOs have led to regulatory gridlock on GM production in the EU that has continued until today (Swinnen and Vandemoortele 2011).

A crucial element was the differential role between the EU and the US that was played by various interest groups, inclusive of activist groups, farmers, biotech innovators, and competing input suppliers (e.g. chemical companies).[8] Graff, Hochman, and Zilberman (2009) argue that the US agribusiness industry has been a much more pro-GM lobbying force than the EU agribusiness industry. One rea-son is because some of the most important GM products have traits that reduce the need for traditional agribusiness products, such as pesticides and insecticides. So, while GM opened up new avenues for profit and commercial avenues in the future, it potentially undermined the agribusiness industry's traditional profits in the short-term. As a result, many of the EU's large agro-pharmaceutical companies were uncertain what side to take in the debate. This underscores that coalitions sometimes depend on calculations of inter-temporal costs and benefits.

By contrast, in the US, some of the key companies, both the new GM start-ups—most of who developed in the US—and some large agribusiness companies, in particular Monsanto, went all out lobbying for GMO. This created a different political coalition in the US than in the EU, contributing to a different regula-tory outcome. Later in the process, some of the European agribusiness companies seem to have changed their mind, with BASF introducing some new GM products and Bayer taking over Monsanto. However, by that time, the EU decision process was stuck in a policy gridlock. Consequently, several European companies have moved much of their GM research capacity and product development to non-EU countries, including the US.

In developing countries as well, coalitions for and against GMOs have pitted input suppliers and the livestock industry against consumers and crop farmers. Kenya, for instance, is an interesting case. Kenya had been considered a leader in GM technology in Africa until the government abruptly banned the import of GM food in 2012 and initiated a moratorium on GM crops (Schnurr and Gore

---

[8] Another key difference between the EU and the US were the regulatory environments and atti-tudes. When GM emerged as a major policy issue the regulatory environment in Washington DC was dominated by the Reagan-era anti-regulation philosophy (Charles 2001). In contrast, in the EU the GM policy issues became most important when food safety crises of the 1990s contributed to growing wariness about new food technologies, including genetic modification (Swinnen et al. 2011).

2015). In the intervening decade, the livestock industry advocated that the government allow GM grain imports for animal feed due to insufficient domestic feed availability, which is a major constraint to expanding production to meet domestic demand. These demands became even more pronounced in 2022 as the Ukraine war further constrained grain supply and as Kenya faced its fourth consecutive year of drought. Consumer and civil society groups, such as the Biodiversity and Biosafety Association of Kenya and the Route to Food, have long opposed lifting the moratorium, as has the influential horticultural sector, which primarily exports to the EU and is one of Kenya's largest sources of export revenue (Resnick et al. 2022). However, when a new government came into office in September 2022, one of its first decisions was to allow GM imports for animal feed.

5.3.3 Biofuels

Biofuels represent another area where the importance of shifting coalitions over time becomes readily apparent. In the 1990s and early 2000s, there were large crop surpluses and low agricultural prices, prompting policymakers to look for ways to support farmers without the burden of huge subsidies. Using crops for alternative uses was one method of removing such surpluses and boosting prices. At the same time, the Gulf War served as a reminder that countries needed to wean themselves from foreign crude oil sources. Increased recognition of climate change stemming from greenhouse gas (GHG) emissions presented yet another rationale for moving away from fossil fuels. As a result, governments in both the EU and the US stimulated the development of biofuels, though it was much stronger in the US (mostly corn-based ethanol) than in the EU (mostly biodiesel).[9] The US biofuels legislation was built on a history of tax exemptions and tariffs (taxes on imports), but the fundamental policy shift was the introduction of mandates for the use of biofuels in transportation—the Renewable Fuels Standard (RFS) in 2005 (Naylor 2012; Lobell et al. 2014; de Gorter et al. 2015).

After 2007, the policy climate on biofuel changed due to two developments. First, while there is disagreement on the size of the impact, biofuels generally have been an important factor in the spiking food prices in 2007–2008 (de Gorter et al. 2013). Second, biofuels were originally thought of as environmentally friendly fuels, due to their decreased carbon impact relative to fossil fuels. However, indirect effects on land use change, particularly through deforestation, may lead to an increase—rather than a decrease—in GHG emissions. These factors transformed the debate on biofuels, triggering what the biofuels industry has described as a policy U-turn. For instance, the EU backtracked from production targets and

---

[9] From 2004 to 2012, the amount of corn used for ethanol increased from about 1.2 billion bushels to about 5 billion bushels. Over 40 percent of U.S. corn use now goes to ethanol.

blending mandates and now seeks to minimize the use of food-crop based biofuels. The new biofuel sustainability requirements of the 2009 Renewable Energy Directive try to limit the impact of biofuels on rising food prices (European Commission 2009). In 2012, the European Commission (EC) published a proposal limiting the use of food-crop based biofuels at 5 percent of consumption of energy for transport in 2020.

However, various organizations with vested interests in biofuels opposed this EC proposal, leading to a postponement of the decision. In general, the growth of biofuels stimulated new alliances that will be difficult to unravel. As biofuels contributed to grain price spikes in the late 2000s, this fostered coalitions of grain farmers and biofuel industries, versus livestock farmers, consumers and other sectors hurt by rising feed and food costs (de Gorter et al. 2015). With the Ukraine war in 2022 and resultant grain and vegetable oil supply shortages, the biofuels debate re-emerged, with some food companies and non-governmental organizations (NGOs) calling for a suspension of mandates for blending biofuels into petrol and diesel even as biofuels companies in both the US and EU argued that the industry has very little practical impact on global food availability (Terazono and Hodgson 2022).

5.4 Cross-Issue Coalitions

Cross-issue coalitions affect agricultural and food actors but often extend well beyond them, and the participants in such coalitions may have several motivations. This section first focuses on coalitions that coalesce around food quality and nutrition and how the contours of those coalitions may vary based on a country's or region's level of economic development. Then, the section considers "legitimacy coalitions," or those alliances that employ narratives to tie their agenda to the broader public interest (Trumbull 2012), including around issues of environmental justice and fair working conditions.

5.4.1 Food Quality and Nutrition

Consumer interests change with economic development. Within OECD countries during the post-war years, stimulating local production to generate sufficient food resonated with consumers, especially those that had faced food shortages during war time. Politicians who had to address their nation's basic concerns, and consumers facing hunger and food shortages during times when food imports and long-distance food supplies were interrupted, supported the domestic production of affordable food.

Although consumers remain concerned about food prices, particularly during recent periods of food price inflation, other qualities beyond price have gained more attention as well. Specifically, consumers increasingly are concerned about the safety and quality of food, as well as with ensuring that the food they consume adheres to environmental and ethical standards. All developed countries have introduced important food safety regulations to protect consumers, often triggered by crises. Two major food safety crises with global implications occurred in Europe. The first, in the mid-19th century, occurred when new technological innovations allowed scientists to test food ingredients—several of which were cheap substitutes and some even poisonous, triggering strong public reactions against, and a wave of regulations imposed on, the food industry (Meloni and Swinnen 2015). The second was in the late 1990s, which triggered major legislative changes such as the Basic Food Law Regulation, including the creation of the European Food Safety Authority (EFSA). The concerns of consumers over food quality and safety also triggered strong reactions from food processors and retailers. This included both the introduction of private standards to address concerns that were/are not addressed by public regulations, the pre-empting of public regulations by private standards, and their lobbying to influence the nature of public food regulations (Winfree and McCluskey 2006; Vandemoortele and Deconinck 2014).

Generating coalitions for food safety can be more challenging in parts of the Global South, such as sub-Saharan Africa, where a large share of the poor depends on the informal sector, including wet markets or street vendors, for affordable food. The combination of costs to adhere to such standards among informal retailers, combined with inadequate regulatory and enforcement capacity in such settings, creates few domestic constituencies for reform despite recurrent cholera outbreaks and food-borne illnesses (see Hoffmann et al. 2019). Poorer consumers, including those who do understand health risks, also cannot effectively use boycotts as a tool to enforce shifts in regulation in the same way that wealthier consumers can in developed countries.

Political institutions can also condition the range of feasible coalitions, sometimes leading to alliances of "strange bedfellows" to support nutrition policies in some countries but not others.[10] For instance, in the US, an unexpected coalition has emerged between nutrition advocates and producers due to the nature of the legislative process and the country's penchant for omnibus bills that attempt

---

[10] Another example of a strange bedfellow coalition includes the peculiar constellation of interests that have aligned historically around food aid programs. Barrett and Maxwell (2005) referred to the "iron triangle of food aid," whereby American millers and processors benefited handsomely from the food aid program due to procurement modalities, and US shipping companies have benefited from legal requirements that most food aid has to be transported by US (private) ships. This coalition of NGOs, agribusiness and maritime transport businesses resulted in USAID spending a higher share of its annual appropriation on food aid on transportation costs for more than 60 years.

to partially satisfy large numbers of interest groups. Specifically, the Supplemental Nutritional Assistance Program (SNAP, earlier known as food stamps) is a major item of the US' Farm Bill. SNAP payments go to families with net incomes less than the poverty line. In the 2022 fiscal year, more than 41 million Americans and 21 million households received SNAP payments, and the US$105 billion consumer package is now the core of US Department of Agriculture's (USDA) budget.[11] For historical and political reasons, this huge, consumer safety net program is located within the USDA's budget rather than within the Department of Health and Human Services, the home for virtually all other welfare programs. Cuellar et al. (2014) claim it is "arguably the most prominent example of coalition politics in American food and agriculture policy," i.e., the cooperative dynamic between supporters of domestic nutrition assistance and supporters of domestic farm subsidies to pass the Farm Bill. This entails an informal understanding whereby members of Congress who support domestic nutrition assistance either vote in favor of, or remain silent on, proposals to subsidize farmers, as long as domestic nutrition assistance programs are also funded adequately. The Farm Bill thus requires the support of both sides.[12] By contrast, in the EU, government support for poor consumers occurs mostly through social spending that is divorced from agricultural policy decisions. Social groups that are particularly vulnerable to food costs, such as the elderly, the unemployed, and the poor, can draw therefore on social security programs.

5.4.2 Environmental Concerns

One critique of Olson's (1965) theory is that individuals are motivated by more than their self-interests, and they may still come together around other issues for which they are passionate, such as environmental sustainability. Environmental organizations have emerged as an important lobby group in agricultural policy discussions. Conservation has a long history in U.S. agricultural policy dating back to the Dust Bowl era of the 1930s (Gardner 2002). Environmental concerns took on new prominence in the 1985 and 1990 Farm Bill: the latter was entitled the "Food, Agriculture, Conservation and Trade Act." Farm groups seeking to limit agricultural production—thereby raising prices—joined a political coalition with environmentalists to establish a Conservation Reserve Program (CRP) for the protection of erodible land (Cuellar et al. 2014). Farmers can place their land in

---

[11] See SNAP data tables available at the USDA Food and Nutrition Service, https://www.fns.usda. gov/pd/supplemental-nutrition-assistance-program-snap (accessed November 11, 2022).

[12] What makes this piece of legislation particularly interesting is that the provision of nutritional assistance provides a safety net for low-income consumers, particularly in times of high or volatile food prices caused in part by agricultural policies like the corn-ethanol program. The convergence of special interests creates a peculiar equilibrium in U.S. food and agricultural policy that is extremely difficult to disrupt.

the CRP in exchange for CRP payments. In 2012, 27 million acres of U.S. crop-land, involving nearly 400,000 farms, were in the CRP (USDA 2013). With higher commodity prices after 2005, CRP payments became less competitive, and fewer farmers are interested in the program.

In the EU, environmental organizations did not have a major impact on agricultural policy until the 2000s. Hopes were high among the environmental organizations that, given the need to address climate change and other environmental concerns, important further changes could be made in the CAP reform to enhance the environmental impact of CAP subsidies. Policy discussions focused on how to reform the farm payments, as increased pressure from taxpayers and demands from environmental groups challenge the current payment structures. One key element was greening the payments so that farm support would be better linked to environmental objectives.

Farm organizations lobbied to secure the payments in the early 2010s. They were supported in these efforts by landowners, who are benefiting from spillover effects of the land-based payments. Farm associations formed a strategic coalition with environmental groups to lobby for as large a CAP budget as possible during the economic and financial crisis. However, as soon as the budget for the 2014–2020 CAP was fixed, the coalition fell apart as farm groups started lobbying to remove or weaken environmental constraints on the payments (Hart 2015; Matthews 2015). In the end, environmentalists were very disappointed with an outcome which some have described as a "green wash" instead of "greening" (Erjavec et al. 2015; Hart 2015).

Food price fluctuations have affected the political outcomes. The global food price spikes during the 2008–2012 period facilitated the successful lobbying of EU farmers against more environmental constraints and contributed to waning interest in the CRP among US farmers in the 2010s. Similarly, food price rises following the Ukraine war in 2022 affected similar policy discussions (see Chapter 13, this volume). The rising food prices caused concern among poor consumers, and producing and securing food suddenly re-emerged as an important policy concern. Environmental concerns gave way to food security and production objectives in political coalitions, and high prices made CRP less attractive to farmers. Both examples underscore how coalitions founded on promoting similar policy instruments but for different reasons can be more unsustainable over time than those encompassing interest groups that are united on the ultimate objectives of those policy instruments.

Coalitions for environmental goals also vary in their strength sub-nationally, leading to uneven implementation of environmental regulations within countries. Milmanda and Garay (2019), for example, uncover that the implementation of Argentina's national forest protection regime (NFPR) varies across the country's provinces. They uncover that in provinces where conservationist coalitions were strong, regulations and enforcement of NFPR was high while in provinces where there was equal strength among coalitions of conservationists and those encompassing large agricultural producers who were demanding more land, governors passed strict regulations but allowed illegal deforestation. And where conservationist coalitions were weak, NFPR regulations were much more permissive. Such studies emphasize that whether a policy issue is localized or not, and who has functional authority over the issue (national or local government) is equally important in identifying coalitions that support sustainable food system reforms.

5.5 Globalization and Transnational Coalitions

Although the chapter thus far has focused predominantly on domestic interests, international organizations, transnational movements, cross-border alliances, and multinational corporations often influence domestic policies. For example, when high import tariffs and export subsidies from the EU were distorting international agricultural markets in the 1970s and 1980s, international pressure increased on policymakers to reduce the distortions. Important outside pressure came from exporting nations, such as the US and Australia, and developing countries, NGOs and international organizations, which accused the EU of causing poverty and hunger in poor rural households. For example, a coalition of the OECD, the World Bank, and NGOs emphasized how the EU (and other countries including the US) were hurting the world's poor by contributing to low agricultural and food prices through their agricultural subsidies (Swinnen 2011). This contributed to significant reforms in the 1990s as part of the General Agreement on Tariffs and Trade (GATT) "Uruguay Round Agreement on Agriculture" (URAA), which was later integrated in the World Trade Organization (WTO).

Another example of international pressure on domestic agricultural and food policies were the structural adjustment programs (SAPs) of the 1980s and 1990s. These programs were introduced in many developing countries under pressure from international institutions, such as the IMF and the World Bank, and resulted in the removal of state intervention in agriculture and food policies. For instance, many countries had to reform or eliminate their marketing boards as well as rescind subsidized inputs. (Anderson et al. 2013). More recently, several countries that have defaulted on their debt have had to return to the International Monetary Fund (IMF) for bailouts and are required to yet again follow austerity programs with implications for agricultural policy. For example, Zambia's 2022 IMF agreement requires the country to significantly reduce its longstanding Farm Inputs Subsidy Program and reform its Food Reserve Agency (IMF 2022). While transnational NGOs, such as the Jubilee Debt Campaign, lobbied against international reform pressures on African countries during the 2000s, coalitions of transnational and domestic interest groups are now lobbying for their governments to demonstrate more transparency in their use of funds. In Kenya, for instance, the International Budget Partnership has joined with the Kenyan Human Rights Commission and the Institute of Social Accountability to demand more information about the contracts that the government signed with international financial institutions.

Moreover, the distinction between domestic interests and foreign interests in traditional trade and political economy models - and in the discourse in many policy discussions – is no longer as clear in today's world of global value chains (Olper, 2017). For example, if companies are sourcing inputs from foreign subsidiaries or contracting with foreign farms or companies for their raw materials, the interests of these (domestic) companies are closely aligned with their (foreign) input suppliers. Traditional trade models do not accurately capture these effects since they implicitly assume costless switching between different producers and consumers if prices or costs change. However, in a world with extensive and elaborate product and process standards, such switching can imply significant transaction costs. For this reason, trading is increasingly integrated in global value chains with elaborate and sophisticated forms of vertical coordination (Nunn 2007; Sexton 2012; Swinnen and Vandeplas 2012; Antras 2015; Swinnen et al. 2015).

The spread of such global value chains thus has implications for the political economy of agricultural and food policies because it changes the incentives of various agents in the value chains to lobby for, or against, import protection and integration in international trade agreements (Blanchard and Matchke 2015; Olper 2017). Blanchard et al. (2016) show that trade protection is lower when the domestic content of foreign produced final goods is higher and (vice versa) for foreign content of domestically produced goods. In other words, the integration of economies and companies in global value chains tends to dampen the incentives for policies that hurt trade. Other recent studies show that more intensive global value chain integrations are associated with deeper trade agreements (Raimondi et al. 2022; Ruta 2017).

Other types of coalitions reveal attempts to rectify asymmetric power dynamics between developing country agricultural producers and multinational corporations. For instance, in 2018, Ghana and Côte d'Ivoire—who produce 63 percent of the world's cocoa—teamed up to create the Ivory Coast-Ghana Cocoa Initiative (ICCIG). The main intention of the ICCIG was to create a living income differential for the two countries' cocoa farmers, who live in abject poverty. In the 2020 cocoa growing season, the countries levied a premium of $400 per ton to prevailing world market prices. Confectionary companies such as Hershey's and Mondelez, in turn, decided to source elsewhere or declared they would begin developing high-yield cocoa plantations in other countries. However, the request of Cameroon and Nigeria to join the group in 2022, who provide an additional 11 percent of the global market share of cocoa, is expected to give the coalition greater bargaining power with the overseas manufacturers.

5.6 Conclusions

Coalitions have received growing prominence in recent years within the development community as a mechanism to transform food systems into healthier and more sustainable entities that result in equitable outcomes. This was underscored by the breadth of coalitions that emerged during the 2021 United Nations Food Systems Summit (UNFSS). Historically, however, coalitions have been just as effective in generating food and agricultural policy reforms as they have for preventing progress that threatens the interests of its members. Consequently, it is necessary to anticipate where coalitions might emerge for different policy instruments relevant to realizing food system transformation and identify whether their points of cohesion are related to shared interests (e.g., higher profits, lower costs, greater market access), or shared outcomes (e.g., less deforestation, safer foods, more decent work).

As this chapter has highlighted, anticipating such points of cohesion or divergence is rarely straightforward and does not necessarily depend on simplistic categorizations of stakeholders as food producers or consumers. Instead, the chapter has emphasized that policy coalitions are much more varied in recent decades due to the relative decline of some sectors in the value chain and the relative growth of others, combined with integration of value chains and consolidation of food industry and agribusiness. New technologies have introduced new players into the value chains while new policy instruments have provided incentives for others to join the lobbying game. Globalization has expanded the range of interested actors and issue areas affecting food systems, including the environment and nutrition, while improved communications augment the possibilities for transnational mobilization.

At the same time, the examples provided in this chapter reveal other factors that explain the rise, or the efficacy, of some coalitions, in some places but not others. Foremost among these are historical path dependence, political institutions, and governments' own development agendas. Shifts in political opportunity structures, including the 2008 and 2022 food price crises, likewise played a role.

Several gaps nonetheless remain in determining the potential and limits of coalitions for food system transformation. First, it remains unclear what are the meaningful boundaries of coalition participation that still enable coalitions to be effective. On the one hand, broader coalitions can facilitate access to more resources, visibility, and legitimacy. On the other hand, just like oversize government coalitions holding together disparate parties, oversize food system policy coalitions may become too unwieldy and risk losing a common goal. Moreover, they can become prone to inequalities that favor the voice of the largest and best-funded interest group. Second, there is scope to better understand which tactics and strategies are most effective for coalitions to employ given the types of policies and the stage of the policy process they aspire to target. Traditional lobbying through peak associations or networks of organizations may be more effective for incremental and iterative reforms while protests, boycotts, or media campaigns may be more useful for raising public attention and getting an issue onto the policy agenda. Third, the potential of collective action depends on the preferences of policymakers who influence not only development and food policy outcomes but also the degree of leverage that organizations exert in the policy sphere. Finally, institutions and political systems matter. Restrictions on freedom of association and speech in more closed political settings may necessarily constrict the breadth of food policy coalitions and their opportunities for mobilization in those countries. Similarly, institutional constraints and arrangements for global agreements obviously affect the success and failure of coalitions, as well as their optimal design.

References

Anderson, K. 1995. "Lobbying Incentives and the Pattern of Protection in Rich and Poor Countries." *Economic Development and Cultural Change* 43(2): 401–423.

Anderson, K. 2009. *Distortions to Agricultural Incentives: A Global Perspective, 1955–2007*. London and Washington, DC: Palgrave Macmillan and the World Bank.

Anderson, K. 2016. *Agricultural Trade, Policy Reforms, and Global Food Security*. New York: Palgrave Macmillan.

Anderson, K., G. Rausser, and J. Swinnen. 2013. "Political economy of public policies: Insights from distortions to agricultural and food markets." *Journal of Economic Literature* 51(2): 423–477.

Antras, P. 2015. *Global Production: Firms, Contracts, and Trade Structure*. Princeton, NJ: Princeton University Press.

Barrett, C.B., and D. Maxwell. 2005. *Food Aid after Fifty Years: Recasting Its Role*. London: Routledge.

Blanchard, E., and X. Matschke. 2015. "US Multinationals and Preferential Market Access." *Review of Economics and Statistics* 97 (4): 839–854.

Blanchard, E.J., C.P. Bown, and R.C. Johnson. 2016. "Global Supply Chains and Trade Policy." NBER Working Paper No. w21883. National Bureau of Economic Research, Cambridge, MA.

Briones, A.E., and J. Swinnen. 2016. "Who Are the Producers and Consumers? Value Chains and Food Policy Effects in the Wheat Sector in Pakistan." *Food Policy* 61: 40–58.

Charles, D. 2001. *Lords of the Harvest. Biotech, Big Money, and the Future of Food*. New York: Basic Books.

Ciaian, P., D. Kancs, and J. Swinnen. 2014. "The Impact of the 2013 CAP Reform on Land Capitalization." *Applied Economic Perspectives and Policy* 36 (4): 643–673.

Ciaian, P., D.A. Kancs, and M. Espinosa. 2018. "The Impact of the 2013 CAP Reform on the Decoupled Payments' Capitalisation into Land Values." *Journal of Agricultural Economics* 69 (2): 306–337.

Ciaian, P., and J. Swinnen. 2009. "Credit Market Imperfections and the Distribution of Policy Rents." *American Journal of Agricultural Economics* 91 (4): 1124–1139.

Clapp, J. 2015. "ABCD and Beyond: From Grain Merchants to Agricultural Value Chain Managers." *Canadian Food Studies* 2 (2): 126–135.

Clapp, J. 2021. "The Problem with Growing Corporate Concentration and Power in the Global Food System." *Nature Food* 2: 404–408.

Coble, K., B. Barnett, and J. Riley. 2013. "Challenging Belief in the Law of Small Numbers." Paper presented at the 2013 Agricultural and Applied Economics Association: Crop Insurance and the Farm Bill Symposium, Louisville, KY, October 8–9.

Cuellar, M., D. Lazarus, W.P. Falcon, and R.L. Naylor. 2014. "Institutions, Interests, and Incentives in American Food and Agriculture Policy." In *The Evolving Sphere of Food Security*, ed. R.L. Naylor, 87–121. Oxford, UK: Oxford University Press

De Gorter, H., D. Drabik, and D.R. Just. 2013. "Biofuel Policies and Food Grain Commodity Prices 2006–2012: All Boom and No Bust?" *AgBioForum* 16 (1): 1–13.

De Gorter, H., D. Drabik, and D.R. Just. 2015. *The Economics of Biofuel Policies*. New York: Palgrave Macmillan.

De Gorter, H., and J. Swinnen. 2002. "Political economy of agricultural policy." In *Handbook of Agricultural Economics* Vol.2, Part B, eds. B. Gardner and G. Rausser: 1893–1943. Amsterdam, The Netherlands: Elsevier Science, 2073–2123.

Erjavec, E, M. Lovec, and K. Erjavec. 2015. "Greening or Green Wash? Drivers and Discourses of the 2013 CAP Reforms." In *The Political Economy of the 2014–2020 Common Agricultural Policy*, ed. J. Swinnen, 215–244. Brussels: CEPS Publications.

European Commission. 2009. *Directive 2009/28/EC of the European Parliament and of the Council of 23 April 2009*. Brussels: European Commission. https://eur-lex.europa.eu/eli/dir/2009/28/oj

Gardner, B.L. 2002. *American Agriculture in the Twentieth Century*. Cambridge, MA: Harvard University Press.

Gawande, K., and B. Hoekman. 2006. "Lobbying and Agricultural Trade Policy in the United States." *International Organization* 60: 527–561.

Graff, G.D., G. Hochman, and D. Zilberman. 2009. "The Political Economy of Agricultural Biotechnology Policies." *AgBioForum* 12 (1): 34–46.

Hart, K. 2015. "The Fate of Green Direct Payments in the CAP Reform Negotiations: The Role of the European Parliament." In *The Political Economy of the 2014–2020 Common Agricultural Policy*, ed. J. Swinnen, 245–276. Brussels: CEPS Publications.

Hoffmann, V., C. Moser, and A. Saak. 2019. "Food Safety in Low and Middle-Income Countries: The Evidence through an Economic Lens." *World Development* 123: 104611.

Holtemeyer, B., J. Thurlow, K. Pauw, and J. Randriamamonjy. Forthcoming. "Measuring Agri-Food Systems: New Indicators and Global Estimates." Washington, DC: International Food Policy Research Institute.

IMF (International Monetary Fund). 2022. *Zambia: Request for an Arrangement under the Extended Credit Facility* No. 22/292. Washington, DC: IMF Country Report.

Ivanova, N., J. Lingard, A. Buckwell, and A. Burrell. 1995. "Impact of Changes in Agricultural Policy on the Agro-food Chain in Bulgaria." *European Review of Agricultural Economics* 22 (3): 354–371.

Josling, T. 2006. "The War on Terroir: Geographical Indications as a Transatlantic Trade Conflict." *Journal of Agricultural Economics* 57: 337–363.

Kirwan, B. 2009. "The Incidence of US Agricultural Subsidies on Farmland Rental Rates." *Journal of Political Economy* 177 (1): 138–164.

La Ferrara, E. 2002. "Inequality and group participation: theory and evidence from rural Tanzania." *Journal of Public Economics* 85(2): 235–273.

Lobell, D.B., R.L. Naylor, and C.B. Field. 2014. "Food, Energy, and Climate Connections in a Global Economy." In *The Evolving Sphere of Food Security*, ed. R.l. Naylor, 238–268. Oxford, UK: Oxford University Press.

López, R.A. 2008. "Does 'Protection for Sale' Apply to the US Food Industries?" *Journal of Agricultural Economics* 9 (1): 25–40.

Matthews, A. 2015. "The Multi-Annual Financial Framework and the 2013 CAP Reform." In *The Political Economy of the 2014–2020 Common Agricultural Policy*, ed. J. Swinnen, 169–192. Brussels: CEPS Publications.

McAdam, D. 1996. "Political Opportunities: Conceptual Origins, Current Problems, Future Directions." In *Comparative Perspectives on Social Movements*, eds. D. McAdam, J. McCarthy, and M. Zald, 23–40. Cambridge, UK: Cambridge University Press.

McKeon, N. 2015. *Food Security Governance: Empowering Communities, Regulating Corporations.* London and New York: Routledge.

Meloni, G., and J. Swinnen. 2015. "Chocolate Regulations." In *The Economics of Chocolate*, eds. M. Squicciarini and J. Swinnen, 268–303. Oxford, UK: Oxford University Press.

Meloni, G., and J. Swinnen. 2018. *Trade and Terroir. The Political Economy of the World's First Geographical Indications.* New York: Mimeo.

Milmanda, B.F. 2019. "Agrarian Elites and Democracy in Latin America after the Third Wave." *Oxford Research Encyclopedia of Latin American Politics.* Oxford, UK: Oxford University Press. https://doi.org/10.1093/acrefore/9780190228637.013.1652

Milmanda, B.F., and C. Garay. 2019. "Subnational Variation in Forest Protection in the Argentine Chacho." *World Development* 118: 79–90.

Naylor, R.L. 2012 "Biofuels, Rural Development, and the Changing Structure of Agricultural Demand." In *Frontiers in Food Policy: Perspectives on Sub-Saharan Africa*, eds. W. Falcon and R.L. Naylor. Palo Alto, CA: Stanford University Center on Food Security and the Environment, 343–376.

Nunn, N. 2007. "Relationship-Specificity, Incomplete Contracts, and the Pattern of Trade." *The Quarterly Journal of Economics* 122 (2): 569–600.

Olper, A. 2017. "The Political Economy of Trade-Related Regulatory Policy: Environment and Global Value Chain." *Bio-based and Applied Economics* 5 (3): 287–324.

Olson, M. 1965. *The Logic of Collective Action: Public Goods and the Theory of Groups.* Cambridge, MA: Harvard University Press.

Paarlberg, R.L. 2001. *The Politics of Precaution: Genetically Modified Crops in Developing Countries.* Washington, DC: International Food Policy Research Institute.

Pinstrup-Andersen, P., and E. Schiøler. 2001. *Seeds of Contention: World Hunger and the Global Controversy over GM Crops.* Washington, DC: International Food Policy Research Institute.

Qaim, M. 2009. "The Economics of Genetically Modified Crops." *Annual Review of Resource Economics* 1 (1): 665–694.

Qaim, M. 2016. *Genetically Modified Crops and Agricultural Development.* New York: Palgrave Macmillan.

Raimondi, V., A. Piriu, J. Swinnen, and A. Olper. 2022. "Global Value Chains, Tariffs, and Non-Tariff Measures in Agriculture and Food." Mimeo.

Resnick, D., S. Haggblade, M. Kamau, and I. Minde. 2022. *The Political Economy of Kenya's Agricultural Transformation: A Comparative Value Chains Approach*. Report prepared for USDA and USAID East Africa Mission.

Ruta, M. 2017. "Preferential Trade Agreements and Global Value Chains: Theory, Evidence, and Open Questions." Policy Research Working Paper No. WPS 8190. World Bank Group, Washington, DC.

Sabatier, P. 1998. "The Advocacy Coalition Framework: Revisions and Relevance for Europe. *Journal of European Public Policy* 5 (1): 98–130.

Salhofer, K., and E. Schmid. 2004. "Distributive Leakages of Agricultural Support: Some Empirical Evidence." *Agricultural Economics* 30 (1): 51–63.

Schnurr, M., and C. Gore. 2015. "Getting to 'Yes': Governing Genetically Modified Crops in Uganda." *Journal of International Development* 27: 55–72.

Schonhardt-Bailey, C. 2006. *From the Corn Laws to Free Trade: Interests, Ideas and Institutions in Historical Perspective*. Cambridge, MA: MIT Press.

Sexton, R.J. 2012. "Market Power, Misconceptions, and Modern Agricultural Markets." *American Journal of Agricultural Economics* 95 (2): 209–219.

Swinnen, J. 1994. "A Positive Theory of Agricultural Protection." *American Journal of Agricultural Economics* 76(1): 1–14.

Swinnen, J. 1996. "Endogenous Price and Trade Policy Developments in Central European Agriculture." *European Review of Agricultural Economics* 23 (2): 133–160.

Swinnen, J. 1999. "Political Economy of Land Reform Choices in Central and Eastern Europe." *The Economics of Transition* 7(3): 637–664.

Swinnen, J. 2009. "The Growth of Agricultural Protection in Europe in the 19th and 20th Centuries." *The World Economy* 32(11): 1499-1537. https://doi.org/10.1111/j.1467-9701.2009.01247.x

Swinnen, J. 2011. "The Right Price of Food." *Development Policy Review* 29 (6): 667–688.

Swinnen, J. 2015. "Changing Coalitions in Value Chains and the Political Economy of Agricultural and Food Policy." *Oxford Review of Economic Policy* 31 (1): 90–115.

Swinnen, J. 2018. *The Political Economy of Agricultural and Food Policies*. New York: Palgrave Macmillan.

Swinnen, J., K. Deconinck, T. Vandemoortele, and A. Vandeplas. 2015. *Quality Standards, Value Chains, and International Development*. Cambridge, UK: Cambridge University Press.

Swinnen, J., L. Knops, and K. van Herck. 2014. "Food Price Volatility and EU Policies." In *Food Price Policy in an Era of Market Instability. A Political Economy Analysis*, ed. P. Pinstrup-Andersen, 457–476. Oxford, UK: Oxford University Press.

Swinnen, J., P. Squicciarini, and T. Vandemoortele. 2011. "The Food Crisis, Mass Media and the Political Economy of Policy Analysis and Communication." *European Review of Agricultural Economics* 38 (3): 409–426.

Swinnen, J., and T. Vandemoortele. 2011. "Policy Gridlock or Future Change? The Political Economy Dynamics of EU Biotechnology Regulation." *AgBioForum* 13 (4): 291–296.

Swinnen, J., and A. Vandeplas. 2010. "Market Power and Rents in Global Supply Chains," *Agricultural Economics*. 41 (S1): 109–120.

Swinnen, J., and A. Vandeplas. 2012. "Rich Consumers and Poor Producers: Quality and Rent Distribution in Global Value Chains." *Journal of Globalization and Development* 2 (2).

Swinnen, J. and S. Vandevelde. 2019. "The Political Economy of Food Security and Sustainability." *Encyclopedia of Food Security and Sutainability* 1: 9-16.

Terazono, E., and C. Hodgson. 2022. "Food vs. Fuel: Ukraine War Sharpens Debate on Use of Crops for Energy." *Financial Times*, June 12. https://www.ft.com/content/b424067e-f56b-4e49-ac34-5b3de07e7f08.

Trumbull, G. 2012. *Strength in Numbers: The Political Power of Weak Interests*. Cambridge, MA: Harvard University Press.

USDA. 2013. *Conservation Reserve Program: Annual Summary and Enrollment Statistics FY 2013*. Washington, DC: United States Department of Agriculture (USDA).

Vandemoortele, T., and K. Deconinck. 2014. "When are Private Standards More Stringent than Public Standards?" *American Journal of Agricultural Economics* 96 (1): 154–171.

Vyn, R.J., Z. Ul Haq, J. Weerahewa, and K.D. Meilke. 2012. "The Influence of Market Returns and Government Payments on Canadian Farmland Values." *Journal of Agricultural and Resource Economics* 37 (2): 199–212.

Winfree, J.A., and J.J. McCluskey. 2005. "Collective Reputation and Quality." *American Journal of Agricultural Economics* 87 (1): 206–213.

Wolfensohn, J. 1999. *Coalitions for Change. Address to the Board of Governors*. Washington, DC: The World Bank Group.

6

Government Response to Ultra-Processed and Sugar Beverages Industries in Developing Nations

The Need to Build Coalitions across Policy Sectors

Eduardo J. Gómez

6.1 Introduction

In recent years, several emerging economies have introduced a host of innovative public health policies in response to the burgeoning growth of non-communicable diseases (NCDs), such as obesity, type-2 diabetes, heart disease, and cancer. Some claim that these ailments are the product of the consumption of unhealthy food products, such as sugary beverages and ultra-processed foods, coupled with increased sedentary lifestyles. Interestingly, it has been in select emerging economies, not wealthier nations, where we have seen the boldest attempts to introduce national policy innovations in response to these healthcare challenges. For example, Mexico's Congress passed a national soda tax in 2014, India adopted a national sin tax on sugary drinks and other unhealthy products in 2017, and South Africa's government created its own tax on sugary beverages in 2018. Furthermore, these are national fiscal policies that are supported by presidents and national congressional and bureaucratic institutions. By contrast, in the United States (U.S.), sub-national governments, particularly major cities, were the first to adopt a soda tax, as seen in San Francisco in 2014. Compared to the U.S., one could argue that the adoption of a national tax in Mexico, India, and South Africa is a far more impressive and an effective way to discourage the public's consumption of these unhealthy products.

These national tax responses emerged within similar political and economic contexts. Mexico, India, and South Africa are federations with strong state economies and political institutions. Though varying in degree, each of these nations have pursued fiscal and administrative decentralization, with local governments playing an increasingly important role in healthcare policy (Nicholson 2001; Arredondo and Orozco 2006; Kaur et al. 2012). Furthermore, all three

Eduardo J. Gómez, *Government Response to Ultra-Processed and Sugar Beverages Industries in Developing Nations*.
In: *The Political Economy of Food System Transformation*. Edited by: Danielle Resnick and Johan Swinnen,
Oxford University Press. © Eduardo J. Gómez (2023). DOI: 10.1093/oso/9780198882121.003.0006

countries experienced the burgeoning rise of soda and ultra-processed, fast-food industries following a rapid turn toward free market reforms during the 1990s.

Mexico's, India's, and South Africa's governments were also successful in introducing several other public health programs in response to NCDs, including informing the public through national health awareness campaigns about the rise of NCDs and revising nutritional guidelines. When it came to regulating the marketing and sale of soda and ultra-processed foods, as well as the introduction of more effective food labels, however, each of these nations were far less successful, though in varying degrees. Mexico introduced, though failed to effectively implement, policies reducing the sale of these products in schools and marketing to children on TV; to this day, no such policies exist in India and South Africa. These regulatory policy outcomes are puzzling when we consider that these nations were the earliest in the Global South to adopt national soda taxes.

Consequently, this chapter asks: why were governments in Mexico, India, and South Africa unwilling to demonstrate equal political resolve across *all* public health prevention and regulatory policy efforts in response to NCDs? Why focus mainly on a soda tax when other regulatory policies were just, if not more, important?

To address these questions, this chapter claims that when compared to regulatory policies, the level of international organizational, philanthropic, and civil societal attention and support emerged earlier and more successfully with respect to soda and snack food taxes. Second, because the tax posed an immediate economic threat to industry and generated resistance among industry actors, it further increased the visibility of the policy debate for governments and among the public; the same could not be said for industry regulations. Finally, with governments seeking economic growth and recovery, the tax's potential to generate fiscal revenue appeared to obtain more government attention and support versus regulations. The broader political economy context for soda taxes in Mexico, India, and South Africa therefore appeared to be much more favorable than regulatory instruments.

Nevertheless, several opportunities exist for international organizations, government, and civil societal actors to build strong coalitions in support of marketing and sales regulatory policies while holding governments accountable for their enforcement. Furthermore, the emergence of soda and snack food taxes has revealed that developing nations can eventually overcome the powerful resistance of food industries.

6.2 The Politics of Policy of the Food Sector: Multiple Streams Analysis and Future Insights

Examining the politics of healthcare policymaking, particularly in the area of junk food, has become an increasingly important scholarly topic. Researchers have been interested in exploring theoretical frameworks in public policy and how they can be applied to public health case studies. Multiple-streams analysis, which was first introduced by John Kingdon in 1984, has been adopted to explain policy reforms across a host of nations, though with vary degrees of success and applicability (Béland and Howlett 2016). Nevertheless, the multiple streams approach provides a good starting point to shed light onto why Mexico, India, and South Africa pursued soda tax policies more aggressively when compared to industry regulation.

At its core, multiple streams analysis addresses the politics of policy-agenda setting processes (Kingdon 1984; Sabatier 2007). According to this approach, the problems (e.g., health, economic, social challenges), politics (e.g., introduction of new elections, general mood in society), and policy streams (policy solutions to these problems) act independently and are brought together by a policy entrepreneur in response to a window of opportunity, such as a change in government and/or national crisis situation (Kingdon 1984; Sabatier 2007). The policy entrepreneur emerges to bring these three streams together through "coupling" processes, which entail building policy consensus among government stakeholders, ultimately prioritizing some policies over others (Kingdon 1984; Sabatier 2007).

As we will see in Mexico, India, and South Africa, each of these nations faced the problem of escalating malnutrition-related diseases, such as obesity and type-2 diabetes; each government confronted a change in political and social context; and each found policy solutions. In addition, policy entrepreneurs, such as a president and senator in Mexico, and civil societal activists and international supporters in India and South Africa, capitalized on this window of opportunity to merge these three streams together and build consensus for reform.

Nevertheless, these three cases studies revealed limitations with the multiple-streams approach, which is that the approach does not appear to address the importance of the international policy community and philanthropists (see also Béland and Howlett 2016 on the limitations with this approach). The initial multiple streams framework was focused mainly on the U.S. domestic agenda-setting process. But in a context of increased economic and global integration, institutions such as the World Health Organization (WHO) and major philanthropic bodies, such as the Bloomberg foundation, can also join civil society and politicians in playing important roles in helping prioritize soda taxes. Furthermore, my comparative analysis of soda taxes versus regulatory policy prioritization reveals that more work needs to be done comparing the international and domestic politics of agenda-setting *between* NCD policy sectors.

6.3 Contrasting Global Attention and Support for NCD Policies

By the late-20th century, in response to a gradual decline in the consumption of sodas and ultra-processed foods in Western industrialized nations, food industries began to invest heavily in emerging markets. While major industries such as

Coca-Cola and Pepsi had established their global footprint early on—as early as the 1930s in South Africa-a myriad of other soda and ultra-processed food companies followed suit during the late-20th century. When combined with other factors, such as increased sedentary lifestyles and stress, sudden access to these foods in the Global South contributed to an increase in weight gain and their associated ailments. This situation caught several governments by surprise, many of which did not have a clear national strategy to respond to NCDs. Further complicating matters was the fact that for some nations, such as India and South Africa, excess body weight was seen as signs of health and prosperity, whereas being too thin and/or underweight suggested poverty and disease. In addition, government officials for the most part viewed excess-weight related challenges as "diseases of luxury," relegated to the wealthy few, with most of the government's attention focused on the larger, enduring problem of poverty, food insecurity, and malnutrition. These cultural and political dilemmas not only hampered the construction of early national policy responses but also gave more time for nutrition-related NCDs to increase, eventually reaching all segments of the population.

The burgeoning rise of NCDs by the early-2000s in developing nations prompted significant attention to addressing these issues at the global level. By 2004, the World Health Organization drafted the Global Strategy on Diet, Physical Activity and Health. The Global Strategy emphasized not only a need for governments to address their growing NCD problems, but also to safeguard the health of vulnerable populations, such as children. Moreover, the 2004 Global Strategy also mentioned country experiences in using fiscal policies, such as a tax, to influence food availability and consumption patterns (WHO 2004). It was a time when the global context shifted in the direction of encouraging nations to be more aggressive in their response to NCDs. By 2013, the WHO Director-General, Margaret Chan, raised alarm about the global rise of NCDs, stressing that preventing their emergence went against the interests of powerful food companies (UN 2013).

6.3.1 Mexico

At a time of heightened international attention and support for national NCD policies, the political economy context in Mexico was noticeably different. The idea of introducing a soda tax existed for several years. Nevertheless, the idea instigated an extensive amount of resistance from not only the soda industry but also from the *Cámara Nacional de la Industria de Azucar* (CNIA), which represented sugar cane producers, who feared a decline in the sale of their products to soda manufacturers (Gómez 2018). At the same time, one could feasibly assume that former president Vincente Fox's (PAN, Partido Acción Nacional, National Action Party, 2000–2006) previous employment history with Coca-Cola, as the corporation's Latin America regional president prior to his arrival into the presidency, incentivized him to refrain from harming the sugary beverage sector. Due to this context, political and social attention to a possible soda tax gradually decreased. During this time the public health activist community favoring a tax was also small in size and influence. However, as academic researchers, such as those from the National Public Health Institute, continued to highlight changes in the Mexican diet, increased sugar consumption and obesity, the government began to increase its attention to the issue (Barquera et al. 2013).

Six years later, under the administration of Enrique Peña Neito (PRI, Partido Revolucionario Institucional, Institutional Revolutionary Party, 2012–2018), the soda tax issue resurfaced. President Neito faced renewed pressures for a sugar tax by a well-organized activist community with strong international support networks. Prior to the tax's adoption, civil societal groups in Mexico started to receive more support, such as US$10 million from the Bloomberg Foundation in New York (as well as the support of academic colleagues), which helped these activists' pay for media campaigns and thereby increase the visibility of their position in favor of a tax (Carriedo Lutzenkirchen 2018). Tax proponents' aggressive media campaigns contributed to the proposed tax's media coverage, generating "over 1,000 media articles in the five-month period (June 1, 2013 through October 31, 2013) leading up to the vote on the tax" (Donaldson 2015, p. 17). This dovetailed nicely with unwavering activist networking, facilitated by philanthropic support, increased public communication campaigns, and improved relationships with government officials (Moodie et al. 2021). Civil society now had the support and connections needed to devise a stronger campaign in favor of a tax.

Furthermore, the international community played an important role in providing policy guidance and research support for the adoption of a soda tax. International health agencies, such as the Pan American Health Organization (PAHO), and philanthropies, such as the Bloomberg Foundation, played important roles prior to the tax's adoption. Indeed, Carriedo Lutzenkirchen (2018, pp. 116–117) mentions that: "Three main ways of involvement of international agencies were identified, including: taking part of advisory committees, such as the case of PAHO with the Senate ... provision of financial support for research; and advocacy groups and support in framing the debate."

Nevertheless, during this period, there also existed a high degree of industry resistance and media attention to the proposed tax. As mentioned earlier, industry and associated labor unions had resisted the idea of a tax for several years. The issue of course was the tax's direct threat to industry profitability. The tax entailed a 1 peso per liter tax on all nonalcoholic beverages with added sugars, with an estimated 11 percent increase in prices for carbonated drinks in 2014 (Colchero et al. 2015). A tax would increase production costs and possibly reduce sugar cane farmers' ability to sell their products to beverage manufacturers, in turn generating tax resistance from this sector (Gómez 2018). This context appeared to instigate a high level of political attention and contestation, fueling media coverage about the controversial policy issue.

The congressional politics surrounding the ultimate vote in support of the soda tax in 2013 was nonetheless favorable to the proponents' position. In September 2013, President Peña Neito introduced the soda tax as part of a broader direct fiscal tax effort under the Impuesto Especial sobre Productos y Servicios (IEPS). Leading up to the congressional vote that fall, President Peña Nieto's political party, the PRI (Partido Revolucionario Institucional, Institutional Revolutionary Party), managed to build a governing coalition which included Mexico's largest political parties, namely the PRI, the PRD (Partido de la Revolución Democratica, Party of the Democratic Revolution), and the PAN (Partido Acción Nacional, National Action Party), which collectively formed the Pacto por Mexico (the Pact for Mexico). In this context, two factors appeared to facilitate the vote's passage. First, Peña Nieto benefited from strong intra-party PRI support for his tax proposal (James et al. 2020). Second, the PRI and its tax idea benefited from the support of some Pacto coalition members, such as the PRD, and garnered support from the PVEM party (Partido Verde Ecologista de Mexico, the Ecological Green Party of Mexico), but not a majority of members from the PAN (James et al. 2020); the latter generally is perceived as a conservative pro-business party.

Interestingly, despite the PAN's resistance, one of the initial proponents of the soda tax was a PAN member, Senator Marcela Torres Peimbert, who was the first to introduce the idea to the Congress in December 2012 (James et al. 2020). Torres Peimbert was selected by the pro-tax coalition mainly because she was from the conservative PAN party, which provided legitimacy to the pro-tax coalition's efforts (James et al. 2020). Eventually, James et al. (2020, p. e1669122-3) reports that because of this pro-tax governing coalition, "... on October 17, 2013, the House of Deputies voted to pass the bill passed [sic] with 317 votes in favor (207 PRI, 73 PRD, and 25 PVEM votes) and 164 votes against (113 PAN and 23 PRD votes). Meanwhile, on October 29, 2013, the Senate voted to pass the bill with 73 votes in favor (54 PRI, 1 PAN, 10 PRD, and 7 PVEM votes) and 50 votes against (36 PAN and 9 PRD votes)."

Yet another factor drawing increased attention and support for a tax was Mexico's economic situation. Facing a decline in the international price of oil, with oil exports being a strong source of government revenue, as well as a global recession in 2013, the soda tax—along with other taxes in the proposed national fiscal package—was viewed as an important source of government revenue (Barquera et al. 2018). When combined with increased widespread support for the tax by 2013, this fiscal situation generated an urgent need to adopt the tax (Barquera et al. 2018).

Eventually the tax was adopted by the Congress in 2014. With this achievement, Mexico became the first nation in the world to introduce a *national* soda tax; this quickly drew a considerable amount of international praise. At an event held in Mexico City on April 2016 on World Health Day, the Director of the Pan American Health Organization (PAHO), Carissa Etienne, commented: "Mexico has shown global leadership by increasing taxes on sugar sweetened beverages, which managed to reduce soda consumption by 6 percent in just one year. This is one component of a comprehensive national strategy adopted by Mexico to fight obesity, overweight and diabetes..." (PAHO 2016, p. 1).

But how successful was Mexico's government when it came to increasing the regulation of the marketing and sale of sugary beverages? In 2014, the Ministry of Health, through the National Strategy for Prevention and Control of Overweight, Obesity, and Diabetes, introduced regulations restricting the advertisement of these products on television for particular hours of the week and weekend (Hennessy, 2014). The National Strategy outlined that unhealthy food products were not to be advertised to children during the weekdays, Monday through Friday, from 2:30 p.m. to 7:30 p.m. and on the weekend, Saturday and Sunday, from 7:30 a.m. to 7:30 p.m. (Hennessy 2014). Furthermore, Vilar-Compte (2018) notes that this advertising regulation was focused on children between the ages of 4 and 12.

These new laws appeared to be significant in Mexico, mainly because previously the government relied on industry self-regulation of advertising through the 2009 Code of Self-Regulation on Advertising Food and Non-Alcoholic Beverages to Children (Latnovic and Cabrera 2013). With time, however, researchers began to question the efficacy of this new regulation. Indeed, research by Vilar-Compte (2018, p. 15) suggests that unhealthy food products are still being advertised despite the introduction of these new laws: "Other studies show that food beverages still advertised on Mexican TV do not meet more stringent nutritional quality, leaving Mexican children exposed to unhealthy food advertisements despite the enacted regulations..." Other regulations introduced through the National Strategy and subsequent policies, such as ensuring the provision of high-quality foods in schools, also have not been adequately enforced (Gómez 2023).

Why was the government less successful when it came to enforcing these regulations when compared to a soda tax? Advertising regulations may be more difficult to adopt than soda taxes because they generally draw less public attention, fall short of instigating the broader public's attention and involvement, and, consequently are often influenced by what Pepper Culpepper (2010) once referred to as quiet, back door politics between business elites and policymakers. This context can gradually facilitate industry's capture of those government agencies seeking to impose regulations. Yet, as mentioned earlier, this was not the case with a soda tax.

Indeed, first, when compared to the soda tax, there appears to have been significantly less international attention and pressures on Mexico to create and enforce marketing and sales regulations of unhealthy products. While international organizations have mentioned the importance of these regulatory efforts (in addition to taxes), direct pressures and technical assistance on these issues appears to have been less apparent in Mexico (Gómez 2021).

Second, the regulation of commercial industry marketing and sales appeared to receive significantly less media attention and discussion within government, especially when compared to the soda tax. In large part this may have been attributed to the highly technical nature of regulatory policy issues, with more technical policy matters often generating "quiet politics" (Culpepper 2010). Furthermore, regulatory efforts may have provided less of a direct economic threat to industries, especially when compared to a tax that would be easier to enforce. As Vilar-Compte (2018, p. 12) notes: "The advertising regulations were less polemical and visible than the SSB tax, but they were criticized by civil society organizations and academia (i.e., *Alianza por la Salud Alimentaria*) ..." With respect to food industry stakeholder's monitoring the SSB tax and advertisement regulations, Villar-Compte et al. (2018) also claims that there was greater interest in doing so for taxes due to its feasibility of adoption compared with advertising regulations.

Moreover, civil society's presence and pressures on the government to strengthen industry regulations were present alongside soda tax advocates; and yet the former's ability to draw policy attention to much needed regulatory reforms and eventually succeed in influencing policy appeared to emerge several years later when compared to the pro-tax coalition. Specifically, activist organizations, such as the Alianza por la Salud Alimentaria (Food Health Alliance), already existed in 2012 to help raise awareness about food marketing toward children, as well as several other issues, such as clear food labels, the provision of healthy foods in schools, access to clean drinking water, and fiscal policies toward junk foods (Vital Strategies 2014). However, it seems that activist organizations, such as the Alianza and El Poder del Consumidor (The Power of the Consumer), and their ability to influence regulatory policies, e.g., front-of-package labeling (FOPL), substantially increased only in 2018 and 2019 after the arrival of external support from the Bloomberg Foundation, UNICEF, and International Development Research Centre (IDRC) Canada (White and Barquera 2020). Given the food industry's historic efforts to influence nutrition policy, improving FOPL policy and avoiding industry involvement was seen as a way to reduce corruption by avoiding conflict of interest. This change in circumstances, inclusive of the influx of vast funds, mass campaign drives, strong networks of FOPL reform activists, and the emergence of a new leftist government led by President Andrés Manuel López Obrador (AMLO) who was committed to anti-corruption efforts, facilitated the introduction of Mexico's new FOPL labeling policy in 2019 (White and Barquera 2020). The new FOPL policy involved the introduction of black octagon warning signs on foods high in sugar, salt, and fat (White and Barquera 2020).

6.3.2 India

Similar to Mexico, by the transition to the 21st century, India encountered a worsening NCD situation, especially with respect to overweight, obesity, and type-2 diabetes. The transition to free market reforms during the 1990s, increased foreign direct investment, the rise of the middle class and changes in dietary patterns were several factors contributing to this situation. India's government was nevertheless considerably delayed in its national policy response to NCDs in general (Gómez 2018). With respect to policy agenda-setting, one of the main challenges was the government's focus on poverty and malnutrition, which was perceived during the 1990s and early-2000s as the biggest public health challenge in the area of nutrition (Khandelwal and Reddy 2013). Overweight and obesity was also seen as a disease of luxury, relegated to the affluent upper-middle classes. National programs focused on nutrition and overweight gradually emerged, however: In 2008, the Ministry of Women and Children's Development (MWCD) created nutritional guidelines to improve diet, exercise, and health, as well as nutritional guidelines for schools (Gómez, 2018). That same year, the government also released its National Program for the Prevention and Control of Diabetes, Cardiovascular Disease, and Stroke (NPCDCS). NPCDCS' goal was not only to call greater attention to these diseases, but also to push for increased prevention through several initiatives, such as the early diagnosis of disease, recommended changes to behavioral lifestyles, improved health system capacity, and early detection and treatment of NCDs (Bloom et al. 2014). Later in 2011, the government, through the National Institute of Nutrition (NIH), also published new dietary guidelines that introduced a food pyramid, recommended a reduction in the consumption of sugary and fatty foods, while advocating for a return to the consumption of traditional foods (CSE 2014).

In 2015, the government of Prime Minister Damodardas Modi (BJP, Bharatiya Janata Party, 2014–present) also introduced the idea of implementing a 40 percent sin tax on aerated drinks (Whitehead 2015), as well as a general "fat tax" on unhealthy foods (Karla 2017). Interestingly, and similar to what we saw in Mexico, the 40 percent tax on drinks was introduced as a broader fiscal policy effort to increase revenue (Wilkes 2015; Gómez 2023).

During this period, the idea of a tax on sugar-sweetened beverages (SSBs) was also supported by several prominent international policy experts (India Resource Center 2016, 2017). These experts claimed that the idea aligned with the World Health Organization's suggested tax on SSBs in 2016 (India Resource Center 2017; Statement in Support of a Sugar Sweetened Beverage Tax 2016). This international support was reported by the India Resource Center, an activist organization (India Resource Center 2017). The media at the same time acknowledged that India's public health advocates supported the idea of a sin tax (Johari 2015). Activists claimed that the tax on aerated soft drinks would join the tax on tobacco in generating the same kind of health benefits (Tandon 2015).

The introduction of a national sin tax was, nonetheless, highly controversial and contested due to the direct threat that it posed to industry. In 2015, major media sources were discussing the proposed tax, mentioning its purpose and that the government was discussing the matter with industry and receiving its suggestions

(The Economic Times 2015). As one would expect, the tax proposal also caused intensive industry attention and opposition. It is important to note, however, that this resistance has been present since 2014, when the parliament Union Budget proposed a 5 percent increase in excise taxes for aerated drinks with added sugar (Coca-Cola India 2014). In fact, KO, the Indian subsidiary of Coca-Cola, stated that if the sin tax passed, it would consider shutting down several of its bottling plants in India (Reuters 2015). Coca-Cola India was of the view that this tax would lead to a reduction in the sale of its products (Reuters 2015). By 2017, the food industry and trade groups were working together to determine how they could effectively lobby against the tax proposal (Karla 2017).

India's economic situation may have also played a role in the government's support of the tax. The sin tax was part of a larger effort by the central government to unify, through a national Goods and Services Tax (GST), its complex, decentralized fiscal tax structure, which, in turn, would help to increase the ease of doing business in the country and thereby augment foreign investment and state revenue (Barry and Kumar 2016). The GST originally was introduced in 2011 and aimed at only taxing goods at point of consumption, thereby deemed a "destination tax." However, it had been opposed for several years by political parties within parliament and larger state governments (Barry and Kumar 2016). Those parties that opposed the idea included the Congress and the Tamil Nadu-based All India Anna Dravida Munnetra Kazhagam (AIADMK) (Gyan Varma 2016). Congress parliamentary members wanted their specific demands addressed first, such as caps on GST taxes, while state-level finance ministers from the Congress party were more willing to accept the tax and were focused more on revenue compensation (Gyan Varma 2016). The AIADMK leaders also wanted Modi's party to accept its specific amendments to the bill prior to the GST's passage (Venkataramakrishnan 2016). The AIADMK argued that since the beginning, they perceived the tax as arbitrary and unconstitutional in its attempts to undermine fiscal federalism and that because Tamil Nadu was a manufacturing state, it stood to lose a lot of revenue (Venkataramakrishnan 2016). The AIADMK also viewed the national tax as a violation of federalism and the states' fiscal autonomy (Venkataramakrishnan 2016). Because of the loss of revenue from the GST tax, the AIADMK asked that 4 percent of revenues allocated to the center be retained for manufacturing states, such as Tamil Nadu (Venkataramakrishnan 2016). Nevertheless, despite this opposition, the constitutional amendment needed to adopt the GST eventually passed within parliament due, it seems, to the BJP political party's efforts to reduce political resistance by obtaining the support of smaller regional opposition parties while the Congress party's majority in parliament was decreasing (Barry and Kumar 2016).

Eventually, Prime Minister Modi's proposed sin tax was adopted in 2017 (India Resource Center 2017). Through the GST, this tax imposed a 28 percent levy on sweetened carbonated drinks, flavored waters, and other unhealthy products, such as tobacco (India Resource Center 2017). Moreover, through its "*compensation cess*," an additional sin tax of 12 percent was imposed on these drinks, along with tobacco and other harmful products (India Resource Center 2017), thus totaling a combined 40 percent tax. This "cess" is imposed in order to compensate the states for the loss of state revenues associated with the centralized GST tax for up to 5 years (Narayan, 2021).

However, the central government appeared far less successful when it came to introducing policies focused on regulating the junk food industry. In 2018, with respect to food labels, the Food Safety and Standards Authority of India (FSSAI), India's chief food regulatory body operating under the Ministry of Health & Family Welfare, created a Draft Food and Safety Standards (Labeling Display) Regulations, with color-coded red visual aids on packages to indicate being high in specific nutritional contents, such as sugar, fat, salt (Srivastava 2019). In general, however, researchers found that food labels in India still provide insufficient and unclear information (Taneja and Khurana 2017), as well as "misleading claims on the amount of trans fat present" (CSE 2014, p. 24; Gómez 2023).

With respect to food marketing and advertising, to this day, no federal regulations exist, especially toward children; only a draft regulation on prohibiting the advertisement of unhealthy foods in and around schools has been proposed by the FSSAI (Anu 2019). Instead, industries engage in a form of self-regulation, which is monitored by the Advertising Standards Council of India (ASCI) (Taneja and Khurana 2017). Hawkes (2004) nevertheless found pundits in India claiming that self-regulatory advertising policies have been ineffective, and that food advertising is often deceptive. However, there are signs that the government is heading in the right direction with respect to the creation of enforceable federal regulations. In 2019, for example, the FSSAI mandated "a fine of up to Rs 10 lakh" (approximately US$14,000) for those companies found guilty of providing misleading advertising of packaged foods high in sugar and salt (Mordani 2019, p. 1).

Finally, limitations also exist with the sale of unhealthy foods. For example, with the exception of a New Delhi High Court ruling in 2015 recommending to FSSAI that the sale of unhealthy foods in schools be restricted and at least 50 meters beyond school borders (Centre for Science and Environment 2015), there are still no federal regulations mandating this requirement.

When compared to the sin tax, the politics surrounding the regulation of food industries was considerably different. Indeed, there appears to have been far less political resolve and attention to these regulatory matters. Why? First, the absence of an early and strong international and domestic support base appears to have been an issue. The author found no evidence suggesting that there were comparatively earlier international and domestic supporters for increasing the sales and marketing regulations of aerated drinks and unhealthy food products in India. The WHO did devise international policy recommendations on the marketing and advertisement of foods and beverages to children, in addition to a report in 2011 by the World Health Organization and the European network on reducing marketing pressure on children on the topic (Bhatnagar et al. 2014). India, along with several other member states, was a signatory to these WHO declarations (Bhatnagar et al. 2014). And in 2020, Shekar and Provo (2020) mentioned that the World Bank has been working with India's regulatory agencies to improve its capacity in the area of food and marketing regulations. However, to the author's knowledge, there was no concerted international effort, either from multilateral organizations or the scientific community, to recommend and impress onto India's government the idea of pursuing industry regulations.

Civil society's pressures for greater industry regulation were nevertheless present, though this appears to have been mainly at the domestic level. A year after the 2004 Global Strategy was adopted, researchers at the Public Health Foundation of India had recommendations for a national plan that would include plans to address food industry advertisements targeting children and vulnerable groups (Varshney 2006). In 2015, researchers in India also called for increased regulations on industry advertising (Balch 2012). However, in general, the absence of robust civil societal pressures for increased regulations on marketing may also have reflected the fact that this issue was just emerging in India and that few efforts had been taken in this area in general (Balch 2012).

When compared to the sin tax, marketing regulations also appear to have been less politically contested within government and society. This may have to do with the fact that some proposed regulations, such as FSSAI's efforts to regulate food advertising (high in fat, salt, and sugar) to children are still under discussion (Yasmeen 2019). There has been no formal proposal and serious attempt to introduce legislation on this topic, and while industries have pushed back against the idea, it is minimal compared to the earlier resistance on sin taxes (Yasmeen 2019). In addition, one must keep in mind that when compared to the sin tax, there is no immediate and substantial financial threat to industries being regulated. In fact, industries may decide to simply ignore regulations, perhaps even willing to pay a small, one-off fine. Under these conditions the proposed regulations may not draw as much industry opposition and thus political attention, especially when compared to the sin tax.

6.3.3 South Africa

As Mexico's and India's emerging economy counterpart in Africa, South Africa also encountered several NCD challenges by the early-2000s. The return to free markets following apartheid rule, nutrition transitions and a rising middle class contributed to the emergence of obesity, type-2 diabetes, and other chronic diseases. Similar to what we saw in India, however, South Africa was faced with the challenge of having to deal with ongoing malnutrition among the poor, which complicated making NCDs a government priority. Overtime, as more data and awareness of NCD challenges emerged, the national government began to focus on introducing several national NCD programs.

Important among them was the 2013 Strategic Plan for NCDs (2013–2017) (Spires et al. 2016). The Strategic Plan focused on several initiatives, such as improving the food environment, interventions to improve diets, advertising regulations toward children, a reduction in trans-fat and salt in foods, and even the possibility of a tax on ultra-processed foods (Spires et al. 2016). The Department of Health soon followed suit with the 2015 Strategy for the Prevention and Controlling of South Africa Obesity, which focused on addressing the broader environmental factors contributing to obesity, the importance of exercise, nutrition, and several other factors, such as increased community awareness and monitoring the prevalence of obesity (Claasen et al. 2016). This plan also introduced the idea of a tax on sugar-sweetened beverages (SSB) (Claasen et al. 2016).

During this time, the international community also provided support for this tax. In 2016, for example, prestigious academics from universities around the world, along with academics from South Africa, published a letter in support of introducing the tax (Cullinan et al. 2020). This letter was also published in South Africa's *Sunday Times* (Cullinan et al. 2020). Moreover, WHO officials, a famous researcher from the University of Illinois at Chicago, Frank Chaloupka, and several other pro-tax advocates gave presentations to the parliament in support of the SSB tax (Cullinan et al. 2020).

Civil societal activists were also fully supportive of the tax. Prior to its implementation, activist organizations, such as HEALA, and other groups, strove to increased public support for the tax through several communication campaigns, which were supported by organizations such as Vital Strategies (Vital Strategies 2019). A total of three national media campaigns were created with the goal of educating the public about the importance of the tax and the harm caused by consuming sugary beverages (Vital Strategies 2019). Furthermore, according to Vital Strategies (2019, p. 1), these campaigns had a successful impact on the public's knowledge and perceptions: "Unconditional support for the levy increased from 42 percent of respondents in October 2016 to 58 percent in July 2017." In addition, academic researchers and statistical analysis from institutions such as PRICELESS (Priority Cost-Effective Lessons for System Strengthening South Africa), a policy think-tank at the University of Witwatersrand, provided evidence that a tax could help to reduce obesity (Cullinan et al. 2020); this information was provided to the Treasury and Presidential office (Cullinan et al. 2020).

However, the proposed SSB tax posed a clear threat to industry's interests, fueling intense opposition. A key argument made by industry was that the tax would generate several economic consequences, affecting not only sugarcane producers but also small shop owners (Karim et al. 2020). Others industry actors claimed that there would be significant job losses in the sugar sector due to the tax (Karim et al. 2020). Aggressive opposition tactics were used, such as the Beverage

Association of South Africa (BEVSA)'s—which represents companies like Coca-Cola and PespiCo—usage of "anti-tax advertisements" in newspapers, as well as BEVSA's meetings with national health officials to emphasize the reformulation of sugary beverages, which analysts claim is often perceived as a proposed alternative to a tax (Cullinan et al. 2020). The tax clearly posed an economic threat to industry. And because of this, it garnered a lot of political and media attention. One must also keep in mind that industry had succeeded in 2002 to lobby and successfully remove a federal tax on sodas and drinking water (Kruger et al. 2021), and this previous success likely further fueled industry's opposition to the 2016 tax proposal.

On the eve of the tax's adoption there was also a considerable amount of media attention to the proposed tax. A content analysis of several media articles between the periods of January 1, 2017 and June 30, 2019 by Essman et al. (2021) revealed that 54 percent of the articles were in favor of the tax, and that most of the arguments in favor underscored the tax's health benefits, while opposing views from industry emphasized the tax's harm to the economy.

South Africa's dire economic situation may have also elevated the importance of the tax. By 2014, Cullinan et al. (2020, p. 7) explains that the economy saw low GDP growth levels, less than 2 percent a year, with high unemployment rates, reaching 27.5 percent by 2017; in this situation introducing a tax could help to provide revenue to the government while meeting public health needs (Cullinan et al. 2020).

By 2017, the stars appeared to align in support of the SSB tax in parliament. South Africa became the first nation in the African continent, after Mauritius in 2013, to introduce a SSB tax (Chutel 2019), receiving praise from the WHO (WHO 2017). In 2018, a tax of 10 percent on sugary beverages was introduced through the Health Promotion Levy (Stacey et al. 2021). Unfortunately, however, Stacey notes that considerable concessions were made to industry prior do the tax's adoption, leading to a reduced taxation rate from 20 percent to 10–11 percent (Stacey et al. 2021).

But the government was less successful when it attempted to introduce industry regulations. For instance, when it comes to advertising unhealthy products, especially toward children, to this day the government has not enacted any legislation. The closest the government came to achieving this was recommending restrictions on advertising to children under the age of 16 in the "draft" Foodstuffs, Cosmetics and Disinfectants Act in 2007 (Igumbor et al. 2012). Instead, and similar to what we saw in Mexico, industries have opted to engage in self-regulatory practices, such as through the 2009 South Africa Pledge on Marketing to Children, which was released by the Consumer Goods Council of South Africa (Claasen et al. 2016).

With respect to food labels, the situation was equally uninspiring. While food labeling is regulated through the 1972 Foodstuffs, Cosmetics and Disinfectants Act via Regulation 146 (Classen et al. 2016), industries are not legally required to provide nutritional labels on their products. Labels are only required if companies make nutritional claims on packages, as stated through the 2010 amendment to Regulation 146 titled Regulations Related to the Labelling and Advertising of Foodstuffs, which took effect in 2012 (Igumbor et al. 2012). Furthermore, by law, industries are not required to disclose the amount of high sugar content on labels (Stacey et al. 2017). Even when labels are provided on packages, research in some areas of South Africa has shown that they are difficult for consumers to understand due to the insufficient amount of nutritional information provided and the way the information is displayed and written (Classen et al. 2016). In 2019, the government did nevertheless state its future intentions of requiring front of package warning labels reporting information on sugar, fat, and salt content (Zama 2019). To date, however, the government has made no effort to introduce this legislation (Nair 2021).

The government's lackluster success at introducing industry regulations when compared to the SSB tax follow a similar pattern observed in Mexico and India: international and civil societal attention and support for SSB taxes pre-dated that for introducing industry regulations in South Africa. In 2010, while the WHO released recommended regulations on the marketing of unhealthy foods and non-alcoholic beverages to children, adopted by the World Health Assembly as WHA 63.14, and the WHO later in 2016 criticized member states through a report for failing to take this resolution seriously (Wicks et al. 2017), the author found essentially no evidence revealing the WHO or any other international agencies' direct support for introducing marketing regulations in South Africa. And with respect to civil society, the author found no evidence suggesting that civil societal actors mobilized early on to pressure the government into adopting regulatory legislation. In general, proactive civil societal activism and influence in the area of nutrition policy has been delayed for many years in South Africa (Gómez 2023). Nevertheless, more recently, NGOs, such as HEALA, have done a commendable job of raising awareness about industries' ongoing violation of the government's marketing policies toward children (HEALA 2021). HEALA in general has also been vocal about the importance of front-of-package warning labels while, as mentioned earlier, being fully supportive of an SSB tax (HEALA 2019, 2021).

In sharp contrast to the SSB tax, government regulations, such as food labeling, also pose far less of an economic threat to industry. This appears to have generated far less industry opposition and, by extension, media attention and political unrest, reaffirming Culpepper's (2010) findings that it is less visible policy issues that are more likely to fall prey to industry capture. Analysts also note that the government has not been fully committed to enforcing existing labeling regulations, such as the Regulation 146 (Sulcas 2022). In this context, why should industries fear failing to adhere to this regulation or even the introduction of new ones?

Finally, the creation and enforcement of regulations does not seem to provide immediate and ongoing benefits to the overall economy. Unlike the SSB tax, regulatory restrictions on industry does not provide additional government revenue. It is instead an entirely public health matter. In a context where the national government does not seem fully committed to enforcing existing regulations, there is little additional economic incentive to focus on them by nutrition and health advocates. Consequently, efforts to introduce improved labeling and advertising restrictions continue to be delayed.

6.4 Conclusion

In recent years, the emerging economies of Mexico, India, and South Africa have demonstrated a new commitment to tackling the rise of NCDs in their countries. While these nations were among the first in the world to create national sugary beverage tax policies as a preventative measure, unfortunately they were not as equally committed to creating effective marketing, sales, and labeling regulations. This is even more puzzling if one considers the myriad of national NCD prevention and nutrition programs recently introduced by these countries.

To explain this puzzle, this chapter suggests that the political economy context was considerably different when it came to introducing food taxes versus industry regulations. For the most part, the introduction of a tax appears to have received earlier and stronger international and domestic civil societal support, posed a more credible economic threat to industry—thus instigating industry opposition, greater political and social attention, while providing economic as well as health benefits. Interestingly, and rather ironically, it seems that vehement industry opposition to the soda tax contributed to the government's focus on this policy and commitment to it. This may be because on such a highly visible and salient policy issue, governments may not want to be perceived as weak and incapable of resisting industry pressures. When combined with the economic motive to garner additional fiscal revenue, this can generate strong government commitment to tax reform. In contrast, when policies are less publicly salient and more technical in nature, such as advertising and food labeling regulations, governments may not feel as threatened by a publicly visible policy issue that is vehemently opposed by industry; here, the latter may be more successful in its efforts to lobby and resist policy change on technical grounds, while at times perhaps engaging in quiet closed door deals with government officials (Culpepper 2010). Regulatory policies have therefore not benefited from the favorable political economy conditions seen with the soda tax. Instead, industry continues to benefit from self-regulation and government inaction.

To better understand the differences in the political economy of reform between the soda tax, advertising, and food labeling regulations, a multiple streams analytical framework was adopted (Kingdon 1984; Sabatier 2007). Applying this framework to the cases of Mexico, India, and South Africa revealed that in addition to all three countries confronting rising NCD challenges (problems stream), a change in political context (political stream), and policy solutions (policy stream), policy entrepreneurs at the domestic and international level were important for coupling these three streams together to build consensus for reform. In Mexico, President Enrique Peña Neito and Senator Marcela Torres Peimbert played key roles in building support for the soda tax, while in India and South Africa, civil societal actors and strong international supporters played this role. Nevertheless, this analysis joins others (Béland and Howlett 2016) in revealing that an important limitation with the multiple-streams framework is its neglect to take seriously the role of international organizations and philanthropic institutions.

As societies in Mexico, India, South Africa, and other developing nations become more aware of the importance of industry regulations, particularly toward vulnerable populations, such as children and the poor, the political economy context in favor of industry regulation may soon improve. Though new, it seems that activists in these nations are becoming more committed to informing the public and calling on government for greater regulatory action. As we saw with the sugary beverage tax, it may only be a matter of time before activists, NGOs, academics, philanthropists, and international agencies work together to build a stronger coalition in favor of effective regulatory policies. This broad coalition certainly facilitated the introduction of national taxes in these countries.

Future research will also need to conduct more work on the comparative political economy of NCD policies. That is, how and why should we compare the complex international and domestic politics of fiscal, regulatory, and broader public health education policies in response to nutrition-related diseases? The success of sugary beverage taxes seems to have generated—and justifiably so—greater attention to this policy endeavor, rather than comparing it to, and at the same time focusing on, other equally important regulatory policies. Going forward, researchers, and more importantly, governments, will need to take a more comprehensive, comparative approach to designing NCD policies. This can help to underscore the similar and different international and domestic stakeholder incentives, interests, and challenges *between* NCD policy sectors. Approaching NCD policy from this perspective will nevertheless require an equal amount of government commitment to fiscal and regulatory policies, while at the same time exploring ways to reduce industry participation and influence in the policymaking process.

References

Anu Anu, M.J.H. 2019. "FSSAI Proposes Ban on Junk Food Advertisements in and Around Schools," *The Times of India*, June 13. https://timesofindia.indiatimes.com/business/indiabusiness/fssai-proposes-ban-on-junkfoodadvertisements-in-and-around-schools/articleshow/69770312.cms

Arredondo, A., and E. Orozco. 2006. "Effects of Health Decentralization, Financing and Governance in Mexico." *Revista de Saúde Publica* 40 (1): 152–160.

Balch, O. 2012. "India: Food, Marketing and Children's Health," *The Guardian*, July 10. https://www.theguardian.com/sustainable-business/fast-food-marketing-childrens-health

Barquera, S., I. Campos, and J. Rivera. 2013. "Mexico Attempts to Tackle Obesity: The Process, Results, Push Backs and Future Challenges." *Obesity Reviews* 14: 69-78.

Barquera, S., K. Sánchez-Bazán, A. Carriedo, and B. Swinburn. 2018. "The Development of a National Obesity and Diabetes Prevention and Control Strategy in Mexico: Actors, Actions and Conflicts of Interest." In *Public Health and the Food and Drinks Industry: The Government and Ethics of Interaction. Lessons from Research, Policy, and Practice*, ed. M. Mwatsama, 18–30. London: UK Health Forum.

Béland, D., and M. Howlett. 2016. "The Role and Impact of the Multiple-Streams Approach in Comparative Policy Analysis." *Journal of Comparative Policy Analysis: Research and Practice* 18(3): 221-227.

Barry, E., and H. Kumar. 2016. "In a Victory for Modi, India Overhauls Its Tangled Tax System," *The New York Times*, August 3. https://www.nytimes.com/2016/08/04/world/asia/india-goods-and-services-tax.html

Bhatnagar, N., R. Kaur, and P. Dudeja. 2014. "Food Marketing to Children in India: Comparative Review of Regulatory Strategies Across the World." *The Indian Journal of Pediatrics* 81 (11): 1187–1192.

Bloom, D.E., C. Fonseca, V. Candeias, E. Adashi, L. Bloom, L. Gurfien, E. Jané-Llopis, A. Lubet, E. Mitgang, C. O'Brien, and A. Saxena. 2014. *Economics of Non-Communicable Diseases in India. World Economic Form*. Boston: Harvard School of Public Health.

Carriedo Lutzenkirchen, AA. 2018. *A Policy Analysis of the 2014 Mexican Soda Tax*. PhD Thesis, London School of Hygiene & Tropical Medicine. DOI: https://doi.org/10.17037/PUBS.046-48204

Centre for Science and Environment. 2015. "CSE Welcomes Delhi High Court Order on Junk Food," March 18. https://www.cseindia.org/cse-welcomes-delhi-high-court-order-on-junk-food–5393

Chutel, L. 2019. "South Africa's Sugar Tax is Pitting Job Losses Against National Health." *Quartz Africa*, March 15.

Claasen, N., M. van der Hoeven, and N. Covic. 2016. "Food Environments, Health and Nutrition in South Africa: Mapping the Research and Policy Terrain." Working Paper 34. PLAAS, UWC and Center of Excellence on Food Security, Cape Town, South Africa.

Coca-Cola India. 2014. "Indian Beverage Association Reacts to the Excise Duty Hike on Aerated Drinks in the Union Budget," Coca-Cola India Newsroom, October 7. https://www.coca-colaindia.com/newsroom/indian-beverage-association-reacts-excise-duty-hike-aerated-drinks-union-budget–2014-2015

Colchero, M.A., J.C. Salgado, M. Unar-Munguía, M. Molina, S. Ng, and J.A. Rivera-Dommarco. 2015. "Changes in Prices After an Excise Tax to Sweetened Sugar Beverages Was Implemented in Mexico: Evidence from Urban Areas." *PLoS ONE* 10(12): e0144408.

CSE (Centre for Science and Environment). 2014. *Junk Food Targeted at Children: Regulatory Action Required to Limit Exposure and Availability*. New Delhi: CSE, 2014. https://www.cseindia.org/junk-food-targeted-at-children–5464

Cullinan, K., L. Maijia, T. Cotter, A. Kotov, S. Mullin, and N. Murukutia. 2020. *Lessons from South Africa's Campaign for a Tax on Sugary Beverages.*

New York: Vital Strategies. https://www.vitalstrategies.org/wp-content/uploads/Lessons-From-South-AfricaCampaign-for-a-Tax-on-Sugary-Beverages.pdf

Culpepper, P. 2010. *Quiet Politics and Business Power*. Cambridge, UK: Cambridge University Press.

Donaldson, E. 2015. *Advocating for Sugar-Sweetened Beverage Taxation: A Case Study of Mexico*. Baltimore, MD: Johns Hopkins Bloomberg School of Public Health.

Essman, M., F. Mediano Stoltze, F. Dillman Carpentier, E. Swart, and L. Smith Tailie. 2021. "Examining the News Media Reaction to a National Sugary Beverage Tax in South Africa: A Quantitative Content Analysis." *BMC Public Health* 21 (454): 1–14. https://bmcpublichealth.biomedcentral.com/track/pdf/10.1186/s12889-021-10460-1.pdf

Gómez, E.J. 2018. *Geopolitics in Health: Confronting Obesity, AIDS, and Tuberculosis in the Emerging BRICS Economies*. Baltimore: Johns Hopkins University Press.

Gómez, E.J. 2018. "Coca-Cola's Political and Policy Influence in Mexico: Understanding the Role of Institutions, Interests and Divided Society," *Health Policy and Planing* 34: 520–528.

Gómez, E.J. 2023. *Junk Food Politics: How Beverage and Fast Food Industries Are Reshaping Emerging Economies*. Baltimore, MD: Johns Hopkins University Press.

Gyan Varma, A. 2016. "GST Bill: ADIADMK, Congress Continue with Opposition." *Mint*, June 15. https://www.livemint.com/Politics/gAIHb0mn3rs1XeatZkBltI/Opposition-to-GST-narrows-to-AIADMK-Congress.html

Hawkes, C. 2004. *Marketing Food to Children: The Global Regulatory Environment*. Geneva: World Health Organization.

HEALA. 2019. "Our Campaigns." https://heala.org/campaigns/

HEALA. 2021. "#NotTodayNestlé: Food Giant Nestlé Flouts SA Law. Again." *HEALA website post*, August 12. https://heala.org/nottodaynestle-food-giant-nestle-flouts-sa-law-again/

Hennessy, M. 2014. "Mexico Restricts Junk Food Ads; Time for Rethink on Advertising?" *Food Navigator*, July 21; https://www.foodnavigator-usa.com/Article/2014/07/22/Mexico-restricts-junk-food-ads-time-for-rethink-on-advertising

Igumbor, E., D. Sanders, T. Puoane, L. Tsolekile, C. Schwarz, C. Purdy, R. Swart, S. Durão, and C. Hawkes. 2012. "'Big Food,' the Consumer Food Environment, Health, and the Policy Response in South Africa." *PLoS Medicine* 9 (7): 1–7. https://doi.org/10.1371/journal.pmed.1001253

India Resource Center. 2016. "Statement in Support of a Sugar Sweetened Beverage Tax in India." http://www.indiaresource.org/documents/SSBTax2016/SugarTaxStatementApril142016.pdf

India Resource Center. 2017. "Press: India Applies Sin Tax on Sweetened Carbonated Beverages." Accessed August 17. http://www.indiaresource.org/news/2017/1007.html

James, E., M. Lajous, and M. Reich. 2020. "The Politics of Taxes for Health: An Analysis of the Passage of the Sugar-Sweetened Beverage Tax in Mexico." *Health Systems & Reform* 6(1): 1-11.

Johari, A. 2015. "'Sin' tax on Colas: Will India Go the Way of Mexico or New York?" *Scroll.in*, December 18. https://scroll.in/article/776281/sin-tax-on-colas-will-india-go-the-way-of-mexico-or-new-york

Karim, S.A., P. Kruger, and K. Hofman. 2020. "Industry Strategies in the Parliamentary Process of Adopting a Sugar-Sweetened Beverage Tax in South Africa: A Systematic Mapping." *Globalization and Health* 16 (116): 1–14.

Karla, A. 2017. "Food, Drink Giants Plot Fightback as India Looks to Tighten Rules." *Reuters*, March 16.

Kaur, M., S. Prinja, P. Singh, and R. Kumar. 2012. "Decentralization of Health Services in India: Barrier and Facilitating Factors." *WHO South-East Asia Journal of Public Health* 1 (1): 94–104. https://doi.org/10.4103/2224-3151.206920

Khandelwal, S., and K.S. Reddy. 2013. "Eliciting a Policy Response for the Rising Epidemic of Overweight-Obesity in India." *Obesity Reviews* 14 (2): 114–125. https://doi.org/10.1111/obr.12097

Kingdon, J.W. 1984. *Agendas, Alternatives, and Public Policies*. Boston: Little, Brown and Company.

Kruger, P., S.A. Karim, A. Tugendhaft, and S. Goldstein. 2021. "An Analysis of the Adoption and Implementation of a Sugar-Sweetened Beverage Tax in South Africa: A Multiple Streams Approach." *Health Systems & Reform* 7 (1): 1–13.

Latnovic, L. and L. Rodriguez Cabrera. 2013. "Public Health Strategy against Overweight and Obesity in Mexico's National Agreement for Nutritional Health." *International Journal of Obesity* 3: S12-S14.

Moodie, R., E. Bennett, E.J. Leung Kwong, T. Santos, L. Pratiwi, J. Williams, and P. Baker. 2021. "Ultra-Processed Profits: The Political Economy of Countering the Global Spread of Ultra-Processed Foods—A Synthesis Review on the Market and Political Practices of Transnational Food Corporations and Strategic Public Health Responses," *International Journal of Health Policy Management* 10 (12): 968–982.

Mordani, S. 2019. "Food Regulatory Upset with Misleading Ads on Foods, Violations to Invite Huge Penalties," *News18*, November 23. https://www.news18.com/news/india/food-regulator-upset-with-misleading-ads-on-foods-violations-to-invite-huge-penalties-2397769.html

Nair, N. 2021. "New Call for Food Warning Labels as SA Steps Up Fight Against Obesity," *Sunday Times*, October 3. https://www.timeslive.co.za/sunday-times/news/2021-10-03-new-call-for-food-warning-labels-as-sa-steps-up-fight-against-obesity/

Narayan, S. 2021. "Extend GST Compensation Payment by 5 Years: States," December 31, Livemint.com; https://www.livemint.com/news/india/extend-gst-compensation-payment-by-5-years-states-11640892930712.html

Nicholson, J. 2001. *Bringing Health Closer to People: Local Government and the District Health System*. Durban, South Africa: The Health Systems Trust. https://www.hst.org.za/publications/HST%20Publications/lg_dhs.pdf

PAHO. 2016. "PAHO Director Lauds Mexico's Soda Tax as a Model Measure to Fight Diabetes." Article published online at: https://www3.paho.org/hq/index.php?option=com_content&view=article&id=11893:paho-director-lauds-mexico-soda-tax-to-fight-diabetes&Itemid=0&lang=en#gsc.tab=0

Reuters. 2015. "This is Coca-Cola's Response to India's 'Sin Tax.'" December 11. https://fortune.com/2015/12/11/coca-cola-india-bottling/

Sabatier, P., ed. 2007. *Theories of the Policy Process*. New York: Routledge.

Shekar, M., and A.M. Provo. 2020. "Business Unusual: How Can Development Partners Support Countries to Fight Obesity?" In *Obesity: Health and Economic Consequences of an Impending Global Challenge*, eds. M. Shekar and B. Popkin, 169–202. Washington DC: World Bank Group. https://openknowledge.worldbank.org/bitstream/handle/10986/32383/9781464814914.pdf

Spires, M., D. Sanders, P. Hoelzel, P. Delobelle, T. Puoane, and R. Swart. 2016. "Diet-related Non-communicable Diseases in South Africa: Determinants and Policy Response." In *South African Health Review 2016*, eds. A. Padarath, J. King, E. Mackie, and J. Casciola, 35–42. South Africa: Health Systems Trust.

Srivastava, A. 2019. "Is Coca-Cola Influencing India's Public Health Policies?" *The Wire*, February 6. https://thewire.in/health/coca-cola-junk-food-companies-are-influencing-indias-public-health-policies

Stacey, N., I. Edoka, K. Hofman, E. Swart, B. Popkin, and S. Wen. 2021. "Changes in Beverage Purchases Following the Announcement and Implementation of South Africa's Health Promotion Levy: An Observational Study," *The Lancet Planetary Health* 5 (4): E200–E208. https://www.thelancet.com/journals/lanplh/article/PIIS2542-5196(20)30304-1/fulltext

Stacey, N., C. van Walbeek, M. Maboshe, A. Tugendhaft, and K. Hofman. 2017. "Energy Drink Consumption and Marketing in South Africa." *Preventive Medicine* 105: S32–S36. https://doi.org/10.1016/j.ypmed.2017.05.011

Statement in Support of a Sugar Sweetened Beverage Tax in India. 2016. Source: http://www.indiaresource.org/documents/SSBTax2016/SugarTaxStatementApril142016.pdf

Sulcas, A. 2022. "Redefining Food Safety: SA's Laws Governing Food Advertising Aimed at Children Need to be Jacked Up." *Daily Maverick*, January 19. https://www.dailymaverick.co.za/article/2022-01-19-redefining-food-safety-sas-laws-governing-food-advertising-aimed-at-children-need-to-be-jacked-up/

The Economic Times. 2015. "'Sin Tax' for Alcohol, Tobacco Industries in GST Regime." October 25. https://economictimes.indiatimes.com/industry/cons-products/tobacco/sin-tax-for-alcohol-tobacco-industries-in-gst-regime/articleshow/49525934.cms

Tandon, A. 2015. "Health Advocates Hail GST Panel's Sin Tax on Aerated Drinks." *The Tribune*, December 14. https://www.tribuneindia.com/news/archive/nation/health-advocates-hail-gst-panel-s-sin-tax-on-aerated-drinks–170592

Taneja, S., and A. Khurana. 2017. "Availability of Junk Food is Changing Children's Diet in India." *DownToEarth*, August 15. https://www.downtoearth.org.in/news/health/spoilt-forchoice–58417

UN (United Nations). 2013. "Global Efforts to Promote Health Face Serious Challenges from 'Big Business.'" *UN News*, June 10.

Varshney, V. 2006. "Corporate Pressure May Put India's Obesity Prevention Plans on Hold," *DownToEarth*, October 15. https://www.downtoearth.org.in/news/corporate-pressure-may-put-indias-obesity-prevention-plans-on-hold–8493

Venkataramakrishnan, R. 2016. "'Unfair, Arbitrary and Unconstitutional': Why Tamil Nadu Opposed the Goods and Services Tax." *Scroll.in*, August 4. https://scroll.in/article/813188/unfair-arbitrary-and-unconstitutional-why-tamil-nadu-opposed-the-goods-and-services-tax

Vilar-Compte, M. 2018. *Using Sugar-Sweetened Beverage Taxes and Advertising Regulations to Combat Obesity in Mexico*. Washington, DC: World Bank Group.

Vital Strategies. 2014. "Mexican Campaign Aims to Protected Children from Junk Food." September 15; https://www.vitalstrategies.org/mexican-campaign-calls-for-children-to-be-protected-from-junk-food-and-suga/

Vital Strategies. 2019. "After 2 Years, South'Africa's Successful Sugar Beverage Tax Still Under Attack." October 15. https://www.vitalstrategies.org/after-2-years-south-africas-successful-sugar-beverage-tax-still-under-attack/

White, M., and S. Barquera. 2020. "Mexico Adopts Food Warning Labels, Why Now?" *Health Systems & Reform* 6 (1): e1752063. https://doi.org/10.1080/23288604.2020.1752063

Whitehead, R.J. 2015. "'Sin Tax' of 40% Proposed to Cover Indian Soft Drinks." *Food Navigator Asia*, December 8. https://www.foodnavigatorasia.com/Article/2015/12/08/Sin-tax-of-40-proposed-to-cover-Indian-soft-drinks#

WHO. 2017. "WHO Commends South African Parliament Decision to Pass Tax Bill on Sugary Drinks." *WHO Africa News*, December 6. https://www.afro.who.int/news/who-commends-south-african-parliament-decision-pass-tax-bill-sugary-drinks

WHO (World Health Organization). 2004. Global *Strategy on Diet, Physical Activity, and Health*. Geneva, Switzerland: WHO. https://www.who.int/publications/i/item/9241592222

Wicks, M., H. Wright, and E. Wentzel-Viljoen. 2017. "Restricting the Marketing of Foods and Non-Alcoholic Beverages to Children in South Africa: Are All Nutrient Profiling Models the Same?" *British Journal of Nutrition* 116 (12): 2150–2159.

Wilkes, T. 2015. "Coca-Cola India Warns of Factor Closure if 'Sin Tax' is Implemented." *Irish Examiner LTD*, December 12.

Yasmeen, A. 2019. "WHO Calls for Tighter Monitoring of Marketing of Unhealthy Foods to Children," *The Hindu*, March 29. https://fssai.gov.in/upload/media/FSSAI_News_WHO_Hindu_01_04_2019.pdf

Zama, Z. 2019 "Visible Warning Labels to be Compulsory on Food Packaging." *7Q2 News*, August 1.

7

Ultra-Processed Food Environments

Aligning Policy Beliefs from the State, Market, and Civil Society

Jonathan Mockshell and Thea Nielsen Ritter

7.1 Introduction

To transition toward nutrition-sensitive food environments, the increasing availability of and access to affordable ultra-processed food products require urgent action (cf. Reardon et al. 2019; Baker and Friel 2016).[1] This action is critical as increasing the availability of ultra-processed food influences food choices and signals to consumers what to purchase, especially in low- and middle-income countries (Herforth and Ahmed 2015; Baker and Friel 2016).[2] For example, in sub-Saharan Africa where increasing food prices and low incomes play a critical role in determining the food basket, the growing trend of increasing ultra-processed food consumption raises a fundamental concern related to food choices and the increasing prevalence of obesity, stunting, and wasting (Laar et al. 2020; Reardon et al. 2021). Estimates suggest that over 40 percent of all men and women (2.2 billion people) are overweight or obese worldwide (Global Nutrition Report 2021). In many African countries, obesity is increasing, ranging from 13 to 31 percent of the population (Global Nutrition Report 2021). In Ghana, between 2007/08 and 2014/15, the prevalence of obesity and overweight increased by 47 percent and 25 percent, respectively, reaching rates of 15 percent and 24.5 percent, respectively (Lartey et al. 2019). Diet-related diseases are also on the rise in Ghana (Ofori-Asenso et al. 2016). This increasing trend in obesity and overweight is associated with the consumption of ultra-processed foods. Analysis by Reardon et al. (2021) suggests that 10 to 30 percent of processed foods are ultra-processed. Similarly, Mockshell et al. (2022) reveals that ultra-processed foods

---

[1] The authors are grateful for feedback and support from Rui Benfica, Kwaw Andam, Collins Asante-Addo and Felix Asante and funding from CGIAR's National Policies and Strategies initiative.
[2] The NOVA classification system categorizes foods as unprocessed, processed culinary, processed, and ultra-processed (Monteiro et al. 2019). "Ultra-processed food products are formulations of several ingredients that, besides salt, sugar, oils and fats, include food substances not used in culinary preparations, in particular, flavors, colors, sweeteners, emulsifiers and other additives used to imitate sensorial qualities of unprocessed or minimally processed foods and their culinary preparations or to disguise undesirable qualities of the final product" (Gibney 2019, p. 3).

Jonathan Mockshell and Thea Nielsen Ritter, *Ultra-Processed Food Environments*. In: *The Political Economy of Food System Transformation*. Edited by: Danielle Resnick and Johan Swinnen, Oxford University Press. © Jonathan Mockshell and Thea Nielsen Ritter (2023). DOI: 10.1093/oso/9780198882121.003.0007

contribute to more than 30 percent of processed foods in Ghana's urban food environment. In Brazil, compared to other types of food, the share of ultra-processed foods and beverages as a proportion of the total value of food purchased at supermarkets is 25 percent higher and prices are 37 percent lower (Machado et al. 2017. The increasing consumption of ultra-processed foods has serious public health implications, especially in developing economies where public health systems are inadequate to deal with emerging health challenges associated with the consumption of ultra-processed foods.

Although this problem has long been a concern to policy and health actors - of relevance is, why is finding solutions to help combat the increasing access to affordable ultra-processed foods so controversial? Analysis of the food environment literature provides clues. Government efforts to regulate and civil society strategies to reduce access to affordable ultra-processed foods have been largely unsuccessful due to limited state capacity, lobbying, and cultural norms (see Baker et al. 2021). While some actors propose the need for more regulations and taxes, others argue that ultra-processed food preferences depend on consumer choices and lobby against such policy instruments (see Popkini et al. 2021). These differing views continue to fuel ultra-processed food versus healthy food debates and have implications for solving the triple burden of malnutrition, i.e., the coexistence of overnutrition, undernutrition, and micronutrient deficiencies in developed and developing economies (cf. Juul and Hemmingsson 2015; Juul et al. 2018; Srour et al. 2019). On the flip side, the ultra-processed food industry's concerns over potential sales and profit losses from regulation lead to financial incentives and market and political actions against reducing ultra-processed foods in the food environment (Fooks et al. 2019; Moodie et al. 2020). The global production network, access to international finance, and global intellectual property rights coupled with hyper-local distribution networks provide leverage and a power base for the ultra-processed food industry to pull strings whenever and wherever possible (Moodie et al. 2020).

These factors constrain state capacity and action by civil society in low- and middle-income countries. The market size of the ultra-processed food industry also plays a significant role in economic development through employment, taxes, infrastructure, technical training, and foreign direct investments in developing economies. For example, policies to regulate or implement a soda tax could lead to revenue losses and counterthreats to governments. For governments aiming to maximize political self-interest for reelection, such policy options are likely not appealing. In contrast, policies focusing on consumer education, food labeling, physical activity, and self-regulation receive more attention from governments and private sector actors. With limited state capacity and high financial incentives from the ultra-processed food industry for lobbyists and political campaign finance, the potential to create and pass policies that aim to reduce the availability and affordability of ultra-processed foods via legislative processes is often thwarted. Through coalitions and constituent building, scientific evidence on ultra-processed foods that could prove instrumental for legislative policy-making processes and raising consumer awareness has not been able to reach the public domain (Moodie et al. 2020). Similar to tobacco use (WHO 2022), obesity is a leading cause of death worldwide and can have devastating health consequences, such as cancer and cardiovascular disease (WHO 2019). Regulations and policies aimed at reducing cigarette use, such as increased prices, warning labels, and bans on television and radio advertisements could serve as templates for the regulation of ultra-processed foods and the impacts of such policies. For example, increased cigarette prices reduce their use (Doogan et al. 2018) and lead to substantial healthcare savings (Contreary et al. 2015).

Prevailing explanations for the increasing availability of ultra-processed foods and the related implications for malnutrition have examined dominant demand-side factors of consumer food choices using rational choice assumption and metabolic and behavioral risk factors (Moodie et al. 2020; Vermeulen et al. 2020). In contrast, supply-side policies relating to the ultra-processed food environment's beliefs, power dynamics, and coalitions have received limited attention in the empirical literature in low- and middle-income countries. In a recent study by Baker et al. (2021), the authors examine the baby food industry using political economy literature, quantitative data, and qualitative literature reviews to unpack the market and political practices of corporate power. Although the behavioral economics literature examines consumer food preferences (cf. Lappalainen and Epstein 1990; Heshmat 2011; Just 2011), there has been limited attention given to ultra-processed foods (Karnani et al. 2016). In the literature, behavioral changes have been conceptualized through the lens of rational choice theory (Vermeulen et al. 2020), which postulates that a consumer has relevant knowledge about the food environment and when faced with options will act rationally by choosing the option that maximizes utility (Simon 1955; Scott 2000). This explanation has some limitations, as consumers do not always act "rationally" as implied by classical economic models due to factors such as information asymmetry and time-inconsistent or "present-biased" preferences (O'Donoghue and Rabin 2000), which often lead people to choose foods based on convenience (Liu et al. 2014). A study conducted in poor neighborhoods of Accra shows a positive association between purchasing food from convenience stores and individual body mass index, implying that access to convenience stores increases the risk of obesity (Dake et al. 2016).

Income also plays a critical role affecting consumer choice with differing effects depending on the level of economic development in the country. Due to differences in food prices, affordability, and accessibility, in high income countries, people with low incomes tend to consume more ultra-processed foods, whereas in middle- and low-income countries such as Ghana people with high incomes tend to consume more ultra-processed foods (Shim et al. 2021; Baker et al. 2020).

High household wealth is associated with higher odds of overweight, obesity, and central adiposity in Ghana (Lartey et al. 2019). In low income and high food price settings, such as in urban environments in Ghana, consumer food choices are constrained to accessible and affordable food options (Mockshell et al. 2022). Food choices are also influenced by a combination of cultural, taste, infrastructure, social, and cognitive processes, including supply-side factors relating to the food environment and policy landscape (Herforth and Ahmed 2015; Vermeulen et al. 2020).

To evaluate such a polarized, complex, and important topic, this chapter takes a step beyond the rational choice assumption and applies a political economy approach by combing the Advocacy Coalition Framework (ACF) developed by Sabatier and Jenkins-Smith (Jenkins-Smith and Sabatier 1994; Weible and Sabatier 2017) with the discourse analysis approach developed by Hajer (1995) and Van Dijk (2004) to unravel policy beliefs and coalitions in the ultra-processed food environment. Although recent literature emphasizes the role of beliefs in agri-food systems (Mockshell and Birner 2015; Resnick et al. 2018), empirical analyses using a political economy analysis to examine the increasing access to ultra-processed foods are limited. By applying a political economy analysis, this chapter aims to unravel the coalitions and beliefs influencing access to affordable ultra-processed foods, using Ghana as a case study. A political economy analysis complements the dominant consumer food choice analysis to pick apart the food environment policy subsystem. The political economy approach is necessary to identify often-neglected issues, namely contestations, power dynamics, beliefs, ideas, interests, coalitions, cooperation, and policy aims of stakeholders in the food environment (Resnick et al. 2018). To identify policy beliefs, discourse is a communicative process in which a set of ideas is expressed as a written or verbal product (Van Dijk 1998). Discourse analysis serves the critical purpose of unveiling the perceptions, goals, beliefs, and value priorities that actors deploy in a policy subsystem (Shanahan et al. 2011). While the self-interest assumption covers components of instrumental and structural policy strategies, the aspect of policy beliefs that are associated with discursive strategies is missing in the empirical evidence (see Baker et al. 2021).

Discursive strategies reveal the underlying policy beliefs embedded in the discourses of actors in the food environment. Examining aspects of discursive strategies provides an opportunity to examine the following questions: Why has achieving alignment among state, market, and civil society actors toward reducing ultra-processed foods not happened yet and what policy options are necessary for policy change? This chapter builds on recent research on urban and informal food environments (cf. Turner et al. 2018; Fooks et al. 2019; Resnick et al. 2019; Laar et al. 2020; Moodie et al. 2020; Gomez 2021), food deserts versus food oases, retail diversity, and nutrition-sensitive value chains (Allen and de Brauw 2018). Ghana provides an applicable case study as the population of this developing economy is growing at an annual rate of 2.2 percent and experiencing urbanization at an annual rate of 3.3 percent (see UN-DESA 2018, 2019) and ranks high among countries with high obesity rates (greater than 20 percent) in Africa. Moreover, urban residency has been found to be associated with higher odds of being overweight, obese, and central adiposity (Lartey et al. 2019). In urban areas in Ghana, the food environment is experiencing a rapid increase in supermarket retail outlets, convenience stores, and fast-food restaurants (Andam et al. 2018), which can be witnessed in many other low- and middle-income countries as well (Monteiro et al. 2013). This chapter focuses on advancing our understanding of the role of policy beliefs and coalitions in ultra-processed food environments in low- and middle-income countries and presenting strategies to reduce the persistent state, market, and civil society organization (CSO) failures. The remainder of this chapter is structured as follows: The next section presents the research methods, the results are presented in Section 7.3 and discussed in Section 7.4, and Section 7.5 provides concluding remarks.

7.2 Research Methods

A political economy approach is employed to answer two key questions of interest: (1) Why is finding solutions to help combat the increasing access to affordable ultra-processed foods so controversial? and (2) Why has achieving alignment among state, market, and civil society actors toward reducing ultra-processed foods not happened and what strategies are necessary for policy change? This analysis aims to advance our understanding of the role of policy beliefs and coalitions in ultra-processed food environments, using Ghana as a case study. To identify the stakeholders and examine coalitions and discourses, an integration of empirical qualitative data and partly transformed quantitative data from in-depth interviews is adopted. The study process involves the following steps: (i) the application of the theoretical framework; (ii) data collection; (iii) theme development; (iv) statistical analysis; and (v) the synthesis of narratives into insights to identify options for policy change.

7.2.1 Theoretical Framework

A theoretical framework that combines the ACF developed by Sabatier and Jenkins-Smith (Jenkins-Smith and Sabatier 1994; Weible and Sabatier 2017) and the discourse analysis approach developed by Hajer (1995) and Van Dijk (2004) is used. Actors with similar perceptions, values, and beliefs form a discourse and advocacy coalition to solve a policy problem. A discourse coalition is defined as an ensemble of storylines, the actors that utter the storylines, and the practices through which the storyline is expressed (Hajer 2006). The ACF provides the theoretical framework to identify advocacy coalitions consisting of different actors who share a set of ideas and policy beliefs in a policy subsystem (Jenkins-Smith and Sabatier 1994). The ACF is particularly suitable to analyze contested food environment policy failures as it embodies the concepts of policy subsystems, policy beliefs, coalitions, policy-oriented learning, and policy change (Jenkins-Smith et al. 2014). The ACF also has a dominant focus on how actors' beliefs, ideas, and interests drive policy preferences (Schlager 1995).

In the ACF, stakeholders who share a belief system form a coalition and work within a policy subsystem (Jenkins-Smith and Sabatier 1994). Coalition members with similar beliefs interact and engage in a significant degree of coordination and planning to influence policy in a subsystem (Weible et al. 2009; Elgin and Weible 2013). A policy subsystem consists of multiple stakeholders: government officials, interest groups, researchers, academia, media, and market sector actors concerned with a problem (Weible 2007). Coalitions in the subsystem form beliefs about practical solutions and coordinate activities in the policy process to influence policy outcomes (Weible 2007). Belief systems can be updated, altered, or changed through policy-oriented learning and crises.

The policy belief system is a fundamental concept in the ACF. A policy belief system includes value priorities, perceptions of world states, and views of the efficacy of policy (Sabatier 1988). In the ACF, beliefs are classified into a hierarchical, tri-partite structure. In the first structure, deep core beliefs involve general normative assumptions and are difficult to change. For example, beliefs about the role of government versus market, and left versus right ideas. In the second structure, core beliefs change more easily than deep core beliefs and represent causal perceptions across an entire policy domain. In general, core beliefs involve the application of deep core beliefs in a policy subsystem. For example, the relative authority of the government versus the market in food policies. In the case of market or government failure, there is an opportunity to change core beliefs related to food policies (Jenkins-Smith and Sabatier 1994). The third and final structure consists of secondary beliefs, which are the easiest to change, are relatively narrow in scope, and address issues within a specific program or policy (Sabatier and Weible 2007). For example, changing budgetary allocations within a food subsidy program requires less evidence and agreement among actors in the food policy subsystem.

In a policy subsystem, learning is critical for coalition members to understand the world and leverage political strategies for achieving policy goals (Jenkins-Smith and Sabatier 1994; Jenkins-Smith et al. 2014). While internal coalition learning is much easier, achieving cross-coalition learning depends on the extent to which actors perceive it as a threat to their core beliefs (Jenkins-Smith et al. 2014). At low and high levels of contested debates, there is little cross-coalition learning (Jenkins-Smith et al. 2014). At a high level of contested debates, actors defend their positions and reject information that undermines their beliefs, while at a low level, stakeholders focus on their own policy sub-system affairs (Jenkins-Smith et al. 2014). An intermediate level of contested policy debates increases cross-coalition learning as opposing coalitions are threatened just enough to pay attention and remain receptive to current information (Jenkins-Smith et al. 2014). Promoting policy-oriented learning is fundamental to achieve policy change. Policy learning can take place in workshops and conferences where coalitions can interact, debate, disagree, and negotiate (Jenkins-Smith et al. 2014. In cases of conflicts among coalitions that hinder policy change, policy brokers can play a mediating role to facilitate cross-coalitions policy learning (Jenkins-Smith and Sabatier 1994; Jenkins-Smith et al. 2014;). Policy change is classified into "minor policy change" involving alterations in secondary aspects of policy beliefs and "major policy change" involving alterations in core aspects of policy beliefs (Jenkins-Smith et al. 2014, p. 201).

7.2.2 Qualitative Data Collection

To apply the ACF and discourse analysis, a set of qualitative in-depth interviews was conducted in the case study country, Ghana. Ghana provides an excellent case study due to its influx of ultra-processed foods, rapid urbanization, and increasing incidence of non-communicable diseases (see Andam et al. 2018; Laar et al. 2020; Mockshell et al. 2022). To examine the ideas, beliefs, and coalitions in the food environment, Yanow's (2000, pp. 26–39) approach of "accessing local knowledge" by combining in-depth interviews and document analysis is applied. The sampling procedure for the respondents started with the enumerator team and the lead researcher mapping the stakeholder organizations that were involved in the food environment policy subsystem by using the stakeholder landscape assessment approach. Through key informant interviews and document analysis, this involved mapping actors engaged in agriculture and food policy, health, nutrition, media, interest groups, and private food industry that are spread across Ghana. Based on the map, interviewees were selected through purposive and snowball sampling techniques that took into consideration their areas of expertise, institutional affiliations, willingness to participate, and geographic location. Additional respondents were identified based on the qualitative research principle of "completeness" (covering the broad spectrum of actors) and "dissimilarity" (respondents with diverse perspectives) (Blee and Taylor 2002). Data and respondent triangulation were employed to check for internal validity and to select more respondents (Golafshani 2003; Guion et al. 2011). The respondents fall into the following categories: state actors, interest groups, industry, knowledge brokers, and media.

Using a semi-structured interview approach, in-depth interviews that lasted one to two hours were conducted with food environment stakeholders. The interview questions were framed around the following questions: (1) Who are the

Table 7.1 Interviewed stakeholders for in-depth interviews

Type	Number
State sector	14
Government ministries and agencies	6
Academia	5
Parliamentarians	3
Civil society organizations (national and international)	5
Private sector food companies	3
Total	22

Note: Out of 15 private food industry sector stakeholders approached, only three were willing to talk to the research team.

main actors and institutions in the food environment policy subsystem?; (2) What are the ideas, incentives, and interests of the actors and institutions in the food environment policy subsystem?; (3) What are the challenges of regulating ultra-processed foods and supplying healthy food options in the food environment?; and (4) What are the policy strategies for transforming the food environment to supply healthy diet options? A total of 22 stakeholders were interviewed throughout Ghana, covering the major regional capitals of Accra, the Cape Coast, Kumasi, and Koforidua. While this sample might seem small, in this context the focus of the qualitative research is achieving a representation of the different stakeholders with knowledge, expertise, and experience in the ultra-processed food policy domain. Based on an assessment of the main actors, this sample adequately covers the main stakeholders. These stakeholders were in the public sector, civil society organizations, and the private food industry (see Table 7.1). State sector actors include policy actors from government ministries and agencies, academia, and parliamentarians. In-depth interviews with the actors were recorded with participant consent and transcribed for analysis. The data collection phase was from September 2020 to November 2020. Although the sample size in each category is small, it represents the main stakeholders who were willing to participate in our study. In a qualitative study, the emphasis of data collection focuses on achieving saturation and richness of various perspectives using participant triangulation approaches. The objective of the study is not to derive statistically significant results, but to examine the policy beliefs of different actors. Thus, the sample size does not necessarily limit the quality of inference from the study. Efforts focused on obtaining a broad spectrum of actors across the different domains in the policy subsystem.

7.2.3 Data Analysis

Transcripts were uploaded into NVivo (Version 12) for analysis. The original texts were coded, and storylines were identified. More codes were identified and aggregated with the initial codes into policy themes (policy beliefs). Overall, a total of 31 policy beliefs were identified following the coding. Table 7.3 describes the policy beliefs in more detail. Major storylines, including specific phrases from the interviews are provided.

To perform factor and cluster analyses, the qualitative data was transformed into quantitative data. The data transformation followed an approach developed by Mockshell and Birner (2015) and further applied by Mockshell and Birner (2020). Each policy belief identified from the content analysis was assigned a binary value (1 = yes, if the policy belief appeared in the narrative of a respondent and 0 = no, if otherwise). From the coding, a total of 31 policy beliefs were found (see Table 7.2). Factor analysis with the principal component extraction method using the oblique rotation method was conducted (see Mockshell and Birner 2015). Factor analysis revealed patterns in the 31 policy beliefs and categorized them into consistent groups (components). After the factor analysis, a two-step cluster analysis using both hierarchical and K-means clustering was conducted to explore how the various actors cluster around the 31 policy beliefs. Cluster membership was determined and cross-tabulated using an identification variable for each actor. Cluster analysis was used to identify coalitions based on shared policy beliefs. Identified policy beliefs were analyzed to examine the discourses of each respondent.

7.3 Identification of Policy Discourse Coalitions

The results show that the identified clusters share similar policy beliefs within and across the cluster groupings (named coalitions), but that these clusters (coalitions) differed on other policy beliefs as illustrated in Table 7.2. Following the conceptual framework described in Section 2, the actors within each cluster are referred to as "coalitions" because they share a similar policy discourse, reflecting similar policy beliefs. The three clusters are labeled "state coalition," "market coalition," and "CSO coalition." These labels were selected to reflect the composition of actors in the three coalitions. However, these labels do not imply that, for example, all state sector actors are members of the state coalition or that all CSOs are members of the CSO coalition. There are also differences within the coalitions. From the analysis, a total of 10 stakeholders belong to the state coalition, which is dominated by actors from the state sector. The 12 remaining actors belong to the CSO, and market coalitions as illustrated by Table 7.2. The next section examines the policy beliefs of the different actors in the food environment.

7.3.1 Food Environment Policy Beliefs

The food environment policy beliefs that emerged from the factor analysis are described in Table 7.3. Bartlett's test of sphericity is significant

Table 7.2 Participants in the discourse coalitions (identified by cluster analysis) (N = 22).

Coalition members	State sector coalition	CSO coalition	Market sector coalition
State	8	3	3
CSOs	2	2	1
Market	0	0	3
Cluster sizes	10	5	7
Cluster distribution (%)	45.5	22.7	31.8

Note: "CSO" refers to civil society organization.
Source: In-depth interviews.

(chi-square = 3,563.413; p < 0.000), showing that the correlation between variables is adequate for factor analysis. Using the Kaiser rule, all factors with eigenvalues greater than 1 were retained (Field 2018). Based on this rule, 10 principal components (i.e., policy beliefs) were extracted, which together explain 83 percent of the error variance. Factor loadings with absolute values of more than 0.30 were initially selected. Using variables with the highest factor loading rule in each component, the policy themes (i.e., policy beliefs) that emerged were labeled to reflect the variables in the component (see Table 7.3). Access to and prevalence of ultra-processed foods, education and awareness, and limited government resources contribute more than 10 percent per component of the explained variance, making them the most dominant policy beliefs. Social classism together with consumer preferences and affordability, weak enforcement, short-term policy focus and profit motivations, and weak institutions contribute a range of 6 to 8 percent per component of the explained variance thereby falling in the middle range of dominant policy beliefs. The high cost of producing healthy foods and lifestyle changes are the least dominant policy beliefs.

7.3.1.1 Shared Food Environment Policy Beliefs

The state, market, and CSO coalitions share a fundamental belief on the increasing presence of affordable ultra-processed foods in the food environment and on the need for more regulation in the food environment. According to an academic respondent in the state coalition, "These energy-dense and nutrient-poor foods are accessible. When you turn left or stretch an arm, you are bound to come across these energy-dense and nutrient-poor foods" (R4).[3] Across the three coalitions, there is also a strongly held belief that lower prices of ultra-processed foods relative

---

[3] "R" stands for "respondent"; "R4" stands for respondent number 4. These labels are used throughout the chapter to protect the respondents' anonymity.

Table 7.3 Food environment policy beliefs identified by factor analysis

Variable	Policies and prevalence of ultra-processed foods	Education and awareness	Limited government resources	Production incentive	Social classism, consumer preference, and affordability	Weak enforcement	Short-term policy and profit motive	Weak institutions and fragmentation	High cost of producing healthy foods	Self-interest and lifestyle changes
High availability of ultra-processed foods	**0.31**	-0.09	**-0.64**	0.22	0.31	-0.04	**-0.42**	0.11	-0.13	0.15
High affordability of ultra-processed foods	**0.31**	0.23	-0.25	-0.01	**-0.73**	0.05	0.08	0.04	-0.01	-0.07
High accessibility of ultra-processed foods	**0.66**	**0.40**	-0.07	-0.08	-0.17	0.00	0.02	-0.26	-0.19	0.08
High cost of producing healthy diet options	-0.09	0.05	-0.18	0.00	0.12	-0.13	-0.01	-0.02	**0.90**	-0.14
Inadequate standards and regulations	0.09	-0.14	0.24	**0.58**	0.19	**0.39**	0.28	0.13	0.23	0.20
Lack of enforcement	0.05	-0.07	-0.03	0.06	-0.09	**0.93**	0.24	0.00	-0.13	-0.05
Limited resources	-0.05	-0.02	**0.77**	-0.21	-0.01	0.02	-0.09	0.12	-0.12	0.16
Policy maker (politician) self-interest	-0.20	-0.13	-0.13	**0.82**	-0.18	0.08	-0.09	-0.12	0.15	**0.34**
Influence of lobby groups	-0.19	**-0.38**	-0.21	0.11	-0.28	**-0.44**	-0.23	0.28	0.13	**0.42**
Lack of policies	**0.48**	0.23	0.16	0.00	0.07	-0.27	0.21	**0.58**	-0.06	0.00
Limited/imperfect information	0.21	0.17	**0.35**	0.01	**0.57**	0.02	**-0.37**	0.14	-0.14	0.26
Policy myopia (short-term fix)	0.12	-0.18	0.18	0.02	0.06	0.18	**0.82**	0.05	-0.04	0.09
Fragmentation and weak coordination	-0.04	**0.84**	0.24	0.17	-0.08	-0.23	-0.03	0.01	-0.08	0.12
Weak institutions	0.14	0.16	0.03	-0.09	-0.03	-0.08	0.10	**-0.86**	0.09	0.08
Lifestyle changes and changing diets of urban residents	0.04	0.10	0.15	0.00	0.06	0.05	0.21	-0.08	-0.07	**0.79**
Convenience and time constraints	0.20	0.15	0.10	-0.20	-0.27	0.10	-0.15	**-0.36**	**0.63**	0.27
Consumer preferences	0.06	0.05	-0.20	-0.08	**0.90**	0.01	0.13	0.06	0.03	-0.09
Education	-0.01	**0.86**	-0.01	-0.07	-0.06	0.06	-0.06	-0.09	0.08	-0.03

Continued

Table 7.3 Continued

Variable	Policies and prevalence of ultra-processed foods	Education and awareness	Limited government resources	Production incentive	Social classism, consumer preference, and affordability	Weak enforcement	Short-term policy and profit motive	Weak institutions and fragmentation	High cost of producing healthy foods	Self-interest and lifestyle changes
Social classism	-0.11	-0.26	-0.11	**-0.34**	**0.51**	0.03	**0.51**	-0.02	-0.05	0.15
High profit motive	-0.03	**0.43**	-0.17	0.17	-0.03	-0.24	**0.60**	-0.15	-0.05	0.28
Aggressive advertisement	**0.39**	0.23	-0.07	0.12	0.07	**-0.61**	0.15	0.03	0.26	0.14
Free market and global trade	-0.19	0.20	-0.09	**0.75**	-0.07	-0.12	0.02	0.07	0.02	**-0.36**
High imports of cheap, ultra-processed foods	0.07	0.06	**-0.60**	-0.17	-0.25	-0.03	0.28	**0.45**	0.06	0.25
Taxes for ultra-processed foods	**0.61**	0.30	-0.07	0.02	0.16	**0.35**	-0.08	**0.38**	0.12	-0.24
Production incentives (subsidies) for healthy food options	0.20	0.03	-0.13	**0.83**	0.00	-0.06	-0.02	0.11	-0.26	-0.05
Education, awareness, and advocacy	-0.28	**0.44**	-0.05	-0.28	0.07	0.20	-0.30	0.24	0.12	0.23
Regulations and standards	-0.09	0.13	-0.15	-0.02	0.10	**0.69**	-0.25	0.04	0.09	**0.31**
Control advertisement	**0.84**	-0.16	0.11	0.17	0.08	-0.14	-0.02	0.17	0.20	0.07
Increase government funds	0.04	0.25	**0.77**	0.01	0.09	-0.14	0.22	-0.13	-0.01	0.15
Government policies	**0.81**	-0.29	-0.21	-0.20	-0.16	-0.05	0.09	-0.15	-0.09	-0.02
Evidence based on research for policy and stakeholder engagements	0.24	-0.40	**0.44**	0.07	-0.20	-0.07	0.11	0.14	**0.50**	-0.02
Proportion explained	*0.14*	*0.13*	*0.11*	*0.10*	*0.08*	*0.07*	*0.06*	*0.06*	*0.04*	*0.04*

Note: Oblimin rotation method (Kaiser normalization) were used for this analysis. Factor loadings over 0.30 appear in bold. Bartlett's test of sphericity (chi-square = 3,563.413; p-value = 0.000).
Source: In-depth interviews.

to healthy and local foods is a major driver of consumer food choices. For example, a government official highlighted that "sugar-sweetened beverages are relatively cheaper than fruits and vegetables, irrespective of the season" (R2). Prevailing low income is highlighted as a driver of consumer demand for ultra-processed foods. A CSO coalition member also highlighted that "they [ultra-processed foods] tend to be cheaper so that even the daily-income wage earner in these urban areas can go in for these highly processed foods" (R14). The easiness of reaching a large population with ultra-processed foods are shared beliefs influencing production decisions of the food processing industry. Institutional weaknesses and fragmentation of policies are other recurring beliefs across the coalitions. A respondent expressed, "I will also talk about the various institutions that are in this sector. Because there is poor coordination, it becomes difficult for the regulatory authorities to take a stand or act" (R15).

7.3.1.2 State Coalition Food Environment Policy Beliefs

Social classism was a recurring metaphor. There was the belief that consuming ultra-processed foods places individuals in an elite and high-income social group. As most ultra-processed foods are imported, the products are considered as western-style convenience foods, which are associated with ideas of "foreign" and "modernity." The growing middle-class demands ultra-processed foods to establish their social identity. According to a state coalition actor, "It looks like people think that if you eat ultra-processed food then you find yourself in the elite bracket" (R7). Over time, consumers develop a taste for ultra-processed foods, which become part of everyday diets and difficult to control. A member of Parliament mentioned, "People have developed the taste for it [ultra-processed foods], so when people are addicted in a way or used to a certain type of food, it is not easy for them to get out of it" (R19).

Profit motives in the processing food industry are highlighted by the state coalition as a factor that increases the supply and availability of ultra-processed foods. A respondent from a government agency noted: "The food industry is driven by, of course, profits... So, they also invest money into the areas that they think will derive the highest benefits possible" (R22). Profit motives drive the food industry to engage in aggressive advertising and deals, as mentioned by an academic respondent: "These food products come in all the time with aggressive advertising. They promote 'buy one, get one free,' and so you are forced to buy stuff that you may not even have thought of buying" (R5). To find solutions to the increasing access to affordable ultra-processed foods, the state coalition share the belief that inadequate capacity of regulatory bodies to provide proper and effective monitoring to ensure strict compliance has been a major challenge. According to a respondent from a government ministry: "I think even though the regulations are there, we all know that sometimes the enforcement is weak" (R12). Without effective enforcement, the private sector, which produces and markets these food products, can easily evade labeling. A respondent from a regulatory agency mentioned, "The standards have been set, but the problem is enforcement, which lies with the metropolitan, municipal, and district assemblies and then the Food and Drugs Authority" (R6).

7.3.1.3 Market Coalition Food Environment Policy Beliefs

The market coalition discourse highlights inadequate infrastructure for storage, transport, distribution, and processing as challenges affecting the availability of healthy food products. These challenges are attributed to the high cost of establishing the relevant infrastructure for healthy foods compared to that for ultra-processed foods. According to a respondent: "Compared to ultra-processed food, the cost that is involved in ensuring that your perishables stay fresh and appealing, is significantly higher than having your ultra-processed food in the pack that can stay for months and sometimes even years" (R2). In the discourse of the market sector coalition, the high cost of producing healthy foods offers a motivating factor for entering the ultra-processed food business. "Short term and quick policy fixes" are highlighted as the reasons for inadequate infrastructure supplying healthy diet options. The market coalition also argues that food policies prioritize food production with less attention to other components of the food system, such as distribution, storage, and consumption (i.e., consumers' nutrition and health outcomes).

Inadequate standards, regulation, and enforcement are metaphors in the market coalition. According to a respondent "there is room for legislation. We need new legislation on how to communicate food information and strengthen the existing ones to prevent unethical marketing of processed foods to our population" (R3). The respondent continued: "There are signboards in many school premises that are sponsored by food companies. That is a challenge, and it needs to be regulated. But the problem is that we currently do not have specific regulations on what kind of restrictions should be in place for marketing unhealthy foods to children" (R3). The market coalition believes that weak enforcement by state institutions is a major challenge. Another respondent added "I think even though the regulations are there, we all know that sometimes the enforcement is weak" (R12).

7.3.1.4 CSO Coalition Food Environment Beliefs

Like the market coalition, CSO actors highlighted that a major factor influencing the shift to more convenient ultra-processed foods is the high cost of producing alternative healthy food options. According to coalition members, production of healthy food options in Ghana is expensive. Some coalition members advocated production incentives for farmers. According to a respondent, "The policy is to try to make healthy foods more affordable and how do you do that? It will mean encouraging more farmers to produce more, by providing them with inputs" (R1). Another respondent from the CSO coalition stressed this point: "In the area of pricing, it is very important for government to implement subsidies that would increase the affordability of healthy foods" (R15).

Policymakers' self-interest was a recurring policy belief in the discourse of the CSO coalition. According to a respondent, "Big private firms have the money to sponsor politicians and ... they sometimes influence politicians, so that they are not able to stop them from producing ultra-processed foods" (R10). Another respondent highlighted, "Frankly, it is quite difficult but, first, looking at the political will and interest, you will be surprised to know that powerful people are behind the importation of such foods in the country. So, if you have such powerful people who are behind these foods getting into the country, the question is how do you stop them from doing their business? ... it is quite difficult" (R8). Another respondent said, "It is particularly important for the government to pass legislation that would regulate the promotion and the advertisement of foods and drinks with all the added sugars. ... There are still a lot of products on the market that do not have labels for you to have confidence that the product you are buying is safe" (R15).

7.3.1.5 Clash of Food Environment Beliefs

The tendency to blame other actors for persistent challenges in the food environment also emerged. Some members in the state sector coalition blamed CSOs for doing little to create the needed public awareness about the health effects of ultra-processed foods. For instance, a regulator from the state discourse coalition mentioned: "We as regulators, we want to see strong advocacy going forward in areas that deal with nutrition because per our mandates, we cannot go out and be preaching against what people should eat. Our job is to ensure safety, once the product is safe, it is safe" (R22). Some CSO coalition members countered this assertion and showed that they are doing a lot in terms of advocacy and putting pressure on the government to ensure a healthy food environment. Instead, they blamed the media for its lack of information dissemination. This was highlighted as: "The media can support the dissemination of information.... This is very key, so we cannot leave them out" (R15). Because of low levels of awareness of ultra-processed foods, improving communications through strong advocacy and increased education are provided as instruments to encourage behavior change. As a member of parliament puts it, "Yes, it is good to regulate, but I think that we must first educate the public. Let them understand the advantages and disadvantages of consuming such [ultra-processed] foods" (R20). While the state coalition believes that their role is to certify food products, the CSO coalition held the belief that the state coalition needs to do more by also checking the nutritional content of the food in the market to ensure labels are accurate.

7.4 Discussion

As discussed in the introduction, the objective of this chapter was to contribute to a better understanding of the prevailing policy beliefs and dissect the coalition landscape influencing access to affordable ultra-processed foods. Combining the ACF and discourse analysis, this chapter reveals a trichotomy of coalitions in the food environment, consisting of state, market, and civil society actors sharing policy beliefs on ultra-processed food environment issues and having independent and divergent policy beliefs on other issues influencing access to ultra-processed foods. As highlighted in the research methods section, beliefs provide a foundation for examining the different perspectives of policy stakeholders and discourse analysis reveals the underlying storyline shaping stakeholders' beliefs. With the increasing prevalence of ultra-processed foods, existing explanations for this persistent problem based on only self-interest assumption of actors as explained in the rational choice theory literature are inadequate. The political economy analysis employed in this study provides additional insights to complement the existing consumer and demand analysis studies to contribute to finding solutions. In this section the discussion will focus on the relevance of the policy beliefs in answering two fundamental questions: (1) Why is finding solutions to the increasing access to affordable ultra-processed food so controversial? and (2) Why is achieving alignment among state, market, and civil society actors toward reducing ultra-processed food not happening and what policy options are necessary for policy change?

7.4.1   Ultra-processed Food Environment Policy Beliefs and Coalitions

As the results highlight, the policy beliefs of the different coalitions reveal that the food industry produces and sells ultra-processed foods because they are more profitable than healthy foods due to their low cost of manufacturing, storage, and transportation. The industry is also guided by consumers' tastes and preferences in producing and selling hyper-palatable, addictive, ultra-processed foods. The food industry is perceived to be driven by profit motives and engaged in more aggressive advertising, as echoed by the discourse of the state coalition (see Monteiro et al. 2013). This criticism can easily be substantiated, especially since profit maximization is the goal of companies in a competitive food market environment. However, profit interests could drive the food industry to lure consumers and influence consumption patterns which would have implications for the triple burden of malnutrition. This behavior in the food industry is explained by Nobel-Prize-winning economists George Akerlof and Robert Shiller in their book *Phishing for Phools: The Economics of Manipulation and Deception*, which challenges the notion that free markets lead to material well-being. They argue that in a market equilibrium and given profit motives, food companies will try to manipulate ("phish") consumers into buying products that they are led to believe will satisfy their preferences but are not in their best interests ("phools") (Akerlof and Shiller 2015). Profits can also drive the ultra-processed food industry to advocate industry narratives that promote alternative solutions to healthy food policies that can shape beliefs and perceptions about their role in the food environment (Global Health Advocacy Incubator 2021). While profits are necessary to food companies' survival, they have implications for combating the increasing availability of ultra-processed foods and growing malnutrition. The fear of losing profits is part of the core belief system of the ultra-processed food industry to use financial incentives, market action, and political practices against the reduction of ultra-processed foods to counter both government regulations and CSO advocacy (see Baker et al. 2021). As the interviews revealed, these actions lead to the belief by the state and CSO coalitions that private food companies engage in lobbying activities. While this is a potential maximization of the political objective function (Swinnen 2010a; 2010b), the effect of lobbying undermines public health promotion efforts and the objective function of CSOs to advocate for a healthier food environment.

Failure of the food market to provide healthy diet options has implications for human health and calls for government legislative intervention to create an environment that promotes healthy foods. Healthy foods depend upon the local context and can be defined by accepted dietary guidelines (cf. Cohen et al. 2016). However, in Ghana, there are no food-based dietary guidelines. Indeed, in Africa, there are only seven countries that have national food-based dietary guidelines. Ghana began the process of developing these guidelines in 2016 but has not yet made them public (Aryeetey and Edd 2022). Such guidelines can influence policies and initiatives, including school feeding programs, nutrition information, and food regulations.

In Ghana, government policy actions in the food environment have been slow to respond and are increasingly challenging to implement due to the growing influence of commercial interests and conflicting policy beliefs among policy stakeholders. As highlighted in the interviews, weak state capacity in Ghana makes it challenging to enforce regulations relating to ultra-processed foods at the national, municipal, and local levels. Some government agencies also hold the belief that their main responsibility is to ensure that "food is safe and thus the nutritional content is of less priority." These beliefs limit the scope of their work and enforcement mechanisms—with implications on the increasing prevalence of ultra-processed foods. As the evidence suggests for the food environment in Ghana, without strong regulations in the free market, the market is left to supply and demand, and self-interests can potentially lead to serious market failures.

In Ghana, CSOs could play a significant role in the food environment by providing consumers information through public discourses and coalitions to make healthy food choices. However, CSOs have also been less effective due to information asymmetry, the influence of lobby groups, and power imbalances. Most consumers are not perfectly rational due to lack of perfect knowledge and because they are subject to bounded rationality (Jolls et al. 1998; Scott 2000; Sunstein and Thaler 2003). When consumers suffer from such cognitive failures, they make choices that may not maximize their welfare. This is particularly the case in developing economies like Ghana, where food choices are constrained by access to healthy food products, income, and food prices (see Mockshell et al. 2022). In such situations, Adam Smith's "invisible hand" argument that firms pursuing their own self-interests incidentally promote the welfare of the society does not apply because private profits and public health interests' clash as revealed by the discourses of the respondents. The consumption of ultra-processed foods suggests that being overweight or obese with the associated burden of diseases resulting from unhealthy food consumption is not simply an individual choice but is also due to differences in the beliefs of the trichotomy in the food environment. Thus, rational choice and bounded rationality arguments are not entirely adequate to explain why consumers choose ultra-processed foods. These arguments contribute to the lack of alignment of the state, market, and CSO beliefs. To contribute to solving this problem, Sunstein and Thaler (2003) proposed an approach based on the concept of "libertarian paternalism." They recommend that with bounded rationality and bounded self-control, libertarian paternalists (i.e., private and public institutions) should steer people's choices to nudge them away from bad choices without eliminating their freedom of choice. In a systematic review, Bucher et al. (2016) conclude that such nudging strategies can influence food choices.

7.4.2. Aligning State, Market, and CSO Coalitions for Food Environment Policy Change

These insights call for examining solutions to reduce the prevalence of ultra-processed foods in the food environment. From the ACF, policy-oriented learning and external shocks provide pathways for achieving policy change (Weible and Sabatier 2017). Policy-oriented learning would require evidence-based research to influence coalition beliefs. The evidence generated from this research highlights some entry points for policy-oriented learning and policy change. While policy belief updating among coalitions would be a gradual process, external shocks such as alarming obesity rates and pandemics could trigger a more rapid policy response in the food environment. These two pathways also provide an opportunity within and across coalitions to identify "policy change packages" (Fesenfeld et al. 2020) that can create incentives to alter stakeholder beliefs and actions in the food environment. Addressing chronic malnutrition requires a corresponding multidisciplinary and multi-sectoral governance response that is lacking in developing economies. Indeed, Gillespie et al. (2019) highlight that nutrition interventions and programs cannot be successful without the political commitment and active support of many actors. Instead of implementing just one silver bullet, there is a need to combine different policy options, such as a tax on unhealthy foods together with a labeling law for such foods, and education awareness (Shah et al. 2013). Below, we elaborate on various policy instruments that could be applied to make food environments healthier.

Subsidies can be used as a bundled policy option to support access to healthy foods. Both the government and CSOs share beliefs on this policy instrument. A subsidy can catalyze a decline in food prices or an increase in real income or purchasing power, thereby enhancing financial and physical access to healthy foods (Mockshell et al. 2022). For example, a systematic review and meta-analysis of prices of healthy and less healthy foods and diet patterns found that healthy foods and diets cost more per day and per calorie than less healthy foods (Rao et al. 2013). Thus, subsidies could be given to local food vendors and convenience stores to encourage them to sell healthy foods at more affordable prices (Holdsworth et al. 2020). While government subsidies have often been spent on protecting and incentivizing the production of staple foods, such as maize and rice (Anderson and Masters 2009), complementarities to staples, such as fresh fruits and vegetables and legumes, have not received much attention. Differences in beliefs on the effectiveness of production subsidies prevail due to past governance challenges in managing input subsidy programs, creating an impasse among policy actors in Ghana (Mockshell and Birner 2015). Since production subsidies can sometimes result in negative environmental externalities, repurposing production subsidies to address dietary concerns while minimizing negative environmental impacts requires recognizing diverse food industry coalitions and reconciling contested policy beliefs to find consensus-oriented approaches (see Chapter 3 of this volume).

A prohibitive tax (sin tax) on ultra-processed foods could increase the price of these unhealthy foods (as producers and suppliers will pass the tax onto consumers) compared to healthy foods and limit their consumption (due to a decline in consumers' purchasing power) (see Mockshell et al. 2019). The belief of using food taxes among the coalitions identified in this chapter has a greater appeal to national governments compared to subsidies because of their revenue-raising potential. Taxes have been used by many countries as part of a broader strategy to reduce the burden of non-communicable diseases (Thow et al. 2018; Popkin 2020). Divergent beliefs on implementing sin taxes are still dominant in the food environment and have caused divisions among different actors. These divergent beliefs are particularly prevalent among private food industry actors as it would increase the cost of their product to consumers. In the case of Ghana, the state coalition has often been criticized for implementing sin taxes for self-interest, rather than for societal interest. This is the case in other developing economies (e.g., Mexico) where sin taxes have met resistance from food industry players.

While a sin tax is a politically unpopular policy, it is also a critical source of revenue for governments in developing economies. The regressive effects of implementing such a tax could also lead to higher food prices and the potential rise of CSO coalitions against national governments. To reduce tensions and align beliefs, one possibility is to invest the revenues generated from sin taxes into subsidy programs and education awareness campaigns promoting healthy foods. The tax could also be targeted at calorie dense foods or specific ingredients (e.g., sugar, fat, and salt) used in producing unhealthy foods instead of the whole food product as has been done in other countries, such as the United Kingdom (cf. Madden 2015; Wright et al. 2017; Thow et al. 2018). Increasing the cost of ultra-processed foods in Brazil has been modeled to decrease consumption of those foods (Pereda et al. 2019)and the prevalence of obesity (Mendes dos Passos et al. 2020).

Food companies can join efforts to provide a healthy food environment through self-regulation or voluntary regulations, awareness, and education. **Voluntary regulations** may help reduce public costs associated with such regulations, particularly in situations in which the government lacks the capacity to design and enforce regulations (Karnani et al. 2016). For example, in France, Siga is a company that indexes foods based on their degree of processing and provides guidance and services to businesses (Siga 2022). However, when there is a divergence between the interests of the food industry and society, self-regulation has unfortunately proven to be ineffective (Karnani et al. 2016). To make self-regulation effective and not self-serving, Sharma et al. (2010) propose a set of basic standards that include: multi-stakeholder engagements (involving scientists, nongovernmental organizations, global governance, and industry) with no single party given disproportionate power; setting relevant aims and targets with codes of acceptable behaviors; and undertaking external and objective evaluations, including mandatory public reporting of adherence to regulations, such as on labeling (discussed below), and oversight by a global regulatory or health authority.

Labeling and advertisement bans are examples of policy options that can play a critical role in reducing the demand of ultra-processed foods and eventually their availability in the food environment. As revealed in the discourses, for these policy options to work, the fundamental challenge of weak state capacity in regulating the food environment in Ghana must be addressed. With a strong state capacity, national governments could enforce food labeling and standards to support consumer decision making. The World Health Organization (WHO) recommends front-of-pack nutrition labels to guide consumers toward healthy foods, which some countries have adopted, such as Chile which uses a system of stop sign labels (see Jones et al. 2019 for a review of nutrition labeling regulations throughout the world). Labeling laws can be effective. For example, a labeling law in Mexico is predicted to reduce ultra-processed foods purchases by an amount equivalent to a 20 percent tax (Langellier et al. 2021). There is a need for international standards in labeling ultra-processed foods. The Codex Alimentarius Commission, which is jointly sponsored by the FAO and WHO, was created to ensure fair practices and consumer protection in global food trade (Heilandt et al. 2013). Its standards are used as references for national standards for consumer protection and include labeling standards (FAO and WHO 2023), yet there is no standard for ultra-processed foods. Thus, the Codex Alimentarius Commission is a possible avenue to establish international standards regarding the labeling of ultra-processed foods, which governments could adopt.

Regulations targeting schools and children are more politically feasible options from the point-of-view of preserving freedom of choice in decisions. Policy options include bans on the sale, promotion, and donation of unhealthy foods at or near schools. There are examples of other countries adopting such regulations targeting children (see Taillie et al. 2019 and Kovacs et al. 2020 for reviews of existing regulations targeting children and schools, respectively). For example, South Korea has "Green Food Zones" where unhealthy foods cannot be advertised, provided, or sold (Bae et al. 2012). More paternal liberalism options have been put forth, such as making tempting foods less accessible or visible at or near schools, which have been found to decrease the amount of these foods being consumed (Wansink et al. 2006). Cohen and Babey (2012) similarly suggest that ultra-processed foods could be sold at the back of stores.

Ghana is headed in the right direction, but more urgent action is needed. For example, the MEALS4NCDs project seeks to measure and support policy actions to create healthy food environments for children in Ghana (Ghana, Ministry of Health and MEALS4NCDs 2021). In addition, Ghana updated a 2012 strategy in 2021 that recognizes interventions such as regulating advertisements of unhealthy foods to children, limiting trans fats and salt in processed foods, and implementing food-related health taxes; however, these interventions have not been made into law (Ghana, Ministry of Health 2021). Also in 2021, Ghana's Ministry of Health hosted a platform for stakeholders to contribute to designing food policies for healthier diets. At the meeting, the Director for Policy, Planning, and Monitoring and Evaluation at the Ministry of Health called for a paradigm shift that repositions the food system in Ghana from "feeding" to "nourishing" (Ghana, Ministry of Health and MEALS4NCDs 2021). Various policy options were discussed, such as controlling advertisements of unhealthy foods and beverages in and near schools and in the media, nutrition labeling, healthy school meal planning, subsidizing healthy foods, educating students and parents about diet-related diseases, and zoning regulations. A major challenge is funding, so selected interventions will likely be driven by cost-effectiveness. However, concern over the cost of such policy options may be offset by the dramatic adverse effects of overweight and obesity on the health and economics of individuals and the total population in Ghana (Lartey et al. 2020).

7.5 Conclusion

The food environment in developing economies is changing rapidly toward the consumption of ultra-processed foods, which is strongly linked to an increased risk of diet-related diseases. Through a case study in Ghana, this chapter focused on advancing our understanding of the role of policy beliefs and coalitions in ultra-processed food environments and the strategies to reduce persistent government and market failures. Findings from this study can be applied to other low- and middle-income countries that share similar policy, social, and food environments as Ghana. For example, like Ghana, other low- and middle-income countries have increasing urbanization (Menashe-Oren and Bocquier 2021), diet-related diseases (Miranda et al. 2019), and prevalence of convenience stores and supermarkets (Barrett et al. 2022). As national contexts are necessary for identifying coalitions and understanding policy beliefs, future research on ultra-processed food environments can focus on other low- and middle-income countries.

The evidence from this analysis highlights the need to unravel beliefs of policy stakeholders to find instrumental, structural, and discursive strategies that align market and state sector beliefs, as well as increase consumer awareness to improve the food environment in low- and middle-income countries. Paying close attention to stakeholder beliefs provides the added opportunity to foster alignments through policy-oriented learning, incentivizing coalitions, and reorienting actions toward a pathway leading to policy change. From the underlining complexities in the food environment, there appears not to be an easy way out as stakeholder beliefs do not align on all fronts. Though useful in shaping the current understanding, existing rational choice explanations for consumer demand and market supply have been inadequate in explaining the complexities and controversies of the ultra-processed food environment in Ghana.

This chapter provides a new perspective based on political economy analysis and the ACF to complement existing studies and contribute to a better understanding of the ultra-processed food environment. Acknowledging the implications of the consumption of ultra-processed foods, it is critical to find solutions that align the policy beliefs of the state, market, and CSO coalitions. As highlighted in the ACF, policy-oriented learning provides options to align policy beliefs of various coalitions to move toward a consensus and find solutions in the food environment. The shared policy beliefs of the actors provide a foundation to start the alignment process, while consensus via policy-oriented learning will be critical for updating policy beliefs of actors holding independent and divergent policy beliefs. It is also critical to examine both intra- and cross-coalition similarities and differences as these also influence how beliefs can be restructured to provide options for policy change in the food environment. Addressing food environment failures and reducing the risk of non-communicable diseases associated with obesity is not only important from a food and nutrition perspective, but also for building resilience to unexpected shocks due to pandemics and accelerating the transformation of food systems.

References

Akerlof, G.A., and R.J. Shiller. 2015. *Phishing for Phools: The Economics of Manipulation and Deception*. Princeton, NJ: Princeton University Press.

Allen, S., and A. De Brauw. 2018. "Nutrition Sensitive Value Chains: Theory, Progress, and Open Questions." *Global Food Security* 16: 22–28. https://doi.org/10.1016/j.gfs.2017.07.002

Andam, K.S., D. Tschirley, S.B. Asante, R.M. Al-Hassan, and X. Diao. 2018. "The Transformation of Urban Food Systems in Ghana: Findings from Inventories of Processed Products." *Outlook on Agriculture* 47 (3): 233–243. https://doi.org/10.1177/0030727018785918

Anderson, K., and W.A. Masters. 2009. *Distortions to Agricultural Incentives in Africa*. Washington, DC: World Bank.

Aryeetey, R., and A.I. Edd. 2022. "Process and Lessons Learned in the Development of Food-Based Dietary Guidelines in Ghana." *African Journal of Food, Agriculture, Nutrition and Development* 22 (2): 19702[-]19726. https://doi.org/10.18697/ajfand.107.21830

Bae, S.G., J.Y. Kim, K.Y. Kim, S.W. Park, J. Bae, and W.K. Lee. 2012. "Changes in Dietary Behavior among Adolescents and Their Association with Government Nutrition Policies in Korea, 2005–2009." *Journal of Preventative Medicine and Public Health* 45 (1): 47–59. https://doi.org/10.3961/jpmph.2012.45.1.47

Baker, P., and S. Friel. 2016. "Processed Foods and the Nutrition Transition: Evidence from Asia." *Obesity Reviews* 15 (7): 564–577. https://doi.org/10.1111/obr.12174

Baker, P., P. Machado, and T. Santos. 2020. "Ultra-Processed Foods and the Nutrition Transition: Global, Regional and National Trends, Food Systems Transformations and Political Economy Drivers." *Obesity Reviews* 21 (12): e13126. https://doi.org/10.1111/obr.13126

Baker, P., K. Russ, M. Kang, T.M. Santos, P.A.R. Neves, J. Smith, G. Kingston, et al. 2021. "Globalization, First-Foods Systems Transformations, and Corporate Power: A Synthesis of Literature and Data on the Market and Political Practices of the Transnational Baby Food Industry." *Global Health* 17: 58. https://doi.org/10.1186/s12992-021-00708-1

Barrett, C.B., T. Reardon, J. Swinnen, and D. Zilberman. 2022. "Agri-food Value Chain Revolutions in Low- and Middle-Income Countries." *Journal of Economic Literature* 60 (4): 1316–1377. https://doi.org/10.1257/jel.20201539

Blee, K., and V. Taylor. 2002. "Semi-structured Interviewing in Social Movement Research. In *Methods of Social Movement Research*, eds. B. Klandermans and S. Staggenborg, 92–117. Minneapolis: University of Minnesota Press.

Bucher, T., C. Collins, M. Rollo, T.A. McCaffrey, N. De Vlieger, D. Van der Bend, H. Truby, and F.J.A. Perez-Cueto. 2016. "Nudging Consumers towards Healthier Choices: A Systematic Review of Positional Influences on Food Choice." *British Journal of Nutrition* 115: 2252–2263. https://doi.org/10.1017/S0007114516001653

Cohen, D.A., and S.H.Babey. 2012. "Cash at the Candy Register—A Risk Factor for Obesity and Chronic Disease." *New England Journal of Medicine* 367 (15): 1381–1383. https://doi.org/10.1056/nejmp1209443

Cohen, J.F.W., M.T. Gorski, S.A. Gruber, L.B.F. Kurdziel, and E.B. Rimm. 2016. "The Effect of Healthy Dietary Consumption on Executive Cognitive Functioning in Children and Adolescents: A Systematic Review." *British Journal of Nutrition* 116: 989–1000. https://doi.org/10.1017/s0007114516002877

Contreary, K.A., S.K. Chattopadhyay, D.P. Hopkins, F.J. Chaloupka, J.L. Forster, V. Grimshaw, C.B. Holmes, R.Z. Goetzel, J.E Fielding, and the Community Preventive Services Task Force et al. 2015. "Economic Impact of Tobacco Price Increases through Taxation: A Community Guide Systematic Review." *American Journal of Preventative Medicine* 49 (5): 800–808. http://dx.doi.org/10.1016/j.amepre.2015.04.026

Dake, F.A.A., A.L. Thompson, S.W. Ng, S. Agyei-Mensah, and S.N.A. Codjoe. 2016. "The Local Food Environment and Body Mass Index among the Urban Poor in Accra, Ghana." *Journal of Urban Health* 93 (3): 438–455. https://doi.org/10.1007/s11524-016-0044-y

Doogan, N.J., M.E. Wewers, and M. Berman. 2018. "The Impact of a Federal Cigarette Minimum Pack Price Policy on Cigarette Use in the USA." *Tobacco Control* 27 (2): 203–208. https://doi.org/10.1136/tobaccocontrol-2016-053457

Elgin, D.J., and C.M. Weible. 2013. "A Stakeholder Analysis of Colorado Climate and Energy Issues Using Policy Analytical Capacity and the Advocacy Coalition Framework." *Review of Policy Research* 30 (1): 114–133.

Fesenfeld, L.P., M. Wicki, Y. Sun, and T. Bernauer. 2020. "Policy Packaging Can Make Food System Transformation Feasible." *Nature Food* 1: 173–182. https://doi.org/10.1038/s43016-020-0047-4

Field, A. 2018. *Discovering Statistics Using IBM SPSS Statistics (5th ed.)*. London and Thousand Oaks, California: SAGE Publications.

FAO and WHO. 2023. *Codex Alimentarius Commission Procedural Manual*. Twenty-eighth edition. Rome. https://doi.org/10.4060/cc5042en

Fooks, G.J., S. Williams, G. Box, and G. Sachs. 2019. "Corporations' Use and Misuse of Evidence to Influence Health Policy: A Case Study of Sugar-sweetened Beverage Taxation." *Global Health* 15: 56. https://doi.org/10.1186/s12992-019-0495-5

Gillespie, S., M.van den Bold, and J.Hodge. 2019. "Nutrition and the Governance of Agri-food Systems in South Asia: A Systematic Review." *Food Policy* 82: 13–27. https://doi.org/10.1016/j.foodpol.2018.10.013

Gibney, M.J. 2019. "Ultra-processed Foods: Definitions and Policy Issues." *Current Developments in Nutrition* 3 (2): nzy077. https://doi.org/10.1093/cdn/nzy077

Ghana, Ministry of Health. 2021. *Developing a Food Policy Package for Healthier Diets in Ghana: A Consultative Meeting*. Post-meeting Report. Accra, Ghana. https://www.meals4ncds.org/en/wp-content/uploads/Report_Developing_Food_Policy_Consultative_Meeting.pdf

Global Health Advocacy Incubator. 2021. "Industry Narratives: How Ultra-processed Food and Beverage Companies Undermine Healthy Food Policies to Protect Their Corporate Image." Industry Alert—June. 2021. Washington, DC: Global Health Advocacy Incubator. https://advocacyincubator.org/wp-content/uploads/2021/07/2021_06_alert_en.pdf

Global Nutrition Report. 2021. *Global Nutrition Report: The state of global nutrition*. Bristol, UK: Development Initiatives.

Golafshani, N. 2003. "Understanding Reliability and Validity in Qualitative Research." *The Qualitative Report* 8 (4): 597–606.

Gómez, E.J. 2021. "The Politics of Ultra-processed Foods and Beverages Regulatory Policy in Upper-middle-income Countries: Industry and Civil Society in Mexico and Brazil." *Global Public Health* 17 (9): 1883-1901. https://doi.org/10.1080/17441692.2021.1980600

Guion, L., D.Diehl, and D.McDonald. 2011. "Triangulation: Establishing the Validity of Qualitative Studies." *EDIS* 8: 3. https://doi.org/10.32473/edis-fy394-2011

Hajer, M.A. 1995. *The Politics of Environmental Discourse: Ecological Modernization and the Policy Process.* New York: Oxford University Press.

Hajer, M.A. 2006. "The Living Institutions of the EU: Analysing Governance as Performance." *Perspectives on European Politics and Society* 7 (1): 41–55.

Heilandt, T., C.A. Mulholland, and M. Younes. 2013. "Institutions Involved in Food Safety: FAO/WHO Codex Alimentarius Commission (CAC)." 10.1016/B978-0-12-378612-8.00006-8.

Herforth, A., and S.Ahmed. 2015. "The Food Environment, Its Effects on Dietary Consumption, and Potential for Measurement within Agriculture-Nutrition Interventions." *Food Security* 7 (3): 505–520. https://doi.org/10.1007/s12571-015-0455-8

Heshmat, S. 2011. *Eating Behavior and Obesity: Behavioral Economics Strategies for Health Professionals.* New York: Springer Publishing Company.

Holdsworth, M., R. Pradeilles, A.Tandoh, M. Green, M. Wanjohi, F.Zotor, G.Asiki, et al. 2020. "Unhealthy Eating Practices of City-Dwelling Africans in Deprived Neighbourhoods: Evidence for Policy Action from Ghana and Kenya." *Global Food Security* 26: 100452. https://doi.org/10.1016/j.gfs.2020.100452

Jenkins-Smith, H.C., and P.Sabatier. 1994. "Evaluating the Advocacy Coalition Framework." *Journal of Public Policy* 14 (2): 175–203.

Jenkins-Smith, H.C., D.Nohrstedt, C.M.Weible, and P.A.Sabatier. 2014. "The Advocacy Coalition Framework: Foundations, Evolution, and Ongoing Research." *Theories of the Policy Process* 3: 183–224.

Jolls, C., C.R.Sunstein, and R.Thaler. 1998. "A Behavioral Approach to Law and Economics." *Stanford Law Review* 50 (5), 1471–1550. doi:10.2307/1229304

Jones A., B. Neal, B. Reeve, C.N.Mhurchu, and A.M.Thow. 2019. "Front-of-Pack Nutrition Labelling to Promote Healthier Diets: Current Practice and Opportunities to Strengthen Regulation Worldwide." *BMJ Global Health* 4: e001882. http://dx.doi.org/10.1136/bmjgh-2019-001882

Just, D.R. 2011. "Behavioral Economics and the Food Consumer." In *The Oxford Handbook of the Economics of Food Consumption and Policy*, eds. J.L.Lusk, J. Roosen, and J.F. Shogren, 99–118. Oxford, UK: Oxford University Press.

Juul, F., and E.Hemmingsson. 2015. "Trends in Consumption of Ultra-processed Foods and Obesity in Sweden between 1960 and 2010." *Public Health Nutrition* 18 (17): 3096–3107. https://doi.org/10.1017/S1368980015000506

Juul, F., E.Martinez-Steele, N.Parekh, C.Monteiro, and V.Chang. 2018. "Ultra-processed Food Consumption and Excess Weight among US Adults." *British Journal of Nutrition* 120 (1): 90–100. https://doi.org/10.1017/S0007114518001046

Karnani, A., B.McFerran, and A.Mukhopadhyay. 2016. "The Obesity Crisis as Market Failure: An Analysis of Systemic Causes and Corrective Mechanisms." *Journal of the Association for Consumer Research* 1 (3): 445–470.

Kovacs, V.A., S.Messing, P.Sandu, P.Nardone, E.Pizzi, M.Hassapidou, K.Brukalo, et al. 2020. "Improving the Food Environment in Kindergartens and Schools:

An Overview of Policies and Policy Opportunities in Europe." *Food Policy* 96: 101848. https://doi.org/10.1016/j.foodpol.2020.101848

Laar, A., A.Barnes, R.Aryeetey, A.Tandoh, K.Bash, K.Mensah, and M.Holdsworth. 2020. "Implementation of Healthy Food Environment Policies to Prevent Nutrition-Related Non-communicable Diseases in Ghana: National Experts' Assessment of Government Action." *Food Policy* 93: 101907.

Langellier, B.A., I.Stankov, R.A.Hammond, U.Bilal, A.H.Auchincloss, T.Barrientos-Gutierrez, L.de Oliveira Cardoza, and A.V.Diez Roux. 2021. "Potential Impacts of Policies to Reduce Purchasing of Ultra-processed Foods in Mexico at Different Stages of the Social Transition: An Agent-Based Modelling Approach." *Public Health Nutrition* 25(6): 1711–1719. https://doi.org/10.1017/S1368980021004833

Lappalainen, R., and L.H.Epstein. 1990. "A Behavioral Economics Analysis of Food Choice in Humans." *Appetite* 14 (2): 81–93. https://doi.org/10.1016/0195-6663(90)90002-p

Lartey, S.T., C.G.Magnussen, L.Si, G.O.Boateng, B.de Graaff, R.B.Biritwum, N.Minicuci, et al. 2019. "Rapidly Increasing Prevalence of Overweight and Obesity in older Ghanaian Adults from 2007–2015: Evidence from WHO-SAGE Waves 1 & 2." *PLoS ONE* 14 (8): e0215045. https://doi.org/10.1371/journal.pone.0215045

Lartey S., L.Si, T.Lung, C.G.Magnussen, G.O.Boateng, N.Minicuci, P.Kowal, et al. 2020. "Impact of Overweight and Obesity on Life Expectancy, Quality-Adjusted Life Years and Lifetime Costs in the Adult Population of Ghana." *BMJ Global Health* 5: e003332. http://dx.doi.org/10.1136/bmjgh-2020-003332

Liu, P.J., J.Wisdom, C.A.Roberto, L.J.Liu, and A.Ubel. 2014. "Using Behavioral Economics to Design More Effective Food Policies to Address Obesity." *Applied Economic Perspectives and Policy* 36 (1): 6–24. https://doi.org/10.1093/aepp/ppt027

Machado P.P., R.M.Claro, D.S.Canella, F.M.Sarti, and R.B.Levy. 2017. "Price and convenience: The Influence of Supermarkets on Consumption of Ultra-Processed Foods and Beverages in Brazil." *Appetite* 116: 381–388. https://doi.org/10.1016/j.appet.2017.05.027

Madden, D. 2015. "The Poverty Effects of a 'Fat-Tax' in Ireland." *Health Economics* 24 (1): 104–121. https://doi.org/10.1002/hec.3006

Menashe-Oren, A., and P.Bocquier. 2021. "Urbanization is No Longer Driven by Migration in Low- and Middle-Income Countries (1985–2015)." *Population and Development Review* 47 (3): 639–663. https://doi.org/10.1111/padr.12407

Mendes dos Passos, C., E.G.Maia, R.B.Levy, A.P.Bortoletto Martins, and R.M.Claro. 2020. "Association between the Price of Ultra-processed Foods and Obesity in Brazil." *Nutrition, Metabolism, and Cardiovascular Diseases* 30 (4): 589–598. https://doi.org/10.1016/j.numecd.2019.12.011

Miranda, J.J., T.Barrientos-Gutiérrez, C.Corvalan, A.A.Hyder, M.Lazo-Porras, T.Oni, and J.C.K. Wells. 2019. "Understanding the Rise of Cardiometabolic Diseases in Low- and Middle-Income Countries." *Nature Medicine* 25: 1667–1679. https://doi.org/10.1038/s41591-019-0644-7

Mockshell, J., and R.Birner. 2015. "Donors and Domestic Policy Makers: Two Worlds in Agricultural Policymaking?" *Food Policy* 55: 1–14. https://doi.org/10.1016/j.foodpol.2015.05.004

Mockshell, J., E.Martey, C.Khoury, and S.Prager. 2019. "Transforming Food Environment to Deliver Healthy Diet Options: Economic Rational and Policy Drivers." CIAT Working Paper 483. International Center for Tropical Agriculture (CIAT), Cali, Colombia.

Mockshell, J., and R.Birner. 2020. "Who Has the Better Story? On the Narrative Foundations of Agricultural Development Dichotomies." *World Development* 135: 105043. https://doi.org/10.1016/j.worlddev.2020.105043

Mockshell, J., S.O.Ogutu, D.Álvarez, C.Asante-Addo, and F.A.Asante. 2022. "How Healthy and Food Secure is the Urban Food Environment in Ghana?" *World Development Perspectives* 26: 100427. https://doi.org/10.1016/j.wdp.2022.100427

Monteiro, C.A., J.C.Moubarac, G.Cannon, S.W.Ng, and B.Popkin. 2013. "Ultra-processed Products are Becoming Dominant in the Global Food System." *Obesity Reviews* 14 (S2): 21–28. https://doi.org/10.1111/obr.12107

Monteiro, et al. 2019. "Ultra-processed Foods: What They are and How to Identify Them." *Public Health Nutrition* 22 (5): 936–941. https://doi.org/10.1017/S1368980018003762

Moodie, R, E.Bennett, E.J.L.Kwong, T.M.Santos, L.Pratiwi, J.Williams, and P.Baker. "Ultra-Processed Profits: The Political Economy of Countering the Global Spread of Ultra-Processed Foods - A Synthesis Review on the Market and Political Practices of Transnational Food Corporations and Strategic Public Health Responses." *International Journal of Health Policy and Management*. 10(12): 968-982. https://doi.org/10.34172/ijhpm.2021.45. PMID: 34124866; PMCID: PMC9309965.

Ofori-Asenso, R., A.A.Agyeman, A.Laar, and D.Boateng. 2016. "Overweight and Obesity Epidemic in Ghana—A Systematic Review and Meta-analysis." *BMC Public Health* 16 (1): 1239

O'Donoghue, T., and M.Rabin. 2000. "The Economics of Immediate Gratification." *Journal of Behavioral Decision Making* 13 (2): 233–250.

Pereda, P., M.A.Christofoletti, S.W.Ng, et al. 2019. "Effects of a 20% Price Increase of Sugar-Sweetened Beverages on Consumption and Welfare in Brazil." Department of Economics Working Papers 2019_33. University of São Paulo, São Paulo, Brazil.

Popkin, B.M., S.Barquera, C.Corvalan, K.J.Hofman, C.Monteiro, S.W.Ng, E.C.Swart, and L.S.Taillie. 2021. "Towards Unified and Impactful Policies to Reduce Ultra-processed Food Consumption and Promote Healthier Eating." *Lancet Diabetes Endocrinol*. 9 (7): 462-470. doi: 10.1016/S2213-8587(21)00078-4. Epub 2021 Apr 15. PMID: 33865500; PMCID: PMC8217149.

Popkin. B. 2020. *Ultra-processed Foods' Impacts on Health*. 2030 - Food, Agriculture and Rural Development in Latin America and the Caribbean, No. 34. Santiago de Chile: Food and Agriculture Organization.

Rao, M., A.Afshin, G.Singh, and D.Mozaffarian. 2013. "Do Healthier Foods and Diet Patterns Cost More than Less Healthy Options? A Systematic Review and Meta-analysis." *BMJ Open* 3: e004277. http://dx.doi.org/10.1136/bmjopen-2013-004277

Reardon, T., R.Echeverria, J.Berdegué, B.Minten, S.Liverpool-Tasie, D.Tschirley, and D.Zilberman. 2019. "Rapid Transformation of Food Systems in Developing Regions: Highlighting the Role of Agricultural Research & Innovations." *Agricultural Systems* 172: 47–59. https://doi.org/10.1016/j.agsy.2018.01.022

Reardon, T., D.Tschirley, L.S.O.Liverpool-Tasie, T.Awokuse, J.Fanzo, B.Minten, R.Vos, et al. 2021. "The Processed Food Revolution in African Food Systems and the Double Burden of Malnutrition." Global Food Security 28, 100466. https://doi.org/10.1016/j.gfs.2020.100466

Resnick, D., S.Haggblade, S.Babu, S.L.Hendriks, and D.Mather. 2018. "The Kaleidoscope Model of Policy Change: Applications to Food Security Policy in Zambia." *World Development* 109 (9): 101–120.

Resnick, D., B.Sivasubramanian, I.C.Idiong, M.A.Ojo, and L.Tanko. 2019. "The Enabling Environment for Informal Food Traders in Nigeria's Secondary Cities." *Urban Forum* 30: 385–405. https://doi.org/10.1007/s12132-019-09371-7

Sabatier, P.A. 1988. "An Advocacy Coalition Framework of Policy Change and the Role of Policy-Oriented Learning Therein." *Policy Sciences* 21 (2): 129–168.

Sabatier, P.A., and C.M.Weible. 2007. *The Advocacy Coalition Framework, Innovations and Clarifications. Theories of the Policy Process, 2nd Edition.* New York: Routledge.

Scott, J. 2000. "Rational Choice Theory." In *Understanding Contemporary Society: Theories of the Present*, eds. G. Browning, A. Halcli, and F. Webster, 126–138. Thousand Oaks, CA: Sage.

Schlager, E. 1995. "Policy Making and Collective Action: Defining Coalitions within the Advocacy Coalition Framework." *Policy Sciences* 28 (3): 243–270.

Shah, A.M., J.R.Bettman, P.A. Keller, J.A.Edell Britton, and P.A. Ubel. 2013. "The Effect of Sin Taxes and Evaluative Labels on Demand for Unhealthy Products." Paper presented at the Theory+Practice in Marketing Conference, London Business School, London, UK.

Shanahan, E., M. Jones, and M.McBeth. 2011. "Policy Narratives and Policy Processes." *Policy Studies Journal* 39 (3): 535–561.

Sharma, L.L., S.P.Teret, and K.D.Brownell. 2010. "The Food Industry and Self-Regulation: Standards to Promote Success and to Avoid Public Health Failures." *American Journal of Public Health* 100 (2): 240–246.

Shim, J-S., S-Y.Shim, H-J.Cha, J.Kim, and H.C.Kim. 2021. "Socioeconomic Characteristics and Trends in the Consumption of Ultra-Processed Foods in Korea from 2010 to 2018." *Nutrients* 13 (4): 1120. https://doi.org/10.3390/nu13041120

Siga. 2022. "Siga, A Scientific Approach to Eat Real and Live Better." Accessed October 12, 2022. www.siga.care

Simon, H.A. 1955. "A Behavioral Model of Rational Choice." *The Quarterly Journal of Economics* 69 (1): 99–118.

Srour, B., L.K.Fezeu, E.Kesse-Guyot, B.Allès, C.Méjean, R.M.Andrianasolo, and M.Touvier. 2019. "Ultra-processed Food Intake and Risk of Cardiovascular Disease: Prospective Cohort Study (NutriNet-Santé)." *The BMJ* 365: l1451. https://doi.org/10.1136/bmj.l1451

Sunstein, C.R., and R.H.Thaler. 2003. "Libertarian Paternalism is Not an Oxymoron." *The University of Chicago Law Review* 70 (4): 1159–1202. https://doi.org/10.2307/1600573

Swinnen, J.F.M. 2010a. "Political Economy of Agricultural Distortions: Literature to Date." In *The Political Economy of Agricultural Price Distortions*, ed. K. Anderson, 81–104. Cambridge, UK: Cambridge University Press.

Swinnen, J.F.M. 2010b. "The Political Economy of Agricultural and Food Policies: Recent Contributions, New Insights, and Areas for Further Research." *Applied Economic Perspectives and Policy* 32 (1): 33–58. https://doi.org/10.1093/aepp/ppp012.

Taillie L.S., E.Busey, F.M.Stoltze, and F.R.Carpentier. 2019. "Governmental Policies to Reduce Unhealthy Food Marketing to Children." *Nutrition Reviews* 77 (11): 787–816. https://doi.org/10.1093/nutrit/nuz021

Thow, A.M., S.M.Downs, C.Mayes, H.Trevena, T.Waqanivalu, and J.Cawley. 2018. "Fiscal Policy to Improve Diets and Prevent Noncommunicable Diseases: From Recommendations to Action." *Bulletin of the World Health Organization* 96 (3): 201–210.

Turner, C., A. Aggarwal, H. Walls, A. Herforth, A. Drewnowski, J. Coates, and S. Kadiyala. 2018. "Concepts and Critical Perspectives for Food Environment

Research: A Global Framework with Implications for Action in Low- and Middle-Income Countries." *Global Food Security* 18: 93–101.

UN-DESA (United Nations, Department of Economic and Social Affairs). 2018. *World Urbanization Prospects: The 2018 Revision.* New York: UN-DESA.

UN-DESA. 2019. *World Population Prospects: The 2019 Revision.* New York: UN-DESA.

Van Dijk, T.A. 1998. *Ideology: A Multidisciplinary Approach.* London and Thousand Oaks, CA: Sage.

Van Dijk, T.A. 2004. "From Text Grammar to Critical Discourse Analysis: A Brief Academic Autobiography." Version 2.0. Unpublished, Pompeu Fabra University, Barcelona, Spain.

Vermeulen, S.J., T.Park, C.K.Khoury, and C.Béné. 2020. "Changing Diets and the Transformation of the Global Food System." *Annals of the New York Academy of Sciences* 1478 (1): 3–17.

Wansink, B., J.E.Painter, and Y.K.Lee. 2006. "The Office Candy Dish: Proximity's Influence on Estimated and Actual Consumption." *International Journal of Obesity* 30: 871–875.

Weible, C.M. 2007. "An Advocacy Coalition Framework Approach to Stakeholder Analysis: Understanding the Political Context of California Marine Protected Area Policy." *Journal of Public Administration Research and Theory* 17 (1): 95–117.

Weible, C.M., P.Sabatier, and K.McQueen. 2009. "Themes and Variations: Taking Stock of the Advocacy Coalition Framework." *Policy Studies Journal* 37 (1): 121–140.

Weible, C.M., and P.A.Sabatier. 2017. *Theories of the Policy Process.* Boulder, CO: Westview Press.

WHO (World Health Organization). 2019. "Obesity and Overweight." *WHO News*, June 9. https://www.who.int/news-room/fact-sheets/detail/obesity-and-overweight

WHO. 2022. "Tobacco." *WHO News*, May 24. https://www.who.int/news-room/fact-sheets/detail/tobacco/.

Wright, A., K.E.Smith, and M. Hellowell. 2017. "Policy Lessons from Health Taxes: A Systematic Review of Empirical Studies." *BMC Public Health* 17: 583. https://doi.org/10.1186/s12889-017-4497-z

Yanow, D. 2000. *Conducting Interpretive Policy Analysis.* New Delhi: SAGE Publications Limited.

8

Asymmetric Power in Global Food System Advocacy

Jody Harris

8.1 Contrasting Food Policy Objectives

Food systems are different things to different people. For farmers and traders of food, and those working to understand jobs and economies, food systems might focus on their provision of livelihoods to billions of people globally (Townsend et al. 2017). For governments and states, food systems might focus on preserving contented electorates and avoiding unrest through maintaining food security (Hossain and Scott-Villiers 2017). For environmentalists, conservationists, and those living in marginal areas, food systems might focus on their interactions with global climate and local ecosystems (Crippa et al. 2021). Or for nutritionists, health professionals, and eaters around the world, food systems might focus on their delivery of healthy and acceptable diets that everyone can access (FAO et al. 2020). Food system policy therefore has multiple legitimate aims, and there have been attempts to understand these as intersecting issues with technical trade-offs and synergies (Willett et al. 2019). Politically however, different policy actors hold different values, beliefs and interests around these different food system outcomes, and will prioritize among them and work toward them differently (Béné et al. 2019; see also Chapter 2 of this volume). This chapter documents what happened when a relatively new set of aims—around reducing malnutrition—was introduced into a relatively stable food policy sub-system—focusing on grain production for rural livelihoods and food security—in Zambia. The chapter draws on studies emerging from a project undertaken between 2011 and 2016 in Zambia, but the findings—on advocacy coalitions, contested framings, and power—are applicable to multiple intersecting food system issues in a range of low- and middle-income country contexts.

8.2 Combining Theories of Public Policy

Food policy coalitions are often invoked but rarely studied. The current research set out to understand the different agendas inherent in Zambian food policy

Jody Harris, *Asymmetric Power in Global Food System Advocacy*. In: *The Political Economy of Food System Transformation*. Edited by: Danielle Resnick and Johan Swinnen, Oxford University Press. © Jody Harris (2023).
DOI: 10.1093/oso/9780198882121.003.0008

processes, and as such takes a broad view of the context in which food system policies are made in terms of scales and sectors involved. The study was framed by policy process frameworks from the field of global health (Table 8.1), used to design the methodology and tools and focus the data collection. The case-study used document review of policies and strategies in the Zambian food system; mapping of policy actor networks through the NetMap method (Schiffer 2007; Schiffer and Hauck 2010); 70 key-informant interviews with 61 different respondents across different levels (international, national, and local) iteratively with abductive analytical coding over time; and participation in and observation of food and nutrition policy processes globally and in Zambia over the five years of the study.

In its empirical analysis, the study then attempted to take on the challenge set by Keeley and Scoones (1999) and Cairney (2012), to combine different approaches and theories in policy process research in order to gain insights from different

Table 8.1 Study design framework

Domain	Description	Sub-domains
Actor power	Strength of individuals and organizations concerned with issue	• Policy community cohesion • Leadership/political entrepreneurship/champions • Guiding institutions, esp. those with coordinating mandates • Civil society mobilization
Ideas	Ways in which those involved with issue understand and portray it	• Internal frame: degree to which policy community agrees on definition of issue, causes and solutions • External frame: Public portrayals of issue by policy community
Political contexts	Environments in which actors operate	• Policy windows / focusing events / political transitions • Governance structures • Resource provision
Issue characteristics	Features of the problem	• Credible indicators • Severity of problem • Effective interventions—existence of effective solutions, easy to explain, etc. • Competing [health] priorities

Sources: Shiffman (2007); Shiffman and Smith (2007).

perspectives, to see what each angle can add to our understanding. This study uses ideas from several policy science approaches, including the concept of a policy cycle in order to understand the different stages in the policy process (Lasswell 1971), though explicitly recognizing that these stages are neither linear nor necessarily always distinguishable from each other; the notion of ideas as input to policy arising from different levels (Kettell and Cairney 2010), including how those ideas are framed by different policy stakeholders and moved over space and time (Marsh and Sharman 2009); the importance of understanding actors working across the policy process and how they coalesce around policy issues (Sabatier and Weible 2016); and the role of power in policy processes (Gaventa 2003).

8.2.1 Framing Narratives: Dominant Ideas

This research used the concept of discourse in the analysis of international nutrition as a branch of international development, and of the historical progression of international nutrition ideas. The work of Foucault (Foucault 1966; Foucault 1975) defines discourse as social construction through language, that allows for the production of knowledge and truth through constructed framings of the world (Hewitt 2009). The production of discourses and normative framings can structure the power to control what is said and how issues are understood, and the study of discourses can therefore reveal power relations in society in order to better understand why history progresses as it does (Considine 2005). The concept of discourse as underlying social action can equally be applied to the field of development and the process of policymaking (Mosse 2011).

8.2.2 Policy Transfer: Setting the Agenda

Every country has policy problems, issues that demand amelioration for a population. While these problems are in some sense unique in terms of the specific history and actors that gave rise to them in a certain context, broad categories of issues and concerns are common across continents (Rose 1991). Policy scholars noticing the tendency to draw policy ideas from other places and times have examined it in various ways: As "lesson drawing" (Rose 1991; Rose 1993); as "policy diffusion" (Basu et al. 2013; Graham et al. 2013); and as "policy transfer" (Dolowitz and Marsh 1996; Dolowitz and Marsh 2000). The policy transfer literature drawn on in this study (Dolowitz and Marsh 1996; Dolowitz and Marsh 2000) is defined by Stone (2004, p. 547) as *"the contested politics of who gets what policy"*—and beyond this, the underlying transfer of ideas, norms, behaviors, and discourses— and is therefore concerned with actors, their agency, and the reasons for their actions.

8.2.3 Advocacy Coalitions: Defining the Alternatives

There are different ways to assess division among actors over policy issues, but a widely used policy science theory that has endured for its holistic vision of the policy process is the Advocacy Coalition Framework (ACF) (Sabatier and Jenkins-Smith 1993). The ACF explicitly uses the concept of policy sub-systems for specific issues, as the grouping of experts and interested parties that have a bearing on policy for a specific issue. The method charts the belief systems, resources, and strategies of actors within the sub-system in order to identify advocacy coalitions, or actor groupings with similar beliefs and policy positions which are likely to advocate in similar directions on policy issues. In advocacy coalitions, it is ideology rather than interests that inspire coalition formation and continuation, and belief systems are a key factor. The sharing of principled values has been identified as a defining feature of transnational advocacy networks in international development, (Keck and Sikkink 1998), such as the international nutrition community (Harris 2019b), thus the concept of beliefs is likely to be a factor particularly in the formation of national coalitions that stem from these international groups.

8.2.4 Theories of Power: Spaces, Forms, and Levels

Finally, policy in the critical tradition is seen through the lens of power, and in particular who has the power to define agendas through power over the ideas and knowledge used in policy systems (Brock et al. 2001). Power is conceived in different ways in policy studies from different fields, conceptualized as a negative and limiting force of "power over" or a positive and enabling force as "power to"; as held by distinct actors (elitism) or as diffuse in different forms across networks (pluralism); as relations based on limiting valid forms of knowledge and language or as capital to be wielded in different fields; or as economic clout or as claim to moral authority (Gaventa 2003; Gaventa 2006; Islam 2009; Cairney 2012; Shiffman 2014; Shiffman 2015). A particularly practical conceptualization of power in the policy process used in this research, which acknowledges a range of different definitions of power while maintaining analytical utility, is the "power cube."[1] This three-dimensional representation acknowledges these different forms that power might take, and adds attention to the different levels at which power dynamics can occur, as well as different spaces in which it might manifest (Lukes 1974; Gaventa 2006).

This chapter calls for explicit analysis of actors, ideas, and power in food policy research and action, and illustrates how existing theories and frameworks can be used.

---

[1] The power cube approach: https://www.powercube.net/

8.3 Evolving Ideas in the International Nutrition Space

Much policy transfer research has been undertaken on more or less voluntary and informed transfer between "developed" countries, particularly between the US and UK and among EU states, and this makes up the majority of policy transfer literature. But globalization has changed the nature of policy making for "developing" countries also, and these countries have many features of political economy and social context different from their Northern cousins. A particular point of difference for low- and middle-income countries is their dependence on international aid for a proportion of national budgets and implementation of specific programs (Fraser 2007). The implication for the policy transfer literature is that donor organizations are key players in policy transfer in aid-dependent countries, with influence over which ideas make it into policy, adding a particular twist that is not present in richer countries (Common 1999; Minogue 2004; Bangura and Larbi 2006).

In modern times, nutrition is an arm of international development that is gaining in visibility and attracting increasing funding, and Zambia is an aid-dependent country receiving large amounts of technical and financial assistance, including in food and nutrition policy. Overwhelmingly in this research, national respondents identified the international community as creating the original awareness, attention, and priority for nutrition policy and action in recent decades. It is therefore necessary to first understand the role of the international community in bringing different interpretations of nutrition to Zambian nutrition policy and practice over time, in order to then understand how Zambian nutrition policy has changed with changing international agendas.

8.3.1 Framing Food Systems

Policy narratives promoting specific ideas are a way that different groups understand, hold, and advance their policy priorities (Berman 2001; Finnemore and Sikkink 2001; Shiffman 2007), with shared beliefs leading groups to a common aim; shared ways of understanding an issue leading to the establishment of certain types of knowledge; and shared ideologies leading to dominant norms or standards of behavior (Cairney 2012). Food policy is no exception, with broad global narratives evolving over time as a result of technical, social, and political change. This has been illustrated in learning from a history of agriculture and nutrition Programing at emblematic international development institutes such as the World Bank: changes in policy focus have been documented from Green Revolution policies in the 1950s and 60s, to agricultural income generation and staple grain production of smallholder farmers in the 1970s, to attempts at multisectoral nutrition planning across agriculture and health sectors in the 1980s, to a focus on direct nutrition interventions separate to agricultural investments almost singularly focused on productivity enhancement and market-led growth in the 1990s, and to policies to address increased globalization and volatility since the 2000s (Herforth and Hoberg 2014). Big-picture policy trends such as these—similar among other dominant global food, agriculture and development institutions—have formed the backdrop to national food policy changes, with global ideas and their narratives as a source of stability and continuity, and instability and change, in national policy processes (Berman 2001; Finnemore and Sikkink 2001).

The issues of agriculture and nutrition, while always inseparable in practice, became disconnected in global discourse and policy over the late 20th century as experts and institutions grew specialist and siloed. This didn't go unnoticed however, and in 2006 the World Bank published a comprehensive report on why and how nutrition should be brought to the fore of rural development after many years in the backwaters (World Bank 2006), citing the alarming scope of the malnutrition problem, the failure of markets to address the issue, and strong development returns on investment as key reasons to reposition nutrition as central to development. This drove a resurgence of interest in reconnecting the issues of agriculture and nutrition through international development practice and funding. In recent years the need for input from multiple sectors to achieve one food system aim—better nutrition—has been re-branded "nutrition-sensitive" action, meaning that policy and programs in several sectors need to be sensitive to nutrition considerations if malnutrition rates are to be reduced. In particular, nutrition-sensitive action in the food and agriculture sector would entail attention to producing and distributing affordable and nutrient-dense diets, not just quantity of grain or increased farmer incomes (Ruel et al. 2013).

In the wake of the 2006 World Bank report on re-linking agriculture and nutrition, the year 2008 is acknowledged as something of a watershed moment for international nutrition. Researchers, many of whom had been working on nutrition issues over long and illustrious careers, recognized that a critical mass of understanding and experience had been accumulated and now needed to be marshaled if the community was to move forward in a coherent manner, with the aim of reducing the burden of malnutrition in some of the world's poorest countries. The resulting publications, the 2008 *Lancet* series on maternal and child undernutrition (Black et al. 2008; Bryce et al. 2008; Morris et al. 2008), presented a summary of current scientific knowledge on the causes and consequences of, and interventions for, undernutrition, with a clear preference for focusing on stunting (chronic malnutrition) as an indicator of multiple development issues. Later in the same year, the Copenhagen Consensus group published its second listing of prioritized development investments based on cost-benefit analyses; five malnutrition interventions featured in the top 10 of 30 efficacious development actions, giving further impetus to the field (Copenhagen Consensus Center 2008). Coming in the same year as the global financial and food price crises and a focus on food security at the 2008 G8 meeting, the role of these normative publications in advocacy efforts by academics and practitioners helped the issue of nutrition to ride the wave of political interest in food security more broadly, to secure a place near the top of food policy agendas by the end of the first decade of the 2000s.

8.3.2 International Actors

These ideas and framings are created and perpetuated by a broad international nutrition community, described as an "international nutrition system" (Morris et al. 2008), a loose grouping of actors and organizations interlinked financially, intellectually, and personally, working broadly to reduce malnutrition globally. The international nutrition system is made up of people affiliated with agencies and programs of the UN; donor organizations such as development banks, bilateral aid agencies, and charitable foundations; international non-governmental organizations (NGOs); major universities and research centers; academic journals and the non-specialist media; and multinational commercial food and nutrition companies.

The United Nations (UN) is broadly tasked with coordinating action on issues of global concern, and nutrition is one such issue with a long history of UN action (Mokoro 2015). In 1977, recognizing the need for specific nutrition action, the UN Standing Committee on Nutrition (UNSCN) was established as the focal point for nutrition policy through the UN system, but without an explicit country coordination mandate; at country level four separate UN agencies (FAO, WHO, UNICEF, and WFP) are tasked with different aspects of nutrition in practice.[2] In 2008, as the international development world more broadly was waking up to nutrition, these agencies established the Renewed Efforts Against Child Hunger and Undernutrition (REACH) mechanism to facilitate joint UN support in countries, and in early 2010 a framework was agreed by broader development partners for the creation of the Scaling Up Nutrition (SUN) movement, aiming to coordinate international nutrition action, by the UN and other development agencies, under country-led agreements. Later in 2010 the UN and the US and Irish governments launched the initiative *1,000 Days—Feed a Child, Feed the Future* with a call to focus on the first 1000 days of life for intervention, and stunting as a primary outcome (Thurow 2016). By the end of 2010, the SUN framework had been turned into a Road Map, the road map had been linked to resources under the 1000 Days Partnership of donors, and the SUN Movement had its first four country members: Ethiopia, Guatemala, Peru, and Zambia.

---

[2] SCN crisis, see: http://www.wphna.org/htdocs/2011_jan_hp4_scn_crisis.htm

8.4 Bringing the Global to the Local

8.4.1 Food Policy in Zambia: Out with the Old…?

Zambia has a long history with food system policy, though not by that name (Figure 8.1). The focus of agricultural policy has for decades been food security, synonymous since colonial times with maize security. In Zambia, food is maize: Maize is the major food security crop, with a large majority of households reporting growing maize each year, including richer urban households who often have a piece of land cultivated in a rural area (Kakeya et al. 2006). A majority of agricultural budgets go to two key food security programs: the Farmer Input Support Program (FISP) and the Food Reserve Agency (FRA). The FRA was set up in 1972 and later amended in 1996 and 2005, to buy maize from farmers at guaranteed prices and form a strategic grain reserve to modulate national grain prices (Chapoto et al. 2015). Building on the idea of maize control boards introduced in colonial times to limit maize production to approved farmers, and continued after independence to provide isolated rural areas with access to a market and the cash economy (Sitko 2008), the FRA is effectively a government output subsidy. The FISP program was introduced as the Fertilizer Support Program (FSP) in 2002 to distribute inorganic fertilizers to farmer groups, and later renamed FISP when other inputs such as hybrid maize seed were included in the distribution. FISP is an input subsidy aimed at improving the asset base of small farmers. These two programs—FRA and FISP—together accounted for upward of 80 percent of the national agriculture budget over the years of this study (Kuteya et al. 2016); and the agriculture budget hovers around 10 percent of the total government budget in Zambia.

Zambian agriculture policies have therefore focused on reducing food insecurity to tackle hunger, but the major FISP and FRA programs do not explicitly tackle malnutrition. Food and health have always been preoccupations of any population, but the framing of nutrition as a discipline or a field of action is very much newer. The first Zambian National Agriculture Policy (NAP), adopted in 2004, mentioned human nutrition three times, in relation to activities of food processing, plant breeding for improved food quality, and fish production; the policy did not mention diets at all, which is arguably the major contribution of the agriculture sector to nutrition.

Separately, nutrition programs have existed in Zambia for decades, largely within the health sector. Written national nutrition policy underpinning programs, however, has only emerged through the early part of the 21st century. Respondents identified the first International Conference on Nutrition (ICN1) hosted by the UN in 1992 as the original encouragement for individual countries, including Zambia, to have a nutrition policy; a large technical and funding push from UNICEF in-country for nutrition subsequent to that; the USAID-funded

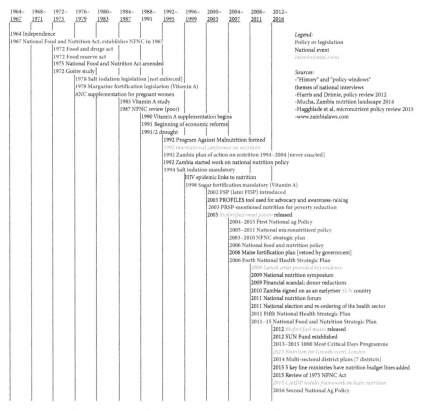

Figure 8.1 Timeline of Zambian food and nutrition policy since independence.
Source: Author's compilation.

Basic Support for Institutionalizing Child Survival (BASICS) project integrating nutrition into national child survival projects in the early 2000s; and international support for supplementation campaigns for decades as vital in keeping aspects of nutrition on the Zambian agenda and in programs. After several decades of program implementation, the National Food and Nutrition Commission's (NFNC) very first five-year Strategic Plan 2005–10 (NFNC 2011) aimed to bring nutrition to the foreground with a mandate for training, monitoring, and research. The 2006 National Food and Nutrition Policy (NFNP) was followed in 2011 by the National Food and Nutrition Strategic Plan (NFNSP) and in 2013 by the 1000 Most Critical Days Program (MCDP), each operationalizing the last. Notably, all of these interventions were within the health sector, where nutrition policy is created and nutrition programs are implemented. More recently, every respondent that mentioned increasing priority of nutrition through international routes attributed it at least in part to the SUN movement.

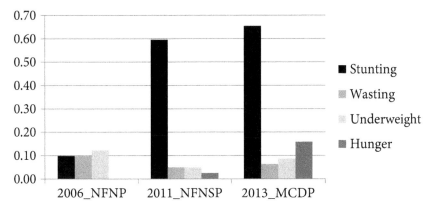

Figure 8.2 Changing national nutrition policy focus over time.

Notes: Mentions of four major nutrition outcome measures in Zambian nutrition policy over time. Calculation: Word count divided by number of pages.
Source: Harris (2019a).

Between 2006 and 2013 the focus of nutrition policy and programs in Zambia crystalized on current narratives of child stunting as the major problem to be addressed. Content analysis of the major nutrition policy and program documents in Zambia (Figure 8.2) shows a marked change in major nutrition focus between the 2006 policy and the 2011 strategic plan, maintained in the 2013 program document, with stunting suddenly outstripping other nutrition issues. Stunting is framed as a catch-all development indicator, an outcome of multiple sectors not being sensitive to the way their work can impact nutrition issues; the agriculture sector is particularly implicated in policy, as a provider of national diets.

8.4.2 Renewed Actor Coalitions in Old Policy Spaces

The idea of stunting reduction was by 2011 dominant within written nutrition policy in the health sector in Zambia, but the multi-sectoral framing of nutrition, brought by the international community as part of its renewed focus on nutrition, required the action of other sectors, and actors outside of the traditional network for nutrition. Dominant international narratives (such as the newer stunting discourse) do not operate in a vacuum at national level; rather they have to interact with myriad established and emerging ideas, interests, preferences, philosophies and beliefs within political, policy, technical, and lay communities in the national political and policy arena. Different coalitions of actors in the food system policy space in Zambia advocate for slightly different food policy outcomes through different narratives reflecting their beliefs on food system priorities.

In all, the network shown in Figure 8.3 makes up the "policy sub-system" for nutrition (Sabatier and Jenkins-Smith 1993). The issue of nutrition in Zambia struggles to find an institutional home, batted about between agriculture (which often does not see its role extending to what people eat), and health (predominantly dealing with the clinical consequences of poor nutrition). Historically, the dominant framing of nutrition in Zambia has been around food security and hunger, and a major coalition within the overall food policy sub-system is an influential group promoting maize production and calorie availability as a core policy response to food insecurity and hunger in Zambia. This *food security coalition* has existed in Zambia for many decades, with FRA and FISP as its primary policies to achieve food security through maize production. Recently however, there has been a change in framing of the complex causes and consequences of malnutrition in parts of the Zambian food policy sub-system, and change is evident in the way people speak about how nutrition was tackled "before" versus "now." Among a second coalition of actors in the food policy sub-system, this change relates to the framing of stunting as the major issue to address, and action by multiple sectors, and particularly the food and agriculture sector, as the route to addressing

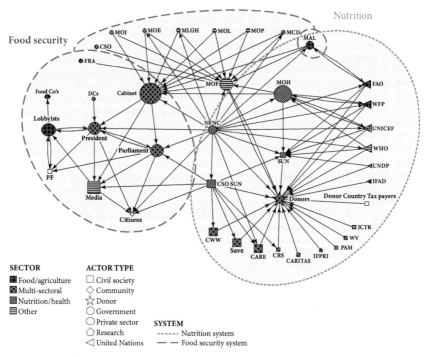

Figure 8.3 Advocacy coalitions in Zambia's food policy subsystem.

Source: Harris (2019a).

it. This *nutrition coalition* is relatively new to the Zambian nutrition policy process. The position of each of these major coalitions—the food security coalition and the nutrition coalition—is overlaid on the policy sub-system figure, based on respondents' own responses and their interpretations of different actors.

With its focus on multi-sectoral action to reduce stunting, the recent nutrition policy narrative impinges directly on an existing food security narrative as it attempts to alter agriculture policy away from maize reliance. The food policy sub-system in Zambia is therefore split between a largely internationally generated coalition promoting action on child stunting, and a largely national coalition focused on food security and hunger, with implications for both sides on progressing a coherent policy agenda (Harris 2019a).

8.4.3 Food Policy in Zambia: In with the New...?

At the same time as the nutrition focus was changing within the nutrition community, economists within Zambia were critiquing the FISP and FRA as inefficient and prone to corruption, even within the limited food security aims of the policies. Assessments of FISP and FRA subsidies have found that while distribution of fertilizer raises maize yields, poor targeting means that it is generally wealthier households and input dealers who gain most benefit (Mason et al. 2013), and centralized government distribution raises program costs so much that cost-effectiveness is negated while potentially more efficient private sector purchases are crowded out (Baltzer and Hansen 2011; Chapoto et al. 2015; Kuteya et al. 2016). There have also been suggestions that the FISP in particular is used as a tool of political patronage to financially reward politically loyal areas of Zambia—though it has not been found to change actual voting patterns in Zambia (Mason et al. 2017).

Because of these negative findings, and also fundamental ideological disagreement with the concept of agricultural subsidies, some financial donors started conditioning their loans on restructuring or removal of these programs. In 2016, Zambia started negotiations with the IMF for a US$1.2 billion loan for instance, which came with a condition on restructuring of FISP and FRA.[3] These changes created a window of opportunity for nutrition advocates to also critique those programs' singular focus on cereal production, and push for a more nutrition-sensitive sector. Zambia's nutrition policy and strategy, although created within the health sector, lays out roles for sectors other than health—and particularly the agriculture sector—in contributing to malnutrition reduction. Thus, the focus on malnutrition reduction in Zambia goes hand-in-hand with a narrative on the need for

---

[3] Source: Bloomberg, accessed August 2016: http://www.bloomberg.com/news/articles/2016-08-18/zambia-imf-reached-broad-consensus-on-imf-package-lungu-says

sectors outside of health to be sensitive to the requirements of nutrition policy, and for multi-sectoral action.

The second Zambian NAP, adopted in 2016, incorporated nutrition more fully into its mandate, including in its over-arching vision, mentioning nutrition 12 times (though still not diets), and dedicating one of its 12 objectives to improving nutrition through the food and agriculture sector. Written agriculture policy therefore started to incorporate nutrition considerations more explicitly. Related to these multiple streams of advocacy, a pilot of an electronic voucher payment system for FISP undertaken in 13 districts in the 2015/16 agricultural season enabled recipients to choose among a wider range of seed and fertilizer options available at local distributors and agro-dealers[4], with around 15 percent of households redeeming the voucher for agricultural inputs other than maize and fertilizer in this first year (Kuteya et al. 2016). Despite a lack of formal impact assessment of the pilot project, successful rollout led to expansion to 39 additional districts in 2016/17. This partial policy reform (Van de Walle 2001) has not revolutionized the FISP, but for now may meet the requirements of the government for a continued patronage platform, some donors for a move toward a more liberalized agriculture sector, and nutrition advocates for a more nutrition-sensitive agricultural policy.

8.4.4 Policy Transfer in Zambia

Driving these "horizontal" multisectoral requirements for other ministries to become involved in nutrition, the changes to nutrition agendas and narratives at an international level created a "vertical" channel for change. Focused on a renewed narrative of stunting reduction as a driver of national productivity and growth, international investments in nutrition shifted; national conversations about nutrition followed suit; and in Zambia, national nutrition advocacy was tailored to the new global post-Millennium Development Goals (MDG) landscape. This research finds that it was this vertical pressure to incorporate nutrition more squarely into national food and agriculture policy discourse, deriving from changes in the global discourse, that drove change in actors and their actions in Zambia's food system, and started to change Zambia's food policy. This work has identified four major mechanisms through which this happened, explained through the theories of advocacy coalitions creating policy transfer (taking advantage of windows of opportunity) mediated by unequal power (Figure 8.4).

---

[4] Musika: http://www.musika.org.zm/article/84-fisp-electronic-voucher-program-to-promote-diversification

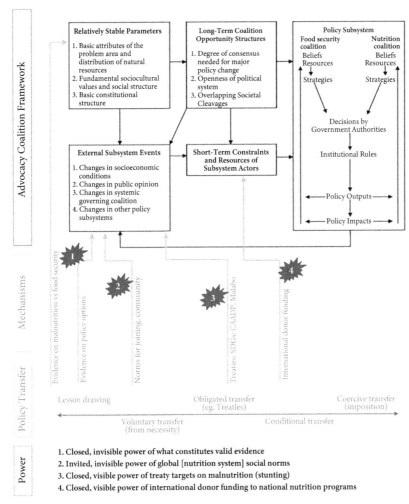

Figure 8.4 Mechanisms and power of policy transfer through advocacy coalitions.

Source: Author's own construction, drawing on (Marsh and Sharman 2009; Gaventa and Martorano 2016; Sabatier and Weible 2016).

Firstly, actors in Zambia's food policy process drew on evidence, created or funded internationally and undertaken both in Zambia and elsewhere. This evidence used global indicators as simple as stunting rates to show the scale of the problem in Zambia through national surveys (Central Statistical Office 2009; Central Statistical Office et al. 2014), and concerted advocacy by global NGOs and SUN partners changed policy actor understanding of the basic attributes of the issue. At the same time, global evidence on the efficacy of multi-sectoral action across the health and agriculture sector, some created in Zambia, was mobilized to show what could be done to address the issue of malnutrition, calling on the food and agriculture sector in particular to include a focus on diverse diets, and move away from maize dominance and the primacy of the FISP. The focus on evidence fed into lesson-drawing for both the food security and nutrition coalitions on how policy could change to become sensitive to nutrition.

Secondly, nutrition's ascendance to an important issue in global development policy and the creation of influential bodies such as SUN, has further strengthened the "pull" for Zambian nutrition actors to align themselves with these global groups. Access to technical assistance, training opportunities, and invitations to participate in global meetings necessitates adherence to global norms shared broadly by the nutrition community, in terms of the language, ethics, and forms of knowledge that are valued (Harris 2019b). This adherence creates a form of voluntary transfer of policy ideas into the national policy arena.

Thirdly, Zambia is a signatory to global and regional food and agriculture covenants that have increasingly oriented toward nutrition, and there is normative international pressure for the agricultural sector to become more sensitive to nutrition. Notable among these is the Comprehensive Africa Agriculture Development Program (CAADP), the continent's over-arching policy since 2003 on economic growth and food security through the agriculture sector, which has a specific focus on reducing hunger and malnutrition. This was reaffirmed in 2014 with the Malabo Declaration which committed participating African countries to bringing down stunting to 10 percent and underweight to 5 percent by 2025; and the African Regional Nutritional Strategy (ARNS) which provides a framework within which to advocate to Africa's leaders on the importance of nutrition for national development. The UN Food and Agriculture Organization (FAO) has since 2011 been running a global task force to integrate nutrition into the CAADP and National Agriculture Investment Plans, adding impetus. Zambia's signing of each of these agreements, and its membership of the FAO, create an obligated policy transfer toward incorporating nutrition goals and targets into food and agriculture policy.

Lastly, while written policies may reflect aspiration, without resources they cannot be implemented. Most resources for agriculture policy in Zambia are allocated through the FISP; and most of the resources for nutrition are allocated through the SUN Fund. This creates an incentive for nutrition actors to align with global discourse, largely on multi-sectoral action through food and agriculture, in order to be able to implement any programs. It also provides an incentive to parts of the agricultural sector, as SUN donors fund agriculture ministries as well in the areas of nutrition-sensitive action. The SUN Fund in particular has a set of actions it is willing to fund, making funding conditional on transferring certain policy ideas into action. While the National Food and Nutrition Commission and its parent Ministry of Health are the formal creators of nutrition policy in Zambia, and the Ministry of Agriculture holds the agricultural mandate, there is therefore an acknowledged role of the international community in shaping nutrition, food, and agriculture policy through these multiple mechanisms.

8.4.5 Power in the Zambian Food Policy Process

Each of these mechanisms of policy transfer (Figure 8.4) is associated with power, and the current research illustrates four key power issues across the different levels, spaces, and forms of power identified in the Power Cube (Gaventa 2006). First, the closed, invisible power of what constitutes valid evidence shaped the issues and options available to be discussed. At the global level, key was the international nutrition system within the field of international development, and within this the epistemic communities focused on multi-sectoral approaches to stunting. An epistemic community can be understood as "networks of professionals (possibly from different disciplines and backgrounds) with recognized-expertise and competence in a particular domain and an authoritative-claim to policy-relevant knowledge within that domain" (Haas 1992). These epistemic communities apply their specialized knowledge and interpretations in providing information to decision-makers, offering-input into policy decisions. Global epistemic communities bring their ideas and beliefs to national level, influencing different groups to share their framings (Keck and Sikkink 1998). Within the nutrition epistemic community, understanding of malnutrition's causes and solutions are seen in similar ways, and members of the community share broad beliefs about how the issue should be framed and therefore how it should be tackled, shaping the policy alternatives seen as valid through power that is not visible but is deducible through research such as this.

Second, the invited, invisible power of global social norms within the global nutrition community created incentives for national nutrition actors to align with global policy ideas for career advancement and acceptance. Connected to the invisible power to shape evidence seen as valid, normative power shapes the actions and even thoughts seen as acceptable within a community (Foucault 1975).

Third, the closed but visible power of treaty targets on malnutrition shaped the framework within which policy was able to be made, and the targets which it, on paper at least, had to engage with. Last, the closed yet visible power of international donor funding to national nutrition programs (and parts of agriculture programs concerned with nutrition) shaped in more concrete ways what could be done, and therefore had the power to shape written policy conditional on that funding.

Notably, this work could not identify any claimed spaces of power (whether through claiming a formal place in previously uninvited spaces or claiming voice through unruly means such as civil disobedience) in the food policy process in Zambia from 2011 to 2016, meaning that the voices and preferences of those not

represented by the most powerful groups (the international community and government) were not factored into policy. Conspicuous in their absence—at the local
or national level, or in claimed or invited spaces of power—are the malnourished-
themselves, or the communities from which they come, who do not seem to have
a clear voice or representative in Zambia's nutrition policy process, and therefore find themselves without power. Appealing to and explicitly including this
broad community constituency—whether framed as the electorate, citizens, or
the malnourished—and including their own understandings and ideas of what is
required to address nutrition issues in their communities, might present options
that those working in the food and nutrition policy space had not previously
considered.

8.5 Conclusion

The story of this research is about how one particular food system issue—
malnutrition—emerged in Zambia's national food policy space, drawing from
international actors and their agendas. Stunting and multi-sectoral action, the
dominant ideas in the international nutrition community throughout this study,
are increasingly evident over time in written nutrition policy within the health
sector in Zambia, largely displacing former framings of nutrition. Changes in the
policy agenda to favor stunting as an outcome and multi-sectorality as a process,
and subsequently in written policy formulation focusing on nutrition through
agriculture, can be shown to result from changes to the international community's
nutrition agenda, transferred to Zambian policy through the normative promotion
of a specific type of evidence and ways of understanding the issue of malnutrition, largely propagated through global norms, regional covenants, and targeted
funding. This agenda has started to impact policy in sectors outside of health,
in particular agricultural policy and the FISP program, with partial reform of
the FISP reflecting the non-dominant but significant power of the relatively new
nutrition coalition in the food policy sub-system.

There remain questions around the extent, implications, and legitimacy of this
international intervention into national policy space that are relevant beyond this
topic and this context. The intervention of international groups in national policy,
and their multiple roles and sources of power as shown above, raise the issue of
legitimacy, concerning the right of a group to be recognized (Habermas 1979)
and to be obeyed (Weber 1922). Legitimacy takes several forms conceptually,
including input legitimacy (fair political process); output legitimacy (performance
on an issue); and normative legitimacy (shaping of discourse to legitimize or
de-legitimize certain actions). In Zambia, a focus on output legitimacy and a
desire to reduce stunting and malnutrition has meant direct international intervention into shaping priorities in food system policy formulation: the promotion

of narratives in support of addressing stunting through multi-sectoral approaches, and the funding of nutrition programs while advocating for the removal of current food security policies. While these may be legitimate policy outputs to advocate, attention must also be paid to power in the process by which this is done (input legitimacy), to ensure that policy processes themselves are fair and equitable.

Questioning by what authority global networks exert their power is particularly pertinent at a time when many international coalitions are moving beyond traditional advocacy and guidance, and toward direct participation in national policy and institutional change (Collingwood and Logister 2005; Shiffman et al. 2016). This has been shown starkly in divisions around the 2021 UN Food Systems Summit, where countries were compelled to participate in Food Dialogues with questionable utility (Canfield et al. 2021), and where the dominance of hegemonic expertise over tacit knowledge and national priorities was sharply questioned through an equity lens (Nisbett et al. 2021). The case of Zambia's evolving food and nutrition policy provides a case-study illustrating the need to understand actors and their power in the process of policy transfer, and to reflect on the legitimacy of direct policy intervention—contrasted to facilitating the participation in policy processes of those most affected by food policy decisions, largely the marginalized and malnourished.

References

Baltzer, K.T., and H. Hansen. 2011. *Agricultural Input Subsidies in Sub-Saharan Africa.* Copenhagen, Denmark: Ministry of Foreign Affairs of Denmark.

Bangura, Y., and G. A. Larbi. 2006. "Introduction: Globlisation and Public Sector Reform." In *Public Sector Reform in Developing Countries*, eds. Y. Bangura and G.A. Larbi, Chapter 1. New York: Palgrave Macmillan.

Basu, S., D. Stuckler, M. Mckee, and G. Galea. 2013. "Nutritional Determinants of Worldwide Diabetes: An Econometric Study of Food Markets and Diabetes Prevalence in 173 Countries." *Public Health Nutrition* 16 (1): 179–186.

Béné, C., P. Oosterveer, L. Lamotte, I.D. Brouwer, S. De Haan, S.D. Prager, E.F. Talsma, and C.K. Khoury. 2019. "When Food Systems Meet Sustainability—Current Narratives and Implications for Actions." *World Development* 113: 116–130.

Berman, S. 2001. "Ideas, Norms, and Culture in Political Analysis." *Comparative Politics* 33 (2): 231–250.

Black, R.E., L.H. Allen, Z.A. Bhutta, L.E. Caulfield, M. De Onis, M. Ezzati, C. Mathers, J. Rivera., et al. 2008. "Maternal and Child Undernutrition: Global and Regional Exposures and Health Consequences." *The Lancet* 371 (9608): 243–260.

Brock, K., A. Cornwall, and J. Gaventa. 2001. "Power, Knowledge and Political Spaces in the Framing of Poverty Policy." Working Paper No. 143. Institute of Development Studies, Brighton, UK.

Bryce, J., D. Coitinho, I. Darnton-Hill, D. Pelletier, and P. Pinstrup Andersen. 2008. "Maternal and Child Undernutrition: Effective Action at National Level." *The Lancet* 371 (9611): 510–526.

Cairney, P. 2012. *Understanding Public Policy: Theories and Issues.* London, UK: Palgrave Macmillan.

Canfield, M.C., J, Duncan, and P. Claeys. 2021. "Reconfiguring Food Systems Governance: The UNFSS and the Battle over Authority and Legitimacy." *Development* 64: 181–191.

Central Statistical Office, Ministry of Health, Tropical Diseases Research Centre, University of Zambia & Macro International Inc. 2009. *Zambia Demographic and Health Survey 2007.* Calverton, MD: CSO and Macro International Inc.

Central Statistical Office, Ministry of Health, Tropical Diseases Research Centre, University of Zambia & Macro International Inc. 2014. *Zambia Demographic and Health Survey 2013–14.* Calverton, MD: CSO and Macro International Inc.

Chapoto, A., O. Zulu-Mbata, B.D. Hoffman, C. Kabaghe, N. Sitko, A. Kuteya, and B. Zulu. 2015. "The Politics of Maize in Zambia: Who Holds the Keys to Change the Status Quo?" IAPRI Working Papers. Michigan State University, Lusaka, Zambia.

Collingwood, V., and L. Logister. 2005. "State of the Art: Addressing the INGO 'Legitimacy Deficit.'" *Political Studies Review* 3 (2): 175–192.

Common, R. 1999. *Public Management and Policy Transfer in Southeast Asia.* Doctoral thesis, Department of Politics, The University of York.

Considine, M. 2005. *Making Public Policy: Institutions, Actors, Strategies.* Cambridge, UK: Polity Press.

Copenhagen Consensus Center. 2008. *Copenhagen Consensus 2008: Results.* Copenhagen, Denmark: Copenhagen Consensus Center.

Crippa, M., E. Solazzo, D. Guizzardi, F. Monforti-Ferrario, F. Tubiello, and A. Leip. 2021. "Food Systems Are Responsible for a Third of Global Anthropogenic GHG Emissions." *Nature Food* 2: 198–209.

Dolowitz, D., and D. Marsh. 1996. "Who Learns What from Whom: A Review of the Policy Transfer Literature." *Political Studies*, 44 (2): 343–357.

Dolowitz, D.P., and D. Marsh. 2000. "Learning from Abroad: The Role of Policy Transfer in Contemporary Policy-Making." *Governance* 13 (1): 5–23.

FAO (Food and Agriculture Organization of the United Nations), IFAD (International Fund for Agricultural Development), UNICEF, WFP (World Food Program), and WHO (World Health Organization). 2020. *The State of Food Security and Nutrition in the World 2020: Transforming Food Systems for Affordable Healthy Diets.* Rome: FAO.

Finnemore, M., and K. Sikkink. 2001. "Taking Stock: The Constructivist Research Program in International Relations and Comparative Politics." *Annual Review of Political Science* 4 (1): 391–416.

Foucault, M. 1966. *Les Mots et Les Choses—Une Archéologie des Sciences Humaines.* Translated as *The Order of Things: An Archaeology of the Human Sciences, 1970.* Paris: Gallimard.

Foucault, M. 1975. *Surveiller et Punir.* Translated as *Discipline and Punish: The Birth of a Prison, 1977.* Paris: Gallimard.

Fraser, A. 2007. "Zambia: Back to the Future?" Paper presented at the 2007 Annual Meeting of the American Political Science Association, Chicago, IL, USA, August 30–September 2.

Gaventa, J. 2003. *Power after Lukes: An Overview of Theories of Power since Lukes and Their Application to Development.* Brighton, UK: Institute of Development Studies.

Gaventa, J. 2006. "Finding the Spaces for Change: A Power Analysis." *IDS Bulletin* 37 (6): 23–33.

Gaventa, J., and B. Martorano. 2016. "Inequality, Power and Participation–Revisiting the Links." *IDS Bulletin* 47 (5): 10.19088/1968-2016.164.

Graham, E., C.R. Shipan, and C. Volden. 2013. "The Diffusion of Policy Diffusion Research in Political Science." *British Journal of Political Science* 43 (3): 673–701.

Haas, P.M. 1992. "Introduction: Epistemic Communities and International Policy Coordination." *International Organization* 46 (1): 1–35.

Habermas, J. 1979. *Communication and the Evolution of Society.* Translated by Thomas McCarthy. Boston: Beacon Press.

Harris, J. 2019a. "Advocacy Coalitions and the Transfer of Nutrition Policy to Zambia." *Health Policy and Planning* 34 (3): 207–215.

Harris, J. 2019b. "Narratives of Nutrition: Alternative Explanations for International Nutrition Practice." *World Nutrition* 10 (4): 99–125.

Herforth, A., and Y.T. Hoberg. 2014. "Learning from World Bank History: Agriculture and Food-based Approaches for Addressing Malnutrition." Agriculture and Environmental Services Discussion Paper No. 10. World Bank Group, Washington, DC.

Hewitt, S. 2009. "Discourse Analysis and Public Policy Research." Centre for Rural Economy Discussion Paper Series No. 24. Centre for Rural Economy, Newcastle, UK.

Hossain, N., and P. Scott-Villiers. 2017. *Food Riots, Food Rights and the Politics of Provisions.* London: Routledge.

Islam, M.S. 2009. "Paradigms of Development and Their Power Dynamics: A Review." *Journal of Sustainable Development* 2 (2): 24–37.

Kakeya, M., Sugiyama, Y., & Oyama, S. 2006. "The Citemene System, Social Leveling Mechanism, and Agrarian Changes in the Bemba Villages of Northern Zambia: An Overview of 23 Years of 'Fixed-Point' Research." *African Study Monographs* 27 (1): 27–38.

Keck, M.E., and K. Sikkink. 1998. "Transnational Advocacy Networks in the Movement Society." In *The Social Movement Society: Contentious Politics for a New Century,* eds. D.S.Meyer and S.G. Tarrow, 217–238. Oxford and New York: Rowman and Littlefield.

Keeley, J., and I. Scoones. 1999. "Understanding Environmental Policy Processes: A Review." *IDS Working Paper 89.* Brighton: Institute of Development Studies.

Kettell, S., and P. Cairney. 2010. "Taking the Power of Ideas Seriously—The Case of the United Kingdom's 2008 Human Fertilisation and Embryology Bill." *Policy Studies* 31 (3): 301–317.

Kuteya, A.N., N.J. Sitko, A. Chapoto, and E. Malawo. 2016. "An In-Depth Analysis of Zambia's Agricultural Budget: Distributional Effects and Opportunity Cost." IAPRI Working Papers. Michigan State University, Lusaka, Zambia.

Lasswell, H. 1971. *A Pre-view of Policy Sciences.* New York: American Elsevier.

Lukes, S. 1974. *Power: A Radical View.* Basingstoke, UK and New York: Palgrave Macmillan.

Marsh, D., and J.C. Sharman. 2009. "Policy Diffusion and Policy Transfer." *Policy Studies* 30 (3): 269–288.

Mason, N.M., T. Jayne, and R. Mofya-Mukuka. 2013. "Zambia's Input Subsidy Programs." *Agricultural Economics* 44 (6): 613–628.

Mason, N.M., T.S. Jayne, and N. Van De Walle. 2017. "The Political Economy of Fertilizer Subsidy Programs in Africa: Evidence from Zambia." *American Journal of Agricultural Economics* 99 (3): 705–731.

Minogue, M. 2004. "Public Management and Regulatory Governance: Problems of Policy Transfer to Developing Countries." Leading Issues in Competition, Regulation and Development Working Papers.University of Manchester Centre on Regulation and Competition, Manchester, UK.

Mokoro. 2015. *Independent Comprehensive Evaluation of the Scaling Up Nutrition Movement: Final Report.* Oxford: Mokoro Ltd.

Morris, S., B. Cogill, and R. Uauy for the Maternal and Child Undernutrition Study Group. 2008. "Effective International Action against Undernutrition: Why Has It Proven So Difficult and What Can Be Done to Accelerate Progress?" *The Lancet* 371 (9612): 608–621.

Mosse, D. 2011. *Adventures in Aidland: The Anthropology of Professionals in International Development.* London: Berghahn Books.

NFNC: National Food and Nutrition Commission. 2011. *National Food and Nutrition Strategic Plan 2011-2015.* Lusaka, Zambia. https://www.nfnc.org.zm/download/national-food-and-nutrition-strategic-plan-2011-2015/

Nisbett, N., S. Friel, R. Aryeetey, F. Da Silva Gomes, J. Harris, K. Backholer, P. Baker, V.B.B. Jernigan, and S. Phulkerd. 2021. "Equity and Expertise in the UN Food Systems Summit." *BMJ Global Health*, 6 (7): e006569.

Rose, R. 1991. "What is Lesson-Drawing?" *Journal of Public Policy* 11 (1): 3–30.

Rose, R. 1993. *Lesson-Drawing in Public Policy: A Guide to Learning across Time and Space.* London: Chatham House Publishers.

Ruel, M., Alderman, H. & Maternal and Child Nutrition Study Group 2013. "Nutrition-Sensitive Interventions and Programs: How Can They Help to Accelerate Progress in Improving Maternal and Child Nutrition?" *The Lancet* 382 (9891): 536–551.

Sabatier, P.A., and H.C. Jenkins-Smith. 1993. *Policy Change and Learning: An Advocacy Coalition Approach (Theoretical Lenses on Public Policy).* Boulder, CO: Westview Press.

Sabatier, P.A., and C.M. Weible. 2016. "The Advocacy Coalition Framework: Innovations and Clarifications." In *Theories of the Policy Process, Second Edition,* ed. P.A.Sabatier, 189–217. New York: Routledge. https://www.taylorfrancis.com/books/edit/10.4324/9780367274689/theories-policy-process-second-edition-paul-sabatier

Schiffer, E. 2007. "The Power Mapping Tool: A Method for the Empirical Research of Power Relations." IFPRI Discussion Paper 00703. International Food Policy Research Institute, Washington, DC.

Schiffer, E. & Hauck, J. 2010. "Net-Map: Collecting Social Network Data and Facilitating Network Learning through Participatory Influence Network Mapping." *Field Methods* 22 (3): 239–241.

Shiffman, J. 2007. "Generating Political Priority for Maternal Mortality Reduction in 5 Developing Countries." *American Journal of Public Health* 97 (5): 796–803.

Shiffman, J. 2014. "Knowledge, Moral Claims and the Exercise of Power in Global Health." *International Journal of Health Policy Management* 3 (6): 297–299.

Shiffman, J. 2015. "Global Health as a Field of Power Relations: A Response to Recent Commentaries". *International Journal of Health Policy Management* 4 (7): 497–499.

Shiffman, J., H.P. Schmitz, D. Berlan, S.L. Smith, K. Quissell, U. Gneiting, and D. Pelletier. 2016. "The Emergence and Effectiveness of Global Health Networks: Findings and Future Research." *Health Policy and Planning* 31 (Suppl 1): i110–i123.

Shiffman, J., and S. Smith. 2007. "Generation of Political Priority for Global Health Initiatives: A Framework and Case Study of Maternal Mortality." *The Lancet* 370 (9595): 1370–1379.

Sitko, N. 2008. "Maize, Food Insecurity, and the Field of Performance in Southern Zambia." *Agriculture and Human Values* 25: 3–11.

Stone, D. 2004. "Transfer Agents and Global Networks in the 'Transnationalization' of Policy." *Journal of European Public Policy* 11 (3): 545–566.

Thurow, R. 2016. "The First 1,000 Days: A Crucial Time for Mothers and Children—And the World." *Breastfeeding Medicine* 11 (8): 416–418.

Townsend, R., R. Benfica, A. Prasann, M. Lee, P. Shah, L. Christiaensen, L. Ronchi, et al. 2017. *Future of Food: Shaping the Food System to Deliver Jobs*. Washington, DC: World Bank.

Van De Walle, N. 2001. *African Economies and the Politics of Permanent Crisis, 1979-1999*. Cambridge, UK: Cambridge University Press.

Weber, M. 1922. *Economy and Society: An Outline of Interpretive Sociology, 1978 Edition*. Berkley: University of California Press.

Willett, W., J. Rockström, B. Loken, M. Springmann, T. Lang, S. Vermeulen, T. Garnett, et al. 2019. "Food in the Anthropocene: the EAT–Lancet Commission on Healthy Diets from Sustainable Food Systems." *The Lancet* 393 (10170): 447–492.

World Bank. 2006. *Repositioning Nutrition as Central to Development: A Strategy for Large Scale Action*. Washington, DC: World Bank.

9

The Political Economy of Bundling Socio-Technical Innovations to Transform Agri-Food Systems

Christopher B. Barrett

9.1 The Imperative and Challenge of Agri-Food Systems Transformation

The world has enjoyed remarkable agronomic, economic, environmental, and nutritional advances thanks to institutional and technological innovations in agri-food systems (AFS) over the past century. A chorus of prominent recent papers and reports nonetheless emphasizes the need to broaden AFS objectives beyond a longstanding, near-singular focus on agricultural productivity growth, the central target of agricultural research and development (R&D) efforts in the high-income world and under the umbrella of the Green Revolution over the past century (IPBES 2019; IPCC 2019; Messerli et al. 2019, Willett et al. 2019, GloPan 2020; Herrero et al. 2020; HLPE 2020; Barrett 2021; von Braun et al 2021; Barrett et al. 2022). The undeniable climate, environmental, health and social justice consequences of consistently prioritizing higher staple crop yields increasingly now compel embrace of multiple AFS objectives, reflecting AFS' central role in driving health and nutrition outcomes, supporting livelihoods, and influencing—and being affected by—natural phenomena. While the exact language varies among documents, the calls are reasonably uniform for accelerating transformation toward what Barrett et al. (2022) term healthy, equitable, resilient, and sustainable (HERS) AFSs. Productivity growth remains imperative, but AFS transformation increasingly must attend to multiple HERS objectives, above all in the low-and-middle-income countries (LMICs) where virtually all food demand growth will occur this century.

AFS transformation is clearly feasible. A vast array of new science-and-engineering-based discoveries exist at various stages of technological readiness, each capable of helping significantly advance one or more of the HERS goals. The promise of these discoveries is manifest in accelerating private investment, with a record US$52 billion of new funding flowing into agrifood tech startups in 2021, an

Christopher B. Barrett, *The Political Economy of Bundling Socio-Technical Innovations to Transform Agri-Food Systems.*
In: *The Political Economy of Food System Transformation.* Edited by: Danielle Resnick and Johan Swinnen,
Oxford University Press. © Christopher B. Barrett (2023). DOI: 10.1093/oso/9780198882121.003.0009

85 percent increase over 2020 and a roughly six-fold increase on the $9 billion flow just five years earlier (AgFunder 2022). Furthermore, a rapidly rising share of those investments occur in LMICs in Asia, Africa, and Latin America. Policy reforms similarly exhibit tremendous capacity to unlock AFS potential, as perhaps manifest most clearly in the dramatic advances China and Vietnam made following significant policy changes from the late 1970s through the late 1990s (Christiaensen 2013; Liu et al. 2020). The opportunities afforded by scientific breakthroughs and institutional and policy reforms create a wealth of exciting options to advance AFS transformation, toward any or several of the HERS objectives.

Interest in and opinions on the desired direction, pace, and mode(s) of AFS transformation differ dramatically, however, as do associated policy prescriptions. These differences of self-interest and opinion pose the thorniest challenge to accelerating AFS transformation. The scientific challenges, though formidable, rarely pose the main obstacles to progress. Rather, the most imposing challenges involve the human relations surrounding the political process of determining whose interests and opinions prevail in the contest to shape AFS transformation.

This is challenging because the embrace of multiple AFS objectives necessarily introduces tradeoffs among competing goals. Not only do different people and organizations stand to benefit or lose differentially from any given policy or technology as regards any one goal, but their preferences also vary among goals. Moreover, an assessment of the impact pathways of a wide range of emerging AFS innovations finds that each one is expected to have adverse impacts on at least one of the sustainable development goals (SDGs), usually through indirect, general equilibrium and/or ecological effects (Herrero et al. 2021). Those who care intensively about an outcome that may be adversely affected by an innovation may mobilize to obstruct its emergence and scaling, even if it yields enormous gains in other dimensions.

Furthermore, new technologies, policies, and institutions do not emerge and scale in a vacuum. They are shaped by prevailing power dynamics within the body politic and the economy. Long-run visions of economic, environmental, or other gains rarely carry the day. Short-run political expediency and profitability dominate the political calculus of most powerful decision-makers in government, business, and even the not-for-profit sector. Thus, the challenge of AFS transformation surrounds not the feasibility of marshaling any of hundreds of scientific or institutional innovations now emerging or on the horizon but rather stems from the complexity of assembling coalitions of parties with sufficient influence to enable the emergence and scaling of contextually appropriate socio-technical innovation bundles (Barrett et al. 2022).

Scientists seeking to help accelerate AFS transformation need to take these inconvenient realities seriously. We must take time to think through the competing interests of different groups and the sociopolitical mechanisms through which those groups interact to shape the incentives and constraints that drive most

AFS transformation. Study of these inherently political phenomena can help us anticipate obstacles to diffusing and scaling innovations that appeal in principle.

The central claim of this chapter is that attention paid to the political economy of innovations can inform strategies to integrate one's favored interventions with other, complementary ones, to build socio-technical innovation bundles (Barrett et al. 2022): the contextually fit-for-purpose combinations of "soft" and "hard" innovations designed keeping firmly in mind with both tradeoffs among objectives and feedback within and among adaptive processes. The (typically large) set of innovations and technologies that satisfy the Kaldor-Hicks compensation criterion offers a menu of options, some combinations of which can motivate concerted support from a coalition of interests sufficient to accelerate AFS transformation. Conversely, AFS transformation is impeded by failure to build such coalitions, sometimes impeded by excessive concentration of power such that some parties do not see a need to compromise or by misinformation that undermines latent coalitions.

9.2 Why Socio-Technical Bundles?

The central message of Barrett et al. (2022) is that bundled innovations are a necessary condition for AFS transformation; magic bullet solutions simply do not exist. Three core reasons drive the need to bundle "socio" and "technical" innovations. First, policies, institutions and culture—the "socio" part—can either enable or impede the diffusion and adaptation of science-and-engineering-based innovations. This naturally turns cultural (e.g., cuisine), institutional (e.g., organizational and contracting forms), and policy innovations into complements to biochemical, digital, ecological, genetic, mechanical, and other technical advances.

Some observers refer to these "softer" cultural, institutional and policy complements as an "enabling environment" for technological change. That framing, however, makes culture, institutions and policies seem exogenous, even immutable, ignoring that they evolve alongside technical innovations through a range of feedback mechanisms. Consider one very current example. As new plant-based and cellular alternative protein products emerge from academic, government and industrial labs and enter grocery stores, institutional cafeterias, and restaurants, incumbent producers of animal-source foods push for restrictions against labeling these new products "meat" and demand that regulators develop new criteria for assuring the safety of novel products, often insinuating the novel products are somehow less healthy or safe than established ones. Meanwhile, alternative protein advocates launch new angel and venture investment vehicles to support startups in this space, generate public service programming around the health, climate, and animal welfare benefits of the new products, and organize cooking shows and widely disseminate recipes to help stimulate grassroots uptake.

The "socio" innovations begotten by scientific innovations are themselves impressive, aimed at either actively reinforcing or obstructing the emergence of a novel biotechnological product.

As elaborated a bit further below, a central lesson of the tremendous success in Green Revolution-era genetic advances in rice concerns the centrality of complementary, bundled rural infrastructure, services, and policies with scientific advances. That reality comes into especially clear focus when one juxtaposes the tremendous successes of the Green Revolution era modern rice varieties with the as-yet-unrealized promise of "golden rice." Although golden rice represents a remarkable scientific advance—the world's first transgenic, biofortified staple cereal—it lacked similar supporting constituencies necessary to bundle enabling institutions and policies to turn exciting science into impactful AFS transformation—and to overcome predictable political opposition from activists protesting the use of transgenic methods.

The second reason bundling is necessary is that rarely does any singular innovation fully solve a problem. Different combinations of institutional, policy and technological innovations will be appropriate among and within distinct contexts. That is true not just at macro scale, e.g., in the rather obvious differences in innovations needed in smallholder dairying systems of the east African highlands, versus northwestern Europe's modest-sized, multifunctional dairy farms, as compared to massive industrial scale dairy farms in the western United States. This structural heterogeneity exists equally within countries. A different form of complementarity arises in this case, wherein distinct subpopulations need different innovations, therefore addressing a macro-scale challenge requires heterogeneous, bundled interventions at more disaggregated, micro- and meso-levels.

A canonical example concerns addressing the micronutrient deficiencies that are the most prevalent diet-based cause of ill health worldwide, affecting more people than hunger (i.e., caloric undernourishment) or obesity and overweight. For example, the best entry point for reducing iron-deficiency anemia (IDA) depends on a target subpopulation's income, dietary and nutritional awareness, age, and gender, whether they farm or not, and conditional on them farming, whether they sell little, most, or all of their harvested output. For some adult subpopulations, income transfers, perhaps coupled with quasi-price incentives, and nutrition education may induce changes in food purchasing and dietary behaviors that remedy IDA.[1] For children, school feeding programs may offer a more direct path to dietary change that boosts iron intake (van Stuijvenberg 2005). But inducing dietary change is hard, so in many contexts industrial fortification of processed

---

[1] A nice example from the United States is the Double Up Food Bucks program, which doubles that portion of government-provided cash-based food assistance (from the Supplemental Nutrition Assistance Program, SNAP) that a beneficiary spends on fresh fruits and vegetables. Currently, only about half of the states employ Double Up Food Bucks. See Wielenga et al. (2020) for evidence on the program's food procurement impacts.

foods appears more impactful at scale (Huma et al. 2007). Other strategies may be needed for more remote, semi-subsistence populations, however, because their dietary intake comes overwhelmingly from home production and consumption. For some, the most cost-effective approach might be to induce acquisition and maintenance of livestock to boost intake of iron-rich animal-sourced foods (Rawlins et al. 2014) or the introduction of biofortified crop varieties that increase iron concentrations in the grains or legumes individuals consume (Finkelstein et al. 2017). Unfortunately, little research has yet explored how best to bundle these various interventions to combat the IDA challenge specifically nor micronutrient deficiencies more generally (Barrett and Bevis 2015).

The third reason to bundle, and the focus of the remainder of this chapter, is political economy. The tradeoffs inherent to every innovation inevitably generate (at least latent) opposition. Conservatism—i.e., resistance to change—is a natural human impulse, a risk averse response to the prospect that change might leave one worse off.[2] Moreover, every innovation in isolation causes some adverse effect somewhere in general equilibrium; that's the macroeconomic lesson of Dutch disease[3] and has been shown in the case of AFS innovations (Herrero et al. 2021). So even those people who enthusiastically favor change will have counterparts who clearly do not favor that same change. This innate conservative tendency is reinforced by humans' greater sensitivity to forces working against them—headwinds—than to those that discreetly favor them—tailwinds (Davidai and Gilovich 2016). If people are more cognizant of potentially bad impacts than they are to potentially supportive processes, then they will resist changes more often than serves their own self-interests.[4] Conservatism therefore works against necessary AFS transformations based on bundling socio-technical innovations.

Hence the need to bundle innovations to form a coalition of parties, each of whom embrace at least one of the bundled innovations and can tolerate the other innovation(s) conditional on getting their preferred innovation included. Bundling innovations can enable the formation of coalitions of a critical mass of

---

[2] Slightly more formally, if there exists some nonzero probability that change will render one worse off as compared to no change, then a rational agent would only favor change over no change under very strong assumptions about the nature of their preferences. The distribution of outcomes under "change" can never stochastically dominate that under "no change." One needs a special case of a particular class of utility function to generate a welfare ordering that favors change for anyone who perceives a chance of an adverse outcome.

[3] "Dutch disease" refers to the economic damage wrought from windfall gains. Its origin comes from the decline of the Netherlands' manufacturing sector following the discovery of massive natural gas reserves that yielded a huge inflow of foreign exchange from the sale of natural gas, which caused the currency to appreciate, making tradable Dutch manufactured (and agricultural) goods less internationally competitive. The concept has been applied to foreign aid and other sources of windfall revenue as well. The point is that what appears an unambiguous gain turns into a mixed bag due to feedback effects through the broader bioeconomy.

[4] This is also a key reason why some policies based on "carrots" commonly succeed politically where analytically superior designs based on "sticks" fail. Consider, for example, the success of subsidy-based policies to reduce greenhouse gas emissions and the failure of analytically superior, tax-based approaches to achieve the same goals.

interested parties, thereby overcoming the tradeoffs inherent to all innovations in a multi-objective, pluralistic body politic, as well as the natural human tendency toward conservativism.

Socio-technical bundling may be essential for the first two reasons, i.e., there exists some sort of complementarity among distinct innovations that makes them more attractive and impactful when implemented together than in isolation, especially within a heterogeneous population. But "identifying and bundling the right innovations is an intrinsically social process, one that demands cooperation that is in shorter supply than are brilliant scientific insights" (Barrett et al. 2022).

9.3 Building Coalitions for Bundling: Insights from the Kaldor-Hicks Compensation Principle

A brief digression into welfare economics can help clarify concepts before I proceed. The original utilitarian philosophers of the 18th, 19th, and early 20th centuries imagined cardinal, interpersonally comparable measures of individual welfare such that one could aggregate individuals' welfare gains or losses from any innovation and thereby identify "socially optimal" (in the utilitarian sense) policies for any given society. In an era in which autocracy was the dominant mode of governance, one could plausibly (if naively optimistic) imagine a technocratic model guiding decisions made by a benevolent dictator. But the combination of the rise of democratic governance—in part because few autocrats proved benevolent!—and advances in economic theory—which evolved to understand that individual welfare is ordinal and not interpersonally comparable—together undermined the old-fashioned, utilitarian approach to political economy. One could no longer assume that the gains of some more than offset the losses of others. Moreover, even were it true that an innovation would yield net societal gains, one could not impose such a result with sufficiently widespread consent among the governed. Arrow's (1950) famous impossibility theorem drove home the central implications that follow from democratic choice and utility theory: all social choice is necessarily a bargain among a range of parties and few policies reach the idealistic welfare standard of Pareto efficiency.

But welfare economics can still offer useful guidance on political economy. In particular, Kaldor (1939) and Hicks (1939) independently developed compensation criteria to address this challenge. The Kaldor-Hicks criterion holds that an innovation is desirable if and only if those who gain can, in theory, at least fully compensate those who would be harmed and remain better off after such compensatory transfers. For this reason, innovations satisfying the Kaldor-Hicks criterion are sometimes labeled "potential Pareto improvements." Kaldor-Hicks still relies on utilitarian reasoning but jettisons the aggregation across individuals and interpersonal comparisons. The weaknesses of the Kaldor-Hicks compensation principle are that (i) no prospective losers will be satisfied by the mere theoretical prospect of being left whole through compensation, and (ii) compensation can be difficult to implement and sequence in a manner that is renegotiation-proof and neither excessively distortionary nor wasteful.

The analytical apparatus of Kaldor-Hicks is nonetheless useful to analyzing the political economy of AFS transformation because it underscores a key benefit of bundling. By bundling multiple innovations, each of which advances the goals of distinct constituencies and thereby de facto compensates for any losses created by another innovation, one can build a sufficiently influential coalition to effect change. Indeed, compensatory transfers to turn the potential Pareto improvements identified by the Kaldor-Hicks criterion into actual Pareto improvements is a special case of bundling, of the innovation and a transfer.[5]

The Kaldor-Hicks compensation criterion thereby provides a means of identifying candidate innovations to bundle. Any AFS innovation that satisfies the Kaldor-Hicks criterion generates sufficient gains for some constituency that some portion of those benefits could be used to compensate other constituencies who would lose from that innovation. But one does not need to design compensation mechanisms—although transfer payments could be one of the innovations in a bundle—if there exist combinations of innovations that accomplish the same goal. Indeed, if one bundles multiple potential Pareto improvements, the net gains are necessarily larger than one realizes under any one of the potential Pareto improvements, made politically feasible with a transfer payment, since transfer payments are intrinsically zero-sum.[6] Hence the political economy appeal of bundling multiple socio and technical innovations. Bundling can enhance gains while overcoming the obstacles to widespread acceptance of any single cultural, institutional, policy, or technical innovation.

Bundling is perhaps especially attractive and feasible among those who share a desire to encourage AFS transformation but who prioritize different outcomes, say better animal welfare and cleaner water and reduced micronutrient deficiencies. Few, if any, single innovations can deliver on all such aspirations, and certainly not in equal measure (Herrero et al. 2021). But a form of compensation can be support for an innovation to which one might object in isolation. Bundle together the right combination of multiple such innovations and one winds up with a critical mass of constituencies that support the bundle of innovations. One can thereby generate Pareto improvement, in which no one is worse off and at least some are

---

[5] A good deal of contemporary agricultural policy in Europe and North America relies heavily on such compensating instruments. See chapter 13 of Swinnen (2018) for a nice exposition and more detailed references.

[6] If transfer payments are distortionary—as is true, for example, of most payments tied to producer behaviors—then transfers could be worse than zero-sum, reducing the scope for potential Pareto improvements and beneficial bundling of transfer payments with other innovations to generate actual Pareto improving policy bundles.

better off (Barrett et al. 2011). The Kaldor-Hicks criterion defines a set of innovations that create a space for political coalition formation to overcome the natural obstructionism of humans' conservative nature.

9.4 The Roles of Institutions, Power, Information, and Trust

The Kaldor-Hicks criterion provides a useful tool for identifying candidate innovations to bundle. But it offers no roadmap for how to craft a bundle that can create a coalition necessary to advance. One must think in terms of how to build political coalitions because human agency is both the main engine of and the primary obstacle to AFS transformation. All humans have both objectives and blind spots. Furthermore, rarely do individuals' varied objectives and blind spots coincide perfectly. Resolving individuals' and organizations' differing interests and blind spots is the task of coalition formation.

Coalition formation necessarily turns on societal institutions, what Douglass North (1991) famously defined as "the humanly devised constraints that structure political, economic and social interaction." We must look to the rules that regulate the sociopolitical processes through which innovation and transformation are negotiated and co-created. Innovation is a strategic game in which differing parties undertake actions aware of, influenced by, and trying to shape prospective responses by others. As with all strategic games, parties' interactions and equilibrium outcomes and disequilibrium dynamics all follow from the incentives and constraints agents face, the information they possess and create, the degree of trust among them—which drives the salience and importance of formal rules—and their power to bring about their preferred outcomes. Thus, institutions (the rules that guide interactions), information, trust, and power ultimately jointly shape the political economy of innovation bundling.

Bundling socioeconomic and technical innovations to transform agri-food systems requires the coordinated exercise of human agency through sociopolitical processes in which diverse AFS actors both empower each other and hold all parties accountable. Arguably the greatest challenge to coalition formation is the excessive concentration of (economic and/or political) power. When power gets too concentrated, the powerful have little incentive to compromise and can too frequently dodge accountability to others for any harms that arise from imposing their will. The powerful may be inclined to impose innovations that suit their interests but harm others because their power obviates the need to build coalitions to bundle innovations that yield Pareto improvements. Or the powerful may obstruct innovations that might threaten their position. The relationship between power and innovation is quite ambiguous. But power commonly obstructs coalition formation of the sort needed to advance bundling that can achieve (or at least approach) Pareto improvements across multiple HERS objectives.

Clear rules to constrain the injurious exercise of power may be less necessary in small communities if community members know and trust their leaders. Strong communities can foster trust, generating mechanisms that endogenously induce good behavior and enforce compliance with the community's unwritten rules (Barrett 1997; Platteau 2000; Fafchamps 2003), although one must be careful not to over-romanticize communities, many of which are disturbingly dysfunctional (Barrett et al. 2001). The gains from trade and associated externalities (e.g., climate change) that span vast distances, however, typically exceed the scope for trust-based interactions at community scale and compel complementing trust with formal rules, as well as accountability and enforcement mechanisms (Platteau 2000). One must trust but verify and enforce.

Hence the foundational importance of the "rule of law" as a check on excessively concentrated power. Of course, the setting and enforcement of rules is itself a political task (Gibson et al. 2005). And rules and the rules-making fora must match the scope of the actors involved, ideally be situated at the minimum scale necessary to internalize the various externalities, following the principle of subsidiarity. Thus, for transnational matters, for example, one necessarily needs multinational fora, such as the Codex Alimentarius or the World Trade Organization. But for subnational watershed scale phenomena, a far more limited scope of participants is optimal.

Myopia is as intrinsic to the human condition as conservativism. The powerful too often underestimate the likelihood that they will eventually fall from power and become passively subject to others imposing their will. It's easy to imagine that behind a Rawlsian veil of ignorance—i.e., in an initial state before one learns one's station in society (Rawls 1971)—all persons would agree to clear, firm limits on the unilateral exercise of power. But once one holds sufficient power that it seems feasible to impose one's preferences, like a utilitarian dictator, then the temptation grows to dismantle or ignore rules. It just takes one deviant dictator who unusually heavily discounts the future in favor of immediate gains to unravel the rules—and who gets away with flouting rules—to degrade the quality of institutions. This is especially true because people naturally follow tit-for-tat strategies in repeated games.[7] Hence the critical importance of holding the relatively powerful accountable for their actions and consequences.

An important, counterintuitive source of power stems from what Olson (1965) labeled "the logic of collective action." The basic idea is that small groups in which each member individually enjoys large prospective gains have stronger incentives to engage in collective action than do the members of far larger groups, who may enjoy massive collective prospective gains but small individual gains. This leads the former, smaller group to organize and achieve collective action that commonly

---

[7] Animal experiments show that behaviors typically follow most recent interactions and fail to integrate remembered experiences over longer timespans (Schweinfurth and Taborsky 2020).

prevails over the latter, larger group, which fails to organize. Thus, a well-organized minority can emerge to dominate political processes, at net cost to society and most of its members.

The logic of collection applies to many individual innovations, the gains from which typically diffuse broadly through general equilibrium price or wage effects or environmental externalities. But a small group of individuals may be highly motivated, e.g., to protect and profit from their intellectual property (IP) rights or favored status in government contracting, or to advance an ideological agenda. They acquire power not because they have the capacity to impose their will unconditionally, but rather because a potentially dominant opposition fails to mobilize itself.

The logic of collective action can be turned to advantage in building coalitions, however. One needs to identify multiple innovations that each satisfy the Kaldor-Hicks criterion—ideally, the innovations are themselves complements, so that the net gains of joint introduction exceed the sum of their independent use—and each of which enjoys a constituency that stands to benefit sufficiently from a particular innovation that it will actively advocate for it. Bundle those innovations together and one has a larger coalition of supporters for the innovation in question. Indeed, the most powerful coalitions commonly combine the strength of organization of small interest groups with the numbers of large, harder-to-organize ones (Swinnen 2018). One can understand creative new ventures like China's Science and Technology Backyards program or the successful emergence and diffusion of Green Revolution rice varieties—both cases described below—as arising from the bundling of innovations that each enjoyed active support from some minority constituency.

Especially as AFS transformation requires increasing uptake of knowledge-intensive innovations, not just technological advances embedded in chemicals, machinery, or seed, the quality of information flow takes on increased importance for ensuring full realization of the prospective gains—and avoidance of prospective harms—from the innovation. But information matters in another, more political way as well. The production and dissemination of information is a very important, specific form of collective action in which those with a strong interest in advancing or opposing an innovation might invest. Information can influence people's opinions about the prospect gains or losses they—or things they care about—face from an innovation. Information can dampen opposition or mobilize support.

The institutional constraints on information matter because of the incentives to produce and circulate misinformation. Some misinformation emerges maliciously, as when an interest group willfully obfuscates as a tactic to gain advantage. But a significant portion arises when untested hypotheses gain a foothold in people's minds and become entrenched through repetition. Indeed, the strongest opinions are often also the most erroneous and held by the least knowledgeable people. That has been shown, for example, in the case of Americans' and Europeans' beliefs about transgenic foods, where "extreme opponents know the least, but think they know the most" (Fernbach et al. 2019). When people are misled as to what serves or does not serve their interests, they can act against their own material interests. That can readily impede accurate identification of options for shared gains following the Kaldor-Hicks criterion.

This matters especially because scientists rarely directly inform policymakers nor even the constituents and lobbyists who nudge policymakers one direction or another. Rather, popular—and increasingly social—media commonly intermediate between scientific and popular discourses. One needs then to recognize that media organizations and individuals have their own interests that condition the description and transmission of information about innovations. For-profit, private media companies will necessarily take short-term profits into consideration in deciding whether or how to cover a story. They may be subject to effective pressure from investors or clients (e.g., major advertisers). Conversely, state-run media can be subject to political pressure from a governing coalition. A free, independent press that is not entirely beholden to commercial interests seems the best bet for reasonably reliable transmission of information. But traditional forms of media are increasingly dwarfed by effectively uncontrolled, private social media, which may leave information especially subject to manipulation.

One explicitly political use of information, perhaps especially misinformation, is to undermine trust in scientific evidence and the scientists who generate both innovations and evidence. Innovations by definition arrive with scant evidence regarding their impacts. Innovations are thus subject to "Knightian uncertainty," meaning there exist unquantifiable, stochastic outcomes rather than a probabilistically quantifiable distribution of outcomes. We economists term the latter "risk" rather than "uncertainty." Knightian uncertainty is important because of humans' inherent conservativism in the face of exposure to a prospective hazard. The precautionary principle formalizes that conservative impulse, holding that one should resist any innovation whose ultimate outcomes are uncertain, especially if there exists any realistic prospect of serious adverse outcomes.

Opponents of innovations therefore work hard to feed prospective opponents' uncertainty, so as to dampen support or even spark active opposition to the innovation in question. Conversely, advocates of innovations must work to reduce uncertainty, hence strict regulatory protocols around what sort of quantifiable evidence must be generated and by what methods in order to secure formal approval of a new innovation.

This leads to the final ingredient behind coalition formation to bundle innovations: trust. People either trust or distrust information and the sources of information. Similarly, they either trust or distrust the producers of and advocates for innovations. The ability to build a coalition depends considerably on the degree of trust among the parties involved because trust sharply reduces the costs of coordination and exchange (Barrett 1997; Platteau 2000; Fafchamps 2003). Coalitions are inherently dynamic, evolving in response to changing conditions, and bundling often requires sequenced implementation or introduction of different innovations. The degree of trust among them affects the likelihood that a coalition forms and persists.

Trust-building is a major advantage of co-creative processes, like participatory plant breeding (Ceccarelli et al. 2009) or China's Science and Technology Backyards program, discussed below. Co-creation can help make more information available to an innovator's partners, but it also builds trust in the information and its source(s). Trust reduces the need for binding, formal rules, and thus lessens the bureaucratic frictions that slow innovative advances. Relative high degrees of trust within southeast Asian societies and their government agencies were arguably part of the recipe for a successful Green Revolution in rice and wheat production, while absence of trust in external scientists, patent holders, and others may have contributed to the slow progress of golden rice, another case discussed below. Transformation accelerators all revolve around human action that generates and shares information and promotes cooperation and trust (Herrero et al. 2020; Barrett et al. 2022). Those who stand to benefit from an innovation that satisfies the Kaldor-Hicks criterion are more inclined to sacrifice some share of their prospective gains with those they trust than with those they do not.

Co-creation processes naturally foster the bundling of socio-technical innovations because different stakeholders join the process with different favored innovations in mind and because each is willing to engage the process because they see the prospective gains from cooperation and compromise. Impactful innovation and bundling can originate among actors anywhere within AFSs, induced by any of a host of motives. So, too, can obstruction. Harnessing the potential inherent to the amazing range of current AFS innovation requires honest, constructive dialogue to co-design contextually appropriate socio-technical bundles of innovations that can enable navigation away from looming dangers and toward a HERS future. Governments and multilateral agencies can try to choreograph some co-creative activities. But most arise serendipitously from decentralized, coordinated actions by public, private, and civil society actors who recognize that they share some common ambitions and opportunities with others.

Co-creative activities necessarily increase human interaction. And increased interaction helps define rules of engagement that constrain the excessive concentration of power, thereby facilitating the flow of (accurate) information, and building and reinforcing trust. Such coalitions can become probabilistically self-reinforcing in the sense that the likelihood of finding common ground increases over time, by both reducing the costs of overcoming distrust and misinformation and facilitating identification of fruitful new opportunities for bundling. Innovations spread more quickly when the technical and economic gains they generate are shared among groups and those groups interact regularly, ideally cooperatively (Rogers 1962; Barrett 1997; Gawande 2013).

9.5 Some Empirical Illustrations

Any of a range of past and current AFS innovations could illustrate the processes described here. Examples from the United States are numerous. For example, one could explore the rise of multifunctional agricultural landscapes in which solar or wind farms combine with crop, livestock, and biogas production, facilitated not just by public subsidies, but at least as much by changes in zoning laws and the regulation of electricity generation along with the extension of rural road and energy infrastructure (Lauer et al. 2018; Pavlenko and Searle 2018). Or one could explore the symbiotic roles played by agricultural and nutritional sciences researchers, the animal welfare lobby, food manufacturers, school systems, and national food regulators in developing alternative proteins to replace animal-sourced products, from the first-generation textured plant-based protein products of the 1970s–80s through more recent plant-based and cell-cultured products (Broad 2019; Neltner 2021; von Kaufman and Skafida 2023). Or how an "Iron Triangle" coalition of agribusiness and shipping industry interests, working with international development and humanitarian nongovernmental organizations (NGOs), reinforced wasteful and relatively ineffective global food aid policies (Barrett and Maxwell 2005) until new scientific evidence and a few courageous NGO leaders dismantled that coalition, engineering rapid advances in humanitarian food assistance (Barrett et al. 2011; Lentz et al. 2013). The following sections draw on three examples from Asia to illustrate the core ideas behind coalitions to build socio-technical bundles.

9.5.1 Example 1: China's Science and Technology Backyards

China's Science and Technology Backyards (STB) program offers a premier example of coalition formation to bundle socio-technical innovations.[8] Starting in 2009, China Agricultural University (CAU) scientists secured support from the central state and the local government in Quzhou, in Zhejiang Province, to launch a participatory research and extension effort aimed at boosting farmers' identification and uptake of yield-improving, resource-conserving farming methods and inputs. Despite China's amazingly rapid technological change, farmers had often been slow to adopt improved production practices, in particular

---

[8] This section draws heavily on the description in Barrett et al. (2022) as well as Shen et al. (2013), Jiao et al. (2019, 2020) and on helpful, informal input from Profs. Jianbo Shen and Fusuo Zhang.

those that improved soil and water management, and especially if such production choices were perceived as demanding added labor, given growing rural labor scarcity as hundreds of millions of Chinese migrated from the countryside to urban manufacturing and services jobs (Christiaensen 2013).

Distinct constituencies sought related, but different goals. University-based agricultural researchers wanted to develop and publish new science. Farmers wanted new tools they could use in their specific contexts—which varied dramatically across a country as vast and heterogeneous as China—with minimal risk and added cost. Commercial input suppliers needed new markets of sufficient volume and prospective profitability to justify the sunk costs of establishing a new distribution channel and relationships. Each group had pushed for its interests with government, with limited success. They ultimately recognized that although each group would need to adapt its prior practices a bit, the net gains from closer collaboration, with clear responsibilities for each party, were sufficiently large to draw them into a coalition that pushed for STB with government and won essential initial financial support. Strong central and provincial government support was essential to finance the bundled intervention and to hold the different constituencies together in the early years. This case is a good example where concentrated (government) power can accelerate innovation when the powerful perceive innovation in their interests, which the Chinese government clearly has in the case of boosting agricultural productivity and sustainability.

The STB design originates in the idea of localized co-creation. University scientists relocated their research programs from the experimental station to rural villages, renting a "backyard" in many villages where they and their students lived, worked, and studied, interacting intensively with farmers and providing regular, intensive training sessions. As farmers began to enjoy improvements on their own farms by applying lessons learned in the backyard research farms, interest spread and more farmers were attracted to the backyards, turning them into technology dissemination focal points. Local governments were supportive because the researchers were no longer outsiders and farmers were allying with the scientists with whom they worked increasingly closely. Input suppliers enjoyed a significant boost in demand for seed, fertilizer, livestock vaccines, and other commercial inputs, which encouraged them to make free samples available when the next backyard opened, enabling faster replication and spread of the model within and across provinces. Companies could also contribute their new technologies for experimentation, getting rapid, low-cost field trial data to identify which products they should scale or abandon. STBs thereby became multi-actor platforms in which each party was able to advance its own objectives, often compromising a bit on its myopically self-interested goals in order to help advance the broader agenda from which it clearly benefitted.

The result was impressive by any standard. By 2020, the initial intervention has scaled to 127 STBs operating in 23 difference provinces and engaging 29 different scientific research institutes and more than 100 different agricultural extension stations, reaching tens of millions of farmers nationwide. Researchers got access to copious amounts of near-real-time data from a range of experimental and observational studies and the ability to adapt research designs quickly in a participatory research and extension system. The scale and scope of data enabled researchers to more accurately and quickly identify which practices and inputs worked well for which farmers under which conditions. Not only did this generate significant scientific insights and publications, it also accelerated crop yield growth and on-farm soil and water conservation (Zhang et al. 2016). The contextualized results from co-created research reinforced farmers' and input suppliers' confidence in the scientific evidence and thus their willingness both to experiment with new methods and inputs—e.g., formulated fertilizers, new sowing technologies, improved soil management practices—and to cooperate with researchers, accelerating both development and diffusion of improved practices, with major productivity and resource conservation gains (Shen et al. 2013; Zhang et al. 2016; Jiao et al. 2019).

9.5.2 Example 2: Genetic Improvements in Rice

The development of improved, high-yielding varieties of rice and wheat in the 1950s and 1960s are widely considered the spearhead of the Green Revolution (Pingali 2012). Crop yields multiplied several times as modern varieties diffused rapidly in places like India, Mexico, and Pakistan, inducing the award of the 1970 Nobel Peace Prize to a plant breeder and pathologist, Norman Borlaug, widely dubbed the Father of the Green Revolution. Careful analyses consistently find dramatic gains to the poor and the natural environment from the bundled innovations of that era based on the development and diffusion of improved crop varieties, especially rice (David and Otsuka 1994; Evenson and Gollin 2003; Gollin et al. 2021).

Political opposition to the Green Revolution nonetheless existed from the outset.[9] But that opposition was overcome by building coalitions of interest groups that supported agricultural modernization and intensification and that coordinated with and largely trusted one another—e.g., CGIAR Centers with national agricultural research institutes, government agriculture ministries, local rural governments, etc. The Green Revolution offers a powerful lesson on the importance of building coalitions that each favor distinct innovations—e.g., in crop genetics, fertilizer formulation, irrigation engineering, labor-saving machinery designs suitable for small farms—with supporting institutions and policies that facilitate the

---

[9] These are my oversimplified summaries of a range of lessons kindly imparted to me over the years by others with far greater in-depth knowledge of the Green Revolution era rice advances than I have, including Randy Barker, Bob Evenson, Yujiro Hayami, Bob Herdt, Kei Otsuka, Prabhu Pingali, Vern Ruttan, Peter Timmer, and Mike Walter.

adaptation of scientific discoveries to specific local AFS contexts and the scaling of impacts.

Many observers at the time openly worried that the introduction of improved Green Revolution crop varieties, irrigation, and agrochemicals would benefit wealthier farmers with more land at the expense of poorer smallholders. Others were concerned that the use of agrochemicals would despoil the natural environment, that higher yielding varieties would lead to monocultures that eliminated agrobiodiversity, or that expanded irrigation would disrupt ecosystems' delicate hydrological cycles. These were certainly not irrational concerns.

The inevitable opposition to IR8, IR36, IR64, and other improved rice varieties was overcome, however, in large measure because those genetic advances were bundled with other agricultural innovations (e.g., irrigation, agrochemicals) in which other commercial or government entities had a strong interest and with complementary institutional (e.g., extension services, marketing boards), infrastructural (e.g., rural roads and electrification), and policy changes (e.g., labor, price, and trade) that independently had support and that helped accelerate diffusion and scale up impact (David and Otsuka 1994). In India, Indonesia, and Pakistan—and a generation later, in China and Vietnam (Pingali and Xuan 1992; Huang and Rozelle 1996; Liu et al. 2020)—a complex web of policies emerged that facilitated the creation and maintenance of political coalitions to support a broad suite of rural development interventions that rapidly transformed those nations' AFSs. The Philippines-based International Rice Research Institute (IRRI) was at the heart of much of this work, with deep, longstanding collaborative relationships with national agricultural research and extension services, national water agencies, local seed companies, and technocratic elites throughout governments in south and southeast Asia. Some of the individual institutional or policy changes (e.g., food price stabilization measures) were themselves contentious and may seem ill-advised when considered in isolation. But such measures often proved politically necessary to build the coalition needed to support more directly impactful interventions, such as in improved irrigation systems to enable more precise water control to realize the full potential of the improved rice varieties and better transport systems to facilitate interregional labor migration and the low-cost evacuation of crop surpluses (David and Otsuka 1994).

Contrast the path and impacts of the early Green Revolution improved rice varieties, such as IR8 and later IR64, with the non-impact of an arguably more momentous scientific advance: transgenic golden rice. In 2000, scientists in Germany and Switzerland published scientific details on a new rice variety that biosynthesizes beta carotene, the precursor to vitamin A, after the introduction of genetic material from a species with which rice cannot naturally cross. Golden rice was, quite unusually for a very technical scientific paper, the cover story for the news magazine *Time* (July 31, 2000), under the title "This Rice Could Save a Million Kids a Year." The fanfare was natural, as golden rice was a far more impressive scientific achievement than the semi-dwarf IR8, IR36, or IR64 varieties of the Green Revolution.

Yet it took more than 20 years after the scientific publication to, in 2021, secure the first regulatory approval in a rice-growing LMIC,[10] the Philippines, to release golden rice for commercial cultivation, processing, and sale. By contrast, within 20 years of its introduction, IR64 became the most diffused cereal seed variety in human history and it and its predecessor lines (especially IR8 and IR36) were widely credited with diffusing so broadly as to rescue south and southeast Asia from the famines the region had episodically experienced from the late 1940s until the early 1970s.

Why such strikingly different outcomes from two episodes of genetic improvements in rice, especially given golden rice's scientific superiority? The difference seems to lie in the political economy of the new varieties' release and attempted diffusion.

Golden rice was popularized as a magic bullet solution but was based on a controversial, transgenic method against which popular distrust was building rapidly in the 1990s and early 2000s.[11] Golden rice was developed by university-based researchers half a world away, without deep, longstanding integration into the economic and political institutions of the region and its AFSs. They were easily (mis)portrayed as outsiders inflicting dangerous science on the poor, a sort of agricultural Dr. Jekyll. Even though much of that (mis)information was produced and propagated by other outsides—e.g., Europe-based environmental NGOs—the lack of trust in or coordination with the external scientists made it relatively easy to sow doubt and uncertainty around this innovation and thereby obstruct its emergence.

Further, the technologies used to create golden rice were subject to a dense thicket of patents that took years to navigate, so golden rice advocates had to divide their time between parrying staunch anti-transgenic opponents, building relationships with local government and business leaders, and navigating a legal quagmire with those disinterested in whether golden rice diffused or not, just with safeguarding their intellectual property rights.

Especially in the 2000s, the technocrats advocating for golden rice failed to build the political coalitions nor to attract the internal, domestic champions to prevail in places like the Philippines, India, and Bangladesh. Notably, over time, as IRRI began to assume greater leadership in the push for golden rice—and as the

---

[10] Golden rice was previously approved by government regulators as safe in Australia (2017), New Zealand (2017), Canada (2018), and the United States (2018).

[11] See Lynas (2018) for a fascinating account by one of the anti-genetically modified foods movement's original leaders about the role of misinformation and political passions in driving opposition to transgenic seeds. One of Greenpeace's self-described co-founders, Patrick Moore, ultimately left and disavowed the organization, launching a counter-campaign called "Allow Golden Rice Now!" and labeling Greenpeace's ardent opposition to golden rice "a crime against humanity" based on disinformation and scare tactics (http://allowgoldenricenow.org/wordpress/about/).

oppositional tactics of anti-transgenic protest groups turned violent and destructive, turning popular opinion away from them and toward golden rice—progress in IRRI's host nation, the Philippines, accelerated. Ultimately, the Philippines became the nation where golden rice first secured full approvals and commercial release for cultivation, consumption, processing, and trade. Elsewhere in the Global South it has proved slower and more difficult to build coalitions and broker the necessary bundles of supporting policies and institutions. Thus, an incredibly promising technology stays largely on the shelf more than two decades later.

The Green Revolution varieties developed using conventional plant breeding methods succeeded with publicly funded R&D and extension in an environment more trusting of science, and less reliant on private funding and intellectual property protections. The juxtaposition of these advances in rice genetics underscores how innovations that advance one or more productivity, health, environmental, or other objective face predictable opposition from other interest groups, with different priorities, in the absence of a concerted effort to build coalitions that bundle multiple innovations together to solve the Kaldor-Hicks problem. And even then, misinformation and the raw exercise of political power can impede progress.

9.5.3 Example 3: The Irony of Bt Brinjal in South Asia

The case of Bt eggplant (also known as aubergine and in South Asia as *brinjal*) in Bangladesh and India brings the political economy of AFS innovation into especially stark relief.[12] Eggplant cultivation is widespread in south Asia, but very vulnerable to the eggplant fruit and shoot borer (EFSB), a pest previously controlled only with multiple applications of expensive and toxic chemical pesticides. Decades of conventional plant breeding had failed to promote adequate EFSB resistance in brinjal. Starting in 2000, scientists with the Indian seed company Maharashtra Hybrid Seeds Company (Mahyco) drew on prior transgenic scientific advances in introducing an insecticidal protein from the soil bacterium *Bacillus thuringeiensis* (Bt) into brinjal. Bt had been successfully introduced into cotton, maize, and other crops similarly vulnerable to borers and the protein is widely used in organic biopesticides. But the Bt brinjal variety is expressly transgenic, just like golden rice.

Transgenic crops require a range of regulatory approvals, including a national biosafety framework. India's approval process involves multiple stages of review, ultimately under the authority of the Minister of Environment and Forests (MEF). India's Genetic Engineering Appraisal Committee (GEAC) had previously

[12] This content draws heavily on informal conversations with experts such as Maricelis Acevedo, Ron Herring, Vijay Paranjape, Tony Shelton, and Usha Barwale Zehr, and on key studies such as Herring (2015), Herring and Paarlberg (2016), Shelton et al. (2018), Brookes and Barfoot (2020a, b), Ahmed et al. (2021) and Shelton (2021). Any errors are entirely mine.

approved Bt cotton for cultivation, yield gains from which led India to become the world's leading cotton exporter, and in October 2009, GEAC approved Bt brinjal for cultivation in India. A formal expert committee reviewed Mahyco's extensive field trials data and concluded that Bt brinjal was both safe and beneficial, as well as likely profitable for small farmers. But anti-GM groups objected vehemently and mobilized India's MEF to overrule GEAC and in February 2010 impose a moratorium on the cultivation of Bt brinjal in India, which remains current today.

It is notable that anti-GM activists prevailed in stopping Bt brinjal when they had failed to stop or rescind approval of Bt cotton. Cotton farmers have long been better organized in India, in part due to the necessity of commercializing fiber harvests, where a large share of perishable brinjal production is auto-consumed by farmers' own families or informally sold locally rather than through formalized marketing channels that feed national and global markets. Cotton exports are strategically important for India's economy, while brinjal is not. The national network of cotton agro-input dealers likewise banded together with farmers and Mahyco to support Bt cotton because the improved cotton seed is relatively profitable for input wholesalers and retailers, even with reduced pesticide sales, due in part to the large volume of seed sales. And Bt cotton was extremely profitable for farmers, so regulators could scarcely contain the spread of the seed even if they had wanted to. By contrast, the commercial incentives for dealer networks were less clear in the case of Bt brinjal, where reductions in pesticide sales were expected to largely offset any gains from the sale of improved seed. Furthermore, the Knightian uncertainty of possible health effects of transgenic food—as distinct from fibers—induced natural conservatism among many groups that further empowered opposition to Bt brinjal relative to the opposition Bt cotton faced. Environmental groups' repeated invocation of the precautionary principle further inflamed that inherent conservativism. As explained earlier, Knightian uncertainty and the precautionary principle leave innovations especially vulnerable to misinformation, of which there has been much concerning Bt crops (Lynas 2018). And because the scale of brinjal production by farmers was typically much smaller than that of cotton, the marginal farm profits at stake were likewise smaller. Cumulatively, while the scientific evidence in favor of Bt brinjal was strong, the politics of opposition were stronger in India.

Meanwhile, Bangladesh, unlike India, had no prior experience with cultivation of transgenic crops. But the favorable field trials evidence—over multiple consecutive years, as had taken place previously in India—convinced the Bangladesh Minister of Agriculture to actively pursue approval of Bt brinjal. Environmental activists were far less well organized and less influential in Bangladesh than in India, and in Bangladesh, the Minister of Agriculture had actively cultivated the support of the Prime Minister. Where India is a major exporter of pesticides, Bangladesh is a large pesticides importer, so the pesticide reductions expected from release of Bt brinjal could save considerable scarce foreign exchange for the country, eliciting support from the Minister of Finance. And the Minister of Environment was satisfied through inclusion of mandatory labeling of Bt brinjal seed packages. Building a coalition of the powerful and bundling in some arguably unnecessary accommodations—e.g., labeling—made a difference. The Bangladesh government approved cultivation of Bt brinjal in October 2013.

Astute readers might wonder why the intellectual property (IP) thickets that partly impeded golden rice's release did not obstruct Bt brinjal. The answer is that Monsanto owned—or already held valid licenses to use—the relevant IP around transgenic Bt crops and also owned a minority stake in Mahyco, the Indian seed company that first developed the variety. So IP issues that often prove problematic with technological innovations today were solved from the outset through commercial and legal agreements.[13]

Rigorous evidence on the impacts of Bt brinjal adoption clearly point to large economic, environmental, and health gains arising from improved yields and sharply reduced applications of toxic pesticides (Brookes and Barfoot 2020a, b; Ahmed et al. 2021). So why was Bt brinjal accepted and diffused broadly in Bangladesh, with favorable agronomic, economic, and environmental impacts, while it failed to secure approval in India, the country in and for which it was originally developed? The answer is clearly politics. In Bangladesh, multiple interests coalesced and bundled multiple innovations (a new seed, labeling) to create a coalition with especially powerful members to prevail against opposition that drew power from the inherent conservativism many have toward new technologies and misinformation that can feed that opposition. The structural situation in India was different, where the logic of collective action enabled a motivated minority of environmental activists, aided by a steady stream of (mis)information, to prevail over the more diffuse interests of millions of brinjal farmers and consumers. In India, the necessary coalitions failed to get built and Bt brinjal remains sidelined, cultivated widely, but illegally to this day.

9.6 Conclusion

Realizing the widely espoused goal of accelerating AFS transformation requires paying at least as much attention to human relationships and to the political economy of coalition formation as it does to sound science. Science can help us identify feasible, impactful innovations, be they technological, institutional, or cultural. But no one-size-fits-all solutions exist; no single innovation will solve the myriad problems confronting the world's AFSs now and into the foreseeable future. Indeed, no innovations exist that do not directly or indirectly pose risks to at least

---

[13] The IP around the technology was nonetheless contested legally when Mahyco and Monsanto were accused of biopiracy for using local brinjal varieties (Peschard and Randeria 2020).

some subpopulations or desired outcomes. For multiple reasons, but especially to overcome the collective action problems inherent to AFS transformation, it is imperative to bundle socio-technical innovations. That is a fundamentally human, and thus political, process.

References

AgFunder. (2022). *AgriFoodTech Investment Report 2022*. San Francisco: AgFunder.

Ahmed, A.U., J. Hoddinott, N. Abedin, and N. Hossain. 2021. "The Impacts of GM foods: Results from a Randomized Controlled Trial of Bt Eggplant in Bangladesh." *American Journal of Agricultural Economics* 103 (4): 1186–1206.

Arrow, Kenneth J. 1950. "A difficulty in the concept of social welfare." *Journal of Political Economy* 58 (4): 328–346.

Barrett, C.B. 1997. "Idea Gaps, Object Gaps, and Trust Gaps in Economic Development." *Journal of Developing Areas* 31 (4): 553–568.

Barrett, C.B. 2021. "Overcoming Global Food Security Challenges through Science and Solidarity." *American Journal of Agricultural Economics* 103(2): 422–447.

Barrett, C.B., T. Benton, J. Fanzo, M. Herrero, R.J. Nelson, E. Bageant, E. Buckler, et al. 2022. *Socio-technical Innovation Bundles for Agri-food Systems Transformation*. London: Palgrave Macmillan.

Barrett, C.B., and L.E.M. Bevis. 2015. "The Micronutrient Deficiencies Challenge in African Food Systems." In *The Fight against Hunger and Malnutrition: The Role of Food, Agriculture, and Targeted Policies*, ed. D.E.Sahn, 61–88. Oxford: Oxford University Press.

Barrett, C.B., A. Binder, and J. Steets, eds. 2011. *Uniting on Food Assistance*. London: Routledge.

Barrett, C.B., K. Brandon, C. Gibson, and H. Gjertsen. 2001. "Conserving Tropical Biodiversity amid Weak Institutions." *BioScience* 51 (6): 497–502.

Barrett, C.B., and D. Maxwell. 2005. *Food Aid after Fifty Years: Recasting Its Role*. London: Routledge.

Barrett, C.B., A.J. Travis, and P. Dasgupta. 2011. "On Biodiversity Conservation and Poverty Traps." *Proceedings of the National Academy of Sciences* 108 (34): 13907–13912.

Broad, Garrett M. 2019 "Plant-based and cell-based animal product alternatives: An assessment and agenda for food tech justice." *Geoforum* 107: 223–226.

Brookes, G., and P. Barfoot. 2020a. "Environmental Impacts of Genetically Modified (GM) Crop Use 1996–2018: Impacts on Pesticide Use and Carbon Emissions." *GM Crops & Food* 11 (4): 215–241.

Brookes, G., and Peter Barfoot. 2020b. "GM Crop Technology Use 1996–2018: Farm Income and Production Impacts." *GM Crops & Food* 11 (4): 242–261.

Ceccarelli, S., E.P. Guimarães, and E. Weltzien. 2009. *Plant Breeding and Farmer Participation*. Rome: Food and Agriculture Organization of the United Nations (FAO).

Christiaensen, L. 2013. "When China Runs Out of Farmers." in *Food Security and Sociopolitical Stability*, ed. C.B. Barrett, Ch. 17, 428–451. Oxford: Oxford University Press.

David, C.C., and K. Otsuka, eds. 1994. *Modern Rice Technology and Income Distribution in Asia*. Boulder, CO: Lynne Rienner Publishers.

Davidai, S., and T. Gilovich. 2016 "The Headwinds/Tailwinds Asymmetry: An Availability Bias in Assessments of Barriers and Blessings." *Journal of Personality and Social Psychology* 111 (6): 835–851.

Evenson, R.E., and D. Gollin. 2003. "Assessing the Impact of the Green Revolution, 1960 to 2000." *Science* 300 (5620): 758–762.

Fafchamps, M. 2003. *Market Institutions in Sub-Saharan Africa: Theory and Evidence*. Cambridge, MA: MIT Press.

Fernbach, P.M., N. Light, S.E. Scott, Y. Inbar, and P. Rozin. 2019. "Extreme Opponents of Genetically Modified Foods Know the Least but Think They Know the Most." *Nature Human Behaviour* 3 (3): 251–256.

Finkelstein, J.L., J.D. Haas, and S. Mehta. 2017. "Iron-Biofortified Staple Food Crops for Improving Iron Status: A Review of the Current Evidence." *Current Opinion in Biotechnology* 44: 138–145.

Gawande, A. 2013. "Slow Ideas." *The New Yorker*, July 29, 36–45. https://www.newyorker.com/magazine/2013/07/29/slow-ideas

Gibson, C.C., Williams, J.T., and Ostrom, E., 2005. "Local Enforcement and Better Forests." *World Development*, 33(2): 273–284.

Global Panel on Agriculture and Food Systems for Nutrition (GloPan). 2020. *Future Food Systems: For People, Our Planet, and Prosperity*. London: GloPan.

Gollin, D., C.W. Hansen, and A.M. Wingender. 2021. "Two Blades of Grass: The Impact of the Green Revolution." *Journal of Political Economy* 129 (8): 2344–2384.

Herrero, M., P.K. Thornton, D. Mason-D'Croz, J. Palmer, T.G. Benton, B.L. Bodirsky, J.R. Bogard, et al. 2020. "Innovation Can Accelerate the Transition Towards a Sustainable Food System. *Nature Food* 1 (5): 266–272.

Herrero, M., P.K. Thornton, D. Mason-D'Croz, J. Palmer, B.L. Bodirsky, P. Pradhan, C.B. Barrett, et al. 2021. "Articulating the Effect of Food Systems Innovation on the Sustainable Development Goals." *The Lancet Planetary Health* 5 (1): e50–e62.

Herring, R., and R. Paarlberg. 2016. "The Political Economy of Biotechnology." *Annual Review of Resource Economics* 8: 397–416.

Herring, R.J. 2015. "State Science, Risk and Agricultural Biotechnology: Bt Cotton to Bt Brinjal in India." *Journal of Peasant Studies* 42 (1): 159–186.

Hicks, John R. 1939. "The foundations of welfare economics." *Economic Journal* 49, 196: 696–712.

HPLE (High Level Panel of Experts on Food Security and Nutrition). 2020. *Food Security and Nutrition: Building a Global Narrative Towards 2030*. Rome: Food and Agriculture Organization of the United Nations (FAO).

Huang, J., and S. Rozelle. 1996. "Technological Change: Rediscovering the Engine of Productivity Growth in China's Rural Economy." *Journal of Development Economics* 49 (2): 337–369.

Huma, N., S-U.-Rehman, F.M. Anjum, M. Anjum Murtaza, and M.A. Sheikh. 2007. "Food Fortification Strategy—Preventing Iron Deficiency Anemia: A Review." *Critical Reviews in Food Science and Nutrition* 47 (3): 259–265.

IPBES (Intergovernmental Science-Policy Platform on Biodiversity and Ecosystem Services). 2019. *Summary for Policymakers of the Global Assessment Report on Biodiversity and Ecosystem Services of the Intergovernmental Science-Policy Platform on Biodiversity and Ecosystem Services*. Bonn, Germany: IPBES Secretariat. https://doi.org/10.5281/zenodo.3553579

IPCC (Intergovernmental Panel on Climate Change). 2019. *Climate Change and Land: An IPCC Special Report on Climate Change, Desertification, Land Degradation, Sustainable Land Management, Food Security, and Greenhouse Gas Fluxes in Terrestrial Ecosystems*. Geneva: IPCC.

Jiao, X., D.S. Feyisa, J. Kanomanyanga, D. Ngula Muttendango, M. Shingirai, A. Ndiaye, B. Kabeto, F. Dapare, and F. Zhang. 2020. "Science and Technology Backyard Model: Implications for Sustainable Agriculture in Africa." *Frontiers of Agricultural Science and Engineering* 7 (4): 390–400. https://doi.org/10.15302/J-FASE-2020360

Jiao, X-Q., H-Y. Zhang, W-Q. Ma, C. Wang, X-L. Li, F-S. Zhang. 2019. "Science and Technology Backyard: A Novel Approach to Empower Smallholder Farmers for Sustainable Intensification of Agriculture in China." *Journal of Integrative Agriculture* 18 (8): 1657–1666. https://doi.org/10.1016/S2095-3119(19)62592-X.

Kaldor, Nicholas. "Welfare propositions of economics and interpersonal comparisons of utility." *Economic Journal* 49,195(1939): 549–552.

Lauer, M., J.K. Hansen, P. Lamers, and D. Thrän. 2018. "Making Money from Waste: The Economic Viability of Producing Biogas and Biomethane in the Idaho dairy Industry." *Applied Energy* 222: 621–636.

Lentz, E.C., C.B. Barrett, M.I. Gómez, and D.G. Maxwell. 2013. "On the Choice and Impacts of Innovative International Food Assistance Instruments. *World Development* 49: 1–8.

Liu, Y., C.B. Barrett, T. Pham, and W. Violette. 2020. "The Intertemporal Evolution of Agriculture and Labor over a Rapid Structural Transformation: Lessons from Vietnam." *Food Policy* 94: 101913.

Lynas, M. 2018. *Seeds of Science: Why We Got It So Wrong on GMOs*. London: Bloomsbury Sigma.

Messerli, P., E. Murniningtyas, P. Eloundou-Enyegue, E.G. Foli, E. Furman, A. Glassman, G. Hernández Licona et al. 2019. *Global Sustainable Development Report 2019: The Future Is Now–Science for Achieving Sustainable Development*. New York: United Nations (UN).

Neltner, T. 2021. "FDA's Short-Sighted Approach to Building Trust in the Safety of Cell-Cultured Meat and Seafood Products." *Environmental Defense Fund blog*, June 17. https://blogs.edf.org/health/2021/06/17/fdas-short-sighted-approach-to-building-trust-in-the-safety-of-cell-cultured-meat-and-seafood-products/

North, D.C. 1991. "Institutions." *Journal of Economic Perspectives* 5 (1): 97–112.

Olson, M. 1965. *The Logic of Collective Action*. Cambridge, MA: Harvard University Press.

Pavlenko, N., and S. Searle. 2018. "Using a Contracts for Difference Program to Support Dairy Biogas in California." *Working paper 2018-04*. International Council on Clean Transportation, Washington, DC. https://www.theicct.org/sites/default/files/publications/Dairy_Biogas_Working_Paper_20180307.pdf

Peschard, K., and S. Randeria. 2020. "Taking Monsanto to Court: Legal Activism around Intellectual Property in Brazil and India." *Journal of Peasant Studies* 47 (4): 792–819.

Pingali, P.L. 2012. "Green Revolution: Impacts, Limits, and the Path Ahead." *Proceedings of the National Academy of Sciences* 109 (31): 12302–12308.

Pingali, P.L., and V-T. Xuan. 1992. "Vietnam: Decollectivization and Rice Productivity Growth." *Economic Development and Cultural Change* 40(4): 697–718.

Platteau, J-P. 2000. *Institutions, Social Norms and Economic Development*. London: Routledge.

Rawlins, R., S. Pimkina, C.B. Barrett, S. Pedersen, and B. Wydick. 2014. "Got Milk? The Impact of Heifer International's Livestock Donation Programs in Rwanda on Nutritional Outcomes." *Food Policy* 44: 202–213.

Rawls, J. 1971. *A Theory of Justice.* Cambridge, MA: Harvard University Press.

Rogers, E. 1962. *Diffusion of Innovations.* New York: Free Press of Glencoe.

Schweinfurth, M. K., and M. Taborsky. 2020. "Rats Play Tit-for-Tat Instead of Integrating Social Experience Over Multiple Interactions." *Proceedings of the Royal Society B* 287 (1918): 20192423.

Shelton, A.M. 2021. "Bt Eggplant: A Personal Account of Using Biotechnology to Improve the Lives of Resource-Poor Farmers." *American Entomologist* 67 (3): 52–59.

Shelton, A.M., M.J. Hossain, V. Paranjape, A.K. Azad, M.L. Rahman, A.S.M.M.R. Khan, M.Z.H. Prodhan et al. 2018. "Bt Eggplant Project in Bangladesh: History, Present Status, and Future Direction." *Frontiers in Bioengineering and Biotechnology* 6: 106. https://doi.org/10.3389/fbioe.2018.00106

Shen, J., Z. Cui, Y. Miao, G, Mi, H. Zhang, M. Fan, C. Zhang, et al. 2013. "Transforming Agriculture in China: From Solely High Yield to Both High Yield and High Resource Use Efficiency." *Global Food Security* 2 (1): 1–8. https://doi.org/10.1016/j.gfs.2012.12.004

Swinnen, J., 2018. *The Political Economy of Agricultural and Food Policies.* New York: Palgrave Macmillan.

van Stuijvenberg, M.E. 2005. "Using the School Feeding System as a Vehicle for Micronutrient Fortification: Experience from South Africa." *Food and Nutrition Bulletin* 26 (2): S213–S219.

Von Braun, J., K. Afsana, L.O. Fresco, and M. Hassan, eds. 2021. *Science and Innovations for Food Systems Transformation and Summit Actions.* Rome: Scientific Group for the UN Food System Summit.

Von Kaufmann, F. and V. Skafida. 2023. "Captive School Markets, Industry Self-Regulation, and Public-Private Partnerships: Narratives Shaping the Development of Alternative Proteins in the United States, 1965–82". *Food Policy*, in press.

Wielenga, V., L. Franzen-Castle, A. Toney, and H. Dingman. 2020. "Nebraska Double Up Food Bucks Increases Purchases of Fresh Fruits and Vegetables among SNAP Users." *Current Developments in Nutrition* 4 (S2): 731–731.

Willett, W., J. Rockström, B. Loken, M. Springmann, T. Lang, S.J. Vermeulen, T. Garnett, et al. 2019. "Food in the Anthropocene: The EAT–Lancet Commission on Healthy Diets from Sustainable Food Systems." *The Lancet* 6736 (18): 3–49. https://doi.org/10.1016/S0140-6736(18)31788-4

Zhang, W.F., G.X. Cao, X.L. Li, H.Y. Zhang, C. Wang, Q.C. Liu, X.P. Chen, et al. 2016. "Closing Yield Gaps in China by Empowering Smallholder Farmers." *Nature* 537 (7622): 671–674. https://doi.org/10.1038/nature19368

10

Sustainable Food and Farming

When Public Perceptions Depart from Science

Robert Paarlberg

10.1 The Political Economy of Science Acceptance in Farming

The acceptance and use of agricultural science has a political economy all its own, one in which farmers and non-farmers often play opposing roles. Many non-farmers who tell us to "follow the science" when it comes to climate change and COVID-19 take the opposite approach when it comes to food and farming, complicating the global pursuit of food system sustainability. This chapter reviews four examples where critical public views emerged that were not supported by science: the Green Revolution, industrial farming, synthetic farm chemicals, and rDNA crops (GMOs). By looking at when the public misgivings emerged—either after a technology was in wide use or before— it is possible to explain why public views did or did not make a difference. GMOs were unique because they triggered public resistance almost immediately, before most farmers had a chance to plant GMO seeds and experience the on-farm benefits, making the technology easier to block.

In the past, resistance to modern science usually came from religious authorities, but this is no longer the case. The influence of religious authorities is much weaker today, partly because of the remarkable stream of material benefits science has been able to deliver (Harrison 2017). Science, however, can never replace religion, because it does not satisfy non-material human needs such as the quest for spiritual or ethical purpose. As alluded to in Chapter 2, values such as these can be just as important as material gain or scientific fact, and some values, such as respect for the natural world and social justice can actually raise new hurdles for science, since unregulated science or science in the wrong hands can damage the natural world and worsen social injustice.

Those motivated to protect natural landscapes, and to protect the vulnerable populations engaged in food production, can therefore mistrust agricultural science today. One central fear has been a replacement of nature's resilient biodiversity with crop monocultures that are chemical-dependent and unsustainable. Another fear is the use of novel methods to alter the genetics of traditional crops and animals, methods of uncertain safety that are mistrusted by non-scientists.

Robert Paarlberg, *Sustainable Food and Farming*. In: *The Political Economy of Food System Transformation*. Edited by: Danielle Resnick and Johan Swinnen, Oxford University Press. © Robert Paarlberg (2023). DOI: 10.1093/oso/9780198882121.003.0010

Protecting the natural environment first emerged as a powerful social movement only a half-century ago. Prior to 1970 there was no Environmental Protection Agency in the United States, and nobody had celebrated an Earth Day. In Europe, Green Parties and advocacy organizations like Greenpeace and Friends of the Earth did not yet exist. The United Nations did not create its Environment Program until 1972, and the first Earth Summit in Rio de Janeiro did not take place until 1992. Today, driven by the universal and accelerating threat of climate change, environmental advocacy has become a fully institutionalized trans-national social movement, with no fewer than 679 separate environmental non-governmental organizations (NGOs) now participating formally in the UN's Rio Conventions. Media-savvy and deeply networked with each other, these organizations speak with a powerful political voice within multiple global governance platforms (Partelow et al., 2020).

Green Parties dedicated to environmental protection have gained considerable strength in many rich countries, especially those in Europe with multi-party systems. They now hold legislative seats in 13 different European countries, and they have become members of ruling coalitions in six (McBride 2021). Farm lobbies in Europe that once dominated politics within the agricultural sector now face growing Green Party opposition.

As an important background change, the virtual elimination of food shortages in rich countries has also undercut the political influence of farm lobbies. Obesity has replaced hunger as the leading dietary health challenge; obesity rates in the United States have tripled since the 1960s, and now stand at 42 percent of adults. Under these circumstances, why do we need more agricultural production, or still more agricultural science? Public support for agricultural science in rich countries has fallen as a result. The growth rate in public spending for agricultural R&D dropped from 9.1 percent in 1960–70 to just 1 percent between 2000–09. In these countries public agricultural research spending actually peaked in 2009, and it has now fallen by 6 percent since then (USDA, Economic Research Service 2020). In the United States, public agricultural R&D has fallen by a third since 2002. Private investments continue to be made in agricultural science, but public funding support has fallen.

In combination, these changes have moved the balance of political power against modern agriculture. As one illustration in Europe, both the Council of Ministers and the European Parliament voted to approve a 2020 European Green Deal "Farm to Fork" strategy designed to reduce farm chemical use and expand the role of organic farming. As discussed in more detail in Chapter 13 of this volume, this Strategy will also fund a variety of "eco schemes" designed to fallow land, promote high-diversity (not high productivity) farming landscapes, and build semi-natural wildlife habitat on farms (European Commission 2021). The German Farmers' Association (DBV) called Farm to Fork a "general attack on the whole of European agriculture" (Appunn 2021), and the EU's general farm lobby,

Copa-Cogeca, pressed hard to weaken the strategy, but Green Party leaders prevailed when the Strategy went before the European Parliament in October 2021, winning approval by a vote of 452 to 170 (Wax and Anderson, 2021).

A stronger political voice for environmental protection has long been needed in the farming sector, where agriculture has been a leading threat to nature, but environmental advocates are wrong to fear that applications of modern agricultural science will make the problem worse. In fact, modern science-based methods usually damage less habitat and pollute less compared to the more traditional methods they replaced, for every ton of food produced. Serious environmental damage continues to be done by farming in rich countries, but this usually reflects how much more is now being produced, not the modern production methods in use.

The practical impact of this growing strength of Green Parties relative to farm lobbies has in most instances been small so far. It has strongly influenced cultural elites and shaped media commentary on what sustainable farming should look like, but it has done little to bend modern commercial agriculture away from a science-intensive trajectory. We see below that only in the case of genetically engineered crops and animals (GMOs) have the non-farmer critics of modern agricultural science been able to keep the latest tools out of farmers' hands.

10.2 Defining Sustainable Food

According to the United Nations Food and Agriculture Organization (FAO), a "sustainable" food system must meet economic, social, and environmental conditions (FAO 2018). A fully sustainable system must be,

- Profitable throughout (economic sustainability)
- Must deliver broad-based benefits for society (social sustainability)
- And must deliver a positive or neutral impact on the natural environment (environmental sustainability).

Clearing all three hurdles at the same time is now difficult due to the continued increases in food demands driven by population growth plus income-linked dietary enrichment, especially in today's low- and middle-income countries (LMICs). This creates a need for better production methods that can reduce the economic, social, and environmental cost of every added ton of output. Fortunately, applications of modern science are now helping to meet this difficult challenge with methods that sharply reduce the amount of land, labor, water, chemicals, and energy required for each bushel produced.

This science-forward "eco-modern" path to sustainability (Asafu-Adjaye et al. 2015) is one that traditional advocates for the environment often miss. They prefer to protect nature not by using science to increase productivity (i.e., more output per unit of input), but instead by preserving the traditional methods they associate with times of less damage, ignoring the much greater harm these methods actually did to nature for every ton produced.

We explore here four cases where non-material values and misrepresentations of agricultural science have created popular resistance to farm production methods that are actually more sustainable than traditional methods. In the first three of these cases—the Green Revolution, "industrial" agriculture, and synthetic chemical use—popular disapproval did little to alter the widespread use of the methods in question, mostly because the popular objections did not increase until after farmers were already using these methods with success and declined to give them up. Only in the fourth case (GMO crops) did popular resistance emerge before most farmers had a chance to try the new seeds and experience their benefits. A technology farmers had not yet learned to value became one that was easy for regulators to block.

A more recent 2012 biotechnology innovation, genome-editing, presents an interesting variation on the GMO case. As with GMOs, gene-edited crops attracted activist opposition almost from the start, before farmers had a chance to experience the benefits, which opened political space for a blockage effort, particularly in Europe. Yet because most gene-edited crops will contain no "foreign DNA" they will be more difficult for governments to detect and regulate, as well as less frightening to ordinary consumers. They are also cheaper, faster, and easier to develop compared to GMOs, both factors will favor widespread uptake.

In reviewing these four cases, several political economy patterns will emerge. In each case, popular resistance to new agricultural science arose first among well-fed citizens in affluent countries. Also in each case, civil society organizations were instrumental in promoting this science resistance, and eventually projecting it into countries that were not yet affluent. But only in the case of GMOs did governmental authorities join the resistance. Civil society objections to the Green Revolution, to industrial farming, and to agricultural chemicals enjoyed less success because they were not launched until after these innovations were in widespread use on farms.

10.3 Case 1: "Green Revolution" Farming

Bringing the latest agricultural science to poor countries was a popular idea in the 1960s. The introduction of high-yielding "Green Revolution" seeds into countries with unmet food needs was hailed initially as a triumph for both science and ethics. Only later did civil society organizations brand it as a source of economic, social, and environmental harm. On the environmental front, they accused the new seeds of requiring "huge amounts of groundwater" (EWG 2009) plus an excessive use of chemicals, including a "sixfold rise in fertilizer use per acre" (Rossett et al. 2000).

Such assertions continue to dominate progressive popular discourse, even though they are scientifically mistaken.

The Green Revolution wheat and rice seeds arrived on farms in Asia beginning in the 1960s. Supported by the Rockefeller Foundation (this was not a corporate initiative), scientists working in Mexico had used conventional crop breeding methods (not GMO methods) to introduce new "dwarfing" traits into wheat plants. Scientists working in the Philippines did the same with rice plants. The dwarfed plants, with shorter stems, devoted less growth energy to producing leaves and straw, and more to producing grain, which roughly doubled grain yields per hectare when adequate water and fertilizer were provided.

This was a yield breakthrough that came at just the right time for India, where lagging grain production and a two-year drought in 1965/66 had brought the country to the brink famine, a tragedy only avoided due to a tripling of wheat imports from the United States. When the new seeds were introduced and spread quickly after 1965, wheat production nearly doubled in just five years. Once India began planting the new rice varieties, production in the states of Punjab and Haryana also nearly doubled, between 1971 and 1976 alone (Paarlberg 1994). India became a small net exporter of rice by 1973, and by 1978 also a net exporter of wheat. Norman Borlaug, the American scientist who led the original wheat breeding effort in Mexico, was awarded the Nobel Peace Prize in 1970.

The Green Revolution package (new seeds, irrigation, and chemicals) was nature-protecting as well as lifesaving. If India had tried to produce its 1993 wheat crop by using the pre-Green Revolution methods of thirty years earlier, it would have had to plow up an additional 36 million hectares of land (Swaminathan 1994). Some environmental advocates did recognize this as a major gain. In May 2002, James Lovelock, the creator of Gaia Theory, and Patrick Moore, the co-founder of Greenpeace, signed a "Declaration in Support of Protecting Nature with High Yield Farming and Forestry." They declared that high yield farming was not just the best way to increase food production to keep pace with market demand; they said it was also good for the "preservation of the natural environment and its biodiversity through the conservation of wild areas and natural habitat." (Russell 2009).

For these reasons, when a powerful new global environmental movement began forming in the 1970s, it should have welcomed the Green Revolution, but instead the opposite happened. Prominent activists, following the lead of Vandana Shiva (identified by *Forbes Magazine* as one of the Seven Most Powerful Women on the Globe), attacked the new seeds. In 1991, Shiva wrote a book-length polemic accusing the Green Revolution of introducing an unsustainable new farming model (Shiva 1991). She said the new seeds required more irrigation water and chemicals, forcing farmers to borrow the money to purchase these inputs, pushing them into debt. Worse, the production gains would be unsustainable because the genetic base of the new seeds was too narrow: "The destruction of diversity and the creation of uniformity simultaneously involves the destruction of stability and the creation of vulnerability... (Shiva 1991, p. 29).

Shiva's influential critique misunderstood several basics. Scientists had shown that the new seeds did not require more water and fertilizer; to the contrary, the yield gains they provided in response to inputs were so large that water and fertilizer requirements per ton of production actually *decreased*. The United Nations FAO confirmed later that the Green Revolution rice varieties increased water productivity—output per unit of water inputs—threefold compared to traditional varieties (FAO 2003). As for fertilizer, the new Green Revolution varieties produced more than 20 pounds of added grain for each added pound of nitrogen, while traditional rice and wheat varieties produced only 10, so the need for fertilizer fell roughly in half for each pound of added grain production (Borlaug 1970).

These gains were hard for non-specialists to appreciate because input use did increase in absolute terms, even though falling relative to total production. In some cases, the increase in water and chemical use was excessive, but the reason was not a requirement of the new seeds. It resulted instead from needlessly high government subsidies designed to promote input use. For example, excessive insecticide spraying became a problem in Indonesia in the 1970s when the government subsidized farm chemical purchases by as much as 85 percent. Indonesia eventually solved this problem by removing the subsidy, but it knew better than to stop using the new seeds themselves (FAO 1988).

Shiva's warning about increased crop vulnerability due to less diversity was also off target. According to a 2019 study in *Global Change Biology*, crop diversity in India, measured both in numbers of different crops grown and the dispersion of those different crops across cultivated area, actually showed a "remarkable increase" after the 1960s (Aizen et al. 2019). Just as important, the genetic base of wheat and rice production in India was not narrowed. Plant breeders value *pedigree complexity*, which is the number of different crop selections originally bred into a variety of wheat or rice (Rosegrant and Hazell 2000). One of the Green Revolution rice varieties ("IR 66") actually had 42 different pre-Green Revolution selections in its parentage, so it had multiple sources of resistance to pests and diseases. As Thomas R. DeGregori has pointed out, a field planted to a monoculture of Green Revolution seeds can actually be more diverse genetically than a polyculture of traditional varieties (DeGregori 2004). In 1996, Melinda Smale and Tim McBride confirmed that "yield stability, resistance to rusts, pedigree complexity, and the number of modern cultivars in farmers' fields have all increased since the early years of the Green Revolution" (Smale and McBride 1996).

The Green Revolution was most of all economically sustainable, since it increased the income of farmers both large and small while reducing food costs for consumers. By one estimate, if the modern seed varieties had not been introduced after 1965, annual crop production in the developing world as a whole in the year 2000 would have been almost 20 percent lower than it actually was, and this would have pushed food prices one-third to two-thirds higher. An added 6 to 8 percent of children in the developing world would have been malnourished (Evenson and Gollin 2003).

Small farmers took up the seeds alongside larger farmers, satisfying an important requirement for social sustainability. The percent of harvested rice area in South Asia under modern Green Revolution varieties increased from zero to 71 percent between 1965 and 2000, and the share of wheat area increased to 95 percent. In East and Southeast Asia, modern variety coverage for rice by 2000 was more than 80 percent, and for wheat nearly 90 percent, indicating broad small farm participation (Gollin et al. 2005). In one study of 30 rice-growing villages in Asia between 1966 and 1972, more than 90 percent of both small and large farms adopted the modern rice varieties within a decade after they became available, with smaller farms actually reaching this cumulative adoption level more quickly than large farms (Ruttan 2004). The seeds worked well on small farms because they could be planted and harvested by hand, with no need for expensive mechanical equipment.

It has now been more than a quarter century since Vandana Shiva branded the Green Revolution unsustainable, yet crop yields have continued to increase. Data from FAO show that average wheat yields in India in 2019 were 52 percent higher than when Shiva wrote in 1991 (FAOSTAT 2019). A 2021 *Journal of Political Economy* study concluded that if the original Green Revolution had simply been delayed for a decade, incomes in the developing world would be 17 percent lower today (Gollin et al. 2021).

Despite these well-documented gains over five decades, Green Revolution approaches continue to be rejected by a preponderance of global civil society organizations. In Rome in 2002, an independent NGO forum blamed the Green Revolution for what it described as a rise in world hunger, even though the only place hunger was rising was Africa, where Green Revolution methods were not in wide use. Two years later, a coalition of 670 separate NGOs attacked the Green Revolution by name once again, this time branding it a "tragedy" (NGO/CSO Forum 2002).

In fairness, the introduction of improved seeds did not bring social sustainability everywhere. In much of Latin America subsistence farmers lacked formal land rights, so when the introduction of profitable new seed and chemical technologies made the land they were squatting on more valuable, it was sold out from under them by large estate owners who gave way to a new class of commercial growers. Poor peasants were pushed off in large numbers and forced to migrate to urban slums (Williams 1986). This was a serious malfunction, but one linked to unjust semi-feudal land ownership patterns, not to the science that had produced the improved seeds.

Civil society organizations have continued to campaign against the Green Revolution. They oppose the Alliance for a Green Revolution in Africa (AGRA), a project launched in 2006 by the Bill and Melinda Gates Foundation (AGRA 2020), and in 2021 they stayed away from the UN Food Systems Summit in part because the Special Envoy to the summit, Dr. Agnes Kalibata, was also the President of AGRA. The alternative they prefer is "agroecology," an approach intended to imitate nature by mixing crops, animals, and trees together, usually based on labor-intensive hand-gardening. Agroecology methods can work well enough at the project level, but they do not scale up with actual farmers because they require too much human labor. Even strong advocates for agroecology acknowledge the high labor costs (Altieri 1999, p. 202).

The Green Revolution lost popular favor in part because it worked so well in Asia. When the widespread famine fears of the 1960s disappeared, it was possible for non-specialists to begin imagining that the new seeds had never been necessary. Fears of environmental damage were replacing fears of food shortage. More agricultural science was actually the proper response to this threat as well, but most environmental advocates embraced artisanal methods instead.

10.4 Case 2: Industrial Farming

Most Green Revolution critics would prefer a return to small local farms producing a wide variety of both crops and animals, a traditional model that dominated even in rich countries prior to the second half of the twentieth century. Yet the greater sustainability of this earlier model is an illusion, because farms then were producing only a small fraction of what is needed today, and they did so at barely a poverty-level income for most farmers.

Modern commercial farm methods not only produce much more food and much higher income for farmers; they also use fewer natural resources per ton of production, making them better for the environment. Precisely because today's commercial farms are large, specialized, and highly capitalized, they can afford new "precision agriculture" technologies that help reduce a wasteful, polluting use of inputs. These precision methods include drip irrigation, no-till seeding, satellite-based global positioning systems (GPS), soil mapping, variable-rate water and chemical applications, unmanned aerial vehicle (UAV) scouting and imaging, artificial intelligence (AI) and robotics, machine learning, and also big data. These tools are all information-intensive rather than resource-intensive; they are now making so-called "industrial" farming into an increasingly post-industrial activity.

As one example, a real-time kinematic (RTK) base station on a modern farm can log small errors detected from incoming GPS satellite data and send correction signals to the roving equipment in the field, via radio or cellular modem. This allows the equipment to know its precise location in real time with *sub-inch* accuracy

(Condliffe 2016). This information is then linked through on-board computers to a digital map of soil moisture and soil chemistry variations, telling the equipment to put down chemicals, water, and seeds at an optimal rate for each specific location. Cutting unneeded applications saves the farmer money, while also reducing polluting runoff.

Modern industrial farms have reduced labor and land use most of all. Total corn production in the United States has increased fivefold since 1940, but the acreage planted to corn has actually declined by one-fifth (Ausubel 2015). Other inputs have also declined. For every bushel of corn produced since 1980, irrigation water use has fallen 46 percent, energy use 41 percent, and greenhouse gas emissions 31 percent (Field to Market 2016).

Chemical use in modern agriculture has also declined over the past four decades. Total fertilizer use in American farming peaked in 1981, and since then it has remained essentially flat, even while total crop production grew 44 percent (USDA, Economic Research Service 2019). The total pounds of pesticide applied to American crops declined by 18 percent in absolute terms between 1980 and 2008, and insecticide use is now more than 80 percent below its 1972 peak (Fernandez-Cornejo et al. 2014).

Modern precision agriculture (PA) methods are also delivering results in Europe. A 2013 study in Hungary found that the overall environmental burden from agriculture declined thirty percent with the embrace of PA. An earlier German study found that PA decreased herbicide use by more than half. A 1996 study of variable rate applications on corn and soybeans in the US and Denmark found insecticide use decreased by roughly one-third, which helped prevent the emergence of insects resistant to the chemicals (Cornell 2016, p. 18).

Considerable environmental damage is still being done by modern farming in rich countries due to today's larger volume of total output, so the gains from PA have gone mostly unrecognized by popular critics. Farms in the United States today are producing nearly three times as much output as in 1948 (USDA 2021a). If output had tripled using 1948 production methods, the environmental damage would have been far greater. In some cases, in fact, total damage was actually greater in the past despite lower production. Early in the twentieth century, American farmers plowed up the drought-prone Southern Plains in order to grow more wheat. When the rains failed in the 1930s, the topsoil blew away creating a disastrous Dust Bowl, forcing 2 million farmers to become environmental refugees.

Fragile lands were saved from this kind of cropping expansion only after new hybrid seeds and fertilizers began boosting yields on less fragile lands already plowed. Farmland area in the United States finally stopped increasing in 1950, and since then total agricultural output has nearly tripled, with no more Dust Bowls.

Modern industrial farming is widely criticized for being economically and socially unsustainable as well, since small farms were consolidated into large farms producing an exodus of rural dwellers and shuttering many small towns. Popular media continue to see this as a problem. In 2019 *Time Magazine* warned that America's rural "decline" was being hastened by a continuing disappearance of small farms (Aemuels 2019).

In fact, returning to a small farm model would be a social and economic step backward, because small farms typically earn far less income. In America in 1910, average household income on farms was less than two-thirds that of non-farm households, and in the 1930s farm income briefly dropped to just one-third the non-farm level (Gardner 2002). This rural poverty problem was not solved until modern "industrial" methods, led by gas-powered mechanization, made it possible to produce food with much less human labor. Farm children could then spend more time in school, graduate, and leave to seek better-paying work in town, including new factory jobs with regular hours, union contracts, and summer vacations. When the older generation eventually stopped farming and sold the land to a neighbor who expanded, a retirement nest egg was the final benefit.

As a result of this consolidation process, America today has many fewer farms, yet very few are poor. The median income for farm families in America in 2021 was 30 percent above the median for all households, and the average net worth of households operating farms was an impressive $2.1 million (USDA, Economic Research Service 2022). Genuine social and economic hardship can be found in rural America today, but it has not been caused by a disappearance of small farms. Instead, it reflects job losses in manufacturing due to outsourcing and automation, which too often leads to family breakdown and substance abuse, but these factors are essentially unrelated to the replacement of small farms by large farms (Green 2020).

Most who are attracted to small farms have never tried to support a family based only on small farm income, or feed a family on what small farms produce. In the United States, New England has a large number of small, diverse farms, often selling directly to consumers through local farmers markets and community supported agriculture (CSA) subscriptions. This model can look appealing, until we consider how little food these farms produce. The commercial sales made by all of the farms, large and small combined, in Massachusetts, Connecticut, Maine, New Hampshire, Vermont, and Rhode Island make up less than one percent of total national farm sales (USDA 2017).

10.5 Case 3: Organic Food

Organic food is a third example of popular opinion departing from science. Foods grown "organically," without synthetic chemicals, are considered by many consumers to be better for the environment, safer to eat (no synthetic pesticide residues), and more nutritious. Roughly 40 percent of Americans say some or most of the food they eat is organic, and this increases to 63 percent among those who claim to eat with a focus on health and nutrition (Pew 2016).

These popular perceptions lack a solid scientific foundation. Science tells us a shift from conventional to organic production would do little or nothing to improve food safety or nutrition, and it would actually harm dietary health by making nutritious fruits and vegetables significantly more expensive. The average retail price (by volume) for organic produce in the United States is 54 percent higher than for conventional (Kang 2019). A scale up of organic methods would also harm the environment, by requiring the use of more land.

In order to be labeled "organic," foods must be grown only using chemicals found in nature, avoiding anything manufactured ("synthetic"). Organic farmers can fertilize crops using the nitrogen found in composted animal manure, but not with nitrogen taken from the atmosphere through the industrial Haber-Bosch process (first introduced in 1909). Synthetic products to help farmers control weeds, crop disease, and insect pests are also barred under the organic rule.

The modern organic food movement was launched in the 1920s by an Austrian mystic philosopher named Rudolf Steiner, who objected to the use of synthetic chemical fertilizers because he said they lacked an imagined "biodynamic" life force (Bechtel and Richardson 1998). Steiner also promoted a number of other ideas not supported by science; he believed in human reincarnation, the lost world of Atlantis, and an earlier lost continent named Lemuria (Steiner 1959).

A second organic advocate early in the twentieth century, an English agronomist named Albert Howard, had been well-trained in agricultural science, but he strayed beyond his scientific competence by making claims connecting soil nutrient replacement to human health (Conford 2001). While working in colonial India, Howard came to believe that composted manures were essential for building the "health" of soils, which he viewed as the essential foundation of human health. In his 1943 book, *An Agricultural Testament*, he endorsed what he called "Nature's farming," based on nurturing plants with composted animal waste, including human waste (Howard 1943).

Objections to the use of synthetic nitrogen fertilizer lack a scientific foundation, because nitrogen is the same chemical element no matter where it comes from. Synthetic nitrogen production soon became essential to feeding the human population, which is now four times larger than when Steiner and Howard formed their views. Vaclav Smil has estimated that without manufactured nitrogen fertilizer, 40 percent of the increase in food production to meet today's population needs would never have taken place. For at least one-third of those living in today's most populous countries, the use of nitrogen fertilizers in the twentieth century made the difference between an adequate diet and malnutrition (Smil 2000).

The mystical organic ban on synthetic materials also does little or nothing to improve food safety. We should always limit exposure to pesticides with toxic properties, but the organic ban doesn't cover naturally occurring toxins (like copper sulfate), and halting chemical use entirely is scientifically unnecessary. This was well understood by Rachel Carson, who criticized the *excessive use* of synthetic pesticides in her 1962 book, *Silent Spring*. As a scientist she knew that "the dose makes the poison," so she never endorsed the rigid organic insistence on going to zero. In *Silent Spring* she said, "The ultimate answer is to use less toxic chemicals so that the public hazard from their misuse is greatly reduced" (Carson 2002, p. 184). When Carson later testified to Congress in 1963, she said, straight out, "I think chemicals do have a place" (Griswold 2012).

The best practice in agricultural pest control is "integrated pest management" (IPM), a method that employs both biological and chemical controls, a method the chemical-prohibiting organic standard makes impossible. Through IPM methods, improved crop genetics, and precision application technologies, the United States has been able—without going organic—to reduce its total applications of insecticide by more than 80 percent since 1972, as noted earlier.

Anxieties persist in rich countries over pesticide residues on food, but toxicologists and food scientists find little or no risk. In the United States in 2003, the FDA analyzed several thousand food samples from the marketplace and found that only half of one percent had chemical residues exceeding regulatory tolerance levels. Those levels had in turn been set conservatively, at only one one-hundredth of an exposure that still did not cause toxicity in laboratory animals. Looking at this evidence, food scientists at the University of California-Davis concluded, "[T]he marginal benefits of reducing human exposure to pesticides in the diet through increased consumption of organic produce appear to be insignificant" (Winter and Davis 2006).

Advocacy organizations nonetheless continue promoting pesticide residue fears. The Environmental Working Group (EWG) issues an annual "Dirty Dozen" report, listing the fruits and vegetables with the highest pesticide residue levels (EWG 2019). This report fails to mention that these "dirtiest" products are all essentially clean. It's like warning patients away from the "dirtiest" operating room in a modern hospital. One paper published in 2011 looked at average pesticide exposures on that year's "Dirty Dozen" products and found all were well below the EPA tolerance level, with the vast majority at less than 0.01 percent of that reference dose (Holsapple et al. 2017).

Advocates for organic foods, including the Organic Trade Association that promotes the industry, also like to claim nutrition benefits, yet independent nutrition scientists do not support this either. In 2012, a review of data from 237 studies conducted through the Center for Health Policy at Stanford University concluded there were no convincing differences between organic and conventional foods in nutrient content or health benefit (Smith-Spangler et al. 2012).

While the public continues to favor organic foods, very few commercial farms have switched to organic methods, mostly because of the higher land and labor costs per bushel of production. Less than one percent of harvested cropland in the United States today is organically certified (OTA 2019). In the European Union, where roughly 9 percent of farmland area is certified organic, a new 2020 "Farm to Fork" strategy wants to convert "at least" 25 percent of farmland to organic methods by 2030 (EU 2020). This is being advanced as a "green" initiative, but organic cereal yields in Europe are only 60–70 percent as high as conventional yields (FAO 2002), so any large switch would require much more European land in farming, releasing more carbon from the soil and causing more forest and habitat loss, hardly a green outcome. In one study of a hypothetical switch to organic in England and Wales, total food output would fall to only 64 percent of the pre-switch baseline (Smith et al. 2018). If Europe goes in this direction, a significant increase in food imports (probably non-organic) would be needed to prevent a steep spike in prices. Organic farming can remain a popular idea in Europe only so long as most farms decline to adopt its restrictive methods.

10.6 Case 4: Genetically Modified Organisms (GMOS)

A fourth example of divergence between scientific consensus and popular perception is GMO crops, which are developed using rDNA genetic engineering. Popular disfavor pushed GMO foods out of the European market soon after they were first introduced in the mid-1990s, and they remain excluded today even though all the leading European science academies have said they are safe. Most other countries around the world followed Europe's path, including countries with poor farmers who might have gained from the new agronomic traits provided by GMO crops.

The scientific consensus on GMO crop safety is remarkably strong. The Royal Society in London, the British Medical Association, the French Academy of Sciences, and the German Academies of Science and Humanities have all said, in writing, they find no convincing evidence of any new risks to human health or to the environment from any of the GMO crops developed so far (DeFrancesco 2013; Nicolia et al. 2013). Even the EU Commission officially endorses this consensus. In 2010, the Research Directorate of the European Union concluded that, "biotechnology, and in particular GMOs, are not per se riskier than e.g., conventional plant breeding technologies" (EU 2010).

Official scientific bodies in the United States say the same thing. In 2016 a committee at the National Academies of Science concluded the following: "The committee carefully searched all available research studies for persuasive evidence of adverse health effects directly attributable to consumption of foods derived from GE [genetically engineered] crops but found none" (NAS 2016).

GMO crops are created by moving genes carrying desired traits from unrelated organisms into the living DNA of crop plants. GMO corn and cotton varieties were originally engineered to contain in their tissues a protein from a soil bacterium that some insects cannot digest (these were called *Bt* crops, after the name of the bacterium). *Bt* crops reduce the need for insecticide sprays, bringing an environmental benefit along with lower production costs. A 2009 USDA study concluded that global plantings of *Bt* corn and cotton between 1996 and 2006 had made possible a 29.9 percent reduction in the use of insecticide active ingredients (Naranjo 2009).

Soybean plants were also genetically engineered in the 1990s, to survive applications of an herbicide named glyphosate. These modified plants made weed control possible without the use of more toxic pre-emergent herbicides, and with less plowing and therefore less burning of diesel fuel. Thanks to the availability of GMO soybeans, the land area under no-till farming in Argentina increased from less than 1 million hectares in 1991 up to 22 million hectares by 2008 (Trigo et al. 2009).

GMO soybeans nonetheless attracted criticism in Europe, because the American company selling the patented seeds, the Monsanto Company, was also selling the patented Roundup herbicide used with the seeds, which raised a concern about corporate control. These new GMO soybeans also began arriving in European ports in March 1996, at exactly the moment when European officials admitted that eating meat from animals with BSE (mad cow disease, unrelated to GMOs) was possibly fatal. Officials had earlier said the meat was safe, so consumers wondered if they could trust assurances from the same officials that the soybeans were safe. It was easy under these circumstances for activists to mobilize popular opposition to GMOs (Bernauer and Meins 2003).

Hoping to calm popular fears, the EU announced in June 1997 that any foods with GMO ingredients would have to carry an identifying label, but this was taken as a sign that there must indeed be a danger. By 1998, popular anxieties forced EU regulators to impose an informal moratorium on new approvals of GMO crops, and by 2004 the EU was requiring all operators in the marketplace to maintain, for five years, a complete "audit trail" record showing where all the GMO products they handled came from, and where they went. To avoid this burden, along with the stigmatizing labels, food companies eliminated any remaining GMO ingredients from their products, including oil from American soybeans and starch from American corn (Levidow and Bijman 2002).

It is revealing that the same Europeans who sought to avoid GMO foods had no objections to GMO medical drugs. Genetic engineering had been widely used in commercial medicine since 1982, when the FDA in the United States first approved a recombinant form of human insulin. European drug companies soon began to incorporate similar genetic engineering techniques, with no popular objections (Paarlberg 2008). What made the GMO drugs acceptable in Europe was not an absence of new risks, since genuine risks were routinely detected during clinical trials and fully disclosed; the key instead was a promise of direct benefits to the consumer.

The first generation of GMO crops introduced in the 1990s did deliver strong benefits to farmers, by making it cheaper and easier to protect against insects and weeds, but for final food consumers the GMO varieties of corn and soy didn't look or taste any better, they didn't have better cooking properties, they weren't any more nutritious, and once mixed into packaged food products they were not noticeably cheaper. Because final consumers did not see any clear benefit from these products, even imagined and unproven risks could turn opinion against them.

A few early and widely publicized research studies did suggest new risks from GMO crops, based on allergic reactions to corn chips, tumors in lab rats, and dead monarch butterfly caterpillars, but when public agencies reviewed these studies, they concluded all were badly designed or otherwise unconvincing. For example, a 2012 study published in the journal *Food and Chemical Toxicology*, found tumors in rats that had eaten GMO corn, but this study had used Sprague-Dawley rats that were unusually prone to tumors. The study was formally dismissed by the European Food Safety Agency (EFSA) and Germany's Federal Institute for Risk Assessment in Berlin, and the journal later retracted the paper (Casassus 2013).

The United States opted not to regulate GMO foods and crops as strictly as in Europe, even though many American consumers—when asked—expressed parallel worries (Hallman et al. 2003). GMOs encountered less official blockage in the United States in part because politically powerful corn, soybean, and cotton farmers quickly learned to value the new seeds. Because fewer European farmers planted these three crops, they did not complain when tight regulations blocked planting. Europe remained willing to import GMO soybeans for animal feed, in deference to its large and influential livestock industries.

GMO corn, soybeans, and cotton were mostly used as animal feed, auto fuel, or for industrial purposes, rather than as human food, so their cultivation spread widely in some countries, but GMO varieties of staple food crops like wheat, rice, and potato, plus GMO fruits and vegetables, have scarcely been planted at all, even in the United States. Some United States growers planted GMO potatoes and tomatoes for a time after 1998, but then they stopped doing so when retailers and fast-food chains began refusing these products in the hopes of avoiding activist protests. Many processed food products in America's supermarkets today do contain oils, starches, and sweeteners from GMO maize, soybean, and also sugar beets, but nearly all the unprocessed foods in these stores are completely non-GMO. So, in the United States, almost as much as in Europe, GMO crops intended for direct human consumption have largely been driven out of the marketplace.

This global rejection of GMO food crops has taken potential benefits away from Africa, where poor farmers are in need of new ways to protect crops against insects, crop disease, and drought. Farmers in Africa struggle every year against stalk borer infestations that reduce their yields of white maize, a leading food crop. If it were legal for them to plant *Bt* maize, crop yields would go up and pesticide use would also go down. For years the Republic of South Africa was the only country in the world to have approved *Bt* white maize for commercial planting, and when small farmers adopted the seeds, their yields roughly doubled (Shew 2021). Kenya finally approved *Bt* maize in 2022, but in much of the rest of Africa, even conducting research on GMO maize has remained illegal. In Tanzania in 2018, a tightly confined government experiment with drought-tolerant *Bt* maize was arbitrarily shut down by official order, and the planting materials had to be destroyed.

The developers of GMO seeds were initially baffled when so many governments with unmet food needs decided not to allow their use. One particularly frustrating moment came in 2002, when southern Africa was struck by a severe drought that left 15 million people across seven different countries in need of international food aid. Yellow corn from the United States—which happened to be GMO—had until then been welcomed in Africa as emergency food aid, but in August 2002 the Government of Zambia turned it down. Zambia's president, Levy Mwanawasa, later explained his decision: "Simply because my people are hungry, that is no justification to give them poison, to give them food that is intrinsically dangerous to their health" (BBC News 2002).

Zambia's mistrust of GMOs had been heavily stoked by civil society groups funded from abroad. At one open meeting, a local NGO leader told her fellow Zambians, "Yes, we are starving, but we are saying no to the food the Americans are forcing on our throats" (Phiri 2002). Her organization received its funding from the Swedish embassy in Lusaka, the Norwegian embassy, and the Danish foreign assistance agency, DANIDA (WFC 2007).

American officials sought to reassure the Zambians by inviting a government delegation on a fact-finding visit to the United States, but the Zambians were also invited to visit Europe. There they met with groups hostile toward GMOs, including Greenpeace, Friends of the Earth, the UK Soil Association (promoting organic), Norway's Institute for Gene Ecology, and an organization named Genetic Food Alert. Greenpeace warned the visiting Zambians that their organic produce sales to Europe would collapse if the nation opened itself up to GMOs, and Genetic Food Alert warned of the "unknown and un-assessed implications" of eating GMO foods. An organization from the UK named Farming and Livestock Concern warned the Zambians that GMO maize could introduce a retrovirus similar to HIV (Wilson 2002). A spokesperson for the Zambian delegation, upon returning home, said the trip had confirmed his anxieties about GMOs (Zambia, Government of Zambia 2002).

Africa's rejection of GMOs was also shaped by "biosafety" training programs funded by European donors, including a highly precautionary "model law" developed for the African Union through a German assistance program (Keetch et al. 2014). Instead of teaching Africans the science of GMOs, these programs taught regulators how to keep the technology out of African hands. Africa's policy-making elites are susceptible to European influence in part because of fears—largely exaggerated—that commercial farm sales into the European market will suffer if any GMO production is allowed (Gruere and Sengupta 2009). A lingering sense of post-colonial deference also plays a role. As one local Kenyan leader said in 2006, "Europe has more knowledge, education. So why are they refusing [GM foods]? That is the question everyone is asking" (Hand 2006). These Africans were seldom told that Europe's own science academies had found no evidence of any new risks from GMOs.

The advocates for GMO crops in Africa—agricultural scientists, for the most part—believe they are now seeing some policy change. In 2018, Nigeria finally approved *Bt* cotton for commercial planting, and it approved insect-resistant *Bt* cowpea in 2021. Kenya approved *Bt* cotton in 2019. Ghana had earlier given technical approval *to Bt* cowpea, yet Ghana's agricultural minister undercut this approval by saying his country didn't really need the technology, mentioning along the way that many of his countrymen were staunchly opposed to GMOs (Gakpo 2019). Late in 2022, under pressure from an extreme drought, Kenya' new president announced the lifting of a 10-year ban on importing and planting GMO maize, yet as also highlighted in chapter 5, a majority of Kenyans continued to express doubts about the safety of GMOs (Kagoe 2022).

10.7 When Will Popular Resistance Block Uptake?

In each of the cases above, agricultural methods based on modern crop science have been met by popular disapproval. This by itself is curious, since most people routinely welcome new applications of science in fields such as transportation, communication, and human medicine. But when will popular disapproval block the uptake of science-based farming practices? It did in only one of these four cases—GMO. What is the explanation?

One key factor is timing. Popular disapproval can prevail if it arises immediately, before most farmers have had a chance to profit from the new science. This was the case with GMOs. But if popular disapproval arises only after farmers have had a chance to taste a science-based benefit, the new science will be nearly impossible to take away. This was the case with the Green Revolution, industrial farming, and also synthetic chemical fertilizers.

The Green Revolution was broadly popular when it was launched, and it enjoyed several decades of rapid and successful uptake before Vandana Shiva galvanized the opposition with her 1991 manifesto. By then, however, millions of farmers had already tasted the benefits and did not want to go back to labor-intensive, low-yield methods. Today's farmers in LMICs have continued to improve on the original Green Revolution, by combining the improved seeds with "sustainable agricultural intensification" (SAI) methods that use inputs with greater precision, and employ IPM, micro-irrigation, and reduced tillage.

These methods scale up because they save labor and reduce input costs without sacrificing yields. Farmers have already put this kind of SAI to use on 453 million acres, or about nine percent of agricultural land worldwide (Pretty et al., 2018).

In similar fashion, "industrial farming" survived popular disapproval because it did not begin coming under strong criticism in rich countries until the 1970s, after the process of small farm consolidation had largely been completed. By then both the farmers remaining on the land and the ex-farmers who had taken jobs in town had seen their incomes rise. The commercial farmers, private investors, regulators who recognized this as progress shrugged off the criticism that came later, mostly from non-farmers. A 2016 review in the journal *Horticulturae* summed it up this way: "Despite the call for alternative methods of production over the years, the paradigm of industrial or conventional agriculture still dominates and permeates most mainstream academic and policy discussions about the future of agriculture" (Valenzuela 2016).

Timing was also an important factor in the failure of organic farming to replace synthetic chemical use. Broad popular anxieties about chemical use on farms did not solidify until after a series of pesticide residue scares in the 1980s, and by then returning to zero use of all synthetic chemicals to become organic was commercially unthinkable. Conventional farmers today remain eager to reduce the unnecessary use of synthetic chemicals to save money, but they know that cutting all the way back to zero, to gain organic certification, will bring costs that organic price premiums cannot cover. This is why less than one percent of harvested cropland in the United States is organic (Bialik and Walker 2019). The EU Farm to Fork strategy hopes to increase organic cropland from 9 percent today up to 25 percent of the total by 2030, but the economic cost to both farmers and consumers, plus the adverse land use implications, will make such a shift improbable. According to one German study, this shift would shrink cereals production in the EU by 21.4 percent. One and a half million hectares of European forest land would be lost, with an additional 5 million hectares lost beyond Europe, where other countries would expand production (mostly non-organic) to meet Europe's new food import needs (Henning and Witzke 2021).

Only in the case of GMO crops did popular resistance to innovative farm science prevail. It was able to do so because it emerged before large numbers of farmers had been given a chance to plant the seeds, and to appreciate the material benefits. In 1996 when popular fears first arose in Europe, most farmers around the world had never used the technology, making it easier for politicians to block uptake. Science academies in Europe did not find any new risks from GMOs, but early popular fears brought on stifling government regulations which kept GMO food crops out of farm fields, not just in Europe but also in most countries hoping to export to the European market. One young environmental campaigner against GMOs in the UK (who later recanted his opposition) observed ruefully that his early anti-GM work was "the most successful campaign I have ever been involved with" (Lynas 2013).

There may be a deeper pattern behind these timing issues. In the case of the Green Revolution, industrial farming, and synthetic chemicals, each of these science-based innovations was introduced and widely taken up before the emergence in the 1970s of a strong global environmental movement. Since we can assume this environmental movement will remain politically strong going forward, maybe crop science breakthroughs will remain more difficult to take up. We are now watching a significant test of this question, with the contested uptake of genome edited crops.

10.8 Will CRISPR Crops Become GMO 2.0?

Since 2012 scientists have mastered a new method to improve crops more quickly and at a lower cost, using genome editing tools such as CRISPR (which stands for Clustered Regularly Interspaced Short Palindromic Repeats). The beneficial edits can be accomplished without introducing any "foreign DNA," so the changes are similar in many ways to common natural mutations. This should have made gene editing more acceptable to the public, but it did not prevent environmental advocates in Europe, led by Friends of the Earth, from mounting a legal against CRISPR crops, branding them "GMO 2.0."

In 2018 these critics secured a ruling from the European Court declaring that gene-edited crops should be regulated just like GMOs, under the same stifling requirements for case-by-case pre-market approval, labeling, segregation in the fields, and audit-trail tracing (Stokstad 2018). The Court said in its ruling that the risks from CRISPR crops "might prove similar" to the risks associated with GMO crops, a puzzling assertion since all of Europe's science academies, and even the EU Commission, had by that time found no new risks from GMOs (EU 2010). One researcher at the Heinrich Heine University in Germany predicted this Court ruling would be "the death blow for plant biotech in Europe" (Stokstad 2018).

In this case resistance to the new science from environmental advocates did raise a legal hurdle well before farmers had a chance to plant any gene-edited crops yet, for other reasons, this new technology should prove more difficult to block than GMOs. The absence of "foreign DNA" makes these crops seem more natural, and with no detectable transgenes they will also be harder for regulators to identify, trace, and segregate. CRISPR techniques in the lab are also much faster, easier, and less costly than transgenic GMO techniques (Chen, Et al. 2019), so beneficial applications are likely to proliferate, and since detection will be nearly impossible some of the improved crops might move into farm fields through simple stealth. This happened even with GMO seeds, when plantings of soybeans in Brazil and cotton in India spread rapidly without official permission, as a fait accompli. The seeds performed so well that government regulators were forced to give permission in the end.

Other factors will also be in play. Countries in Asia and Africa are less likely to follow Europe's regulatory lead with genome-editing, compared to transgenic GMO crops two decades ago, because they now have a much greater scientific capacity—better labs and more molecular biologists—to take advantage of this new crop science. The fact that genome editing is faster and cheaper compared to rDNA will also make the technology harder for big corporations to monopolize. Non-corporate scientists will be able to develop improved varieties of the "orphan crops" ignored until now because they are only locally significant, or only planted by poor farmers who can't afford to buy commercial seeds.

Because most gene-edited crops will have no foreign DNA and will not have to come from large profit-making companies, they will also be easier for both farmers and consumers to trust. They are less likely to be locked up by patents. In September 2021, Wageningen University in the Netherlands, a world leader in agricultural research, announced it would waive its patent rights on CRISPR technologies for non-commercial use to help get these technologies more quickly into the hands of the poor (Van der Oost, J., and Fresco, L., 2021).

The political geography of crop science regulation has also changed over the past two decades. The Western Hemisphere, led by the United States, Canada, Argentina, and Brazil, has remained friendly to new crop science, including genome editing. Argentina was among the first to set in place permissive regulations for gene-edited crops, along with the United States, and as early as 2013 Canada commercialized a gene-edited variety of canola. The UK, which left the EU in January 2020, is going forward with gene edited crops as well. Meanwhile Europe has lost influence and China, a strong supporter of gene editing, has gained global influence through its Belt and Road Initiative. In agriculture, specifically, China hosted a Forum on China-Africa Cooperation (FOCAC) in Beijing in 2000 and created 25 Agricultural Technology Demonstration Centers in individual African countries.

China still hasn't commercialized transgenic rice, maize, or soy, but it has shown little hesitation on genome editing. As early as 2018 China had nearly as many CRISPR patent applications and published scientific papers on CRISPR as the United States. China's interest in the latest crop science was clear in its recent purchase of the international biotech company Syngenta. Eager to capture CRISPR's benefits, China's Ministry of Agriculture and Rural Affairs released preliminary guidelines early in 2022 that exempted gene-edited crops from GMO regulations, so long as they had no "foreign" DNA (FAO 2022). Few of China's agricultural exports go to Europe, so it will worry less about market risks from commercializing CRISPR crops.

Other important Asian countries that previously followed Europe on GMO regulations are also being more open to CRISPR crops. Japan has decided that genome-edited crops must be registered, but they don't need to undergo separate safety or environmental testing, and in December 2020 Japan explicitly approved the sale to consumers of a genome-edited tomato (Houser 2022). In India, at least seven institutes and universities are now using gene-editing to improve rice, banana, groundnuts, wheat, soybean, and maize. India still prohibits the planting of any transgenic GMO crops other than cotton and mustard, but in 2020 its National Academy of Agricultural Sciences recommended that gene-edited crops without foreign DNA should be exempt from GMO regulations (FAO 2022).

Even in Africa, both Nigeria and Kenya have now published guidelines for scientists working with CRISPR, indicating that crops (and animals) with no foreign DNA will probably not be regulated as GMOs. Kenya's Biosafety Authority has even granted approval to seven different gene-editing research projects.

10.9 Conclusion: Even Unpopular Science Reaches Farmers, Most of the Time

The historical record shows that even when agricultural science becomes unpopular with cultural elites, it can go forward in the field. Sometimes this happens because the new science only encounters cultural resistance after it has already reached farm fields, by which time farmers will refuse to give it up. This was the case with Green Revolution seeds, highly capitalized industrial farming, and synthetic chemicals. GMO food crops were blocked from a broad uptake because cultural resistance arose before most farmers got the seeds. The new political power of environmental organizations might seem to make such outcomes more probable in the future.

On the other hand, agricultural science is learning to protect itself from elite cultural resistance by finding a home in countries where food production imperatives are still strong, and where the grim realities of pre-modern, pre-industrial farming are a more recent memory. Twenty years ago, Asia mostly followed Europe's lead in blocking the uptake of GMO crops, but today Asia is turning away from Europe's example and joining the Western Hemisphere in clearing a path for genome editing. Even Africa, much of which missed out on both the Green Revolution and GMOs, is joining this camp. Europe's resistance to modern crop science is thus becoming politically isolated. This will likely prove uncomfortable for Brussels. Green Parties in Europe attracted to pre-industrial, artisanal crop farming may have to accept compromise in the end.

In the future, it is likely that popular misgivings toward agricultural science will continue to arise, especially among the well-fed urban dwellers in rich countries who have little first-hand exposure to commercial farming. But the resulting suspicions will not have to alter outcomes on farms around the world, so long as scientists continue to deliver new tools that are safe to use, sustainable, and most of all profitable for farmers. It will be farmers, more often than not, who get the last word.

References

Aemuels, A. 2019. "'They're Trying to Wipe Us Off the Map.' Small American Farmers are Nearing Extinction." *Time*, November 27.

AGRA (Alliance for a Green Revolution in Africa). 2020. *False Promises: The Alliance for a Green Revolution in Africa (AGRA)*. New York: Rosa Luxemburg Stiftung, July.

Aizen, M.A., S. Aguiar, J.C. Biesmeijer, L.A. Garibaldi, D.W. Inouye, C. Jung, D.J. Martins, et al. 2019. "Global Agricultural Productivity Is Threatened by Increasing Pollinator Dependence Without a Parallel Increase in Crop Diversification." *Global Change Biology* 25 (11): 3516–3527.

Altieri, M.A. 1999. "Applying Agroecology to Enhance the Productivity of Peasant Farming Systems in Latin America." *Environment, Development, and Sustainability* 1 197–217.

Appunn, K. 2021. "EU's Farm to Fork Strategy Impacts Climate, Productivity, and Trade." *Clean Energy Wire*, March 5. https://www.cleanenergywire.org/factsheets/eus-farm-fork-strategy-impacts-climate-productivity-and-trade

Asafu-Adjaye, J., L. Blomqvist, S. Brand, B. Brook, R. Defries, E. Ellis, C. Foreman, et al. 2015. *An Ecomodernist Manifesto*. Available online www.ecomodernism.org

Ausubel, J. 2015. "The Return to Nature: How Technology Liberates Environment." *The Breakthrough Institute*, May 12. https://thebreakthrough.org/images/elements/Figure_1.png

BBC News. 2002. "Zambia Refuses GM 'Poison.'" September 3.

Bechtel, W., and R.C. Richardson. 1998. "Vitalism." In *Routledge Encyclopedia of Philosophy*, ed. E. Craig. London: Routledge. https://www.rep.routledge.com/search?searchString=vitalism&newSearch=

Bernauer, T., and E. Meins. 2003. "Technological Revolution Meets Policy and the Market." *European Journal of Political Research* 42 (5): 643–683.

Bialik, K., and K. Walker. 2019. "Organic Farming on the Rise in the United States." Pew Research Center, January 10. https://www.pewresearch.org/fact-tank/2019/01/10/organic-farming-is-on-the-rise-in-the-u-s/

Borlaug, N, 1970. "The Green Revolution, Peace, and Humanity." Nobel Peace Prize Lecture, December 11.

Carson, R. 2002. *Silent Spring*. New York: Houghton Mifflin Company.

Casassus, B. 2013. "Study Linking Genetically Modified Corn to Rat Tumors Is Retracted." *Scientific American*, November 29. https://www.scientificamerican.com/article/study-linking-genetically-modified-corn-to-cancer/#:~:text=The%20study%20found%20that%20rats,added%20to%20their%20drinking%20water

Chen, K., Y. Wang, R. Zhang, H. Zhang, and C. Gao. 2019. "CRISPR/Cas Genome Editing and Precision Plant Breeding in Agriculture." *Annual Review of Plant Biology* 70: 667–697.

Condliffe, J. 2016. "A New Technique Makes GPS Accurate to an Inch," *Gizmodo*, February 11.

Conford, P. 2001. *The Origins of the Organic Movement*. Glasgow, UK: Floris Books.

Cornell University. 2016. *Digital Agriculture in New York State: Report and Recommendations.* Ithaca, NY: Cornell University. https://blogs.cornell.edu/ccefield cropnews/files/2016/11/StateonPrecisionAgFinalReport110716-1o99jgm.pdf

DeFrancesco, L. 2013. "How Safe Does Transgenic Food Need to Be?" *Nature Biotechnology* 31:794–802

DeGregori, T.R. 2004. "Green Myth vs. the Green Revolution," *Butterflies & Wheels*, February 5. http://www.butterfliesandwheels.org/2004/green-myth-vs-the-green-revolution/

EU. 2010. *A Decade of EU-funded GMO Research (2001–2010).* Report No. 24473. Brussels: European Commission. https://ec.europa.eu/research/biosociety/pdf/a_decade_of_eu-funded_gmo_research.pdf

EU (European Union). 2020. "A Farm to Fork Strategy: For a Fair, Healthy, and Environmentally-Friendly Food System." Brussels: European Commission. https://eur-lex.europa.eu/legal-content/EN/TXT/?uri=CELEX:52020DC0381

European Commission. 2021. "List of Potential Agricultural Practices That Euro-Schemes Could Support." Brussels: European Commission. https://ec.europa.eu/info/sites/default/files/food-farming-fisheries/key_policies/documents/factsheet-agri-practices-under-ecoscheme_en.pdf

Evenson, R.E., and D. Gollin. 2003. "Assessing the Impact of the Green Revolution, 1960 to 2000." *Science* 300 (5620): 758–762. https://www.ncbi.nlm.nih.gov/pubmed/12730592

EWG (Environmental Working Group). 2019. "EWG's 2019 Shopper's Guide to Pesticides in Produce." https://www.ewg.org/foodnews/dirty-dozen.php

EWG (Environmental Working Group), 2009. "Not so green—Green Revolution." April 15. https://www.ewg.org/news-insights/news/not-so-green-green-revolution

FAO. 1988. *Integrated Pest Management in Rice in Indonesia: Status after Three Crop Seasons.* Jakarta: FAO.

FAO, 2002. "Certified Organic Agriculture—Situation and Outlook." In *Organic Agriculture, Environment and Food Security*, eds. S. El-Hage Scialabba and C. Hattam, Chapter 3. Rome: FAO. https://www.fao.org/3/Y4137E/y4137e03.htm

FAO, 2003. *Unlocking the Water Potential of Agriculture.* Rome: FAO. https://www.fao.org/publications/card/en/c/406af8d8-f9bb-4814-bc69-d8a69abbfc72/

FAO. 2018. *Sustainable Food Systems: Concept and Framework.* Rome: FAO.

FAO. 2019. FAOSTAT database. http://www.fao.org/faostat/en/#data/QC/visualize

FAO. 2022. *Gene Editing and Agrifood Systems.* Rome: FAO.

Fernandez-Cornejo, J., C. Osteen, R. Nehring, and S.J. Wechsler. 2014. "Pesticide Use Peaked in 1981, Then Trended Downward, Driven by Technological Innovations and Other Factors." *Amber Waves*, June 2. https://www.ers.usda.gov/amber-waves/2014/june/pesticide-use-peaked-in-1981-then-trended-downward-driven-by-technological-innovations-and-other-factors/

Field to Market. 2016. *Environmental and Socioeconomic Indicators for Measuring Outcomes of On-Farm Production in the United States.* Third Edition. Washington, DC: Field to Market. http://fieldtomarket.org/media/2016/12/Field-to-Market_2016-National-Indicators-Report.pdf

Gakpo, J.O. 2019. "Ghana's Scientists, Farmers Reject Claim that GMO Crops Aren't Needed." *Alliance for Science Blog*, March 20. https://allianceforscience.cornell.edu/blog/2019/03/ghanas-scientists-farmers-reject-claim-gmo-crops-arent-needed/#:~:text=Ghana's%20science%20community%20and%20farmers,foods%20to%20ensure%20food%20security.

Gardner, B. 2002. *American Agriculture in the Twentieth Century: How it Flourished and What it Cost.* Cambridge: Harvard University Press.

Gollin, D., C.W. Hansen, and A.M. Wingender. 2021. "Two Blades of Grass: The Impact of the Green Revolution." *Journal of Political Economy* 129 (8): 2344–2384.

Gollin, D., M. Morris, and D. Byerlee. 2005. "Technology Adoption in Intensive Post-Green Revolution Systems." *American Journal of Agricultural Economics* 87 (5): 1310–1316.

Green, G.P. 2020. "Deindustrialization of Rural America: Economic Restructuring and the Rural Ghetto." *Local Development & Society* 1: 15–25.

Griswold, E. 2012. "How 'Silent Spring' Ignited the Environmental Movement." *New York Times Sunday Magazine*, September 21.

Gruere, G., and D. Sengupta, 2009. "Biosafety Decisions and Perceived Commercial Risks." IFPRI Discussion Paper 00847. International Food Policy Research Institute, Washington, DC.

Hallman, W., W.C. Hebden, H.L. Aquino, C.L. Cuite, and J.T. Lang. 2003. *Public Perceptions of Genetically Modified Foods: A National Study of American Knowledge and Opinion.* New Brunswick, NJ: Food Policy Institute.

Hand, E. 2006. "Africa in the Middle of the U.S.–EU Biotech Trade War." *GM Watch*, December 12. https://www.gmwatch.org/en/news/archive/2006/5572-africa-in-the-middle-of-us-european-trade-war-post-dispatch-12122006

Harrison, P. 2017. "Science and Secularization." *Intellectual History Review* 27 (1): 47–70.

Henning, C., and P. Witzke. 2021. "Economic and Environmental impacts of the Green Deal on the Agricultural Economy." Unpublished Manuscript, University of Kiel.

Holsapple, M.P., H.E. Dover, and K. Ayoob. 2017. "Don't Believe Everything You Hear About Pesticides on Fruits and Vegetables." *The Conversation*, April 12.

Houser, K. 2022. "7 ways CRISPR is shaping the future of food." *Freethink*, November 5. https://www.freethink.com/science/crispr-food

Howard, A. 1943. *An Agricultural Testament.* New York: Oxford University Press.

Kagoe, R. 2022. "Why Kenya is Turning to Genetically Modified Crops to Help with Drought." *BBC News, Nairobi*, November 9. https://www.bbc.com/news/world-africa-63487149

Kang, J. 2019. "Grocers Pick Produce for Healthy Growth." *Wall Street Journal*, December 27.

Keetch, D.P., D. Makinde, C.K. Weebadde, and K.M. Maredia. 2014. *Biosafety in Africa: Experiences and Best Practices.* East Lansing: Michigan State University.

Levidow, L., and J. Bijman. 2002. "Farm Inputs under Pressure from European Food Industry." *Food Policy* 27 (1): 31–45.

Lynas, M. 2013. "Lecture to Oxford Farming Conference." Oxford Farming Conference, Oxford, UK, January 3.

McBride, J. 2021. "How Green Party Success is Reshaping Global Politics." *Council on Foreign Relations Backgrounder*, July 7.

Naranjo, S.E. 2009. "Impacts of *Bt* Crops on Non-target Invertebrates and Insecticide Use Patterns." *CAB Reviews* 4 (11): 1–23. https://www.ars.usda.gov/ARSUserFiles/4056/naranjocabreview2009.pdf

NAS (National Academies of Sciences). 2016. "Genetically Engineered Crops: Experiences and Prospects- New Report." *News Release*, May 17. https://www8.nationalacademies.org/onpinews/newsitem.aspx?RecordID=23395

NGO/CSO Forum. 2002. "'Profit for Few or Food for All' Revisited Five Years Later." Paper presented at the 2002 Rome NGO/CSO Forum for Food Sovereignty, Rome, Italy, June 10.

Nicolia, A., A. Manzo, F. Veronesi, and D. Rosellini. 2013. "An Overview of the Last 10 Years of GE Crop Safety Research." *Critical Reviews in Biotechnology* 34 (1): 77–88.

Van der Oost, J., and L. Fresco. 2021. "Waive CRISPR Patents to Meet Food Needs in Low-Income Countries." *Nature*, 597: 178. https://doi.org/10.1038/d41586-021-02397-7

OTA (Organic Trade Association). 2019. "We're the Organic Trade Association." Accessed May 17, 2019. https://www.ota.com/

Paarlberg, R. 2008. *Starved for Science: How Biotechnology is Kept Out of Africa.* Cambridge: Harvard University Press.

Paarlberg, R. 1994. *Countrysides at Risk: The Political Geography of Sustainable Agriculture.* Washington, DC: Overseas Development Council.

Partelow, S., K.J. Winkler, and G.M. Thaler. 2020. "Environmental Non-governmental Organizations and Global Environmental Discourse." *PLoS One* 15 (5): e0232945.

Pew Research Center. 2016. *The New Food Fights: U.S. Public Divides over Food Science.* Washington, DC: Pew Research Center. https://www.pewresearch.org/science/2016/12/01/the-new-food-fights/

Phiri, B. 2002. "US Comes Under Attack Over GMOs," *The Post Zambia*, August 13. https://allafrica.com/stories/200208130100.html

Pretty, J., T.G. Benton, Z.P. Bharucha, L.V. Dicks, C.B. Flora, H.C.J. Godfray, D. Goulson, et al. 2018. "Global Assessment of Agricultural System Redesign for Sustainable Intensification." *Nature Sustainability* 1: 441–446.

Rosegrant, M.W., and P.B.R. Hazell. 2000. *Transforming the Rural Asian Economy: The Unfinished Revolution.* Hong Kong: Oxford University Press for the Asian Development Bank.

Rosset, P., J. Collins, and F.M. Lappe. 2000. "Lessons from the Green Revolution: Do We Need New Technology to End Hunger?" *Tikkun Magazine* 15 (2): 52–56.

Russell, C. 2009. *Autonomy and Food Biotechnology in Theological Ethics.* Bern, Switzerland: Peter Lang.

Ruttan, V.W. 2004. "Controversy about Agricultural Technology: Lessons from the Green Revolution." *International Journal of Biotechnology* 6 (1): 43–54.

Shew, A.M. 2021. "Yield Gains Larger in GM Maize for Human Consumption than Livestock Feed in South Africa." *Nature Food* 2: 104–109.

Shiva, V. 1991. *The Violence of the Green Revolution: Third World Agriculture, Ecology, and Politics.* London: Zed Books.

Smale, M., and T. McBride. 1996. "Understanding Global Trends in the Use of Wheat Diversity and International Flows of Wheat Genetic Resources." CIMMYT Economics Working Paper. International Maize and Wheat Improvement Center (CIMMYT), Mexico City, Mexico.

Smil, V. 2000. *Enriching the Earth: Fritz Haber, Carl Bosch, and the Transformation of World Food Production.* Cambridge, MA: MIT Press.

Smith, L.G., P.J. Jones, G.J.D. Kirk, B.D. Pearce, and A.G. Williams. 2018. "Modeling the Production Impacts of a Widespread Conversion to Organic Agriculture in England and Wales." *Land Use Policy* 76: 391–404.

Smith-Spangler, C., M.L. Brandeau, G.E. Hunter, J.C. Bavinger, M. Pearson, P.J. Eschbach, V. Sundaram, et al. 2012. "Are Organic Foods Safer or Healthier than

Conventional Alternatives? A Systematic Review." *Annals of Internal Medicine* 157 (5): 348–366.

Steiner, R. 1959. *Cosmic Memory: Prehistory of Earth and Man.* New York: Rudolf Steiner Publications.

Stokstad, E. 2018. "European Court Ruling Raises Hurdles for CRISPR Crops," *Science*, July 25. http://www.sciencemag.org/news/2018/07/european-court-ruling-raises-hurdles-crispr-crops

Swaminathan, M.S. 1994. Letter to Environment Magazine, Vol. 36, No. 3 (April), pp. 3-4.

Trigo, Eduardo, E. Cap, V. Malach, and F. Villareal. 2009. "Innovating in the Pampas: Zero-tillage Soybean Cultivation in Argentina." In *Millions Fed: Proven Successes in Agricultural Development*, eds. D.J. Spielman and R. Pandya-Lorch, Chapter 8, 59–64. Washington, DC: International Food Policy Research Institute. https://www.ifpri.org/publication/innovating-pampas-zero-tillage-soybean-cultivation-argentina

USDA. 2021a. "A Look at Agricultural Productivity Growth in the United States: 1948–2017." *USDA Blog*, July 29. https://www.usda.gov/media/blog/2020/03/05/look-agricultural-productivity-growth-united-states-1948-2017

USDA (United States Department of Agriculture). 2017. "Cash Receipts by Commodity, State Ranking." Economic Research Service Data. https://data.ers.usda.gov/reports.aspx?ID=17844

USDA, Economic Research Service. 2019. "Fertilizer Use and Price." https://www.ers.usda.gov/data-products/fertilizer-use-and-price/summary-of-findings/

USDA, Economic Research Service. 2020. "Agricultural Research and Productivity." https://www.ers.usda.gov/topics/farm-economy/agricultural-research-and-productivity/

USDA, Economic Research Service. 2022. "Farm Household Well-being: Income and Wealth in Context." https://www.ers.usda.gov/topics/farm-economy/farm-household-well-being/income-and-wealth-in-context/

Valenzuela, H. 2016. "Agroecology: A Global Paradigm to Challenge Mainstream Industrial Agriculture." *Horticulturae* 2 (1): 2.

Wax, E., and E. Anderson. 2021. "The Transatlantic Relationship Descends into a Food Fight." *Politico Pro*, September 29.

WFC (Women for Change). 2007. "Women for Change: WFC Networking." www.wfc.org/zm/networks.htm

Williams, R.G. 1986. *Export Agriculture and the Crisis in Central America.* Chapel Hill: University of North Carolina Press.

Wilson, M. 2002. "Will Their Protests Leave Her Hungry?" *The Telegraph*, November 23.

Winter, C.K., and S.F. Davis. 2006. "Organic Foods." *Journal of Food Science* 71 (9): R117–R124. https://doi.org/10.1111/j.1750-3841.2006.00196.x

Zambia, Government of Zambia. 2002. "Report of the Factfinding Mission by Zambian Scientists on Genetically Modified Foods." Lusaka, Zambia.

11

Enabling Positive Tipping Points in Public Support for Food System Transformation

The Case of Meat Consumption

Lukas Paul Fesenfeld and Yixian Sun

11.1 Introduction

Today's food production and consumption has large consequences for the environment and human health. With respect to climate change, our food system is now responsible for at least a third of the global anthropogenic greenhouse gas (GHG) emissions (Crippa et al. 2021). In particular, the production of red meat has become the largest source of methane, which is a powerful short-lived GHG (Fesenfeld et al. 2018). Livestock production is also the single largest driver of habitat loss, and a leading cause of soil erosion, water, and nutrient pollution across the world, which increasingly compound pressures on ecosystems and biodiversity (Machovina et al. 2015). In addition, scientific evidence suggests strong associations between meat consumption and health risks including total mortality, cardiovascular diseases, colorectal cancer, and type 2 diabetes (Battaglia Richi et al. 2015; Zheng et al. 2019). This issue of overconsumption is particularly salient for developed countries and large emerging economies where meat consumption is high (i.e., >20–30kg per person per year). Recent systematic reviews suggest that domestic demand in countries with tropical rainforests cause a significant proportion of agriculturally driven tropical deforestation (Pendrill et al. 2022). Hence, rapid dietary changes toward more plant-based diets are a critical component of global food system transformation as they hold the promise to make important contributions to solving health, climate, and ecological crises (Springmann et al. 2018). Without such changes, achieving the Paris Agreement targets and many Sustainable Development Goals (SDGs) is unlikely, even if all other sectors were to achieve rapid transition toward sustainability (Clark et al. 2020).

However, political economy dynamics often delay or derail policy interventions on this issue. In fact, many governments remain unwilling to take strong actions to reduce meat consumption as related policies may cause public backlash by intervening in people's everyday life (Fesenfeld 2020). How can policymakers overcome barriers in promoting ambitious policies to minimize the climate and

Lukas Paul Fesenfeld and Yixian Sun, *Enabling Positive Tipping Points in Public Support for Food System Transformation*. In: *The Political Economy of Food System Transformation*. Edited by: Danielle Resnick and Johan Swinnen, Oxford University Press. © Lukas Paul Fesenfeld and Yixian Sun (2023). DOI: 10.1093/oso/9780198882121.003.0011

environmental impacts of the food system? Drawing upon the literature on public opinion, transition, and policy studies, we develop a theoretical framework,
which identifies three factors to shift public opinion on transformative policy
change—policy framing, policy design, and policy feedback (Fesenfeld 2020, 2023;
Fesenfeld, Rudolph and Bernauer, 2022). We argue that ambitious transformative
food policies, such as measures to transition toward more plant-based diets, are
likely to gain public support when government interventions are carefully framed
to appeal to popular narratives, different types of policies are strategically combined, and positive feedback of policies are created over time. We use evidence
gathered from survey experiments with 4,874 respondents in China, Germany,
and the United States (US) to illustrate this argument. While focusing on public
opinion, we recognize that citizens' support for policies is only one dimension in
the political economy of food system transformation. Hence, to understand the
dynamics in the whole sectoral transformation, the insights drawn from public
opinion research should be combined with the analysis of the broader political
economy context (as outlined in other chapters of this book).

The rest of this chapter is structured as follows. Section 11.2 provides a brief
review of the existing literature on public opinion on sustainable food transition
and identifies research gaps. Section 11.3 introduces our theoretical framework,
which takes into account the roles of policy framing, design, and feedback in promoting food system transformation. After briefly explaining our methodological
approach, we present results from several survey experiments conducted since
2017 and show how they lend support to our argument. To conclude, we discuss
policy implications of our findings and important directions for future research.

11.2 Existing Literature on Public Opinion on Sustainable Food Policy

To understand how the public in different countries perceives and reacts to policies aimed at transforming the food system toward greater sustainability, especially
reducing meat consumption or promoting more plant-based diets, we first conducted a scoping review of the academic literature on public opinion regarding
sustainable food policy. Through keyword searches and screening, we identified
86 peer-reviewed publications related to public opinion of food policy (see our
methodology in Appendix). Over 90 percent of these studies were conducted in
developed countries and only 12 reviewed studies focus on meat-related policies.
Using cross-sectional survey data, most studies provide a snapshot of public support at one point in time without considering potential feedback of policies over
time. Our review identified several patterns. First, public opinion varies across different types of government policies. More importantly, support for policies that
add costs to consumers such as food taxes tend to be low. Abundant evidence
supports this. For instance, a study on taxes of sugar-sweetened beverages in the

US found that the majority of study participants opposed this policy because they believed that taxes are a quick way for politicians to fill budget holes, an unacceptable intrusion of government into people's lives, and harmful to the poor (Barry et al. 2013b). Likewise, a study on obesity prevention policy in Australia demonstrated that 90 percent of the respondents supported mandatory nutrition labelling, 83 percent supported zoning restrictions of unhealthy food shops, but only 40 percent supported taxes on unhealthy food because people are generally concerned about government overreach through taxation and the effectiveness of taxes in changing behaviors remains questionable (Farrell et al. 2019). A similar pattern also exists in the United Kingdom (UK) as a recent study showed that food place and promotion policies (e.g., supermarkets positioning healthier products at the end of aisles and checkouts and retailers restricting promoting on high-calorie food and drinks) were much more supported by the public than tax policies (e.g., taxes on sugary drinks or high-fat content foods) (Fatemi et al. 2021).

Moreover, policies that impose restrictions on consumers receive lower support as many citizens are concerned about their freedom of choice and therefore unwilling to accept more government interventions in their daily lives. For instance, Kwon et al.'s (2019) online survey measuring support for 13 food policies to promote healthy diets by 19,857 adults in Australia, Canada, Mexico, the UK, and the US found that across all countries, the highest level of support was for policies that provided incentives (e.g., price subsidies) or information (e.g., calorie labeling on menus), and the lowest level of support was for those that imposed restrictions (e.g., restrictions on food company sponsorship of sport events). Likewise, when studying consumer support for supermarkets' initiatives to promote healthy foods in these five countries, Gómez-Donoso et al. (2021) found that "more shelf space for fresh and healthier foods" received the highest support (from 72 percent of the respondents), whereas "checkouts with only healthy products" received the lowest support (from only 48.6 percent of the respondents). Research on different types of "nudges"—behaviorally motivated interventions that steer people in certain directions but maintain freedom of consumer choice—by national governments showed that the policy of having a meat-free day per week has been perceived highly intrusive in people's lives and accordingly received low approval rates in countries like Denmark (Loibl et al. 2018). Pechey et al. (2022) showed that in the UK, policies targeting meat consumption were less supported than policies targeting unhealthy food. They also found that labels and information campaigns were the most accepted policies to reduce meat consumption, followed by measures to reduce availability and provide incentives for plant-based diets. Increasing prices and banning advertising for meat, however, were the least supported measures. Yet, similar to Fesenfeld et al. (2020), Pechey et al. (2022) found that there is substantial scope to increase support for meat reduction policies. All in all, the existing literature sheds light on the importance of policy design when promoting sustainable food as public support for different types of policies varies significantly.

Second and related, the messages provided when introducing a policy can affect public support for that policy. In other words, policy framing matters as campaigners can use messages to alter individuals' preferences through changes in the presentation of the issue in question (Chong and Druckman 2007). For instance, research on the debate about meat taxes in UK media found that the arguments on meat taxes were categorized into five major topics (i.e., climate change and environment, human health, effects on animals, fairness, and acceptability of government intervention), which are associated with different values (Simmonds and Vallgårda 2021; see also Chapter 2 of this volume). The implication is that policy advocates can strategically use certain frames to highlight specific arguments and thus appeal to targeted segments of the population. For instance, research on policies targeting child obesity showed that, regardless of how the cause of childhood obesity was framed, when a news report frames the problem using individualized depictions of a specific child, survey respondents were less likely to support prevention policies than when the report described the problem in more general terms (Barry et al. 2013a). Meanwhile, research found that highlighting policies' effectiveness to protect human health could increase public demand for the relevant policies aiming to reduce unhealthy food (Reynolds et al. 2019). On reduction of meat consumption, Graça et al.'s (2020) study in Portugal showed that individuals who read a news piece about a law approving meat curtailment policies were more likely to support such policies, irrespective of individual differences in ideology and consumption. Also, Perino and Schwickert (2023) showed that framing meat taxes as an animal welfare tax can significantly increase public support for adopting meat taxes in Germany. Hence, we expect that public support for policies to transform the food system can be significantly affected by policy framing.

Third, individuals' awareness of, and concerns about, the sustainability impacts of food are likely to influence their support for relevant policies. For example, research on the food-energy-water nexus in the US consistently showed that individuals' knowledge about such nexus issues as well as their concern for the environment increases their support of policies for managing food, energy, and water resources (Bullock and Bowman 2018; Portney et al. 2018). Likewise, a study in Australia found that support for environmental food policies is positively associated with people's concerns over environmental impacts of food, and their pro-environment purchasing intentions are positively linked to concerns over nutritional, environmental, food safety, and animal welfare impacts of food (Worsley et al. 2015). Hence, building awareness on the sustainability impacts of food consumption and production can be an important pathway to increasing public support for policy interventions.

Fourth, some studies have also paid attention to the dynamic process of dietary transition and potential feedback of peoples' changing opinion and behavior on policy. For instance, research has identified the links between projections about the future of a plant-based society and current support for policies to promote plant-based diets. By investigating support of university students in New Zealand for social changes toward plant-based societies, Judge and Wilson (2015) found that for a vegetarian future, the strongest predictor of current support for social change was the expectation that widespread vegetarianism would reduce societal dysfunction, whereas for a vegan future, the strongest predictor of support for social change was an expectation of increased interpersonal warmth in a vegan society.[1] Sparkman and Walton (2017) showed that dynamic social norms, i.e. information about how people's behavior changes over time, can lead to strong meat consumption shifts. These findings suggest possible feedback effects across society as dietary changes accelerate. This reinforces Carlsson et al. (2022) research in Sweden, which found that people's growing experiences with meat alternatives can increase their willingness to pay for such substitutes. Therefore, changes in behaviors and respective social norms may have positive feedback effects on public support for food system transformation.

In summary, although empirical research on public support for policy promoting more plant-based diets remains limited, the evidence provided by recent studies has shown promising signs of the possibility to trigger such changes. For example, Perino and Schwickert (2023) showed in a recent referendum choice experiment that a majority of German citizens clearly supported an animal welfare meat tax rate of €0.39/kg (or €50/t CO_2). This finding suggests that citizens in some developed countries have become more conscious of their meat consumption and are willing to accept higher taxes on meat compared to other countries. Likewise, in the US, partisanship does not necessarily seem to be a barrier to food system transformation as the differences between Democrats and Republicans converge on issues of organic and local food as well as affordable food (Biedny et al. 2020). Therefore, as pointed out by Happer and Wellesley (2019), there is significant potential to develop and reinforce a positive narrative around the benefits of dietary change, and the most effective levers for action are likely to be those that resonate with everyday concerns and that stress the co-benefits of dietary change such as improved health and wellbeing.

11.3 Theoretical Argument

Our scoping review shows that the scientific community has paid increasing attention to the question of public support for the sustainability transition in the food sector. However, the up-to-date knowledge on pathways to food system

---

[1] "Warmth" is a concept in psychology, which refers to "a constellation of traits related to perceived favourability of the other person's intentions toward us, including friendliness, helpfulness, and trustworthiness" (Williams and Bargh, 2008: 606).

transformation remains fragmented. Here we propose a theoretical framework that combines three key factors—policy framing, design, and feedback—to understand dynamics in public support for food policies aimed at rapid transformation aligned with the goal of the Paris Agreement and the 2030 Agenda for Sustainable Development.

The first factor in our framework is policy framing, which is often seen as a popular communication strategy with identity-protective reasoning (Druckman and McGrath 2019). By "framing," we refer to the instances where actors use messages to alter people's preferences by changing the presentation of an issue or an event (Chong and Druckman 2007). In other words, when promoting a new regulation or government intervention, policymakers and their supporters can tailor messages emphasizing specific subsets of arguments to certain population subgroups in order to gain their support. In the past decade, a large number of studies were produced to examine framing effects in the area of environmental and climate policy. Most of these studies have found significant effects of different types of framing on public opinion. Notwithstanding some caveats to framing research (Bernauer and McGrath 2016; Fesenfeld et al. 2021, Fesenfeld et al, 2022), the importance of framing in the policy cycle is key since providing additional and tailored information can change citizens' understanding on the issue, and consequently their policy support and behaviors.

Beyond framing, the second, and probably more important, factor for changing public support is policy design. The premise of this factor is that food system transformation is likely to require mixing various types of policies including those at the supply- and demand-sides that induce both behavioral and technological innovations (Geels et al. 2017; Fischer, 2018; Poore and Nemecek 2018; Springmann et al. 2018). Past research has shown that many citizens perceive supply-side regulations and pull measures (e.g., discounts for environmentally friendly food products) as less intrusive and costly and thus support them more; in contrast, demand-side market-based push measures and regulations, like meat taxes or restrictions in public cafeterias, receive lower support (Fesenfeld 2020; Fesenfeld et al. 2020; Fesenfeld 2022; Pechey et al. 2022; Perino and Schwickert 2023). For many citizens, the material and immaterial costs (compared to the benefits) of such demand-side push measures are more salient and visible. Besides higher financial costs and restrictions in their personal lives, citizens also often perceive such demand-side push measures as unfair and not effective. Earmarking revenues from taxes to compensate for low-income groups in society as well as for green investments could partially address these concerns and enhance public support. Moreover, the level of policy stringency, i.e., the increase in the policy ambition vis-à-vis the status quo, can affect public support. More stringent policies often also imply higher perceived costs, especially for more visible demand-side policies, and thus can lead to lower support levels. As outlined in previous studies (Fesenfeld et al. 2020; Fesenfeld 2022), we expect that the strategic packaging of different types of policies with different levels of stringency can increase public support for food policies. This expectation rests on the assumption that positively valued policy design features can compensate for the negative support effects of policy design features with high cost visibility for citizens (Häusermann et al. 2018; Fesenfeld 2020).

The third factor in our proposed framework is policy feedback, which has not yet been a focus of empirical studies on public opinion about food policy. "Policy feedback" broadly refers to the variety of ways in which existing policies can shape key aspects of politics and policymaking (Béland and Schlager 2019). More specifically, feedback effects occur through two mechanisms: first, policies provide resources and incentives that encourage political actors as well as individuals to act in ways that lock in a particular path of policy development since policies cannot be easily reversed and generate increased returns; second, policies also have cognitive consequences by providing actors with information and cues that encourage particular interpretations of the political world (Pierson 1993, 2000). In other words, by changing material incentives, perceptions, and social norms, certain policies or interventions may, over time, trigger transformative changes. Over the past three decades, policy feedback has become an important research topic in the field of public policy and transition studies, as well as with respect to environmental and climate policy (Rosenbloom et al. 2019). However, it has so far received scant attention from food policy researchers.

Research on feedback requires attention to sequencing and ratcheting-up dynamics in the policy lifecycle (Levin et al. 2012; Pahle et al. 2018; Farmer et al. 2019). Harnessing positive policy feedback via a strategic sequence of policies over time is likely to be a critical enabler for transformative food policy change in the face of scarce political and economic resources. In the case of meat system transformation, one can expect that the current political-economic equilibrium and the respective public discourse around meat consumption and production can shift if change-oriented actors identify sensitive intervention points to gradually booster public support for ambitious sustainable food policies, and ultimately trigger non-linear, often abrupt changes toward a more sustainable food system (so-called positive tipping points [Sharpe and Lenton 2021; Fesenfeld et al. 2022]). For instance, actors can destabilize the existing meat system through adopting first politically less controversial supply-sided pull policies that foster innovations and offer new income sources to potential losers of more stringent policies (e.g., governmental support for the diffusion of sustainable meat substitutes and consumer discounts for plant-based alternatives, etc.). These policies may gradually shift public opinion on meat and its regulations by changing social norms and consumer behaviors. Moreover, such policy sequencing may also create changes in interest group coalitions (e.g., new meat substitute industries), which seek to change the framing and public narratives around meat and respective policies. This, in turn, may generate feedback in public support for more stringent policy actions to transform food systems.

Overall, taking a political economy approach that incorporates policy framing, design, and feedback effects on public support is helpful to understanding food policymaking decisions. Yet, this political economy perspective needs to also account for the relative role of public support in shaping food policy design choices compared to other factors, like interest groups power, political institutions, and broader economic developments and external shocks. These factors can moderate the relative effects of public opinion on food policymaking. Swinnen's (2018) review shows that different agents along value chains—from farmer groups and processors to retailers and consumers—influence agricultural and food policymaking. According to Culpepper (2011), the public salience of different policy options moderates the relative influence of different interest groups and public opinion on policymaking. In general, we can expect that public opinion matters more for very salient and visible policy decisions compared to more technical, less salient decisions. Past research has also indicated that political institutions including regime types, electoral rules, and bureaucrats' position can influence governments' choices of agricultural and food policies. For example, farmer or consumer groups have more influence on governments' policy choices (e.g., tax on a commodity) in democratic systems (Olper 2007). Within democracies, Olper and Raimondi (2013) have found that agriculture is more protected (or less taxed) under a proportional electoral rule or a presidential system than under a majoritarian rule or a parliamentary system. Among OECD countries, right-wing governments are on average more protectionist in agriculture than left-wing governments (Olper 2007), but this effect is conditioned by the political power of key interest groups in each country. In the case of autocracies, economic development can also shift communist regimes from taxing to subsidizing agriculture as shown by the case of China (Rozelle and Swinnen 2010). Additionally, dramatic changes in agricultural and food policy in many countries have been triggered by large external shocks (e.g., economic crises or pandemics), which can overcome policy inertia and change dominant actor coalitions (Anderson 2009). Thus, governments' food policy choices result from the dynamic interactions between public opinion and the broader political economy environment.

Figure 11.1 summarizes how the three factors, policy framing, design, and feedback, are likely to influence public support for sustainable food transition. We expect that sustainable food transformation can gain public support when government interventions are carefully framed, strategically designed by combining different types of policies, and positive feedback effects are harnessed. We also assume that variation in the broader political economy environment and institutional setting (e.g., power of different interest group coalitions, ideologies, regime types, electoral systems, etc.) will moderate the relative effects of these three factors in shaping public support for transformative food policies.

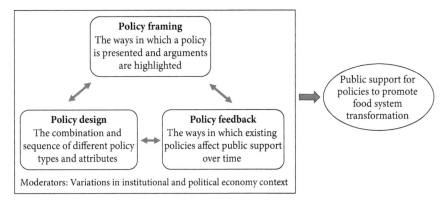

Figure 11.1 A framework of framing, design and feedback for food system transformation.

11.4 Methods Used in Survey-Embedded Experiments

To illustrate our argument, we present here initial evidence from a large survey in China, Germany, and the US that we conducted in 2017–2018. We used quota sampling to ensure representativeness in terms of age, employment status, gender, income, and region (please see details in our related publications Fesenfeld et al. 2020; Fesenfeld et al. 2021). These countries were selected for two reasons. First, they are among the world's largest producers and consumers of meat products, hence exerting a major environmental impact (Global Footprint Network 2018; OECD 2018). Second, the three countries have very different political economy systems: authoritarian state-led economy in China, coordinated market economy in Germany, and liberal market economy in a bipartisan system in the US. The structure and power of the interest groups supporting the meat industry are likely to vary across these cases. Moreover, the salience of the issue of meat consumption in these countries seem to also vary. For instance, with strong support of civil society, reduction of meat consumption has been put on the government's agenda of climate policy in Germany, but the issue was much less considered in the US, and almost not at all in China. Hence, the three country cases provide a good sample to investigate how different political economy contexts shape public support for food system transformation. Finally, the three countries vary in their current rates of meat consumption. While the US has the highest per capita meat consumption of all three countries (128 kg/person in 2019), also Germany (76 kg/person in 2019) has a higher per capita meat consumption than China (64 kg/person in 2019). Nevertheless, in the US and Germany, per capita meat consumption is stagnating or slightly falling while in China it has been rising sharply over the last years.[2]

---

[2] The data are from the UN Food and Agricultural Organization, see also respective interactive visualization on OurWorldInData at https://ourworldindata.org/meat-production.

11.4.1 Sampling

The survey was conducted in collaboration with Ipsos. In total, we conducted our survey-embedded experiments with 4,874 respondents in China (n=1626), Germany (n=1624), and the United States (n=1624). All experiments were internet-based, and participants were recruited via the online panels that Ipsos maintains in each country. For our survey, Ipsos pre-selected respondents from their panels according to quotas and constructed samples that were representative of the national voting age population in the three countries. More specifically, we used hard quotas in our sampling in an attempt to match distribution by gender, age, and region according to each country's latest census data. Quotas for gender and age were combined to ensure that each age group was nationally representative in terms of gender distribution. We also employed soft quotas for education, income, rural-urban population, and occupation to ensure that the samples are not too skewed toward certain socio-demographic groups.

The quotas worked well in Germany and the US such that our samples in these two countries closely followed distribution by income, education, rural–urban divide and occupation in the national population. The sample from China was more skewed toward a higher educated, higher income urban population because sampling rural, low-income populations in China is currently not feasible through internet-based surveys. Yet, given the particularly significant uneven economic development in China and the country's political regime, we believe that our sample represents well that subgroup of the Chinese population—namely, the urban middle-class—whose consumption has the most significant impact (Wiedenhofer et al. 2017; Zhang et al. 2016). In our robust check analyses (see further details in Fesenfeld et al. 2020, 2021), we also included various socio-demographic and political control variables and repeated the analyses for the urban middle-class, higher educated segments of respondents in Germany and the US. These analyses indicate that our results are robust and not substantially affected by the sample differences across China and the two other countries. The survey was conducted in the three countries during February 2018.

The outcome variables of interests for this chapter focus on policy support. The first outcome variable concerned willingness to pay more for meat products as part of increasing taxes; we assumed that higher prices would discourage meat consumption. We first showed respondents an indicative average price for meat in their country and asked them to indicate on a scale from 0 to 100 percent how much more they would be willing to pay for meat (compared to current prices) as part of a tax increase. To increase the external validity of our findings and reduce potential social desirability bias, we connected respondents' responses (as percentages) to the respective price increase and showed them how much money they would personally have to pay for meat under the related scenario. The second outcome variable concerned support for public policy that promotes reduction of meat consumption and the consumption of meat alternatives. We differentiated here between three prominent types of meat alternatives, namely plant-based meat substitutes, insect-based meat substitutes, and lab-based meat substitutes. Here, we asked respondents to indicate their level of support for policies for reducing meat consumption or promoting meat alternatives in their country on a 7–point Likert scale (ranging from "strongly oppose" to "strongly support").

11.4.2 Combined Framing and Conjoint Experiments

To overcome the limits of simple surveys in terms of social desirability bias and test policy framing and design effects, the survey also included combined framing and conjoint experiments. In a first framing experimental step, in each of the three country samples we randomly varied four different policy frames to compare their effects on policy support. Based on our prior expert interviews in these countries, we identified four broad types of arguments in favor of shifting meat consumption and respective policy change. They are the protection of (1) animal welfare, (2) the global climate, (3) the local environment, and (4) personal health. We hence designed our treatments for the experiment along the lines of these real-world arguments to create realistic policy implications concerning the effects of policy framing on public support for dietary shifts. To ensure that participants read and looked carefully at the framing text and graphical illustrations, they could not move on from the treatment page for a minimum of ten seconds before continuing the survey. We then employed a manipulation check to ensure that participants had understood the essential information in the related frames and that the treatment worked as expected.

As our primary outcome variable of interest, we here use respondents' policy support for differently designed policy packages as measured in a conjoint experiment that was administered to respondents after the framing experiment. Conjoint experiments ask respondents to evaluate profiles that combine multiple randomly assigned attributes. We used a conjoint design of fully randomized paired profiles in which each respondent was shown profiles of two different hypothetical policy packages displayed side-by-side. Hence, each policy measure constituted an "attribute" in the package to which it belonged, and the attribute values were randomly assigned such that the two policy packages in each pair differed in one or more attribute values (Hainmueller et al. 2014). Each policy-package contained six types of policies (i.e., new tax on meat, rules for public cafeteria, animal welfare standards, information campaigns, discount for vegetarian alternatives, and reducing subsidies for meat products) and an additional attribute related to earmarking for the tax policy. We choose these six policy instruments based on expert interviews and a review of the existing food policy literature (Fesenfeld et al. 2020). Table 11.1 provides an overview of the policy instruments and stringency levels

Table 11.1 Overview of policy design attributes in the conjoint experiment.

Policy Instrument	Policy Stringency (high, medium or no change to status quo)	Policy Type and Primary Target Group	Perceptions of Policy-Induced Costs and Benefits by Majority of Citizens	Expected Policy Design Effects on Support for Policy Packages
"Taxes"—New tax on meat and fish products	• Increase prices by 30% • Increase prices by 15% • No new tax	• Market-based push instrument targeting consumer demand	• Low Benefits & Moderate to High Costs	Moderate to Strong Negative Effects on Support for Packages
"Regulations"—Rules about minimum share of vegetarian meals in public cafeterias	• At least 75% vegetarian meals • At least 50% vegetarian meals • At least 25% vegetarian meals • No such rules	• Command-and-control pull instrument targeting consumer demand	• Low to Moderate Benefits & Moderate to High Costs	
"Campaigns"—Information campaigns	• Frequent campaigns • Occasional campaigns • No campaigns	• Information-based pull instrument targeting consumer demand	• Moderate Benefits & Low Costs	Moderate to Strong Positive Effects on Support for Packages

Continued

Table 11.1 *Continued*

Policy Instrument	Policy Stringency (high, medium or no change to status quo)	Policy Type and Primary Target Group	Perceptions of Policy-Induced Costs and Benefits by Majority of Citizens	Expected Policy Design Effects on Support for Policy Packages
"Discounts"—Discounts for low-emission (vegetarian) alternatives	• Reducing prices by 30% • Reducing prices by 15% • No discounts	• Market-based pull instrument targeting consumer demand	• Moderate to High Benefits & Low Costs	
"Producer subsidies"—Reduction of subsidies for meat and fish producers	• Eliminating subsidies • Halving subsidies • Keeping subsidies at current level	• Market-based push instrument targeting supply side	• Moderate to High Benefits & Low Costs	
"Standards"—Animal farming standards	• Organic standards/free range • Higher animal farming standards • Standards kept at current level	• Command-and-control push instrument targeting producer supply	• Moderate to High Benefits & Low Costs	

Note: Please also compare to Fesenfeld et al. 2020 for more details on the experimental design. In our conjoint experiment, the policy stringency of each policy instrument randomly varied between three levels, i.e., no difference from the status quo, a medium level of stringency, and a high level of stringency. We expect citizens' perceived policy-induced costs and benefits and thus also their support level to vary according to the type of instrument and the level of policy stringency.
Source: Fesenfeld et al. (2020); reproduced with permission.

that we randomly varied in the conjoint experiment as well as the expected support effects among the majority of respondents based on previous research and the arguments outlined in the theory section (Fesenfeld et al. 2020). Respondents then indicated which of the two presented policy packages they would choose and to what extent they supported or opposed each package using an ordinal scale of seven degrees ranging from "strongly oppose" to "strongly support." These ratings resulted in a numerical variable from 1 to 7 for participants' level of support for each package.

In this chapter, we go beyond our previous publications (Fesenfeld et al. 2020, 2021) and combine the framing and conjoint experiments to discuss policy framing and design effects simultaneously. Moreover, this combination of experiments allows us to test for potential interactions between policy framing and design.

11.5 Results

Turning to the empirical findings, Figure 11.2 illustrates the observed variation in consumers' willingness to pay more for meat as part of a tax increase in the three countries. In China and Germany, participants indicated the greatest willingness to pay more for meat products. This is a significantly higher willingness to pay than the willingness of American respondents. Overall, these results show substantial average support for increasing taxes on meat to reduce meat consumption.

This finding is buttressed by our results of the average support for policies to reduce meat consumption and promote meat alternatives in the three countries. Figure 11.3 below shows that in China, a majority of respondents clearly supports public policies to reduce meat consumption and promote certain meat alternatives. However, the support for public policies to promote meat alternatives varies by meat substitute type. In China policies promoting plant-based alternatives receive the highest support, followed by policies promoting lab-based meat and insect-based meat. In Germany, on average respondents accept public policies to reduce meat consumption and promote plant-based meat alternatives. Yet, German respondents clearly oppose public policies promoting lab-based and insect-based meat. In the US, we find the same pattern. Also, here respondents on average accept (but not actively support) public policies to reduce meat consumption and promote plant-based meat alternatives, but not other types of meat alternatives.

Although we do not empirically explore the reasons for these differences here, socio-political and cultural differences between China and the other two countries are likely to account for these differences in public attitudes. Broadly speaking,

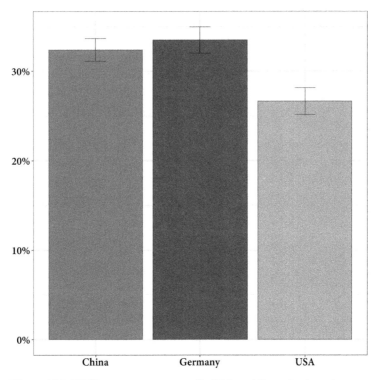

Figure 11.2 Willingness to pay more (in %) by adding a tax to reduce meat consumption.

Note: The graph shows the mean willingness to pay more for meat as part of a tax increase in China, Germany, and the US. The lines indicate 95 percent confidence intervals. Willingness to pay more for meat as part of a tax increase was measured on a scale from 0 percent to 100 percent meat price increases (compared to current prices), where higher values imply greater willingness to pay more for meat. In China, respondents are, on average, willing to pay 32.5 percent higher prices for meat than today due to a respective tax increase, while in Germany the average accepted price increase due to higher taxes was 34 percent. In the US, the average accepted price increase for meat due to higher meat taxes is 27 percent (compared to current prices) and thus significantly lower than in the two other countries.

China has a more collectivist culture valuing a strong role of the state, while Germany and the US have a rather individualistic and more liberal culture (Hofstede 2001). Moreover, food traditions in China differ strongly from the other two countries (Happer and Wellesley 2019; Fesenfeld 2020). For instance, plant-based meat sources, such as soy protein, have a long tradition in China, while such alternatives traditionally have been less prominent in Germany and the US. The explanatory factors of these cross-country differences warrant further investigation.

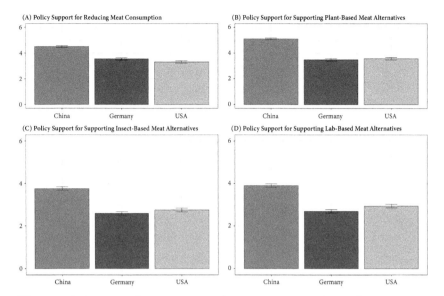

Figure 11.3 Average policy support to reduce meat consumption and promote different types of meat alternatives in China, Germany, and the United States.

Note: The lines indicate 95 percent confidence intervals. Support for policy reducing meat consumption and promote meat alternatives was measured on a scale from 1 to 7, where higher values imply stronger policy support.

11.6 Combined Framing and Policy Design Effects

Nevertheless, simple stated preference measures for general policy support might overestimate true support due to social desirability biases. Also, as outlined in our literature review citizens are likely to hold varying preferences for different types of policy instruments and the specific policy design is thus an important factor to consider. Moreover, as highlighted in our theoretical argument, policy design and framing might interact and jointly affect public support for policies to transform the food system.

Our framing and conjoint experiments can reduce such social desirability risks and yield more externally valid results (Hainmueller et al. 2015). In the following, we present the results of combining two conjoint and framing experimental studies.[3] As outlined in the Method section above, respondents had the choice between different pairs of food policy packages consisting of six different types of food policies. In addition, prior to rating the support for these policy packages, respondents were randomly confronted with four different types of policy frames. This design

---

[3] As outlined in the Method section, we here combine two experiments that we discuss in more detail in Fesenfeld et al. (2020, 2021).

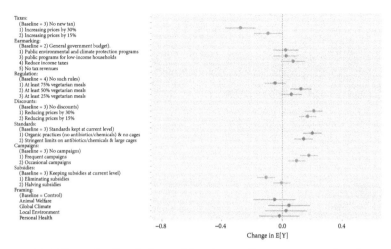

Figure 11.4 Effects of policy design and framing attributes on respondents' support rating (China).

Note: Scale is from 1 to 7, where higher values imply stronger policy support on policy packages to reduce meat consumption. Data points with horizontal lines indicate average marginal component effects for medium and high policy design stringency and different framing treatments with cluster-robust 95 percent confidence intervals from linear least squares regression. The dashed vertical line at 0 on the y-axis denotes the baseline category (that is, no design change to the status quo and no framing). The figure is based on data collected for Fesenfeld et al. (2020, 2021).

thus allows us to estimate the average marginal component effects on policy support of both different policy design attributes and policy frames as well as their potential interactions.

In contrast to the more generic policy support items outlined in Figures 11.2 and 11.3 above, here we test the support for specific types of policy instruments. In addition to the advantages of conjoint experiments to reduce social desirability risks (Hainmueller et al. 2015), the measurement of specific policy instruments arguably increases the external validity of results because individuals are less likely to overstate their support for specific instruments compared to general policy goals (Fesenfeld 2020).

Figure 11.4 shows the average marginal component effects of the different policy design and framing attributes on respondents' support rating on policy packages to reduce meat consumption in China. As expected, including a tax in a policy package that increases the prices of meat by 30 percentage points on average reduces support for a proposed policy package by about 0.28 points (on a 7–point Likert scale) in China, while a tax that would increase prices by 15 percentage points reduces support by around 0.1 points (on a 7–point Likert scale). However, against our expectations, earmarking the tax revenues for social or environmental purposes does not significantly affect support levels in China. Interestingly, demand-side regulations that define a minimum share of vegetarian meals in public cafeterias also do not negatively affect support levels in China. A minimum share of 50 percent vegetarian meals would even significantly increase support levels in China. This finding contradicts our expectation about the negative support effects of demand-side restrictions outlined in the theory section and Table 11.1 above.

In line with our expectations, we find that adding discounts for plant-based meat alternatives and stricter animal welfare standards can significantly increase support levels for a proposed policy package in China. For example, adding discounts for plant-based meat alternatives to a policy package would increase support by about 0.22 points (on a 7–point Likert scale) in China. While adding information campaigns also increase the average support levels for a proposed policy package, eliminating subsidies for meat producers significantly reduces support. Surprisingly, the policy framing attribute, compared to the policy design attributes, does not significantly affect support levels in China.

As illustrated in Figure 11.5, similar to China, we also find in Germany that the combination of different positively and negatively valued policy design attributes can increase support for ambitious food policy packages. In Germany, we find that strong tax increases reduce support levels by 0.49 points (on a 7–point Likert scale) and thus more than in China. However, in contrast to the Chinese case, we can observe small but statistically significant positive effects of earmarking

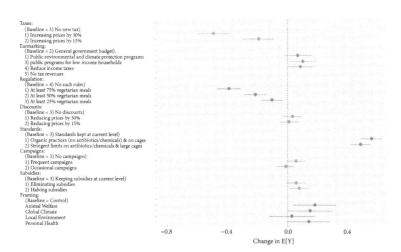

Figure 11.5 Effects of policy design and framing attributes on respondents' support rating (Germany).

Note: Scale is from 1–7, where higher values imply stronger policy support on policy packages to reduce meat consumption. Data points with horizontal lines indicate average marginal component effects for medium and high policy design stringency and different framing treatments with cluster-robust 95 percent confidence intervals from linear least squares regression. The dashed vertical line at 0 on the y-axis denotes the baseline category (that is, no design change to the status quo and no framing). The figure is based on data collected for Fesenfeld et al. (2020, 2021).

tax revenues for public programs for low-income households. Also, in contrast to the Chinese case, stringent rules about the minimum share of vegetarian meals offered in public cafeterias reduce support for a proposed policy package by about 0.39 points (on a 7–point Likert scale). This is in line with our expectation on the negative support effects of stringent demand-side push measures. While unexpectedly discounts for plant-based meat alternatives do not significantly affect support levels in Germany, adding stricter animal welfare standards would increase support by about 0.56 points in Germany. Also, reduced subsidies for meat producers would slightly increase support levels while information campaigns do not have any significant effects on the support for a proposed policy package. Finally, in contrast to China, in Germany the policy framing attribute has a significant positive effect on policy support but not for all policy frames. The animal welfare, personal health, and global climate change frame increases support by almost 0.2 points (on a 7–point Likert scale), while the local environment does not have a significant support effect.

We also investigated potential interactions between the policy frames and policy design attributes (see Figure 11.6). In contrast to China, for the German case, we find that higher taxes on meat are supported significantly more if framed via the animal welfare argument (i.e., the marginal mean of respondents' support is

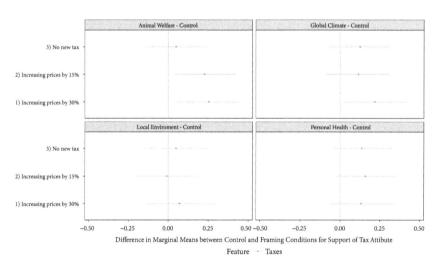

Figure 11.6 Difference in marginal means between the control and framing conditions for different tax levels on meat (Germany).

Note: We estimated the difference in marginal means for the different framing attributes and tax levels with cluster-robust 95 percent confidence intervals using the R cregg package developed by Leeper et al. (2020). If the error bars do not overlap with the dashed vertical line at 0 on the y-axis, we find a significant difference in the marginal means between the control and respective framing conditions for the support rating of the respective tax level. The figure is based on data collected for Fesenfeld et al. (2020, 2021).

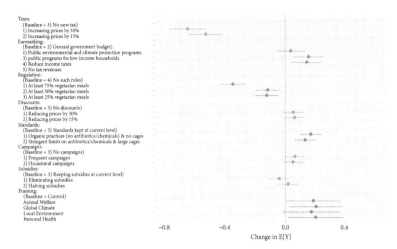

Figure 11.7 Effects of policy design and framing attributes on respondents' support rating (United States).

Note: Scale is from 1 to 7, where higher values imply stronger policy support on policy packages to reduce meat consumption. Data points with horizontal lines indicate average marginal component effects for medium and high policy design stringency and different framing treatments with cluster-robust 95 percent confidence intervals from linear least squares regression. The dashed vertical line at 0 on the y-axis denotes the baseline category (that is, no design change to the status quo and no framing). The figure is based on data collected for Fesenfeld et al. (2020, 2021).

around 0.25 points higher on the 7-point rating scale for the animal welfare condition compared to the control condition without a frame). This result is in line with recent evidence from a referendum choice experiment in Germany conducted by Perino and Schwickert (2023). In addition, the global climate change frame also has a significant positive effect on respondents' support for taxes that increase meat prices by 30 percent, while the other framing conditions do not significantly increase support for higher taxes compared to the control condition.

Finally, for the US sample (Figure 11.7), we uncover very similar findings to the German case and in many regards also to the Chinese case. In the US, strong tax increases reduce support levels even significantly more (by 0.65 points on a 7-point Likert scale) compared to the German and Chinese cases. Similar to Germany, earmarking tax revenues for programs for low-income households significantly increases support in the US.

In contrast to China, but similar to Germany, stringent rules about the minimum share of vegetarian meals offered in public cafeterias would reduce support for a proposed policy package by about 0.35 points (on a 7-point Likert scale). Like in Germany, against our expectation, discounts for plant-based meat alternatives do not significantly increase support. Yet, as in China and Germany, stricter animal welfare standards can significantly increase support levels for a proposed policy package.

While adding information campaigns or subsidy reductions to a policy package does not significantly affect support in the US, policy framing can have positive support effects. In the US, all frames (except the local environment frame) significantly increase support by a magnitude of 0.2 points. Like in Germany, also in the US the animal welfare and global climate change frames significantly increase respondents' support for policy packages, including higher taxes (see Figure 11.8). In fact, the marginal mean of respondents' support is around 0.30 points higher on the 7-point rating scale for the animal welfare and climate condition compared to the control condition without a frame. However, in contrast to Germany and China, the personal health frame also significantly increases support for higher meat taxes in the US. In sum, justifying meat taxes via the animal welfare and climate change argument seems a promising way of increasing support levels for meat taxes in the two democracies, while in the US the health frame also has positive support effects. In China, none of the frames increase support for taxes any further. Yet, for the Chinese case, it is noteworthy that support for packages including higher meat taxes is already significantly higher than in Germany and the US (see Figure 11.9 below).

All three country cases clearly support our expectation that the combination of different types of policies within policy packages is key for explaining majority support for policies to reduce meat consumption. To illustrate the importance of

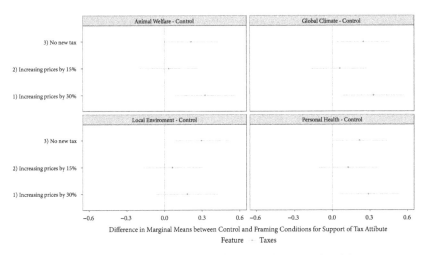

Figure 11.8 Difference in marginal means between the control and framing conditions for different tax levels on meat (US).

Note: We estimated the difference in marginal means for the different framing attributes and tax levels with cluster-robust 95 percent confidence intervals using the R cregg package developed by Leeper et al. (2021). If the error bars do not overlap with the dashed vertical line at 0 on the y-axis, we find a significant difference in the marginal means between the control and respective framing conditions for the support rating of the respective tax level. The figure is based on data collected for Fesenfeld et al. (2020, 2021).

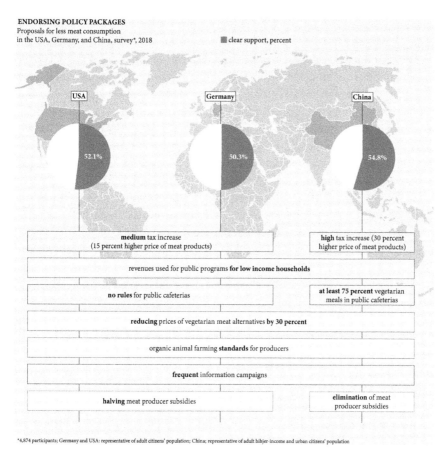

ENDORSING POLICY PACKAGES
Proposals for less meat consumption
in the USA, Germany, and China, survey*, 2018   ■ clear support, percent

*4,874 participants; Germany and USA: representative of adult citizens' population; China; representative of adult hihjer-income and urban citizens' population

Figure 11.9 Most stringent policy package proposals in China, Germany, and US receiving clear public support (i.e., a rating of 5 or higher on a 7-point scale).

Note: Figure is based on predicted support for differently designed policy packages as published in Fesenfeld et al. (2020). To estimate the share of support we recoded the seven-point Likert scale into a binary oppose/support variable. In essence, the values 1–4 indicate opposition to the proposed policy-package, while the values 5–7 indicate support for the policy-package. This coding scheme provides conservative estimates of feasible policy packages given that we only consider packages respondents clearly support (i.e., awarded a rating of 5 or higher) rather than packages respondents would also accept (i.e., awarded a rating of 4 or higher).
Source: Bartz/Stockmar, CC BY 4.0 https://creativecommons.org/licenses/by/4.0/

policy packaging, we also predicted respondents' share of clear support for policy packages (i.e., a rating of 5 or higher on a 7-point scale) that include specific policy attributes. For example, Figure 11.9 outlines the most stringent but still clearly supported policy packages in the three countries. Here we can see that in Germany and the US packages including moderate taxes are only clearly supported by more than 50 percent of respondents if combined with discounts for plant-based meat alternatives, stricter animal farming standards and public programs.

In China, however, we find broader public support—even for packages including larger tax increases.

Overall, policy design seems to be the substantially more important factor in shaping public support compared to policy framing. Nevertheless, our results also indicate that policy framing can affect support levels to some degree and that the interactions between specific policy frames and design attributes (e.g., animal welfare frame and meat taxes) can be essential for garnering majority support. Overall, as we discuss in more detail below, we conclude that more research is needed to investigate the effects and interactions of different policy frames and policy designs in shaping public opinion about food system transformation.

Finally, given the cross-sectional nature of our survey, we cannot directly assess policy feedback, which should be a focus of future research. Nevertheless, in several recent studies, we gathered preliminary evidence about potential feedback effects on public support for food system transformation. First, in a recent survey experimental study in China and the US (Fesenfeld et al. 2023), we find that more tasting experiences per week with plant-based meat substitutes, such as vegetarian burger patties, is an important predictor for public support of costly demand-side policies to reduce meat consumption, such as higher taxes on meat. Using different machine learning-based methods,[4] we find that the strong predictive effects of meat substitute experience have an independent effect on policy support and are unlikely to be an artifact of third variables (e.g., ideology, environmental awareness, knowledge, gender, etc.) that correlate with meat substitute experience. These findings also resonate with evidence from another study that shows that being familiar with meat substitutes is an important predictor of the willingness to pay for substitutes and thus potentially also for support of tax-based policies to incentivize a switch from meat-to-meat substitutes (Carlsson et al. 2022). Second, in a recent study in Switzerland, we employed a novel combination of vignette and conjoint experiments to test for the joint effect of policy framing, design, and feedbacks on public opinion (Fesenfeld, Maier et al. 2022). Here we find that private industry initiatives can have positive feedback effects on public support for governmental regulations to improve the sustainability of the food sector.

In sum, these studies indicate that pull policies that seek to increase the availability and consumer experience with plant-based meat alternatives (e.g., targeted discounts, innovation programs, and less intrusive nudges in public cafeterias) are more publicly acceptable at an earlier point of time than push policies at the demand-side, like higher meat taxes. That said, over time, positive feedback effects of such supply-side policies—both public policy and private initiatives— are likely to increase public support for the subsequent introduction of more

---

[4] Please refer to the original study for further details on the methodological approach (Fesenfeld, Maier, et al., 2023).

stringent demand-side food policies. Hence, more empirical research is needed to investigate such policy feedback and sequencing strategies in the political economy of food system transformation.

11.7 Discussion and Research Outlook

Reflecting upon the results presented above, we identify some limitations of the existing literature and provide an outlook for further research on food system transformation. Overall, policy framing, design, and feedback effects have, so far, been studied mainly in isolation and hence also in different survey and/or country populations. However, in reality these three factors are likely to interact with each other (Fesenfeld 2020, 2023; Fesenfeld, Rudolph and Bernauer, 2022). For example, policy framing can make specific policy design factors more salient in the public discourse and thus alter the public support effects of different policy package attributes. In addition, the specific labeling of policies (e.g., tax versus levy or animal welfare tax versus meat tax) can create interacted policy framing and design effects (Fesenfeld 2023; Perino and Schwickert 2023). Moreover, the complexity of policy designs can also make public support more prone to framing effects (Fesenfeld 2022). Finally, the specific combination of different policies is likely to alter potential feedback effects and thus change public support for transformation over time. In fact, recent research has started to look at all three factors simultaneously and provides evidence on their synergetic relationships in moving public support for sustainability policies in the food sector (Fesenfeld, Rudolph and Bernauer, 2022).

Considering the dynamism of food policies, future research can move beyond cross-sectional survey experiments and instead combine field- and survey-experiments in a panel design to gather preference and behavioral data over time. For example, in a combined longitudinal survey- and field experiment in supermarkets or public cafeterias, one could randomly vary the availability of sustainable meat substitutes and provide different policy design and framing treatments to compare combined effects on individuals' shopping behaviors, perceived social norms, and policy attitudes over time. Moreover, such settings would also allow to estimate social norm diffusion and social contagion effects by testing for potential spillover effects from treated to non-treated individuals in the same social context (e.g., in work-place cafeterias or families).

Such research designs would be helpful to examine positive tipping dynamics, which could play a crucial role in accelerating food system transformation. A tipping point occurs when change in part of a system becomes self-perpetuating beyond some threshold, leading to substantial, widespread, often abrupt and irreversible impacts. At a positive tipping point in a socio-technical-natural system, such as a food system, a relatively small intervention can shift the system toward a qualitatively new state that is predominantly beneficial to humans and the natural systems on which we rely (Sharpe and Lenton 2021; Fesenfeld et al. 2022). For instance, a critical mass of consumers that start to shift to a more plant-based diet could make investments into the development of new meat alternatives profitable and thus decrease substitute prices over time. At a certain price and quality level, meat alternatives thus also become more attractive to other (less conscious) consumer segments and their increasing experience with and information about the sustainability benefits of substitutes helps to shift social norms and public discourses. This, in turn, increases investments into new markets and shifts interest group positions about food policies, such as meat taxes and producer subsidies. Potentially, this then enables policy change that can further accelerate meat consumption shifts. Eventually, this could reduce demand for natural resources linked to meat production and lower the risks of crossing dangerous tipping points in natural systems, such as the dieback of the Amazon rainforest. Thus far, however, we lack knowledge about whether and how such tipping dynamics exactly take place in the food sector and which types of policies can trigger them (Fesenfeld et al. 2022).

In terms of geographic coverage, as outlined by our scoping literature review in Section 11.2, the majority of public opinion research on food policymaking still focuses on Western industrialized countries, particularly the US and the European Union (EU). However, given the rising meat consumption and dietary changes in many developing countries and emerging economies, more cross-cultural and comparative research on public opinion about food system transformation is needed (Resnick 2020). We thus encourage more public opinion research in the developing world, especially large emerging economies where the impacts of food consumption and productions continue to grow.

Finally, we would like to highlight the need for research on the interactions between opinions of citizens and political elites on food system transformation. So-called second-order beliefs (i.e., beliefs of actors about the beliefs of other actors and the public) could yield misperceptions among citizens and key political stakeholders about each other's opinions (Fesenfeld 2020). Also, the relationship between the opinions of the public and those of elite actors is likely to be dynamic and endogenous. While policymakers, businesses, non-governmental organizations (NGOs), and scientists seek to strategically communicate to and influence public opinion, public opinion in turn also affects stakeholder positions. For example, parties in democratic countries are likely to shift their positions as result of major public opinion changes, and companies may alter their product offerings and lobbying positions as result of shifts in public discourses.

11.8 Conclusion

Our chapter provides an overview of the existing public opinion research on food system transformation, which shows that most of the existing studies have focused on health-related issues (e.g., sugar taxes) rather than a holistic food system transformation perspective in line with different SDGs (e.g., environment-related goals such as biodiversity protection and climate mitigation or social outcomes such as ending hunger and improving livelihoods and wellbeing). Based on our scoping review and the broader transition literature, we propose a theoretical framework for structuring future research on the subject. Specifically, we highlight that policy framing, design, and feedback effects should be studied as important factors for shaping public opinion about food system transformation and policy change.

We present survey-experimental evidence, which support the importance of these factors, especially policy design and feedback, for shifting public opinion. More specifically, our surveys in China, Germany, and the US show that public support for ambitious policies to reduce meat consumption—arguably one of the most important goals to transform the food system in line with the SDGs—is already high in large meat consuming and producing countries. However, the results also show that support for stringent policy measures such as higher meat taxes strongly depend on policy design and specific packaging—e.g. moderate tax increases can be accepted if combined with stringent producer standards and discounts for plant-based meat substitutes. Thus, careful policy packaging can be a useful strategy to garner majority support. At the same time, we also find that simple policy framing (e.g., emphasizing health, animal welfare, or climate mitigation and local environmental protection arguments) does only slightly alter public support for ambitious policies to reduce meat consumption. Lastly, policy sequencing—e.g., first introducing pull policies to increase consumer experience with meat alternatives and then demand-side push policies like meat taxes—has the potential to increase public support for ambitious food policies and alter social norms, which may ultimately enable positive tipping points in public support for food system transformation.

Linking our chapter to other chapters in this book (e.g., Chapter 3, 7, and 9), we also believe that such sequencing strategies might be effective at shifting both public opinion and elite actor coalitions. As outlined in the introduction, increased public support for food system transformation is only one of the factors that determine political feasibility of transformative policy initiatives. Here, we suggest that our framework on policy framing, design, and feedback can also be useful to understand combined public opinion and actor coalition shifts and thus estimate the political feasibility space for food system transformation.

For example, the rise of new meat substitutes might offer an opportunity for creating an integrative policy frame around green growth jointly supported by a coalition of change-oriented food industry and civil society actors. Such a novel narrative could combine traditional civil society frames around food system sustainability (e.g., climate protection, animal welfare, and health) with new innovation and technology arguments pushed by meat substitute producing companies. This actor coalition could use the positive and integrative policy frame to shift public opinion in favor of transformative policy initiatives and jointly lobby policymakers in favor of the adoption of (currently less opposed by citizens) pull policies. Such strategic policy framing and design efforts could then help shifting resources to the new actor coalition and trigger feedback for altering public discourse and opinion in favor of stringent demand-side food policies (currently more opposed by citizens).

Overall, while the chapter focuses on the role of public opinion in the political economy of food system transformation, our framework and preliminary evidence shed light on the interactions between policy framing, design, and feedback in the broader processes of sustainability transition. Looking ahead, researchers of food policy need to conduct more time-series analysis to compare countries with different socioeconomic and political systems. For addressing the limitations of existing research, future research should also employ more field-experimental and panel designs that increase external validity and allow to better study the interactions between policy framing, design, and feedback over time. We also need more research on the interactions between public opinion and the broader political economy environment. Integrating novel computational social science methods with experimental and case studies thus offers new opportunities for moving beyond existing limitations in analyzing the political economy of food system transformation.

References

Anderson, K. 2009. *Distortions to Agricultural Incentives: A Global Perspective*, 1955–2007. London/Washington, DC: Palgrave Macmillan/World Bank

Barry, C.L., V.L. Brescoll, and S.E. Gollust. 2013a. "Framing Childhood Obesity: How Individualizing the Problem Affects Public Support for Prevention." *Political Psychology* 34 (3): 327–349. https://doi.org/10.1111/pops.12018

Barry, C.L., J. Niederdeppe, and S.E. Gollust. 2013b. "Taxes on Sugar-Sweetened Beverages: Results from a 2011 National Public Opinion Survey." *American Journal of Preventive Medicine* 44 (2): 158–163. https://doi.org/10.1016/j.amepre.2012.09.065

Battaglia Richi, E., B. Baumer, B. Conrad, R. Darioli, A. Schmid, and U. Keller. 2015. "Health Risks Associated with Meat Consumption: A Review of Epidemiological Studies." *International Journal for Vitamin and Nutrition Research*. 85 (1–2): 70–78. https://doi.org/10.1024/0300-9831/a000224

Béland, D., and E. Schlager. 2019. "Varieties of Policy Feedback Research: Looking Backward, Moving Forward." *Policy Studies Journal* 47 (2): 184–205. https://doi.org/10.1111/psj.12340

Bernauer, T., and L.F. McGrath. 2016. "Simple Reframing Unlikely to Boost Public Support for Climate Policy." *Nature Climate Change* 6 (7): 680–683. https://doi.org/10.1038/nclimate2948

Biedny, C., T. Malone, and J.L. Lusk. 2020. "Exploring Polarization in US Food Policy Opinions." *Applied Economic Perspectives and Policy* 42 (3): 434–454. https://doi.org/10.1002/aepp.13053

Bullock, J.B., and A.O. Bowman. 2018. "Exploring Citizens' Support for Policy Tools at the Food, Energy, Water Nexus." *Environmental Progress & Sustainable Energy* 37 (1): 148–154. https://doi.org/10.1002/ep.12727

Carlsson, F., M. Kataria, and E. Lampi. 2022. "How Much Does It Take? Willingness to Switch to Meat Substitutes." *Ecological Economics* 193: 107329. https://doi.org/10.1016/j.ecolecon.2021.107329

Chong, D., and J.N. Druckman. 2007. "Framing Theory." *Annual Review of Political Science* 10 (1): 103–126. https://doi.org/10.1146/annurev.polisci.10.072805.103054

Clark, M.A., N.G.G. Domingo, K. Colgan, S.K. Thakrar, D. Tilman, J. Lynch, I.L. Azevedo, and J.D. Hill. 2020. "Global Food System Emissions Could Preclude Achieving the 1.5° and 2°C Climate Change Targets." *Science* 370 (6517): 705–708. https://doi.org/10.1126/science.aba7357

Crippa, M., E. Solazzo, D. Guizzardi, F. Monforti-Ferrario, F.N. Tubiello, and A. Leip. 2021. "Food Systems Are Responsible for a Third of Global Anthropogenic GHG Emissions." *Nature Food* 2 (3): 198–209. https://doi.org/10.1038/s43016-021-00225-9

Culpepper, P. 2011. *Quiet Politics and Business Power: Corporate Control in Europe and Japan.* Cambridge: Cambridge University Press.

Druckman, J.N., and M.C. McGrath. 2019. "The Evidence for Motivated Reasoning in Climate Change Preference Formation." *Nature Climate Change* 9 (2): 111–119. https://doi.org/10.1038/s41558-018-0360-1

Farmer, J.D., C. Hepburn, M.C. Ives, T. Hale, T. Wetzer, P. Mealy, R. Rafaty, S. Srivastav, and R. Way. 2019. "Sensitive Intervention Points in the Post-carbon Transition." *Science* 364 (6436): 132–134. https://doi.org/10.1126/science.aaw7287

Farrell, L.C., V.M. Moore, M.J. Warin, and J.M. Street. 2019. "Why Do the Public Support or Oppose Obesity Prevention Regulations? Results from a South Australian Population Survey." *Health Promotion Journal of Australia* 30 (1): 47–59. https://doi.org/10.1002/hpja.185

Fatemi, M., R. Murray, and T. Langley. 2021. "Public Acceptance of Obesity Prevention Policies in the UK." *Journal of Cancer Policy* 27: 100256. https://doi.org/10.1016/j.jcpo.2020.100256

Fesenfeld, L. 2020. "The Political Feasibility of Transformative Climate Policy–Public Opinion about Transforming Food and Transport Systems." Doctoral thesis, ETH Zürich, Zürich, Switzerland. https://doi.org/10.3929/ethz-b-000425564

Fesenfeld, L. 2023. Political economy of meat taxing. *Nature Food* 4, 209–210. https://doi.org/10.1038/s43016-023-00716-x

Fesenfeld, L., L. Rudolph, and T. Bernauer. 2022. "Policy Framing, Design and Feedback can Increase Public Support for Costly Food Waste Regulation." *Nature Food.* 3, 227–235. https://doi.org/10.1038/s43016-022-00460-8

Fesenfeld, L., Y. Sun, M. Wicki, L. Beiser-Mcgrath, and T. Bernauer. 2022. "Systematic Review Raises Doubts about the Effectiveness of Framing in Climate Change Communication." *Preprint,*. https://doi.org/10.21203/rs.3.rs-445613/v1

Fesenfeld, L., Y. Sun, M. Wicki, and T. Bernauer. 2021. "The Role and Limits of Strategic Framing for Promoting Sustainable Consumption and Policy." *Global Environmental Change* 68: 102266. https://doi.org/10.1016/j.gloenvcha.2021.102266

Fesenfeld, L.P. 2022. "The Effects of Policy Design Complexity on Public Support for Climate Policy." *Behavioural Public Policy.* 1–26. https://doi.org/doi:10.1017/bpp.2022.3

Fesenfeld, L.P., M. Maier, N. Brazzola, N. Stolz, Y. Sun, and A. Kachi. 2023. "How information, social norms, and experience with novel meat substitutes can create positive political feedback and demand-side policy change." *Food Policy* 117 (May): 102445. https://doi.org/10.1016/j.foodpol.2023.102445

Fesenfeld, L.P., N. Schmid, R. Finger, A. Mathys, and T.S. Schmidt. 2022. "The Politics of Enabling Tipping Points for Sustainable Development." *One Earth* 5 (10): 1100–1108. https://doi.org/10.1016/J.ONEEAR.2022.09.004

Fesenfeld, L.P., T.S. Schmidt, and A. Schrode. 2018. "Climate Policy for Short- and Long-Lived Pollutants." *Nature Climate Change* 8 (11): 933–936. https://doi.org/10.1038/s41558-018-0328-1

Fesenfeld, L.P., M. Wicki, Y. Sun, and T. Bernauer. 2020. "Policy Packaging Can Make Food System Transformation Feasible." *Nature Food* 1 (3): 173–182.

Fischer, G. 2018. "Transforming the Global Food System." *Nature* 562 (7728): 501–502. https://doi.org/10.1038/d41586-018-07094-6

Geels, F.W., B.K. Sovacool, T. Schwanen, and S. Sorrell. 2017. "Sociotechnical Transitions for Deep Decarbonization." *Science* 357 (6357): 1242–1244. https://doi.org/10.1126/science.aao3760

Global Footprint Network. 2018. "Global Footprint Network." https://data.footprintnetwork.org/#/

Gómez-Donoso, C., G. Sacks, L. Vanderlee, D. Hammond, C.M. White, C. Nieto, M. Bes-Rastrollo, and A.J. Cameron. 2021. "Public Support for Healthy Supermarket Initiatives Focused on Product Placement: A Multi-country Cross-sectional Analysis of the 2018 International Food Policy Study." *International Journal of Behavioral Nutrition and Physical Activity* 18 (1): 78. https://doi.org/10.1186/s12966-021-01149-0

Graça, J., S.G. Cardoso, F.R. Augusto, and N.C. Nunes. 2020. "Green Light for Climate-friendly Food Transitions? Communicating Legal Innovation Increases Consumer Support for Meat Curtailment Policies." *Environmental Communication* 14 (8): 1047–1060. https://doi.org/10.1080/17524032.2020.1764996

Hainmueller, J., D. Hangartner, and T. Yamamoto. 2015. "Validating Vignette and Conjoint Survey Experiments against Real-World Behavior." *Proceedings of the National Academy of Sciences* 112 (8): 2395–2400.

Hainmueller, J., D. Hopkins, and T. Yamamoto. 2014. "Causal Inference in Conjoint Analysis: Understanding Multidimensional Choices via Stated Preference Experiments." *Political Analysis* 22 (1): 1–30.

Happer, C., and L. Wellesley. 2019. "Meat Consumption, Behaviour and the Media Environment: A Focus Group Analysis across Four Countries." *Food Security* 11 (1): 123–139. https://doi.org/10.1007/s12571-018-0877-1

Häusermann, S., T. Kurer, and D. Traber. 2018. "The Politics of Trade-Offs: Studying the Dynamics of Welfare State Reform with Conjoint Experiments." *Comparative Political Studies* 52 1059–1095.

Hofstede, G. 2001. *Culture's Consequences: Comparing Values, Behaviors, Institutions and Organizations across Nations.* Thousand Oaks, CA: Sage Publications.

Judge, M., and M.S. Wilson. 2015. "Vegetarian Utopias: Visions of Dietary Patterns in Future Societies and Support for Social Change." *Futures* 71: 57–69. https://doi.org/10.1016/j.futures.2015.07.005

Kwon, J., A.J. Cameron, D. Hammond, C.M. White, L. Vanderlee, J. Bhawra, and G. Sacks. 2019. "A Multi-country Survey of Public Support for Food Policies to Promote Healthy Diets: Findings from the International Food Policy Study." *BMC Public Health* 19 (1): 1205. https://doi.org/10.1186/s12889-019-7483-9

Leeper, T.J., Hobolt, S.B. and Tilley, J., 2020. "Measuring subgroup preferences in conjoint experiments." *Political Analysis*, 28 (2), pp.207–221.

Levin, K., B. Cashore, S. Bernstein, and G. Auld. 2012. "Overcoming the Tragedy of Super Wicked Problems: Constraining Our Future Selves to Ameliorate Global Climate Change." *Policy Sciences* 45 (2): 123–152. https://doi.org/10.1007/s11077-012-9151-0

Loibl, C., C.R. Sunstein, J. Rauber, and L.A. Reisch. 2018. "Which Europeans Like Nudges? Approval and Controversy in Four European Countries." *Journal of Consumer Affairs* 52 (3): 655–688. https://doi.org/10.1111/joca.12181

Machovina, B., K.J. Feeley, and W.J. Ripple. 2015. "Biodiversity Conservation: The Key is Reducing Meat Consumption." *Science of The Total Environment* 536: 419–431. https://doi.org/10.1016/j.scitotenv.2015.07.022

OECD (Organization for Economic Co-operation and Development) and FAO (Food and Agriculture Organization of the United Nations). 2018. *OECD-FAO Agricultural Outlook 2018–2027.* Paris: OECD. https://doi.org/10.1787/agr_outlook-2018-en

Olper, A. 2007. "Land Inequality, Government Ideology, and Agricultural Protection." *Food Policy* 32: 67–83.

Olper, A., and V. Raimondi. 2013. "Electoral Rules, Forms of Government and Redistributive Policy: Evidence from Agriculture and Food Policies." *Journal of Comparative Economics* 41 (1): 141–158.

Pahle, M., D. Burtraw, C. Flachsland, N. Kelsey, E. Biber, J. Meckling, O. Edenhofer, and J. Zysman. 2018. "Sequencing to Ratchet up Climate Policy Stringency." *Nature Climate Change* 8 (10): 861–867. https://doi.org/10.1038/s41558-018-0287-6

Pechey, R., J.P. Reynolds, B. Cook, T.M. Marteau, and S.A. Jebb. 2022. "Acceptability of Policies to Reduce Consumption of Red and Processed Meat: A Population-Based Survey Experiment." *Journal of Environmental Psychology* 81: 101817.

Pendrill, F., T.A. Gardner, P. Meyfroidt, U.M. Peterson, J. Adams, T. Azevedo, M.G. Bastos, Lima, et al. 2022. "Disentangling the Numbers behind Agriculture-Driven Tropical Deforestation." *Science* 377 (6611): eabm9267. https://doi.org/10.1126/science.abm9267

Perino, G., and H. Schwickert. 2023. "Animal Welfare Is a Stronger Determinant of Public Support for Meat Taxation than Climate Change Mitigation in Germany." *Nature Food.* 4, 160–169. https://doi.org/10.1038/s43016-023-00696-y

Pierson, P. 1993. "When Effect Becomes Cause: Policy Feedback and Political Change." *World Politics* 45(4), 595–628. https://doi.org/10.2307/2950710

Pierson, P. 2000. "Increasing Returns, Path Dependence, and the Study of Politics." *The American Political Science Review* 94 (2): 251–267. https://doi.org/10.2307/2586011

Poore, J., and T. Nemecek. 2018. "Reducing Food's Environmental Impacts through Producers and Consumers." *Science* 360 (6392): 987–992. https://doi.org/10.1126/science.aaq0216

Portney, K.E., B. Hannibal, C. Goldsmith, P. McGee, X. Liu, and A. Vedlitz. 2018. "Awareness of the Food–Energy–Water Nexus and Public Policy Support in the United States: Public Attitudes among the American People." *Environment and Behavior* 50 (4): 375–400. https://doi.org/10.1177/0013916517706531

Resnick, D. 2020. "Political Economy of Food System Reform." *Nature Food* 1: 2642. https://doi.org/10.1038/s43016-020-0049-2

Reynolds, J.P., S. Archer, M. Pilling, M. Kenny, D.J. Hollands, and T.M. Marteau. 2019. "Public Acceptability of Nudging and Taxing to Reduce Consumption of Alcohol, Tobacco, and Food: A Population-Based Survey Experiment." *Social Science & Medicine* 236: 112395. https://doi.org/10.1016/j.socscimed.2019.112395

Rosenbloom, D., J. Meadowcroft, and B. Cashore. 2019. "Stability and Climate Policy? Harnessing Insights on Path Dependence, Policy Feedback, and Transition Pathways." *Energy Research & Social Science* 50: 168–178. https://doi.org/10.1016/j.erss.2018.12.009

Rozelle, S., and J.F. Swinnen. 2010. "Why Did the Communist Party Reform in China, But Not in the Soviet Union? The Political Economy of Agricultural Transition." "*China Economic Review*" 20 (2): 275–287.

Sharpe, S., and T.M. Lenton. 2021. "Upward-Scaling Tipping Cascades to Meet Climate Goals: Plausible Grounds for Hope." *Climate Policy* 21 (4): 421–433. https://doi.org/10.1080/14693062.2020.1870097

Simmonds, P., and S. Vallgårda. 2021. "'It's Not as Simple as Something like Sugar': Values and Conflict in the UK Meat Tax Debate." *International Journal of Health Governance* 26 (3): 307–322. https://doi.org/10.1108/IJHG-03-2021-0026

Sparkman, G., and G.M. Walton. 2017. "Dynamic Norms Promote Sustainable Behavior, Even if It Is Counternormative." *Psychological Science* 28(11), 1663–1674. https://doi.org/10.1177/0956797617719950

Springmann, M., M. Clark, D. Mason-D'Croz, K. Wiebe, B.L. Bodirsky, L. Lassaletta, W. de Vries, et al. 2018. "Options for Keeping the Food System within Environmental Limits." *Nature* 562: 519–525. https://doi.org/10.1038/s41586-018-0594-0

Swinnen, J.F.M. 2018. *The Political Economy of Agricultural and Food Policies*. Palgrave Macmillan. https://doi.org/10.1057/978-1-137-50102-8

Wiedenhofer, D., Guan, D., Liu, Z., Meng, J., Zhang, N., & Wei, Y.-M. 2017. Unequal household carbon footprints in China. *Nature Climate Change*, 7(1), 75–80. https://doi.org/10.1038/nclimate3165

Williams, L.E., and J.A. Bargh. 2008. "Experiencing Physical Warmth Promotes Interpersonal Warmth." *Science* 322 (5901): 606–607. https://doi.org/10.1126/science.1162548

Worsley, A., W.C. Wang, and M. Burton. 2015. "Food Concerns and Support for Environmental Food Policies and Purchasing." *Appetite* 91: 48–55. https://doi.org/10.1016/j.appet.2015.02.040

Zhang, L., Xu, Y., Oosterveer, P., and Mol, A.P.J., 2016. Consumer trust in different food provisioning schemes: evidence from Beijing, China. *Journal of Cleaner Production*, 134, 269–279. https://doi.org/10.1016/j.jclepro.2015.09.078

Zheng, Y., Y. Li, A. Satija, A. Pan, M. Sotos-Prieto, E. Rimm, W.C. Willett, and F.B. Hu. 2019. "Association of Changes in Red Meat Consumption with Total and Cause Specific Mortality among US Women and Men: Two Prospective Cohort Studies." *BMJ* 365: l2110. https://doi.org/10.1136/bmj.l2110

12

Urban Food Systems Governance in Africa

Toward a Realistic Model for Transformation

Gareth Haysom and Jane Battersby

12.1 Introduction

This chapter focuses on African cities and problematizes emerging food system and urban system trends and actions in these cities. The focus on Africa is deliberate. While other areas of the Global South are encountering dramatic urban transitions (UN-DESA 2018), Africa's dramatic demographic shift raises important political economy challenges. Specifically, Africa's median age is only 19 years, and 41 percent of the population is 14 years of age or younger (Saleh 2021); the continent will become increasingly younger over the next 30 years (UNICEF 2017). Given past demographic trends and rates of urbanization, the majority of those born in Africa will be born in cities (UNICEF 2017). Ensuring that the urban food system guarantees the attainment of optimal developmental and health outcomes is therefore essential, both to ensure the youth dividend and for society at large.

The rapid transformation of both Africa's cities and food systems demands new and novel forms of governance. Until recently, Africanists have largely ignored, or were openly hostile to, almost all aspects of a wider urban agenda, focusing instead on issues such as the peasantry, agriculture, natural resource use or national sovereignty (Pieterse et al. 2018). Food insecurity therefore has been framed as predominantly experienced in rural areas, and to be addressed by increased agricultural production (Crush and Frayne 2010), and food and cities are seldom seen as being spatially connected and mutually dependent on one another in African food system discourses. Beyond being the recipient of food produced in rural areas, urban areas have largely been neglected in food security policy and governance.

This predominantly rural and production bias framing of food insecurity has meant that many African cities lack a holistic mandate over food systems governance. African cities might have policies and mandates to manage components of the urban food system, such as waste management or public health (Smit 2016), or informal food vending (Duminy 2018), but a wider and deliberative focus and engagement in urban food system governance is largely absent. Moreover, urban

Gareth Haysom and Jane Battersby, *Urban Food Systems Governance in Africa*. In: *The Political Economy of Food System Transformation*. Edited by: Danielle Resnick and Johan Swinnen, Oxford University Press. © Gareth Haysom and Jane Battersby (2023). DOI: 10.1093/oso/9780198882121.003.0012

food system governance encompasses multiple framings of both the food system and governance (Smit 2016). In this chapter, we position governance as encompassing, but extending beyond, state-centered institutions. In particular, while the state plays a role as the *authorizing environment* in African cities, societal actors, including civic bodies, the private sector and the general public at large, are part of the *activating environment*. In other words, institutional and societal actors all have equally important—albeit different—governance functions.

Drawing on these observations, this chapter presents three main arguments. First, as mentioned, we highlight that urban food governance requires not only focusing on traditional government-led policies and projects but also a systematic focus on societal relationships and processes. Secondly, ambitious, emerging food systems agendas need to be commensurate with extant governance structures and the allocation of power across multi-level structures, from local, to regional to national, but at times, also global processes, such as the UN Sustainable Development Goals (SDGs). Third, given the preceding considerations, we conclude by arguing that it is inappropriate and generally not useful to import models for food systems governance that do not suitably correspond to citizen and state capacities, especially in those cities that have inadequate fiscal and political authority to effectively govern their food systems.

This chapter begins with a reflection on the historical approaches to governance of urban food in Africa. The chapter then reflects on the food and governance vacuum that exists in African cities, stressing that for food and nutrition security to be achieved, governance processes are needed for both urban systems and food systems to connect in mutually beneficial ways. Several approaches to urban food governance subsequently are discussed, highlighting emergent processes and actions, as well as the actors involved in such actions. In turn, we reflect on the manner in which global governance and development processes are misaligned to the emergent African urban reality, specifically in terms of contextual governance needs, and how these processes intersect with emerging urban governance actions. The chapter uses these reflections to call for alternative approaches to urban food governance, whereby the state at both national and urban levels (i.e., the authorizing environment) and society (the activating environment) play far more active and mutually supporting roles.

12.2 Governance of African Urban Systems and Food Systems

Although rarely acknowledged in academic or policy dialogue, the history of control of urban space and urban populations in Africa is inherently and fundamentally linked to the control of food. Historical work on urban food governance in Africa focused on the functioning of market systems or on urban food supply (Duminy 2018). Far less attention was directed at official responses to urban food issues in relation to problems such as nutrition, poverty, and labor unrest (Clayton and Savage 1974; Cooper 1987). Research focusing on African colonial town planning shows official interest in controlling disease and migration and, coupled with the colonial project, of promoting racial segregation (Duminy 2018).

Building on the control position and the manner in which control, and governance, over urban food was asserted, Duminy (2018: 84) suggests the emergence of a "dual mode of addressing the urban food system ... on one hand, in concerns over food contamination and the spread of disease, ... and anxiety over urban food supply and nutrition, understood as a wider economic problem involving food production, distribution, pricing, and income." This resulted in what Duminy (2018: 84) describes as colonial Africa's urban governance being "limited to regulating and preventing certain kinds of food preparation, supply, and trade." Such governance approaches remain, as demonstrated through by-laws controlling food vending, food market regulation and control, and even zoning regulations prohibiting urban food growing (Battersby and Muwowo 2018).

However, as Tacoli and Vorley (2015: 1) correctly note, "our food security narratives are outdated: urban dwellers are not all 'over-consumers'; rural communities are not exclusively producers." As Lang and Barling (2012: 313) point out, food security responses have "suffered from more than just the common policy ailment of a mismatch between evidence and policy. It is dominated by a discourse emanating from an analysis first charted scientifically in the early to mid-20th century. This is that food insecurity must be centrally addressed by producing more food." The focus on agriculture in food security policy discourses has remained even more pronounced in Africa due to the enduring perception of African societies as predominantly rural and the relatively high percentage of employment and Gross Domestic Product (GDP) in the agricultural sectors of African countries (Crush and Riley 2018: 46). This production orientation has created a rural bias in food security programming and policy (Battersby and Haysom 2018; Crush and Riley 2018). This bias has its origins in earlier framings of the role of cities in development, specifically the urban bias theory.

Under the urban bias framing (Lipton 1977), it was argued that urban consumers and industry were able to exert political pressure on government to ensure cheap food to the cities, at the expense of appropriate prices for rural farmers. The neglect of urban food security is the residual effect of this urban bias, which saw cities as parasitic on rural areas (Baker and Pedersen 1992). Agricultural terms of trade were, according to this argument, tipped to favor urban areas over rural (Bates 1981), what Lipton referred to as price twists (Lipton 1977). A rural development agenda arose in the wake of this urban bias, supported by UN architecture, the Consultative Group structures and the Food and Agriculture Organization of the United Nations (Battersby and Njogu 2023).

The resultant focus on rural areas and production has meant that both food security research and policy responses in Africa have disregarded urban areas beyond being viewed as sites of consumption. The focus has instead been on rural household food insecurity or mechanisms to improve national food security through production (Battersby and Njogu 2023).[1] The production focus has been to grow staples to ensure base level food security across urban and rural areas, thus feeding urban populations. This need is not disputed, but such approaches have failed to actually address food and nutrition insecurity in urban areas, enabled poor diets in urban areas, and led to an extremely limited set of policy tools to engage urban food systems.

This framing has had at least three consequences on urban food governance and wider food governance policy, programming, and resourcing. First, interventions and policies focus on the individual or household, often resulting in efforts to improve livelihoods or encourage household food production (Battersby and Haysom 2018). Second, the production and livelihood interventions have a distinct project focus, missing the systemic drivers of food and nutrition issues. Thirdly, because of these two framings, wider food system failings are overlooked, even occluded, in policy and programming. Such issues are compounded when challenges associated with the urban food system intersect with the multiple other modes of urban functioning (Battersby and Haysom 2018). As a result, governance interventions that emerge are what Kirsten (2012) has termed "second class" interventions, interventions that seek to mitigate the negative impacts of the prevailing food system but fail to directly engage the structural problems of the urban food system.

In the last twenty years there has been an increased focus on the role played by local government in food systems governance. Globally, cities are attempting to develop new approaches to urban food governance with concepts such as food policy councils (FPCs) and other localized governance processes emerging as possible options to connect cities to their food systems (MacRae and Donahue 2013; Haysom 2015). However, in the African context, food governance has remained largely confined to the state and government.

In Africa, colonial, racialized control measures reinforced through apartheid-type planning approaches (see Duminy 2018), as well as more recent legacies linked to the impacts of structural adjustment policies (Maxwell 1999) and the rolling back of social safety nets (McClintock 2014), make governance shifts in urban Africa all the more challenging. In African cities, the policy and subsequent governance landscape often undermines urban food governance and neutralizes re-imagined urban food system governance processes, despite dramatic demographic and economic changes. It is necessary that these legacies are considered when analyzing the applicability of emerging urban food governance approaches.

---

[1] In a review of the rural bias in research, in a search on the Scopus database in February 2022 using the search terms "Africa" and "Food Security" Battersby and Njogu (2023: 164) "found 5,603 publications between 1980 and 2021, just 528 of these mentioned the term 'Urban.'"

12.3 Food Governance in African Cities

Added to these dynamics is the fact that although many African countries have decentralized over the last 20 years, governmental hierarchies and allocated mandates and the associated fiscal allocations still reflect a national, government-dominated orientation to governance. This is particularly evident in the case of food security, and food systems more broadly. Past colonial or structural governance approaches of centralized control remain deeply entrenched. In urban areas, the role of centralized governance has taken on a new dimension given the shifting political landscape in Africa's urban areas with the rise in power of opposition parties in urban areas. For this, and other reasons, devolution is more of a work in progress than a reality. Combined, this means that from a food governance perspective, the historical sites of food struggle—rural areas—still dominate perceptions and understandings of need (Crush et al. 2020).

Despite an absent urban food system-specific governance and policy mandate, city management activities intersect directly with the urban food system. Many cities govern urban food markets (Battersby and Muwowo 2018), approve development plans for new food-oriented developments, like supermarkets (Peyton, Moseley, and Battersby 2015), collect license fees and permits from market food vendors, regulate informal food traders, manage market infrastructure, and build and regulate local transportation infrastructure (Smit 2016).

Local governments are governing components of the food system, but most governance actions fail to actively connect the urban system and the urban food system. Local government departmental mandates and structures dictate that governance takes the form of managing compliance, often operationalized through urban by-laws and policies. These processes are unable to keep pace with rapidly growing African cities. Equally, most urban food system governance activities disregard the majority of African urban food system users, such as the informal food vending sector. African cities are sites of continual hybridity, of contingent processes intersecting with governance in varied and unclear ways.

12.4 Disrupting Food and Urban Governance—Misalignment in Global Processes

Given this context, multilateral processes seem disconnected from the contemporary urban food governance needs in African cities. On the one hand, the SDG approach to the "food goal"—SDG2—further affirms not only the siloed nature of these goals but also existing food perspectives and governance agreements, amplifying a production-focused and a rural orientation to food (Crush and Battersby 2016; Battersby 2017). The dominance of production-focused and availability-oriented perspectives of, and responses to, food security presents an urban governance challenge because it directs food policy and governance to scales of government beyond the urban milieu. This becomes incongruent with Africa's urban demographic trends.

On the other hand, multilateral processes that center on urban issues have incorporated a focus on food in an equally unsatisfying fashion. For instance, the UN-Habitat New Urban Agenda (NUA), adopted in Quito in 2016, inserted food into urban governance processes (UN-Habitat 2016) and framed food within a wide group of inalienable rights. Accordingly, the NUA

> [e]nvisage[s] cities and human settlements that [f]ulfil their social function, … with a view to progressively achieving the full realization of the right to adequate housing as a component of the right to an adequate standard of living, without discrimination, universal access to safe and affordable drinking water and sanitation, as well as equal access for all to public goods and quality services in areas such as food security and nutrition, health, education, infrastructure, mobility and transportation, energy, air quality and livelihoods.
>
> (UN-Habitat 2016: 5)

Cities will deliver on this aspirational position through support for

> urban agriculture and farming, as well as responsible, local and sustainable consumption and production, and social interactions, through enabling and accessible networks of local markets and commerce as an option for contributing to sustainability and food security.
>
> (UN-Habitat 2016: 24)

And when considered in context and spatially, the NUA would

> promote the integration of food security and the nutritional needs of urban residents, particularly the urban poor, in urban and territorial planning, in order to end hunger and malnutrition. … promote coordination of sustainable food security and agriculture policies across urban, peri-urban and rural areas … [and] further promote the coordination of food policies with energy, water, health, transport and waste policies.
>
> (UN-Habitat 2016: 32)

Such statements present a significant urban governance challenge because the NUA articulates an approach to both urban governance and urban food governance that is at odds with current governance processes and regimes in Africa, presenting positions that lack any grasp of the political economy of urban food and urban governance systems in Africa. These goals reflect political, spatial and mandate ambiguity, espousing flawed assumptions about urban governance authority, voice and local politics, resourcing, and the centrality of mandates, and associated fiscal flows, in ensuring governance action. Such articulations, which reinforce and justify the actions of global multilateral organizations and international non-governmental organizations (INGOs), divert focus and attention to ideas and concepts disconnected from everyday forms of governance, both formal and informal, in African cities.

12.5 Emerging Global Urban Food Governance Processes

In parallel to these multilateral processes, there is a global trend that seeks to decentralize food governance, a trend that sees urban areas, regardless of their governance domain or type (government, society, or both) attempting to reclaim control of the city food system (Ilieva 2017; Raja, Morgan, and Hall 2017; MacRae and Donahue 2013). These emerging trends are, however, largely confined to the Global North (Haysom 2015). Urban food governance trends are varied, including processes linked to devolution of food governance that are seen as part of a wider reclaiming of the urban food space. Such processes include a focus on food system embeddedness (Hinrichs 2000), localism and localization (Winne 2009), and a focus on urban agriculture (McClintock 2010). These are processes and actions through which citizens aim to reclaim a measure of urban food system agency while actively seeking to activate urban food systems change.

While simplified, current urban food governance processes can be divided into three categories": city-led food governance interventions, pluralistic governance processes, and issue-specific actions. First, cities innovate and initiate direct food system actions such as Belo Horizonte in Brazil or the City of Cape Town in South Africa. Second, there is a broad category of efforts whereby diverse actors come together in a democratic and egalitarian manner to co-create a food governance agenda, through, for example, food policy councils (FPCs). These efforts encompass pluralistic local food governance structures, seeking to engage food governance through multi-stakeholder groups that adopt different food system governance roles at scale (per Koc and Bas 2012). Third, there are distinct issue-oriented processes whereby activities focus on a specific problem or an aligned collection of issues and champion these under the banner of urban-scale processes; in this third category, interventions fall under the mandate of a single governance actor or related department rather than the wider urban governance domain.

Some of these processes are externally initiated by organizations such as the Food and Agriculture Organization (FAO), the Milan Urban Food Policy Pact (MUFPP), and Local Governments for Sustainability (ICLEI), all of which are engaging African cities in an effort to stimulate urban specific food governance approaches.[2] Often donor-funded development organizations drive processes, frequently in partnership with cities or key urban stakeholders. All offer opportunities and have limitations. City-led processes offer great promise, particularly when policies and actions can align to fiscal allocations to ensure effective programmatic resourcing. Activities led by external actors, often from global governance or development organizations offer prestige, may bring additional funding and can draw on lessons from other cities and engagements. Some of these externally driven processes also promote and advocate for food policy council approaches. Pluralistic multistakeholder approaches can offer different benefits, such as potentially increasing agency and enhancing the influence of non-state actors on the food system.

Each category of urban food system governance efforts also brings its own politics, own views of food system needs, and different forms of convening authority and legitimacy. However, all three domains make specific assumptions about participation, agency, and stakeholder voice. Some processes, such as city-led processes generally operate through top-down governance processes. Equally, project actions generally operationalize actions according to a specific agenda with associated authority and budget-aligned prescripts.

12.5.1 City-led Efforts

Some examples of city-led and city-governed approaches to urban food governance include those in Belo Horizonte, Brazil, or the transversal governance experiment emerging in the City of Cape Town and its wider region (FAO 2022). These processes reflect city-led change whereby the city leads the process but at times crowd in other, non-city, processes. Specifically, Belo Horizonte, a city of nearly three million residents and capital of south-eastern Brazil's Minas Gerais state, was the first Brazilian city to successful adopt a specific urban food system governance agenda (Göpel 2009; Rocha and Lessa 2009). A central consideration in Belo Horizonte was an emphasis on urbanizing a national mandate pertaining to the realization of the right to food and wider programmatic activities linked to the country's Zero Hunger (Fome Zero) strategy (Rocha and Lessa 2009). Food was therefore seen as a tool to enable development, and to ensure health and well-being, drawing on a wider national scale authorizing environment to legitimize the devolution of food governance to the urban scale. By viewing food as an essential public good, the city adopted a direct obligation to respond to the identified need. Food and nutrition were also governance tools to engage a wide array of urban

---

[2] Local Governments for Sustainability was previously named the International Council for Local Environmental Initiatives.

activities from land use to education, from skills development to urban health, from food retail to equity (Rocha and Lessa 2009).

National-scale processes are often blind to the urban food system challenge and miss key urban food and nutrition issues. Most importantly, the national-scale processes are ill equipped to effectively govern the intersection between the urban system and the urban food system. While the Belo Horizonte example is not from Africa, what this does show is the utility of drawing on national policy frameworks and policy positions to enact city-scale processes that speak to specific contextual needs.

Within Africa, the city of Cape Town has sought to embed a form of food systems governance in the city's internal processes through a phased approach that started with detailed research, identification of food system challenges, the integration of these into its resilience strategy (CoCT 2019) and finally, inclusion into the Integrated Development Plan (IDP). The IDP is the mechanism through which longer term fiscal allocations can be directed at specific actions. Cape Town is showing evidence of a new form of transversal urban food governance, driven through the City's Resilience Department, but with increasing political and operational support, across over 40 ongoing city programs or policies (Faragher 2021). Here, a variety of actions have coalesced to legitimize the process and amplify need. Although officials in the City of Cape Town have been working on urban food issues since the early 2000s (Battersby et al. 2014), further alignment to networks such as C40, ICLEI, and the MUFPP have served to legitimize processes (CoCT 2019). Partnerships and networks with academic institutions have deepened engagement and enabled critical reflections. Importantly these emergent actions were then amplified through two crises, first the protracted drought of 2016–2019 (Ziervogel 2019) and then the extreme food crises that emerged as a result of COVID-19 (Battersby 2020).

The Cape Town case reflects four factors. Firstly, the transversal mandate of the Resilience Department facilitated processes across many mandates and silos in local government. Secondly, it leveraged inputs from international networks, as opposed to adopting these uncritically. Thirdly, a specific government department took on the food mandate in the city. Finally, similar to the case in Brazil, the overarching legal obligation of the Right to Food served to ground actions in the country's overarching legal framework. While Cape Town does not have a proactive process to understand and engage the food insecure, it interfaces with parallel processes like a Community of Practice on urban food governance hosted by a local university and a civil society food forum hosted by a local not-for-profit organization.

Drawing on the four factors evident in the Cape Town case, many African governments, specifically city and county governments, can act in similar ways. African governments, both local and national, have a far greater role to play in responding to urban food system challenges. Cities in Africa are increasingly becoming sites of struggle. These issues frequently escalate to become national issues. When development challenges, such as high levels of informality, inequality, joblessness, increasing food costs, aligned to other increases in costs for essential items such as infrastructure combine, situations become volatile, as seen in the case of food riots (Moseley 2022). It is in these circumstances where people's necessities require their political representatives to act. And if leaders, both national and urban fail to act, this can provide the urban poor with the political leverage to act in their own interest. It is here where the politics of provisions—those moments when it is safe to challenge the state, even actively protest and disrupt wider societal needs—will certainly become far more evident in African cities (Bohstedt 2014: 3; Hossain and Scott-Villiers 2017).

12.5.2 Food Policy Councils (FPCs)

International development support organizations, such as the Resource Centre on Urban Agriculture and Food Security (RUAF), the Humanist Institute for Development Cooperation (HIVOS) and others, have been active in food systems change in Africa for several decades. RUAF works seeks to create sustainable, equitable and resilient food systems in African cities. One of the ways in which these processes are enacted is through a form of FPC. The initiatives of the MUFPP are aligning with these engagements. International organizations such as ICLEI have worked with African cities and run several city-focused food programs, working with cities to develop city-scale food visions, supporting city-to-city food system exchanges and increasingly focusing on urban food system governance innovation. A specific area of focus for ICLEI has been to support certain African cities in the development of FPCs, drawing on international examples. Cities where such food policy structures are being developed include Antananarivo (Madagascar), Arusha (Tanzania), and Stellenbosch (South Africa) (Haysom and Currie 2023), as well as similar multistakeholder processes in Lusaka (Zambia) and Fort Portal and the Kabarole District (Uganda) (Chirwa and Yossa 2019).

Internationally, food policy councils (FPCs) have gained increased attention since the early 1980s (Harper et al. 2009). MacRae and Donahues' (2013: 16) account of the increase in initiatives in Canada demonstrate a clear escalation from the initiation of the Toronto Food Policy Council in 1990 to over 55 such councils by 2012. Innovations are not confined to North America alone, with structures emerging across Europe (Moragues-Faus and Morgan 2015; Sonnino 2017; Sieveking 2019) and Latin America (Dubbeling et al. 2017). A 2015 review of localized FPC governance structures in North America demonstrated diverse governance positions, ranging from structures officially embedded within city government, enacting food policy processes at the urban scale, to structures actively seeking to engage food system issues independent of government processes (Haysom 2015). A similar trend was identified by Gupta et al. (2018: 12) who "noted structural autonomy—being organized outside of the government while maintaining strong collaborations with the government [that] helps food policy councils retain their independence while promoting more inclusive policy making processes that link community members to the government." The overarching theme of such processes is broader urban food system participation, as the pluralistic terminology denotes, to actively engage the governance of the food system in context.

FPCs, while focusing on a variety of urban food system related issues, are increasingly argued to be more than just governance processes. FPCs are increasingly seen as levers to shift the wider food system but are also places where different politics are enacted and given life. FPCs have been celebrated for their democratic potential (Sieveking 2019), espousing inclusive democratic processes associated with voice and participation. While most still directly support policy-related activities and food systems change (Gupta et al. 2018), increasingly FPCs are seeking ways to expand urban governance mandates, at times even seeking change beyond the urban food system (Schiff 2008; Harper et al. 2009; Moragues-Faus and Morgan 2015), engaging wider issues such as sustainability, climate change, and urban governance writ large.

Yet, while FPC-type processes espouse far greater participation and a democratic ethic, some have challenged such processes for de-politicizing urgent issues that are inherently political (Swyngedouw 2005). Examples of such issues include avoiding policy failures that result in certain societal groups experiencing severe hunger and food related vulnerability, such as migrants, disproportionate leeway to private sector actors, and adverse treatment of informal food vendors. It has been cautioned that such governance processes are characterized by processes "based on spurious participation that disregards dissent and champions consensual modes of decision-making led by dominant economic and political interests" (Moragues-Faus 2020: 76). These critiques challenge the articulation of multi-actor partnerships, such as food policy councils, as a democracy-enhancing process (Levkoe 2011). Dissenting voices call for a deeper examination of the values and politics at play in these governance mechanisms (Moragues-Faus and Morgan 2015). Such politics include the frequent exclusion of informal food vendors, as Skinner (2008) and Young (2018) show in the cases of Durban, South Africa and Kampala, Uganda, respectively. Swyngedouw (2005: 1991) raises essential questions about the assumption that such processes are inherently democratic and aligns with the caution that "emerging innovative horizontal and networked arrangements of governance-beyond-the-state are decidedly Janus-faced," further pointing out that the "arrangements of governance have created new institutions and empowered new actors, while disempowering others. ... that this shift from 'government' to 'governance' is associated with the consolidation of new technologies of government, on the one hand, and with profound restructuring of the parameters of political democracy on the other, leading to a substantial democratic deficit."

These cautions are important in the context of African urban food governance actions. Given the levels on inequality in African cities and the historical marginalization of certain groups, claims of democratization of the urban food system might not translate in practice. Despite claims of inclusion and democracy, most emerging local food governance actions remain ensconced in elite enclaves speaking for the poor and of the poor, but not with the poor and marginalized (Haysom 2020).

12.5.3 External and Issue-Oriented Interventions

Different actors outside city-led or bottom-up governance processes also shift the nature of the urban food system. Many private sector development funders and global funding agencies are actively investing in Africa's urban food systems. These actors often bring a specific operational and ideological view of where the food system challenge lies. Such actions at times disrupt and destabilize existing food system activities, and even lobbying the state for food system actions that might serve the interests of specific lobby groups, but not always the needs of the most food insecure. These urban food system engagements, including the development of shopping malls with supermarkets as their anchor tenants resulting in the clearance of traditional food vendors from the area, or the closure and relocation of traditional wet markets to areas peripheral to the city, are altering African urban food systems (Battersby 2017; Joubert et al. 2018). International development finance-driven developments of both shopping malls and multi-story trader malls further disrupt traditional urban food system processes and networks (Young 2018).

Relatedly, urban food systems can be disrupted by issue-led interventions that address distinct bottlenecks in a disconnected manner. The identification of the issues to prioritize may emerge from bottom-up processes or from donor-funded actions and concerns. Issue-led actions might include urban greening, school gardens, early childhood development center support, and urban food growing projects, among others. Although issue-led processes bring benefits and can facilitate wider urban food engagements, such as witnessed in the case of Stellenbosch, South Africa (Haysom 2015), this is generally not the case. Instead, such interventions typically lead to a project-oriented approach, which prevents tackling the wider systemic drivers of the issues being addressed.

12.5.4 Summary

As a result of the convening authority and the increasing importance placed on local or city governments by devolution aspirations, many donor- and INGO-funded programs target local governments as the key agents of change. Some of these nascent city-level food systems governance processes are often presented as inclusive and participatory. Yet, many urban actors, particularly the poor and those disaffected by under-performing urban food systems, are not part of these processes (Moragues-Faus 2020). Given the marginalization of so many in African cities, it is doubtful that the poor would ever be able to be part of such processes. In addition, given the remaining rural bias and production focus of national governments, many city governments lack effective autonomy and resources to implement the food systems policies envisioned by donors. The fiscal vacuum has other consequences. External donors, development agencies and equity funders can bring much needed resources, and prestige, but this skews power relations and frequently redirects attention away from more democratically determined processes, to enclave-type developments for more affluent communities that can siphon limited resources to support their needs as opposed to the urban majority (Pieterse et al. 2018).

12.6 Combining Authorizing and Activating Environments

Drawing on the examples provided above, there are at least five reasons why urban food governance processes that originated in the Global North may not be fully effective for transforming urban food systems in African cities. First, in Global North contexts, many urban food governance processes are domestically driven and have their roots in longer-term activism, but in the African context, these processes are often created by outsiders. Second, the scope of engagement is informed by the experiences and world views of these external actors. These perspectives may negate or dilute actions around wider urban systems change informed by local contexts. Third, Northern food system governance is linked to the agency and voice of the various stakeholders. The ability to actively engage in democratic governance processes is often absent in African cities: colonial histories, post-independence self-sufficiency programs, structural adjustment, and neoliberal economic policies have resulted in a particular type of food system. Most problematically, many African cities are not in democratic countries and therefore pluralistic models do not align with the broader restrictions on civic space. There is often active protest demonstrated at components of these food system issues, such as food price and food quality, but far fewer opportunities to challenge wider food system issues and the historical underpinnings of these issues, and resultant outcomes such as hunger (see Moseley 2022). Fourth, from a policy perspective, food system issues are generally not the exclusive mandate of local/urban governments. Many devolution reforms give local governments authority over agriculture and food but many of these powers are shared concurrently with national actors. This creates significant challenges, and it is here where the problem of accountability and authority for actions comes into play. Fifth, processes that avoid questions of scale, be these hyper-local or regional interventions, or concepts such as nexus actions (e.g., Weitz et al. 2014), miss the politics of scale and the essential governance question of authority and mandate. Clearly there is a need for wider engagement across scales but from an urban food governance perspective, each scalar governance entity needs to hold authority over the actions within their area of responsibility. If other governance actors dictate for other scales, actions are diluted.

Combined, these challenges reduce the potential for governance actions that are truly representative across all city food system actors. Mirroring Swyngedouw's (2005) concern, many of the current urban food governance structures and associated processes reflect both new technologies of government and profound restructuring of the parameters of political democracy. These are often facilitated through INGOs and development organizations. Although convenors of these groups attempt to make these inclusive structures, existing networks and trust relationships mean that in many cases the structures include small groups of connected officials and individuals and groups with histories of working with the state or INGO sector. These groupings may not be responsive to the needs of the urban majority.

Given the high levels of urban food insecurity, and the increasingly challenging food system outcomes (Frayne et al. 2010), urban food systems in African cities require fundamental change. The need for democratic processes that enact input, voice, and participation across the urban majority in change processes is not disputed. The inclusion of agency and wider sustainability as dimensions of food security are essential (Clapp et al. 2021). The food insecure in African cities need to be able to engage with the governance of the food system. Over and above negative food security outcomes of hunger, food insecurity, and under-nutrition, the trend lines in the rise in diet related non communicable diseases and overweight and obesity, are already shifting in the wrong direction (Global Nutrition Report 2020).

Governance responses require a deliberate activation of different actors and scales of action. The state does not hold absolute franchise over food system actions. Equally the state does not hold all urban food system knowledge. Significant knowledge, strategic thinking, as well as legitimacy vests at the community scale, which we refer to as the activating environment. Bottom-up processes that draw on actors and processes that elevate voice and participation are as important to urban food governance as policies. At the same time, urban governments need to act with other governmental tiers, such as county, provincial, regional, or national, to reclaim governance authority over urban food systems and engage issues in a manner aligned to political and policy mandates. We refer to this governance scale of action as the authorizing environment. Figure 12.1 depicts a stylized view of the activating environment and the authorizing environments.

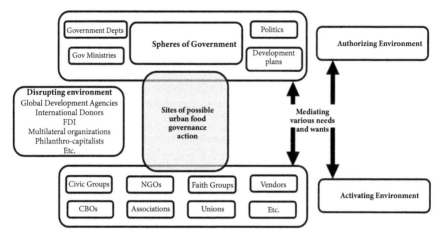

Figure 12.1 Stylized view of urban food governance through activating and authorizing environments.

Source: Authors' own representation.

Most examples of urban food governance from cities from the Global North have been cases where the activating environment—the sites of struggle within communities, key stakeholder groups and community level activists—have sought out ways to engage and shift the urban food agenda. These activating environment actions generally engage processes located within the authorizing environment— the sites of policy, power, and fiscal allocations—to enact context specific food systems transformation.

Currently in African cities, most food systems change processes either focus on single sites of struggle, at the activating environment (e.g. through urban agriculture projects). Other actions focus solely on the authorizing environment, through, for example, high level networks driven by city leadership actors. Urban food governance processes across African cities seldom engage both environments to enact change.

The essential question is whether both environments, activating and authorizing, are able to effectively engage the other? We suggest that the political economy of both the state and civic actions often limits or constrains the ability of either to engage systematically. Engagements are generally confined to processes between one actor from the authorizing and another form the activating environment. Central to this model is the key role played by those who facilitate processes that mediate the various needs and wants to enable change. These actions require very specific skills and attributes, such as the ability and experience to engage the messy politics of the contested food space. Facilitators also need to be trusted and respected by all actors involved in governance processes, often informed by past actions and resumés from similar processes. These actions often come with costs associated with such roles, and it is here that external donor and development actions might be better directed. Further, we suggest that it is when the needs, wants, and practices of these two different environments are not attended to that the fertile ground for the proliferation of the actions of the disrupting environment, external actors, vested interests, and sites of system capture, emerge.

Such a framing, we propose, demands far deeper engagement in how urban food systems governance might be operationalized and enabled. This requires nuance, contextual specificity and a multi-scalar and multi-mandate approaches. Almost all discussions on urban food governance in the African context have focused on food alone. Key to the food system challenge is the intersection between the urban system and the food system.

Roberts suggested that "more than with any other of our biological needs, the choices we make around food affect the shape, style, pulse, smell, look, feel, health, economy, street life and infrastructure of the city" (Roberts 2001: 4). Equally, the choices made about urban infrastructure shape the economy and food environments of the city and will affect the food system, health system, social system, and overall wellness outcomes of a city. These intersecting systems are the sites of required urban food system governance in African cities, expanding the governance actors in such processes. Arguably, urban infrastructure is the "keystone" where the urban system and the food system intersect. Given that local governments often have a greater infrastructure mandate than a food mandate, engaging a wider remit, and including key urban aspects, such as infrastructure, can offer greater legitimacy to more localized urban food engagements.

As a general framing, this calls for approaches that differentiate between food sensitive governance actions and food specific governance actions. Many urban governance activities, from planning to education can inculcate a food sensitive approach. But equally, food specific approaches need to espouse and align with a sensitivity to urban system needs.

Histories of the city's and the country's food systems, of power relationships, in both government and society, and of approaches to and styles of governance all require far greater consideration when enacting urban food governance processes in African cities. Attempting to replicate food governance processes copied from contexts removed from a city's history, politics and power dynamics is naïve and dangerous given that it sets the process up to fail, and in so doing often disenfranchises those facing the greatest need.

Given the development challenge in Africa, and specifically in African cities, we have argued for a different approach to urban food systems governance. We have suggested that current urban food governance models active in African cities have not necessarily paid due attention to entrenched power and processes of exclusion (as highlighted by Moragues-Faus et al. 2023). Differentiating between the modes of urban food governance (formal or less formal) and the approaches and practices of actual governance of urban food systems is a pre-requisite in understanding the agency at play and their power (Moragues-Faus and Battersby 2021). Similar concerns have been voiced pertaining to wider food system governance and the dominant role of vested interests in governance processes (McKeon 2017). In the case of urban food governance, similar concerns around unequal power relationships and the impact of these on agency are evident. As Moragues-Faus et al. (2023: 14) caution, "despite wide acknowledgement of the importance of considering and engaging with multiple stakeholders in urban food governance transformation, there is an increasing critique that multistakeholderism does not clearly contend with power." It is essential that governance processes avoid creating the democratic deficit described by Swyngedouw (2005) and enable greater participation, embracing the politics of urban food.

Traditionally, cities have not had an explicit mandate to govern the urban food system. However, as the urban transition unfolds, an essential urban food system governance approach must be one that connects the urban food systems needs to the urban system. It is here where city governments have an essential role to play. However, urban government is not the only food system actor in African cities. The Cape Town case showed how cities adopt a far more transversal and integrated approach to understanding, and potentially governing, the urban food system. Nongovernmental organizations, civic groups and general citizens, among others, have detailed food systems knowledge, understand local needs, and often hold greater legitimacy than the state in site specific contexts. There exists significant food systems knowledge at the community scale that is yet to be included in the longer-term governance.

We argue here that for the variety of reasons discussed, in African cities, neither the authorizing environment or the activating environment are as yet suitably equipped to engage novel urban food governance processes. For this reason, those able to facilitate engagement across the authorizing and activating domain are essential in laying the foundation of robust urban food systems governance in Africa. Such mediated structures and approaches differentiate the emergent processes from more traditional FPCs.

12.7 Conclusion

Given the transition to a predominantly urban world, many external actors and development actors, such as development agencies, funders, and researchers, are turning their attention to cities. The historical anti-urban bias discussed earlier that typified African development discourse and policy is receding (Myers 2014) with a diverse range of urban issues attracting attention. A similar city-centric reworking is evident in the shifting focus of global governance institutions, multi-lateral institutions, and global philanthropic actors. This shift in focus has allowed urban food to become an area of governance focus.

At the same time, current governance processes are ill-equipped to engage Africa's dual challenge of rapid urbanization and negative urban food system outcomes. Both challenges are escalating, requiring urgent governance responses. This chapter has questioned the utility of existing urban food governance approaches to meet the urban, urban food system, and wider food system needs of Africa.

Cities have always been sites of experimentation, particularly in different forms of governance. Urban food governance offers a unique opportunity to engage in such experimentation. In African cities, urban food governance actions that engage the physical, material, and relational properties of urban place and space are urgently required. In this context governance is about more than just policies, but active processes and agents shaping the nature of development and enactment of these processes, as sites of complex socio-spatial and material relations that engage both food and urban system needs.

Such a relational view requires far deeper engagement in three intersecting processes that determine the nature and form of urban food governance: agency and voice, power, and policy. This requires contextual specificity directly aligned to a governance mandate. Both the state and society need to be actively involved in such a process. For successful governance to be achieved, it is essential that politics, power, convening authority, and voice are recognized and embedded in processes and by governments across all tiers. Equally, external and multi-scalar interventions that portend to support the urban system offer certain benefits. However, if urban food systems are not actually governed at the urban scale—but rather only dictated by national authorities, overseen by discrete local government departments, or ignorant of diverse societal actors in the city—urban food systems *governance* will remain elusive.

References

Baker, J. and P.O. Pedersen, 1992. *The Rural–Urban Interface in Africa*. The Scandinavian Institute of African Studies, Uppsala.

Bates, R. 1981. *Markets and States in Tropical Africa*. University of California Press, Berkely, CA.

Battersby, J. 2017. "Food System Transformation in the Absence of Food System Planning: The Case of Supermarket and Shopping Mall Retail Expansion in Cape Town, South Africa." *Built Environment* 43 (3): 417–430.

Battersby, J. 2020. "South Africa's Lockdown Regulations and the Reinforcement of Anti-informality Bias." *Agriculture and Human Values* 37: 543–544.

Battersby, J., and G. Haysom. 2018. "Linking Urban Food Security, Urban Food Systems, Poverty, and Urbanisation." In *Urban Food Systems Governance and Poverty in African Cities*, eds. J. Battersby and V. Watson, 56–67. Abingdon, UK and New York: Routledge for Taylor & Francis.

Battersby, J., G. Haysom, G. Tawodzera, M. McLachlan, and J. Crush. 2014. *Food System and Food Security Study for the City of Cape Town*. Cape Town, South Africa: City of Cape Town.

Battersby, J., and F. Muwowo. 2018. "Planning and Governance of Food Systems in Kitwe, Zambia: A Case Study of Food Retail Space. In *Urban Food Systems Governance and Poverty in African Cities*, eds. J. Battersby and V. Watson, 128–140. Abingdon, UK and New York: Routledge for Taylor & Francis.

Battersby, J., and E. Njogu. 2023. "Does Scholarship on African Food Insecurity Have a Rural Bias?" In *Debating African Issues: Conversations Under the Palaver Tree*, eds. W.G. Moseley and K.M. Otiso, 164–176. Abingdon, UK and New York: Taylor and Francis.

Bohstedt, J. 2014. "Food Riots and the Politics of Provisions in World History." IDS Working Papers No. 444. Institute of Development Studies, Brighton, UK.

Chirwa, M., and I. Yossa. 2019. Food Change Labs Transform Local Food Systems in Uganda and Zambia. In *Urban Agriculture Magazine #36: Food Policy Councils*, RUAF, October 2019.

Clapp, J., W.G. Moseley, B. Burlingame, and P. Termine. 2021. "The Case for a Six-Dimensional Food Security Framework." *Food Policy* 106: 102164.

Clayton, A., and D.C. Savage. 1974. *Government and Labour in Kenya, 1895–1963*. London: Frank Cass.

CoCT (City of Cape Town). 2019. *City of Cape Town Resilience Strategy*. Cape Town, South Africa: CoCT. https://resource.capetown.gov.za/documentcentre/Documents/City%20strategies%2C%20plans%20and%20frameworks/Resilience_Strategy.pdf

Cooper, F. 1987. *On the African Waterfront: Urban Disorder and the Transformation of Work in Colonial Mombasa*. New Haven, CT and London: Yale University Press.

Crush, J., and J. Battersby, eds. 2016. *Rapid Urbanisation, Urban Food Deserts and Food Security in Africa*. Cham, Switzerland: Springer.

Crush, J., and B. Frayne. 2010. "The Invisible Crisis: Urban Food Security in Southern Africa." Urban Food Security Series No. 1. Queens University and AFSUN, Kingston, Ontario and Cape Town, South Africa.

Crush, J., B. Frayne, and G. Haysom, eds. 2020. *Handbook on Urban Food Security in the Global South*. Cheltenham, UK and Northampton, MA: Edward Elgar Publishing.

Crush, J., and L. Riley. 2018. "Rural Bias and Urban Food Security." In *Urban Food Systems Governance and Poverty in African Cities*, eds. J. Battersby and V. Watson, 44–55. Abingdon, UK and New York: Routledge for Taylor & Francis.

Dubbeling, M., G. Santini, H. Renting, M. Taguchi, L. Lançon, J. Zuluaga, L. De Paoli, A. Rodriguez, and V. Andino. 2017. "Assessing and Planning Sustainable City Region Food Systems: Insights from Two Latin American Cities." *Sustainability* 9 (8): 1455.

Duminy, J. 2018. "Ecologizing Regions; Securing Food: Governing Scarcity, Population and Territory in British East and Southern Africa." *Territory, Politics, Governance* 6 (4): 429–446.

FAO (Food and Agricultural Organisation of the United Nations). 2022. *From Crisis to Transformation: Strengthening Urban Food Governance in Cape Town during a Pandemic*. Rome: FAO. https://www.fao.org/in-action/food-for-cities-programme/news/detail/en/c/1472942/

Faragher, T. 2021. "City of Cape Town Food System Programme Food Governance Overview of the Pilot Food Systems Programme." Presentation by the City of Cape Town Resilience Department, South Africa, July 6.

Frayne, B., W. Pendleton, J. Crush, B. Acquah, J. Battersby-Lennard, E. Bras, E., A. Chiweza, et al. 2010. "The State of Urban Food Insecurity in Southern Africa." Urban Food Security Series No. 2. Kingston, Ontario and Cape Town, South Africa: African Food Security Urban Network (AFSUN).

GNR (Global Nutrition Report). 2020. "Africa: The Burden of Malnutrition at a Glance." Accessed October 13, 2021. https://globalnutritionreport.org/resources/nutrition-profiles/africa/

Goöpel, M. 2009. Celebrating the Belo Horizonte Future Policy Award 2009: Solutions for the Food Crisis Food Security Programme. World Future Council, Hamburg, Germany.

Gupta, C., D. Campbell, K. Munden-Dixon, J. Sowerwine, S. Capps, G. Feenstra, and J.V.S. Kim. 2018. "Food Policy Councils and Local Governments: Creating Effective Collaboration for Food Systems Change." *Journal of Agriculture, Food Systems, and Community Development* 8 (Suppl 2): 11–28.

Harper, A., A. Shattuck, E. Holt-Gimenez, A. Alkon, and F. Lambrick. 2009. *Food Policy Councils: Lessons Learned*. Oakland, CA: Food First.

Haysom, G. 2015. "Food and the City: Urban Scale Food System Governance." *Urban Forum* 26 (3): 263–281.

Haysom, G. 2020. "Perspectives on Urban Food-System Governance in the Global South." In *Handbook on Urban Food Security in the Global South*, eds. J. Crush, B. Frayne, and G. Haysom, 363–379. Cheltenham, UK: Edward Elgar.

Haysom, G., and P. Currie. 2023. "Food Policy Councils and Governance Partnerships in African Urban Contexts". In *Routledge Handbook of Urban Food Governance*, eds. A., Moragues-Faus, J.K. Clark, J. Battersby, and A. Davies, 196–209. Abingdon, UK: Routledge.

Hinrichs, C.C. 2000. "Embeddedness and Local Food Systems: Notes on Two Types of Direct Agricultural Market." *Journal of Rural Studies* 16 (3): 295–303.

Hossain, N., and P. Scott-Villiers. 2017. *Food Riots, Food Rights and the Politics of Provisions*. Abingdon, UK: Routledge.

Ilieva, R.T. 2017. "Urban Food Systems Strategies: A Promising Tool for Implementing the SDGs in Practice." *Sustainability* 9 (10): 1707.

Joubert, L., J. Battersby, and V. Watson. 2018. *Tomatoes and Taxi Ranks: Running Our Cities to Fill the Food Gaps*. Cape Town, South Africa: African Centre for Cities.

Kirsten, J.F. 2012. "The Political Economy of Food Price Policy in South Africa." Working Paper No. 2012/102. UNU-WIDER, Helsinki, Finland.

Koc, M., and J.A. Bas. 2012. "The Interactions between Civil Society and the State to Advance Food Security in Canada. In *Health and Sustainability in the Canadian Food System: Advocacy and Opportunity for Civil Society*, eds. R. MacRae and E. Abergel, 173–205. Toronto: University of British Columbia Press.

Lang, T., and D. Barling. 2012. "Food Security and Food Sustainability: Reformulating the Debate." *The Geographical Journal* 178 (4): 313–326.

Levkoe, C.Z. 2011. "Towards a Transformative Food Politics." *Local Environment* 16 (7): 687–705.

Lipton, M. 1977. *Why Poor People Stay Poor*. Harvard University Press, Cambridge, MA.

MacRae, R., and K. Donahue. 2013. *Municipal Food Policy Entrepreneurs: A Preliminary Analysis of How Canadian Cities and Regional Districts Are Involved in Food System Change*. Toronto: Toronto Food Policy Council.

Maxwell, D. 1999. "The Political Economy of Urban Food Security in Sub-Saharan Africa." *World Development* 27 (11): 1939–1953.

McClintock, N. 2010. "Why Farm the City? Theorizing Urban Agriculture through a Lens of Metabolic Rift." *Cambridge Journal of Regions, Economy and Society* 3 (2): 191–207.

McClintock, N. 2014. "Radical, Reformist, and Garden-Variety Neoliberal: Coming to Terms with Urban Agriculture's Contradictions." *Local Environment* 19 (2): 147–171.

McKeon, N. 2017. "Are Equity and Sustainability a Likely Outcome When Foxes and Chickens Share the Same Coop? Critiquing the Concept of Multistakeholder Governance of Food Security." *Globalizations* 14 (3): 379–398.

Moragues-Faus, A. 2020. "Towards a Critical Governance Framework: Unveiling the Political and Justice Dimensions of Urban Food Partnerships." *The Geographical Journal* 186 (1): 73–86.

Moragues-Faus, A., and J. Battersby. 2021. "Urban Food Policies for a Sustainable and Just Future: Concepts and Tools for a Renewed Agenda." *Food Policy* 103: 102124.

Moragues-Faus, A., J.K. Clark, J. Battersby, and A. Davies. 2023. "Towards Urban Food Governance for More Sustainable and Just Futures." In *Routledge Handbook of Urban Food Governance*, eds. A. Moragues-Faus, J. K. Clark, J. Battersby and A. Davies. Abingdon, UK and New York: Routledge for Taylor & Francis.

Moragues-Faus, A., and K. Morgan. 2015. "Reframing the Foodscape: The Emergent World of Urban Food Policy." *Environment and Planning A: Economy and Space* 47 (7): 1558–1573.

Moseley, W. 2022. "The Trouble with Drought as an Explanation for Famine in the Horn and Sahel of Africa." *The Conversation*, February 15. https://theconversation.com/the-trouble-with-drought-as-an-explanation-for-famine-in-the-horn-and-sahel-of-africa–177071

Myers, G. 2014. "From Expected to Unexpected Comparisons: Changing the Flows of Ideas about Cities in a Postcolonial Urban World." *Singapore Journal of Tropical Geography* 35 (1): 104–118.

Peyton, S., W. Moseley, and J. Battersby. 2015. "Implications of Supermarket Expansion on Urban Food Security in Cape Town, South Africa." *African Geographical Review* 34 (1): 36–54.

Pieterse, E., S. Parnell, and G. Haysom. 2018. "African Dreams: Locating Urban Infrastructure in the 2030 Sustainable Developmental Agenda." *Area Development and Policy* 3 (2): 149–169.

Raja, S., K. Morgan, and E. Hall. 2017. "Planning for Equitable Urban and Regional Food Systems." *Built Environment* 43 (3): 309–314.

Roberts, W. 2001. *The Way to a City's Heart is through Its Stomach: Putting Food Security on the Urban Planning Menu*. Crackerbarrel Philosophy Series. Toronto: Toronto Food Policy Council.

Rocha, C., and I. Lessa. 2009. "Urban Governance for Food Security: The Alternative Food System in Belo Horizonte, Brazil." *International Planning Studies* 14 (4): 389–400.

Saleh, M. 2021. Median Age of the Population of Africa 2000–2020." Statista. Accessed October 22. https://www.statista.com/statistics/1226158/median-age-of-the-population-of-africa/#:~:text=In%202020%2C%20the%20median%20 age,it%20was%20around%2018%20years

Schiff, R. 2008. "The Role of Food Policy Councils in Developing Sustainable Food Systems." *Journal of Hunger & Environmental Nutrition* 3 (2-3): 206–228.

Sieveking, A. 2019. "Food Policy Councils as Loci for Practising Food Democracy? Insights from the Case of Oldenburg, Germany." *Politics and Governance* 7 (4): 48–58.

Skinner, C. 2008. "The Struggle for the Streets: Processes of Exclusion and Inclusion of Street Traders in Durban, South Africa." *Development Southern Africa* 25 (2): 227–242.

Smit, W. 2016. "Urban Governance and Urban Food Systems in Africa: Examining the Linkages." *Cities* 58: 80–86.

Sonnino, R. 2017. "Urban Food Geographies in the Global North." In *A Renewed Reading of the Food-City Relationship*, eds. E. Dansero, G. Pettenati, and A. Toldo, 39–46. Rome: Società Geografica Italiana.

Swyngedouw, E. 2005. "Governance Innovation and the Citizen: The Janus Face of Governance-Beyond-the-State." *Urban Studies* 42 (11): 1991–2006.

Tacoli, C., and B. Vorley. 2015. "Reframing the Debate on Urbanisation, Rural Transformation and Food Security." IIED Briefing Paper No. 17281. International Institute for Environment and Development, London, UK.

UN-DESA (United Nations, Department of Economic and Social Affairs). 2018. *World Urbanization Prospects: The 2018 Revision, Online Edition.* https://population.un.org/wup/Download/

UN-Habitat (United Nations Human Settlements Programme). 2016. *New Urban Agenda.* Quito: United Nations. http://habitat3.org/wp-content/uploads/NUA-English.pdf

UNICEF (United Nations Children's Emergency Fund). 2017. *Generation 2030 Africa 2.0: Prioritizing Investments in Children to Reap the Demographic Dividend.* New York: UNICEF.

Weitz, N., M. Nilsson, and M. Davis. 2014. "A Nexus Approach to the Post-2015 Agenda." *The SAIS Review of International Affairs* 34 (2): 37–50.

Winne, M. 2009. "Local and State Food Policies: What Can We Do?" In *Food Policy Councils: Lessons Learned*, eds. A. Harper, A. Shattuck, E. Holt-Gimenez, A. Alkon, and F. Lambrick, 13–16. Oakland, CA: Food First.

Young, G. W. 2018. *Informal vending and the State in Kampala, Uganda* (Doctoral dissertation, University of Cambridge).

Ziervogel, G. 2019. "Unpacking the Cape Town Drought: Lessons Learned." Cities Support Programme Climate Resilience Paper. Cape Town, South African: African Centre for Cities.

13

The Political Economy of Food System Transformation in the European Union

Alan Matthews, Jeroen Candel, Nel de Mûelenaere,
and Pauline Scheelbeek

13.1 Introduction

The European Union (EU)'s food system is under pressure for reform. Agriculture production alone is responsible for 10 percent of the EU's greenhouse gas emissions (EEA 2020), while the EU's food system as a whole contributes about three times as much emissions (Crippa et al. 2021) when measured on a territorial basis. Current modes of food production in the EU are strongly linked to biodiversity loss, water and air pollution, animal welfare concerns, and the exploitation of people working in the food chain. Diet-induced increases in the number of Europeans suffering from overweight and obesity have contributed to the rapid spread of non-communicable diseases, such as diabetes type II, cardio-vascular disease and various types of cancer, amounting to approximately 16 million healthy lives lost in the EU in 2017 (GBD 2017 Disease and Injury Incidence and Prevalence Collaborators 2018). Furthermore, there are ongoing concerns and debates about the EU food system's impacts on ecosystems and livelihoods outside of the continent, especially in the Global South.

To tackle these and additional food system challenges, the European Commission in 2020 launched its ambitious Farm to Fork and Biodiversity Strategies, which are embedded within its overarching Green Deal policy that aims for climate neutrality by 2050, the decoupling of economic growth from resource use, the protection of biodiversity and zero pollution. The Farm to Fork (F2F) strategy is a first step toward an EU food policy that covers the whole food chain and includes both quantified and more generic targets for 2030 and beyond. The Biodiversity Strategy as well as the EU Climate Law and recent proposals to apply sustainability criteria to EU supply chains add further objectives, as summarized in Table 13.1.

Importantly, whereas the Green Deal strategies have put food system sustainability on top of the EU political agenda, the degree to which they will result in actual policy change and novel governance approaches remains to be seen. European Commission strategies do not carry legal weight, and to become effective,

Alan Matthews et al., *The Political Economy of Food System Transformation in the European Union*. In: *The Political Economy of Food System Transformation*. Edited by: Danielle Resnick and Johan Swinnen, Oxford University Press.
© Alan Matthews et al. (2023). DOI: 10.1093/oso/9780198882121.003.0013

Table 13.1 Green Deal food system objectives

Farm to Fork Strategy	– Reduce by 50% the use and risk of both chemical and more hazardous pesticides by 2030 – Reduce nutrient losses by at least 50% by 2030, while ensuring no deterioration on soil fertility – Reduce fertilizer use by at least 20% by 2030 – Reduce by 50% the sales of antimicrobials for farmed animals and in aquaculture by 2030 – Achieve 25% of total farmland under organic farming by 2030 – Halving per capita food waste at retail and consumer levels by 2030 – Create a healthy food environment which makes the healthy and sustainable choice the easy choice – Promote the global transition toward sustainable food systems
Biodiversity Strategy	– Expand the Natura 2000 network so that 30% of EU's land is protected – Place at least 10% of agricultural area under high-diversity landscape features
Climate Law	– Zero net emissions by 2050 – Net 55% reduction in emissions by 2030 compared to 1990
External dimensions	– Ensure only deforestation-free and legal products (according to the laws of the country of origin) are allowed on the EU market, currently covering soy, beef, palm oil, rubber, wood, cocoa, and coffee – Due diligence requirements for companies to ensure their supply chains are free of human rights, environmental, and forced labor abuses – Carbon Border Adjustment Mechanism for selected industrial products including fertilizer – Mirror clauses for selected agricultural practices

Source: Authors' own tabulation.

they must first be translated into legislation. Various legislative initiatives are proposed in the F2F strategy which will have to pass through the Council of the EU, constituted by the member state governments, and the European Parliament, which is directly elected by the EU's citizens. It is here that the commitment to food systems transition will really be tested.

In a recent reflection, Schebesta and Candel (2020) discuss four overarching governance challenges in the implementation process of the Farm to Fork Strategy. First, there is considerable ambiguity about what a "sustainable food system" means, with (potential) trade-offs existing between interventions aimed at different sustainability-related objectives. Second, there is a large discrepancy between the objectives set out in the strategy and the legal actions and instruments that are proposed, partly due to the limited competences that the EU has over some relevant issues and domains. Third, there are considerable institutional disagreements between and within the EU's institutions, partly fueled by deeper differences in worldviews and policy preferences. Fourth, there is a multi-level coordination challenge, as realizing many of the Green Deal's goals is dependent on stepped-up efforts at national, local, and international levels.

In this chapter, we pick up on these governance challenges and explore them in more depth for the two sides of the food system that have been particularly central to recent debates about an EU food system transition: changing agricultural practices and fostering healthier and more sustainable diets. The central question is under what conditions the EU and its member states may be able to bring about behavioral change among thousands of food producers and millions of consumers, so as to realize the Green Deal's overarching objectives. We reflect on the policy, political and institutional challenges, and opportunities in this pursuit, drawing on recent insights and debates from across a range of relevant disciplines. The consequences for food, fertilizer, and energy markets of Russia's invasion of Ukraine in February 2022 has only increased the salience of this debate.

13.2 Food Systems Transition in the EU—State of Play

Understanding the institutional framework that could bring about behavioral change in EU food systems is the starting point for our political economy analysis. The EU is a unique actor in this volume because of its multi-level governance framework that determines the scope for action at different levels—EU-wide, national and local. The EU only has the competences conferred on it by its member states through its founding Treaties, the Treaty on European Union (TEU) which sets out the objectives and principles of the EU, and the Treaty on the Functioning of the European Union (TFEU) which provides the organizational and functional details. Of the domains that are of particular importance for the transition to a more sustainable food system, trade policy, the conclusion of certain international agreements, and the conservation of marine biological resources under the common fisheries policy are exclusive competences of the Union. Climate, environment, agriculture, food safety and public health are shared competences between the Union and national governments.

EU decision-making is unique as compared to states in that only the Commission can propose legislation (though it may do so at the request of either the Council or Parliament). The role of the President of the Commission is thus much more than the role of the head of the civil service in national jurisdictions. The Commission, in turn, is divided into a number of Directorate-Generals, each headed by a Commissioner with responsibility for an area of policy. However, all legislative proposals must be agreed by the College of Commissioners as a whole.

Another relevant feature is that the EU has very limited budget resources—amounting to about 1 percent of its gross national income—but strong regulatory powers. Of its budget resources, around one-third are allocated to agricultural policy objectives. Member states can also allocate national budget resources to agriculture within rules decided at the Union level, but agricultural policy stands out as one spending area where the Union is the dominant actor. For most other policy areas, the EU's influence comes mainly from its regulatory powers.

The complex and fragmented character of EU decision-making procedures highlights the need for vertical coordination (between Union and member states) alongside the traditional problem in all states of ensuring horizontal coordination (between different Directorate-Generals and policy domains) when addressing a policy challenge such as the transition to a more sustainable food system. How these coordination issues underpin some of the political economy dynamics and affect the pace and design of strategies intended to transform food production and consumption practices in the EU, is discussed in the remainder of this chapter.

13.2.1 The EU Food Policy Framework

In the EU, much of the debate around the transition to a more sustainable agriculture revolves around the role of the EU's Common Agricultural Policy (CAP). The obligation to pursue a joint agricultural policy is laid down in the Treaties. Although formally a shared competence with the member states, the CAP framework and budget is largely determined at the EU level. The CAP is organized in two Pillars. Pillar 1 finances direct payments to farmers as income support as well as market management expenditure. Direct payments mostly take the form of decoupled payments paid per hectare of eligible land regardless of what the farmer produces or indeed if they produce at all (provided the land is maintained in a way that it could produce food). Farmers in receipt of direct payments are required to observe a set of statutory management requirements set out in EU legislation as well as various standards of good agricultural and environmental practice (a system known as cross-compliance). Non-compliance can lead to a reduction in the payment received. Pillar 2 finances rural development activities including aids to modernize agriculture, the promotion of business activity in rural areas and agri-environment-climate schemes that compensate farmers for adopting more environmentally and climate-friendly practices that go beyond the minimum standards required under cross-compliance. Around three-quarters of CAP expenditure is allocated to Pillar 1 measures, and the remaining one-quarter to Pillar 2.

Environmental objectives have been gradually integrated into the CAP over the past 25 years (Feindt 2010; Matthews 2013). The entry into force of the Single European Act (1987) added a title on the environment to the European treaties and, for the first time, gave a legal basis for EU environmental policies. The growth in environmental awareness led to the introduction of a raft of environmental legislation affecting agricultural practices. Among the more important were the Nitrates Directive (1991), the Pesticides Regulation (1991), the Habitats Directive (1992), the Water Framework Directive (2000), and the National Emissions Ceiling Directive (2001). These regulations and directives sought to protect water quality across Europe by preventing nitrates from agricultural sources polluting ground and surface waters and by promoting the use of good farming practices, to reduce the risks and impacts of pesticide use on human health and the environment, to ensure the conservation of particular habitats important for rare or threatened animal or plant species or important in their own right, to improve the governance of water quality and quantity issues through an integrated river basin management approach, and to limit emissions of air pollutants.

The EU has also developed an extensive body of food legislation, mostly devoted to ensuring a high level of food safety and protection for consumers. The General Food Law was adopted in 2002 in the wake of a series of food-related incidents including the outbreak of bovine spongiform encephalopathy (BSE) in cattle. This legislation developed an integrated approach to food safety "from farm to fork" covering all sectors in the food chain. EU rules also define requirements on subjects like market authorization for food additives, novel foods and genetically modified foods, chemical, and biological contaminants in food, food hygiene, tracking and tracing, withdrawal and recall, food labeling, and nutritional claims. The Green Deal initiatives extend this approach from food safety to include a broader sustainability perspective.

13.2.2 Modest Results to Date

Despite this extensive body of EU agricultural and food legislation, the EU food system is far from sustainable. Intensive agricultural practices are largely responsible for a substantial decline in biodiversity in agricultural ecosystems as reflected in a drop of farmland birds and losses of insect populations in parts of the EU. There has been only limited progress in reducing the risks of pesticide use, which is one of the causes of this decline (European Commission 2020). Soil health and fertility are rapidly degrading. Around 45 percent of the mineral soils in Europe have low or very low organic carbon content (0–2 percent) and 45 percent have a medium content (2–6 percent) and soil loss through erosion continues (EEA 2019). Where there has been some progress (for example, in reducing greenhouse gas (GHG) emissions, ammonia emissions, and nitrogen fertilizer use) much of this reduction occurred during the 1990s decade. GHG emissions and nitrogen use have flat-lined in recent years and further reductions will require additional interventions. On average across Europe, about a 40 percent reduction in nitrogen inputs would be needed to prevent exceedance of the critical values beyond which eutrophication can be expected (EEA 2019). Sustainability does not only cover environmental issues but also has a social dimension. Seasonal agricultural workers are an important part of the EU agricultural labor force but their living and working conditions are sometimes unacceptable (Augère-Granier 2021). A recent reform of the CAP regulations in 2021 introduced an element of social conditionality for the first time by including compliance with national labor and employment law as one of the eligibility requirements for receipt of CAP direct payments.

On the consumption side, the availability of food has not been perceived as an immediate, major concern in Europe although the response to the COVID-19 pandemic revealed limitations in the Union's preparedness to deal with short-term shocks. In response, the Commission established a European Food Security Crisis Preparedness and Response Mechanism (Official Journal 2021/C 461 I/01) to improve coordination between member states, third countries whose food systems are closely integrated with the Union, and food chain stakeholders. This new mechanism was activated in March 2022 to address the food security implications of Russia's war in Ukraine. Food poverty remains a concern in many European countries, with the situation worsening as the Ukraine war has exacerbated food price inflation. There are also major challenges regarding ecological sustainability and public health arising from the dietary choices of European consumers, with up to 20 percent of all food produced in the EU ending up as food waste.

The General Food Law introduced in 2002 and complemented by subsequent legislation on hygiene of foodstuffs, food contamination, food labeling, and food additives generally has been seen as a success in ensuring a supply of safe food to consumers but less adequate to address broader sustainability issues (European Commission 2018). The general regulation established the European Food Safety Authority, tasked with assessing and informing on all risks related to the food chain. It stresses the "precautionary principle," sets out a risk assessment approach and establishes general provisions to ensure the traceability of food and feed. A Rapid Alert System for Food and Feed allows member states and the Commission to exchange information rapidly and to coordinate their responses when a health threat due to food or feed is notified.

Several EU policies and initiatives exist that aim to foster healthy diets. These include Commission initiatives such as the EU Platform on Diet, Physical Activity, and Health, regulatory measures on food information to consumers and nutrition and health claims, strategies to address nutrition and obesity, and specific instruments such as CAP measures to supply milk, fruits and vegetables to schools. Initiatives have also been taken at city government level to design more sustainable food policies, for example, under the Milan Urban Food Policy Pact (Candel 2020). But it is mainly member states that have the ability to leverage dietary change. Most EU countries publish official dietary guidelines, including food-based guidelines, and an increasing number explicitly consider sustainability as well as health considerations in their recommendations. However, adherence to these dietary guidelines remains very low (Scheelbeek et al. 2020) and there remains a large gap between observed and recommended intakes. Fiscal measures to promote healthier and more sustainable diets (e.g., taxes on sugar, fats, or meat, or lower taxes on fruits and vegetables) have been used to only a very limited extent (mainly on sugar-sweetened beverages) (Jensen and Smed 2018).

There are some encouraging signs of changes in consumer attitudes. There is greater awareness of sustainable eating, especially among the younger generation. Per capita meat consumption has plateaued or shows a gentle decline in most EU countries, with an even faster substitution of white meat for red meat. For example, between 2005 and 2021 annual beef consumption per capita in the EU fell from 12.0 kg to 9.7 kg and annual pig meat consumption from 34.0 kg to 31.0 kg, but these decreases were offset by an increase in poultry meat consumption from 18.6 kg to 24.8 kg (European Commission 2021a). But these figures also demonstrate that this increased interest has not yet translated into the necessary level of dietary behavior change, leaving us far behind on reaching our targets on sustainable and healthy eating.

13.2.3   Farm to Fork Strategy

Against this background, the publication of the European Green Deal and its agri-food and nature protection elements in the F2F and Biodiversity Strategies represents a step change in rhetoric and ambition and has injected a new sense of urgency into the debate. It is also the first time that the production (agriculture) and consumption (food) dimensions of the food system have been considered together at EU level, thus paving the way for a more holistic and coordinated approach to its transformation. The F2F Strategy is built around three central planks: ensuring the food chain has a neutral or positive environmental impact; ensuring food security, nutrition, and public health; and preserving the affordability of food while generating fair returns for the supply chain. Among the strategy's aims are stimulating sustainable production and processing, ensuring food security, promoting sustainable consumption, reducing food waste, and combatting food fraud.

The F2F and Biodiversity Strategies include a range of ambitious targets intended to put the EU food system on a transformative path to greater sustainability. In addition to the targets for agricultural production outlined in Table 13.1, the F2F strategy also underlines the importance of consumer behavior change in food system transformation and climate change mitigation. Among the measures advocated are empowerment of consumers by better front-of-pack nutrition labeling; strengthening of educational messages in schools around sustainable eating;

promotion of food-based dietary guidelines that incorporate sustainability aspects and encouragement to use fiscal policy tools to promote healthy and sustainable diets; an active change in food environments in institutions, including minimum mandatory criteria for sustainable food procurement by schools, hospitals, and other public institutions; and setting a legally binding target to reduce food waste.

The F2F strategy was published as a Commission Communication and is not a legislative proposal. This means that it was not accompanied by an impact assessment examining a range of alternative scenarios and targets and evaluating their impacts for production and the environment that would normally be required for new legislation. While a Farm to Fork strategy on sustainable food along the whole value chain was highlighted in the political guidelines announced by Commission President Ursula von der Leyen when seeking support for her nomination in the summer of 2019 (see below), this was not further elaborated until the strategy was published in May 2020. Thus, the targets in the strategy were the outcome of a process of intra-Commission negotiation and bargaining and were not the subject of in-depth consultation with member states, stakeholders, or experts prior to their announcement. Although the main EU institutions subsequently welcomed the broad direction of travel set out in the strategy, dissatisfaction with the way the strategy was launched has led to a steady stream of demands for a full impact assessment, which was reinforced by the perceived consequences of the Russian war in Ukraine (European Parliament 2022). The Commission responded that an impact assessment would accompany each of the legislative initiatives foreseen in the strategy designed to translate its high-level goals into concrete policies in the coming years.

The strategy also recognizes the importance of complementing domestic actions with an external dimension designed to protect domestic producers from competition with imported products produced to lower standards (the level playing field argument), to avoid externalizing the negative environmental impacts of EU consumption and to use access to the EU market as leverage to raise global standards. The extent to which the Green Deal strategy will succeed in accelerating the move to a more sustainable food system will depend on the pace and ambition of these follow-up initiatives.

An initial test of the EU's commitment to the Green Deal objectives in the agricultural sector was seen in the negotiations to restructure the rules of the EU's agricultural policy for the period 2023–2027. The Commission put forward its proposal in July 2018 built around a new governance model for the CAP. Specific objectives for the CAP would be set at the Union level as well as a range of broadly defined interventions. Member states would then draw up strategic plans setting national targets for these objectives based on a needs assessment, and would have greater flexibility to design the interventions needed to achieve these targets. Union oversight would be ensured by requiring Commission approval for the initial plans as well as through regular monitoring of progress toward the targets.

When the Commission published its F2F targets in May 2020, the negotiations on the future CAP were still ongoing between the Council and Parliament. The Commission wanted member states to commit to national targets for the goals set out in the F2F strategy and proposed to make approval of the national CAP plans conditional on this happening. However, member states pushed back, insisting that the F2F targets had as yet no legal basis and they could not be obliged to include corresponding national targets in their plans. The Commission ultimately accepted that the inclusion of any such national targets would be on a voluntary basis. When the new CAP legislation was finally agreed in November 2021, there were mixed assessments regarding its ability to drive the required changes in agricultural practices or whether it largely represented a continuation of business-as-usual (Candel, Lakner, and Pe'er 2021; Matthews 2021). While the legislation allocates a higher share of spending to support farmers to meet environmental and climate objectives, the fear is that the measures proposed by member states will require little change to current farm practices and will be designed mainly as a support to farm incomes. A summary of the observations that the Commission sent to 19 member states following receipt of their draft plans highlighted that many member states have been asked to redraft their plans to show higher environmental ambition and to better clarify how the interventions they propose will achieve the national values they propose for F2F targets (European Commission 2022a). A full evaluation of the CAP strategic plans has been promised by the Commission toward the end of 2023.

The F2F strategy recognizes the health and environmental benefits of moving to a more plant-based diet with less red and processed meat and with more fruits and vegetables. Although environmental footprints vary greatly depending on natural conditions, inputs, management, and machinery at farm level (and to a lesser extent on processes beyond the farm gate), there is overwhelming evidence that animal-source foods are typically associated with higher carbon, land, water, and biodiversity footprints than plant-based sources of protein. However, a major weakness in the strategy is the limited discussion on how to bring about this shift, which puts primary emphasis on labeling and giving consumers better information to make informed food choices. We return to this issue later in this chapter.

The strategy appears to assume that the emergence of alternative proteins will in itself bring about the desired change in consumer behavior. The strategy emphasizes the role of research in increasing the availability and sources of alternative proteins and "novel foods" such as plant, microbial, marine, and insect-based proteins and meat substitutes. However, regulatory obstacles remain. Dairy terms or names such as milk, cheese, butter, and yogurt are protected for use in the animal-source foods sector. Plant based dairy alternatives must use alternative names such as "drink," "beverage," etc. (Annex VII of Regulation (EU) 1308/2013). The use of terms such as "alternative" or "replacement" on packaging if directly referring to an animal-source food that the manufacturers aim to replace is prohibited. The introduction of more "futuristic" novel foods appears still far away: lab-grown meat is subject to major challenges in terms of cost of production and scale-up, while food safety approvals form another hurdle. Development of regulations for the widespread introduction of insect-based foods on EU markets is equally in its infancy. A first assessment of an insect product as legal novel food on EU markets was only conducted by the European Food Safety Authority in 2021 (Lähteenmäki-Uutela et al. 2021).

13.3 Political Economy Explanations for Change (or the Lack of It)

13.3.1 New Voices Reflected in Decision-Making Fora

The previous discussion has shown that significant changes have taken place at EU level in terms of agenda-setting with the legitimization of a broader role for agricultural policy to contribute to environmental sustainability (especially biodiversity, soil health, water and air quality) objectives, climate stabilization, and to public health objectives.[1] At the same time, only modest progress has been made in reversing some of the negative environmental and health impacts of agricultural production. There remains a very large gap between rhetoric and action. From a political economy perspective, both of these phenomena require explanation.

Studies of the political economy of agricultural policy reform in the EU emphasize the interplay between the incentives for farmers to demand protection, the strength of the opposition to farm protection from the rest of society, as well as the importance of political-institutional changes that influence how farmers and other interest groups interact when decisions are taken (Swinnen 2008, 2015, 2018). Political scientists have long used agricultural policy-making as the classic empirical example of a compartmentalized and "exceptionalist" policy-making process (Skogstad 1998; Daugbjerg and Feindt 2017). This refers both to the arguments that justify treating agriculture as a sector in need of exceptional treatment, and also to a policy process in which policy outcomes are decided through bargaining between powerful sectoral interest groups and policy-makers who mostly see their role as defending and promoting the interests of the sector. At the heart of this traditional policy agenda has been supporting and maintaining food production (often justified as necessary to ensure continued food security), farm incomes, and farm numbers. Daugbjerg and Feindt put forward the idea that this traditional

---

[1] Food safety has been a long-standing concern, as has sustainable use of pesticides, there is growing awareness of the contribution of agriculture to air pollution through emissions of ammonia and methane, while the adoption of the "One Health" approach has focused attention on the problem of antimicrobial resistance.

model may be giving way to policy post-exceptionalism resulting from the demand for more market-oriented and performance-based policies. They highlight how new institutions and actors (international trade rules, consumer activism, environmentalists, animal welfare advocates, retailers) have succeeded in introducing new norms, values, and interests into the agricultural policy debate.

The broadening of the agricultural policy agenda has been driven, in part, by the growing weight of scientific evidence that has made it increasingly difficult to ignore the pressures that agricultural production is putting on the environment. Youth activism stimulated by the iconic leadership of Greta Thunberg played a very important role in pushing the need for climate action. The international commitments that the EU has signed up to, including the UN 2030 Sustainable Development Goals, the Paris Agreement on climate change and the goals set out in the Convention on Biological Diversity, have also been important at the rhetorical level. But transforming these concerns and commitments into a new policy agenda has required the widening of EU decision-making to include new stakeholders, actors, and constituencies.

Elections to the European Parliament in May 2019 shifted the balance of forces. For the first time, the two largest political groups in the Parliament, the center-right European People's Party and the center-left Socialist and Democrats group, no longer had an absolute majority of the seats between them. Significant gains were made by two groups, the liberal Renew Europe (with close associations to President Macron's party in France) and the Greens/EFL, and for both of these groups environmental and climate issues had a higher priority. The incoming Commission President, Ursula von der Leyen, whose appointment depended on getting the approval of the Parliament, recognized the significance of these changes and made the European Green Deal the centerpiece of her political guidelines when seeking its support for her nomination (von der Leyen 2019).

In the new Commission that took office in December 2019, key responsibilities for implementing the agri-food aspects of the Green Deal were given to the Commissioners for Environment, and Health and Safety, rather than to the Commissioner for Agriculture and Rural Development. In addition, a more hierarchical Commission structure was introduced creating a new post of Commission Executive Vice-President (filled by the Dutch Commissioner Frans Timmermans). Timmermans was given overall responsibility for implementing the Green Deal and other Commissioners whose portfolios would play a major role, including agriculture, reported to him. In the inter-institutional trilogue negotiations between the Council, Parliament, and Commission where the final CAP agreement was hammered out, and where normally the Commission would be represented only by the Agriculture Commissioner, Timmermans played an active role bringing to the table the voices calling for greater environmental and climate action which would not normally be present in negotiations on agricultural policy.

Barriers to the representation of non-farm interests such as consumer, environmental, and Global South activists in agricultural policymaking remain. In the Parliament, responsibility for developing the Parliament's position on agricultural policy matters is usually given to its agricultural committee which always has a high proportion of farmer members. On this occasion, the Parliament's environmental committee was given associated status on those parts of the legislation with environmental relevance. Although it was an indication that agricultural policy is no longer seen as the preserve of farmers, the innovation turned out to have little practical impact. In the Council, CAP negotiations are handled by the member state agricultural ministers. The business of the agricultural Council is prepared, uniquely, by a special committee of member state representatives whose sole interest is agriculture whereas other dossiers are prepared by member state representatives with oversight over several areas. Farmer organization representatives often have privileged access to Council meetings, an access not extended to other representative groups. However, when looking at the list of legislative actions attached to the F2F strategy, what is striking is that most of them fall under the responsibility of and will be initiated by the Commissioners with responsibility for the environment, health and safety, or climate action, rather than by the Agriculture Commissioner. These dossiers will then be handled by different Council formations (for example, environment or health ministers) and different Parliamentary committees. This underlines the conclusion that the EU's agricultural policy agenda is increasingly determined by a wider range of interests and policy concerns than in the past, and that farmers no longer have the sole prerogative in setting this agenda.

13.3.2 Negative Impacts on Production and Farm Incomes

Although there is no doubting the change in rhetoric and framing around agrifood policy objectives, implementation on the ground is by no means guaranteed. Significant obstacles to change need to be overcome. Farm groups perceive these new demands as conflicting with their values (to produce as much food as possible to satisfy market demand) and interests (where pursuing other objectives is perceived to threaten their income). Governments worry that higher environmental standards and climate targets will have a negative impact on agricultural output and employment both on-farm and in ancillary processing industries, which may particularly disadvantage rural areas that are often lagging behind in any event in terms of economic activity and employment opportunities. They also worry that pursuing the sustainability agenda will have adverse distributional impacts if it leads to higher food prices particularly for low-income households. Input suppliers and food industry actors fear that their business models are being undermined and that greater regulation will lead to higher costs and reduced profits. Environmentalists worry that higher environmental standards and climate targets will simply lead to domestic production being replaced by imports, shifting pollution effects and emissions abroad to exporting countries, and exacerbating the competition for land and water that is already causing environmental stresses in these countries.

A series of modeling studies simulating the impact of implementing several Green Deal targets concur that production would fall, although they disagree on the farm income effects (Beckman et al. 2020; Barreiro-Hurle et al. 2021a; Bremmer et al. 2021; Henning et al. 2021; Wesseler 2022). In some studies, market price responses to the projected fall in production are sufficiently strong to result in an overall increase in farm income. The value of these studies as guides to outcomes has been called into question (Barreiro-Hurle et al. 2021b; European Commission 2021; Candel 2022). The ability of market models to simulate changes in production practices of the magnitude envisaged in the Green Deal with parameters calibrated on the basis of the marginal changes seen historically can be questioned. The measures simulated leave out many of the complementary initiatives foreseen in the Strategy, particularly on the demand side or in terms of trade policy. The studies can be seen as unbalanced as they fail to quantify, and in some cases even to recognize, the value of the environmental and health benefits that the Strategy is seeking to achieve. They also adopt a business-as-usual baseline against which to compare their results, without attempting to assess the strength of the negative feedback loops between ecosystem damage and future potential yields.

These weaknesses indeed suggest that these studies are not a good basis for planning the food system transition, but it is unlikely that their central insight will be overturned. Moving toward a more sustainable agriculture with lower use of external inputs, greater reliance on more extensive production systems, and deliberately taking land out of agricultural production in order to make room for nature, will reduce EU production. Also, none of the studies specifically include targets for reducing agricultural emissions that will likely require reductions in animal agriculture that go beyond those simulated in these studies or consider the competitiveness implications of the higher animal welfare standards that have been flagged by the Commission. It is not surprising that farmers worry about the potential impact on their incomes. Although some studies suggest that farmers will be able to compensate for lower production through higher prices, farmers as price-takers in the food chain remain skeptical of this outcome. Previous research has noted that agricultural policy reform is easier in periods of relative prosperity for farmers (Swinnen 2018). The price shocks resulting from the Russian war in Ukraine, notably the sharp increase in feed and fertilizer costs and fears over the adverse effect on farm income, have led to a noticeable softening in the political support for making a radical change in farming practices at this time (Farm Europe 2022). Reconciling this tension between the economic and environmental dimensions of sustainability will be critical to the success of the food system transition.

13.3.3 Differing Understandings of Sustainability

The transition in agriculture is further complicated by differences in understanding of what is meant by sustainable agriculture. Previous analyses have shown how different actor groups problematize overarching objectives such as "food security" or "resilience" in different terms, resulting in conflicting policy preferences (Candel et al. 2014). In the case of sustainable agriculture, this has partly to do with the production technology seen as compatible with sustainability. The productivist view (shared by several of the EU's trading partners) emphasizes that global land use constraints require the pursuit of higher yields through sustainable intensification and puts a heavy emphasis on the role of technology to reduce external inputs and to mitigate associated environmental externalities. Agroecological advocates, on the other hand, emphasize the importance of minimizing external inputs by working with natural systems and adopting more extensive production methods. They also tend to be suspicious of modern technologies, opposing techniques such as gene-editing and emphasizing instead the precautionary principle. Others argue that EU policy agendas still tend to approach food exclusively as a commodity, whereas alternative framings, such as food as a human right or as a commons, may open up new policy pathways (Jackson et al. 2021). Moreover, growing concerns about animal welfare among European citizens have spurred scholarly debates about the dominance of anthropocentrism, raising questions about the "rights" of animals or even natural ecosystems in the food system. The fact that the F2F strategy has advocated for an extensification rather than intensification approach remains a strongly contested issue.

The other contested issue in discussing sustainable agriculture in the EU concerns the future role for animal agriculture. Animal agriculture contributes 40 percent of the value of agricultural output in the EU but that grossly underestimates its significance given that two-thirds of EU cereals production is used for animal feed. The off-farm employment in terms of slaughterhouses, feed mills, and other inputs is also significant, particularly in rural areas. The scientific evidence says that this level of animal production is unsustainable, but neither the EU nor member states have endorsed this view, and there are no plans in place to help livestock farmers in this transition.[2] Reducing EU livestock production, say, by half in the decade to 2030 as some advocate, would be an even bigger transition than

---

[2] In early 2022, the Dutch government was considering plans to buy out livestock farms in an effort to reduce livestock numbers to comply with court orders to reduce ammonia emissions.

the phase-out of coal in Europe (in 1950, employment in coal mines in the main producers UK, Germany, France, and Netherlands numbered around 1.6 million workers while in 2016 there were 2.6 million holdings in the EU specialized in livestock production and a further 2.2 million holdings with some livestock). Farmers producing feed grains would also have to adjust to find new uses for their land. The parallel may be misleading given the very skewed distribution of livestock numbers. Almost three-quarters of all holdings with livestock in the EU have less than 5 livestock units (LSU), while just 9 percent of holdings with livestock—around 458,000 out of the 10.5 million holdings in the EU—account for 80 percent of LSU. Yet no serious consideration has been given either in policy circles or in the academic literature to what a reduction in livestock numbers would mean for land use or how to provide a "just transition" for these farmers.

13.3.4 Challenges in Changing Food Environments and Consumer Behavior

Food systems cannot transform without substantial and population-wide consumer action. The collective change of consumers with regards to dietary choices, food group substitutions and waste management are pivotal in accelerating food system transformations and reaching food system related climate change mitigation goals. Successfully facilitating behavior change proves to be challenging within all sectors, as humans naturally resist change, but the process of dietary behavior change is subject to some particular obstacles. Where other public health initiatives, for example, those relating to reduced consumption of sugar-sweetened beverages or smoking cessation, were dealing with consumer choices that could be completely eliminated without health concerns, the anticipated targets in dietary change toward sustainable diets are subtler. The aim is not necessarily the complete removal of certain food groups in people's diets, but rather a rebalancing in the overall proportions of food group contributions to daily consumption. This complicates the application of "conventional" behavior change mechanisms and interventions.

First, the rebalancing—rather than removing—food groups from people's diets makes the use of stringent legislation and/or tax regimes to encourage consumer behavior toward sustainable diets complicated. Food is a basic human right and hence diets should still be affordable for all after implementation of rigorous measures. There is a danger of diets becoming unhealthier rather than healthier if affordability steers consumers in the wrong direction, for example, away from meat or other animal-source foods, but toward refined grains, foods with high salt or sugar contents or otherwise unhealthy energy dense foods. Furthermore, changing consumption patterns in food outlets does not necessarily lead to healthier diets: knowledge on correct preparation of "new foods," cooking skills or the creativity to fit them into daily meals can be a real challenge for consumers and could (unintentionally) lead to adverse effects, such as reduced availability of food/meals in the household, lower enjoyment of meals, and increased food waste.

Second, while food choices are often regarded as autonomous consumer decisions, the reality is far from that. Food environments, from the number of food outlets in the local area to the placement of products in the supermarket, as well as access and exposure to foods at school, work, and public service environments, shape—if not predominantly determine—the purchase patterns of consumers. Hence, facilitating dietary behavior change when only targeting consumers in food outlets will likely be unsuccessful. It requires a much more coherent food system wide approach and necessitates transformational change of all aspects of the food environment with which people interact on a daily basis. This might include strategies such as banning advertisements of unhealthy foods during the day or early evening to reduce exposure to younger audiences, having "buffer zones" around educational institutions where fast food outlets are banned, and "sugar free" checkout lanes in supermarkets where customers are not tempted into impulse buying of high-sugar snacks while awaiting their turn in the check-out queue. Taxes and subsidies can be effective interventions but have mostly been used to date in a health rather than sustainability context (Latka et al. 2021). The evidence suggests that, if used alone, high rates of tax may be necessary to induce significant changes in consumer behavior (Bonnet et al. 2018) and care needs to be taken to avoid undesired substitution effects and trade-offs between nutrition and environmental sustainability (Revoredo-Giha et al. 2018).

Third, sustainable eating is a rather complex concept for the average consumer. The majority of the population use/consider front-of-package labeling in their purchase behavior and understand the meaning of various traffic light systems that are used in different European countries. However, these labels only highlight one dimension of "informed" decision-making. The sustainability angle brings in several additional, and sometimes contradictory, dimensions of informed purchasing, including carbon footprints, water use, land use, and biodiversity loss. These are complex concepts to accurately communicate to consumers. They also require some time investment from the consumer to avoid misunderstanding or feeling overwhelmed. Despite guidelines on healthy and sustainable diets rapidly accumulating in the scientific literature, and which in a limited number of countries have been translated into food-based dietary guidelines, a solid mechanism to present this in an understandable and practical way to consumers has not yet been found.

Food systems transformation will also require the active participation, and in many cases, regulation, of food companies. The pursuit of short-term profitability has misdirected manufacturing and processing toward the use of unhealthy ingredients (e.g., palm oil, trans fats, excess sugar, and excess salt). The Commission has introduced a Code of Conduct on Responsible Food Business and Marketing

Practices that actors "between the farm and fork" can voluntarily commit to. However, the literature on such public–private partnerships suggests that in practice they struggle to make much impact. The Netherlands National Institute for Public Health and the Environment (RIVM), for example, found that an agreement between the Dutch government and industry on product reformulation toward lower salt, sugar, and fat levels (2014–2020) had only a minor effect (ter Borg et al. 2021). Similar findings have been reported for the English 2011 Public Health Responsibility Deal, which was criticized for its low ambition and lack of monitoring and sanctioning (Panjwani and Caraher 2014). At the same time, it should be noted that the evidence base about public-private partnerships in the field of nutrition is relatively limited, and their effectiveness is likely to be dependent on the broader governance configurations in which they are embedded (Fanzo et al. 2021). The evidence on the effectiveness of voluntary sustainability standards is also limited and context-specific (Marx et al. 2022). Political scientists have in this respect argued that the effectiveness of public–private agreements may be conditional on the presence of a "shadow of hierarchy," i.e. a threat of more stringent government intervention in case of non-compliance (Börzel and Risse 2017).

13.3.5 Overcoming Consumer Reluctance to Change

Fatty, salty, sugary and "ultra-processed" food products feature highly in EU diets because they are designed to appeal but also because they are cheaper. Animal-source foods are also central to many aspects of European food culture. For example, many products protected by a geographical indication in the EU that indicates a high-quality product linked to a particular territory are meats and cheeses. EU member states have therefore been reluctant to go beyond general messages to eat these products in moderation (as reflected in national dietary guidelines) to more interventionist measures based on regulations or fiscal measures. Aligned with the demand that governments "should keep out of the bedroom" that accompanied the relaxation of sexual mores in the 1970s and 1980s, we now hear demands that governments should "keep out of the kitchen."

Throughout history, however, food interventionism has been the rule rather than the exception. As Peter Scholliers pointed out, public food consumption has been as much the result of politics as from economy, culture and individual preferences (Scholliers 2021, p. 194). In the first half of the twentieth century, for example, European consumption patterns changed considerably, with a rebalancing of food groups. Meat, dairy, and fruit replaced the previously dominant wheat products and potatoes. This was the result of a rise in living standards, but also of targeted public interventions. During the First World War, food scarcity had become an urgent societal problem that demanded economic, political, and social measures. In the years that followed, scientists discovered the link between diet deficiencies and pathology, especially in children, and urged governments to focus on food in public health initiatives (de Mûelenaere 2021). Additionally, new processed foods (e.g., sugar, milk) necessitated more a centralized safety and quality control system. In response, states became—as Josep L. Barona aptly described— "regulating, stabilizing, disciplining and civilizing" agents in the transformation of eating habits, and set out a strategy to make populations more healthy and more resilient in the face of war (Barona 2010, p. 17).

These measures explicitly focused on food consumption, safety, and quality. An alliance of scientists, food industries and policy makers developed nutritional standards and outlined a range of actions geared toward promoting certain foods (e.g., meat, dairy, and fruit), while warning against others. This was part of an international movement that emphasized nutrition as a matter of social and political importance, as described by The League of Nations' Health Committee advisory commission on nutrition (Barona 2010). Along with social policies, governments provided tax relief, price control, food subsidies, family allowances, free seeds, and free school meals. In addition, educational programs, advertising, cookbooks, articles in women's magazines, and dietary propaganda directly targeted children and women. These measures, part of the emergence of the social welfare state, fundamentally altered food habits of Western middle-class populations. Food choices became increasingly influenced by what was considered nutritious instead of what provided the most energy (Veit 2013).

Today, the need for more sustainable food systems receives some support from consumers/citizens but survey results show that this is still relatively soft and focused strongly on health-related aspects such as the absence of pesticides (BEUC 2020; Eurobarometer 2020). Citizens support specific interventions (e.g., using public procurement, better labeling, incentivizing more sustainable practices among farmers and food companies) but there is little appetite for raising the price of unhealthy foods. Stronger interventionist measures are controversial because of their potential effects on income distribution and health inequalities. Lower-income households are already more likely to purchase foods of poorer nutritional value, whose prices may be lower than those of more nutritious foods. Thus, limiting the supply of such foods or raising their price through a food tax risks affecting disproportionately the poorer parts of populations, who already spend a greater proportion of their incomes on food purchases as compared to the expenditure patterns of higher-income households. Governments with an eye to re-election are well aware of this. Consumer support for sustainability initiatives may be a fair-weather phenomenon. With food price inflation gathering pace in the EU in 2021 and 2022 as a result of high energy prices and the conflict in Ukraine, EU member state governments are even more reluctant to push initiatives that will lead to an increase in the price of food.

13.3.6 The Need to Reflect the External Dimension

A significant argument against change, particularly when it affects production, is that reducing production inside the EU will simply shift pollution and emissions and low standards to third countries who get to increase their exports to make up for the gap in supply. This effect is referred to as leakage. In the case of GHG emissions leakage, because EU production is on average less emissions-intensive per kg of product that production elsewhere, there is even the possibility that reducing emissions from agriculture in the EU could increase global emissions if production increases outside the EU. Another example might be where more extensive production in the EU leads to increased imports, for example, of water-intensive fruit and vegetable production from water-stressed countries (Scheelbeek et al. 2020) or of animal feed which might lead to increased deforestation in exporting countries. In a food transitions framework, shifts in diets should take place simultaneously with the shifts in production to minimize such leakages. The impact on global sustainability also depends on whether it is the EU alone that is making the transition or whether there is a generalized effort to raise standards across many countries. Finally, complementary instruments such as trade policy and development assistance can be used to minimize the extent of these leakage effects. In practice, these necessary conditions are still largely absent, so these leakage effects and negative external impacts in third countries are an important barrier to change.

13.3.7 Changing Market Conditions and the War in Ukraine

Previous work on the political economy of food and agricultural policy reform has emphasized the role of changes in commodity prices in influencing the trajectory of reform. For example, Swinnen (2015) explores the impact of the 2008–2009 price spike on the outcome of the negotiations for a new CAP for the 2014–2020 programming period. We also observe how the dramatic changes in agricultural output and input prices in the course of 2022 which have followed the Russian invasion of Ukraine in February 2022, also reflected in food price inflation, have altered the discourse around the food system transition in the EU. The situation on world markets in 2008–2009 and 2022–2023 cannot be directly compared, but the spike in commodity prices in both instances led to greater prominence for discourses that emphasized the need to ensure and safeguard food security and not to risk or undermine food production. As the availability of food supplies for EU consumers has not been directly at risk following the Ukraine war, the food security argument has been framed in terms of the need to maintain EU production in order to make up for the shortfall in Black Sea supplies on world markets and thus to dampen the impact of food price increases particularly for importing low-income developing countries.

Specifically, the Commission permitted member states to derogate from the conditions for eligibility for the greening payment by allowing farmers to cultivate fallow land declared to meet the conditions for crop diversification or ecological focus areas in 2022. This derogation from the rules on crop rotation and maintenance of non-productive features on arable land was temporarily extended also to 2023 to encourage the production of cereals "to help increase food security worldwide."

Despite these temporary deviations, the Commission has underlined that "The current crisis lays bare the dependency of the EU food system on imported inputs, such as fossil fuels, fertilizer, feed and raw materials, confirming the necessity of a fundamental reorientation of EU agriculture and EU food systems toward sustainability, in line with the Green Deal and the reformed CAP..." (European Commission 2022c). However, we have already noted the softening of political support for pursuing the agricultural leg of the Farm to Fork strategy as a result of the changed market outlook. This particularly reflects the very significant food price inflation (on average, food prices increased by 18 percent in the EU in the year to November 2022) which, in conjunction with much higher energy prices, has put severe pressure on the spending power particularly of low-income households. Governments have been reluctant to contemplate measures that might put further upward pressure on food prices. This hesitation is reflected in attempts to slow down the passage of legislative proposals designed to implement specific targets in the F2F strategy. For example, the Commission proposed a revised Sustainable Use of Pesticides Regulation in June 2022 that would set national targets for the reduction in pesticide use (European Commission 2022b) accompanied by an impact assessment. Both member states in the Council and the AGRI Committee of the European Parliament have called for an additional impact assessment taking into account the impact of the war in Ukraine on global food security, which would delay further consideration of this proposal. We see clearly that the outlook for commodity prices, and the implications for both farm income and food price inflation, can act as a brake on pursuing the food system transition. At the same time, the food system vulnerabilities revealed by the Ukraine war also help to make the case why the transition to a more circular, less input-intensive farming system is even more urgent as a way to improve food system resilience in addition to limiting its negative impacts on climate, biodiversity and the natural environment.

13.4 Opportunities to Catalyze the Transition

The European Commission put forward its Green Deal proposal in December 2019 and its Farm to Fork strategy in May 2020. Both the agricultural Council of Ministers and the European Parliament have expressed support for the general direction of travel. However, this chapter emphasizes the dissonance between the dramatic change represented by the rhetorical commitment to a healthier and more sustainable food system in the Green Deal, and the significant obstacles that emerge when specific steps toward that objective are proposed and which mean that only modest progress has been made to date. This is of course not unique to the agri-food policy area. Given the urgent need for food system transformation, accelerating progress requires an understanding of the political economy obstacles to change and how they can be addressed.

As noted above, the biggest obstacle to change is the tension between the economic and environmental dimensions of sustainability, reflected both in the concerns of the farming community over the potential negative impact on their income, and the concerns of consumers and governments around higher food prices. The fact that agricultural output may drop as the sustainability requirements demanded of agriculture are increased reflects the standard response developed in the theory of negative externalities in economics. In the longer term, the changed incentives for innovation will help to foster disruptive innovation, including the scaling up and cost reductions of novel, possibly more sustainable, modes of production (agroecological practices, microbial fermentation, in vitro meat, etc.). However, requiring producers to internalize the costs that until now they have been able to pass on to society at large—the polluter pays principle, which incidentally is enshrined in the EU Treaties—will in the short-term lead to a reduction in production. EU farmers already receive a lot of public support, but many farmers still have relatively low household incomes. On equity grounds, EU governments may feel it is unfair to push the polluter pays principle. Are there other sources of revenue to ease the transition? How should such payments be designed to facilitate transition and not just maintain the status quo?

Several mechanisms suggest themselves. One potential route is to repurpose existing EU agricultural subsidies, shifting payments to farmers from simple income support to providing positive incentives for change. As noted, the 2021 CAP reform represents a modest step in that direction, but the size of that step can only be assessed when the national CAP strategic plans are fully evaluated. It is not costless for farmers, as tying payments to taking active steps to develop more sustainable farm businesses will reduce their value as income support. However, the Green Deal can create new income streams for farmers, e.g., through the production of industrial raw materials for the bio-economy, biomass or biogas for energy, or through payments for ecosystem services including carbon farming.

Improving resource efficiency (e.g., nitrogen use efficiency) and promoting a circular economy (thus valorizing waste streams) can also be a win–win situation both for farmers and the environment. Some EU member states that have imposed a carbon tax (e.g., Ireland) are using some of the proceeds of that tax to provide additional incentives to farmers to take climate action. To the extent that farmers have access to technical and management options that allow them to reduce the adverse environmental impacts of their activities while maintaining production, the easier it is to manage the tension between economic and environmental sustainability. This implies that investment in research and innovation to enlarge the toolbox of environmentally friendly practices available to farmers should be urgently ramped up. Innovation is needed in nature-based solutions, data-driven farming, as well as more high-tech solutions based on molecular genetics, vertical farming, and alternative proteins.

From a consumer perspective, there are underexplored opportunities to integrate knowledge on mechanisms and pathways of successful dietary change in the past, which could be used to strengthen current and future behavior change interventions. While average European diets are far from any definition of a "sustainable and healthy diet," at an individual or household level there are numerous examples of pathways where people have successfully shifted their dietary choices from conventional or average diets (typically unhealthy and unsustainable) to healthy and sustainable diets. Such positive dietary change patterns seem to have intensified over the COVID-19 pandemic (and associated severe social disruption), though unfortunately alongside several patterns of dietary change patterns associated with worsening diets. Studying pre- and peri-pandemic dietary change patterns and unraveling what determinants facilitated the shifts toward, and also the long-term adherence to, sustainable and healthy diets would likely yield pivotal insights from a consumer perspective that may prove crucial in future dietary change strategies. Supermarket panel or loyalty card data could, for example, be a helpful resource in such analysis.

Funding for the green transition cannot only come from the public sector. Consumers must also be prepared to pay a higher price for more sustainable production. This highlights two of the other political economy obstacles to change: the difficulty of recouping the higher costs of more sustainable production in a trading economy where firms and consumers continue to have access to lower-cost imports; and the reluctance of governments to contemplate higher food prices, not least because of the difficulties they create for low-income households. With food bills rising due to the knock-on effects of the war in Ukraine, governments are even more reluctant to contemplate measures that would add fuel to the flames.

Given the unique nature of multi-level governance in the EU identified at the outset of this chapter, there is also a need to ensure coherence between the different levels of governance, particularly between the EU and member states given their very different competences. As regards agricultural policy, the CAP agreed for the 2023–2027 programming period introduces a new governance model with a very different allocation of responsibilities between the EU and member states. Under the new performance-based delivery model, member states are responsible for setting targets for several economic, social, and environmental objectives in their national strategic plans, choosing the interventions to meet these targets and allocating EU and national funding appropriately. An indicator-based performance monitoring framework allows the European Commission to follow how EU funding is being used. But early evaluations of the draft strategic plans of member states indicate that it is difficult to assess the real level of environmental ambition and the extent to which the plans will accelerate the transition to more sustainable agricultural systems. The need for improved vertical coordination is even clearer on the food policy side, where the EU's competences in the area of sustainability are more limited and largely confined to some (limited) budgetary resources, setting standards, and regulating food labels while member states are responsible for interventions around public procurement, food environments, fiscal policy, and dietary guidelines and there is also a significant role for local actors (e.g., urban food councils). The Sustainable Food Systems Framework Law which the Commission will propose toward the end of 2023 (European Commission 2021c) will be crucial in enabling greater coordination across levels of government to achieve the Green Deal objectives.

Another area where greater coherence is required is the need to complement domestic actions to improve sustainability with a strengthened external dimension including trade policy measures. The EU has proposed a carbon border adjustment mechanism to apply to six industrial commodities (including fertilizer, but not food) to avoid carbon leakage due to the potential loss of competitiveness in those sectors. In the case of agri-food, it is considering the use of "mirror clauses" that would require imported products to meet the same sustainability standards as required of EU producers. These latter proposals are still at a very early stage of consideration and much remains to be decided on the possible coverage of these mirror arrangements and how they might operate in practice.

The mantra when it comes to food pricing is that the most sustainable food must ultimately become the most affordable. There may be some possibilities to subsidize the consumption of more healthy and sustainable foods, e.g., by reducing the value-added tax (VAT) rate on fruits and vegetables to zero, but most of the heavy lifting will be done by making less healthy foods and those with heavy environmental footprints more expensive. Complementary targeted income support policies will be needed to offset the regressive impacts on poorer households who both spend a higher share of their household income on food, and also consume a higher share of unhealthy foods within that basket. Modeling studies suggest that the tax rates required to achieve the consumption shifts necessary to replicate desired dietary intakes, if used alone, can be very high (Latka et al. 2021). Complementary efforts to change consumer preferences through information campaigns and labeling, the use of public procurement, and mandatory regulation of food manufacturing to reduce the use of undesirable ingredients and to control marketing strategies, will also be required. Research and development into alternative proteins to enhance their attractiveness and reduce their cost must also be continued.

The debate in the EU on policy responses to the consequences of the war in Ukraine for food, energy, and fertilizer prices has highlighted the tension between these several objectives but also the fragility of the political consensus supporting the green transition in agriculture as laid out in the F2F strategy. Despite no evidence that food security at the EU level is threatened (it is of course a different matter for low-income households where high food prices will exacerbate existing situations of food insecurity), the EPP, the largest political group in the European Parliament, called on the Commission President to "refrain from tabling any new proposal that could undermine our ability to feed ourselves" and for the postponement of key legislative initiatives foreseen in the F2F strategy.[3] The European Parliament adopted a resolution in which it supported the temporary planting of fallow land intended to safeguard biodiversity with protein crops, while also stating that the F2F target to allocate 10 percent of agricultural land to non-productive features to maintain biodiversity cannot be implemented in current market circumstances (European Parliament 2022).

Political leadership is required to avoid the unraveling of the plans for food system transformation in the EU. While the Commission has provided this leadership in formulating the Green Deal package, national governments more exposed to the vagaries of electoral fortune are often more hesitant. We commented earlier on the lack of a common understanding of what a sustainable food system means and how it can be interpreted very differently in the light of different value systems. We argue that the politicization of future food system directions along these different value systems is inherent, or even a precondition, to a transition process. Whereas EU food policymaking has for a long time been low in salience and left to a closed policy community, the recent emergence of new players and views marks its rise to the top of EU political agendas. Channeling these different views through democratic fora is likely to increase the quality and legitimacy of the Green Deal's food system ambitions. It could be valuable to make greater use of deliberate institutions such as food policy councils or citizens' assemblies for this purpose. At the same time, it will be a central challenge to avoid the spread of disinformation causing "dialogues of the deaf" and an erosion of basic rules of the game, such as respecting scientific evidence and legal commitments.

References

Augère-Granier. 2021. *Migrant Seasonal Workers in the European Agricultural Sector*. Brussels: European Parliamentary Research Service.

Barona, J. 2010. *The Problem of Nutrition: Experimental Science, Public Health, and Economy in Europe, 1914-1945*. New York: P.I.E. Peter Lang.

---

[3] https://www.eppgroup.eu/newsroom/news/increase-european-food-production-now.

Barreiro-Hurle, J., M. Bogonos, M. Himics, J. Hristov, I. Pérez Domínguez, A. Sahoo, G. Salputra, F. Weiss, E. Baldoni, and C. Elleby. 2021a. *Modelling Environmental and Climate Ambition in the Agricultural Sector with the CAPRI Model.* Luxembourg: Publications Office of the European Union.

Barreiro-Hurle, J., M. Bogonos, M. Himics, J. Hristov, I. Pérez-Domínguez, A. Sahoo, G. Salputra, F. Weiss, E. Baldoni, and C. Elleby. 2021b. "Modelling Transitions to Sustainable Food Systems: Are We Missing the Point?" *EuroChoices* 20 (3): 12–20. https://doi.org/10.1111/1746-692X.12339

Beckman, J., M. Ivanic, J. Jelliffe, F. Baquedano, and S. Scott. 2020. *Economic and Food Security Impacts of Agricultural Input Reduction under the European Union Green Deal's Farm to Fork and Biodiversity Strategies.* Economic Brief Number 30. Washington, DC: United States Department of Agriculture Economic Research Service.

BEUC. 2020. *One Bite at a Time: Consumers and the Transition to Sustainble Food Food: Analysis of a Survey of European Consumers on Attitudes towards Sustainable Food.* Brussels: BEUC The European Consumer Organisation.

Bonnet, C., Z. Bouamra-Mechemache, and T. Corre. 2018. "An Environmental Tax towards More Sustainable Food: Empirical Evidence of the Consumption of Animal Products in France." *Ecological Economics* 147 (May): 48–61.

ter Borg, S., M. Beukers, H. Brants, I. Milders, and E. Wilson-van den Hooven. 2021. *Het Geschatte Effect van Het Akkoord Verbetering Productsamenstelling Op de Dagelijkse Zout- En Suikerinname in Nederland.* Eindrapportage 2014–2020. Utretcht, the Netherlands: Rijksinstituut voor Volksgezondheid en Milieu (RIVM). https://doi.org/10.21945/RIVM-2020-0173

Börzel, Tanja A., and Thomas Risse. 2017. "Public–Private Partnerships: Effective and Legitimate Tools of Transnational Governance?" In *Complex Sovereignty*, 195–216. Toronto: University of Toronto Press. https://doi.org/10.3138/9781442684201-011

Bremmer, J., A. Gonzalez-Martinez, R. Jongeneel, H. Huiting, R. Stokkers, and M. Ruijs. 2021. *Impact Assessment of EC 2030 Green Deal Targets for Sustainable Crop Production.* Report 2021-150. Wageningen, the Netherlands: Wageningen Economic Research.

Candel, J. 2020. "What's on the Menu? A Global Assessment of MUFPP Signatory Cities' Food Strategies." *Agroecology and Sustainable Food Systems* 44 (7): 919–946. https://doi.org/10.1080/21683565.2019.1648357

Candel, J. 2022. "Current Impact Studies Are Unfit for Food System Transitions." *Paper under Review.*

Candel, J., G. Breeman, S. Stiller, and C. Termeer. 2014. "Disentangling the Consensus Frame of Food Security: The Case of the EU Common Agricultural Policy Reform Debate." *Food Policy* 44: 47–58. https://doi.org/10.1016/j.foodpol.2013.10.005.

Candel, J., Sebastian Lakner, and G. Pe'er. 2021. "Europe's Reformed Agricultural Policy Disappoints." *Nature* 595 (7869): 650–650. https://doi.org/10.1038/d41586-021-02047-y

Crippa, M., E. Solazzo, D. Guizzardi, F. Monforti-Ferrario, F.N. Tubiello, and A. Leip. 2021. "Food Systems Are Responsible for a Third of Global Anthropogenic GHG Emissions." *Nature Food* 2: 198–209. https://doi.org/10.1038/s43016-021-00225-9

Daugbjerg, C., and P.H. Feindt. 2017. "Post-Exceptionalism in Public Policy: Transforming Food and Agricultural Policy." *Journal of European Public Policy* 24 (11): 1565–1584. https://doi.org/10.1080/13501763.2017.1334081

de Mûelenaere, Nel. 2021. "Still Poor, Still Little, Still Hungry? The Diet and Health of Belgian Children after World War I." In Justin Nordstrom (ed.), *The Provisions of War: Expanding the Boundaries of Food and Conflict, 1840-1990.* University of Arkansas Press, 207-217.

EEA (European Economic Area). 2019. *The European Environment—State and Outlook 2020.* Luxembourg: Publications Office of the European Union on behalf of the European Environment Agency.

EEA. 2020. "Annual European Union Greenhouse Gas Inventory 1990-2018 and Inventory Report 2020." Copenhagen: European Environment Agency.

Eurobarometer. 2020. *Making Our Food Fit for the Future—Citizens' Expectations.* Special Report 505. Brussels: European Commission.

European Commission. 2018. *The REFIT Evaluation of the General Food Law (Regulation (EC) No 178/2022.* SWD(2018) 38. Brussels.

European Commission. 2020. *Revision of the Sustainable Use of Pesticides Directive: Combined Evaluation Roadmap/Inception Impact Assessment.* Brussels: European Commission.

European Commission. 2021a. *EU Agricultural Outlook for Markets and Income 2021–2031.* Brussels: European Commission Directorate-General for Agriculture and Rural Development.

European Commission. 2021b. *Sustainable Food System Framework Initiative—Inception Impact Assessment.* Brussels: European Commission.

European Commission. 2022a. *CAP Strategic Plans and Commission Observations: Summary Overview for 19 Member States.* Brussels: European Commission.

European Commission. 2022b. *Proposal for a Regulation of the European Parliament and of the Council on the Sustainable Use of Plant Protection Products and Amending Regulation (EU) 2021/2115.* COM(2022) 305. Brussels: European Commission.

European Commission. 2022c. *Safeguarding Food Security and Reinforcing the Resilience of Food Systems.* COM(2022) 133. Brussels: European Commission.

European Parliament. 2022. *Resolution of 24 March 2022 on the Need for an Urgent EU Action Plan to Ensure Food Security inside and Outside the EU in Light of the Russian Invasion of Ukraine (2022/2593(RSP)).* Brussels: European Parliament.

Farm Europe. 2022. "The Farm to Fork: In Need of a New Political Consensus." *Farm-Europe Blog*, April 11, 2022. https://www.farm-europe.eu/news/the-farm-to-fork-in-need-of-a-new-political-consensus/

Fanzo, J., Y. Ribhi Shawar, T. Shyam, S. Das, and J. Shiffman. 2021. "Challenges to Establish Effective Public-Private Partnerships to Address Malnutrition in All Its Forms." *International Journal of Health Policy and Management* 10 (Special Issue on Political Economy of Food Systems): 934–945. https://doi.org/10.34172/ijhpm.2020.262

Feindt, P.H. 2010. "Policy-Learning and Environmental Policy Integration in the Common Agricultural Policy, 1973–2003." *Public Administration* 88 (2): 296–314.

GBD 2017 Disease and Injury Incidence and Prevalence Collaborators. 2018. "Global, Regional, and National Incidence, Prevalence, and Years Lived with Disability for 354 Diseases and Injuries for 195 Countries and Territories, 1990–2017: A Systematic Analysis for the Global Burden of Disease Study 2017." *The Lancet* 392 (10159): 1789–1858. https://doi.org/10.1016/S0140-6736(18)32279-7

Henning, C., P. Witzke, L. Panknin, and M. Grunenberg. 2021. *Economic and Environmental Impacts of the Green Deal on the Agricultural Economy: A Simulation Study of the Impact of the F2F-Strategy on Production, Trade, Welfare and the Environment*

Based on the CAPRI-Model - English Summary. Kiel and Bonn, Germany: Institut für Agrarökonomie and Eurocare.

Jackson, P., M.G. Rivera Ferre, J. Candel, A. Davies, C. Derani, H. de Vries, V. Dragović-Uzelac, et al. 2021. "Food as a Commodity, Human Right or Common Good." *Nature Food* 2 (3): 132–134. https://doi.org/10.1038/s43016-021-00245-5

Jensen, J. D., and S. Smed. 2018. "State-of-the-Art for Food Taxes to Promote Public Health." *Proceedings of the Nutrition Society* 77 (2): 100–105. https://doi.org/10.1017/S0029665117004050

Lähteenmäki-Uutela, A., M. Rahikainen, A. Lonkila, and B. Yang. 2021. "Alternative Proteins and EU Food Law." *Food Control* 130: 108336. https://doi.org/10.1016/j.foodcont.2021.108336

Latka, C., M. Kuiper, S. Frank, T. Heckelei, P. Havlík, H-P. Witzke, A. Leip, et al. 2021. "Paying the Price for Environmentally Sustainable and Healthy EU Diets." *Global Food Security* 28: 100437. https://doi.org/10.1016/j.gfs.2020.100437

von der Leyen, U. 2019. "Opening Statement in the European Parliament Plenary Session by Ursula von Der Leyen, Candidate for President of the European Commission." European Parliament, July 16. https://ec.europa.eu/commission/presscorner/detail/pt/speech_19_4230

Marx, A., C. Depoorter, and R. Vanhaecht. 2022. "Voluntary Sustainability Standards: State of the Art and Future Research." *Standards* 2 (1): 14–31. https://doi.org/10.3390/standards2010002

Matthews, A. 2013. "Greening Agricultural Payments in the EU's Common Agricultural Policy." *Bio-Based and Applied Economics* 2 (1): 1–27.

Matthews, A. 2021. "Can the New CAP Help EU Agriculture to Meet the Targets in the European Green Deal?" *Journal of the European Court of Auditors* 2: 13–19.

Panjwani, Clare, and Martin Caraher. 2014. "The Public Health Responsibility Deal: Brokering a Deal for Public Health, but on Whose Terms?" *Health Policy (Amsterdam, Netherlands)* 114 (2–3): 163–173. https://doi.org/10.1016/j.healthpol.2013.11.002

Revoredo-Giha, C., N. Chalmers, and F. Akaichi. 2018. "Simulating the Impact of Carbon Taxes on Greenhouse Gas Emission and Nutrition in the UK." *Sustainability* 10 (1): 134. https://doi.org/10.3390/su10010134

Schebesta, Hanna, and Jeroen J. L. Candel. 2020. "Game-Changing Potential of the EU's Farm to Fork Strategy." *Nature Food* 1 (10): 586–588. https://doi.org/10.1038/s43016-020-00166-9

Scheelbeek, Pauline, Rosemary Green, Keren Papier, Anika Knuppel, Carmelia Alae-Carew, Angela Balkwill, Timothy J. Key, Valerie Beral, and Alan D. Dangour. 2020. "Health Impacts and Environmental Footprints of Diets that Meet the Eatwell Guide Recommendations: Analyses of Multiple UK Studies." *BMJ Open* 10 (8): e037554.

Scholliers P. 2021 *Brood. Een Geschiedenis van Bakkers en Hun Brood*. Antwerp, Belgium: Uitgeverij Vrijdag.

Skogstad, Grace. 1998. "Ideas, Paradigms and Institutions: Agricultural Exceptionalism in the European Union and the United States." *Governance* 11 (4): 463–490. https://doi.org/10.1111/0952-1895.00082

Swinnen, J., ed. 2008. *The Perfect Storm: The Political Economy of the Fischler Reforms of the Common Agricultural Policy*. Brussels: Centre for European Policy Studies.

Swinnen, J., ed. 2015. *The Political Economy of the 2014-2020 Common Agricultural Policy: An Imperfect Storm*. London: Rowman & Littlefield International, Ltd.

Swinnen, J., 2018. "Policy Reform in History: Europe, the USA, and China." In *The Political Economy of Agricultural and Food Policies*, Chapter 7. New York: Palgrave Macmillan.

Veit H. 2013. *Modern Food, Moral Food: Self-Control, Science, and the Rise of Modern American Eating in the Early Twentieth Century*. Durham: The University of North Carolina Press.

Wesseler, Justus. 2022. "The EU's Farm-to-Fork Strategy: An Assessment from the Perspective of Agricultural Economics." *Applied Economic Perspectives and Policy* 44 (4): 1826–1843. https://doi.org/10.1002/aepp.13239

14

Tracking Progress and Generating Accountability for Global Food System Commitments

Stella Nordhagen and Jessica Fanzo

14.1 Introduction

Central to understanding the political economy of food systems transformation is clarifying the systems that enable—or prevent—monitoring progress on transformation, setting evidence-based commitments for improvement, and ensuring accountability for delivering on them. Prior chapters in this volume have elucidated the role of data and evidence in settling fact-based policy disagreements (Chapter 2) and described some of the challenges that arise when disinformation and bias instead dominate policy discussions (Chapter 1). They have also given specific examples of how evidence can galvanize attention to an issue, as in the case of obesity prevention (Chapters 6 and 7) or environmental sustainability (Chapter 11), or support the case for policy change, as in the case of agricultural subsidies or direct payments (Chapters 3 and 4). And they have highlighted the need to track how well policies are implemented (Chapter 6) as well as their intended and unintended consequences (Chapter 3). Jointly, the prior chapters have made clear that monitoring food system transformation can play a central role in several different political economy spaces described in the first chapter of this volume, such as policy mobilization, design, and adaptation.

This chapter thus builds on this foundation to examine prior attempts at monitoring food systems and ensuring accountability. After highlighting existing gaps and why new approaches are needed, we present selected options for filling these gaps. We then conclude with a discussion of what else, besides information, is needed to foster the broader accountability cycle—and thus to support the process of food system transformation amid the types of political economy challenges described in the prior challenges.

Stella Nordhagen and Jessica Fanzo, *Tracking Progress and Generating Accountability for Global Food System Commitments*. In: *The Political Economy of Food System Transformation*. Edited by: Danielle Resnick and Johan Swinnen, Oxford University Press. © Stella Nordhagen and Jessica Fanzo (2023). DOI: 10.1093/oso/9780198882121.003.0014

14.2 The Need for Transformation, Commitments, and Accountability

As explained in the introduction to this volume, food systems transformation is an urgent priority. Food systems are essential for supporting human health, make major contributions to livelihoods, and provide essential ecosystem services (FAO 2009, 2013, 2017; Christiaensen et al. 2011; Barrett et al. 2020), and their ability to produce increasing amounts of food has enabled global population growth and prosperity for decades (Evenson and Gollin 2003; Pingali 2012). They are central to achieving many global commitments and goals, including the Sustainable Development Goals (SDGs). At the same time, they are currently failing to provide affordable, healthy diets to much of the global population, particularly in lower-income countries, and are contributing to a large and growing burden of diet-related ill health, including undernutrition and diet-related non-communicable diseases (NCDs) (GBD 2017; Diet Collaborators 2019; FAO et al. 2020). Malnutrition in all its forms is associated with annual economic costs of up to $3.5 trillion (GloPAN 2016). Food systems currently give rise to 600 million cases of foodborne illness annually (Havelaar et al. 2015) and play a role in driving antibiotic resistance (WHO 2017) as well as zoonotic and other infectious diseases (Rohr et al. 2019; UNEP and ILRI 2020).

Food systems also contribute about one third of global greenhouse gas (GHG) emissions and drive various other negative environmental impacts, including through land use change, biodiversity loss, and localized pollution (Herrero et al. 2009; Rockström et al. 2009; Kummu et al. 2012; Lennox et al. 2018; FAO and UNEP 2020;). While food systems support the livelihoods of billions, many of these producers and other food systems workers remain marginalized, unable to earn a living wage in a safe environment (Anderson; Fleischer et al. 2013; Christiaensen et al. 2021). Finally, food systems' resilience to climate, geopolitical, and economic shocks is limited, and they are under increasing pressure from conflict and extreme weather events (FAO, IFAD, UNICEF, WFP, and WHO 2018, 2021; Loboguerrero et al. 2019; Barrett et al. 2020; Rockström et al. 2020).

Addressing these intertwined challenges requires urgent, diverse, and coordinated action across many levels of food systems—from global to local, and throughout food supply chains as well as food environments, policies, and other influencers of individual behavior (Blesh et al. 2019; Barrett et al. 2020; Webb et al. 2020). Much evidence already exists on how to do this, including on specific interventions to improve nutrition (Bhutta et al. 2008, 2013; Keats et al. 2021) and reduce hunger (Cornell University et al. 2020) as well as broader food systems transformation (Barrett et al. 2020; Gerten et al. 2020). However, as made clear in many of this book's prior chapters, this evidence will not translate into impact without specific commitments to specific actions by specific actors—backed up by the needed resources and political will.

Once those commitments are in place, accountability mechanisms will be needed to ensure they are actually acted upon. For the purposes of this chapter, *accountability* refers to being answerable for actions and able to give a clear explanation for action (or inaction). It involves "the recognition of achievements and enforcement of performance through the application of sanctions for poor performance or non-compliance" and requires that a key actor (e.g., a political decision-maker) be bound to answer to another entity who is empowered to assess how well the first actor fulfills their obligations (Kraak et al. 2014; Swinburn et al. 2015). This can be depicted through a cycle (Figure 14.1): *setting* the account by defining the objectives and measurable targets for action; *taking* the account by collecting, analyzing, and evaluating relevant available evidence; *sharing* the account by deliberative, participatory stakeholder engagement; *holding* to account by providing incentives and disincentives to decision-makers; and *responding* to the account by taking action (Kraak et al. 2014). *Accountability mechanisms* facilitate this cycle to occur—providing and disseminating the evidence needed to set, take, and share the account, then establishing processes through which actors can held to account and spurred to respond.

The food and nutrition community is currently at an important juncture for ensuring accountability for such commitments: 2021 featured the United Nations

Figure 14.1 The accountability cycle.

Source: Reproduced from (Accountability Pact 2021) with author's permission; adapted from (Kraak et al. 2014)

Food Systems Summit, the Nutrition for Growth Summit, and the 26th United Nations Climate Change Conference of the Parties. Some potentially important commitments emerged from these summits, but such commitments are mere platitudes if not followed up by action. Strong and independent tracking of actions and progress toward transformation, as well as accountability mechanisms to ensure commitments are respected, will be needed.

14.3 Prior Work on Food Systems Accountability and Monitoring

There are numerous prior and existing efforts to improve accountability and monitoring of food systems outcomes and commitments. The vast majority of these focus on "taking" and "sharing" the account, either based on an account "set" through international processes or without reference to specific targets, are not linked to a mechanism for "holding to account." While many of these also exist at the level of a specific country, organization, or project, we focus on those that are global and highlight major contributions as opposed to providing an exhaustive list.

14.3.1 Recurring High-Level Reports

The first set of such initiatives is a set of recurring reports (see examples in Figure 14.2).

Flagship United Nations Food and Agriculture Organization (FAO) reports. The FAO, in collaboration with other UN organizations, puts out numerous flagship recurring reports on food systems issues. The FAO's original annual flagship report is the State of Food and Agriculture (SOFA), launched in 1947 as an input into an FAO conference and based on data contributed by member states (FAO 1947).[1] Early reports were geared toward member state governments and consisted mainly of agricultural statistics. Over time they transitioned to more analysis and discussion on specific thematic focuses (e.g., livestock, water scarcity). They no longer include standard annual indicators, which are instead published separately online. From 1999, SOFA was joined by a second flagship report, The State of Food Insecurity in the World (SOFI), which began with the aim of reporting on progress toward the 1996 World Food Summit goal of halving undernourishment (FAO 1999). The United Nations Children's Fund (UNICEF), the World Health Organization (WHO), the International Fund for Agricultural Development (IFAD), and

---

[1] The FAO's predecessor, the International Institute of Agriculture, began reporting government-provided agricultural statistics around 1910.

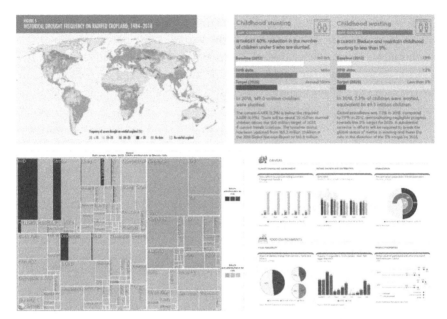

Figure 14.2 Examples of data presented in high-level reports (top) and online dashboards (bottom).

Sources: Top left: SOFA (FAO 2021), reproduced under a CC BY-NC-SA 3.0 IGO Creative Commons license; https://creativecommons.org/licenses/by-nc-sa/3.0/igo Top right: GNR (Development Initiatives 2020) Bottom left: Country dashboard from the Food Systems Dashboard. Global Alliance for Improved Nutrition (GAIN) and Johns Hopkins University (2020). https://www.foodsystemsdashboard.org. https://doi.org/10.36072/db. Bottom right: GBD Compare data on disability-adjusted life years attributed to dietary risks (IHME 2021), reproduced under a CC BY-NC-ND 4.0 International license, https://creativecommons.org/licenses/by-nc-nd/4.0/

the United Nations World Food Progamme (WFP) later joined FAO as publishers, and the series was renamed to the State of Food Security and Nutrition in the World, with a greater focus on monitoring progress toward "globally agreed food security and nutrition targets, providing analytical interpretation of trends and in-depth analysis on emerging issues to inform decision making and contribute to the achievement of ending hunger, food insecurity and malnutrition." SOFI reports are thematic and provide updated estimates for core indicators, particularly undernourishment prevalence, and sometimes present new indicators—such as the 2020 report's food affordability estimates (FAO et al. 2020). Other major recurring FAO reports include the State of the World's Forests; State of World Fisheries and Aquaculture; and State of Agricultural Commodity Markets.

Global Nutrition Report (GNR). The GNR was launched following the first Nutrition for Growth (N4G) summit in 2013, with the aim of tracking progress against global nutrition targets along with the financing and commitments to reach them. It is developed by an Independent Group of Experts with various external contributors. Specific to nutrition, GNR tracks progress against World Health Assembly global nutrition targets, other nutrition indicators, and N4G commitments. Each report has a theme, providing an overall perspective plus country-by-country profiles. The GNR has recently initiated the Nutrition Accountability Framework to minimize the burden of reporting on commitments following the 2021 N4G summit (GNR 2021).

Global Food Policy Report (GFPR). Published by the International Food Policy Research Institute (IFPRI) since 2011, the GFPR aims to "provide a comprehensive, research-based analysis of major food policy challenges at the global, regional, national, and local levels." Each report contains chapters from different IFPRI researchers and others on various topical themes as well as regional focuses and tables of food policy indicators to track change over time.

The Global Access to Nutrition Index. This index, originally created by the Global Alliance for Improved Nutrition (GAIN) and now put out by the non–profit Access to Nutrition Initiative (ATNI), focuses exclusively on the private sector. Published every 2–3 years, the Index rates major global food and beverage manufacturers (e.g., Nestlé, Unilever) in contributing to addressing obesity, diet-related NCDs, and undernutrition. Each company is scored across seven dimensions: governance, products, accessibility, marketing, lifestyles, labeling, and environment. Main audiences targeted are the companies and their investors, with a goal of encouraging more private-sector action to improve nutrition.

***Lancet* Countdowns.** A collaboration between the WHO, the non-profit NCD Alliance, and Imperial College London, the biennial *Lancet* NCD Countdown 2030 aims to be an independent mechanism for countries to monitor progress to achieving SDG target 3.4, a reduction in mortality from NCDs (many of which are diet-related)—and for other stakeholders to hold them accountable for doing so. Similarly, the annual *Lancet* Countdown on Climate Change and Health monitors key areas of health and climate change, some of which are relevant to food systems.

In addition to these reports that are regularly reporting on topics of direct relevance to food and nutrition, other major recurring reports, such as UNICEF's "State of the World's Children," the World Bank's "World Development Report," and the Intergovernmental Panel on Climate Change's (IPCC) assessment reports, regularly include coverage of food and nutrition topics, including tracking indicators. Periodic reports from the High-level Panel of Experts on Food Security and Nutrition (HLPE) of the Committee on World Food Security (CFS) and the Global Panel on Agriculture and Food Systems for Nutrition also highlight important issues and steer thought and action within the food systems space, but do not have a specific tracking and accountability purpose.

14.3.2 Online Databases and Dashboards

Second, a growing set of online databases and dashboards provide data and information on food and nutrition (see examples in Figure 14.2). Compared to the abovementioned reports, these tend to be more regularly updated, interactive, and visual, with less in-depth analysis and interpretation.

Food Systems Dashboard. Launched in 2020, this initiative is led by GAIN and Johns Hopkins University, with FAO and other partners, and aims to give users a comprehensive view of food systems by bringing together data from multiple sources in visualizations that enable cross-country comparisons and tracking across time. Based around a food systems framework, it combines data for over 200 indicators from over 40 sources for over 230 countries (about 630,000 data points), encompassing health and environmental aspects. To help decision makers prioritize ways to sustainably improve nutrition through improving food systems, the Dashboard plans to add functionalities to diagnose food systems issues and identify policies to address them (GAIN and Johns Hopkins University, 2020; J. Fanzo et al. 2020).

FAOSTAT. This FAO-run database provides country-level data on 245 countries and territories, including food production, food security, prices, climate change, and employment. Data can be visualized online or downloaded and can be compared across countries or over time.

Global and Local Burden of Disease. These dashboards, hosted by the Institute for Health Metrics and Evaluations (IHME), include certain key nutrition and diet-related indicators (e.g., stunting, diet low in various beneficial nutrients), which can be visualized in various different ways.

World Food Programme Hunger Map LIVE. This visualization tool aims to monitor and predict the magnitude and severity of hunger in near real-time for lower- and lower-middle-income countries. It includes food security monitoring data and machine learning-generated predictions and allows for identifying areas with high prevalence of insufficient food consumption, with overlays for different types of hazards and conflicts. It also includes a visualization of vegetation levels and recent rainfall.

WHO Nutrition Landscape Information System (NLiS). This platform provides profiles for different countries, including non-interactive visualizations and tables, including malnutrition, health services, food security, and government commitments.

Other online efforts specific to food and nutrition data but with fairly narrow focuses include the Global Fortification Data Exchange, FAO Global Individual Food Consumption Data Tool, Global Dietary Database, State of Acute Malnutrition dashboard, Vitamin A Supplementation interactive dashboard, AQUASTAT, and the UNICEF-WHO-World Bank Joint Child Malnutrition Estimates dashboard. There are also several online databases with a broader focus but coverage of food systems data, including the World Bank Open Data platform, Our World in Data, and the SDG Tracker.

It is difficult to assess whether and how these reports and databases change behavior of food system actors, particularly governments. While reports can have a large readership measured by downloads and media coverage (Bou-Karroum et al. 2017), whether they are read thoroughly and if their data and recommendations are used to inform policymaking is challenging to measure. A survey of approximately 500 policy stakeholders across Africa, Latin America, and South Asia found that printed and online publications and databases were the most effective tools that informed national policymaking (as compared to policy briefs, events, and media) (Evans 2015). IPCC reports have formed the scientific basis of the Conference of the Parties (COP) negotiations (Howarth and Painter 2016). Oxfam's Behind the Brands report ranked the behaviors of food companies and helped prompt further engagement (as opposed to alienation) (Mayne et al. 2018; Sahan 2016). Similar reports that use indices to rank the performance of countries or companies can serve to motivate or de-incentivize, but this is often political.

Data-based communication has been shown to be powerful in some contexts. For example, bringing together concepts and using data to describe the magnitude of a challenge helps frame knowledge for policymakers and has been shown effective in nutrition (Gillespie and van den Bold 2017; IFPRI 2014). However, despite an increase in data visualization tools in the food systems space, many lack a theory of change of how they will change decisions and actionable indicators, making them less powerful advocacy tools (Manorat et al. 2019). Overall, evidence on how prior reports and data-sharing efforts have been used to change behavior is very limited; more research on the topic is needed, including that which looks into which types of evidence (e.g., rankings, policy briefs) are the most impactful.

14.4 Gaps in Food Systems Monitoring Work

The progress made on food systems monitoring since 1947's original SOFA report is impressive. From an 18-page, text-only monograph with a handful of statistics on food supplies (sold at a cost of 20 cents), the global food and nutrition community now benefits from multiple high-quality reports and near-real-time data-visualization websites. Indicator coverage, quality, and timeliness have increased considerably, and many initiatives are working to make data increasingly useful to stakeholders.

At the same time, there remain opportunities for improvement. First, most reports and dashboards focus on only one aspect of food systems and their effects (e.g., nutrition outcomes, NCDs). Even among the most comprehensive existing efforts, such as FAOSTAT and the Food Systems Dashboard, key aspects of food systems are omitted. For example, indicators related to livelihoods and equity are largely absent; while one can find numbers on employment and productivity, they are largely limited to agricultural production (omitting the post-farm value chain) and say nothing about employment quality or respect for workers' rights. Indicators for food systems resilience are largely lacking and require additional work, both conceptual and practical (Béné 2020; J. Fanzo et al. 2021). The informal economy is rarely captured, despite playing an essential role in livelihoods and food security (Resnick 2017). Large monitoring gaps also exist for indicators related to policy and governance, such as market power of international food corporations (J. Fanzo et al. 2021). And when diverse data on different food systems aspects *are* provided jointly, they are often presented in parallel, without examining the feedbacks and interactions that occur among them.

Second, the question of which data to include, and which stakeholders to engage, becomes more challenging when thinking not about tracking for tracking's sake but rather monitoring to foster accountability. Food system outcomes are influenced by many factors, rarely with a single, clear actor responsible for them; significant change instead requires coordinated action across sectors. As a result, it may be unclear *whom* to hold to account for action—there is a risk that "everyone and no one" becomes responsible. To mitigate this, indicators could be chosen that are clearly linked to specific actions (e.g., enacting a carbon or sugar-sweetened-beverage tax). However, such an approach is no panacea as it could lead to a bias toward focus on inputs and outputs (e.g., funding provided) without verifying whether they lead to intended changes in outcomes. Moreover, there will be some cases (e.g., diet quality) where essential indicators cannot be tied to any single action or actor.

Third, even for existing data, there are often gaps in quality and coverage (Marshall et al. 2021). For example, aside from data on young children collected through the Demographic and Health Surveys, there is little high-quality, representative information available on diets. Knowledge of what people eat is essential for understanding how to intervene to improve health and environmental impacts of food, but the best-available estimates of dietary intake rely on proxy data and modeling that is subject to inconsistencies (Beal et al. 2021).

Fourth, many indicators are monitored only at the national level, not for subnational regions where policy decisions are often made (Marshall et al. 2021). In addition, data are often irregularly updated, with a long lag between data collection and reporting, making them less actionable.

Finally, not all monitoring initiatives have transparent processes led by independent, diverse stakeholders, and it is not always clear how local stakeholders' voices are integrated. There are rarely obvious data inclusion/exclusion criteria or a well-articulated process for indicator identification. This lack of transparency and clarity can be particularly problematic in a context where information is increasingly seen as subject to interpretation (i.e., through "alternative facts"). For example, after the 2021 Global Hunger Index ranked India low, the Indian government alleged that the data were inaccurate and biased (Chadha 2021)—*despite* the Index using a consistent, transparent process. And the once-influential World Bank Ease of Doing Business Index was recently discontinued after losing credibility due to evidence of data irregularities that sought to favor certain countries, as opposed to consistently following a transparent and formalized process (Machen et al. 2021).

Future efforts at food systems monitoring need more comprehensive approaches, looking across food system sectors to bring together analyses often presented in silos. Doing so will require forging new coalitions of experts, cutting across disciplines and geographies and with the independence to hold stakeholders accountable and the diversity to stave off complaints of bias. It will be essential to use a systems approach, as opposed to an isolated sectoral vision. This will require understanding and tracking key trade-offs and feedback loops among outcomes across sectors to identify impactful entry points and holistic approaches that leverage interactions—while avoiding unintended consequences (Ingram 2011; Griggs 2015; Lade et al. 2020; Golden et al. 2021).

Monitoring will need to be done in a way that is useful for stakeholders. Doing so will first necessitate defining who the key stakeholders are—which should consider who, within a given context, which decision-makers are able to undertake the desired actions (e.g., tax sugar-sweetened beverages, cap GHG emissions from food production) and which are able to hold decision-makers to account (e.g., legal mechanisms where existing, civil society, industry groups). Once such stakeholders are determined, it will be essential to ensure that the indicators tracked are relevant for each stakeholder's decisions.

At the level of the data, quality and coverage will need to be improved for certain indicators—but this will be a long-term process, contingent on resource availability, and should not become a roadblock to improving monitoring in the short term. It will also be essential (and a long-term project) to make data available more quickly, aiming at near-real-time information for key fast-changing indicators (e.g., food prices). Indicators and interpretation will need to focus not only at the national scale, particularly for large countries and food systems aspects that are strongly shaped by local cultures (e.g., diets) and ecological systems (e.g., environmental impacts). Data must be interpreted within context, including targets and commitments (e.g., the 2030 Agenda, Paris Climate Accords) where relevant. Alongside quantitative data, it will be useful to include case studies that represent the nuance of local contexts and perspectives—and that showcase *process*, not just outcomes.

14.5 Efforts to Fill These Gaps

Several initiatives are trying to fill these gaps. In particular, the Global Food Systems Countdown to 2030 Initiative is working to build a globally comprehensive, independent, science-based system to monitor food systems to guide decision-makers and hold those in power to account for transformation (J. Fanzo et al. 2021). Based on a food systems framework modified from (HLPE 2017), the Countdown covers five thematic areas, including food systems outcomes and cross-cutting issues critical to their transformation, with a set of indicator domains under each area as shown in Figure 14.3.

Under each thematic area, a set of high-quality indicators will be tracked over time. A consultative process involving over 50 researchers was used to identify the five areas and a preliminary set of indicator domains. Indicators were identified based on a set of criteria: relevance, high quality, interpretable, and useful to support policymaking. For example, within the domain of "Diets, Nutrition, and Health," it was decided to focus on diets and their determinants, rather than indicators of nutrition outcomes, as the latter are already widely tracked and influenced by factors extending beyond the food system (e.g., sanitation, healthcare) (UNICEF 1990). Instead, the tracking will likely focus on indicators of diet quality, food security, and food environments and policies influencing them, which were identified as important levers for change. While some indicators within the thematic area are already tracked by other efforts (e.g., SOFI), tracking them through the Countdown is thought to add value by being integrated with indicators for other thematic areas (e.g., environment).

As a second example, the domain of livelihoods, poverty, and equity is rarely tracked in depth in existing food systems-related monitoring. It plans to consider livelihoods *in any part* of the food system—not just, for example, farmers—and to track employment, incomes, poverty, and welfare. It is also expected to monitor social protection coverage for food system workers (including through informal sources) and respect for their human rights. While the indicators for diets are comparatively well-defined, additional work will be needed to define indicators within

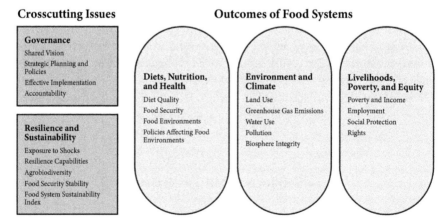

Figure 14.3 Framework for the Global Food Systems Countdown to 2030 Initiative.
Source: Authors' compilation.

livelihoods, poverty, and equity and high-quality data. Filling such conceptual and practical gaps across thematic areas is one goal of the Countdown.

The Countdown includes experts from all inhabited continents and nearly 30 different organizations, spanning academia, civil society, and the UN, and plans to expand to a more diverse set of stakeholders engaged via transparent and inclusive consultative processes. Tracking is projected to begin in 2023 and continue in biannual publications thereafter. Where established targets exist, indicators will be compared to these to support accountability. The overall aim is to offer food system actors and stakeholders (e.g., civil society, governments) actionable evidence to hold governments, consumers, and the private sector accountable for food system transformation. The *actionable* point is key: indicators will be specifically chosen as those impactable by the engaged stakeholders, helping facilitate holding them to account for action.

A second recently launched food systems monitoring initiative is the International Pact on Monitoring for Accountability for Action on Food Systems. This pact focuses on the need to strengthen food systems by monitoring evidence generated by researchers, translating this into the real-world food systems context, and advocating for evidence-based food systems transformation (Accountability Pact 2021). As of September 2021, over 250 experts had signed the pact. While such initiatives may not generate data on their own, they can galvanize members to do so—for example, the work of the Countdown collaboration is very much in line with the ethos of the pact. However, both initiatives are primarily focused on the *taking* and *sharing* stages in the accountability cycle. While the Pact is commendable for its strong focus on communicating results and holding food systems actors to account, it is not clear that the actors signing it (primarily researchers) have the power to actually hold decision-makers accountable. The Countdown prioritizes communication on results but includes no mechanism to sanction or reward.

14.6 Moving from Data and Information to Accountability

With numerous existing reports and databases as well as new initiatives in the works, there is an incredible opportunity to expand evidence to support accountability to meet global commitments. Evidence is a key input into the efforts of civil society organizations, investors, funders, and others advocating for improved food systems (Kraak et al. 2014) but is only one part of ensuring political commitment and action. The initiatives discussed in this chapter so far focus heavily on only one step in the accountability cycle: *taking* the account. We recommend five areas in which more effort is needed to ensure stronger accountability for food systems transformation.

Co-creation and collective action: Because food systems involve all of society, their transformation cannot be dictated top-down or by any single stakeholder group. There is instead a need for co-creation, to create and harness a shared vision and responsibility for collective action (Barrett et al. 2020). This should cut across all steps in the accountability cycle but is particularly important for setting objectives and targets and holding decision-makers to account. It must be done in an inclusive way that brings together diverse food systems actors with interest in how food systems are governed—and prevents the voices of the powerful, including major food corporations, from overwhelming the debate (Canfield et al. 2021). At the same time, it will be essential to ensure that a distributed, inclusive process does not exacerbate the "everyone and no one" challenge of accountability mentioned above: those responsible for acting must be clearly designated. Moving forward, it will be essential to create a global food system architecture that is not only inclusive and equitable, rebalancing power within it, but also innovative in how it moves the food system toward bold transformation (Nisbett et al. 2021). Structured bottom-up processes like communities of practice and dialogues could be used to change the social narrative and co-produce not only research but also the action that follows from it—aiming to reframe power, empower excluded voices, and navigate different ideologies (Chambers et al. 2021). Leveraging social media to understand popular opinions and leverage constituent voices is also a possibility (Delmastro and Zollo 2021).

Investments and funding: More funding has significant potential to reduce hunger and improve other food systems outcomes (Chichaibelu et al. 2021). Investments in food systems and nutrition remain significantly low and "traditional," with overseas development assistance providing a very minor amount of funding toward agriculture and nutrition (Byerlee and Fanzo 2019). For example, less than 1 percent of development donors' investments are in nutrition, whereas 22 percent of adult deaths are attributable to dietary risks and 45 percent of child deaths are attributable to undernutrition (GBD 2017; Diet Collaborators 2019; Baker 2021)—making nutrition one of the development sectors with the largest gap between level of investment and potential impact. There is also little innovative financing to support the sector (Covic et al. 2021; Development Initiatives 2021). Without funding to support food systems transformation, transformative potential is limited—particularly for low-income countries, for which short-term investments could allow them to "leapfrog" certain historical transitions (e.g., toward greater reliance on intensive, high-input farming) and avoid the mistakes that high-income countries have made as their food systems transitioned (Elzen et al. 2020). Moreover, investment mechanisms can also support *holding* to account, as investors have leverage to pressure company leaders to act and may even be able to include binding commitments within financial contracts. For example, the Farm Animal Investment Risk & Return Initiative (FAIRR) is a network of major investors that focuses specifically on improving environmental, social, and governance aspects of the livestock sector. In addition to investment in facilitating transformative action, investments in information systems and data platforms that provide information related to different policy scenarios and pathways could better empower policymakers to carve a path forward.

Capacity building for systems thinking: Food systems are complex and interact with many systems and actors, and systems thinking is not easy. In this transdisciplinary space, professionals need to be fluent in discussing the concepts and constructs of other disciplines to effectively engage with decision makers in other sectors and seize opportunities to influence policies and programs (Fanzo et al. 2015). Yet many individuals are instead trained in specialized, niche areas such as agronomy, nutrition, global health, or food biotechnology. Systems approaches and thinking are rarely taught in, and many food systems decision-makers lack the tools to examine feedback loops, synergies, and trade-offs of decisions across the food system (Babu and Blom 2014). This does not mean that every policymaker or donor must be a systems expert, but having key ministries (for example) staffed with some systems analysis capacity could greatly help stakeholders navigate the complexity of food systems and translate the aforementioned monitoring data into action and accountability.

Scientific consensus generation and evidence translation: Another way to improve accountability is ensuring that the vast amount of science generated goes through a process of consensus: policymakers and other non-science actors cannot be expected to sort through a cacophony of technical voices or weed through enormous amounts of data that may contradict. Some policymakers may also see a perceived lack of scientific consensus as a reason for inaction. Divergent views among scientists, or consensus that stems merely from a homogenous group, can also be used to support claims of bias from those who seek to discredit uncomfortable results. Instead, providing action-oriented and consensus-based syntheses of scientific evidence can help policymakers translate data into action (Oliver and Cairney 2019). Consensus needs to be built in a way that focuses on the evidence most relevant for policymaking and makes its implications clear. This could be done through a science-policy bridging body that validated available evidence and built consensus on global food system performance, actions needed, and potential solutions (Nature Editorial 2021). What such a body might look like is being debated—with some controversy around establishing a new body to take on a role that some argue the CFS and its High-Level Panel of Experts currently serve (see Box 14.1) (European Commission 2021).

Box 14.1 An IPCC for Food?

The debate around an "IPCC for Food" (i.e., a new body that would serve as a food systems analogue to what the Intergovernmental Panel on Climate Change is for climate change) highlights some of the challenges in food system monitoring: determining what to monitor (including what types of science and knowledge should be included), who should monitor it (including what "independence" means within this context), and what should become of that data (i.e., how it translates into accountability). Those in favor of an IPCC for Food argue that existing systems have led to a fractured, under-resourced, and undervalued voice for science in the food policy-making process. A more comprehensive approach, in terms of both subjects covered (particularly environmental aspects) and voices represented, is needed, they say, to strengthen the science-policy interface for food and forge more science-based policies, accounting for the diverse aspects of food systems and trade-offs among them (GloPan 2020; von Braun and Kalkuhl 2015). Those opposed generally argue that the HLPE already fills this role, with a clear mandate and an accountability structure linked to the CFS; some also assert that proposals for a new body represent business interests and lack transparency (Clapp et al. 2021). Instead of creating a new structure, they argue, commitment to and investment in the HLPE should be increased (Anderson et al. 2021; Clapp et al. 2021).

The IPCC example offers both an encouraging example and a cautionary tale. Bringing together hundreds of scientists and 195 member states, the IPCC is generally regarded as impartial, inclusive, and able to resist pressures from lobbying groups (Nature Editorial 2021). Though not without criticism, its reports are seen as the comprehensive synthesis of evidence on climate change and carry an authoritative voice that is widely respected and flows directly into climate policy processes. Central to this success was the group's structure and clear, well-defined mandate (Nature Editorial 2021). At the same time, its ever-more-dire reports have thus far failed to galvanize the serious efforts needed to limit human-induced warming to a manageable level (UNEP 2019)—highlighting the challenge of transforming even the most robust of monitoring systems into policy action in the face of entrenched political interests. Whether expanded monitoring powers end up with the HLPE or a new body, that entity will need to navigate this tension.

Holding Decision-Makers to Account: Inclusivity, funding, capacity, and scientific consensus can set a strong foundation for ensuring that monitoring data are correct and holistic, forming a foundation for action. To follow through on that action by ensuring decision-makers and implementers are accountable for progress requires mechanisms focused on actually *holding to account* to meet set objectives and targets. This requires mechanisms that can voice praise and mete out sanctions—and for such mechanisms to work, they must be independent, transparent, and free of conflicts of interest. In the case of private-sector or civil-society action, government can play an important role in holding to account; in the case of governments, this largely falls to civil-society organizations and the voting public, or international mechanisms where they exist (Swinburn et al. 2015). Domestically, civil society play an important role as watchdogs, calling out power asymmetries and conflicts of interest but may not always have sufficient power to influence change. Indeed "holding to account" is often the weakest part of the accountability cycle (Kraak et al. 2014; Swinburn et al. 2015) and is made more complicated by the distributed nature of responsibility when it comes to food systems issues. Internationally, food systems accountability mechanisms should not be created as new efforts outside of agreed-upon goals or commitments, as this could weaken, or even undermine, global processes. Rather, they should be tethered to existing accountability mechanisms, for example, related to the SDGs, the Convention of Parties Climate Agreement, or the Convention on Biological Diversity—all of which have time-bound targets or goals. However, these could be strengthened by establishing a common, agreed-upon framework that incentivizes countries to be ambitious in their actions to address these interlinked "wicked" challenges within food systems, brings donors to a joint table, and spurs epistemic communities to come together around common issues. Such a joint effort will not be easy: global goal-setting can be plagued with overambition and ambiguity, paired with unquantifiable measures of impact (J. Fanzo 2018). Food systems accountability could easily fall victim to these pitfalls, given the vast range of issues upon which food systems touch, the diversity of actors that engage with them, and the limited data to track progress. However, the potential benefits of a joint accountability mechanism for spurring action outweigh these potential risks.

14.7 Conclusion

Food systems are fundamental to human and planetary health. They support nutrition, provide essential ecosystem services, house key natural resources, and provide livelihoods for over a billion people. Yet they are currently far from achieving their full potential. Instead, considerable amounts of environmental degradation and climate change are caused by food systems while they simultaneously contribute to rising diet-related NCD incidence and stubbornly persistent hunger and malnutrition as well as poor-quality livelihoods. Shifting this trajectory requires radical action for food systems transformation—and transforming food systems requires understanding where they are at present on key indicators, as well as how they are changing over time. As this chapter has shown, there is a truly impressive amount of data available in the food systems space, and there are exciting initiatives already underway to improve food systems monitoring to make it more comprehensive, multi-disciplinary, and inclusive.

These efforts at food systems monitoring have laid a strong foundation for transformation. Ensuring that actions are built upon that foundation will require translating data into action-oriented scientific consensus and building capacity for systems thinking to interpret it; fostering inclusive co-creation and collective action for change that balances the influence of vested interests, then making more funding available to enable those changes to happen; and finally—and particularly crucially—ensuring strong, independent, and transparent mechanisms are in place to actually hold decision-makers to account. Gathering, translating, and using data entail one set of challenges, but ensuring accountability for commitments made is another thing altogether—the most difficult. But without doing so, the vision to transform food systems will be just that, an unfulfilled vision.

References

Accountability Pact. 2021. "An International Pact on Monitoring for Accountability for Action on Food Systems." https://www.accountabilitypact.org/

Anderson, M.D. 2008. "Rights-Based Food Systems and the Goals of Food Systems Reform." *Agriculture and Human Values* 25 (4): 593–608. https://doi.org/10.1007/s10460-008-9151-z

Anderson, M. et al. 2021. "Open Letter to Policy Makers: No New Science-Policy Interface for Food Systems." Open Letter. https://drive.google.com/file/d/1axLNs6Ck1FA_T8WjQbmxKAQavT_5l9fI/view.

Babu, S.C., and S. Blom. 2014. "Capacity Development for Resilient Food Systems: Issues, Approaches, and Knowledge Gaps." Paper prepared for the Building Resilience for Food & Nutrition Security 2020 Conference, Paper No. 6, May 17–19, Addis Ababa, Ethiopia. http://ebrary.ifpri.org/cdm/ref/collection/p15738coll2/id/128151

Baker, S. 2021. "Global Financing for Nutrition: 45% ≠ 1%." *LinkedIn Blog*, March 22. https://www.linkedin.com/pulse/global-financing-nutrition-451-shawn-baker-/

Barrett, C.B., T.G. Benton, K.A. Cooper, J. Fanzo, R. Gandhi, M. Herrero, S. James, et al. 2020. "Bundling Innovations to Transform Agri-food Systems." *Nature Sustainability* 3 (12): 974–976. https://doi.org/10.1038/s41893-020-00661-8

Beal, T., A. Herforth, S. Sundberg, S.Y. Hess, and L.M. Neufeld. 2021. "Differences in Modelled Estimates of Global Dietary Intake." *The Lancet* 397 (10286): 1708–1709. https://doi.org/10.1016/S0140-6736(21)00714-5

Béné, C. 2020. "Resilience of Local Food Systems and Links to Food Security—A Review of Some Important Concepts in the Context of COVID-19 and Other Shocks." *Food Security* 12 (4): 805–822. https://doi.org/10.1007/s12571-020-01076-1

Bhutta, Z.A., T. Ahmed, R.E. Black, S. Cousens, K. Dewey, E. Giugliani, B.A. Haider, et al. 2008. "What Works? Interventions for Maternal and Child Undernutrition and Survival." *The Lancet* 371 (9610): 417–440. https://doi.org/10.1016/S0140-6736(07)61693-6

Bhutta, Z.A., J.K. Das, A. Rizvi, M.F. Gaffey, N. Walker, S. Horton, P. Webb, A. Lartey, and R.E. Black. 2013. "Evidence-based Interventions for Improvement of Maternal and Child Nutrition: What Can Be Done and at What Cost?" *The Lancet* 382 (9890): 452–477. https://doi.org/10.1016/S0140-6736(13)60996-4

Blesh, J., L. Hoey, A.D. Jones, H. Friedmann, and I. Perfecto. 2019. "Development Pathways toward 'Zero Hunger.'" *World Development* 118: 1–14. https://doi.org/10.1016/j.worlddev.2019.02.004

Bou-Karroum, L., F. El-Jardali, N. Hemadi, Y. Faraj, U. Ojha, M. Shahrour, A. Darzi, et al. 2017. "Using Media to Impact Health Policy-Making: An Integrative Systematic Review." *Implementation Science* 12 (1): 52. https://doi.org/10.1186/s13012-017-0581-0

Braun, Joachim von, and Matthias Kalkuhl. 2015. "International Science and Policy Interaction for Improved Food and Nutrition Security: Toward an International Panel on Food and Nutrition (IPFN)." ZEF Working Paper Series, No. 142. Bonn: University of Bonn, Center for Development Research (ZEF).

Byerlee, D., and J. Fanzo. 2019. "The SDG of Zero Hunger 75 Years On: Turning Full Circle on Agriculture and Nutrition." *Global Food Security* 21: 52–59. https://doi.org/10.1016/j.gfs.2019.06.002

Canfield, M., M.D. Anderson, and P. McMichael. 2021. "UN Food Systems Summit 2021: Dismantling Democracy and Resetting Corporate Control of Food Systems." *Frontiers in Sustainable Food Systems* 5: 661552. https://doi.org/10.3389/fsufs.2021.661552

Chadha, S. 2021. "Global Hunger Index: India's Position and Why Govt Is So Upset." *Times of India*, October 18. https://timesofindia.indiatimes.com/business/india-business/global-hunger-index-indias-position-and-why-govt-is-so-upset/articleshow/87101322.cms

Chambers, J.M., C. Wyborn, M.E. Ryan, R.S. Reid, M. Riechers, A. Serban, N.J. Bennett, et al. 2021. "Six Modes of Co-production for Sustainability." *Nature Sustainability* 4: 983–996. https://doi.org/10.1038/s41893-021-00755-x

Chichaibelu, B.B., M. Bekchanov, J. von Braun, and M. Torero. 2021. "The Global Cost of Reaching a World Without Hunger: Investment Costs and Policy Action Opportunities." *Food Policy* 104: 102151. https://doi.org/10.1016/j.foodpol.2021.102151

Christiaensen, L., L. Demery, and J. Kuhl. 2011. "The (Evolving) Role of Agriculture in Poverty Reduction—An Empirical Perspective." *Journal of Development Economics* 96 (2): 239–254. https://doi.org/10.1016/j.jdeveco.2010.10.006

Christiaensen, L., Z. Rutledge, and J.E. Taylor. 2021. "Viewpoint: The Future of Work in Agri-food." *Food Policy* 99: 101963. https://doi.org/10.1016/j.foodpol.2020.101963

Cornell University, IFPRI (International Food Policy Research Institute), and IISD (International Institute for Sustainable Development). 2020. *Ceres2030: Sustainable Solutions to End Hunger. Summary Report.* Ithica, NY: Cornell University. https://ceres2030.org/wp-content/uploads/2021/03/ceres2030_en-summary-report.pdf

Covic, N., A. Dobermann, J. Fanzo, S. Henson, M. Herrero, P. Pingali, and S. Staal. 2021. "All Hat and No Cattle: Accountability Following the UN Food Systems Summit." *Global Food Security* 30: 100569. https://doi.org/10.1016/j.gfs.2021.100569

Clapp, Jenifer E., M Anderson, M Rahmanian, and S Monsalve Suárez. 2021. "An 'IPCC for Food?' How the UN Food Systems Summit Is Being Used to Advance a Problematic New Science-Policy Agenda." Briefing Note 1 on the Governance of Food Systems. International Panel of Experts on Sustainable Food Systems.

Delmastro, M., and F. Zollo. 2021. "Viewpoint: Social Monitoring for Food Policy and Research: Directions and Implications." *Food Policy* 105: 102147. https://doi.org/10.1016/j.foodpol.2021.102147

Development Initiatives. 2020. *2020 Global Nutrition Report: Action on Equity to End Malnutrition*. Bristol, UK: Development Initiatives.

Development Initiatives. 2021. *Global Nutrition Report 2021*. Bristol, UK: Development Initiative. https://globalnutritionreport.org/

Elzen, B., W. de Haas, S. Wigboldus, B. Bos, and M. Dijkshoorn-Dekker. 2020. *Transition Pathways-Contours of an Analytical Framework*. Report WPR-839. Wageningen, the Netherlands: Wageningen University & Research.

European Commission. 2021. *Everyone at the Table: Co-creating Knowledge for Food Systems Transformation*. Brussels: European Commission. https://www.au-plovdiv.bg/docs/Novini/2021/m.08/EK-FOOD-SYSTEM-EXPERT-GROUP-2021-REPORT.pdf

Evans, D. 2015. "Do Policy Briefs Change Beliefs?" *World Bank Blogs*, February 9. https://blogs.worldbank.org/impactevaluations/do-policy-briefs-change-beliefs

Evenson, R.E., and D. Gollin. 2003. "Assessing the Impact of the Green Revolution to 2000." *Science* 300 (5620): 758–762. https://doi.org/10.1126/science.1078710

Fanzo, J. 2018. "Does Global Goal Setting Matter for Nutrition and Health?" *AMA Journal of Ethics* 20 (10): e979–e986. https://doi.org/10.1001/amajethics.2018.979

Fanzo, J., L. Haddad, R. McLaren, Q. Marshall, C. Davis, A. Herforth, A. Jones, et al. 2020. "The Food Systems Dashboard Is a New Tool to Inform Better Food Policy." *Nature Food* 1 (5): 243–246. https://doi.org/10.1038/s43016-020-0077-y

Fanzo, J., L. Haddad, K.R. Schneider, C. Béné, N.M. Covic, A. Guarin, A.W. Herforth, et al. 2021. "Viewpoint: Rigorous Monitoring is Necessary to Guide Food System Transformation in the Countdown to the 2030 Global Goals." *Food Policy* 104: 102163. https://doi.org/10.1016/j.foodpol.2021.102163

Fanzo, J.C., M.M. Graziose, K. Kraemer, S. Gillespie, J.L. Johnston, S. de Pee, E. Monterrosa, et al. 2015. "Educating and Training a Workforce for Nutrition in a Post-2015 World." *Advances in Nutrition* 6 (6): 639–647. https://doi.org/10.3945/an.115.010041

FAO. 1999. *The State of Food Insecurity in the World*. Rome: FAO.

FAO. 2009. *The State of Food and Agriculture 2009: Livestock in the Balance*. Rome: FAO.

FAO. 2013. *The State of Food and Agriculture: Food Systems for Better Nutrition*. Rome: FAO. www.fao.org/docrep/018/i3300e/i3300e.pdf

FAO. 2017. *Food Systems for Healthy Diets*. Policy Guidance Note No. 12. Rome: FAO.

FAO. 2021. *State of Food and Agriculture 2020: Overcoming Water Challenges in Agriculture*. Rome: FAO. https://www.fao.org/documents/card/en/c/cb1447en

FAO (Food and Agriculture Organization of the United Nations). 1947. *The State of Food and Agriculture: 1947*. Rome: FAO.

FAO and UNEP (United Nations Environment Programme). 2020. *The State of the World's Forests 2020: Forests, Biodiversity and People*. Rome: FAO and UNEP.

FAO, IFAD (International Fund for Agricultural Development), UNICEF (United Nations Children's Fund), WFP (United Nations World Food Programme) and WHO (World Health Organization). 2018. *The State of Food Security and Nutrition in the World 2018: Building Climate Resilience for Food Security and Nutrition*. Rome: FAO, IFAD, UNICEF, WFP, and WHO. https://doi.org/10.4060/ca9692en

FAO, IFAD, UNICEF, WFP and WHO. 2021. *The State of Food Security and Nutrition in the World 2021*. Rome" FAO, IFAD, UNICEF, WFP, and WHO. https://doi.org/10.4060/ca9692en

FAO, IFAD, UNICEF, WFP, and WHO. 2020. *The State of Food Security and Nutrition in the World 2020*. Rome: FAO, IFAD, UNICEF, WFP and WHO. https://doi.org/10.4060/ca9692en

Fleischer, N.L., H.M. Tiesman, J. Sumitani, T. Mize, K.K. Amarnath, A.R. Bayakly, and M.W. Murphy. 2013. "Public Health Impact of Heat-Related Illness among Migrant Farmworkers." *American Journal of Preventive Medicine* 44 (3): 199–206. https://doi.org/10.1016/j.amepre.2012.10.020

GAIN (Global Alliance for Improved Nutrition) and Johns Hopkins University. 2020. *The Food Systems Dashboard*. Global Alliance for Improved Nutrition (GAIN) and Johns Hopkins University. https://doi.org/10.36072/db

GBD 2017 Diet Collaborators. 2019. "Health Effects of Dietary Risks in 195 Countries–2017: A Systematic Analysis for the Global Burden of Disease Study 2017." *The Lancet* 393 (10184): 1958–1972. https://doi.org/10.1016/S0140-6736(19)30041-8

Gerten, D., V. Heck, J. Jägermeyr, B.L. Bodirsky, I. Fetzer, M. Jalava, M. Kummu, W. Lucht, J. Rockström, S. Schaphoff, and H.J. Schellnhuber. 2020. "Feeding Ten Billion People Is Possible within Four Terrestrial Planetary Boundaries." *Nature Sustainability* 3 (3): 200–208. https://doi.org/10.1038/s41893-019-0465-1

Gillespie, S., and M. van den Bold. 2017. "Stories of Change in Nutrition: An Overview." *Global Food Security* 13: 1–11. https://doi.org/10.1016/j.gfs.2017.02.004

GloPAN (Global Panel on Agriculture and Food Systems for Nutrition). 2016. *The Cost of Malnutrition. Why Policy Action Is Urgent*. Technical Brief No. 3. London: GloPAN.

GloPan. 2020. "Future Food Systems: For People, Our Planet, and Prosperity." London: Global Panel on Agriculture and Food Systems for Nutrition (GloPan).

GNR (Global Nutrition Report). 2021. "The Nutrition Accountability Framework." https://globalnutritionreport.org/resources/nutrition-accountability-framework/

Golden, C.D., J.A. Gephart, J.G. Eurich, D.J. McCauley, M.K. Sharp, N.L. Andrew, and K.L. Seto. 2021. "Social-Ecological Traps Link Food Systems to Nutritional Outcomes." *Global Food Security* 30: 100561. https://doi.org/10.1016/j.gfs.2021.100561

Griggs, D. 2015. "Sustainability Science: Exploiting the Synergies. *Nature* 519 (7542): 156. https://doi.org/10.1038/519156a

Havelaar, A.H., M.D. Kirk, P.R. Torgerson, H.J. Gibb, T. Hald, R.J. Lake, N. Praet, et al. on behalf of World Health Organization Foodborne Disease Burden Epidemiology Reference Group. 2015. "World Health Organization Global Estimates and Regional Comparisons of the Burden of Foodborne Disease in 2010." *PLOS Medicine* 12 (12): e1001923. https://doi.org/10.1371/journal.pmed.1001923

Herrero, M., P.K. Thornton, P. Gerber, and R.S. Reid. 2009. "Livestock, Livelihoods and the Environment: Understanding the Trade-Offs." *Current Opinion in Environmental Sustainability* 1 (2): 111–120. https://doi.org/10.1016/j.cosust.2009.10.003

HLPE (High Level Panel of Experts on Food Security and Nutrition). 2017. *Nutrition and Food Systems*. Rome: Committee on World Food Security.

Howarth, C., and J. Painter. 2016. "Exploring the Science–Policy Interface on Climate Change: The Role of the IPCC in Informing Local Decision-Making in the UK." *Palgrave Communications* 2 (1): 16058. https://doi.org/10.1057/palcomms.2016.58

IFPRI (International Food Policy Research Institute). 2014. *POSHAN (Partnerships and Opportunities to Strengthen and Harmonize Actions for Nutrition in India):*

Overview. Washington, DC: IFPRI. https://poshan.ifpri.info/files/2014/04/BR001-POSHAN-Overview_102214.pdf

IHME (Institute for Health Metrics and Evaluation). 2021. "GBD Compare." https://vizhub.healthdata.org/gbd-compare/

Ingram, J. 2011. "A Food Systems Approach to Researching Food Security and Its Interactions with Global Environmental Change." *Food Security* 3 (4): 417–431. https://doi.org/10.1007/s12571-011-0149-9

Keats, E.C., J.K. Das, R.A. Salam, Z.S. Lassi, A. Imdad, R.E. Black, and Z.A. Bhutta. 2021. "Effective Interventions to Address Maternal and Child Malnutrition: An Update of the Evidence." *The Lancet Child & Adolescent Health* 5 (5): 376–384. https://doi.org/10.1016/S2352-4642(20)30274-1

Kraak, V.I., B. Swinburn, M. Lawrence, and P. Harrison. 2014. "An Accountability Framework to Promote Healthy Food Environments." *Public Health Nutrition* 17 (11): 2467–2483. https://doi.org/10.1017/S1368980014000093

Kummu, M., H. de Moel, M. Porkka, S. Siebert, O. Varis, and P.J. Ward. 2012. "Lost Food, Wasted Resources: Global Food Supply Chain Losses and Their Impacts on Freshwater, Cropland, and Fertiliser Use." *Science of The Total Environment* 438: 477–489. https://doi.org/10.1016/j.scitotenv.2012.08.092

Lade, S.J., W. Steffen, W. de Vries, S.R. Carpenter, J.F. Donges, D. Gerten, H. Hoff, T. Newbold, K. Richardson, and J. Rockström. 2020. "Human Impacts on Planetary Boundaries Amplified by Earth System Interactions." *Nature Sustainability* 3 (2): 119–128. https://doi.org/10.1038/s41893-019-0454-4

Lennox, G.D., T.A. Gardner, J.R. Thomson, J. Ferreira, E. Berenguer, A.C. Lees, R. Mac Nally, et al. 2018. "Second Rate or a Second Chance? Assessing Biomass and Biodiversity Recovery in Regenerating Amazonian Forests." *Global Change Biology* 24 (12): 5680–5694. https://doi.org/10.1111/gcb.14443

Loboguerrero, A., B. Campbell, P. Cooper, J. Hansen, T. Rosenstock, and E. Wollenberg. 2019. "Food and Earth Systems: Priorities for Climate Change Adaptation and Mitigation for Agriculture and Food Systems." *Sustainability* 11 (5): 1372. https://doi.org/10.3390/su11051372

Machen, R.C., M.T. Jones, G.P. Varghese, and E.L. Stark. 2021. *Investigation Findings and Report to the Board of Executive Directors*. Report to the World Bank. Washington, DC: WilmerHale. https://thedocs.worldbank.org/en/doc/84a922cc9273b7b120d49ad3b9e9d3f9-0090012021/original/DB-Investigation-Findings-and-Report-to-the-Board-of-Executive-Directors-September-15-2021.pdf

Manorat, R., L. Becker, and A. Flory. 2019. "Global Data Visualization Tools to Empower Decision-Making in Nutrition." *Sight and Life Magazine* 33: 108–114.

Marshall, Q., A.L. Bellows, R. McLaren, A.D. Jones, and J. Fanzo. 2021. "You Say You Want a Data Revolution? Taking on Food Systems Accountability." *Agriculture* 11 (5): 422. https://doi.org/10.3390/agriculture11050422

Mayne, R., D. Green, I. Guijt, M. Walsh, R. English, and P. Cairney. 2018. "Using Evidence to Influence Policy: Oxfam's Experience." *Palgrave Communications* 4 (1): 122. https://doi.org/10.1057/s41599-018-0176-7

Nature Editorial. 2021. "Does the Fight against Hunger Need Its Own IPCC?" *Nature* 595 (7867): 332. https://doi.org/10.1038/d41586-021-01904-0

Nisbett, N., S. Friel, R. Aryeetey, F. da Silva Gomes, J. Harris, K. Backholer, P. Baker, V. Blue Bird Jernigan, and S. Phulkerd. 202). "Equity and Expertise in the UN Food Systems Summit." *BMJ Global Health* 6 (7): e006569. https://doi.org/10.1136/bmjgh-2021-006569

Oliver, K., and P. Cairney. 2019. "The Dos and Don'ts of Influencing Policy: A Systematic Review of Advice to Academics." *Palgrave Communications* 5 (1): 21. https://doi.org/10.1057/s41599-019-0232-y

Pingali, P.L. 2012. "Green Revolution: Impacts, Limits, and the Path Ahead." *Proceedings of the National Academy of Sciences* 109 (31): 12302. https://doi.org/10.1073/pnas.0912953109

Resnick, D. 2017. "Governance: Informal Food Markets in Africa's Cities." In *Global Food Policy Report 2017*, 50–57. Washington, DC: International Food Policy Research Institute. https://doi.org/10.2499/9780896292529_06

Rockström, J., O. Edenhofer, J. Gaertner, and F. DeClerck. 2020. "Planet-Proofing the Global Food System." *Nature Food* 1 (1): 3–5. https://doi.org/10.1038/s43016-019-0010-4

Rockström, J., W. Steffen, K. Noone, Å. Persson, F.S. Chapin, E.F. Lambin, T.M. Lenton, et al. 2009. "A Safe Operating Space for Humanity." *Nature* 461 (7263): 472–475. https://doi.org/10.1038/461472a

Rohr, J.R., C.B. Barrett, D.J. Civitello, M.E. Craft, B. Delius, G.A. DeLeo, P.J. Hudson, et al. 2019. "Emerging Human Infectious Diseases and the Links to Global Food Production." *Nature Sustainability* 2 (6): 445–456. https://doi.org/10.1038/s41893-019-0293-3

Sahan, E. 2016. *The Journey to Sustainable Food: A Three-Year Update on the Behind the Brands Campaign*. Oxford, UK: Oxfam. https://doi.org/10.21201/2016.605193

Swinburn, B., V. Kraak, H. Rutter, S. Vandevijvere, T. Lobstein, G. Sacks, F. Gomes, T. Marsh, and R. Magnusson. 2015. "Strengthening of Accountability Systems to Create Healthy Food Environments and Reduce Global Obesity." *The Lancet* 385 (9986): 2534–2545. https://doi.org/10.1016/S0140-6736(14)61747-5

UNEP. 2019. "Emissions Gap Report 2019: Executive Summary." Nairobi: United Nations Environment Programme (UNEP).

UNEP and ILRI (International Livestock Research Institute). 2020. *Preventing the Next Pandemic—Zoonotic Diseases and How to Break the Chain of Transmission*. Nairobi: UNEP. https://wedocs.unep.org/bitstream/handle/20.500.11822/32316/ZP.pdf

UNICEF. 1990. *Strategy for Improved Nutrition of Children and Women in Developing Countries*. New York: UNICEF.

Webb, P., T.G. Benton, J. Beddington, D. Flynn, N.M. Kelly, and S.M. Thomas. 2020. "The Urgency of Food System Transformation is Now Irrefutable." *Nature Food* 1 (10): 584–585. https://doi.org/10.1038/s43016-020-00161-0

WHO. 2017. *Guidelines on Use of Medically Important Antimicrobials in Food-Producing Animals*. Geneva: WHO. https://apps.who.int/iris/bitstream/handle/10665/258970/9789241550130-eng.pdf

15

Conclusions

Danielle Resnick and Johan Swinnen

While the need for policy reforms to generate more equitable, healthier, and sustainable food systems increasingly is acknowledged by policymakers and the public, the political economy dynamics to achieve this will remain sizeable in the years to come. This is particularly true given the range of polarizing factors affecting decisions over the food system at domestic and international levels—from debates over values and (mis)information, to concerns over food self-sufficiency, corporate influence, and human rights. By prioritizing political economy issues in the food and agricultural policy arena, this volume has aimed to delineate the range of incentive structures, mobilizational forces, policy designs, and implementation concerns that either propel or derail reforms. This chapter summarizes key messages from the volume, highlighting promising options to achieve food system transformation as well as areas that are likely to be more intractable.

15.1 Reconciling Trade-Offs Generated by Different Incentive Structures

A core thread throughout the volume is that transforming food systems often involves trade-offs across development objectives, among policy instruments, and over time, thereby resulting in different distributional effects across interest groups. For instance, Chapters 3 and 4 discussed policy options for repurposing agricultural support, including more investments in agricultural research and development, rural infrastructure, "green conditionality" direct payments to farmers for lowered input use, and ecosystem services. Such repurposing can have large gains for environmental sustainability and diets, and several countries have pursued reforms, precipitated by international commitments and concerns about reigning in financial expenditures. At the same time, such reforms may not only disproportionately affect some groups—including very well-organized ones—more than others but also involves weighing the benefits of current policy familiarity, even if socially sub-optimal, against future policy uncertainty and possible unintended consequences. Vehement resistance by Indian farmers to proposed market reforms in 2020 or the impacts of US biofuels mandates on increased

Danielle Resnick and Johan Swinnen, *Conclusions*. In: *The Political Economy of Food System Transformation*.
Edited by: Danielle Resnick and Johan Swinnen, Oxford University Press. © Danielle Resnick and Johan Swinnen (2023).
DOI: 10.1093/oso/9780198882121.003.0015

GHG emissions due to land expansion represent examples of these distributional and temporal trade-offs.

Deconinck (Chapter 2) offers a useful reminder that trade-offs may not be easily reconcilable when they involve value polarization, and drawing on Goldgeier and Tetlock (2008), points to the existence of "routine," "taboo," and "tragic trade-offs." While traditional policy instruments may be able to address routine and taboo trade-offs, which involve conflicts over two interests or between interests and values, respectively, tragic trade-offs pit two values against each other. In such cases, intransigence among groups is more likely because any concession infringes upon a group's identity and worldview. This tendency can be further exacerbated depending on different groups' access to, and preference for, certain types of information and media outlets. As noted in Chapter 1, a proclivity to accept information that resonates with extant beliefs, and dismiss that which does not, is a major contributor to value polarization.

In Chapter 6, Gómez offers a useful example of routine trade-offs that revolve around costs, benefits, and public salience. He shows how two types of interests—the profit considerations of beverage companies and the nutrition priorities of civil society groups—clashed in the cases of Mexico, India, and South Africa. Governments in all three countries ultimately chose to side with nutrition advocates by adopting sugar-sweetened beverage (SSB) taxes, which complemented their own interest to increase fiscal revenue. The cases offer examples of how health goals can be achieved, despite corporate resistance, through alignment with decisionmakers' own preferences. This likely explains why the policy instrument has become more accepted over time (Popkin and Ng 2021), with 54 countries now having a SSB tax and 41 of those countries adopting such a measure since 2014.[1] The chapter also noted that along with considerations of costs and benefits of policies to different groups, decisionmakers need to be cognizant of the salience of different policy instruments to the public. Indeed, regulatory approaches and labeling could also result in similar goals—reducing consumption of unhealthy foods—but their technical nature and tendency to be negotiated behind closed doors reduces their visibility, thereby affecting the level of engagement and mobilization by the public.

Paarlberg's chapter (Chapter 10) on the role of science in agriculture offers several examples of taboo trade-offs. For instance, he discusses that while organic farming methods involve higher land and labor costs that increase consumer prices, they are not necessarily scientifically proven to be better for human health. Nonetheless, in his view, organic foods appeal to consumers who prioritize "naturalness" among other values. Fesenfeld and Sun's analysis (Chapter 11) tackles

---

[1] See   https://www.obesityevidencehub.org.au/collections/prevention/countries-that-have-implemented-taxes-on-sugar-sweetened-beverages-ssbs#:~:text=Over%2050%20countries%20have %20implemented,SSBs%20has%20been%20extensively%20studied, accessed November 14, 2022.

tragic trade-offs related to meat consumption, which can be viewed by some as morally irresponsible for the planet and seen by others as their personal prerogative. Like Gómez, they believe salience affects the degree of public support for different policy options, but they find that policy framing can shift an intervention to be more visible to the public if it resonates with their values; in other words, framing a levy on meat consumption as necessary for protecting "animal welfare" rather than simply labeling it as a "meat tax" can give such an intervention broader appeal. Fesenfeld and Sun, as well as Deconinck, further highlight how values over the food system vary cross-nationally. Similarly, Andrews, Candel, de Mûelenaere, and Scheelbeck (Chapter 13) note that even understandings of concepts like "sustainability" can be interpreted differently by disparate constituencies within the same region.

As noted in the introduction, institutions often mediate interests and ideas. Despite declining faith in multilateralism and a growing range of new global actors (Chapter 1), multilateral institutions remain one of the few mechanisms for driving internationally concerted reforms that will have the largest positive impacts on sustainability. The Paris Climate Agreement helped drive some policy reforms in diverse contexts, including China and the EU (Chapter 3). Yet, Anderson and Strutt (Chapter 4) are more skeptical about the role of the WTO in addressing agricultural trade issues given that they are increasingly intertwined with a range of environmental and biodiversity concerns. The EU has a complex institutional structure with several areas of exclusive competencies relative to food system transformation and several—such as on climate, environment, food safety and public health—that are shared between the Union and national governments (Chapter 13). Federal structures at the national level likewise can lead to conflicts among states over a reform agenda, as the example of India's failed market procurement reforms in 2020-2021 illustrated (Chapter 3).

Several of the chapters further elucidate how the incentives space influences the perceived degree of power and agency that stakeholders can exert. Indeed, corporate power in certain agricultural and food industries, and its effects on policy coalitions, were discussed broadly by Swinnen and Resnick (Chapter 5) as well as specifically in Ghana by Mockshell and Ritter (Chapter 6). Harris (Chapter 8) emphasizes in her chapter on Zambia how the combined economic power of donors and the epistemic power of the international development community, which increasingly promotes the idea of dietary diversity over food self-sufficiency, is re-shaping national food policies. This leads to important questions about how the principles of the Paris Declaration on Aid Effectiveness, which stress country ownership (OECD 2005), are upheld in national food and agricultural strategies and whether commitments to food system transformation in those documents, and in the national food system pathways anticipated from the UNFSS, genuinely reflect domestic priorities or external pressures.

Collectively, the chapters also provide a useful reminder that it is problematic to ascribe a normative interpretation to stakeholders' interests and ideas. Civil society and transnational advocacy networks may, for instance, be focused on improving social welfare in some settings (Chapter 6) but undermine government policy ownership in others (Chapter 8), or interpret scientific information through a biased lens in still others (Chapter 10). Actors in the agriculture and food industry, both large corporations and small family farms, may sometimes resist reforms that rescind their economic protections (Chapter 3) or undermine their profits (Chapters 6 and 7). However, they can also be a major generator of innovation (Chapters 9 and 10) and food safety, quality, and labor standards (Chapter 5). Consumers in some parts of the world are still perceived as motivated mostly by affordability, thereby preferring cheaper ultra-processed foods (see Chapter 7); in others, they express a willingness to try new options, such as alternative proteins (Chapter 11) and, especially among younger generations, show a greater awareness of sustainable eating (Chapter 13). And governments too are not monolithic in their interests and ideas; different ministries, subnational authorities, and political parties hold diverse viewpoints about the food system (e.g., Chapters 8, 10, 11, 12, 13). Avoiding simplistic characterizations of the motivations of interest groups can mitigate further polarization around needed food system reforms.

15.2 Mixed Modes of Mobilization

Many of the book's chapters addressed examples of mobilization, with an emphasis on coalitions. Such coalitions have become increasingly expansive in food systems as agricultural value chains have become more complex and, as noted in Chapter 1, food and agricultural policy increasingly touches on non-traditional issues. Sometimes coalitions result from alignments among farmers with processors, such as the EU sugar quotas discussed by Swinnen and Resnick in Chapter 5. At other points, these coalitions rely on constituencies of domestic and international actors who share similar interests and values, such as those who formed to support SSB taxes (Chapter 6). In still others, coalitions may unite around similar policy instruments but for different reasons, such as examples of farmers and environmentalists who supported biofuels or ecosystem payments (Chapters 3 and 4). When policies favored by coalitions begin to have unintended consequences, however, a coalition's strength is tested; those with different objectives—or different "core beliefs" in the language of Sabatier's advocacy coalition framework (1988)—may achieve a short-term policy gain but fail to transform into a broader movement due to internal conflicts within the coalition.

Transnational coalitions supporting SSBs, biotechnology, child nutrition, and environmental sustainability can be a source of strength by offering domestic allies with more resources and visibility for their advocacy efforts

(Chapters 5, 6, 8, 9, 10). At the same time, the credibility of such transnational advocacy can be undermined if it brands such coalitions as elitist, detached, and imposing outsider preferences that fail to resonate with local populations. As noted by Nordhagen and Fanzo (Chapter 14), these observations are equally true for data-driven initiatives led by epistemic communities of development professionals. Even how one measures progress toward food system transformation requires careful attention to whether the indicators of progress are perceived as credible by targeted stakeholders.

The marshaling of information to forge particular policy narratives is a common tactic by coalitions that repeatedly appears in the volume. In some cases, information is purposely distorted by using provocative marketing that downplays more nuanced evidence, such as the "Dirty Dozen" report noted in Chapter 10. In many cases, information is filtered to update preferences in a way that reinforces extant biases; as highlighted by Barrett (Chapter 9), evidence about the benefits of biotechnology is differentially perceived by national regulators depending on how pronounced the precautionary principle has become in a particular country. At other times, information can be framed to help with consumer or policy acceptance. By framing input subsidies for maize as ineffective for addressing childhood stunting, rather than just being economically wasteful, international donors and domestic nutrition advocates in Zambia countered the government narrative around food self-sufficiency (Chapter 8). Different types of frames around animal welfare and climate change also showed promise for consumer willingness to accept taxes on meat in Germany and the US (Chapter 11). Probing such narratives, such as done by Mockshell and Ritter, and where these narratives originate is a fruitful pathway for considering opportunities for consensus and negotiation. This option is reinforced by Deconinck (Chapter 2) who references deliberative forums in Ireland focused on climate mitigation policy and the *Convention Citoyenne pour le Climat* in France examining options to reduce GHGs.

15.3 Addressing Divergent Coalition Preferences through Strategic Policy Design

Recognizing the diversity of food system coalitions and their disparate interests and power allows for a more considered approach to designing politically feasible reforms. Since policies are rarely static and unidimensional, there are several strategies for addressing trade-offs and responding to interest group mobilization. Barrett (Chapter 9) promotes the idea of policy bundling, which he argues is not only essential for the technical changes needed for transformation but also to overcome political economy bottlenecks. Specifically, bundling can amass the policy concerns of multiple groups simultaneously, reducing the efforts of any one group to stymie reforms. Focusing on consumer food choices, Fesenfeld and

Sun (Chapter 11) suggest policy packaging that includes combinations of taxa-tion, regulation, subsidies, and consumer awareness efforts can generate support for decreased meat consumption.

Policy sequencing is so critical because if done poorly, it can erode confidence in governments' future reform efforts, and fuel misinformation. This is particularly true the greater the perceived uncertainty about the reform's health or economic consequences. However, if done well, governments can create positive policy tip-ping points (Chapter 11) whereby consumer confidence increases due to positive exposure to a technology or to a reform. Such sequencing appears several times in the case studies reviewed in the volume, especially with respect to GMOs (Chapter 10) where anti-GMO groups were better organized than the potential beneficia-ries of reform and therefore had a first-mover advantage in shaping the discourse around the health and environmental risks of the technology.

While the volume's chapters indicate many advantages of bundling, packaging, and sequencing, they do generate path dependencies. On the one hand, this miti-gates against policy volatility. On the other hand, it can make future reforms more difficult due to the range of constituents whose concurrence is needed for change. For instance, if bundling required a complex negotiation to win over an array of different veto players, it may have entailed building coalitions of strange bedfel-lows who may support similar policies for different reasons. Policy refinements over time therefore will require consistently getting the same group of stakehold-ers on board, complete with their divergent objectives. An example is the alliance between farmers and nutrition advocates who both need to be onboard for reforms to the US Farm Bill, which encompasses both farmer subsidies and SNAP benefits (Chapter 5).

15.4 Policy Adaptation and Implementation

As noted in Chapter 1, path dependencies can be disrupted by critical junctures. In Mexico, India, and South Africa, Gomez (Chapter 6) describes how fiscal crises increased the attractiveness of SSB taxes, which previously had received minimal traction with government in those countries. In the EU, the growing inroads of green parties in the European Parliament created a window of opportunity for the Farm to Fork strategy but an unexpected crisis—the Ukraine war—has been among several factors that has delayed implementation (Chapter 13). Paarlberg (Chapter 10) further notes that the window of opportunity to introduce GM soy-bean crops to Europe was partially shut by a food safety crisis, namely the mad cow disease scare in 1996.

Policy diffusion and cascades can also upend traditional policy pathways, but their efficacy sometimes can be disrupted by a mismatch between policy instruments and administrative capacities (Wegrich 2021). As noted in Chapter

1, policy diffusion refers to the uptake of an innovation from one country or context to a another (Weyland 2005). Yet, while external examples encourage domestic policymakers of possible success, diffusion can sometimes just result in isomorphic mimicry—reforms that outwardly look the same but operate fundamentally differently in the imported context (Andrews et al. 2013). This is observed by Haysom and Battersby (Chapter 12) with regards to the importation of food policy councils into urban Africa, which they see as sometimes incongruent with local realities and exacerbating some of the weaknesses of multi-stakeholderism that were noted in Chapter 1. Indeed, while devolution reforms in the region have given local governments more authority on food issues, many of these powers are shared with national actors. This not only creates significant challenges for accountability but also can be problematic given that local governments lack sufficient fiscal resources to meet their mandates. They further observe that while local governments remain essential for managing urban food markets, collecting license fees, and regulating informal food traders, such roles are largely about managing compliance with extant laws rather than facilitating transformation.

A similar challenge of multi-scalar and cross-sectoral implementation is particularly clear in the case of the EU's Green Deal and Farm to Fork (F2F) strategy (Chapter 13), which tries to address several goals simultaneously: ensure the food chain avoids a negative environmental impact, promote food security and nutrition, preserve food affordability, and provide fair returns to those working in the supply chain. The F2F is equivalent to a cascade initiative that emerges from a supranational body and expected to be implemented nationally. Yet, it does not fully align with the national goals and realities of all its members states. Moreover, the F2F has no legal backing; while the EU wanted states to commit to the targets set out in the F2F and proposed to make approval of national Common Agricultural Policy (CAP) plans conditional on this, the member states refused to do so, noting that the lack of legal backing meant they should not be obliged to so.

The UNFSS and its push for national food system pathways symbolizes another cascade effort. Given the multi-faceted nature of food systems policy, implementation, and enforceability of food system commitments at the national and subnational levels will be challenging. Nordhagen and Fanzo discuss the potential of the Global Food Systems Monitoring Countdown as a way to hold those in power to account for transformation by simultaneously tracking indicators in five domains: nutrition and health, environment, livelihoods, governance, and resilience. This approach also draws on policy diffusion, drawing on several other initiatives that employ data tracking to encourage better performance among governments and ideally provides policy actors and civil society a holistic view of where their countries excel and where they are lagging (Kelley 2017). Yet, they further stress that such indicators are inconsequential on their own without other interventions, such as capacity building for systems thinking that goes beyond the narrow silo disciplinary training that both public sector officials and development practitioners traditionally receive.

Beyond these issues, there are the traditional challenges of public sector coordination that influence implementation. Regulatory policies, for instance, may need to go through approvals from multiple agencies, creating several opportunities for opponents to derail progress. In the case of Bt brinjal adoption in Bangladesh (Chapter 9), there was a confluence of interests among the ministries of agriculture, finance, and environment over productivity, revenue generation, and product labeling, respectively, which made bundling feasible. By contrast, there were more sources of opposition among regulatory actors in India, where approval for Bt brinjal failed. A similar disconnect is observed by Mockshell and Ritter (Chapter 7) who find that fragmented coordination among institutions impedes effective regulatory action on the urban food environment in Ghana; standards may be established by the Food and Drugs Authority but then not enforced or prioritized by the local government administration, known as the Metropolitan, Municipal, and District Assemblies. These and other examples in the volume highlight that identifying incentives structures within public sector bureaucracies for overcoming coordination challenges is as central to the political economy of food system reform as reconciling differential societal interest group preferences. Moreover, they underscore that implementing food system reforms requires a more sophisticated understanding of administrative capacity gaps, with focused attention to what Lodge and Wegrich (2014) call the four problem-solving capacities of the modern state: delivery, regulation, coordination, and analytics.

15.5 Conclusions, Limitations, and Ways Forward

As this current volume illustrates, identifying the large array of political economy issues that permeate the food system is not possible using only one disciplinary lens or methodological tool. Instead, the rich set of issues uncovered and addressed by this volume's authors relied on the traditional fields of economics, political science, public policy, and history while also drawing on critical concepts from psychology, philosophy, and sociology. Moreover, despite the geographical breadth of the authors' expertise, some themes and dilemmas frequently re-emerged.

The volume also touched on, but did not fully explore, several topics that are worthy of additional consideration to expand cumulative knowledge on the political economy of food system transformation. One is that while there are several policies that, through diffusion across multiple countries, have proved to be useful in addressing a particular concern about the food system, the ideal constellation of policies to actually transform the entire food system are relatively unknown and, of course, likely to be context dependent. In other words, the volume has addressed certain issues discretely—such as repurposing subsidies, bundling on-farm innovations, and reducing over-consumption of sugar and meat—but the policy options to simultaneously advance progress in all these areas and more remains unidentified. This impedes political economy analysis to some extent because without knowing what the optimal food system transformation policy package consists of, it is impossible to fully uncover the true winners and losers from reforms.

A second area relates to the tactics of negotiation between interest groups or coalitions with political actors and how those have, and will continue to, change with the rise of new political configurations. As noted in the introduction, there has been a growth in both populist (right- and left-wing) and green parties in certain parts of the world; while there is sometimes surprising alignment in these party movements regarding some parts of the food system (e.g., Buzogány and Mohamad-Klotzbach 2021), polarization prevails elsewhere. These shifts, alluded to in parts of Chapters 10 and 13 with respect to environmental sustainability, should be kept in mind when considering how different types of evidence, policy objectives, and coalitions may rise and fall in the food systems space in the years to come due to shifting partisan attachments.

A third topic is the importance of citizen trust in their governments, which is paramount for reforms that involve intertemporal trade-offs and uncertainty (Kyle 2018). Barrett (Chapter 9) discusses the role of trust, highlighting the utility of co-creation processes to improve trust and pointing to China's Science and Technology Backyards program. Sometimes the process of arriving at a policy decision often matters as much as the final adopted policy instrument when building trust. Matthews et al. (Chapter 13) note that the lack of in-depth consultations with member states, stakeholders, or experts on the targets underlying the EU's Farm to Fork strategy led to high levels of dissatisfaction with the strategy. Focusing on process, Nordhagen and Fanzo (Chapter 14) mention the need for co-creation and structured bottom-up processes to co-produce trusted research on food systems. In general, greater learning is needed about scalable efforts to foster public trust in comprehensive reform efforts, drawing on but expanding beyond some of the examples offered by Deconinck (Chapter 2).

A fourth area relates to how to generate politically influential constituencies for needed reforms. Among other areas, this challenge is particularly relevant to the issue of repurposing agricultural subsidies for research and development, which is mentioned several times in the volume and is frequently emphasized in the broader literature (e.g., Alston and Pardey 2014; Goyal and Nash 2016). Globally, the share of agriculture related activities within total research and development (R&D) is small, but the gap between low-income countries versus middle- and high-incomes countries is notable (Pardey et al. 2016). Particularly in low-income countries, where there is less private sector investment in agriculture R&D, governments still play a central role (Fuglie 2016). Yet, governments often underinvest in this area because of its high uncertainty, low salience to voters, and the long temporal lag between allocation and final delivery of service (Mogues 2015; Cai et al. 2017). Several studies indeed affirm a preference of both political elites and smallholder farmers for short-term, visible investments in infrastructure or subsidies over longer-term investments in agricultural research and development (Mogues and do Rosario 2016; Mason et al. 2019; Resnick 2022).

Finally, the linkages between global, regional, and local policies are undeniable, especially with respect to issues with cross-jurisdictional impacts, such as climate change and biodiversity. Some of these linkages were examined in the book's chapters (3, 4, 13). However, more detailed studies are needed that show the simultaneous international and domestic political economy dynamics that surround policies with large externalities. For instance, the new sustainability standards incorporated into the EU's Farm to Fork strategy, which require reduced pesticide and fertilizer use and harmonization of phytosanitary regulations, will have impacts on major African exporters of agricultural products into the EU. This will potentially generate a new set of lobbying between value chain actors and their governments in certain African countries for policy reforms to meet these new standards. Two-level game frameworks, which traditionally have been used to analyze trade and conflict resolution policies (Putnam 1988), offer one tool for understanding cross-border and multi-scalar decisionmaking around food systems.

Despite these and other potential areas for further research, the current volume has nonetheless offered a holistic compilation of the political economy considerations that must be confronted to meaningfully transform food systems in ways that resonate with local livelihoods and global realities. Indeed, while the needed policies to achieve a food system that contributes to human and planetary health might be technical, the pathways to those policies will almost always be political.

References

Alston, J.M., and P.G. Pardey. 2014. "Agriculture in the Global Economy." *Journal of Economic Perspective* 28: 121–146.

Andrews, M., L. Pritchett, and M. Woolcock. 2013. "Escaping Capability Traps through Problem Driven Iterative Adaptation (PDIA)." *World Development* 51: 234–244.

Buzogány, A., and C. Mohamad-Klotzbach. 2021. "Populism and Nature- The Nature of Populism: New Perspectives on the Relationship between Populism, Climate Change, and Nature Protection." *Zeitschrift für Vergleichende Politikwissenschaft* 15: 155–164.

Cai, Y., A.A. Golub, and T.W. Hertel. 2017. "Agricultural Research Spending Must Increase in Light of Future Uncertainties." *Food Policy* 70: 71–83.

Fuglie, K. 2016. "The Growing Role of the Private Sector in Agricultural Research and Development Worldwide." *Global Food Security* 10: 29–38.

Goldgeier, J., and P. Tetlock. 2008. "Psychological Approaches." In *The Oxford Handbook of International Relations*, eds. C. Reus-Smit and D. Snidal, Ch. 27, 462–480. Oxford, UK: Oxford University Press.

Goyal, A., and J. Nash. 2016. *Reaping Richer Returns: Public Spending Priorities for African Agriculture Productivity Growth*. Washington, DC: World Bank.

Kelley, J. 2017. *Scorecard Diplomacy: Grading States to Influence Their Reputation and Behavior*. Cambridge, UK: Cambridge University Press.

Kyle, J. 2018. "Local Corruption and Popular Support for Fuel Subsidy Reform in Indonesia." *Comparative Political Studies* 51 (11): 1472–1503.

Lodge, M. and K. Wegrich. 2014. "Introduction: Governance Innovation, Administrative Capacities, and Policy Instruments." In *The Problem-solving Capacity of the Modern State: Governance Challenges and Administrative Capacities*, eds. M. Lodge and K. Wegrich. Oxford, UK: Oxford University Press.

Mason, N., A. Kuteya, D. Resnick, V. Caputo, and M. Maredia. 2019. "Smallholder Farmers' and Other Agricultural Sector Stakeholders' Priorities for Government Spending: Evidence from Zambia." Feed the Future Innovation Lab for Food Security Policy Research Paper 155. Michigan State University, East Lansing, MI. https://www.canr.msu.edu/resources/smallholder-farmers-and-other-agricultural-sector-stakeholders-priorities-for-government-spending-evidence-from-zambia

Mogues, T. 2015. "Political Economy Determinants of Public Spending Allocations: A Review of Theories, and Implications for Agricultural Public Investment." *European Journal of Development Research* 27: 452–473.

Mogues, T. and D. do Rosario. 2016. "The Political Economy of Public Expenditures in Agriculture: Applications of Concepts to Mozambique." *South African Journal of Economics* 84: 20–39.

OECD (Organization for Economic Co-operation and Development). 2005. *Paris Declaration on Aid Effectiveness*. Paris, France: OECD.

Pardey, P.G., C. Chan-Kang, S.P. Dehmer, and J.M. Beddow. 2016. "Agricultural R&D Is on the Move." *Nature* 537: 301–303.

Popkin, B., and S. Ng. 2021. "Sugar-Sweetened Beverage Taxes: Lessons to Date and the Future of Taxation." *PLoS Medicine* 18 (1): e1003412. https://doi.org/10.1371/journal.pmed.1003412

Putnam, Robert. 1988. "Diplomacy and Domestic Politics: The Logic of Two-Level Games." *International Organization* 42(3): 427–460.

Resnick D. 2022. "Does Accountability Undermine Service Delivery? The Impact of Devolving Agriculture in Ghana." *European Journal of Development Research* 34 (2): 1003–1029

Sabatier, P. 1988. "An Advocacy Coalition Framework of Policy Change and the Role of Policy-Oriented Learning Therein." *Policy Sciences* 21: 129–168. https://link.springer.com/article/10.1007/BF00136406

Wegrich, K. 2021. "Policy Instruments and Administrative Capacities." In *Oxford Research Encyclopedia*, ed. William Thompson. Oxford, UK: Oxford University Press.

Weyland, K. 2005. "Theories of Policy Diffusion: Lessons from Latin American Pension Reform." *World Politics* 57 (2): 262–295.

Index

For the benefit of digital users, indexed terms that span two pages (e.g., 52–53) may, on occasion, appear on only one of those pages.

Tables, figures and boxes are indicated by an italic *t*, *f*, and *b* following the paragraph number.

accountability
  cycle 340*f*, 340
  definition 340
  food system transformation 338, 353
  high-level reports 341, 342*f*, 345
  mechanisms 16, 22, 340
  moving towards 349
  and need for transformation 339
  online databases and dashboards 344–345
  and prior work on food systems 341
ACF *see* Advocacy Coalition Framework (ACF)
activist organizations 20, 136–137, 140, 141, 145, 147
adaptive space for policy reform 11*f*, 15, 21–22
advertising 139–140, 143–144, 146, 167–168, 174–175
Advocacy Coalition Framework (ACF) 19, 158, 159–160, 170, 176–177, 197*f*, 187
advocacy coalitions 159–160, 187, 193, 194*f*, 197*f*
Africa
  CRISPR crops 250
  food policy councils (FPCs) 297, 365–366
  food systems 288, 304
  GMOs 244–246
  nutrition 198
  obesity 155–156, 158–159
  population 288
Africa Agriculture Transformation Scorecards 16
African Regional Nutritional Strategy (ARNS) 198
African urban food governance
  authorizing and activating environments 300
  in cities 292
  city-led 296–297
  emerging global approaches 294
  external and issue-oriented interventions 299
  food systems 21
  historical approaches 289
  and misalignment in global processes 292

AFS transformation *see* agri-food systems (AFS) transformation
agenda-setting 3, 135, 186, 200, 320–321
"agricultural exceptionalism" 44
Agricultural Produce and Livestock Market Committee (APMC) 66–67
agricultural production
  global inefficiencies 80–81
  multifunctionality 85–86
  negative impacts 321
  and reforms in China 1–2, 68*f*
  small influence of support 58
agricultural support policies
  case studies of reforms 64, 68*f*
  contributions of various instruments 90
  by country 56*f*, 92*t*, 93*f*, 94*t*
  current 55
  and global costs 96
  impacts of current 57
  by main types 55*f*
  nominal rates 91*f*
  and policy instrument choices 82
  political economy 54, 60, 61*f*, 72, 73*t*
  price-distorting 81
  from reinstrumenting to repurposing 80, 101
  relative rate of assistance (RRAs) 95*f*
  removal 58, 72–74
  repurposing 56–57, 59*f*, 59, 72–74, 100, 360–361
  and welfare economics 87
agri-food systems (AFS) transformation
  and bundling 212–213
  challenge 206
  and Kaldor-Hicks 212
  and knowledge intensive innovations 215
  and socio-technical bundles 208, 225
agroecology 237, 323
Akerlof, George 170–171
Alianca por la Salud Alimentaria (Food Health Alliance) 140
Alliance for a Green Revolution in Africa (AGRA) 237

All India Anna Dravida Munnetra Kazhagam
　(AIADMK) (India) 142
All India Kisan Coordination Committee 67
American Beverage Association 46–47
animal agriculture 322–324
animal welfare 86, 259, 260, 273–276, 322–323,
　361–362
Argentina 124–125, 243, 249
Australia 8–9, 82–85, 257–259

Bangladesh 224–225, 367
Belgium 116, 118
Belo Horizonte, Brazil 295–296
Beverage Association of South Africa
　(BEVSA) 145–146
Bharatiya Janata Party (BJP) 66–67, 142
Bharatiya Kisan Union (Indian Farmers
　Union) 67
bias
　and consensus 351
　data 346–347
　and evidence-based policymaking 7–8, 63
　interest groups 37, 46
　media 12–13
　rural 288–292, 299–300, 304
　and science 363
　urban framing 290
　and values 43–44
biodiversity habitats 2, 314–315, 333
Biodiversity strategy 310, 311t, 316–317
biofuels 70, 120, 360–361
biotechnology 118, 364
Black Sea 1
Black Sea Grain Initiative 1
Bloomberg Foundation 135, 137, 140
Bolsonaro, Jair 8–9
Borlaug, Norman 220, 234
Brazil 8–9, 117, 155–156, 173–174, 295–296
Brazilian Agrarian Caucus 117
BRICS countries (Brazil, Russia, India, China,
　South Africa) 9–10
Bt brinjal 223, 367
Bt crops 242–246

campaigns 46–47, 137, 145, 237, 247–248, 267t,
　273–274, 276
Canada 34, 38–39, 85, 297–298
CAP see Common Agricultural Policy (CAP)
Cape Town, city of 296–297, 304
carbon sequestration 86, 104
carbon taxes 330–331
Carson, Rachel 240–241
CFS see Committee on World Food Security
　(CFS)

chemical use 238
children 139, 143–144, 146, 147, 175, 209–210,
　235–236
China
　agricultural priorities 67
　agricultural productivity 1–2
　agricultural support 56, 67, 68f
　farm income growth 67
　policy support to reduce meat consump-
　　tion 269, 270f, 271f, 272f, 272–273,
　　277f
　political economy dynamics 73t
China Agricultural University (CAU) 218–219
citizens' forums 45–46
city-led food governance 294–295
civil society activities
　coalitions 14
　growth and inclusion 6–7
　holding decision-makers to account 352–353
　and nutrition priorities 137, 140, 144, 147,
　　361, 363
　and science resistance 236–237, 363
　and ultra-processed food 156–157, 170
civil society organizations (CSOs) 164t, 164,
　168, 169–171
climate change 2, 72, 102, 256, 274–276
Climate Law (EU) 310, 311t
coalitions
　advocacy 159–160, 194f, 187, 193, 197f
　building for bundling 211
　cross-issue 18, 112, 121, 160–161
　discourse 159–160, 163, 164t, 169
　and food environment policy change 172, 176
　formation 213
　importance 111, 127
　increasingly expansive 363
　and negotiation 368
　policy 113
　and potential policy reforms 13, 18–19, 363
　state 163, 164t, 164–167, 169, 170–171,
　　173–174, 288–289
　and strategic policy design 364
　in support of reform 39
　transnational 18, 112, 125, 363–364
　and ultra-processed food 170
　and unintended consequences 363
　vertical policy 18, 112, 115
Coca-Cola 135–137, 141–142
cocoa production 126
co-creative processes 217–219, 349–350, 368
Codex Alimentarius Commission 174–175
collective action 113, 349–350
Committee on World Food Security (CFS) 343,
　351b

commodity prices 328–329
Common Agricultural Policy (CAP) 69, 85,
    124, 313, 314–315, 317–318, 320–321, 330,
    331–332, 366
Comprehensive Africa Agriculture Development
    Program (CAADP) 16, 198
Congress Party 4, 142
conjoint experiments 266, 267t, 271–272, 278
Conservation Reserve Program (CRP) 123–124
conservatism 210, 212–213, 216
consumer behavior 316–317, 324, 326
consumer boycotts 9
consumer spending 2
consumer support estimates 90
corn production 238, 241–242
"corporate political activities" 37–38
corporate power 362
corporate social responsibility (CSR) 5–6
costs and benefits 11–12, 43, 361
Côte d'Ivoire 126
cotton production 224
Covid-19 pandemic 3–4
CRISPR (Clustered Regularly Interspaced Short
    Palindromic Repeats) crops 248
critical junctures 15–16, 365
culture 208–209, 250

databases and dashboards 342f, 344–346
decentralization initiatives 5, 133–134
Denmark 83
design space for policy reform 11f, 14, 19–21
dietary guidelines 34, 38–39, 140–141, 171,
    315–317, 325
direct payments 17–18, 67–68, 72–74, 85, 92,
    313, 360–361
"Dirty Dozen" report (Environmental Working
    Group) 241, 364
discourse analysis approach 158–160, 170, 186
discourse coalitions 159–160, 163, 164t, 169
dis/misinformation 7–9, 37, 46, 215–216, 222,
    225, 333, 338
Doha Round trade negotiations (2005) 9–10
Dutch disease 210

Ease of Doing Business Index (World
    Bank) 346–347
economic growth 40–41f, 82, 90
ecosystem services 85–86, 96–97, 104, 360–361
Ecuador 1
education 82, 89, 102–103, 149, 165t, 169
employment in agriculture 2, 58, 91, 114,
    321–324
Enabling the Business of Agriculture Index 16

environmental policies 90, 102, 104–105,
    313–314
environmental protection see also welfare
    economics
    and agricultural science 230, 250
    and CAP 313–314
    in China 69
    coalitions 123
    and CRISPR crops 248
    and economic growth 40–41f, 90
    and ecosystem services 104
    and ensuring policies in place 102, 104–105
    in Europe 70
    and GMO crops 242
    and Green Revolution farming 233
    in India 65
    and industrial farming 237
    and negative impacts 321
    and organic food 239
    and policy decision-making 319
    and popular resistance to science 246
    and public opinion 259
    and R&D investment 330–331
    and societal demands 86
    and sustainable food 232
    in US 70–71
Europe
    and CRISPR crops 248–249
    and food safety 122
    and GMO foods 103–104, 119, 242–248, 250
    and Green Parties 231
    and land rental 118
    and organic farming 241–242
    and policy coalitions 116
    protectionist trade policies 85
European Commission (EC) 120–121, 310–312,
    320, 329–330
European Commission Group of Chief Scientific
    Advisors 34
European Economic Community (EEC) 84
European Food Safety Authority (EFSA) 122,
    315, 318–319
European Food Security Crisis Preparedness
    and Response Mechanism 315
European Parliament 310–311, 320, 329–330,
    333
European Union (EU)
    agricultural support 56, 69, 84
    Common Agricultural Policy (CAP) see
        Common Agricultural Policy (CAP)
    decision-making procedures 312, 319,
        331–332
    environmental concerns 124

European Union (EU) (*Continued*)
  Farm-to-Fork strategy *see* Farm to Fork (F2F)
    strategy
  food policy framework 313
  and GMO foods 242
  opportunities for transition 329
  and organic crops 241–242
  policy instruments 91–92
  political economy 73*t*, 310, 319, 362, 365
  re-instrumenting 85
  sugar quota 116
evidence translation 351
export subsidies 69–70, 81, 85, 87–88, 91–93,
    97, 99*t*, 99*t*, 100*t*, 100*t*, 125
external dimension 21–23, 140, 294–295,
    299–301, 304, 311*t*, 317, 328

facts 14, 17, 32–33, 35*t*, 47
FAOSTAT 344–346
Farm Animal Investment Risk & Return
    Initiative (FAIRR) 350–351
Farm Bill (US) 122–124, 365
Farmer-Citizens Movement (Boer Burger
    Beweging, BBB) party 7–8
Farmer Input Support Program (FISP) 191,
    194–196, 198–200
farmers
  government support 80–81
  and landowners 117
  numbers 114
  real incomes 95, 96*t*
  share of consumer spending on food 2
  support 95
Farmers Defense Force (FDF) 7–8
farm incomes 65, 67, 68–69, 82–83, 85, 87–88,
    96*t*, 239, 321
Farm Inputs Subsidy Program 125–126
farm lobbies 85–86, 231
farm support policies *see* agricultural support
    policies
Farm to Fork (F2F) strategy
  approval 231–232
  dissatisfaction with 368
  governance 310–312
  impact on value chains 369
  and inflation 329
  launch 310
  objectives 311*t*
  and organic farming 241–242, 247
  as policy cascade 16
  postponement 333, 365
  and sustainable aims 70, 316, 329–330, 366
fertilizer use 2, 235, 238, 240
FISP *see* Farmer Input Support Program (FISP)

Food and Drugs Authority (Ghana) 167–168,
    367
food choices 9, 33, 155–158, 164–167, 325, 327,
    364–365
food environment policy beliefs 163–164, 165*t*,
    167–170, 324, 367
food governance
  in African cities 292
  authorizing and activating environments 300
  emerging global processes 294
  urban 289
"foodies" 45
food prices *see also* market price support (MPS)
  and change in farming practices 322–323,
    327, 328–329, 331
  and environmental concerns 70, 124
  and green transition 331
  inflation 329
  and sustainability 332
food quality 121
Food Reserve Agency (FRA) (Zambia) 125–126,
    191, 194–196
food safety 34, 122, 240–241, 314
Food Safety and Standards Authority of India
    (FSSAI) 143
food security
  in Africa 290–294, 301
  and agricultural support 84
  definition 89–90
  in Europe 315–316, 328–329, 333
  and policy objectives 184
  and political economy 1–2
  in Zambia 191, 194*f*, 194–195–C823, 198
food shortages 1–2, 121, 231
food sovereignty 6, 89
Food Systems Dashboard 342*f*, 344–346
Food Systems Dialogues 45
food system transformation
  and coalitions 111–112, 127–128
  complexities underlying 3
  and monitoring 338, 353
  and political economy 1, 23, 367–369
  and political economy drivers of policy
    choice 10
  and public support 259–260, 264*f*, 261–262,
    279–282
  ways forward 367
Forum for Democracy 7–8
Fox, Vincente 136–137
FRA *see* Food Reserve Agency (FRA) (Zambia)
France 34, 36, 45, 116, 174
funding 46, 350–351

General Agreement on Tariffs and Trade (GATT) 83–85, 125 *see also* Uruguay Round Agreement on Agriculture (URAA)

General Food Law (2002) 314–315

genetically modified organisms (GM/GMOs)
and coalitions 112–113, 118
and policy controversies 46
and policy sequencing 20, 365
and politics 223–225
and regulation 118–119
and reluctance to allow 103–104
and science resistance 34, 230, 233, 242, 246–250

genome editing technologies 103–104, 233, 248, 250

Germany
coalitions 116
meat consumption 264
policy framing 259, 364
policy support 20–21, 260, 269–270*f*, 271*f*, 273–278, 273*f*, 274*f*, 277*f*

Ghana
Bt crops 246
as case study 158–159, 161–162
civil society organizations 168–169, 171–172
coalitions 19, 362
cocoa production 126
dietary guidelines 171
food choices 155–156
government policy actions 171, 367
obesity and overweight 155–159
regulations targeting children 175
sin taxes 173–174
subsidies 173
ultra-processed foods 155–158, 176–177

GHGs *see* greenhouse gas emissions (GHGs)

Global Access to Nutrition Index 343

Global and Local Burden of Disease 344

Global Food Policy Report (GFPR) 343

global food system advocacy
bringing the global to local 191
combining theories of public policy 184
contrasting policy objectives 184
evolving ideas in the international nutrition space 188
and food policy space 200

Global Food Systems Countdown to 2030 Initiative 347–349, 348*f*, 349, 366–367

Global Hunger Index 346–347

globalization 18, 126, 127, 188

globally traded calories 1

Global Nutrition Report (GNR) 342*f*, 342–343

Global Strategy on Diet, Physical Activity and Health (WHO) 136

Global Trade Analysis Project(GTAP) Data Base 96–97, 98*t*

Global Trade Analysis Project(GTAP) model 17–18, 99*t*, 99*t*, 96, 99–100*t*, 100*t*, 101

GMOs *see* genetically modified organisms (GM/GMOs)

golden rice 209, 217, 221–223

Goods and Services Tax (GST) 66, 142–143

governments
agricultural support 17, 57, 67–69, 72, 80–83, 191, 219
and coalitions 18–19, 116
and environmental policies 102, 104–105
and food governance 21
and genetically modified organisms (GM/GMOs) 245–248
meeting multiple demands 86, 100, 363
and multiple streams analysis 134–135
and non-communicable diseases policy 135
and policy reforms 65–67
and policy support 20–21, 256–259, 263
and R&D investment 368–369
responses to ultra-processed industries 133, 135–136, 148, 156–157, 167–168, 171, 326–327, 329, 361
and sustainable food 321–322, 333
and trust 368
and urban food governance 292, 296–297, 299–300

green conditionality 72–74, 360–361

Green Deal policy 310–312, 311*t*, 314, 316, 317, 320, 322, 329–330, 333, 366

greenhouse gas emissions (GHGs)
agriculture production contribution 57, 127, 310
in China 69
and corn production 238
in Europe 314–315, 328
food system contribution to 256, 339
impact of adopting GM crops 103–104
impact of taxing 102
and impacts of agricultural support 57
and land use expansion 2
need for reduction 57–58
need for reduction of 60
and repurposing agricultural support 60
and subsidies 65

Green Parties 7, 231, 232, 365, 368

Green Revolution 19–20, 209, 217, 220–223, 233, 246–248, 250

GTAP Data Base *see* Global Trade Analysis
    Project(GTAP) Data Base
GTAP model *see* Global Trade Analysis
    Project(GTAP) model

HEALA 145, 147
health awareness campaigns 134, 140, 147, 169,
    339
Health Canada 34, 38–39
Health Promotion Lev 4, 146
health services 103
healthy, equitable, resilient and sustainable
    (HERS) objectives 206–207
High-Level Panel of Experts on Food Security
    and Nutrition 343, 351*b*
high-level reports 341, 342*f*, 345
Howard, Albert 240

ideas
    evolving in nutrition 188
    and incentives space 11
    and information 62
    and interests 62–63
    and political economy dynamics 73*t*
    and potential policy reforms 12
    study design framework 185*t*
import tariffs
    and coalitions 111–112
    as farmer support 91
    global welfare cost 81
    and government revenue 93
    in GTAP database 98*t*
    and inequality 88
    international pressure 125
    lowering 83–84, 87
    removal 97, 99*t*, 99*t*, 100*t*, 100*t*
    and vertical policy coalitions 115–116
incentives space for policy reform 11*f*, 11,
    17–18, 81, 362
incentive structures 13, 22–23, 360
incentive subsidies 63–64
India
    agricultural support 65
    challenges of market reform 65, 72, 74, 362
    data transparency 346–347
    GMO crops 223–225, 249–250, 367
    Goods and Services Tax (GST) 66, 142–143
    Green Revolution farming 234–236
    political economy dynamics 73*t*
    sugar sector 4
    sugar-sweetened beverage taxes 18–19, 133,
        140, 148–149, 361, 365
India Resource Center 141
Indonesia 235

industrial farming 237, 247
information
    and AFS transformation 215–218
    and agricultural support policies reform 73*t*
    and coalitions 14–15
    communication 37
    dis/misinformation 7, 37, 46, 215–216, 222,
        225, 333, 338
    and interests 63
    lack of availability 33
    and policy framing 261, 276, 364
    and political economy dynamics 73*t*
    and potential policy reforms 14
    role 213
    and sustainable food policies 258, 273–274
INGOs *see* international non-governmental
    organizations (INGOs)
innovations
    agri-food systems (AFS)
        transformation 207–208, 225
    and coalitions for bundling 211, 213
    and power, information and trust 213
    and socio-technical bundles 208
institutions
    academic 34
    and agricultural support policies reform 73*t*
    and bundling 213
    influence 12–13
    and mediation 362
    and misinformation 215–216
    multilateral 9–10
    political 122–123
    and political economy dynamics 73*t*
    and political economy of agricultural support
        policies 62
    and potential policy reforms 12–13
    and socio-technical bundles 208–209
"integrated pest management" (IPM) 241
interest groups
    and agricultural support policies reform 64,
        73*t*
    in dynamic food system 4
    negotiation 368
    and policy coalitions 111–112, 117
    and political economy 263
    and political economy dynamics 73*t*
    and political economy framework 61
    and potential policy reforms 12
    pressure 37–38
    and values 46–47
interests
    commensurable and incommensurable 42–43
    disagreements 32, 35*t*, 37
    and policy input 36–37

versus values 41
vested 12
Intergovernmental Panel for food 12–13, 351*b*
international actors 190
international community 137, 145, 188, 193
International Conference on Nutrition
   (ICN1) 191–192
International Covenant on Economic, Social,
   and Cultural Rights (ICESCR) (1976) 6
International Food Policy Research Institute
   (IFPRI) 343
International Monetary Fund (IMF) 125–126
international non-governmental organizations
   (INGOs) 10, 293–294, 299–301
International Pact on Monitoring for
   Accountability for Action on Food
   Systems 349
International Rice Research Institute
   (IRRI) 221–223
investment
   for accountability 350–351
   agrifood tech startups 206–207
   capital 103
   education 103
   and funding 350–351
   health 103
   R&D 64, 71–72, 103–104, 330–331, 368–369
   rural infrastructure 103
Ireland 118, 364
Irish Citizens' Assembly 45
iron-deficiency anemia (IDA) 209–210
issue linkage 5, 39
Ivory Coast-Ghana Cocoa Initiative
   (ICCIG) 126

Japan 83, 91, 249–250
Jubilee Debt Campaign 125–126

Kaldor-Hicks criterion 211–213, 217, 222
Kenya 119–120, 125–126, 244–246, 250
Knightian uncertainty 216, 224

labelling 113, 140, 143, 146–148, 174–175, 243,
   325, 361
Lancet, The 189–190
Lancet Countdowns 343
landowners 117, 124
Latin America 117, 236
"learning by doing" 36
livestock production *see* animal agriculture
local governments 5, 21, 219, 291, 292, 299–300,
   365–366
Local Governments for Sustainability
   (ICLEI) 294–297

logic of collective action 113–114, 214–215, 225
low-and-middle-income countries
   (LMICs) 206–207, 246–247

Maharashtra, India 4
Maharashtra Hybrid Seeds Company
   (Mahyco) 223–225
maize production 191, 194–195, 244–245
Malabo Declaration 198
malnutrition
   , and agriculture 189–190
   databases and dashboards 344–345
   economic costs 339
   in India 140–141
   in South Africa 144–145
   and ultra-processed food 156, 170–171
   in Zambia 184, 191, 194–196, 199, 200
market coalitions 163, 164*t*, 164, 168
market price support (MPS) 55–57
mass media 12–14, 63, 101
MEALS4NCDs project 175
meat consumption
   in China 272*f*, 272–273
   and disinformation 8
   in Europe 316
   and food safety 243
   in Germany 273–275, 273*f*, 274*f*
   and literature on policy support 257
   and need for food system
      transformation 256
   and policy framing 361–362, 364
   and policy support 20–21, 270*f*, 262, 269,
      271*f*, 276–279, 277*f*, 281
   and removal of tariffs 99–100
   and survey methods 264
   and sustainable eating 316
   in US 275–276, 275*f*, 276*f*
meat substitutes 8, 20–21, 115–116, 208–209,
   262, 278–280, 318–319, 363
Mexico 18–19, 133, 136, 148–149, 174–175, 234,
   361, 365
Milan Urban Food Policy Pact (MUFPP) 5,
   294–297, 315–316
misinformation *see* dis/misinformation
mobilizational space for policy reform 11*f*, 13,
   18–19, 22–23, 363
Modi, Damodardas 141–143
monitoring
   efforts to fill gaps 347
   food system transformation 338, 353
   gaps in food systems 345
   prior work on food systems 341
Monsanto 119, 225, 243
moral foundations 40, 42

motivated reasoning 32, 36–37
MUFPP *see* Milan Urban Food Policy Pact
    (MUFPP)
multifunctionality 85–86, 104
multilateralism 9, 83–84, 101–102,
    293–294, 362
multiple streams analysis 134, 148–149

National Food and Nutrition Commission
    (NFNC) 198–199
National Food and Nutrition Security Council
    (CONSEA) 8–9
national taxes 133–134, 138–139, 141–142
NCDs *see* non-communicable
    diseases (NCDs)
Neito, Enrique Peña 137–138, 148–149
Netherlands 7–8, 74, 118
New Zealand 82–83, 91, 259–260
NGOs *see* non-governmental organizations
    (NGOs)
Nigeria 14, 62–63, 246, 250
nitrogen use 7–8, 235, 240, 314–315
nominal rates of assistance (NRAs) 68f, 91f,
    9192t, 95f
non-communicable diseases (NCDs) 2, 18–19,
    133, 135, 148, 310
non-governmental organizations (NGOs) 46,
    218, 231, 236, 304
novel foods 318–319
nutrition
    accountability 16
    and agriculture 188
    and domestic assistance 122–123
    evolving ideas 188
    high-level reports 341–343
    in India 140–141
    and international actors 190
    investments and funding 350–351
    online databases and dashboards
        for 344–345
    and populism 8–9
    security 89
    in South Africa 144–145
    standards 327
    and stunting 19
    in Zambia 191–200, 192f, 193f, 200, 364

obesity 2, 4, 140–141, 155–159, 231, 257–259,
    310
Olson, Mancur 113–114, 123–124, 214–215
organic food 40, 239, 361–362
Organization for Economic Development
    (OECD) 102

Organization for Economic Development
    (OECD) countries 39, 91, 92, 263
overweight 135–136, 140–141, 155–156, 310

Pan American Health
    Organization (PAHO) 137
Paris Climate Agreement 9–10, 69, 74, 256, 320,
    362
Paris Declaration on Aid Effectiveness 362
Pepsi 135–136
pesticides 2, 34, 36, 69, 224–225, 238, 240–241
Pew Research Centre 34
Philippines 221–223, 234
*Phishing for Phools: The Economics of Manip-
    ulation and Deception* (Akerlof and
    Shiller) 170–171
polarization 7–9, 361
policy beliefs
    and data analysis 162–163
    and discourse analysis 158–159
    identification of coalitions 163
    understanding 176
policy bundling
    and China 218
    coalitions 212–213
    and Green Revolution farming 220
    and potential policy reforms 14–15, 19–20,
        22–23
    and role of institutions 213
    socio-technical 208, 364–365
    and transgenic crops 223
policy capture 37–39, 48–49
policy cascades 16, 365–367
policy characteristics 63
policy choices 10
policy coalitions *see* coalitions
policy controversies 33, 35t, 36–37, 46, 48
policy design
    addressing coalition preferences 364
    attributes in meat production
        experiment 267t
    and coalitions 364
    and meat consumption research 261–263,
        264f, 272f, 281
    and policy framing 271, 279
    and policy support 273f, 275f
policy diffusion 16, 22–23, 186, 365–367
policy disagreements
    over facts 33
    over interests 37
    over values 39
    and policy controversies 46
    and policy reforms 32, 35t, 48, 338
policy feedback 15, 262, 264f, 278

policy framing
and meat consumption research 259, 261, 264f, 266, 272f, 276f, 278–279, 281–282
and policy design 271
and policy support 273f, 274f, 275f, 361–362, 364
policy instruments *see also* campaigns; subsidies; taxes
and coalitions 115, 124, 127, 363
contributions to national producer and consumer support estimates 90, 91f, 93f, 94t, 95f
evolving objectives 82
and healthier food environments 172
and incentives space 11–12
inefficiencies 104
and policy characteristics 63–64
and political economy dynamics 73t
and public support 81–82, 361
and trade-offs 361
used in sustainable food policy experiment 266–269, 267t, 272
and welfare economics 87
win-set 60–61f
policymaking, evidence-based 7, 14, 33–34, 36
policy objectives 184
policy packaging 15, 20–21
policy process 38–39, 185t, 184–186
policy reform spaces
adaptive 11f, 15, 21–22
design 11f, 14, 19–21
for food systems transformation 10–11, 22–23
incentives 11f, 11, 17–18
mobilizational 11f, 13, 22–23
policy sequencing 15, 20–21, 262, 281, 365
policy support
in China 272f
combined framing and policy design effects 271
in Germany 273f, 274f
literature 257
reducing meat consumption 269, 271f, 277f, 281, 361–362
theoretical argument 260
in US 275f, 276f
willingness to pay more 270f
policy transfer 19, 186, 188, 196, 197f
political economy
considerations for food systems reform 11f
drivers of policy choices 10
dynamics 73t, 256–257
and food security 1–2
food system transformation 1

frameworks 60
influences 61f
issues 367
polluter pays principle 330
pollution taxes 63
poor agrarian economies (PAEs) 95, 96t
poor consumers 57, 65, 88, 122–123, 157
popular resistance 246
populism 7, 9, 368
power
and incentives space 13
and potential policy reforms 13
role 213
theories 187
in the Zambian Food Policy process 19, 190
precision agriculture (PA) 237–238
price stabilization 84–85
producer support estimates (PSEs) 90, 93f, 94t
profits 167–168, 170–171, 361, 363
property rights 103
"prophets" worldviews 47
protectionist trade policies 83–86, 89, 90–91f, 117, 126
public opinion research
combined framing and policy design 271
discussion and research outlook 279
literature on sustainable food policy 257
and meat consumption 256
and methods used in survey-embedded experiments 264
overview 281
results 269
and theoretical argument 260
public policy 184
public-private partnerships 325–326
public relations companies 8–9, 14
public views 8–9, 34

R&D (research & development) 46, 59, 64, 69, 72, 74, 103, 231, 360–361, 368–369
Rapid Alert System for Food and Feed 315
rational choice theory 157, 170
Razoni cargo ship 1
reciprocity 39
Regulatory Impact Assessments 34
regulatory policies 64, 134, 139–140, 143–149, 156–157, 174–175, 248–250, 267t, 361, 367
relative rates of assistance (RRAs) 95f
Renewable Energy Directive (2009) 120
Renewable Fuels Standard (RFS) (2005) 120
research and development *see* R&D (research & development)
resistance
to agricultural support policies reform 64, 74

resistance (*Continued*)
  and bundling 19–20
  and CRISPR crops 248–249
  cultural 250
  and GMO crops 230
  popular 233, 246
  religious 230
  science 34, 233–234, 236, 237, 242, 246–251,
    363
  and science resistance 233–234
Resource Centre on Urban Agriculture and Food
    Security (RUAF) 297
resource efficiency 330–331
rice 65–66, 68, 83, 217, 220, 234–236
rich industrial economies (RIEs) 82–83, 95, 96t
"right to food" 6, 8–9, 295–296
routine trade-offs 42–43, 361
rural bias 288–292, 299–300
rural infrastructure 103, 114, 360–361
Russia 1

Scaling Up Nutrition (SUN) movement 190,
    198–199
science
  acceptance in farming 230
  and bias 363
  consensus generation and evidence
    translation 351
  and CRISPR crops 247–248
  and GMO resistance 34, 230, 233, 242,
    246–250
  and GMOs 242–C1057, 248
  and Green Revolution farming 233–234
  and organic food 239–240, 361–362
  and popular resistance 246–248, 250–251
  and regulation 249–250
  and religious resistance 230
  role 361–362
  and sustainable food 232–233
  unpopular 250
Science and Technology Backyards (STB)
    program (China) 218, 368
scientific advisory bodies 34
SDGs *see* Sustainable Development Goals
    (SDGs)
self-regulation 37–38, 139, 143, 174
shared food environment policy beliefs 164
Shiller, Roger 170–171
Shiva, Vandana 234–236
sin taxes 141–143, 173–174
SNAP payments *see* Supplemental Nutritional
    Assistance Program (SNAP)
social media 7–9
social welfare 363

societal actors 288–289, 367
socio-technical innovation bundles 14–15,
    19–20, 208, 217–218
soda taxes 133, 136, 145–146, 148–149
soil health 33–34, 314–315
South Africa 4, 133, 144, 244–245, 361, 365
SSB *see* sugar-sweetened beverage (SSB) taxes
stakeholders 6–7, 10, 13, 34, 38
standards 363, 367
state coalitions 163, 164t, 164–167, 169,
    170–171, 173–174, 288–289
State of Food and Agriculture (SOFA) 341–342f
State of Food Insecurity in the World
    (SOFI) 341–342, 348
State of Food Security and Nutrition in the
    World 341–342
Steiner, Rudolf 240
structural adjustment programs (SAPs) 125–126
structural separation 43–44
stunting 189–190, 193–196, 198, 200–201
subsidies
  agricultural 17, 118, 330, 365, 368–369
  consumer 55–56
  elimination 99t, 99t, 100t, 100t
  in EU 69–70
  export *see* export subsidies
  and healthier food environments 173
  incentive 63–64
  in India 65–66
  in Indonesia 235
  by region 98t
  removal 58, 60, 64, 97–100
Sugar Industry Value Chain Masterplan 4
sugar quotas 116, 363
sugar sector 4, 116
sugar-sweetened beverage (SSB) taxes
  in developing nations 133, 148, 361, 365
  implementation 18–19
  in India 140
  and interest groups 46–47
  in Mexico 136
  in Nigeria 14
  and social media 8–9
  in South Africa 144
  in US 257–258
Supplemental Nutritional Assistance Program
    (SNAP) 122–123, 365
sustainability
  challenges for change 324, 326
  and changing market conditions 328
  and contrasting worldviews 47
  and CRISPR crops 248
  defining sustainable food 232
  differing understandings 323

and economic growth 90
in Europe 310–316
and GMOs 242
and Green Revolution farming 233
and industrial farming 237
and literature on public opinion 257
and negative impacts 321
opportunities for transition 329
and organic food 239
and popular resistance to science 246
and public support 279, 281
and R&D investment 74
and repurposing 59f
and science acceptance 230, 250
tension with economic dimensions 330–333
and theoretical argument 260
sustainable agricultural intensification (SAI)
    methods 246–247
Sustainable Development Goals (SDGs) 2, 207,
    256, 292–293, 310–311, 343
sustainable eating 316–317, 325, 363
systems thinking 351, 366–367

taboo trade-offs 42, 47, 361–362
Tamil Nadu state, India 142
Tanzania 244–245
taxes
    and agricultural support 55–56
    carbon 330–331
    Goods and Services Tax (GST) 66, 142–143
    meat 267t
    national 133–134, 138–139, 141–142
    pollution 63
    sin 141–143, 173–174
    soda 133, 136, 145–146, 148–149
    sugar-sweetened beverage see sugar-sweetened
        beverage (SSB) taxes
thinktanks 34–36
Timmermans, Frans 320
tobacco 142–143
Torres Peimbert, Marcela 138, 148–149
trade liberalization 17–18, 39, 97–99t, 100t, 101
trade-offs 42, 47, 360–362
tragic trade-offs 42, 361–362
transgenic crops 209, 215–216, 221–225,
    248–250
transnational advocacy networks 5–7, 363–364
transparency 38–39
transport costs 87
trust 213–214, 216–218, 368
Tunisia 1
Twitter 8–9

Ukraine war 1, 119–121, 124, 315, 322–323,
    328, 365
ultra-processed foods
    and affordability 363
    concerns 8–9, 155, 176
    dominance 2
    in EU diets 326
    and food environment policy beliefs 170
    in the Global South 135–136
    and policy discourse coalitions 163, 165t
    policy responses 133–134
    research methods 159, 162t
uncertainty 36, 47
underweight 198
UN Food and Agriculture Organization
    (FAO) 8–9, 198, 232, 341–342, 344
UN Food Systems Summit (UNFSS) 16, 18,
    362, 366–367
(2021) 2, 10, 17, 111, 127, 201
UN-Habitat New Urban Agenda
    (NUA) 293–294
United Kingdom (UK) 84, 116, 118, 249,
    257–259
United Nations (UN) 9–10, 190
United States (US)
    AFS innovations 218
    agricultural output 238
    agricultural support 56, 69–70, 91
    biofuel policies 70, 120–121, 360–361
    chemical controls 241
    coalitions 122–123
    corn production 238, 241–242
    environmental concerns 123–124
    GMO foods 118–119, 244–245
    obesity rates 231
    organic crops 247
    organic food prices 240
    policy support 257–260, 269, 270f, 271f,
        275–278, 275f, 276f, 277f
    political economy dynamics 73t
    R&D support 231
    re-instrumenting 85
    small farms 238–239
    soda tax 133
    tariffs 68
Universal Declaration of Human Rights
    (1948) 6
urban bias framing 290
urban food governance
    activating environment 288–289
    in Africa 288, 292, 304
    authorizing and activating
        environments 288–289, 300, 302f
    emerging global processes 294

urban food governance (*Continued*)
  historical approaches 289
  misalignment in global processes 292
Uruguay Round Agreement on Agriculture
    (URAA) 39, 70, 80–81, 83–85, 125
US Department of Agriculture (USDA) 122–123

value chains 13, 112–113, 115, 126–127
values 32, 35*t*, 36–37, 39, 41, 361–362
vegans 8
Vital Strategies 145
voluntary regulation *see* self-regulation
von der Leyen, Ursula 317, 320
voting 44

wealth inequality 88
welfare costs 17–18, 81–82, 101
welfare economics 87, 211–212
wheat production 1, 84–85, 234, 236, 238
WHO Nutrition Landscape Information System
    (NLiS) 344
"wizards" worldviews 47
working conditions 314–315
World Bank 9–10, 93, 143–144, 189–190,
    346–347

World Food Programme Hunger Map LIVE 344
World Food Summit (1996) 6
World Health Organization (WHO) 136, 141,
    143–144, 147, 174–175, 341–342, 344
World Trade Organization (WTO) 9–10, 73*t*,
    68, 80–81, 97, 101–102, 125, 362
World Value Survey 40–41
worldviews 36–37, 47

Yavapai Indians 42–43

Zambia
  changing nutrition policy 193*f*
  coalitions 193, 194*f*
  evolving policy ideas 188, 200, 362
  food policy 191
  GMOs 245
  IMF agreement 125–126
  new food policy 195, 364
  policy transfer 196, 197*f*
  power in the food policy process 199
  theories of public policy 184
  timeline of food and nutrition policy 192*f*